INSIDERS' GUIDE®

INSIDERS' GUIDE® SERIES

INSIDERS' GUIDE® TO
THE POCONO MOUNTAINS

FOURTH EDITION

JANET BREGMAN-TANEY AND KENNETH R. CLARK

INSIDERS' GUIDE®

GUILFORD, CONNECTICUT
AN IMPRINT OF THE GLOBE PEQUOT PRESS

The prices and rates in this guidebook were confirmed at press time. We recommend, however, that you call establishments before traveling to obtain current information.

INSIDERS' GUIDE®

Text design by LeAnna Weller Smith
Maps by XNR Productions, Inc © The Globe Pequot Press

ISSN 1541-048X
ISBN 0-7627-3458-2

Manufactured in the United States of America
Fourth Edition/First Printing

Waterfall in Delaware Water Gap. COMSTOCK

[Top] *East Stroudsburg area high school marching band.* JANET BREGMAN-TANEY
[Bottom] *Open-air concert at Church of the Mountains, Delaware Water Gap.* JANET BREGMAN-TANEY

[Top] *Farmers' Market on Main Street in Stroudsburg.* JANET BREGMAN-TANEY
[Bottom] *Main Street, Stroudsburg.* JANET BREGMAN-TANEY

Indian Head, Delaware Water Gap. JANET BREGMAN-TANEY

Delaware River from Shawnee-on-Delaware. JANET BREGMAN-TANEY

Antelao Restaurant on Main Street in Delaware Water Gap. JANET BREGMAN-TANEY

Shawnee Falls Art Studio in Shawnee-on-Delaware. JANET BREGMAN-TANEY

[Top] *Scenic golfing in the Poconos.* JANET BREGMAN-TANEY
[Bottom] *Driving range in Delaware Water Gap.* JANET BREGMAN-TANEY

[Top] *Playful whitewater rafting.* POCONO MOUNTAINS VACATION BUREAU
[Bottom] *Waterskiing Lake Wallenpaupack.* JIM MCELHOLM/POCONO MOUNTAINS VACATION BUREAU

Shawnee Church. JANET BREGMAN-TANEY

St. Luke's Church on Main Street, Stroudsburg. JANET BREGMAN-TANEY

Fort Depuis. JANET BREGMAN-TANEY

[Top] *The Stroud Mansion.* JANET BREGMAN-TANEY
[Bottom] *The Dutot.* JANET BREGMAN-TANEY

At the annual Balloon Festival, Shawnee-on-Delaware. JANET BREGMAN-TANEY

CONTENTS

CONTENTS

Directory of Maps

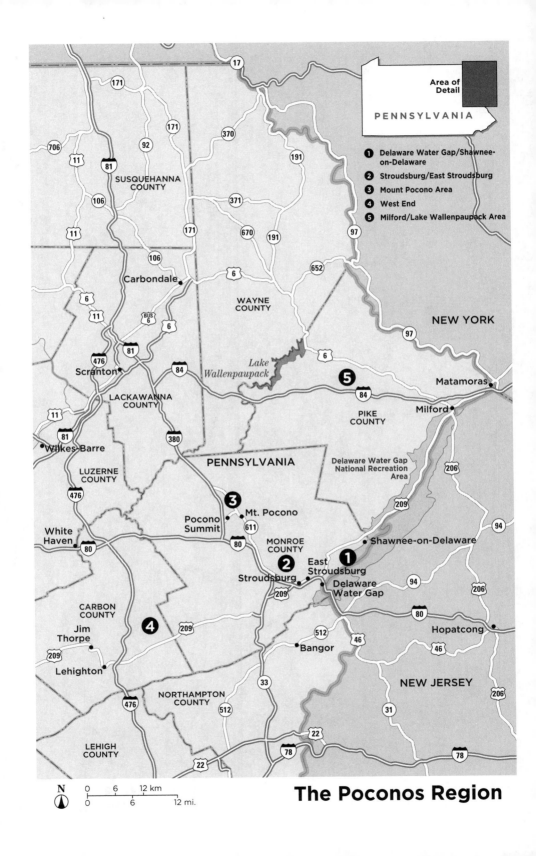

The Poconos Region

PENNSYLVANIA

Area of Detail

1. Delaware Water Gap/Shawnee-on-Delaware
2. Stroudsburg/East Stroudsburg
3. Mount Pocono Area
4. West End
5. Milford/Lake Wallenpaupack Area

NEW YORK

SUSQUEHANNA COUNTY

WAYNE COUNTY

Carbondale

Lake Wallenpaupack

Scranton

LACKAWANNA COUNTY

PIKE COUNTY

Matamoras

Milford

Wilkes-Barre

LUZERNE COUNTY

PENNSYLVANIA

Delaware Water Gap National Recreation Area

White Haven

Pocono Summit

Mt. Pocono

MONROE COUNTY

Shawnee-on-Delaware

East Stroudsburg

Stroudsburg

Delaware Water Gap

CARBON COUNTY

Jim Thorpe

Hopatcong

Lehighton

Bangor

NEW JERSEY

NORTHAMPTON COUNTY

LEHIGH COUNTY

N

0   6   12 km

0   6   12 mi.

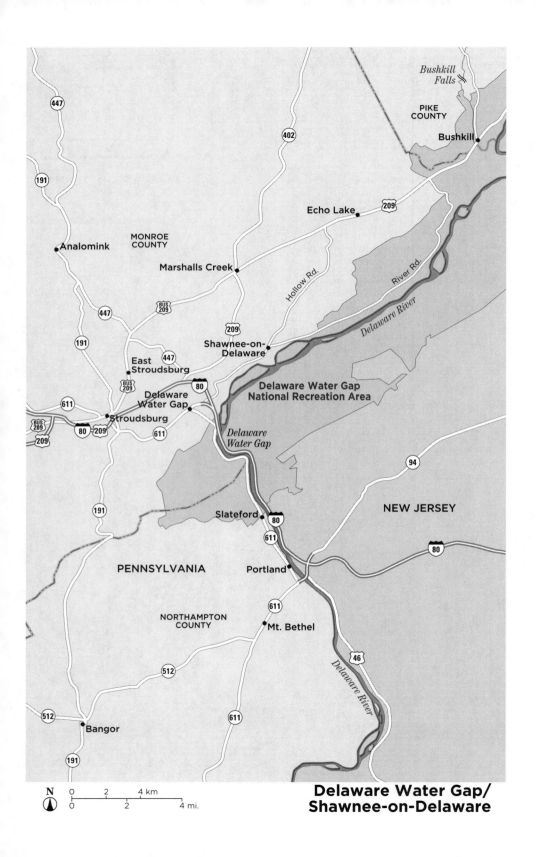

Bushkill
Falls

PIKE
COUNTY

447

Bushkill

191

402

209

Echo Lake

MONROE
COUNTY

Analomink

Marshalls Creek

Hollow Rd.

River Rd.

447

BUS
209

209

Delaware River

Shawnee-on-
Delaware

East
Stroudsburg

447

Delaware Water Gap
National Recreation Area

BUS
209

80

Delaware
Water Gap

611

Stroudsburg

BUS
209

80   209

611

Delaware
Water Gap

94

209

191

Slateford

80

611

NEW JERSEY

PENNSYLVANIA

Portland

80

611

NORTHAMPTON
COUNTY

Mt. Bethel

46

512

Delaware River

512

611

Bangor

191

N   0   2   4 km

           0   2   4 mi.

**Delaware Water Gap/
Shawnee-on-Delaware**

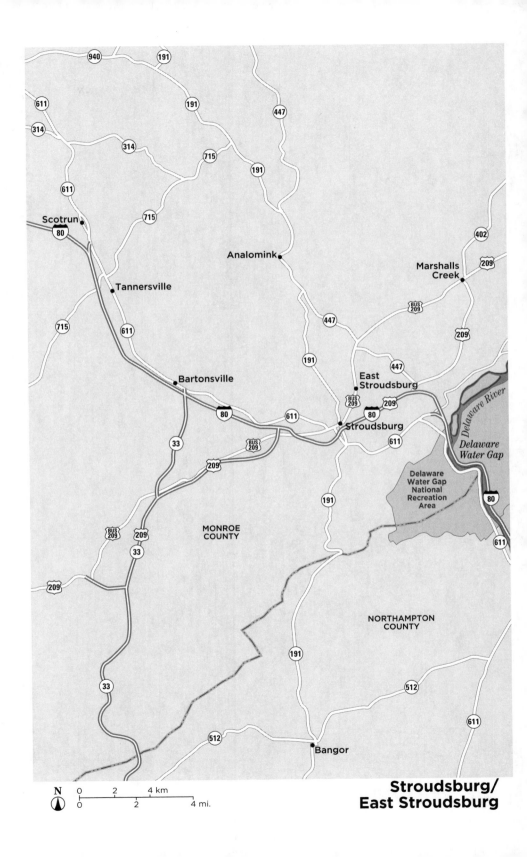

Stroudsburg/
East Stroudsburg

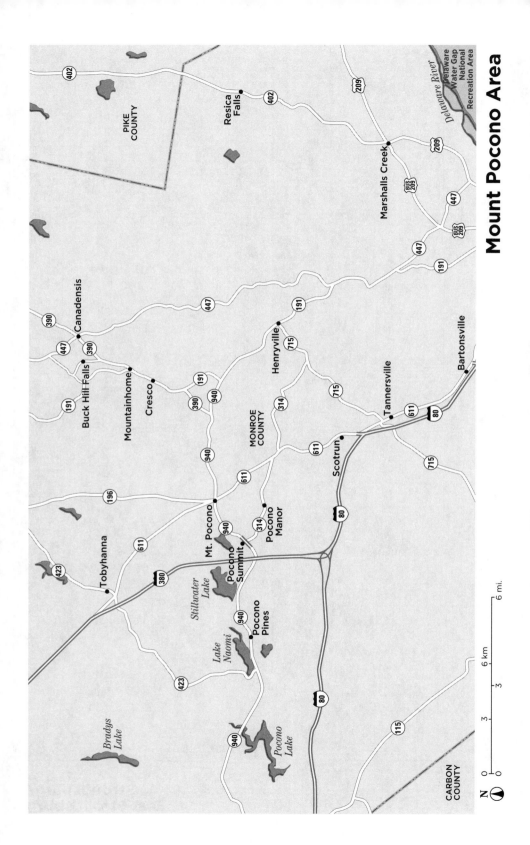

Mount Pocono Area

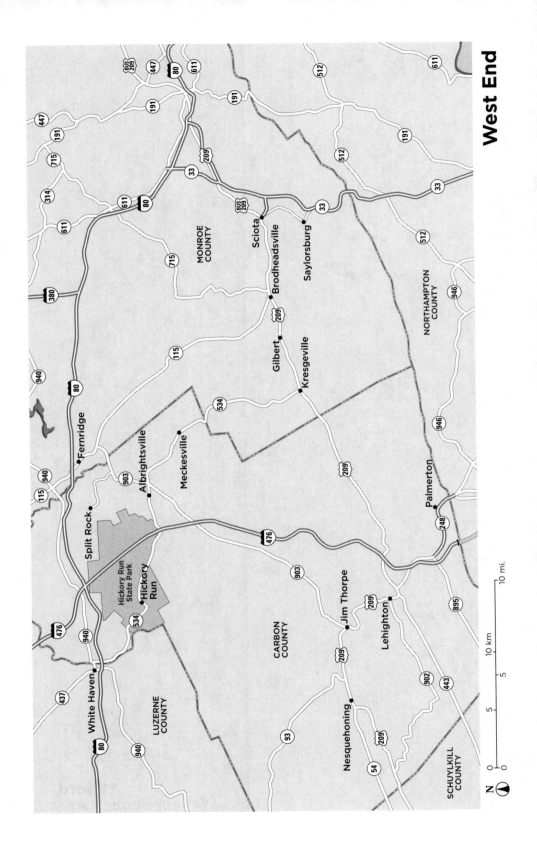

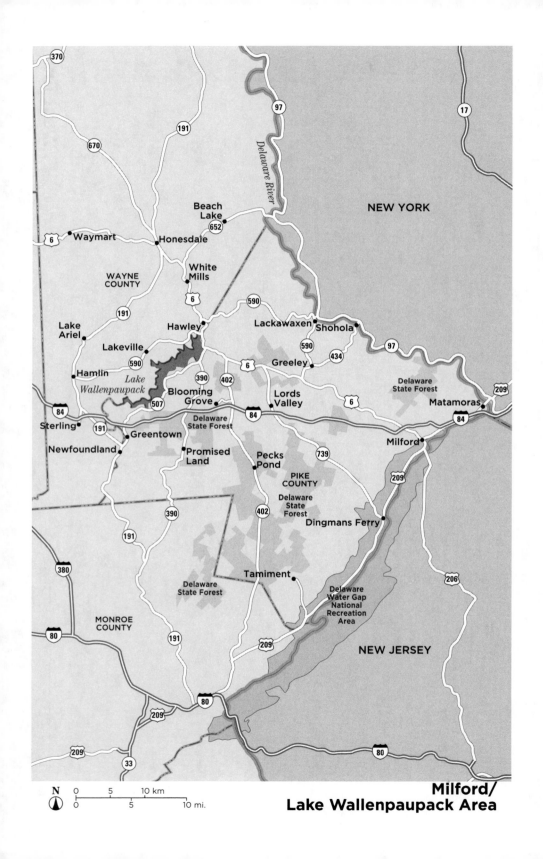

**Milford/
Lake Wallenpaupack Area**

PREFACE

One of the great joys of living in the Poconos comes just prior to Memorial Day, Labor Day, Thanksgiving, or Christmas when friends who live elsewhere ask, "Are you going away for the holidays?" How deliciously smug it is to be able to answer, "I don't have to; I'm already there."

Out-of-towners often say of New York City, "It's a great place to visit, but I wouldn't want to live there." The Poconos are a great place to visit too—a point made clear by the approximately 8 million vacationers who come here each year. But the region also is a great place to live, as its burgeoning population will attest. Sooner or later, everybody wants to come to the Poconos, and with this, the fourth edition of *The Insiders' Guide to the Pocono Mountains,* we hope to show you how to maximize your visit across the widest range of preferences, from those heart-shaped tubs and Jacuzzis for honeymooners, about which you've heard so much, to some things of which you may have heard altogether too little.

The first question a newcomer usually asks is "What and where are the Poconos?" Those questions will be answered in detail in the Overview and in the Getting Here, Getting Around chapters. The short answer is that the Poconos constitute a breathtaking panorama of lakes, streams, forests, rolling farm fields, winding back-country roads, wildlife, nightlife, and the good life in the midst of a literal eruption of arts, crafts, and culture. In short, the Poconos are less a place than a state of mind.

Despite the national spotlight long focused upon the Poconos' still-flourishing honeymoon resorts, there really is a great deal more to do here than luxuriate in private tubs for two.

If you love the outdoors, check out our chapters on Parks; Recreation; In, On, and Around the Water; Fishing and Hunting; Golf; Our Natural World; and Winter Sports. We have horseback riding, swimming, whitewater rafting, canoeing, snowboarding, ice-skating, fishing, golf—both regulation-size and miniature—and virtually any other conceivable outdoor activity you can imagine. Golfers here can play a different course every day for three weeks and still not play them all. Anglers can fish for weeks and never tap all of the hidden hotspots. If you like to camp, the national and state parks provide tremendous opportunities, as do the private campgrounds throughout the area.

If you are artistically inclined, our Arts and Annual Events chapters highlight art galleries, choral and orchestral groups, music festivals, craft festivals, state performances, concerts, and more for your artistic pleasure.

If you like to shop, you'll find our Shopping chapter full of great places to spend some time—and money. We have outlets, antiques shops, crafts stores, collectibles shops, and Christmas shops, even a special teddy bear shop! Many festivals noted in the Annual Events and Festivals chapter offer some shopping opportunities in the way of arts and crafts, not to mention fun-filled activities. And Pocono wineries are great places to buy new wines for your collection.

If you are a history buff, you will find that this area is full of remnants and recollections from days gone by. In our Arts and Culture, History, Attractions, and Native Americans chapters, you will find many places to satisfy your penchant for the past. Annual events and festivals sometimes are tied into historical themes, as are day trips and attractions, so check

Quirks and Colloquialisms

"Up the mountain" refers to the area of the Pocono Plateau—Mt. Pocono, Cresco, Mountainhome, Tobyhanna, Gouldsboro, Skytop, and other villages around there. Up the mountain is usually five degrees colder than down by the river.

"Eastburg" is our way of saying East Stroudsburg.

ESU = East Stroudsburg University, PMC = Pocono Medical Center, our hospital

Because of the rural nature of postal delivery, many homes must suffer two addresses—one, a mailing address to a post office box, though the box sits at a small post office or the community entrance, and a physical address for FedEx and UPS delivery.

out those chapters as well as the cross-referencing that ties the whole thing together.

If you have the kids, we have lots for you to consider. The Kidstuff, Camps and Conference Centers, and Education chapters are great resources to help young people discover the Poconos.

Wondering what we eat here? Great food! Our Restaurants and Nightlife chapters present a fine selection of places where you can discover just how good eating in the Poconos can be. Our Shopping chapter also points out some fun, quick eateries where you can stop while you shop.

If an evening's entertainment is what you seek, we have that too. The Nightlife chapter lists a plethora of places to spend your late-night hours. Arts and Culture also offers nighttime entertainment

opportunities in the way of plays, performances, and art exhibits.

We know that once you visit us, you probably will want to move here, so we've included a Relocation chapter to help you find your dream home in the Poconos. In addition to real estate, it covers retirement, health care, child care, and worship.

And, for help in navigating all of this, our Getting Here, Getting Around chapter tells you where to find the country roads that lead to all the wonderful places about which we have written. We aren't a city; we are the country; and one way to get around is to get lost on our beautiful back roads. So kick back, relax, and enjoy discovering that all these routes intermingle; you can completely circle the Poconos by traveling only the country roads—an exciting prospect if you have some time.

ACKNOWLEDGMENTS

JANET BREGMAN-TANEY

When we took on this book, neither Ken nor I had any inkling of the scope of the assignment and how many hours we would put into exploring the Poconos and singing its praises. Therefore, I am absolutely in awe of the job the authors of the first edition—Leona Adamo Maxwell and Brian Hineline—did on the book. The work they did is simply unimaginable, and a little of their prose remains in this edition. Ken Clark, my co-author, is a joy to work with—I couldn't ask for a better writing partner. I've benefited from his experience, and I've thoroughly enjoyed his company. Thanks also to Ken's wife Dorothy for cheering us both on. I'm thrilled to be able to count Ken and Dorothy among my friends.

There are two kinds of editors, the ones who ruin your fabulous prose, and the ones who make it even better. The editors I have worked with on this book, Dan DeGregory, Pat Von Brook, Shelley Wolf, and Steve Bedney (earlier editions), as well as Liz Taylor (for this edition), have contributed to this book and made it better than we could have alone. I thank them, and I thank the folks at the *Pocono Record,* who originally got me started on this project. Thanks also to Armand Whitehead, who helped with some of the research in the third edition. A huge thank you goes to the Pocono Mountain Vacation Bureau, and especially to Melissa Bilé, who supplied so many of the photos in this book.

Many friends old and new have contributed a great deal to this book. Thanks with all my heart to the following: John McLaughlin and Jamie Downs for talking us into moving to the Poconos, also for Jamie's insights into Pennsylvania Dutch food; Rachel Val Cohen, constant consultant, who knows everything I don't about the Poconos (or so it seems); Bridget Kelly, one of the most dedicated educators I've ever met, for her thoughts on the local education scene; all the winemakers—Bonnie Pysher, Sid Butler, Mary Sorrenti, and Dominic Strohlein—who spent so much time with me and poured so much wine; Jack Richardson for his insights on contemporary Native Americans; Leslie Smoke for her ideas on day trips in New York; Scott Leeds, the voice on the tape at the National Park Service, for finding answers to all the weird questions I posed; and the many other Pocono people who have been so helpful and so kind to me.

Most importantly, I want to thank my husband, Peter Taney, and my daughter Joy. They put up with a messy house and a mom who had no time to cook or swim or take a walk. They never complained about being dragged along on one of my forays (in fact, they claimed they enjoyed themselves), and they happily ate endless meals with me at restaurants across the region. For all the support, suggestions, and good cheer they gave me, thank you.

KEN CLARK

At the risk of sounding like a trombone-tooting charter member of the Mutual Admiration Society when this appears next to kudos offered by my colleague, Janet Bregman-Taney, I must, of necessity, place her at the top of my thank-you list. I can say with confidence that she would walk tall in the company of the best reporters and writers with whom I have been privileged to work in the highest ranks of daily journalism for the past 45 years. One could not ask for a better companion in the adventure involved in putting together a detailed guide to just about everything worth doing, seeing,

ACKNOWLEDGMENTS

experiencing, and enjoying in a region like the Poconos.

There are, of course, a lot of people who must be thanked in any endeavor such as the one in which Janet and I have just been engaged. Jennifer Call at the Pocono Mountains Vacation Bureau is one of them. I salute her for research above and beyond the call of duty—always done cheerfully, accurately, and without complaint. Laura Goss at the Pocono Arts Council is another, as are Kristina Anzini at Jacob Stroud Corporation for Downtown Development, and Randy Turner and Scott Leeds, at the National Park Service, who patiently filled me in on every aspect of recreational opportunity in our great outdoors. Thanks also are due Louis Herfurth, at the Wacky Worm bait and tackle shop in Gilbert, who regaled me with the lore of field and stream, and to Jack Weaver, of the Pennsylvania Game Commission's Northeast Region, who patiently filled me in on the minutia of the law regarding hunting and trapping. Appreciation is also due Kerry Messerle, manager of the Fish and Boat Commission's Northeast Region, who taught me all I now know about lakes in the Poconos, the fish that live there, and laws governing the use of both. I also must honor Betty Lou McBride at the Old Jail Museum in Jim Thorpe for her colorful insight into the infamous Mollie Maguires, some of whom were hanged in what now is her establishment, and Janet Mishkin, at the Monroe County Historical Society, for guidance in research of the Walking Purchase that dispossessed the Lenape Indians and opened the Poconos to white settlers in the 18th century.

Most of all, however, I want to thank my wife, Dorothy, for putting up with me and my "deadline mentality," not only for the duration of the current project, but also for a lifetime in pursuit of the next story. Hers, as I'm sure she would assure you, is the greatest burden of all.

There are many others to whom I have neglected to render thanks due simply for the warmth and civility with which they greeted me in their shops and restaurants during my quest for information. If you are one of them, please accept my apologies. You know who you are; know also that you are appreciated.

HOW TO USE THIS BOOK

This book is designed to be your owner's manual to the Poconos. Whether your time in our region is measured in days or years, you will find here all you need to know to visit or reside in one of the most desirable areas in the northeastern United States.

Do not feel daunted by the hundreds of pages. This is a guide, not a novel. You do not need to read it cover to cover in one sitting. Our book is intended to be used every day—strap it to your bike, throw it in the back of the car, read it in your hotel room, put it in your backpack, take it in your canoe. Use it and abuse it as you see fit.

Each chapter exists independently. Need a good Japanese restaurant? Just fly past the History and Accommodations chapters, and you can find one in the Restaurants chapter. Want to know how Pike County got its name (it has nothing to do with fish)? Turn back to the History chapter. But note that as you read the chapter specific to your desire or need of the moment, you will find it cross-referenced to other chapters calculated to pique your interest. A listing in the "Fine Arts and Crafts Galleries" section of the Arts and Culture chapter, for instance, might correlate with references to shopping or galleries. The Restaurants chapter also may lead you to Accommodations where applicable, and the chapter on Native Americans might refer you back to an entry in the History chapter.

We hope you will start by reading a chapter that suits your initial interest and then turn to other parts of the book. Total content is designed to inform those unfamiliar with the Poconos and supplement the knowledge of longtime residents.

Newcomers to the Poconos might want to begin with the History, Overview, or Relocation chapter to familiarize themselves with the towns and lifestyles of the different parts of the region.

The Poconos cover a four-county area stretching from Wayne, which borders New York State to the north, all the way through Pike and Monroe Counties to Carbon County, where true mountains spill their sparkling rivers into the Lehigh Valley to the south. Individual subdivisions of each region have their own distinct characteristics. If shopping is your goal, you'll want to check out the factory outlets at Tannersville; antiques are found all over the West End; the burgeoning artistic community is primarily in Stroudsburg, East Stroudsburg, and Delaware Water Gap; and anglers will want to cast their lures into the Delaware River or Lake Wallenpaupack (see appropriate chapters for details). For this reason, we have broken the geographic area down into the following subregions: Delaware Water Gap/Shawnee-on-Delaware; Stroudsburg/East Stroudsburg; Mount Pocono area; West End, with Carbon County included for the sake of brevity; and the Milford/Lake Wallenpaupack area, which covers the northernmost section of the Poconos.

Like most of the rural political subdivisions in Pennsylvania, the Poconos are infamous for the lack of signs. Most villages seem loath to admit their identity to the outsider, almost reflecting the attitude that if you don't know where you are, you shouldn't have come here in the first place. To make matters worse, "city limits" often exceed the "city" by miles. You may find yourself wandering amid open fields with scarcely a farmhouse in sight, and still be 2 or 3 miles inside Lehighton or Brodheadsville. Any hostile implications, however, are quickly erased by the people, who are among the friendliest on earth. If you are lost—and if you're a newcomer, you will be, often—never hesitate to stop and ask for directions. Meanwhile, keep the maps at the front of the book close at hand and refer to them frequently. And don't forget to check out the tidbits of insiders' knowledge (look for the ▣).

While we have spent long days and nights driving, talking, dining, sampling, and exploring, it's possible we have overlooked some worthwhile spot that you will discover. If you find something you believe should be included in future editions of this book, we'd love to hear from you.

If you have a suggestion or comment regarding our book, please write The Globe Pequot Press, Reader Response, Editorial Department, P.O. Box 480, Guilford, CT 06437. You can also send us e-mail at editorial@GlobePequot.com.

HISTORY 🏛

The Pocono Mountains, which really are not mountains at all, constitute a paradise of rolling green golf courses, sparkling lakes and streams in deep summer-green or autumn-painted forests, and rural landscapes that are living postcards. Ski resorts lure thousands to their snowy slopes every winter, while other resorts of romantic persuasion lure honeymooners to their heart- and champagne glass–shaped bathtubs in every season.

But the paradise of the Poconos was born in a bloodbath, and if local folklore bears any measure of truth, the ghosts of its dark and brutal past still walk the hills and haunt certain houses built when life was charged not with vacation joy but with terror and death. Between a series of Indian massacres in the 18th century and the emergence 100 years later in the coal fields of an Irish terrorist gang called the Mollie Maguires, the tale of the Poconos makes the more storied opening of the American West, with its mythic gunslingers and square-jawed lawmen in Dodge City and Tombstone, look like a lawn party.

The Pocono region was a paradise unsullied by the nightmare to come when Nicholas DePuis, a French Huguenot seeking a place to practice his religion in peace, arrived in 1725. Like William Penn, who founded Penn's Woods, the region that was to become the Commonwealth of Pennsylvania, on a land grant from the King of England, DePuis was a gentle man living among peaceful Native Americans from whom he bought 3,000 acres of land along the river north of the Delaware Water Gap. Though there is no record that he actually gave anything to the Lenape Indians for the land, he was welcomed and lived there in peace with his wife Wyntie Roosa DePuis for many years, siring four sons and five daughters in a large house bounded by an apple orchard and a grist mill. The land was fertile, the crops abundant, and the Lenape friendly. Naturally, it could not last.

THE WALKING PURCHASE

When William Penn died, administration of the vast, barely settled territory north of Philadelphia fell to his son, Thomas. While the son inherited the mantle of governor, he did not seem to have been in the will where his father's legendary personal integrity was concerned. Land-hungry English and German settlers were coming to the New World in droves, and given the chaotic nature of the frontier, no one was sure who owned what part of lands occupied by Native Americans for 10,000 years. DePuis, the original European settler of the Poconos, eventually had to re-buy the land he already had bought once, this time from an entrepreneur named William Allen who had purchased 10,000 acres—including the DePuis homestead—from a group of Philadelphia proprietors who claimed ownership of the entire territory. Unfortunately for the Native Americans, they were divided by centuries of intertribal warfare, and powerful tribes of the Iroquois confederacy thought nothing of selling out the interests of lesser tribes, such as the Lenape, that they had subjugated. The internecine maneuvering played right into the hands of Thomas Penn.

He wanted more land to develop, and he wanted the Native people out of it, but he was more of a conman than a conqueror. Indian hegemony of the Poconos already had been endangered in 1736, when chiefs of what was known as the Six Nations, along with the Susquehannas and the Lenape, were persuaded to deed to Pennsylvania officials a vast block of land drained by the Susquehanna River. The arrangements ignored a previous treaty under which the Shawnee had been given permission to live on some of the land—a sleight that put the fierce tribe in French ranks against the English in the bloody French and Indian wars to come. To complicate matters, William Penn had earlier signed a treaty with the Native people calling for sale of a tract of their land already encroached upon by white farmers north of the Blue Mountains. The acreage, set by what would come to be known as the Walking Purchase, was to be established by the distance a man could walk in a day and a half, with a line then drawn from that terminus east to the Delaware River.

William Penn never got around to implementing the agreement, but in 1737 his son resurrected it as a means of taking the Poconos away from the Lenape. These Native people, who already had ceded Bucks County, south of the Poconos, were led to believe the new line established by the Walking Purchase treaty would end in the vicinity of the Delaware Water Gap and never actually impinge upon the Pocono region. Such might have been the case had Penn hired just one walker to set the boundary. Instead of one, however, he hired a team of what today probably would be regarded as marathon runners. That way, he figured, even if most of them dropped out along the way, the last to fold would gain the greatest mileage and hence, the largest territory. Penn offered $5.00 and 500 acres of land to the one who prevailed and walked the farthest.

The walk was launched from beneath a chestnut tree near Wrightstown in Bucks County at sunrise, September 19, 1737. By nightfall all walkers save two— Edward Marshall and James Yeates—had dropped out. Marshall and Yeates forged on until early on the second day when Yeates, exhausted by the pace, quit the trek, leaving Marshall. Marshall reportedly ran part of the way, to finish alone on Big Pocono Mountain near what now is the town of Jim Thorpe at the present Monroe–Carbon county line. In the time allotted,

Marshall had covered 68.6 miles—twice the distance the Lenape had been led to believe would be achieved. The line was drawn not directly east, as agreed, but northeast to the Delaware River, thus ending at Lackawaxen, some 40 miles north of the Delaware Water Gap. The land grab—for it can be called nothing else— legally evicted the Lenape from all of what was to become Monroe County and a large portion of the future counties of Carbon and Pike.

The Lenape, belatedly realizing that they had been duped by the wily governor, cried foul. For several years thereafter, legal appeals to the commonwealth went nowhere, and when finally they were ordered to leave their ancestral homes, they took to the warpath. For the next decade, in massacre after massacre, white farm families throughout the region were subjected to wholesale butchery. At one point 500 refugees from the bloodbath poured into the villages of Easton, Nazareth, and Bethlehem south of the Poconos. An early chronicler wrote, "They came like hound-driven sheep, a motley crowd of men, women, and children . . . with clothes not fit to be seen by mankind . . . and some with scarce a sufficiency of rags to cover their nakedness."

Retaliation finally came under the direction of a Philadelphia printer named Benjamin Franklin, who was called upon to plan a defense of the northern frontier. He constructed a string of forts across the region and sent a contingent of 500 to 600 men to Upper Smithfield township north of Shawnee-on-Delaware to battle the marauders. The militiamen's pay was a scant $6.00 a month plus subsistence, but the lure to battle was enhanced by a bonus of $40.00 for every Native scalp collected.

But if the Lenape were out to kill white people in general, they had in mind one man in particular. Edward Marshall, the champion walker whose sprint had handed the Poconos to the white man, never was to be forgotten or forgiven. In 1748 a band of warriors ambushed and killed his son, sending the family fleeing into New Jersey. Eight years later, however, the Marshalls returned, only to learn that the Lenape in the region where Edward had earned his 500 acres had long memories. The family was singled out for attack again, and this time, the war party shot Marshall's daughter and killed and scalped his wife. Marshall, who gave his name to the present village of Marshalls Creek, had many more narrow escapes before the rampage was ended by a 1758 peace treaty brokered by the Quakers. He eventually died of natural causes—something of an unnatural way to go in those days.

In 1763, with a horde of settlers pouring into the region, the Native people rose once again. The new governor, John Penn, son of the architect of the Walking Purchase, issued a proclamation forbidding newcomers to violate Indian treaty rights, but it was ignored by the land-greedy pioneers, who thought no more of evicting a Native American than getting rid of a groundhog or a raccoon. As a result, Native war parties once again took the field, prompting Penn to post a new bounty on their scalps—$134 for that of a Native male and $30 for the scalp of a woman. Extra pay was offered for kidnapped children. The local battle ended with the end of the overall French and Indian wars before any of the blood money could be paid.

GROWTH AND EARLY INDUSTRY

With subsidence of the Indian war terror, a measure of peace and vigorous prosperity came to the Poconos. Out of a totally agrarian landscape, industry began to emerge. The War of 1812 fostered a new industry, the manufacture of firearms. A factory at Kunkletown turned out weapons for the American army from 1812 through 1830. Ice harvesting from the region's many lakes became a winter staple; vast fields of hard, clean-burning,

anthracite coal were opened, largely to fuel railroads spreading west, and following construction of one of the first tanneries, by the Stroud family in Stroudsburg, the industry boomed, giving its name to Tannersville, which became its center.

The tanners' need of certain tree barks as a source of the acid used in tanning hides, coupled with a growing demand for lumber spurred both by a local building boom and the popularity of such plentiful hardwoods as oak, beech, maple, and hickory, resulted in the virtual deforestation of the Poconos, as trees from the once magnificent primeval forest were cut, lashed into rafts, and floated to markets down the Delaware River.

On a raw and essentially roadless frontier, waterways offered the only ready access to distant urban markets, and Philip Hone, for whom Honesdale is named, took advantage of the fact by becoming a canal owner. With growth in demand for the coal being mined in Carbon County and surrounding areas, he established the western terminus for Hone's Delaware & Hudson Canal Company in 1826. Coal was brought to Honesdale from mines in the Lackawanna Valley by gravity railroad for transport by canal boat to New York. In 1855 and 1856 more than a million tons of coal passed through Honesdale on canal boats, each of which carried approximately 130 tons of the precious carbon.

One of the earliest means of crossing the Delaware River was via a ferry built in 1735 near what now is Dingmans Ferry. The privately owned bridge linking New Jersey and Pennsylvania at Dingmans Ferry stands at the site of the original connector. People have crossed the river at this point, either by bridge or ferry, for more than 260 years. At least eight other ferries operated on the Delaware between Delaware Water Gap and Port Jervis, New York. All had been replaced by bridges by the early 1900s.

As the area grew, new counties and townships were sliced from old established precincts. Of the four counties that make up the bulk of the area, Wayne was first to be formed, on March 21, 1798, from a slice of Northampton County. The county was named after Revolutionary War general "Mad Anthony" Wayne. Pike County, named for Col. Zebulon Pike, a hero of the War of 1812 who gained later immortality by giving his name to a mountain peak in Colorado, was established on March 26, 1814, from land in Wayne County.

Monroe County, named for President James Monroe, was formed on April 1, 1836, from land taken from Pike and Northampton Counties. Northampton and Monroe Counties contributed the land for Carbon County on March 13, 1843.

THE MOLLY MAGUIRES

Jim Thorpe, Carbon County's seat, originally existed as two towns, Mauch Chunk and East Mauch Chunk. The community merged in 1954 and was renamed in honor of the famed athlete, who, though he never lived there, is buried there.

The town, with its aura of Victorian charm, sits in a deep V-shaped valley and has justifiably been dubbed "The Switzerland of America." But thanks to its location in the center of the Carbon County coalfields, its early history presented a much darker metaphor. After a century of peace, terror and bloodshed once again loomed over the Pocono region with the emergence of a murderous gang of Irish immigrant cutthroats known as the Mollie Maguires.

The secretive terrorist group, named for a Celtic woman short of temper and swift to murder, was formed in Ireland to strike back at hated English landlords who kept the peasants on their lands at starva- tion levels of poverty. Many Irish immigrants were coal miners, and when 19th-century coal barons started acting like English landlords, they were begging the Mollies to be born again on American soil.

Certainly any coal miner of the day earned more grievances than pay for a day's work. With no federal regulation and a fierce anti-labor union bias on the part of courts and Congress, mine owners were a law unto themselves. By a collusion that would have landed them in prison today, they kept the price of coal artificially inflated while paying the men who dug it out of the earth for them as little as 50 cents a day. Then, by restricting the miners' commerce to company-owned stores and driving them ever deeper into debt for the bare necessities of life, the barons reduced them to virtual slavery.

The Mollie Maguires fought repression with violence, targeting for assassination anyone connected with mine management, from local pit bosses to general managers, threatening even the barons themselves. Through sheer terror they controlled local elections, putting their own candidates into governmental offices ranging from school districts and county commissions to law enforcement and even local judgeships. So great did their power become, that from 1862 through 1877, they burned homes and businesses and murdered their enemies with impunity.

The Mollies loved to warn their chosen victims, whose ranks soon were expanded to include law enforcement officers and even people simply disliked by the rank and file of a terrorist cell, of impending death with "coffin notices." These were notes bearing crude drawings of skulls and crossbones and coffins, with or without corpses, giving the condemned a choice: Get out of town or die. A sample of one such notice, enlarged and on display now at the Mollie Maguires Pub in Jim Thorpe (see our Nightlife chapter), put it this way: "Henry Morgan your [sic] a marked man. Prepare your [coffin drawing] at once or else leave this place. Your life is doomed and youll [sic] die like a dog if you stay here any longer as mine boss. Take warning."

It is not recorded whether Henry Morgan got out of town or fell, as did so many of his colleagues, at the hands of the Irish assassins. So great did fear of the Mollie Maguires become, that they frequently carried out their assassinations by daylight in the presence of scores of witnesses who later could be guaranteed to testify that they had seen nothing. Jack Kehoe, a prominent terrorist leader, once boasted that if ever he were convicted of murder, "the old man up at Harrisburg," which was to say the governor, never would allow him to be hanged.

But hubris alone was not enough to keep terror in power. The excesses of the Mollie Maguires finally turned public sympathy—initially fostered by the excesses of the mine owners—against them. In 1873 the famed Pinkerton Detective Agency of Philadelphia was called in to put an end to the siege. A young Irish detective, James McParlan, went undercover, infiltrated the group, and eventually brought them down with his testimony.

With the organization broken, its exposed members went en masse to the gallows, but one of them left a haunting calling card at the Carbon County jail in Jim Thorpe. The record is unclear whether it was Alexander Campbell, who was hanged for murder in 1877, or Thomas Fisher, who followed him a year later, who left the mysterious handprint on the wall of cell No. 17, in which both men had been held prior to execution. According to legend, one of them, upon being led to the gallows, defiantly slapped his hand against the cell wall, proclaiming that the resulting print would stand forever as proof of his innocence. Over the years dozens of coats of paint and plaster have covered the handprint, but always it bleeds through, and it is there now in a jail that has become a museum of another dark and dangerous era in the Poconos (see our Attractions chapter).

TOURISM, THE FLOOD OF '55, AND TOCKS ISLAND

As the 19th century rolled toward its conclusion, tourism gradually replaced farming and industry as the backbone of the Poconos' economy. Delaware Water Gap became a visitors' mecca, with a half-million traveling from eastern urban centers coming by train every year to stay all summer in more than 20 grand hotels. As Delaware Water Gap filled up, wealthy summer visitors looked elsewhere in the region for luxury lodging, giving rise to the construction of such accommodations as the Inn at Buck Hill Falls, the Inn at Shawnee, and Skytop Lodge. (See our Accommodations chapter.)

With tourism came entertainment on a national scale. Stars ranging from John Philip Sousa through Enrico Caruso to Fanny Brice played Delaware Water Gap. Fred Waring, leader of the famed Pennsylvanians, made Shawnee-on-Delaware his headquarters, broadcasting his shows, first on radio and later on television, from Worthington Hall, now the Shawnee Playhouse.

At that point the Poconos were well into the 20th century, but despite the passing of the bad old days, the region still was not immune to disaster, as residents learned during the week of August 13, 1955, when back-to-back hurricanes dumped 25 inches of rain on the region. More than 200 people, 80 in Monroe County alone, died in the resulting flood, as homes and businesses were inundated and bridges washed away.

Broadhead Creek roared over its banks on the morning of August 19, sending its waters through Canadensis and Analomink, where 38 people were killed at Camp Davis. All bridges leading to East Stroudsburg were washed away, cutting off the town and the hospital. Thirty-two people died in homes in the Lincoln Avenue "Flats" area now occupied by the Pocono Plaza and Wal-Mart. Survivors were evacuated from attic windows into rowboats.

The Switchback Railroad: America's First Roller Coaster

Josiah White, founder of the Lehigh Coal & Navigation Company, designed and invented many devices for the operation of his canal and mines. As his business prospered during the 1820s, White needed a more efficient system to transport his coal from the mines in Summit Hill to the Lehigh River and the canal docks at Mauch Chunk, now Jim Thorpe.

White's solution became his most fabled enterprise—the Switchback Railroad. It was the second railroad in the United States, and many people consider it to be the first and longest roller coaster ever built.

The 9-mile Gravity Road was completed in April 1827. Ten wagons, each carrying 1.5 tons of coal, traveled down Summit Hill powered entirely by gravity. A brake attached to a cable was the only means of control. Mules pulled the empty cars back up the hill and then rode down with the coal in a car of their own. With the mules' help, the trip up Summit Hill took three hours; the gravity-assisted descent lasted 35 minutes.

The Industrial Revolution of the 19th century increased the demand for coal, especially in New York City and Philadelphia, so White looked to increase the productivity of his railroad.

In the 1840s, the old track was expanded to become a continuous 18-mile figure eight, thus allowing empty cars to travel back to the mines while, simultaneously, full ones descended to the canal.

Two inclined planes, at Mount Jefferson and Mount Pisgah, were used to transport the cars up the sides of the mountains. Stationary steam engines at the top of each plane supplied power. Cars were pushed uphill by a "safety car," which was attached to a steam engine by bands of Swedish steel. The rest of the trip, approximately 17 miles, was powered by gravity. The entire journey took about an hour and 20 minutes.

This wild, scenic ride began to catch the eyes of tourists. Soon, all afternoon trips were reserved for passengers (coal was hauled in the morning). Locals used

The worst flood in the history of the Poconos destroyed 42 highway bridges, 17 railroad bridges, most water mains, and telephone lines. Electric power was cut, and more than 20,000 homes were lost. But that was not the full extent of the damage. Publicity generated by the disaster dropped tourist occupancy rates from 96 percent to 20 percent immediately

after the storm. An estimated 8,500 people saw the flood wash their jobs away as damages in Monroe County hit $28.5 million. Pike County suffered $5.3 million in damages and Wayne County $3.3 million.

Rebuilding efforts, emphasizing flood control for the future, resulted in a fiasco called the Tocks Island Dam project. The 1962 plan, purportedly designed to curb

the Switchback as a means of commuting between Mauch Chunk and Summit Hill. The return trip became legendary for its remarkable views and fast pace, with speeds exceeding 50 miles per hour.

By the mid-1870s, major railroads began to service the mines; the Switchback became exclusively a tourist attraction. Rail excursions from nearby cities were scheduled to coincide with its operating hours. Among the highlights of the trip were the trestle spanning the ravine at Mount Pisgah, the views from the cliffs and summits, the entrance to the Hacklebernie Mines, and the Indian Stairway, reportedly built by Native Americans as a means of crossing the mountains.

The Switchback became the second-leading tourist destination in America, behind only Niagara Falls. It attracted 75,000 people annually, each of whom paid $1.00 for the ride. On holidays and other occasions, trains departed every six minutes.

Noteworthy riders included Thomas Edison, who marveled at the technological wonder and pronounced that he would not change any part of its operation. Another visitor fashioned an amusement park ride after the Switchback—the roller coaster. Tourism soon competed with coal as the region's primary industry.

The Switchback prospered until ridership steadily declined during the 1920s. The popularity of the automobile hastened the ride's demise, and the Great Depression sealed its fate. The last car ran October 31, 1933. On September 2, 1937, the entire operation was sold as scrap for $18,000. The metal eventually ended up in Japan, which was improving its military preparedness.

Restoration efforts occasionally were discussed over the next few decades, but none materialized. In 1986, however, the Switchback Gravity Railroad Foundation was formed. Studies have concluded that complete restoration is feasible and environmentally safe. (Currently, most of the old track beds are used as hiking and cross-country skiing trails.) This nonprofit organization is raising funds to bring back this amazing part of history for future generations of tourists to enjoy.

To learn more about the Switchback Railroad and to stay abreast of the Switchback Gravity Railroad Foundation's progress, go to www.switchbackgravity rr.org/index.html.

floodwaters and provide hydroelectric energy, called for construction of a dam on the Delaware River north of Shawnee. The result would be a lake stretching all the way to Milford. The government purchased thousands of acres of land both on Pennsylvania and New Jersey sides of the river and forced residents to relocate. Once-thriving small towns, such as Bushkill, lost their business districts to the government and never have recovered economically. Resorts, farms, and boarding houses were bought up and demolished, and at one point, long-haired protesters (remember the "hippies" of the '60s?) moved into evacuated buildings, vowing to hurl their bodies into the paths of bulldozers to stop the project. When it was over, many of their ranks settled in and just outside the area.

The dam never was constructed, not because of the demonstrators but because the lake it was to form finally was deemed not viable. But to this day, foundations of demolished houses, curbs that once lined village streets, and even flowers planted by homeowners who once landscaped their yards remain there as ghostly reminders of communities killed by "progress." On the upside, from an environmental standpoint at least, land evacuated by the project became the Delaware Water Gap National Recreation Area in 1965. Today the once-settled area is gradually reverting to nature as a haven for hundreds of species of migrating songbirds. But many of those who were forced from their homes to provide it still view the scene with bitterness.

With the advent of the 21st century, a measure of déjà vu has come to the Poconos. Once again hordes of settlers are pouring in from New York and New Jersey as white-collar workers, weary of life in urban pressure cookers, turn the region into a bedroom community. And once again longtime residents, finding themselves in the position of Native Americans nearly 300 years ago, view the encroachment with alarm, as the well-paid urbanites drive property values and taxes upward. But for all the residual resentment, at least there is a difference.

This time nobody is taking scalps.

DELAWARE WATER GAP/ SHAWNEE-ON-DELAWARE

Antoine Dutot, a French refugee from Santo Domingo who came to the Poconos, bought land and founded Dutotsburg in 1793, preceded the first tourist by 17 years, but he still may be regarded as the father of the vacation industry that dominates the area economy today.

Dutot, whose name is no longer attached to Delaware Water Gap, which is what his town subsequently was rechris-

tened, started construction on Kittatinny House, the area's first resort hotel, in 1829. By the time it was finished in 1833, it could accommodate 25 guests, and an expansion in 1884 raised capacity to 275.

Early access to the town was provided by a ferry across the Delaware River to a wagon road, and the first vacationers, who actually arrived in 1820, stayed in private homes. Their presence may have inspired Dutot's construction of Kittatinny, which has long since burned down, leaving only parts of its old foundation visible on Resort Point.

Resort Point offers a panoramic view of the Water Gap and the river that carved it over the millennia. Early tour guides called it one of the 15 most spectacular scenic wonders of the nation. The only major changes from the early days have been the addition of the highway (Interstate 80) and the toll bridge that now connects Pennsylvania and New Jersey.

Kittatinny House had a rival, Water Gap House, farther up the mountain, but it, too, burned to the ground—a fate suffered by many of the original hotels in the area, which were constructed of wood, easily set ablaze in kitchens using wood or coal as fuel. The hotels were also too far from readily available water supplies for the firemen to save. But for every resort hotel that burned, others were constructed, and as the 20th century approached, a half-million people a year were visiting the area, with a choice of more than 20 luxurious places in which to stay. Early recreational activities included burro rides, scenic walks, golf, boating on nearby Lake Lenape (now a stagnant pond near the entrance of the Appalachian Trail), steam boat rides on the Delaware, and swimming in the river. Soon a large wooden pier was installed. Tourists also could take a trolley to Stroudsburg and East Stroudsburg.

President Theodore Roosevelt vacationed in Delaware Water Gap August 2, 1910, and stayed at Water Gap House, raising the town's profile to a national level.

The Delaware, Lackawanna, and Western railroad station was the point of arrival for most tourists. Built in 1853, the station was once the scene of constant activity, with hundreds regularly arriving and departing. Today the station is in need of restoration. The Lackawanna Chapter of the Railway and Locomotive Historical Society has been raising money to that end and has even mentioned the possibility of an excursion train.

At the heart of downtown Delaware Water Gap was Hauser's, a large souvenir store; the Central House, today home to the Deer Head Inn's outstanding live jazz concerts; and the Castle Inn, which is still the headquarters for renowned band leader Fred Waring's publishing enterprise, Shawnee Press.

The Castle Inn became the region's central entertainment showcase in the 1900s. John Philip Sousa's band performed there for a crowd of 875 on August 20, 1912. He was followed through the years by Enrico Caruso, Fanny Brice, and a host of other stars of their eras. Fred Waring bought it in 1952 and used the space to rehearse his Pennsylvanians as well as to run summer workshops for youths and for music teachers. The main concert hall of the Castle Inn burned down, torched by an arsonist who tried to eliminate many buildings in the area, but today, the beat goes on. An open-air stage has been erected as the site of the town's annual jazz festival. World-famous jazz performers Phil Woods and Urbie Green live in the village, and such other jazz greats as Phil Markowitz, John Coates, and Bob Dorough (jazz singer and composer for ABC television's *School House Rock*) are regulars at the festival, which runs the weekend after Labor Day.

STROUDSBURG/EAST STROUDSBURG

The county seat of Monroe County, Stroudsburg was founded by Jacob Stroud, who laid out the town in 1799. The house he built on Main Street for his son John is known as Stroud Mansion, now the headquarters of the Monroe County Historical Association.

One of the earliest hotels was the Stroudsburg House, 700 Main Street, which was built in 1833. A hotel has occupied that corner ever since. After modernizing the façade in 1971, the owners of the former Penn Stroud Hotel reopened as the Penn Stroud Hilton. The hotel became the Best Western Pocono Inn in 1981.

Another early, large Main Street hotel was the Indian Queen. The first automobile to visit the Poconos stopped there August 23, 1899. Mellon Bank has assumed its spot in the business district. A portion of the Indian Queen still stands next door. The national variety store chain Newberry's was founded in the town, but, pulled down by competition from shopping malls and superstores, the original anchor store closed for good in 1997. Today a Dollar General operates in part of the original building. Stroudsburg possesses a beautiful traditional main thoroughfare filled with boutiques, eateries, nightclubs, banks, and retail stores.

Stagecoach routes were scattered throughout the Poconos in the late 1800s. The fare from Brodheadsville to Stroudsburg was 35 cents in 1889. Gone since 1928, trolleys and streetcars once commuted regularly between Stroudsburg and East Stroudsburg. In 1870 mules pulled passenger cars through Stroudsburg, but were replaced by a steam engine that was used from 1892 to 1902. After that, electric cars traveled through Stroudsburg, East Stroudsburg, and Delaware Water Gap, and during the 1920s Crystal Street in East Stroudsburg was crowded with streetcars, trolleys, and automobiles. Trolleys were discontinued in 1928 because the increased automobile traffic made them dangerous, and the tracks were removed by 1930.

Rail travelers arrived in East Stroudsburg at the Delaware, Lackawanna, and Western Station, built in 1856. This significant structure was restored and opened to the public as the Dansbury Depot Restaurant. (See our Restaurants chapter.)

Train service peaked in 1900 with the arrival of the legendary Phoebe Snow, "the finest passenger transportation vehicle in the world," according to advertising. Its comfortable sleeping cars and lavish dining and lounge cars were well publicized. D. L. & W advertising pictured a woman stylishly dressed in white to show how clean and sootless anthracite coal was when burned in locomotive fire boxes.

Fronting the station, Crystal Street businesses thrived, and several hotels were successful. One, the Lackawanna Hotel, still operates as a bar and coffee shop with small apartments on the upper floors. The Lackawanna is the bar with the strange sticks in the window. Called boom-bas, the sticks are a Northeast Pennsylvania instrument probably of German origin, played to polka music (cymbals and a tambourine built onto the sticks provide most of the sound). Drop by on a weekend night, and if you ask and you're lucky, Stanley, the owner, will give a demonstration. (See our Nightlife chapter.)

A coal station and turntable for locomotives were on Stokes Avenue in East Stroudsburg until 1950. As winter sports became popular, a special "ski train" was added on weekends in the 1930s, and the stations in East Stroudsburg and Cresco were jammed with tourists carrying skis. The D. L. & W. merged with the Erie Railroad in 1960 and became known as the Erie Lackawanna Railroad. Passenger rail service ended on January 5, 1970, and freight trains ran far less often.

The local railroad with the most colorful history was the Delaware Valley Railroad (DVR). It puffed along from the East Stroudsburg station to Bushkill, following roughly the course of the present U.S. Highway 209. Because of the lack of a turntable, the train, known locally as "the Dink," ran backward to Bushkill and forward to East Stroudsburg.

From 1901 to 1938 the Dink carried everything from tourists and school children to such staples as coal, ice, grain, and produce. Without the train, many children in rural areas would not have had the opportunity for an education beyond grade school, because no transportation was provided for them to reach the high school in town. The availability of a train helped develop more of the river region for tourists and summer camps. Vacationers could arrive at the station in East Stroudsburg and board the Dink for resorts along the river. They no longer were required to stay close to East Stroudsburg and Delaware Water Gap.

Ironically one of the DVR's last missions was hauling concrete to build US 209, the highway that made the Dink obsolete.

Early industries in the Stroudsburgs—breweries, glass factories, silk mills, a cigar factory, duck farm, shoe peg factory, tanneries, and brick factories—catered to the leisure needs of folks in New York and Philadelphia. The ghost of a former livery stable and blacksmith shop still overlooks Lower Main Street in Stroudsburg in the form of a building frieze proclaiming the sale of wagon shafts, wheels, hubs, and spokes. The building now houses a collection of small shops and boutiques.

A portion of East Stroudsburg was, and is, known as Bricktown because most of its buildings are constructed of bricks made by the Zacharias family, still in business at Zacharias Pond near North Courtland Street. The area also was home to a tannery that, when in operation near the train station in East Stroudsburg, filled the air with the noxious aroma of animal hides floating in huge vats of water.

Stroudsburg retains much of its elegant past. The houses along Sarah, Thomas, and Scott Streets are mansions of remarkable architectural diversity displaying styles from Victorian to Gothic. Main Street has not changed drastically.

Some of its buildings still contain evidence of the Underground Railroad, which was used to shuttle slaves to freedom in the North during the Civil War.

Another historical footnote concerns J. Summerfield Staples. This Stroudsburg resident was chosen by lottery to be President Abraham Lincoln's official representative soldier during the Civil War. Staples is buried in the cemetery on Lower Main Street where a monument explains his noteworthy if not spectacular place in Civil War history. Staples never actually fired a shot in battle.

MOUNT POCONO AREA

Even more than the Stroudsburgs, the Mount Pocono region became the playground of the rich. As Delaware Water Gap became overcrowded, and passenger rail service to Cresco north of Mount Pocono exploded, the mountain area became the new popular spot in the Poconos. The resorts here were first-class, particularly the Inn at Buck Hill, Pocono Manor, and Skytop.

Built near Buck Hill Falls, the Inn at Buck Hill boasted the Poconos' first golf course, which opened in 1904. It also first introduced the region to such winter sports as skiing and tobogganing. Because it was founded by Quakers, no drinking was allowed on the premises. The inn has closed, but its main building still stands, and many residents still live in magnificent cottages on the grounds. While the inn was featured as a haunted hotel in an episode of MTV's *Fear* (March 11, 2001), the owners claim that MTV made up scary stories when they found little but happy memories at the Buck Hill Inn.

The equally elegant Pocono Manor also offered recreational opportunities early in the resort history of the Poconos. The manor still is open and is discussed in detail in our Accommodations chapter.

Also thriving today is the legendary Skytop, an opulent hotel of European-style sophistication. Perched on a spot over-looking much of the region, the five-story, stone hotel boasts large porches and an observation deck to maximize the view.

Skytop brought hotel entertainment to new levels. In addition to golf, tobogganing, skating, and skiing, guests enjoyed such activities as winter carnivals, rodeo shows, dog shows, polo matches, boxing matches, and hunting parties. Guests could ice-skate while being pulled across the lake by tractors, or ski with the assistance of an airplane. Called "ski joring," this daring skiing adventure involved guests being pulled across the snow by the Skytop Auto Gyro. Ski cycling, skiing behind a motorcycle, also was popular. During the 1930s, commuters in a hurry could be flown from New York to Skytop by the lodge's private plane.

Aside from such outdoor recreation, there never was a need to leave the main building. Everyday necessities such as a barber, hairdresser, drugstore, laundry, grocery, health staff, post office, photographer, tailor, stenographer, and bootblack were provided. There was even a separate building to house servants, if they had traveled with guests who planned an extended stay.

Naturally, all Pocono accommodations were not this lavish. More typical hotels catered to weekend tourists and the early honeymoon trade.

Fishing hotels, such as the Henryville House, opened to accommodate the many sportsmen who discovered the outstanding fly-fishing in the mountain streams. First opened in 1836, the Henryville House hosted such celebrities as Annie Oakley, John L. Sullivan, Lily Langtry, and Buffalo Bill Cody. Presidents Grover Cleveland, Benjamin Harrison, Calvin Coolidge, and Teddy Roosevelt also signed the guest register.

Civil War hero General Phillip Sheridan was so impressed by the surroundings that he dubbed the area "Paradise Valley," a name that has stuck to this day.

The major industries all catered to the city populations. Lumbering, farming, and ice harvesting thrived because of rail service to large markets.

Much of the timber that was used in the coal mining areas as supports to hold up the roofs of tunnels after anthracite had been removed came from around Mount Pocono. Farmers also grew produce, and locals picked huckleberries and wintergreen for shipment to New York and Philadelphia.

During winter, ice harvesting became a source of income for the region's farmers. The huge lakes left behind when the glaciers retreated, as well as those created by loggers who had dammed streams to make log-holding areas, produced a bounty of ice that was transported on rail lines built for the coal industry. Workers, laboring through 10-hour days while constantly battling frostbite and the risk of falling into icy water, earned 30 cents an hour. They handled blocks of ice weighing approximately 300 pounds. This ice was stored in enormous buildings roughly 50 feet wide, 50 feet high, and nearly 300 feet long. Sawdust and hay provided insulation. You can see an icehouse in Bethlehem that has been restored and turned into a performing arts space. (See our Day Trips chapter.)

The ice industry peaked in the early 20th century, when more than a million tons of ice were harvested annually. During a typical summer more than 100 railroad cars filled with ice left the Poconos each day.

As refrigeration in private homes became more common in the 1930s, the ice industry declined. Many of the icehouses burned or simply collapsed and rotted away. The only evidence now of their existence are foundations visible near most of the lakes throughout the region.

Another industry of lesser but noteworthy importance involved the growing of Christmas trees and decorative rhododendrons, which also were shipped to the cities.

The Tobyhanna Army Depot, which still is a significant employer in the region, has a long history. It first was used by the Army as a training ground for troops and artillery in the summer of 1913. During World War I, ambulance and tank personnel were given combat training there, and from 1935 to 1937 it was a Civilian Conservation Corps camp accommodating 400 men. They planted trees and performed many government construction projects in a national project to provide work during tough economic times.

When the United States entered World War II, the depot was used by the Air Service Command. Gliders assembled and packaged there were used in the Normandy invasion in 1944. Near the end of the war, the depot became a camp for German prisoners of war. Since the 1950s Tobyhanna Army Depot has stockpiled, repaired, and distributed communications equipment.

WEST END

The southern part of the Poconos differs greatly from other regions because of its lack of a significant tourist industry. This is farming country full of flat land and good soil.

There was no big draw for outsiders, other than Saylors Lake, which hosted all the famous Big Bands in its pavilion and provided swimming, boating, and fishing facilities. Today the Beltsville Dam provides outdoor recreational activities.

Tourists driving along US 209 south from Stroudsburg will see a greatly changed West End, as the southwestern portion of Monroe County locally is known. For this guide's purposes, the West End also includes all of Carbon County south of I-80. Housing developments cover former farmlands made available as farmers saw their land become more valuable than the crops they could raise on it. Strip malls line either side of the road through Kresgville and Brodheadsville, and though hints of days gone by remain in the form of numerous century-old barns that delight the hearts of sketch artists, few residents speak the Pennsylvania Dutch that once was more popular than English in the area.

Continuing farther south on US 209, the traveler comes to Highway 248, the route to Palmerton and the Lehigh Gap. Like the Delaware Water Gap, the Lehigh Gap was created by the river that bears its name. Ostensibly as beautiful as its more famous rival on the Delaware, it would still be an equal draw for scenery-lovers had not the New Jersey Zinc Company chosen to build its factory near Palmerton, creating an unfortunate eyesore in an otherwise attractive natural setting.

When the West Plant of the New Jersey Zinc Company was constructed in 1898, it was heralded as a welcome boost for the local economy. Palmerton's namesake, Steven Squires Palmer, was the original president. Demand for the company's oxides and sulfuric acid was so great that a second factory, called the East Plant, was completed in Palmerton in 1912.

World War I created more business. During the hostilities, New Jersey Zinc Company's entire output contributed to the manufacture of arms and ammunition.

Even after the war the factory employed 3,000 men and was the largest manufacturer of zinc products in the world.

The downside was the poisonous sulfur dioxide smog these factories emitted into the air. As a result, more than 10,000 acres of vegetation was killed during the company's 82-year production history. Today the barren landscape surrounding the East and West plants resembles a war-torn countryside more than a tourist area.

The United States Environmental Protection Agency began investigating the plant in 1980 and forced it to shut down in 1985. As it is a Superfund cleanup site, efforts have been made to reclaim the hillsides. Green patches are visible again on Lehigh Gap, but there is still much work to be done. Most of the mountainsides remain barren, and fertilizing and replanting will take years to bring the valley back to anything resembling its former natural beauty.

Farther up the Lehigh River a former industrial town has successfully embraced the transition to tourism. The former

Mauch Chunk, the original name of the current town of Jim Thorpe, was the Indian phrase for Bear Mountain. Indians believed the humped ridge across the Lehigh River from the town resembled a sleeping bear.

Mauch Chunk, renamed Jim Thorpe in 1955 when the town became the final resting place of the famed Native American athlete, more resembles a European hamlet than a typical Poconos town.

Travelers descending winding US 209 along the Lehigh River are suddenly greeted by a pocket of Victorian mansions, steep narrow streets, and tightly packed stone row houses.

The town, seemingly ignored by the passage of time, was developed in the mid-19th century to accommodate the nearby mining industry. Coal was hauled from the mines to Mauch Chunk where it was placed on canal boats—and later, trains—for transport to cities.

Millionaire Asa Packer, founder and president of the Lehigh Valley Railroad, owned the mining operation as well and used the fabled Switchback Railroad (see this chapter's related Close-Up) to move his coal to Mauch Chunk.

Packer's mansion, an ornate Victorian home built in 1868, is open to tourists and well worth a visit. In addition to his industrial exploits, Packer, a generous philanthropist, founded Lehigh University and ran for U.S. president in 1868. His daughter, Mary Packer Cummings, lived in the mansion until her death in 1912. Her most cherished possession, a Welty Cottage Orchestrion, still stands and, with its spiked piano rolls twirling, plays for visitors touring the place. The Orchestrion—sort of an early home-entertainment center—is 10.5 feet tall and 8 feet wide, yet Mary had it broken down and packed into crates whenever she traveled so that she could take it with her.

The opera house, built in 1881, still hosts performances and art exhibitions.

Race Street, developed in 1849, got its name from the race, or channel, of water that cascades down the hill beneath the pavement to the Lehigh River. Along this street Asa Packer built 16 stone row houses as homes for the artisans and engineers he hired to work on his various enterprises. These buildings are now occupied by an assortment of boutiques and art galleries.

At the end of Race Street, the Gothic-style St. Mark's Episcopal Church boasts a unique combination of interior features such as a wrought-iron elevator, Tiffany windows, a baptismal font with gas standards, and a tile floor made in England. It is open to the public for tours. (See our Attractions chapter for details.)

The entire town and much of the Pocono Mountains region can be seen from the top of Flagstaff Mountain, a former tourist attraction where, in the Big Band era, Tommy Dorsey occasionally played. It still is accessible to the public.

Lovers of the supernatural should visit the Carbon County Jail, where the famous handprint detailed earlier in the history of the Mollie Maguires still is visible on the cell wall. The jail, built in 1871, now serves as a museum. (See our Attractions chapter.)

MILFORD/LAKE WALLENPAUPACK AREA

Like other resort communities during the early 20th century, Milford, the seat of Pike County, parlayed its location and scenic beauty into a profitable enterprise. Large hotels employed many of the townspeople. Other residents provided laundry services and such staples as eggs, milk, butter, and produce. As in much of the rest of the Poconos, most of Milford's lavish old hotels are long gone. Prior to the invention of the automobile, most people vacationed for long periods—often an entire summer. The advent of the automobile offered the temptation to see more places in the same amount of time.

One of Milford's early resorts hosted D. W. Griffith, film director of the famous 1915 silent film, *Birth of a Nation*. Prior to its filming, Griffith arrived at the Sawkill House in 1912 to shoot the films *The Informer* and *A Feud in the Kentucky Hills* (even then the movie industry fudged locations to save money).

Among the 60 people accompanying Griffith were actresses Mary Pickford, Dorothy Gish, and Lilian Gish. Griffith reportedly lauded the Milford area as "one of the greatest locations I have ever visited for the making of moving pictures . . . the entire troupe is in ecstasies over the beautiful natural scenery."

The primary industry in the Milford area was bluestone mining. The bluestone quarried here was shipped to Boston, New York City, Philadelphia, Trenton, Scranton, and Wilkes-Barre. Many of the sidewalks, building blocks, hitching posts, and cemetery markers in those cities were built with stone from nearby Pond Eddy and Parker's Glen.

Although the quarries near Parker's Glen alone employed nearly 1,000 men in 1887, the industry died before the start of the 20th century when cheaper, more easily transported building materials such as concrete were developed. In Milford the Tom Quick Monument, Grey Towers, and Forest Hall all are made of bluestone.

The Tom Quick Monument commemorates a man known as "The Indian Slayer" or "The Avenger of the Delaware." After Quick's father, the first white settler in Milford, was killed by Indians in 1756, Quick made it his mission to avenge the death—hence his nickname. Quick's bones were placed in the cornerstone of the monument.

Historians are split on whether Quick Jr., the first white child born within present-day Milford, was a hero or a villain. While the rest of the Quick family settled into society, he carried on his one-man vendetta, killing a reported 99 Native Americans. Robert Ripley, in "Ripley's Believe It or Not," claims that Quick died of smallpox—and went right on killing. The Ripley report said Native Americans, still bitter over Quick's campaign against them, dug up his grave to defile it and contracted the disease from his corpse.

Grey Towers is the former estate of legendary conservationist and two-term Pennsylvania governor Gifford Pinchot. The lavish home and grounds are maintained by the United States Forest Service and are open to the public.

On his property Pinchot established the first successful forestry school in the United States, The Yale School of Forestry. An earlier venture launched at Cornell University in 1898 had failed by 1903. The previously mentioned Forest Hall, which still stands today at the corner of Broad and Harford Streets, housed the classrooms and today houses several shops. The medallions on its side are likenesses of artist-sculptor Bernard Palissey, 19th-century tree expert Andre Michaux, and soldier statesmen Lafayette. Forest Hall's architect, Richard Morris Hunt, also designed the base on which the Statue of Liberty stands.

On September 24, 1963, President John F. Kennedy visited Milford to dedicate Grey Towers as the Pinchot Institute for Conservation Studies.

Another historic attraction, Rohman's Inn, in Shohola, is one of the truly unique inns of the Poconos. Rohman's Inn has hosted Gloria Swanson, Charles Lindbergh, Jean Harlow, Bette Davis, Babe Ruth, and Paul Newman. During the Civil War, the inn temporarily became a hospital in 1864 when a trainload of Confederate prisoners crashed nearby. Some of the men escaped and settled in the area. In the 1940s a four-lane bowling alley was installed on the second floor. Although still in operation, it is not automated, so expect to set your own pins. Rohman's still has the 19th-century wooden barstools that pull down from the bar.

Western novelist Zane Grey dined regularly at Rohman's while living in nearby Lackawaxen from 1905 to 1918. His home is maintained as the Zane Grey Museum and contains many original manuscripts and memorabilia. (See our Attractions and Arts and Culture chapters for more information.)

One access to Lackawaxen is the Roebling Aqueduct, designed by John Roebling, who patterned the Brooklyn Bridge after what he learned in Lackawaxen. Originally built in 1848 for the canal industry, the bridge now carries cars across the Delaware River, making it the country's oldest suspension bridge still in service.

Honesdale, in Wayne County, was created as a direct result of the Delaware & Hudson Canal's presence. The company's 108-mile canal flowed from Kingston, New York, to Honesdale, Pennsylvania. Coal from the anthracite mines near Scranton traveled by rail to Honesdale where it then was loaded onto the canal boats. More than 900 tons of coal were delivered to Honesdale each day. In the 19th century Honesdale was an industrial hub of activity. In fact, the town is named for Philip Hone, the first president of the canal company.

Washington Irving, author of *Rip Van Winkle* and *The Legend of Sleepy Hollow*, traveled with Hone on the canal in 1841. Irving visited Honesdale on this trip and admired a nearby mountainside, which became known as Irving Cliff as a result of his casual interest. More than 150 years later, its name remains.

In 1884 a magnificent hotel was built on the cliff; it never opened. Financial setbacks left the completed building idle. New owners had prepared for a grand opening on June 22, 1889, but a fire on May 28 of that year—possibly caused by someone who lost money on the venture—destroyed the building. The town's water hoses could not carry water up the 300-foot cliff. Salvaging what they could, firefighters moved furniture as the fire burned methodically. The only financial benefit the people of Honesdale ever received from the Irving Cliff Hotel, which, according to newspaper accounts, might have been the grandest hotel ever constructed in northeastern Pennsylvania, were the doors, beds, desks, chandeliers, linens,

During the winter of 1951, Les Paul and Mary Ford vacationed near Stroudsburg. While there, Paul designed his famous Gibson Les Paul Standard guitar, and the couple recorded many songs, including "Bye Bye Blues" and "Take Me in Your Arms and Hold Me."

and silverware carried out during the fire. Instead of greeting hundreds of money-spending tourists, the residents were left with trinkets from an enterprise that could have made the town a major resort.

Both Honesdale and nearby Hawley contain many wonderful Victorian homes, the style of choice of those towns' wealthy industrialists. On the outskirts of Hawley is the Castle, the largest bluestone structure in the United States. In former lives, this building was a silk mill, a glass-cutting factory, and an electric power plant. It currently houses an antiques/reproductions shop. (See our Shopping chapter.)

The area changed dramatically when Pennsylvania Power & Light Company (PP&L) constructed a hydroelectric power plant and dam on Wallenpaupack Creek. As a result, Lake Wallenpaupack was born.

Around 1924 the company purchased 12,000 acres of land at the going rate of $20 per acre. Much of this land comprised the town of Wilsonville, named for James Wilson, a signer of the Declaration of Independence. Wilsonville was the Wayne County seat; Honesdale is today. Contrary to popular local rumor, no intact houses exist at the bottom of the lake, according to PP&L.

The dam is up to 70 feet high, 1,280 feet long, and includes a huge pipe to control the flow of water from the dam to the power plant 3.5 miles away.

The 5,700-acre Lake Wallenpaupack offers extensive recreational opportunities both on and around it. (See our In, On, and Around the Water chapter.) Tourists have embraced Lake Wallenpaupack, and it has become an essential part of the local economy.

Railroad buffs should plan a visit to the Wayne County Historical Society's museum in Honesdale to see the Stour-bridge Lion (see our Attractions chapter), a replica of the first locomotive ever run on a commercial track in the United States. It made its first (and only) trip from Honesdale on August 8, 1829. The original engine is housed in the Smithson-ian Institution in Washington, D.C.

AREA OVERVIEW

When we moved to the Poconos, we were hit hard with a strange affliction called "new residents' disease." Suffering from this ailment meant that every time we walked out the door, we were overcome by an intense sense of wonder and joy that we had somehow landed in such an amazing corner of Pennsylvania. Seeing the constant stream of tourists, we were awed by the fact that we lived in a place where people come to spend their vacations.

It's no wonder we suffered from new residents' disease. We can look out our window and see a waterfall flanked by an early 19th-century home, little changed from its original aspect. We can take a short walk and discover a hillside smothered with orange tiger lilies. At twilight we can go down to the river and, if we're lucky, see a bald eagle circling overhead. On a snowy night, we can look out the window and see a family of deer nibbling on some winterberry bushes. Every day in the Poconos brings new surprises from the natural world and from the cultural life of the community.

The Poconos are bounded to the east by the Delaware River. While 100 miles south, in its tidal section, the river is large enough to support international shipping, here it's ankle deep in spots and meanders past unspoiled shoreline and around numerous islands before it cuts through the most dramatic water gap in the eastern half of the country. The region is dotted with hills, ridges, and knobs almost tall enough to pass for mountains. Around every bend, you'll find lakes gouged out by glaciers.

Parts of the Poconos are so wild they are literally unmapped, while other parts are infested with houses. In a 15-minute drive, you can go through unspoiled forest, past farms, and into an urban-style neighborhood.

A more convenient location for such a paradise is hard to imagine. The Poconos are 45 minutes by car from the Allentown/Bethlehem region, one and a half hours from New York City, and two hours from Philadelphia. Within six hours of driving, you can reach most of the major metropolises in the Northeast. The area is an easy vacation destination for one third of the population of the United States, and it's an almost reasonable commute for people working in Allentown/Bethlehem, Scranton, Wilkes-Barre, New York City, southern Connecticut, and most of northern New Jersey. Judging by the number of people we know who commute, almost reasonable is good enough.

While there are still descendants of the original French Huguenot and Dutch settlers here, you will also find lots of Pennsylvania Dutch families. That's Dutch for "Deutsch," people of German descent, not Netherlanders. These are not the Amish or Mennonites who eschew most aspects of modern technology and style out of religious conviction. You won't be able to spot most of our Pennsylvania Dutch, except by their surnames. German, however, was once more common than English here, and the first local schools taught in German. The older folks may still speak a little German or may use English phrases based on German grammatical structures. Some Pennsylvania Dutch foods, like chowchow and apple dumplings, show up occasionally on menus, and if you look hard, you'll find plenty of people who love to polka.

Over the course of the last few decades, people from many other backgrounds have settled here too. Some who built second homes in the Poconos or vacationed in these mountains have come to live year-round. Artists and musicians have found that they can pursue their craft in a beautiful setting and still live close enough to major cities to advance

Poconos Vital Statistics

Size: 2,400 square miles

Counties: Monroe, Pike, Wayne, and Carbon Counties

Population: Monroe County—145,000, Pike County—49,000, Wayne County—48,000, Carbon County—60,000

Highest point: 2,131 feet above sea level at Pocono Knob within Big Pocono State Park on Camelback Mountain

Lowest point: The Delaware River, at approximately sea level

Climate: Temperate, four distinguishable seasons, summer: 70–95 degrees F, cooler at night; winter: 0–50 degrees F, some snow; 5–7 degrees cooler in the higher parts of the region.

Average yearly rainfall: 49 inches/year

Mean annual snowfall: 50 inches

Major towns: Stroudsburg, East Stroudsburg, Milford, Honesdale, Hawley, Jim Thorpe

Major rivers: Delaware, Lehigh, and Lackawaxen Rivers

Important agricultural crop: Garlic

Food you'll find growing wild: Blackberries, raspberries, blueberries, morels, puffballs

National parks: Delaware Water Gap National Recreation Area and Upper Delaware Scenic and Recreational River

State parks: Big Pocono State Park, Gouldsboro State Park, Promised Land State Park, Tobyhanna State Park, Hickory Run State Park, Lehigh Gorge State Park, Beltzville State Park

Places of special interest: Delaware Water Gap, Bushkill Falls, Tannersvillle Cranberry Bog, Big Pocono State Park, The International Pocono Raceway (NASCAR), and The Crossings Outlet Shopping

their careers. College students who come to East Stroudsburg University fall in love with the area and settle here. Between the local artists, tourism, and the university, we have a remarkably rich cultural life for such a rural area.

Since the 1970s, the population of the region has tripled, and today an estimated 145,000 people live in Monroe County, the area around Stroudsburg; 49,000 live in Pike County, the area around Milford; 60,000 live in Carbon County encompassing the region around Jim Thorpe; and 48,000 live in Wayne, the county around Lake Wallenpaupack. Pike and Monroe Counties are the first and second fastest growing counties in the state. Many New Yorkers have traded tiny apartments for spacious Pocono homes, figuring that a country lifestyle and the difference in what they paid for real estate was worth the long commute. Some of these former New Yorkers are now active members of our community, while others found they couldn't take all the travel and moved back eastward. With the influx of people used

Visitors: Approximately 8 million tourists visit the Poconos each year.

Airports: In the Poconos—Pocono Mountains Municipal Airport and Stroudsburg-Pocono Airpark, for general aviation; Near the Poconos—Lehigh Valley International Airport and Wilkes-Barre/Scranton International Airport, small airports with flights linking to national and international destinations; almost two hours away—Newark International Airport

Sales tax: 6 percent, no sales tax on grocery items and clothing

Colleges and universities: East Stroudsburg University, Northampton Community College

Daily newspapers: *The Pocono Record* (Stroudsburg), *The Wayne Independent* (Honesdale), *The Times News* (Lehighton)

Major interstates: Interstate 80, Interstate 380, Interstate 81, and Interstate 84

Alcohol sales: Bottled wine and spirits are available at State Liquor Control Board Stores; bottled beer may be purchased by the six-pack from some bars and by the case from beer distributors.

Room count: 14,000 rentable rooms

Tourist specialties: Honeymoon resorts with heart-shaped bathtubs or champagne-tower bathtubs; outdoor activities including canoeing, rafting, hiking, skiing, tubing, and more; world-class musical performances, especially jazz

Major employers: The tourist industry, East Stroudsburg University, Tobyhanna Army Depot, Pocono Health Systems, Aventis Pasteur, Weiler Corporation

Famous residents: J. Summerfield Staples (President Lincoln's "substitute-in-uniform" during the Civil War), A. Mitchell Palmer (congressman, United States Attorney General under Woodrow Wilson, and unsuccessful Democratic presidential candidate), S. S. Kresge (department store and foundation founder), Fred Waring (choral innovator and inventor), Phil Woods (jazz saxophonist), Bob Dorough (composer and singer of many of the *Schoolhouse Rock* tunes), Dave Liebman (avant garde saxophonist), Paul Sorvino (actor)

to city life, has come a demand for a greater variety of restaurants, better shopping and services, as well as busier roads and an increase in property values and taxes. Longtime residents speak longingly of the days when a dog could sleep all afternoon on the warm road in the middle of what, today, is a busy intersection.

Where there are lots of people in the Poconos, most of the available jobs are generally lower paying and require fewer skills than those in the surrounding regions. The largest industry here is tourism. Commuters and people who own second homes here make significantly higher incomes than those who work locally. Don't decide to move to the Poconos to find work without taking a look at the Sunday classified section of the *Pocono Record*. If you're used to big-city wages or the variety of jobs a more populous region offers, you're in for a surprise. On the other hand, if you're a telecommuter or work in a field where it doesn't matter where you live, the quality of life here is hard to beat.

www.poconosbest.com is a comprehensive Web site devoted to the Poconos. You'll find listings, coupons, and some fun articles there. They give "Poconos Best" awards to area businesses chosen by a panel or by the authors of the Web site. Make sure you read "You Know You're a Pocono Native When."

The Poconos are the outdoors. We have two federal recreation areas and seven state parks as well as some world-class environmental centers. We have some of the most dramatic scenery in the nation at the Delaware River Gap as well as unique environmental pockets like the Tannersville Cranberry Bog. (See the Natural World chapter.) You can live in the Poconos all your life and neither conquer all the trails nor exhaust the many recreational opportunities available. If you're a dedicated golfer, you can play a different course every day and not repeat yourself for nearly a month. In winter you don't have to curl up by the fire and wait for spring. You can ski down the mountains and across trails, drive snowmobiles, ride in old-fashioned sleighs, clomp around in snowshoes, sled, tube, skate, and go tobogganing.

If you're planning a vacation in the Poconos, you'll want to know what the weather is like. The region is large and varied, and often there's at least a five-degree difference between Stroudsburg and Mount Pocono. The Pocono Mountains are actually a high plateau that drops 1,000 feet, making the Mount Pocono area significantly colder than the lowlands around Stroudsburg. You can visit the Stroud Mall during a winter rainstorm and observe cars with a foot of snow on their roofs. Insiders always know how heavy the snow is "up the mountain," or around Mount Pocono, by the depth of snow on the cars at the mall.

If you live in New York City or Philadelphia, figure the warmer parts of the Poconos are about five degrees cooler

than the city, with areas up the mountain averaging five degrees cooler still. Spring comes a couple of weeks later in the Poconos. The old-timers don't plant before Memorial Day and laugh at newcomers who can't wait to set out their tomatoes and then fret about late frost. During the summer, the days can get as warm around Stroudsburg as anywhere else in the Northeast, but when the sun goes down, the air cools quickly, making the nights pleasant. We say our cool nights make for good sleeping weather. Of course, we don't mind the heat here; we have plenty of rivers and lakes, so we just jump in the water. If you go up the mountain, summer days can be lovely and cool even when we're broiling down by the river.

You won't find any line around the Poconos on a map, and definitions of the region vary. For the purposes of this book, we will put the eastern boundary at the Delaware River and the western boundary running past Jim Thorpe. To the south, the Poconos logically follow the southern borders of Monroe and Carbon Counties. The northern reaches of the Poconos follow the Delaware River in Pike County and cut across Wayne County just above Beach Lake and Waymart.

We have divided the Poconos into five regions that largely reflect our own patterns of daily activity. If you live in Stroudsburg, you go to the West End to eat or shop only on special occasions.

DELAWARE WATER GAP/ SHAWNEE-ON-DELAWARE

Originally, Delaware Water Gap was the vacation destination of choice in the Poconos, because trains went there directly and the scenery was—and is—magnificent. The town's proximity to New York City and Philadelphia made it one of the top vacation spots in the country during the early 20th century.

Today Delaware Water Gap is a relatively quiet community, Expanded rail service and the invention of the automobile made other areas of the Pocono Mountains more accessible to vacationers, siphoning off many of the tourists who flocked to Delaware Water Gap. Most of the town's celebrated wooden hotels burned down. The magnificent train station was abandoned 'though today a group of railroad enthusiasts is raising money to restore it.

Delaware Water Gap is a haven for artists, who draw inspiration from the scenery, the Victorian architecture, the small-town community spirit, and the rich history of the area. Commuters also look for property near the town because of easy access to Interstate 80. Fewer than 800 people live in Delaware Water Gap.

Main Street boasts some excellent restaurants and shops. Local artists display their works at the Antoine Dutot Schoolhouse. (See Attractions and Arts and Culture.) Internationally recognized jazz musicians live in the area and perform at the Deer Head Inn. (See our Restaurants, Nightlife, and Arts and Culture chapters.) Artists, performers, and chefs come together each year in early September for the Delaware Water Gap Celebration of the Arts held on the grounds of the Castle Inn. (See our Annual Events and Arts and Culture chapters for more information.)

The Appalachian Trail cuts through town, and you'll frequently see huge backpacks leaning by the doorway of a restaurant. The trail is popular with locals and tourists as well as ambitious hikers, and the Presbyterian Church of the Mountain provides an excellent shelter for long-distance hikers. Now the tenth-most-visited park in the National Park System, the Delaware Water Gap National Recreation Area hosted more than 5 million visitors in 2002. Even though these figures may sound incredible, the park is close to enormous centers of population, making it a good day trip destination or a reasonable spot to spend the weekend.

Below Delaware Water Gap, following Highway 611 along the river, you'll find a few pretty little towns including Portland,

The **Pocono Record** *puts out a supplement full of great suggestions for summer fun twice during the summer and once during the fall, as well as a supplement called "What You Need to Know to Live in the Poconos." Watch for these useful publications.*

whose Main Street is devoted to antiques shops.

North of Delaware Water Gap, still following the river, is Shawnee-on-Delaware, with a grand old inn built at the turn of the century. The Shawnee Inn started as an exclusive resort for friends and employees of industrialist C. C. Worthington, became popular with the show-business set when Fred Waring (see our History chapter) owned it, and has expanded tremendously over the last two decades. Shawnee Resort–related businesses now include timeshares, town houses, the Shawnee Mountain Ski Area, and Shawnee Place water park.

Continuing up the river, you'll find Bushkill, the ghost of a once-thriving village, in the Delaware Water Gap National Recreation Area. Bushkill is beginning to pick up steam again, as it is the home of the new Mountain Laurel Center for the Performing Arts, an ambitious project that has begun to present world-class performances (see our Arts and Culture chapter). West of Shawnee, Marshalls Creek, along U.S. Highway 209, is the center of lots of new building. It seems as though businesses, shops, town houses, and restaurants sprout up there on an almost daily basis.

STROUDSBURG/EAST STROUDSBURG

Stroudsburg and East Stroudsburg, the largest towns in the Poconos, provide services for many of the smaller communities. The Census figures for 2000 are 9,900 for East Stroudsburg and 5,800 for Stroudsburg.

In addition to our hospital, the Pocono Medical Center (see our Relocation chapter), East Stroudsburg is home to East Stroudsburg University, one of 14 universities in the Pennsylvania State System of Higher Education. Approximately 5,100 undergraduate and 1,000 graduate students are enrolled in more than 80 degree programs. (See our Education chapter for more information.)

Crystal Street, East Stroudsburg's main business district, is seeing a return of commercial activity following a devastating fire in 1996. The former train station, built in 1856, is now home to a popular local restaurant, the Dansbury Depot (see our Restaurants chapter). East Stroudsburg was once known as Dansbury, in honor of its founder, Daniel Brodhead.

Stroudsburg serves as the county seat for Monroe County, its courthouse sitting on one side of a square just off Main Street.

Main Street in Stroudsburg is a traditional business area—a long, tree-lined street sprinkled with a mix of financial institutions, shops selling essentials, restaurants, galleries, and boutiques offering fine clothing, handcrafted jewelry, and assorted gift items. Near Main Street, on Ann Street, is a complex of outlet shops. If you prefer the comfort of familiar mall-style stores, Stroud Mall is on Ninth Street. (See our Shopping chapter for more information.)

Following Ninth Street (a.k.a. Highway 611) past the mall, you'll go past lots of small strip malls, through Bartonsville, home to an enormous truck stop and a well-known candle outlet, and Tannersville, a popular destination for the Crossings

---

There are no Pocono Mountains! The Pocono region is actually a large plateau averaging nearly 1,500 feet above sea level. The plateau dramatically drops, creating what we call mountains. At many points in the abrupt drops you will find one of the delights of Pocono scenery—waterfalls.

---

outlet mall (see Shopping) and Camelback Mountain, which hosts skiing, a water park, and a state park with hiking trails and incredible views. (See our Parks, Recreation, and Winter Sports chapters.)

MOUNT POCONO AREA

Many of the Poconos' largest resorts and employers are in this region northwest of Stroudsburg. While Skytop Lodge in Skytop provides the finest in vacation elegance, couples resorts such as Caesar's offer heart-shaped bathtubs and other honeymoon accouterments. The Poconos have been a leading honeymoon destination for decades, primarily because of the resorts near Mount Pocono. (See our Accommodations chapter for details.)

For those who like their romantic activity a little more subdued, the Mount Pocono region has dozens of inns and bed-and-breakfasts sprinkled along beautiful country roads. (See our Bed-and-Breakfasts and Country Inns chapter for more information.) State parks scattered throughout the region offer hiking, fishing, swimming, cross-country skiing, snowmobiling, and more.

The Tobyhanna Army Depot has a fascinating past. (See our History chapter.) Today it is an important source of electronics and communications equipment for American soldiers. Aventis Pasteur Inc., in Swiftwater, is part of an international company that is the world's leading supplier of human vaccines. Aventis specializes in vaccines for polio, diphtheria, tetanus and pertussis, flu, yellow fever, meningitis, rabies, and typhoid fever.

Mount Pocono, with a population of 2,700, has a charming main street as well as fast-food restaurants and major discount chains. Nearby towns such as Mountainhome, Cresco, and Canadensis have retained the flavor of the old Poconos, with streamside motels and inviting antique and specialty shops. (See our Shopping chapter.) They are all accessible by taking a scenic drive along Highway 191.

WEST END

Southwest of Stroudsburg, the view along US 209 has changed dramatically. Housing developments have sprouted on farmlands; small businesses and strip malls line the road; traffic clogs the stretch near Brodheadsville, particularly on weekends.

Following US 209, you can turn off toward Palmerton or continue on to Lehighton and Jim Thorpe, the seat of Carbon County. The first two towns are close-knit communities with few tourist activities. However, Jim Thorpe, an enclave known as the "Switzerland of America" for its steep, twisty streets lined with interesting shops, has made a remarkable transition into a travel destination along the order of New Hope, Pennsylvania. You will be amazed as the narrow, winding valley along the Lehigh River suddenly opens up to reveal Jim Thorpe sitting on a hillside. The streets and alleys of the town are inviting, and when you tire of exploring, you can eat at one of the excellent restaurants. Scenery lovers, mountain bikers and hikers, whitewater rafters, shoppers, and railroading buffs all flock to Jim Thorpe for its unique ambience and attractions Purists may argue that Jim Thorpe is beyond the West End, but we like it so much, we had to find some way to include it in this book.

MILFORD/LAKE WALLENPAUPACK AREA

Milford, the county seat of Pike County, is a classic, well-kept Victorian town with inviting restaurants, galleries, boutiques, and bed-and-breakfasts. Walk down almost any street and you'll find some whimsical Victorian creation, lovingly restored. Milford residents find convenient commuting to jobs in New Jersey and New York City via Interstate 84 or the Metro-North Commuter Railroad, which stops in nearby Port Jervis, New York. The town sits in the middle of vast state forest and game lands adjacent to the Delaware

Pick up your tourist information at the Vacation Bureau Information Centers or look in the lobbies of hotels and restaurants. Many Pocono travel brochures include coupons for restaurants, shops, and attractions that may save you significant amounts of money.

River, which makes it ideal for outdoor enthusiasts of all persuasions.

Milford's most famous resident was Gifford Pinchot. In 1905 he became the first chief of the Forest Service established by President Theodore Roosevelt. Pinchot was elected governor of Pennsylvania in 1923 and 1931. In 1963 President John F. Kennedy visited Milford to dedicate Grey Towers, Pinchot's estate, as the Pinchot Institute for Conservation Studies. Less than two months later, Kennedy was assassinated. Grey Towers is open to the public for tours of the mansion and surrounding grounds (see our Attractions and Arts and Culture chapters).

Pike County is the fastest growing county in Pennsylvania. Though the location would seem ideal for commercial growth, industry is not a major factor in the Pike County economy. Of Pike's total land area of 350,000 acres, more than 140,000 acres are designated as state forests and game lands. This not only protects the environment but also limits opportunities for large corporate projects.

Wayne County's major towns were built to service the coal mining industry. The region's economy is no longer based on coal, but rather on a mix of health care, government, resort, and manufacturers. Six hundred and forty small farms operate in Wayne County, mostly in the northern areas.

Honesdale, with a population of 4,900, is the largest municipality in this rural county. (See our History chapter for some interesting notes on Honesdale's past.) The best-known business in Honesdale is *Highlights for Children* magazine. Founded in 1946, this monthly's circulation of more

"Pocono" is a Lenape word meaning "stream between two mountains."

VISITOR RESOURCES

than 2 million is the largest of any national periodical for children. Offices are at 803 Church Street. Honesdale has a wonderful history museum (see Attractions and Arts and Culture) and the nearby Dorflinger-Suydam Sanctuary and Glass Museum offers world-class concerts in the summer and a beautiful display of locally made glass.

Hawley, population 1,300, was named for Irad Hawley, first president of the Pennsylvania Coal Company. Waymart's name was derived from that town's former use as a place to stockpile coal and weigh it—a "weigh mart"—before transport to Honesdale. Waymart has a population of 1,400.

Tourism was not a major factor in this area before construction of Lake Wallenpaupack (see our In, On, and Around the Water chapter) in 1926. Built by Pennsylvania Power & Light Company to generate hydroelectric power, the lake has lots of recreational opportunities and is popular with tourists and locals.

As the northernmost part of the Poconos, this region is also the coldest. In winter, the average temperature is 25 degrees, with a record low of 27 below zero. The average annual snowfall is 57 inches, and there is at least an inch of snow on the ground an average of 52 days a year.

If you're planning a trip here, be sure to contact the Pocono Mountains Vacation Bureau. Visit their excellent Web site (www.800poconos.com) and order brochures online, or call ahead (800-762-6667), and the staff will send you a package of information. Staff can assist visitors with referrals, reservations, and answers to travel-related questions.

The Vacation Bureau operates the following drop-in information centers where you can get lots of brochures and advice. Look for information centers at:

- Delaware Water Gap, exit 310 off I-80, (570) 476-0167
- Crescent Lake, I-80 east after Pennsylvania 380 junction, before exit 299 (brochure distribution only; center is not staffed).
- Hickory Run, I-80 East between exits 262 and 273, (570) 443-8626
- I-84 east and west (both directions) between exits 20 and 26
- Lake Wallenpaupack, U.S. Highway 6 just west of junction of US 6 and U.S. Highway 507, (570) 226-2141
- Carbon County Visitors Center in Jim Thorpe at the Railroad Station, Route 209, (570) 325-3673
- White Haven, Route 940 and Northeast Extension of Pennsylvania Turnpike (WAWA), (570) 443-8429

GETTING HERE, GETTING AROUND

We find it highly amusing that we jump on the interstate to go the mall and buy shoes, while the next car over may be on the road to Oregon. By contrast, our trip to the grocery store is along a twisting country road, past a lake, a ski mountain, and a barn with a fading Pennsylvania Dutch hex sign.

The major interstate highways that get you to, and in most cases through, the Poconos are Interstate 80, from the east and west; Interstate 380, from Scranton, heading southeast and merging with I–80 west of Tannersville; Interstate 84 from the east and west; Interstate 81 from the northeast and southwest; Interstate 78 from the southeast and southwest; and Interstate 95 from the north and the south. (See the "By Auto" section for a more detailed look at each of these highways.)

Interstates 81, 78, and 95 never actually enter the Poconos, but get you to the outskirts or to appropriate feeder highways.

While there is some public transportation and some taxi service (see subsequent sections), most people rent a car when they fly into the area. If you're staying at a resort, talk with the people at the resort to see if you need a car. If you're staying anywhere else, you'll need wheels. It's always wise to reserve a car ahead of time when you plan to rent. Otherwise you could end up paying for a luxury Lincoln when all you wanted was a little Focus. See our "By Plane" section for phone numbers of rental companies that serve the airport where you plan to arrive.

BY AUTO

Get very clear directions to wherever you're going and pick up a good map. It's fun to discover new country roads, but when you're really lost, it's hard to maintain that sense of enjoyment. Many of our roads are twisting, steep, and narrow. Observe the speed limits and be alert for wildlife that wants to share the road with you. Hitting a deer can spoil your day—and your car. (See the following "Drivers' Safety Tips" section for advice negotiating Pocono roadways.)

This section tells you about the major primary and secondary roads in the Pocono region as well as the important feeders. When it comes to navigating, however, a picture really is worth a thousand words. Get yourself a map and study it religiously.

Drivers' Safety Tips

We've compiled the following list to help alert you to potential hazards:

- Believe in the posted speed limits. We have some wildly winding roads that regularly eat the cars of nonbelievers.
- For some reason, almost every car that passes us in a no passing zone has out-of-state plates. We have a sneaking suspicion that if it were safe to pass, the locals would do it too.
- We have lots of big, fuzzy wildlife here, and they don't know the rules of the road. Be ready to stop for deer and bear especially.

Some interstate highways allow a 65 mph speed limit; most highways in the Poconos don't. In fact, the speed limit for I-80 through Stroudsburg is only 50 mph (it's a high-accident zone). Please observe area speed limits carefully.

- Country roads don't have streetlights. When it's dark in the Poconos, it's really dark. It's a good idea to burn your headlights from dusk 'til dawn and in inclement weather.
- After it snows, main roads (interstates, U.S. highways, and ski mountain access roads) are plowed quickly and covered with cinders, but our state and county highways can be treacherous. Driving up and down hills in the snow requires caution. It's very easy to slide off the road if you accelerate too quickly. Even a little bit of snow causes lots of accidents here. If you can, cuddle up with a book in front of the fire, and avoid driving until the snow stops and the roads are clear.
- We have "black ice" in the Poconos. Black ice looks like a wet spot on the road, but it's really slippery. Whenever the temperature is near freezing, treat all "wet" spots as if they were ice and drive carefully. If you are heading into higher elevations, be aware that the town you are leaving may be warmer than your destination, so even if ice isn't a problem when you depart, it may become one en route. Bridges (we have lots of them) ice over quickly when the temperature plummets.
- Fog is common at higher elevations and in the river valleys. This is especially true on secondary roads such as Highways 940 and 314 as well as on River Road in the Delaware Water Gap National Recreation Area. Fog also profoundly affects travel on the interstates. It's often hard to tell when fog will occur; it might be perfectly clear in one spot, then you'll

go over a ridge and find yourself in pea soup. Mist comes up off the river when the temperature changes quickly, so the foggiest times tend to be at dawn and dusk. If you find yourself surrounded by a white cloud, drive slowly, turn on your low beams, and use extra caution.

Interstates and U.S. Highways

INTERSTATE 95

I-95 doesn't enter the Poconos, but if you are coming from south of the Philadelphia area on this interstate, catch Interstate 476 to the Northeast Extension of the Pennsylvania Turnpike. Actually, just to confuse you, the Northeast Extension is now I-476 too, but it was renamed recently, and many maps still show that part of the turnpike as Highway 9 or the Northeast Extension. Proceed on I-476 to Lehighton or Blakeslee if you're going to the western corner of the Poconos, or catch U.S. Highway 22 near Allentown and take it along the northern edge of Allentown and Bethlehem. Just before Easton, when you think you've gone too far, take Highway 33 north to the Stroudsburg area. If you're going to Stroudsburg or points east, pick up U.S. Highway 209 north to Stroudsburg, which will take you to I-80. Don't exit any version of US 209 until you see the sign for Stroudsburg, or you may end up deep in the country. If you're heading to Bartonsville or points west, you can continue on Highway 33.

INTERSTATE 78

I-78 parallels I-80 but remains south of the Poconos, traversing the Allentown area. To reach the Poconos from I-78, take the exit for Highway 33 North, then follow the directions in the I-95 section from Highway 33 to get to your Poconos destination.

INTERSTATE 81

I-81 skirts the Poconos west of the Blakeslee area. It travels north through Wilkes-Barre and Scranton, connecting with all of the major interstates that run through the Poconos.

INTERSTATE 84

I-84 comes into the Poconos in the north from Matamoras to Scranton, running south of Lake Wallenpaupack. It goes past Milford and the Newfoundland area and below Hawley. Quite a few residents use I-84 to commute to jobs in Waterbury and Danbury, Connecticut. I-84 is a good alternative to I-80 if you're going to points north of New York City.

INTERSTATE 80

I-80 goes right through the heart of the Poconos—the areas surrounding Delaware Water Gap, Marshalls Creek, Stroudsburg, East Stroudsburg, Mount Pocono, and Blakeslee. It provides immediate access to Interstates 380 and 81, which will link you with I-84. It also provides access to most of the Pennsylvania highways that run through the Poconos. If you're crossing the I-80 bridge from New Jersey to Pennsylvania there is a toll of 75 cents. You may also use an EZ Pass.

INTERSTATE 380

I-380 connects I-80 to Interstates 84 and 81. It peels off from I-80 between Tannersville and Lake Harmony and takes you up the distinctive Pocono Plateau past Pocono Summit, Tobyhanna, and Gouldsboro straight to Scranton.

U.S. HIGHWAY 209

US 209 runs from Milford south and west to Jim Thorpe. It passes a lot of towns on the way and crosses I-80 at Marshalls Creek. From Bushkill and north, it is part of the Delaware Water Gap National Recreation Area. In the park, you'll pass farms, meadows, and woods, catching glimpses of the Delaware River along the way. US 209 is often congested between Stroudsburg and Marshalls Creek. A bypass has been planned and may be finished by 2007, but for now, you can avoid the congestion by taking an alternate route.

If you're heading south from Milford, you can get off US 209 at the stoplight at Fernwood. Turn left on River Road past Treetops, some of Fernwood's villas; it leads to the town of Delaware Water Gap and I-80. If you plan to travel north on US 209 and want to avoid a traffic delay on the weekends, take River Road from Delaware Water Gap and I-80 (exit 310) past Shawnee-on-Delaware. You can turn left on Hollow Road by the Shawnee Playhouse, which will take you to US 209 just south of the Foxmoor shopping area, neatly avoiding the congestion around US 209, Highway 402, and the Pocono Bazaar Flea Market. US 209 Business connects Marshalls Creek and Sciota; so, if you prefer, you can travel through the Stroudsburgs and small villages instead of zipping along an interstate. Just avoid this route on a weekend unless you like heavy traffic.

Try to avoid driving during a snowfall. Our roads are winding and can be very slick when there's snow and ice. The wisest strategy is to wait until the plows have been through. If you must drive in icy conditions, leave yourself lots of extra time and go slow.

U.S. HIGHWAY 6

National Geographic magazine calls US 6, which runs along the length of Northern Pennsylvania, "one of America's most scenic drives." In the Poconos, it lives up to that claim, going from north of Scranton through Waymart, Honesdale, Hawley, past Shohola Falls, and through Milford. A brochure on US 6 is available from the Pocono Mountains Vacation Bureau at their information centers and online at www.800poconos.com. (See our Overview chapter.)

Secondary Roads

PENNSYLVANIA HIGHWAY 611

Highway 611 takes you from Tobyhanna, in the northwest, past Mount Pocono through Delaware Water Gap and south toward Philadelphia. It's a beautiful drive the entire way, especially from Delaware Water Gap and south where you go right along the river almost all the way to New Hope.

Get a map of Monroe or Pike County and study it. When you encounter traffic, there's often a country road that will take you around it. A map will help you find the way.

PENNSYLVANIA HIGHWAY 903

The "Highway to Adventure," can be reached from I-80 or Highway 940 via Highway 115. It leads to Jim Thorpe and is a lovely road that takes you through unspoiled country and across a ridge that was part of the infamous Walking Purchase. (See our History chapter.) Along the road you can see forest to the west as well as valleys and hills that fill the range from this point to the Delaware Water Gap. Highway 903 is also the access road for Big Boulder Ski Area and Split Rock Resort.

PENNSYLVANIA HIGHWAY 715

Highway 715 begins in Brodheadsville. From Brodheadsville north, Highway 715

If you hate traffic jams, avoid these congested spots (especially on weekends):
- *Highway 611 between Stroudsburg's Main Street and the Mall*
- *The intersection of US 209, US 209 Business, and Highway 402 in Marshalls Creek*
- *The intersection of Fifth and Main Streets in Stroudsburg*

leads to I-80, or you can cross the interstate and continue on to Highway 191. The road takes you past forests, lakes, streams, restaurants, accommodations, and new housing developments.

PENNSYLVANIA HIGHWAY 33

Highway 33 is your connecting route running straight through the State Belt to the Lehigh Valley area, including Lehigh Valley International Airport via US 22. If you're coming from Allentown/Bethlehem, Highway 33 connects with US 209 North, which takes you to I-80. Don't be fooled by the way US 209 dovetails with and departs from Highway 33. Follow the signs to Stroudsburg and you won't wind up lost in Sciota.

PENNSYLVANIA HIGHWAY 191

Highway 191 cuts across the Poconos from Honesdale to Newfoundland, through East Stroudsburg and Stroudsburg and heading over Bangor Mountain to Bangor. This highway takes you all over the Poconos from north to south, dovetailing with Highway 390, in Mountainhome, for a spell.

PUBLIC TRANSPORTATION

Monroe County Transit Authority Highway 611, Scotrun (570) 839-6282 www.geocities.com/capitolhill/lobby/ 5240
MCTA is the only substantial public transit system in the Poconos, running 12 buses between Mount Pocono, Stroudsburg, and Brodheadsville. Shared Ride, also operated by MCTA, is available to anyone in Monroe County who needs transportation and lives more than 0.25 mile from an MCTA bus route. To schedule a ride, you must call (570) 839-8210 by noon of the previous day. Shared Ride is about the price of a taxi cab, but senior citizens pay only 50 cents for most trips. Regular MCTA buses are free to those 65 and older during off-peak hours, on weekends, and during spe-

cific holidays. (See our Relocation chapter for more on this option.)

TAXIS

We've seen the occasional taxi in the Poconos, but don't expect to hail one from the street. You'll need to call ahead.

Milford Tri-State Taxi
115 East Hartford, Milford
(570) 296-TAXI, (800) 926-TAXI
www.milfordtaxi.com
Tri-State provides service to Milford, Dingmans Ferry, Lords Valley, and the surrounding area, covering Pike County and parts of Wayne. If you're going between two points in the general Milford area, you'll pay $3.00 for a ride, but once you get past the Texaco station, your fare will be determined by zones and the car's odometer. Tri-State Taxi runs from 6:30 A.M. to 9:00 P.M. Monday through Friday, 8:00 A.M. to 9:00 P.M. on Saturday, and 9:00 A.M. to 6:00 P.M. on Sunday. During the summer, service is offered until 1:00 A.M.

Road Runner Taxi
Mountain Drive, Mt. Pocono
(570) 839-1500
Road Runner serves Mt. Pocono, Tobyhanna Township, and Coolbaugh. They charge $2.75 for the first mile or any part of a mile and $1.80 for each additional mile. They are open 9:00 A.M. to 9:00 P.M.

Time Saver Taxi
Beartown Road, Cresco
(570) 595-9545
Time Saver can pick you up only in Canadensis, Barrett, Mountainhome, Buck Hill, Cresco, or Skytop. They charge $2.00 for the first mile and $1.50 for each mile after that. Call seven days a week between 6:00 A.M. and midnight. If you have a flight that is outside of those times, call ahead and make a reservation. Time Saver Taxi is a family business and they'll be happy to accommodate you.

WGM Transportation
9074 Franklin Hill Road, East Stroudsburg
(570) 223-9289, (877) WGM-TAXI
www.wgmtransport.com
WGM, with headquarters in Stroudsburg, covers all of Monroe, Pike, and upper Northampton Counties. WGM charges $3.20 for the first mile and $1.75 for each additional mile, and 25 cents per minute wait time.

LIMOUSINE SERVICE

Hire a limousine (make advance reservations) to go to the airport, New York City, Atlantic City, or Philadelphia, or get one for a special occasion. Each company has its own special touches.

A & G Limousine
230 Koehler Road, Sciota
(570) 992-7027, (866) 992-7027
A & G serves the Poconos, and most of their business is transportation to and from airports. The owner wants you to know he's an Irish bachelor, and he's the main driver, though he has two other drivers, and if demand is high, he has access to many other limousines and drivers. There's always a limo available, but you must make advance reservations at least two days in advance.

Champagne Limousine Service
8 East Webster Street, Roseto
(610) 863-5994, (800) 634-5466
Champagne Limousine Service provides shuttles to the airport as well as luxury

School buses carry the Poconos' most precious cargo. Please drive carefully and watch for buses on winding mountain roads. State law requires that you stop when a school bus stops, whether you are behind the bus or driving toward it. That way, you won't hit any students who cross the road.

CLOSE-UP

Crossing a Span of Centuries—Dingmans Ferry Bridge, One of the Few Privately Owned Bridges in the United States

One of the delights of the Poconos is the bridge at Dingmans Ferry. This small, two-lane bridge is made from sections of a railroad trestle that traversed the Susquehanna River before the turn of the century. It was originally the crossing point of a ferry operated by Andrew Dingman, who claimed the spot in 1735 as part of a land grant from William Penn. The ferry was in Lenape tribal land and provided an escape route during occasional Indian raids. The bridge is owned by Dingman's descendants and others who bought into the Dingmans Choice & Delaware Bridge Company in 1836. The company's name is derived from the local legend that Andrew Dingman declared his land saying, "This is my choice."

The bridge has existed in various incarnations since 1836 and is owned by

cars for special occasions. They even have a service that provides guided tours to New York City via limo, and they know all the best restaurants in New York.

J & J Luxury Transportation
445 Business Park, Allentown
(800) 726–5466
www.jjtransportation.com
J & J provides airport transport and luxury service around and beyond the Poconos 24 hours a day, seven days a week. Their luxury cars, buses, and vans are ready to go to any major airport or city you require.

Pocono Limousine Service Inc.
Highway 611, Swiftwater
(570) 839–2111, (800) 537–4667
www.poconolimousine.com
Pocono Limousine provides airport shuttles and luxury cars as well as tours to Atlantic and New York Cities, and a Pocono dinner tour.

Xpres-Limo
RR 3, Box 353, Greentown, PA 18426
(570) 253–3383, (800) 346–2168
www.xpreslimo.com
Express offers airport transportation and special occasion luxury cars in Wayne, Lackawanna, Luzerne, and Pike Counties. If you have tickets to a show in New York City and want to go in style, Express Limousine offers classy transportation into the city.

BUS LINES

You can get to the Poconos by Greyhound or Martz Trailways buses. They come into the region from New York, Scranton, and Philadelphia.

Greyhound
Highway 611, Delaware Water Gap
(570) 421–3040
www.greyhound.com

the same originating families, though members now live all over the United States. Every October they get together for a board meeting.

The storied span has been the subject of a Charles Kuralt special. In April 1996 a Japanese news show featured a story about it. And it remains one of the few privately owned bridges in the country.

Turn east off U.S. 209 in Dingmans Ferry to reach the bridge. Suddenly you'll find yourself in another setting—almost another time. The bridge exudes a charming otherworldly quality. Bridge keepers walk out to your car to collect the 75-cents toll (it has been the same amount for as long as we can remember), talk about the weather or the bridge and, if they get to know you, inquire as to how you and your children are doing. The toll collectors are also great sources of bridge history.

It's a treat to simply cross the bridge and come back, but the drive on the New Jersey side is lovely. The road runs along the river, through the Delaware Water Gap National Recreation Area. There are lots of old houses to see, riverside spots to access for swimming and fishing, and trails to hike. Leave yourself some time to explore this wonderful road.

You can take a Greyhound directly to Philadelphia at 8:05 A.M. or 5:10 P.M. and make connections to anywhere in the United States. The fare to Philadelphia is $30 round trip. Greyhound also runs two buses a day to Scranton/Wilkes-Barre, leaving at 1:45 P.M. and 7:40 P.M. for $11 one way.

Martz Trailways
Highway 611, Delaware Water Gap
(570) 421-3040

Pennsylvania Highway 447 and US 209
Marshalls Creek
no phone

7 Fork Street, Mount Pocono
(570) 839-7611
www.martztrailways.com
Martz provides buses to New York City and Scranton/Wilkes-Barre for commuters and casual travelers. Between 4:45 and 6:45 A.M.—prime commuting time—buses run every 15 minutes. After that, buses run every two to three hours until 7:40 P.M. You'll pay $39.85 for the round trip from Delaware Water Gap to New York City, or you may buy a commuter pass for 10 one-way trips for $107 that must be used within three weeks or for 44 one-way trips for $351 (must be used within 31 days). The buses go to the Port Authority. On Saturdays, catch the Shoppers' Special that takes you to Rockefeller Center in New York City (by reservation only—reserve a week in advance). This $30 round trip leaves Delaware Water Gap at 8:30 A.M. and Rockefeller Center at 7:00 P.M.

No tickets are sold at the Marshalls Creek Bus Station; you must buy them elsewhere. If you plan to use this terminal, get a parking permit when you buy your ticket—a permit is required to leave your car there. Parking at the Martz terminals costs $3.00 per day.

Shortline Bus/Coach USA
Fluffs Deli, 215 Main Street, Hawley
(570) 226-8801

Gulliver's Travel
959 Main Street, Honesdale
(570) 253-3871
www.shortlinebus.com
Believe it or not, Shortline operates a mainly commuter bus line from the Hawley/Honesdale area, through Matamoras and ending 3 hours later at the Port Authority in New York City.

Eight buses leave from Hawley, starting at 4:00 A.M. The last one leaves at 6:23 P.M. If you want to go from Honesdale, you'll have to wait until 8:18 A.M. to catch the bus. Eight daily buses leave the city for Hawley between 8:15 A.M. and 11:00 P.M.; six of them go on to Honesdale.

BY PLANE

The major area airports are outside the Pocono region. The two closest airports are Lehigh Valley International Airport and Wilkes-Barre/Scranton International Airport. Lehigh Valley International is in the Allentown/Bethlehem area, which is south of the Pocono region but only an hours' drive from its heart. Wilkes-Barre/Scranton International is in Avoca, which is west of the Poconos, also about an hour's drive from most Pocono destinations. Newark (NJ) International Airport is a two-hour drive east. Lehigh Valley and Wilkes-Barre/Scranton airports are good, small facilities that will get you to many of your destinations with none of the stress you may encounter in their big-city counterparts. If

If you're driving to Lehigh Valley International to catch a plane, leave yourself an extra 40 minutes. US 22 often becomes jammed and sometimes comes to a complete halt. If you give yourself extra time, you'll make that plane.

you are averse to changing planes to reach a destination not directly accessible by these airports, you may prefer to make the trek to Newark.

Many of the larger resorts will arrange to pick you up from and deliver you to area airports, so if you're booked in a resort, ask about shuttle service.

Lehigh Valley International Airport
US 22 and Airport Road, Allentown
(610) 266-6000, (800) FLY-LVIA
www.lvia.org
This is a clean, pleasant airport. It's a short walk from the parking area to the terminal. Display cases throughout the airport showcase the area's business—Martin Guitars; Daytimer; and Just Born Candies, makers of Marshmallow Peeps, Hot Tamales, and Mike and Ike. A gift shop carries newspapers from around the world, magazines, books, gifts, and the requisite Pennsylvania hex signs. There's a hoagie concession and the Valley Cafe, which offers salads, sandwiches, pizza, and hot dogs. The counter takes a 90-degree turn, and you go from croissants to a full bar. A newer terminal adds to the concourses as well as providing more restaurant and newsstand space.

Forty-eight daily nonstop flights serve 18 cities, some of which are hubs where you can make connections to nearly every United States and many international destinations. This airport is serviced by: U.S. Airways Express (800-428-4322), United Express (800-241-6522), Northwest Airlines and Northwest Airlink (800-225-2525), Continental Express and Continental Connection (800-525-0280), Delta Connection (800-221-1212), Air Canada-Ontario's Air Georgian (888-247-2262), and Southeast Airlines (800-359-7325). When you land, you can take a cab or a bus right outside the baggage area, but if you are heading for the Poconos, your best bet is a rental car. Agencies include Alamo/National (610-264-5535), Avis (610-264-4450), Budget (610-266-0667), Dollar (610-231-8785), and Hertz (610-264-4571).

Wilkes-Barre/Scranton
International Airport
Off I-81, Avoca
(877) 2-FLYAVP
www.flyavp.com

Wilkes-Barre/Scranton is a regional airport that provides direct jet/commuter service to hubs including Cincinnati, Philadelphia, Pittsburgh, Atlanta, Cleveland, and Chicago. One-stop service is available to more than 450 cities. The major airlines that service this airport are: U.S. Airways/U.S. Airways Express (800-428-4322), United Express (800-241-6522), Continental Connection (800-525-0280), and Delta Connection (800- 354-9822). To get to the Poconos once you land, you'll need to rent a car or take a cab. Arrange airport pickups with the individual car rental companies: Alamo (800-462-5266), Avis (800-331-1212), Hertz (800-654-3131), National (800-227-7358), and Budget (800-527-0700).

Smaller Airports

Pocono Air Center
Highway 611, 1.5 miles north
of Mount Pocono
(570) 839-6080
www.poconoaircenter.com

Pocono Mountains Municipal Airport has a small, comfy lounge with a friendly staff and a few snacks available from honor boxes. The field is uncontrolled (which, for the uninitiated, means there's no air-traffic control). Services include tie-downs, fueling, and storage. Tie-down fees vary. If you purchase fuel (100 LL and Jet A are available), the daily fees are waived, but overnight fees still apply. Fees run from $6.00 for a single-engine plane to $12.00 for a turbine jet. If you're landing at night, the runway lights are pilot-controlled. Use Unicom frequency 122.7 to light up the runway. Rental cars can be arranged through Northern Car Rental (570-839-2215). If you want a car, call ahead for a reservation.

Stroudsburg-Pocono Airpark
Off US 209 Business, 3 miles north of
East Stroudsburg
(800) 722-3597

This airport is primarily a tourist attraction for sightseeing flights and daytrips (see our Attractions chapter for details). However, hanger space and tie-downs are available here—$60 per month or $5 per night. The field is uncontrolled and has pilot-controlled runway lights at Unicom frequency 123.0. Only 100 LL fuel is sold here. A picnic pavilion is available for those who want to fly in and have a cookout.

ACCOMMODATIONS

In any season of the year, the Poconos are as big as all outdoors. That's because outdoors is where so much of the action lies. Subsequent chapters, therefore, will tell you how to rough it by hiking, biking, skiing, camping, golfing, rafting, and pursuing other calls of the wild, but this chapter is concerned with the softer, more luxurious side of your vacation.

In this chapter, we'll tell you where to kick back, unwind, and be pampered and waited on in any number of establishments ranging from the little motel around the corner to resorts and honeymoon havens where the Sultan of Brunei might feel right at home. We'll also touch upon timesharing options, housekeeping cottages, and campgrounds. Because there are so many bed-and-breakfasts and country inns in the Poconos, we dedicate a special chapter to them. Here, however, is the rest of the spectrum on accommodations. Those presented here—and certainly our list does not cover the total lineup—offer a wide range of price and design, ensuring there are some to suit every budget and every taste.

As an added guideline, the Pocono Mountains Vacation Bureau has adopted a system of voluntary inspection called the Quality Assurance Program. Under its terms, resorts, motels/motor inns, and other accommodations in the area agree to be inspected annually by a Florida firm that certifies that they have met strict standards of excellence for cleanliness, housekeeping maintenance, management, and guest services. We will not attempt to list the establishments that have the Quality Assurance Seal, but if you want to check up on any given facility, call the Vacation Bureau at (800) 762-6667.

Before we begin our journey through the lobbies and past the registration desks, let's get some business concerns out of the way.

Major credit cards generally are accepted—we note any exceptions. If you wish to know about a specific credit card's acceptability, contact individual establishments that interest you.

Pets usually are not allowed, but this policy of exclusion is not etched in stone. Several motels and motor inns welcome your four-legged traveling companions, though you may have to pay a security deposit to cover any damage left behind. In this chapter, we'll tell you where the welcome mat is out; otherwise please make other arrangements for Fido and Fluffy.

As a general rule, smoking is permitted only in designated areas, though most hostelries still have smoking and non-smoking rooms. If an establishment is entirely nonsmoking, or if there are no no-smoking accommodations, we'll tell you.

Wheelchair accessibility is a consideration for some people, and most establishments comply with the Americans with Disabilities Act. We suggest, however, that you check with the ones that interest you for information about their facilities and restrictions.

Many of the accommodations in this section have convention and conference facilities. Even the top-of-the-line resorts do a great deal of business catering special events, and most have meeting rooms, separate convention facilities, and dedicated staffs. If you're planning a group meeting of any size, contact any of the resorts, hotels, and motels in our area for available opportunities.

A final word about price: Because of the range of options, pricing varies. Some rates are for the week, some for the night, and all may vary from season to season, or even from month to month. Figures quoted here are based on 2004 peak-season rates and may go up, or even down as special promotional discounts are instituted. Many establishments offer packages that include midweek discounts as weekend bonuses.

Wherever possible, we include price codes for each category that reflect the type of pricing used, so even with seasonal variations, we are able to give you a general gauge of cost levels you might expect. Pennsylvania also has a 6 percent sales tax that is not included in the quoted rates. Some places add a gratuity to the bill; we note that where applicable.

Now let us explore the premises.

RESORTS

Delaware Water Gap/ Shawnee-on-Delaware

Fernwood Resort and Country Club
U.S. Highway 209, Bushkill
(888) FERNWOOD
www.resortusa.com
Did you say you like action and want to feel in the middle of things? Did you say a vacation for you means not only mountains and trees, but also lots of activities? Well Fernwood is action.

Fernwood's 175 acres flank US 209 and River Road, which separate Fernwood's tubing area and golf course from the lodges. It's this separation that gives Fernwood that right-in-the-middle-of-things feel. Everywhere you look, people are on their way to activities—and there you are on "Main Street" in the mountains! There are three themed restaurants— Mama Bella's casual Italian restaurant; the Jukebox Diner, a '50s-style classic; and the Trolley Stop Pub, a sport enthusiast's dream with big screen TV and satellite televisions broadcasting your favorite sporting events (as well as a good pub menu); Wintergreens, a snack bar, is conveniently located for golfers in the summer and snow tubes in the winter, and there's even a small food court with chicken, Pizza Hut, and a coffee bar. There are also banquet and conference facilities for meetings,

parties, and weddings. Don't expect to eat in peace—musical productions, children's shows, and dinner entertainment are on the menu at Mama Bella's, and live bands are featured at the Trolley Stop. Check Fernwood's calendar for big events, too. We've seen advertisements for well-known bands such as K.C. and the Sunshine Band as well as some WXW wrestling matches.

Winter activities such as snow tubing, ice-skating, and horseback riding abound (see our Winter Sports chapter for details), but summer, spring, and fall are activity filled too. Fernwood's grounds are great for biking and hiking and include a private lake for fishing or paddleboating. Golfing options include an 18-hole championship course. (See our Golf chapter.) You can swim indoors or outdoors and then take advantage of the sauna and whirlpool. The state-of-the-art fitness center rounds out the complement of amenities. Nautilus workout equipment, an on-call masseuse, a great video arcade, miniature golf, paddle and bumper boats, and paintball are all available. Equipment rentals and some activities require an additional fee, but most activities are free.

Kids' activities for ages 4 to 12 are available all day. Depending on the season, there are games, contests, and all kinds of planned group activities. You'll get a guidebook when you check in, so you'll know what's going on at all times.

Accommodations range from standard to deluxe and include guest rooms and villas. Some rooms have Jacuzzis, saunas, or separate living areas. Rates depend on the type of room, the time of stay, and length of stay. Rates range from $129 per night for a room with two double beds, which will sleep up to four people, to $295 for a villa with kitchen and, in some cases, Jacuzzi, sleeping four to six.

Mountain Manor Inn & Golf Club
off Highway 402, Marshalls Creek
(570) 223–8098, (800) MANOR47
www.mountainmanor.com

Mountain Manor is a Pocono establishment that attracts families year after year. The cozy 450-acre resort is owned and operated by the Scott family. Lovely hiking trails on the grounds lead you along streams, over bridges, and through the woods. The main lodge has a white-columned central entrance that leads to the lobby, gift shop, and dining room. Some of the guest rooms at this country resort are in the wings of this building.

Golf is the main activity here. There are four nine-hole regulation courses and one nine-hole executive course. (See our Golf chapter.) Golf season packages include complimentary greens fees, breakfast, and dinner. The Scotts' inn also features tennis; indoor and outdoor swimming; indoor ice-skating, cross-country skiing, and tobogganing in the winter (see our Winter Sports chapter); a fitness center with Nautilus equipment; a game room with video games and a pool table; an indoor gym for basketball, tennis, and volleyball; and Thunder Creek (see our Kidstuff chapter), a play park with an arcade, bumper boats, go-karts, miniature golf, and an in-line skate park. (Thunder Creek is subject to additional fees.)

Stays at Mountain Manor include dinner and breakfast, hayrides in-season, and a full schedule of daily activities, such as unlimited golf, horseshoes, softball, weenie roasts, and more. Breakfast and dinner are served in the dining room, or you can enjoy lunch specials and dinners (five nights a week) in the Club. There is a snack shop on the golf course too.

Mountain Manor offers packages based on golf, weather, themes, sports, holidays, shopping, or nothing at all. The shopping package is great for those who want to take advantage of all the retail opportunities in the Stroudsburg and Mount Pocono areas.

Accommodations are available in duplex units, townhouses, and motel units—Creekside, East Wing, West Wing, and Golf Club—with private baths and cable TVs. Duplex accommodations include two floors, a living room with fireplace and fold-out couch, a kitchenette, and a bedroom. Motel units include two double beds, a full bath, cheery decor, a refrigerator, and balconies overlooking the golf course. Price for a motel room for two adults is $139 per night; a duplex is $159, and a town house is $189. Kids younger than 4 stay free, while kids 4 to 11 cost $29 and those 12 to 17 cost $55.

If you want the room and golf, you get a real bargain. One night at midweek in a motel room, including golf, dinner the night of check-in, and breakfast the following morning, is $105 per night for two in a room; two nights midweek cost $196; three nights midweek cost $279. The rates for a duplex or town house go up accordingly. Midweek and package rates are lower. Mountain Manor's brochure is extensive, and there are many variables; call for a copy.

Mountain Manor is only 0.5 mile from US 209 in Marshalls Creek.

Pocmont Resort
Bushkill Falls Road, Bushkill
(570) 588–6671, (800) 762–6668
www.pocmont.com

Pocmont has recently undergone major renovations that have added facilities and improved the resort. The health club has floor-to-ceiling windows that overlook the outdoor pool. The indoor pool is close to the fitness center, sauna, whirlpool, and steam rooms. A Manhattan-style deli offers overstuffed sandwiches, and a multilevel nightclub pumps up the evening excitement. In all the rebuilding, special attention has been paid to the needs of people with disabilities, and new areas meet the requirements of the Americans with Disabilities Act.

Activities abound: tennis, boat rides on the lake, archery, boccie, miniature golf, ice-skating, a game room, and volleyball. We did mention the Olympic-size outdoor pool, didn't we? Planned activities are available throughout the day, and guests can enjoy dancing and entertainment nightly. Fun-filled theme weekends offer special packages. A fully supervised day camp keeps the kids happy. Gourmet meals are served in a lovely dining room. In winter you can ride the resort's snow-mobiles; in summer, walk its miles of trails.

Accommodations are in suites, with luxuries including Jacuzzis, hydromassage whirlpools, and in some cases, fireplaces or terraced balconies. There are also standard rooms in the hotel plus one- and two-bedroom cottages, some with king-size beds and separate living rooms.

Rates depend on the type of accommodation but range from $84 to $155 per person per night, double occupancy, and include breakfast and dinner daily. Children 2 and younger are free; ages 3 to 12 cost $25 to $48, depending on the season and the plan; and ages 13 to 17 cost $40 to $68 per night.

Shawnee Inn and Golf Resort
River Road, Shawnee-on-Delaware
(570) 424-4000, (800) SHAWNEE
www.shawneeinn.com

When C. C. Worthington, a turn-of-the-century industrialist and inventor, built and ran the Shawnee Inn (originally called the Buckwood Inn), its guests were leaders in industry and other powerful people. When Fred Waring owned it, his showbiz pals populated its halls. (Fred Waring and his Pennsylvanians, a Big Band chorus, were known worldwide. Fred was an inventor too; his Waring Blendor was the first successful version of an appliance that is in almost everybody's kitchen today.) Those who remember Shawnee in Waring's heyday tell stories of his radio broadcasts from Worthington Hall, now the Shawnee Playhouse (see our Arts and Culture chapter); Jackie Gleason's pool shark shenanigans; and Mickey Mantle and the New York Yankees, who looked so gigantic to the children of the village that when they jumped into the pool, all the water seemed to splash out. Shawnee's present owners, Charlie and Ginny Kirkwood, have many overseas interests (Ginny was once head of the Peace Corps in Thailand), and today as you stroll through the grounds, you'll hear a babble of different languages.

Shawnee is an impressive turn-of-the-century grande dame—a historic site—with lawns meandering to the Delaware River's edge. Activities on the grounds and a few minutes away by car include hiking trails, an A. W. Tillinghast-designed 27-hole golf course mostly on an island in the Delaware River (see our Golf chapter), a golf academy, ski slopes (see our Winter Sports chapter), a miniature golf course, canoeing, rafting, tubing (see our In, On, and Around the Water chapter for rental information), fishing (licenses and equipment required), indoor and outdoor pools, tennis, basketball, bike riding, and relaxing down by the river or on the inn's gracious verandah that overlooks the river and the Kittatinny Ridge. There's also a lovely riverside grill (the only restaurant for 40 miles along the Delaware); a lounge with entertainment (see Nightlife); and a coffee shop with great views of the river, excellent coffee, and the most sinful desserts imaginable.

Shawnee has undergone extensive renovation, and the lobby and rooms have been restored to the elegance that made this inn famous. The public areas in the inn are now WiFi compatible. Bring your WiFi-compatible laptop, and you can log right on to a lightning-speed Internet connection.

A lovely village on one side of the resort provides pleasant lanes for walking. Jackie Gleason once owned a cottage here, and Mr. Greenjeans, of Captain Kangaroo fame, lived in the white bungalow that is the second house from the river on Worthington Avenue. While most of the village was built by Worthington 100 years ago, it was the first spot in the area settled by Europeans, and parts of it are much older. (See our History and Relocation chapters.)

Around the second week of October, Shawnee hosts an annual balloon festival (see Annual Events) with hot-air balloon launching, music, food, crafts, and games. It's an event that draws many people to this usually quiet spot.

The rooms have been redecorated, and the phones even provide modem plugs. A shuttle runs between all the scattered Shawnee spots, so you can park your car and leave it, if you wish.

Shawnee Inn rooms run from $69 to $300 per room, depending on the season and whether you're getting the breakfast and dinner plan or just a room. There are also a variety of packages, including ski packages, golf packages, and bus tour packages.

Children younger than 18 stay for $30 a night; those younger than 5 stay and eat free. Shawnee can also accommodate group meetings or conferences; call for details.

Many Pocono residents rent their homes on a weekly or monthly basis, particularly in private communities and near recreation areas such as Lake Wallenpaupack. These are discussed in our Real Estate chapter. Consult a real estate agent for rates and availability in the region you desire.

Tamiment Resort & Conference Center
Bushkill Falls Road, Tamiment
(570) 588–6652, (800) 233–8105
www.tamiment.com
Tamiment, a four-season resort, surrounds a beautiful mountain lake, which you'll see as you drive in toward the main lodge. From the lakefront, the rolling hills, woods, and Robert Trent Jones–designed 18-hole golf course (see our Golf chapter) make you feel like you're being cradled by nature. Amenities here include six lighted outdoor tennis courts and two indoor courts, indoor and outdoor basketball, volleyball, indoor racquetball, and boccie. Fitness amenities include a full fitness room with state-of-the-art equipment, Ping-Pong, Jacuzzi, and sauna. Swim in the enormous lakeside pool or lovely indoor pool. The spectacular spring-fed lake offers boating and fishing. Tamiment's 2,200 acres provide ample room to hike, ride horses, or, in winter (weather permitting), go cross-country skiing.

Breakfast and dinner are served in the formal dining room overlooking the lake. Lunch is available at a cafe or poolside snack bar. There is a nightclub here with live entertainment every night during the summer and weekends the rest of the year. Recreation programs for adults and children are offered all day long. There are also meeting rooms and facilities large enough to hold the most demanding convention, corporate meeting, or family reunion. Golf outings are popular too. The staff is ready to help plan group activities such as meals and team-building programs.

Accommodations include guest rooms and suites, ranging from standard to deluxe. They are available in the Tamiment House Hotel or Golf Clubhouse. All are carpeted, color-coordinated, climate-controlled, and equipped with private baths, color TVs, and telephones. Rates run from $66 to $108 per person per night for double occupancy on the Modified American Plan. Children ages 5 to 12 are $19.84 per night (MAP); children 13 to 16 are $24.60 per night if staying in the same room (MAP). Winter rates are less, and special packages are available.

Water Gap Resort
Main Street (Highway 611 South)
Delaware Water Gap
(570) 476–0010
www.watergapresort.com
The venerable Glenwood Resort has new owners and a new name. Now the Water Gap Resort, it is walking-distance to all the happenings in town. It is one of two hotels from the heyday of Delaware Water

Gap that is still operating (the other is the Deer Head Inn, which no longer operates as a hotel but as a jazz club and restaurant; see Nightlife and Restaurants). The Water Gap Trolley, part of the ambiance here, takes visitors on a tour of the area and historic points of interest. (See our Attractions chapter.)

The Water Gap Resort has a minigolf course, indoor and outdoor pools, a sauna, shuffleboard, tennis courts, an exercise room, and a restaurant.

Three types of accommodations are available: main lodge rooms, motel rooms (park at your door), and cabanas. All rooms have color TVs, private baths, telephones, and refrigerators. Motel rooms have two full-size beds, and the main lodge rooms include some single cabanas and motel rooms. The cabanas have full- to king-size beds, and some have a Jacuzzi.

Rooms run from $55 to $75 per person per night, double occupancy, Modified American Plan, or $60 to $125 per room, with no meal plan. Children younger than 10 stay free but pay $15 a day for food. Children 10 and older, add $20 a day to stay; children 11 and older, add $25 a day to eat.

Stroudsburg/East Stroudsburg

Hillside Inn
Frutchey Drive, East Stroudsburg
(570) 223-8238
www.poconohillside.com
This 109-acre resort holds the distinction of being the first and only resort in the Poconos owned by an African-American family. It was opened to cater to the black community when other Pocono hotels still were segregated. Its founder, retired Federal Judge Albert Murray Sr., already had beaten the segregation mind-set of his day by rising to the top in a legal career essentially closed to Blacks. The doors are

> *Modified American Plan, or MAP, means your room comes with breakfast and dinner, while European Plan, or EP, is for the room only, no meals.*

open now, and Judge Murray's son, Albert Jr. is now in charge. Sonny, as his friends know him, has had a stellar career in law. Among his legal coups was a decision by the IRS to take a percentage of Sammy Davis Jr.'s future royalties rather than leave his widow penniless. The Hillside Inn prospers with guests of all races who come to enjoy this 30-room, modern resort and two-bedroom villas.

Amenities include an indoor exercise room, game room, swimming pool with hot spa, and live entertainment that draws locals as well as guests. Hillside features the best in jazz, gospel, and dance music. (The Sunday gospel programs are a real treat.) Outdoor activities include tennis, round robin golf course, basketball, volleyball, softball, shuffleboard, ping pong, horseshoes, hiking, walking, and jogging. Fishing is available in the private lake.

Rooms feature king, queen, or double beds, and all contain wall-to-wall carpeting, color TVs, telephones, private baths, and air-conditioning. The larger rooms have sitting areas with sofas. Suites and townhouses offer options for families. Rates, based on double occupancy and including breakfast and dinner, run $68 to $109 per person per night, depending on the season. Better prices for weekend, midweek, and full-week stays are available. Townhouses, which sleep up to six, are a bit higher and can be rented with or without a meal plan. Children ages 6 to 11 stay for half price, and those 5 and younger stay free.

The dining room specializes in Southern, Caribbean, and traditional American cuisine served family-style at several large tables so that guests get to know each other. The motto of this lovely hillside resort is "old-fashioned warmth, good

Deerfield Spa, the Friendly, Affordable Spa Experience

So you weigh a little more than you'd like, and you'll admit, you're out of shape. You have fantasies of going to a spa, but everyone knows they're only for the hopelessly wealthy. Not so. The Poconos' own Deerfield Spa is a top-quality spa that won't make your bank account thinner than your tummy.

Deerfield Spa is a homey, friendly place. The main building is in a large, white country house decked with porches and plenty of flowers. In an earlier lifetime, it was a small hotel called the Humble Rest. (Ironically, the Humble Rest was known for its fattening Pennsylvania Dutch food.) Inside the main house and annex, the carpets are thick, the walls white, and the fabrics floral. The simplicity of the décor accents the exquisite art you'll find on walls all over the spa.

The spa was established by Frieda Eisenkraft, and when she died, her daughter Joan Wolff took over. Deerfield was a welcoming, friendly place in Frieda's time, and Joan has continued the tradition. With only 33 guests at any one time, you can be sure that staff will learn your name quickly, and lots of the customers return year after year; some even visit two or three times a year. The staff also is loyal. Many have been working here for more than a decade.

What is a day in a spa like? You start at 7:15 A.M. with yoga. Breakfast is next, at 8:15 A.M., and then you spend the day taking fitness seminars in aerobics (in a beautiful dance gym), interval circuit training (in a gym equipped with all the latest high-tech exercise machinery), stretching, body sculpting, water aerobics, dance, taichi, sports, hiking (either at the Delaware Water Gap or one of the other beautiful area trails) and more. Deerfield Spa offers classes in more than 30 different disciplines, so you can find the ones that are right for you, and emphasizes moderation, free choice, and personalized programs. After dinner, an evening program might be a lecture on nutrition, an astrology or tarot reading, or a cooking class.

Of course, you don't have to do everything. You can mix and match programs to suit your own needs, or you can

food, and personal service." Accordingly, the inn provides shuttle service for guests to and from the bus station.

Hillside is a high-water mark in the Poconos for its groundbreaking past. The inn is close to Delaware Water Gap National Recreation Area as well as golf courses in Shawnee, Delaware Water Gap, Marshalls Creek, and Analomink—seven courses in all within a 20-minute drive, which those who know the family say is a good thing because the Judge loves his golf. The inn also is a scant 5-minute drive from Shawnee Mountain and about 15 minutes from Alpine Mountain and Camelback ski areas.

add extras to your day, including massages, facials, body wraps, manicures, psychic readings, and fitness consultations.

What about the food? Will you get tiny portions of rabbit food and be hungry all week? Deerfield's meals, served in a wood-paneled dining room with lots of windows overlooking the pretty grounds, are mostly organic, mostly vegetarian, but include chicken and fish options every day. Everything is made fresh by the highly skilled chef who emphasizes whole foods and lots of vegetables. All foods are calorie counted and very low fat. The presentation is stunning. As Frieda used to say, "You eat with your eyes, first." Colorful sauces are drizzled over an entrée, and edible flowers often grace your plate. This is food you expect to see in California or at a particularly upscale restaurant in New York. Since the cuisine emphasizes vegetables, portions are fairly substantial, and no one looks hungry at Deerfield Spa. Dinner is often four courses—salad, a main course, vegetables, and a dessert of fruit or fat-free frozen yogurt.

The spa holds its own on a national level. It has been rated highly in Zagat's U.S. Hotel and Resort Spas survey and was named one of the top 25 destination spas by *Spa Vacations* magazine, right up there with the Golden Door and Canyon Ranch. And yes, you may find yourself rubbing shoulders with celebrities. Actors, authors, and politicians' wives have been guests at Deerfield Spa.

So what does all this cost? A week, which includes all kinds of classes, a massage, all meals, evening programs and follow-up materials, can run from $800 to $1,295 depending on the room your choose—no more expensive than a stay at many of our resorts. Day and weekend rates are available; early- and late-season special packages lower the rates even more. You can send for a brochure (650 Resica Falls Road, East Stroudsburg, Pennsylvania 18301), call (570) 223–0160 or (800) 852–4494, or go to www.deerfieldspa.com for more information.

The result of your week at a spa? "You may lose a few pounds," said Frieda, "but we promote good health. We show you what you can eat, how much you can eat, and how plentiful the right kind of food can be. You go home motivated because you've had a lot of days of exercise and a lot of different kinds of exercise. You can pick something you like and keep doing it at home. A week at a spa is a beginning."

Mount Pocono Area

Caesars Brookdale
Highway 611, Scotrun
(570) 839–8844, (877) 822–3333
www.caesarspoconoresorts.com
Caesars Brookdale is one of four famed Caesars resorts in the Poconos. While the others cater to couples only, Brookdale has facilities for families, too. Brookdale is lovely, surrounded by woods on a 250-acre estate on the corridor between Stroudsburg and Mount Pocono. It includes a trout-stocked lake as well as hiking and bicycling trails. The atmosphere is rustic, relaxed, and comfortable. Cou-

ples can enjoy the heart-shaped tubs and champagne towers (7.5-foot-tall, champagne glass–shaped whirlpools), big enough for two.

The whole family can take part in activities such as indoor roller skating; outdoor ice skating; tennis; miniature golf; billiards; indoor and outdoor swimming; exercising at the health club; and playing outdoor basketball, volleyball, and softball. On the lake, enjoy canoes, paddleboats, and sailboats.

The Caesars group has an option called the Key Around Club, which offers adult guests free use of facilities at the other Caesars resorts. (As the other three Caesars resorts are for adults only, the Key Around Club is not available to children.) With the Key Around Club, you can cross-country ski at Pocono Palace (see the subsequent "Couples/Honeymoon Retreats" section), toboggan at Cove Haven, play indoor racquetball at Paradise Stream and Cove Haven, golf at Pocono Palace, use the golf driving ranges at Pocono Palace and Cove Haven, and water-ski at Pocono Palace and Cove Haven. Brookdale is only minutes away from the Camelback and Alpine ski areas. (See our Winter Sports chapter.) The new "Kids Kamp" provides supervised, age-appropriate activities for children grouped by age—5 to 7, 8 to 12, and 13 and older. As the Kamps run midmorning to early afternoon, parents may sign their children in and out at any time.

Entertainers perform in the resort's nightclub, the Applause. Breakfast and dinner all-you-can-eat buffets are part of your accommodations package; for honeymooners there is a breakfast in bed.

Rates are per couple and include two meals daily and free use of all facilities

plus Key Around Club options for adults. They are based on a minimum of three nights, but you can add to the base package in daily increments. Rates start at $161.25 per room and go up based on additional in-room amenities, such as pools and spas. The most expensive are the Champagne Towers from Rome, luxurious two-story accommodations including a downstairs living room with fireplace and cathedral ceiling, a dining area, a private heart-shaped pool, and a loft area with bedroom. The bedroom contains a king-size round bed with a starlight ceiling. The Roman Tower also includes a sauna and the Champagne Tower whirlpool, which you enter from the loft level. Rates run from $292.50 per night. At Brookdale, children older than 12 are $75 daily; children 5 to 12 are $60 daily, and children 4 and younger are free.

The Chateau at Camelback
300 Camelback Road, Tannersville
(570) 629–5900, (800) 245–5900
www.chateauresort.com
The Chateau is at the base of Camelback Ski Area, which makes it a great choice for skiers who want to be as close as possible to the slopes but in a hotel rather than a townhouse or condominium. This hotel looks like a modernized French chateau set among mountains and nestled against its own little swan-filled lake. One side of The Chateau is all glass, affording views of the mountains in four-season splendor from the lounge, main lobby, indoor swimming pool, Jacuzzi, and dining room. The outdoor pool and surrounding gardens, gazebo, and multi-level sun decks also have mountain views. You can play boccie, volleyball, and shuffleboard; hike in nearby Big Pocono State Park (see our Parks chapter); hang out in the game room, heat up in the sauna, and tone-up in the exercise room.

The rooms are large and comfortable with two double beds; some have lofts, and all have wonderful views. Poolside rooms have balconies overlooking the pool and pond with Camelback as the backdrop. High season rates per room (double occupancy) run from $87.50 to $159.00 per person per night, depending on the time of week and the type of room. Children stay free. Great package deals for golfing or skiing are available. Conferences, conventions, and groups are welcome. And weddings outside by the pool or in the poolside, Ledges, or Mountainview dining rooms are truly lovely. This hotel is up the mountain from the Crossings Factory Stores (see our Shopping chapter)—a great option if some in your group want to shop while others ski.

Chestnut Grove Resort
Upper Swiftwater Road, Swiftwater
(570) 839-3656
www.chestnutgrove.com

Chestnut Grove is an active, happy family resort. When you walk in the lobby of the main building, a gracious old white inn, the first thing you see is an activity board with trips to various Pocono attractions every day. Social directors keep everyone busy, especially the kids who can participate in a fishing contest, play volleyball, make arts and crafts, or join in one of the many other diversions here. Two pools, one indoor and one out, each have a wading area for the little ones. The indoor pool includes a hot tub with a waterfall cascading down some rocks. There's a playground, picnic tables, a pretty lake with a bridge leading to a picturesque island, paddleboats, tennis courts, a softball field, basketball, boccie, a bonfire with music and a wienie roast, hayrides, and a game room. The small lake has incredible catch-and-release fishing for largemouth bass.

The resort is run by Chick Daniels, who started Daniels Top-O-The Poconos Resort (see subsequent entry), and he knows how to keep his guests happy. Hearty breakfasts and dinners, included in your stay, are served in a lovely green and white dining room with lace curtains. On a nice day, many guests take their food to the tables on an outdoor deck. A bar off

the dining room is decorated with pretty white Christmas lights and offers live entertainment every night in July and August and weekends the rest of the year. A set of boom-bas sticks (see our Nightlife chapter) gives guests a chance to try a local "musical" oddity.

Chestnut Grove offers cottages and rooms in the lodge. Cottages, some sleeping up to six, are decorated in Pocono rustic style with lots of wood and simple furnishings. They have a sitting room with a pullout couch, air-conditioning, and color TV. Most include a fireplace. The most luxurious cottages are the Vistas with sunken living rooms, stone fireplaces, and terraces overlooking the lake. These have sumptuous modern furnishings.

Chestnut Grove is a reasonably priced resort. A family of four can stay for $1,045 for the week, which includes breakfast and dinner; a two-night weekend stay costs $250–$325 for a couple with breakfast and dinner depending on the season.

Daniels Top-O-The-Poconos Resort
Highway 447 North, Canadensis
(570) 595-7531, (800) 755-0300
www.danielsresort.com

Being at Daniels is like spending Christmas in the home of a large family. There are children, lots of activity, laughing, and events going on all the time. The facilities include three outdoor pools, an indoor pool with hot tub and sauna, a softball field, a full-size lighted basketball court, lighted boccie courts, three tennis courts, an archery range, playgrounds, a videogame room, volleyball, laser karaoke, and more than 80 beautiful country acres to walk, hike, take hayrides across, or cross-country ski in winter. Other activities include talent nights, tournaments in all the sports, arts and crafts, nature walks, bingo, live entertainment, and more. There are oodles of family-oriented activities all summer. After Labor Day, when the little ones are in school, many couples and singles come for a romantic getaway or a quiet retreat, and on winter weekends

Make sure you check a hotel, resort, or campground's Web site for special deals and special dates.

before Christmas, Daniels allows guests to cut their own free trees from the resort's property to take home for the holidays.

Food is excellent and plentiful. Guests are served a hearty breakfast each morning and a full-course dinner each night. Breakfast includes eggs or omelettes, home fries, bacon or sausage, pancakes, French toast or waffles, and hot or cold cereal. Lunch is available at the snack bar, although most guests say they're usually too full from breakfast to eat lunch. Dinner might be baked Virginia ham, sweet and sour chicken, roast beef with gravy, chicken cordon bleu, or Chinese pepper steak, each with potatoes and vegetables.

Daniels is a family place that folks come back to year after year—and bring all their friends. It's a place where everybody knows your name, and it's a great place for family reunions.

Accommodations include inn rooms, poolside cottages, and the Hilltop Lodge and Cottages. Hilltop, with a separate outdoor pool and play area, is tucked away in a quieter spot 0.75 mile from the inn—for those who want to get away from it all. Rates depend on the number of people in your family. For Friday through Sunday, you pay $120 to $185 per adult, depending on the weekend, which includes all meals. The cost per child is $40 to $65, depending on the weekend. Their weekly rates are equally reasonable. (*Note:* Bring your own towels.)

Daniels advertises the cheapest rates in the Poconos; call for a brochure to survey specific options. It also offers weekend getaway packages, themed weekends, and special rates for groups, including reunions. Daniels is near many Poconos delights. (See the "Mount Poconos Area" sections of each chapter.) If you want a break from the scheduled activities here, daily or hourly excursions to local attractions are available.

Hillside Lodge Resort Motel and Cottages
Highway 390, Canadensis
(570) 595-7551, (800) 666-4455
www.hillsidelodge.com

Hillside is a quiet, cozy family resort of suites and cottages in the hills near Canadensis. The emphasis is on family and activities to suit your entire clan. Nature walks, volleyball, horseshoes, boccie, minigolf, a game room, and swimming in the indoor and outdoor pool are some of the many activities. Don't miss the weekly bonfire—it's fun! A whitewater rafting adventure is planned each week for adults and children six and older.

Buffet-style meals are served in the colorful dining room, with a private table for each family or group.

Accommodations include large spacious suites or cottages, some with fireplaces and some with sunken heart-shaped tubs or two-person whirlpools. The cottages have refrigerators and separate living rooms and bedrooms. One cottage is even decorated with a Penn State theme, for Nittany Lions fans.

Depending on the season, you can book the resort on the Modified American Plan, or no meals. Rates are based on double occupancy. Options include daily and weekend rates and monthly rates. Weekend packages offered throughout the year include theme events and discounted rates. Special weekends are offered throughout the year, so check the Web site, or inquire when you're making reservations. Honeymoon packages are also available.

The daily base room rate with Modified American Plan is $185 to $225 for a suite, and for the most extravagant cottage with king-size bed, fireplace, and two-person whirlpool, $275. Monthly rates run from $2,250 to $3,999. Rates for children begin at $20 daily for ages 2 to 5 and range up to $40 daily for ages 13 to 17. Children younger than 2 stay free.

Laurel Grove Inn & Resort
Highway 447, Canadensis
(570) 595-7262, (800) 842-0497

Laurel Grove looks like your quintessential old-time resort—like something from the movie *Dirty Dancing*. The 117-year-old white wooden inn boasts a great porch with a row of green rockers facing the road and the woods beyond. Around the side of the porch, a series of tables sits under outdoor ceiling fans, and if you look carefully, you'll see some swallows' nests on a special shelf that seems to have been built for them. Inside are large, old-fashioned sitting and dining rooms—functional and simple, but comfortable. A series of cabins runs behind the main inn. The rooms are standard hotel rooms with a variety of sleeping arrangements, mostly two double beds, a television, and a private bath. The assumption is that you'll spend your time at the swimming pool, tennis court, nine-hole golf course, pool table, basketball court, volleyball court, or indoor shuffleboard. You can also use the grill and picnic tables. A trail behind the resort leads to a pretty stream and across the road, the resort has a lovely picnic grove under a stand of tall pine trees. Laurel Grove has several conference rooms and can accommodate large-scale gatherings and church retreats.

The restaurant doesn't open regular hours but will provide breakfast, lunch, and dinner for guests who want it.

Laurel Grove, in season, costs $80 to $100 for two people. A third person in the room costs $15 more; meals are extra and by arrangement only. Pets are allowed in some rooms.

Pocono Manor Inn and Golf Resort
Highway 314 West, Pocono Manor
(570) 839-7111, (800) 233-8150
www.poconomanor.com

Pocono Manor, a comfortable, welcoming historic retreat built by Quakers in 1902 is on the National Register of Historic Places as a designated historic district. It sits on top of a ridge like a fairy tale castle surrounded by privately owned "cottages" right out of Philadelphia's wealthy Main Line. It has evolved from a 65-room summer retreat into a beautiful inn with 257 guest rooms and suites, meeting rooms, banquet facilities, and a dining room with a breathtaking view of the misty hills beyond. Pocono Manor is a golf resort and has two excellent 18-hole courses. (See our Golf chapter.) In 1966 the inn and its accompanying 3,500 acres were bought by the late Samuel Ireland, owner of the Ireland Coffee Company. The property is still owned by the family today.

You'll encounter a friendly atmosphere as soon as you walk into the comfortable lobby. Here, as in other sitting rooms throughout, are large, stone fireplaces that blaze all winter surrounded by lots of easy chairs and couches. A nice touch is the ever-present coffee table in the lobby, with fresh java for guests any time of day.

Winter or summer you'll find little nooks, indoors and out, where you can relax. The Irelands have renovated and refurbished this historic inn. The main public areas have been recarpeted and redecorated in wonderful combinations of green, burgundy, and taupe; the rooms have been redecorated with historically representative yet modern functional decor. The custom, handcarved wood furniture is from the Bethlehem Furniture company; the dining room features solid cherry, comb-back chairs made by the famous Duckloe Furniture Company. (See our Shopping chapter.)

There are about 190 rooms in the main lodge, all with lovely views of the surrounding mountains and some with views of the Delaware Water Gap. Across from the front entrance (beautifully restructured in stone) are about 60 rooms in the Laurel and Spruce buildings, which guests access via covered walkway. These rooms surround the outdoor swimming pool, where guests can enjoy a lunch of hot dogs and hamburgers cooked on a large stone grill. The delightful Fireside Lodge—also with access to the outdoor grill—hosts private events for as many as 150 people.

For indoor eating, the light and airy main dining room offers mountains of wonderfully prepared food. Outdoors, beneath this dining room, is a large barbecue area for summer events.

Renovated and updated amenities include indoor and outdoor pools, a kiddie pool, saunas, a world-class spa, a Nautilus fitness center and, of course, the two 18-hole championship golf courses. Other activities include indoor and outdoor tennis courts, racquetball courts, horseback riding on the beautiful trails that grace the wooded grounds, hay or sleigh rides, ski and skate rentals, a driving range, biking, snowmobiling, snow tubing, and trap shooting. In addition, Pocono Manor has been endorsed by Orvis as an official hunting and fishing lodge with sporting clays. Some of these activities and the ones that follow are complimentary with your room; others require an additional charge. Other on-site activities include dancing and playing games in the game room. For less strenuous pursuits, The Old Lamplighter Lounge features a library with a pool table and large-screen TV, live music, and movies on weekends.

Winter activities include cross-country skiing, ice-skating at a delightful outdoor rink nestled at the base of the main lodge, and sledding and tubing on a special hill. There is always some type of live entertainment.

There are plenty of facilities for groups, organizations, conventions, seminars, family reunions, and such. If you are planning a wedding, we suggest you look at the Horizon Room and the Terrace Ballroom. Both have lovely views of the surrounding mountains and grounds of Pocono Manor, and both are beautifully decorated. Each also adjoins a lounge that can be used as a private reception area.

Standard high-season room rates are $170 per couple per night, excluding meals. For a standard room plus meals on the Modified American Plan, the rate is $268 per couple. Children younger than eight stay for $37 per night; this includes breakfast and dinner. Packages are available, and their golf and spa packages are super.

Skytop Lodge
Highway 390, Skytop
(570) 595-7401 or (800) 617-2389
www.skytop.com

Drive toward Skytop along a winding country road that leads to the sudden view of a grand, stone bridge over an enormous, beautiful lake. Continue up the driveway to what appears to be an incredible English country estate. As you walk from your car into Skytop's impressive main building, and you're greeted by the helpful doorman, you feel you have entered another dimension, an enchanted place where people and place exceed your expectations. Everything about Skytop, from the physical plant to its wonderful staff, bolsters this impression. Skytop is an especially elegant resort that was built in the 1920s as a members-only hunting and fishing lodge. It was designed to be a top-flight accommodation.

The circular drive in front of the grand, stone portico entrance (where you are met by stately, jacket-clad bellhops) is surrounded by beautiful gardens and expansive lawns. From the wooden rocking chairs on the elegant South Porch, you can see the Delaware Water Gap. From any room in the European-style grand lodge, Skytop's 5,500 acres spread out before you, across meadows, down mountains, into woods, along streams, beneath waterfalls, and around a lake. The land encompasses a gentle ski slope suitable for beginning and intermediate skiers with four trails, two lifts and 100 percent snowmaking; cross-country skiing trails; an 18-hole championship golf course (see our Golf chapter); pro-caliber tennis courts; an outdoor pool; a bathing beach on the sparkling lake; jogging and hiking trails and a weather-protected ice-skating pavilion. The grounds also include lovely guest cottages and a new inn and convention center. The lodge is the centerpiece of a private community of astonishing homes.

Skytop is the choice for an elegant, Old World–style weekend getaway, a mid-week escape, or a week-long family vacation. Guests dress up—men wear sport jackets, ladies don appropriate attire (no shorts, bathing suits, tank tops, or jeans)—for dinner in the distinguished dining room. Casual attire is fine for breakfast and lunch. Floor-to-ceiling windows look out over the south lawn and provide a backdrop of foliage and views in every season that only nature could design. Waiters (many of them) attend to your every need, serving and pampering you at each meal.

The main lobby of the lodge intensifies the feeling of luxury with its huge fireplace, Oriental rugs, wingback chairs, and lovely seating groups. Pickled pine beams rib the ceilings and form the huge columns in the grand ballroom-size entrance. More floor-to-ceiling windows look out on the South Porch and beyond. Afternoon tea can be enjoyed in the lobby.

In summer, abundant activities for the entire family are included in your stay: concerts in the South Courtyard; miniature golf; archery; movies; dancing; bridge; hiking; nighttime deer watches; stargazing; relaxing in the sauna, whirlpool, kiddie pool, indoor or outdoor pool; lake swimming in July and August; table tennis; and picnicking. An expanded health club with treadmills, stair-step machines, and Marcy gym stations are part of the fitness facilities.

For a modest charge you can have a massage, facial, or pedicure at the health spa; play tennis; golf; go mountain biking; go boating (kayaking, rowboating, and canoeing); attend the children's summer day camp (providing you're young enough, mid-June to Labor Day) or participate in a Skytop tradition—lawn bowling.

Traveling with little ones? Take them to Skytop's new toddler room, set up with foam pads for them to climb, books, toys, and toddler-size tables and chairs.

A 6-percent accommodations tax applies in Pennsylvania. Don't forget to figure this amount into your vacation budget.

Skytop is now affiliated with Orvis, the world leader in fly-fishing schools and equipment. You can study with Orvis instructors, March through October, or cast out on your own along one of Skytop's trout-filled streams. The lakes offer trout and bass, and some world-class fishing spots, including Zane Grey's beloved Lackawaxen River, are a short drive away. Skytop has also introduced clay shooting to its amenities. Beginners can learn on a straightforward course, while more-experienced shooters will enjoy a challenging 12-station course. Instruction for all levels is available. There are miles of hiking trails to see beautiful mountain vistas, ancient forests, sparkling lakes, cascading waterfalls, and other beauties of nature. Trails take you close to native fauna, such as minks, bobcats, black bears, coyotes, river otters, and more than 175 kinds of birds. Naturalist John Serrao leads nature walks, and the *Skytop Trail Guide* and other publications explain trail characteristics in great detail.

Accommodations in the lodge itself include double rooms, minisuites, and VIP suites. Four-bedroom cottages are within walking distance of the lodge. One set of cottages adjoins the fairway—perfect for golfers; the other set adjoins a children's playground—perfect for families. A 20-room inn right on the golf course provides luxury accommodations for golfers.

A number of rooms at Skytop reflect the cozy comfort of an accessorized sitting room rather than simply a sleeping room in a hotel. A nice feature is adjoining rooms for children—separate yet convenient.

There are many ways to enjoy Skytop. You can come to experience a theme weekend (how about a Dickens Christmas Weekend, a Country Weekend, an Edgar

Since most people now travel over the weekday rates are usually lower. If you're thinking of taking three or four days and can do so between Monday and Thursday, you'll save money.

Allan Poe Weekend, or a Mad Hatter's Weekend?); enjoy a romantic getaway; appreciate an Autumn Nature Weekend or a Golf Getaway package for unlimited golf on the 18-hole course or play tennis all weekend long.

Rates at this retreat, which include three meals a day, vary based on type of accommodation and length of stay. There are family plans, senior-citizen plans, mid-week packages, even conference packages for groups and family reunions. The basic parameters of each money-saving option are available on request.

High-end weekend rates start at $226 per person, per night, double occupancy. The family plan allows children 16 and younger to stay in their parents' room for $30 per child per night (no more than two children). Additional children cost $45 each. Children occupying their own room receive a $100 discount. A 15 percent service charge is added to your bill in lieu of gratuities for regular lodge services.

If you are looking for an elegant place at what feels like the top of the world, you should treat yourself to a stay at Skytop.

West End

The Mountain Laurel Resort & Spa
off I-80 exit 42, White Haven
(570) 443-8411, (800) 255-7625
www.mountainlaurelresort.com
This resort in the western Poconos is a relaxed getaway with a focus on "Leave the kids with us." Facilities include indoor and outdoor swimming pools, three lighted tennis courts, sauna, archery, horseback riding, and nature trails for hiking and walking, a miniature golf course, and, in winter, sledding and ice-skating.

Skiing is available nearby at Jack Frost and Big Boulder.

A new spa and fitness area offers massages by appointment (there's an extra charge). Meals may be purchased in the on-site restaurant a Touch of Vanilla, Molly Maguire's snack shop, or Tavern on the Terrace, a bar and nightclub.

"Just Us Kids" provides activities for children age 3 to 12 in two sessions daily and a third, evening session, on the weekend. The evening session includes dinner, giving the folks a chance to eat kid-free. Arts and crafts are included in every session, and, depending on the weather, kids might also play games, pet some farm animals at the stable, play mini-golf or bubble gum bingo. The cost is $3.00 per session, and children will be divided into age groups, depending on how many children attend each session.

The nightly rate for a double-occupancy room ranges from $59 to $99, depending on the season. Children 5 and older, who stay in the room with their parents, cost $15 each, per night. Those 4 and younger stay free. Mountain Laurel is serious about a no pets rule. If they discover a pet in your room, they will charge $250 for fumigation. This resort allows you to combine on-site activities with the myriad attractions in Jim Thorpe.

The Resort at Split Rock
1 Lake Drive, Lake Harmony
(570) 722-9111, (800) 255-7625
This resort once was a hunting and camping retreat for executives of the Lehigh Coal and Navigation Company. It originally was developed by company president Robert V. White in 1941 as a lodge surrounded by five private cottages. In 1946, White turned Split Rock into the nation's first ski resort. Split Rock, which quickly became a favorite weekend retreat, also was the first ski resort in the nation to try snowmaking. (See related Close-up in our Winter Sports chapter.)

Today, after passing through other owners and surviving a devastating fire that nearly destroyed it in 1970, Split Rock has become a premier family resort with a 27-hole golf course, a lake for swimming and boating, and several types of accommodations. Rooms are available in the lodge, suites in the Galleria complex and at slopeside, cottages are offered near the lake, and villas near the golf course. This is an energetic, casual, activities-oriented resort.

When you enter the complex through the private toll road, you are on your way to the ultramodern Galleria. There are two restaurants, a massage facility, a movie theater, the Pit Lounge, and the Galleria Night Club, with entertainment almost nightly. A fitness center and sports complex with indoor tennis and racquetball courts and an indoor pool also are available for health-conscious guests.

After you have passed the Galleria and a series of casual vacation homes (A-frames and lodges, both with lots of decks), you'll find yourself heading for the lodge, just past Westwood Villas and the golf course, and farther on, the minigolf course, outdoor tennis courts, and an outdoor pool.

The lake, with its swimming lagoon and boat dock, is the backdrop for the main lodge. Its amenities include Bell'ago, a fine Italian restaurant, overlooking Lake Harmony, for indoor, cozy, fireside dining in winter and alfresco dining on the deck in summer. The Rock Bar, a coffee shop, the Old Fashioned Ice Cream Parlour in the Galleria, and the Harmony Pizza Shop in the lodge area offer fast food for guests on the go.

Something is always happening here: the Pocono Blues Festival, the Pocono Country Music Festival, and the Pocono American Roots Festival (two events in one) are nearby, and such food-related events as the Great Tastes of Pennsylvania Wine and Food Festival and the Great Brews of America Classic Beer Festival are held at the resort. The resort is near Pocono Raceway, which makes it a great place for race fans to stay. The town of Jim Thorpe is about a half-hour drive if you are interested in enhancing your vacation with a cultural turn in a museum or art gallery.

Family fun is a focus, with Kids' Korner in morning, afternoon, and evening sessions for children 3 and older. Family activities also include the 18-hole championship miniature golf course, softball, bumper boats, archery, and much more, including fabulous activities for everyone by social director Doc Holiday. Swimming is available indoors (in the main lodge and the Galleria) and outdoors, as well as in the lagoon, flanked by a sandy beach on the lake. For the times you'd rather be on the water than in it, you can go boating in paddleboats or rowboats.

Other outdoor amenities include volleyball, croquet, badminton, shuffleboard, boccie, a children's playground, and hiking and biking trails. Indoor facilities include an eight-lane bowling alley, a video game room, billiards and Ping-Pong tables. Indoor fitness options are enhanced by whirlpools and a massage center. There is also a salon to keep your hair in shape.

In winter, ski, snowboarding, and snow tubing packages are offered with tickets for nearby Big Boulder and Jack Frost ski areas. The Split Rock shuttle can take you there. Sledding is available at Split Rock.

The resort also offers event planners, 23 meeting rooms, and extensive exhibit space in an area of more than 77,000 square feet, one of the largest group meeting facilities in northeastern Pennsylvania. Staff members are pleased to assist in planning your event and attending to details while it is in progress. Costs depend on the type of accommodations and length of stay.

If you and your family group are looking for an energetic, activity-filled vacation, Split Rock is a good option. Rates in July and August 2004 range from $184 to $314 per couple, plus tax and service charges per night, with meals on the Modified American Plan. Children ages 5 to 15 are $45 per night (MAP); kids 16 and older, or an extra person in a room, $55 (MAP). Children younger than 5 stay free, but meals are not included.

The Resort at Split Rock is conveniently located just 4 miles from Interstate 80 and the Pennsylvania Turnpike.

Milford/Lake Wallenpaupack Area

Malibu Ranch
351 Foster Hill Road, Milford
(570) 296-7281, (800) 8-MALIBU
www.malibududeranch.com
Malibu is a dude ranch, specializing in horses and trail riding.Guests are entitled to unlimited horseback riding, swimming, fishing (bring your own equipment), and boating. Instruction is provided so novice riders can enjoy the wooded trails on horseback. Those who are more experienced can take an all-day trail ride if they happen to be at Malibu on a Tuesday in the fall. Always wondered what it would be like to be in a rodeo? Visit Malibu on a holiday, and take part in a guest participation rodeo. Call them or visit their Web site for more details. Other outdoor activities include whitewater rafting nearby on the Delaware River, tennis, archery, and shooting at the rifle range. The ranch provides guns for kids and adults who know how to shoot but you pay for the bullets. It also offers an indoor pool, sauna, a petting zoo, and arcade.

Accommodations are in the main lodge, which has suites as well as double rooms (all rooms have double beds); a motel; stone house; chalets; and cabins. The cost is $80 a day per adult, based on double occupancy. The price goes down as you add more days to your stay or more adults to your room. Children 6 to 16 stay for half price, and children 5 and younger are free. (See our Kidstuff chapter for additional information.) The rate includes three meals a day, horseback riding, and all scheduled activities.

Woodloch Pines Resort Inc.
Highway 590 East, Hawley
(570) 685-8000, (800) 572-6658
www.woodloch.com

This resort has been recognized three times by *Better Homes & Gardens* as one of the top family resorts in America, and it has become a family tradition for many. Woodloch Pines is a first-class winter and summer playland. From its highly rated golf course (see our Golf chapter) to its Broadway-style theme shows, Woodloch Pines provides a first-rate informal family fun fest and a variety of accommodation options.

The resort surrounds an enormous crystal-clear mountain lake that offers boating (sailboats, rowboats, paddleboats, scenic boat rides, and canoes), swimming, water skiing, fishing (licenses are sold at Woodloch; bring your own equipment), and, in winter, ice-skating and ice-fishing. A beautiful outdoor pool stretches alongside the lake, increasing the feeling of "water, water everywhere."

Each week, staff arrange different activities and package options designed with the entire family in mind. With few exceptions, nearly all resort activities and amenities are included in your family's stay, as well as three meals a day. Two meals are an option at some times of the year. Holiday specials include Thanksgiving and Christmas midweek, miniweek, and weekend options. There also are winter getaways plus a full lineup of spring and summer feature packages, including Easter. There are additional specials for school holidays and St. Patrick's Day. Spring and summer feature full-fledged weeklong fun fests, with entertainment, weekend tournaments, and events focused on families doing fun things both together and apart. Fall events celebrate the change of season and include Halloween festivities. Children's activities such as arts and crafts are available winter or summer, and special facilities for the young ones include a children's playground, climbing wall, kiddie pool, kiddie cars, toddler room, video game rooms, and a miniature golf course.

Other general activities include basketball, volleyball, bingo, boccie, bicycling, bumper cars, a water slide, IROC go-karts, shuffleboard, nature trails, scavenger hunts, trap shooting (extra charge), Ping-Pong, racquetball (extra charge), tai chi classes, family olympics, batting cages (extra charge), tennis, and hayrides. Additional on-site winter options are snowmobiling (extra charge), and snow tubing. You'll also find a rifle range and a shooting gallery (extra charge).

Accommodations include an impressive array of comfortable and homey rooms, suites, and houses—all decorated in rustic country décor, or country-refined. Basic rooms with a private bath, two double beds, and color TV are available in lodges near the lovely woods that surround Woodloch. Larger rooms with separate areas for family privacy also are near the lodges, and some overlook the lake. Rooms adjoining the main lodge—all with private balconies—afford lovely views of the lake and are suitable for families or couples. Suites, attached to the indoor swimming pool complex, feature varying degrees of luxury and are set up for extended families—at least two bedrooms, full baths, and TVs. Two- to five-bedroom homes are available about 2 miles from the main facilities.

Prices vary considerably here, depending on the accommodation, season, time of the week, and any package options you might elect. Overall, the low end for rooms is $375 per person (double occupancy) for a spring or fall weekend (winter weekends are less expensive; holiday weekends are more expensive); the high is $440. For a week in summer, rates range from $1,295 per person to $1,589. Rates for children staying with two adults for a week range from $322 to $714 (age increments are 3 to 6, 7 to 12, and 13 to 19; children younger than 3 stay free). High season weekend children's rates vary according to holiday.

You have many options here, so be sure to look at the Web site or the elaborate brochure that spells out what's available week by week, weekend by weekend, all year long. All rates include access to all resort amenities, except for the previously

noted few that require an additional fee. Most packages include three meals a day, although there are some other options available. There is excellent country cooking—a choice of appetizers, two entrees, desserts, all served family style all you can eat. On special weekends and at Tuesday dinner and Sunday lunch a spectacular all-you-can-eat smorgasbord is featured. A la carte options are available with some of the other packages.

Nearby activities include cross-country skiing, downhill skiing at Tanglwood, Big Bear, Mount Tone, Jack Frost, or Big Boulder (the latter two are about an hour's drive, the former three closer; see our Winter Sports chapter) and all the goings-on in the Hawley area. (See the Milford/Lake Wallenpaupack Area section of our Arts and Culture, Shopping, and Attractions chapters.)

COUPLES/HONEYMOON RETREATS

The Pocono Mountains are world famous as a honeymoon resort area, complete with heart-shaped bathtubs and other romantic accouterments. Although, of course, the area is much more than a retreat for newlyweds, there are several resorts that cater to couples. Some have great couples' accommodations while allowing all ages, but the following resorts are for couples only.

Delaware Water Gap/Shawnee-on-Delaware

Caesars Pocono Palace
US 209, Marshalls Creek
(570) 588-6692, (877) 822-3333
www.caesarspoconoresorts.com
Caesars Pocono Palace offers a country club setting with the amenities of a Caesars couples resort. It has a nine-hole golf course and specializes in sports activities. It's set off US 209 and is surrounded by

woods, so it's secluded yet close to the corridor between Stroudsburg and Milford. Water skiing is a favorite activity on the 430-acre lake, or you can go boating by rowboat or paddleboat, fish, hike, or bike the lovely wooded grounds.

Rooms range from literally over-the-top, with 7-foot champagne glass-shaped whirlpool bathtubs for two, heart-shaped heated swimming pools, vaulted ceilings and arches, dry sauna, steam shower, king-size round bed with a starry ceiling—that's all in one room, the Roman Towers—to merely sumptuous, with a king-size bed, whirlpool for two and great view. They also offer "Fantasy Apple" suites with a heart-shaped whirlpool bath for two, private heated pool and sauna, fireplace, king-size bed with mirrored headboard, and more.

A Champagne Honeymoon program here and at the other Caesars resorts employs a Honeymoon Concierge to make sure your honeymoon is perfect. Honeymooners also get a bottle of champagne and a time capsule including a scrapbook, T-shirts, and a single-use camera.

A sports arena offers indoor racquetball, basketball, billiards, an arcade, an exercise spa, a pool, whirlpools, miniature golf, and roller-skating.

Amenities here and through the Key Around Club, which allows access to the other three Caesars in the Poconos, include indoor roller skating; outdoor ice-skating; tennis; racquetball; cross-country skiing; indoor and outdoor miniature golf; billiards; archery; indoor and outdoor pools; a health club and spa; and outdoor basketball, volleyball, and softball. You can toboggan at

---

Honeymooning before the wedding? You must be at least 18 and single to marry in Pennsylvania (younger people can wed with parental consent). Apply at a courthouse for your license; there's a mandatory three-day waiting period. If you're divorced, you'll need a copy of the divorce decree.

Cove Haven, use the golf driving ranges here and at Cove Haven and water-ski here and at Cove Haven and Brookdale.

Pocono Palace's nightclub features comics, dance bands, and theme nights. Two full-course meals daily are part of your package as are pre-dinner hor d'oeuvres and midnight snacks. Honeymooners can enjoy champagne breakfast in bed.

Per couple rates for a one-night stay, high season, with two meals a day start at $260.15 for a merely sumptuous Club Lodge room and go all the way up to $574.75 for the incredible Roman Towers. Watch the Web site for special discounts.

Guests who have stayed here and at the other Caesars three or more times get special discounts and benefits.

Stroudsburg/East Stroudsburg

Penn Hills Resort
Highway 447 North, Analomink
(570) 421-6464, (800) 233-8240
www.pennhillsresort.com
Located in the heart of the Pocono Mountains, this four-season couples' resort offers a superb combination of exciting things to do or quiet spaces to experience together. Featured on-site is the full-service Arcadia Spa, with indoor and outdoor pools and Jacuzzis. Tennis and fishing also are available. Take a walk and enjoy nature's beauty at the Rainbow waterfalls, streams, and lakes.

Minutes from Penn Hills, enjoy great winter outdoor excitement at Alpine Mountain Ski and Ride Center, where you'll find skiing, snowboarding, snow tubing, and lessons by professional trained ski instructors (see our chapter on Winter Sports).

During spring, summer, and fall, have fun golfing at Evergreen Golf Club (see our Golf chapter). Bordered by scenic streams and ponds, the course features rolling hills, dramatic fairways, finely manicured greens among sand traps, and water. A fleet of well-maintained golf carts, club rentals, and pull carts are available. Groups and outings are always welcome at Evergreen.

Newly redecorated accommodations offer special packages from $190 midweek and $215 per night on weekends and holidays for two people, including use of all resort facilities, and breakfast and dinner. Breakfast only packages also are available. Call or visit the Web site for more information.

Penn Hills offers discounts for many Poconos attractions and shopping, located minutes from the resort.

Mount Pocono Area

Caesars Paradise Stream
Highway 940, Mount Pocono
(570) 839–8881, (877) 822–3333
www.caesarspoconoresorts.com
Paradise Stream is another of the famed Caesars resorts in the Poconos for couples only. The winding stream and bridges that weave through this property make it a romantic spot for lovers to wander. Its prime location is notable: Mount Pocono to the west, Stroudsburg to the east, Tannersville to the south and Cresco and Canadensis to the north. That means it's close to Alpine Mountain and Camelback as well as many restaurants and attractions. Paradise Stream is also part of the Caesars Key Around Club, allowing adults to use the amenities at all four Pocono Caesars, and other Caesars resorts are easily accessible from here.

The atmosphere and accommodations range from comfortably relaxed to exciting, with villas, suites, and champagne towers. Amenities available here and through the Key Around Club include indoor roller-skating; outdoor ice-skating; tennis; racquetball; indoor and outdoor miniature golf; billiards; archery; indoor and outdoor pools; a health club and spa; and outdoor basketball, volleyball, and softball. On the lake here, as well as at Cove Haven and Brookdale, you'll find

canoes, paddleboats, and sailboats. With the Key Around Club, you can cross-country ski at Pocono Palace, toboggan at Cove Haven, play indoor racquetball here and at Cove Haven, golf at Pocono Palace, use the driving ranges at Pocono Palace and Cove Haven and water-ski at Pocono Palace and Cove Haven.

Entertainment is always available at the resort's Red Apple Lounge. There are always festivities, often with a theme like Mardi Gras, tropical beach, and Roman nights. Two generous buffets are part of your package, and a champagne breakfast in bed is available to honeymooners.

Rates are per couple, with two meals and free use of all facilities including Key Around Club options.

Nightly rates per couple vary according to in-room amenities. The most expensive lodging is in Champagne Towers by Cleopatra, a suite offered for $400 a night at three of the four Caesars Resorts in the Poconos (this one is reduced to $390 at Brookdale On-the-Lake). Other rates are as follows: Jacuzzi Suite, $270; Lakeside Villa, $300; the new Diana's Oasis, $300, Garden of Eden Apple, $380. Ask about special programs and discount options.

Milford/Lake Wallenpaupack Area

Caesars Cove Haven
Highway 590, Lakeville
(570) 226–4506, (877) 822–3333
www.caesarspoconoresorts.com
Cove Haven, near Hawley, is the farthest north and largest of the Caesars resorts. It's a top-notch facility on the shores of Lake Wallenpaupack, with the lake as its focal point and woods all around. Wallenpaupack provides the ultimate in fishing and boating opportunities, including water-skiing and speed boating. The lovely wooded grounds feature trails for hiking and biking, and in winter, spots for snowmobiling and tobogganing. The atmosphere is casual.

> *When venturing out onto Lake Wallenpaupack or any other lake in the Poconos, always wear a life jacket, not only because life jackets are mandated by law, but also because even the strongest swimmers have been known to drown in boating accidents. In early spring, when the water is cold, hypothermia can paralyze a swimmer in minutes.*

You'll find many activities for couples. Of course, heart-shaped tubs and champagne glass towers adorn some rooms. Amenities here and through the Key Around Club, which allows Casears' guests access to facilities at all four Pocono Caesars, include indoor roller skating; outdoor ice-skating; tennis; racquetball; indoor and outdoor miniature golf; billiards; archery; indoor and outdoor pools; a health club and spa; and outdoor basketball, volleyball, and softball. With the Key Around Club, you can row on the smaller lake at Brookdale; cross-country ski at Pocono Palace; play indoor racquetball here and at Paradise Stream; golf at Pocono Palace; use the golf driving ranges here and at Pocono Palace; and water-ski here and at Pocono Palace.

Big-name entertainers, such as Bobby Vinton, Shirley Reeves, and the Shirelles, are featured in the nightclub; ask about the performers scheduled to appear. Packages include two full-course meals, and for honeymooners, a champagne breakfast in bed. Honeymooners also get special presents and the use of Caesars' Honeymoon Concierge. Caesars coordinates packages with USAir that include air transportation for guests coming from a distance.

Rates are per couple with two meals and free use of all facilities here and at other Pocono Caesars resorts. Nightly rates, per couple, increase depending upon in-room options, such as pools and spas. At the most economical end is a room in the Harborette, adjacent to the spa, which costs $215. In ascending order,

room costs are: Harbor towers, $270; the new Juliette wing, $290; Cove Harbor, $290; Cove Fantasy, $330; Garden of Eden Apple, $380, and, most expensive of all, Champagne Towers by Cleopatra, $400. Ask about specials. Seniors, for example, are eligible for discounted rates.

MOTELS/MOTOR INNS, CABINS, AND COTTAGES

The Pocono region is dotted with all manner of standard nightly accommodations, and we include a sampling in this section. Unless otherwise specified, basic in-room amenities apply (standard bath, telephone, TV, heat/air-conditioning unit, and wheelchair accessibility). You will be paying for a place to spend the night, close to all the great Pocono opportunities we discuss in other chapters such as Shopping; Winter Sports; In, On, and Around the Water; Day Trips; Attractions; and Arts and Culture. Any extra charge for children is noted.

PRICE-CODE KEY

The following key represents the average rate for a double-occupancy room during peak season.

$75 or less	$
$76 to $100	$$
$101 to $125	$$$
$126 and more	$$$$

Delaware Water Gap/ Shawnee-on-Delaware

Ramada Inn $
101 Broad Street
Delaware Water Gap
(570) 476-0000, (888) 298-2054
www.theramada.com
The Ramada Inn, right off I-80, features 104 deluxe rooms with free HBO, a game room, and indoor and outdoor pools. We have met people who stay here again and

again, raving about the rooms and the service. This Ramada is walking distance to Delaware Water Gap's attractions, including shopping, live entertainment (the Deer Head Inn is a must stop for jazz lovers; see our Nightlife chapter), eateries, and cultural events, such as the Delaware Water Gap Celebration of the Arts and art shows at the Dutot Museum (see our Arts and Culture chapter for details). Children 18 and younger stay free.

Stroudsburg/East Stroudsburg

Best Western Pocono Inn $$$
700 Main Street, Stroudsburg
(570) 421–2200, (888) 508–BEST
www.bestwesternpa.com
The Best Western is in the heart of Stroudsburg, so you can walk to anything happening on Main or Lower Main streets. (See our Arts and Culture as well as Shopping chapters for some ideas.) There are 90 large rooms, each with two double beds and free HBO, and in-room movies are available. Amenities include a lovely indoor pool with whirlpool spa on the side. The popular Brownie's in the 'Burg Restaurant and Front Row Sports Bar (with live bands on weekends) are part of this hotel. Children 16 and younger stay free with adults.

Budget Motel $$
I-80 exit 308, East Stroudsburg
(570) 424–5451, (888) 233–8144
www.budmotel.com
Insiders talk about this place for its great food. Everyone comes to eat at the on-site J.R.'s Green Scene restaurant, even if they aren't staying here (see our Restaurants chapter for details). The lovely greenhouse dining room overlooks the Stroudsburgs and features a menu with delicious contemporary American cuisine. All 115 rooms have guest-controlled heating and air-conditioning and 25-inch remote color TVs, dataport telephones,

and in-room movies. Rooms have two double beds or one king-size bed. Budget Motel is convenient to Poconos shopping, winter sports, watersports, and attractions. Pets are accepted, but a $20 refundable security deposit is required. There is no extra charge for children. This is the only AAA Three Diamond Rated property of its kind in the Poconos.

Clarion Hotel $$$$
1220 West Main Street, Strousdburg
(570) 424–1930,
(800) 274–8884 (ext. 290)
www.clarionhotel.com
With 133 rooms surrounding an indoor tropical courtyard complete with heated pool and bar, and spitting distance from Interstate 80, the Clarion is a popular choice. You have a choice of a king or two queen-size beds, and there's a 25-inch TV in each room. Most rooms have a computer hookup, and some rooms have a Jacuzzi, a microwave oven, and a refrigerator. Free continental breakfast and a *USA Today* are included in your stay.

Evergreens Restaurant, featuring a Sherpa chef specializing in Indian cuisine, overlooks the tropical courtyard, and Whispers Lounge often has live entertainment. There's an exercise room and some meeting rooms for parties or conferences. Children stay free with their parents, but no pets are allowed.

The Clarion is conveniently located just west of the center of Stroudsburg, within sight of I–80, on US 209 Business and close to Highway 611. You'll find lots of things to see and do within a very short distance.

Days Inn $$
100 Park Street, Stroudsburg
(570) 424–1771
www.hotel-chains-online.com
This Days Inn is just a few blocks from Main Street. All 55 rooms are equipped with television and premium cable. There is an outdoor pool, and coffee and doughnuts are available for guests every morning. Rates fluctuate with activities in the

region so call ahead to confirm. There's no charge for children staying in the room with their parents.

Echo Valley Cottages $$
1 Lower Lakeview, East Stroudsburg
(570) 223-0662
http://come.to/EchoValley
This rustic spread of eight cottages, each accommodating from two to eight people, has an East Stroudsburg address, but it actually lies between Marshalls Creek and Bushkill north of US 209, so be sure to call and ask directions. Cottages have fully equipped kitchens, television sets, and basic cable. The grounds boast a basketball court, pool, and pond where you can fish if you have a license (bring your own tackle). Echo Valley is open weekends only September to June, with a two-night minimum, and rents by the week only during the summer.

As remote as Echo Valley seems to be, it is a scant five-minute drive from the Foxmoor shopping center on US 209 (see our Shopping chapter). Echo Valley is great for family reunions.

Shannon Inn $$
US 209, East Stroudsburg
(570) 424-1951, (800) 424-8052
This motel is right off I-80 Marshalls Creek exit. It has 118 guest rooms with cable TVs, an indoor pool with a tropical motif, and complimentary continental breakfast. Children 12 and younger stay free in their parents' room. Call for group rates.

Werry's Cottages, Motel & Pub $$
5049 Milford Road, East Stroudsburg
(570) 223-9234
Closer to Bushkill than East Stroudsburg, Werry's is attached to a pub that provides bar food, live bands on weekends, and lots of games. The rooms are comfortably furnished, standard motel rooms. The cabins have picnic tables, and some have kitchens. Guests can relax at a pool next to the pub. Werry's offers a number of packages, including ski and golf packages. Children younger than 12 stay free.

Mount Pocono Area

Alvin's Log Cabins $$
Highway 715, Henryville
(570) 629-0667
Alvin's charming log cabins include efficiencies and housekeeping units with kitchens, sitting rooms with fireplaces, and cable TV. The units sleep 2 to 14 people. Each cabin has a porch, and each porch has a picnic table. There's a swimming pool, swing sets, badminton, shuffleboard, and ping pong for guests' entertainment. Alvin's is minutes from the Camelback Ski Area (see our Winter Sports chapter) and the Tannersville Crossing Outlets (see our Shopping chapter). If you're renting by the week, the rates are substantially lower. Summer weekend reservations usually require a minimum of two nights. Credit cards and personal checks are not accepted here.

Howard Johnson $$$-$$$$
Highway 611, Bartonsville
(570) 424-6100, (866) 787-6767
www.poconohotel.com
Howard Johnson is easily accessible off I-80 in Bartonsville. It has a heated indoor pool as well as a lounge, restaurant, and fitness center to complement its rooms, which have standard or king-size beds, 25-inch TVs with HBO, in-room coffeemakers, small refrigerators, microwaves, and dataports on the phones. Children 12 and younger stay free with parents. Banquet facilities are available.

Kuebler's Mountain Hotel $
Main Street, Tobyhanna
(570) 894-8291
Many small towns, especially in the west, have a hotel/tavern in the center of town that caters to the working class traveler—the traveling salesman or the young woman who's on her way to somewhere else to make it big. Kuebler's epitomizes this tradition. While the furnishings are basic and most of the bathrooms are semiprivate or shared, the rooms are sparkling clean and the owners are constantly remodeling this very old building.

Your pets can stay with you, but call ahead to make arrangements. The church across the street chimes lovely bells, adding to the old-fashioned feel of the place. If you're starved for decor, visit the cocktail lounge, which offers snacks and pizzas. It's friendly and clean—owner Edie Kuebler says, "It's the kind of place you can bring your grandmother." Twinkly lights and stars poke through the ceiling tiles. Edie says be sure to stop by at Christmas when the lounge is so heavily decorated that people travel in from all over to see it.

Martinville Streamside Cottages $$$$
Highway 390, Canadensis
(570) 595–2489
www.martinvillestreamsidecottages.com
Martinville Streamside Cottages boast the charm of 1930s housekeeping cottages with the luxurious amenities of the new millennium. Built by Grandfather Martin, once maitre d' at Buck Hill, the cottages have been passed down through the family to identical twins Kitty and Molly. The cottages are gorgeous, set along a bubbling stream amid beautiful flowers in beds and boxes. Every one has thick carpeting, air-conditioning, a television, a full kitchen with microwave, tasteful furniture, a fireplace, a porch filled with flowers in the front, and a deck out back with a grill. The decks hang over the stream so you can fish right off your deck. Some of the cottages have cathedral ceilings, some have queen- and king-size beds. They run from one bedroom to three. Some of their newest options are impressive. The "Love Shack is awesome," says Kitty, listing its king-size loft bed, two-person Jacuzzi, fireplace, and deck over the stream. Treetop Cottage has a kitchen, two-person Jacuzzi, two bedrooms, and a balcony built around a tree. Mountain View House, 5 miles north of the cottages, is a four-bedroom house with stone fireplace and a cedar hot tub on secluded acres with, of course, a great view.

A slide will dump you right into a lake, but it can be cold, and you might prefer

While cottages and cabins may sound like interchangeable terms, usually a "cottage" is beautifully decorated and luxurious while a "cabin" is rustic and basic. (You will find some cabins that claim to be cottages, but no cottages that call themselves cabins.) "Housekeeping" means there's a kitchen in the unit.

to fish, paddle around in the paddleboats, or swim in the heated pool. The lake is so good for fishing that one guest caught 10 trout in a day here.

The way Grandfather Martin's son Jim tells it, on the day Grandfather decided to make a lake, he forgot to tell Grandmother Martin. The sound of dynamite at five in the morning was something of a surprise to her.

Trails from the back of the property lead up the mountain. Children stay for free. A good discount is available for stays of a week or more.

Naomi Village $$$$
Highway 390, Mountainhome
(570) 595–2432, (800) 336–2664
www.naomivillage.com
Naomi Village straddles the line between housekeeping cottages and resorts. The village is made up of 29 beautifully decorated cottages, and the owners are constantly renovating them on a rotating basis. When number 29 is finished, they start again with number one. The cottages, scattered among attractive plantings, have different layouts and range from studio cottages for two to a four-bedroom house that can sleep 10. Each is individually decorated, and all have beautiful, fully equipped kitchens, microwaves, VCRs, fireplaces, thick carpeting, and porches with tables. One employee paints furniture, and you will find a few very interesting pieces in the cottages. Many cottages have Jacuzzis, and some have saunas.

Guests can swim in the heated outdoor pool; fish in the pond; play shuffleboard, tennis, basketball, or volleyball; use the barbecue and picnic tables by the pond; hike on trails behind the village; work out in the fitness center, or relax in the hot tub. A playground is provided for children.

Naomi Village is in the heart of Mountainhome, a pretty tourist village with lots of restaurants and interesting shops. Check their Web site for seasonal specials.

Super 8 Motel/Pocono Mountain $-$$$
Highway 611 South, Mount Pocono
(570) 839-7728, (800) 800-8000
www.super8.com

Right on Highway 611, this 37-room motel has an outdoor pool; rooms with Jacuzzis; waterbeds; double, queen-, and king-size beds; and free HBO. There's no extra charge for children in the room, but if you need a cot, it's $10. This Super 8 has truck parking.

West End

The Country Place Motel $$
Highway 903, Jim Thorpe
(570) 325-2214

This quaint, country motel has 12 rooms, each with air-conditioning, color TV, and basic cable. The large rooms are decorated with country antiques and old-fashioned country schemes of plaids and flowers. The rooms all have full baths and double or king-size beds.

Pets are welcome at no additional charge or security deposit. Each additional adult is $15.00; each child, $7.50. From April to October a free continental breakfast is available.

This spot is about 3 miles from the Jim Thorpe Mausoleum, burial place of the legendary Jim Thorpe, and 13 and 17 miles, respectively, from the twin ski and recreational areas of Jack Frost and Big Boulder. It's also just a 20-minute drive from the Pocono International Raceway. (See the Close-up in our Attractions chapter.)

Harmony Lake Shore Inn $$
Highway 903, Lake Harmony
(570) 722-0522

This little motel offers only basic in-room amenities but is right on Lake Harmony. Some rooms have one queen-size bed, while others have a double and a single. Boating, fishing, and swimming are available at the lake. In winter there's ice-skating (weather permitting) and snowmobiling. Any more than two people in the room cost $5.00 each.

Pocono Ramada Inn $$$
Highway 940, Lake Harmony
(570) 443-8471, (800) 251-2610
www.poconoramada.com

This Ramada is close to Lake Harmony and, in winter, good skiing at Big Boulder or Jack Frost. The 139 rooms include standard units (some with king-size beds) and suites. Rooms have two double beds and color TVs.

Amenities include an indoor pool, saunas, an indoor sun deck with sun lamps, a miniature golf course, and game room. The pool is shaped like a snowman! Children 18 and younger stay free with their parents, and pets are welcome but require a $50 refundable deposit. Pets that bark may not be left alone in the room.

The Garden Terrace Restaurant, overlooking the pool, offers breakfast and lunch, while the Stable serves dinner. The Copper Penny Lounge offers a pub-style menu.

Milford/Lake Wallenpaupack Area

Babbling Brook Cottages $$-$$$
Silver Lake Road, Dingmans Ferry
(570) 828-9175

Tucked away on a lane right next to Childs Falls, Babbling Brook Cottages are totally charming. Garden enthusiasts will love the beautiful English-style gardens surrounding the office and scattered around the five cottages. The cottages are gorgeously decorated and immaculate. Two have cathedral ceilings, one has log-cabin walls, and another tongue-in-groove paneling; each has a kitchen with everything including a microwave, coffeepot, bookshelves stocked with good books, and terrific art you can buy right off the walls. The great fireplace in one cottage makes it a popular choice. There are outdoor lounge chairs, fire pits, barbecues, picnic tables, and horseshoes. You can walk right through the back of the property to Childs Falls, with three large waterfalls and lots of hiking trails.

Best Western Inn at Hunt's Landing $$$$
900 U.S. Highways 6 and 209
Matamoras
(570) 491-2400
www.bestwestern.com

This is a super motel. It has wonderful views of the mountains and the Delaware River from its Hunt's Landing location on the river. The 109 guest rooms include kings, suites, and doubles, some with Jacuzzis. Each room has two vanity sinks in separate rooms, in-room coffee, and a wide-screen TV. Children younger than 12 stay free.

Continental breakfast is included in the price of the room. The inn features a tropical indoor pool, saunas and on-site fishing in their stocked pond. They have meeting rooms suitable for parties and conferences, and their monthly themed festivals draw busloads of seniors. Meals are served in the gracious Edgewater Restaurant overlooking the grounds; its Sunday brunches are especially popular—make reservations ahead of time, or you may not get a table. Annie's Cafe offers after-dinner cocktails and dancing.

Blue Spruce Motel $-$$
US 6 and US 209, Matamoras
(570) 491-4969
www.bluesprucemotel.com

Blue Spruce features beautifully decorated rooms, some in a motel section, some as pretty white cottages with flower boxes at the windows. All the rooms are immaculate. Children stay for $5.00 to $10.00 each, depending on their age. You can get complimentary morning coffee in the office after 7:30 A.M. This quiet motel is especially popular with senior citizens.

Cherry Ridge Campsites and Lodging $$
Camp Road, Honesdale
(570) 488-6654
www.cherryridgecampsites.com

This big RV park boasts 7 fully equipped housekeeping cottages and 20 individual rental rooms in two buildings. Some of the rooms have private baths, while others share a community facility. A community kitchen also is available to all guests. Cottages have one, two, and three bedrooms, all with kitchen, living room, and bath, and one single-room efficiency apartment is available. Kitchens are equipped with stoves, refrigerators, pots, pans, dishes, and silverware. Weekly rates are available.

Cherry Ridge specializes in dance weekends all season long, featuring workshops, and square, round, and country line dancing.

To get to Cherry Ridge, take U.S. Highway 191 south from Honesdale, or Highway 296 south from Waymart, to State Road 3028 and follow the signs.

Comfort Inn $$$
Highway 191, Lake Ariel
(570) 689-4148, (800) 523-4426
www.comfortinn.com

This is the only chain hotel in the lake region. It is a great stop for parents taking their children to one of the area's camps and, for this reason, is generally booked heavily on summer weekends. The 124 rooms include doubles or kings (some with Jacuzzis) with satellite TVs. There is a suite with a whirlpool and wet bar. Meals are available at the Twin Rocks Restaurant open 24 hours a day except Saturday night. Cocktails are served in the Prince Edward Island Lounge. An excellent complimentary continental breakfast is included in your room rate. Children 18 and younger stay free with parents. General amenities include an exercise room with a sauna and Jacuzzi. Your pet is welcome, but you must pay an additional nonrefundable $15.

Ehrhardt's Waterfront Resort $$$
Highway 507, 1 mile south of US 6
Hawley
(570) 226-4388, (800) 678-5907
www.ehrhardts.com

This lovely motor inn offers 24 motel rooms, some with balcony decks overlooking Lake Wallenpaupack, and six family units, each with one large bedroom facing the lake and a smaller adjoining bedroom for children. All rooms have small refrigerators, family units have fully equipped kitchens. Guests may sign up for rooms only or (summer only) rooms with meals on the Modified American Plan, catered by Ehrhardt's Restaurant (see our Restaurants chapter) next door. Weekly rates, with and without meals, also are available. Children older than three are $5.00.

Amenities include a boat slip for guests bringing their own craft; paddleboats, rowboats, and canoes; shuffleboard, and an outside pool. Ehrhardt's has been owned and operated by the same family for nearly 60 years.

Gresham's Lakeview Motel $$
US 6 and Highway 507
Hawley
(570) 226-4621, (888) 845-6760
www.greshams.net

This stately two-story motel is on the shore of Lake Wallenpaupack and consequently offers boat slips to guests with boats for a rental of $15 per day. Twenty-one rooms are available, with air conditioning, cable TV, patios that face the lake, and handicapped accessibility. Gresham's is now a completely smoke-free motel. Gresham's Chophouse Restaurant, part of the motel, provides fine American dining overlooking the lake. There's live entertainment here on weekends. In addition to being immediately adjacent to Lake Wal-

lenpaupack's only white sand public beach, Gresham's is minutes away from horse stables and two 18-hole golf courses and offers daily boat rides as well as a small shopping mall. The motel caters to skiers in winter and anglers in spring.

The Myer Country Motel $$
US 6 and US 209, Milford
(570) 296-7223, (800) 764-MYER
www.myermotel.com

Myer has a series of sweet white cottages arranged around a green, looking for all the world like a small village. Every cottage has a porch with chairs. One cottage has a full kitchen. The green, a great place for the kids to play, has barbecue grills and picnic tables shaded by tall pine trees. Inside, the cottages are beautifully decorated. Some have wooden wainscoting accenting dark green walls; others have floral wallpaper artfully arranged to simulate wainscoting. Much of the furniture is especially lovely. Some cottages have king-size beds and sitting areas. Most are no-smoking. A significant number of the guests at this delightful motel are repeat customers.

Pocono Pines Motor Inn $$
Highway 507 at Lake Wallenpaupack
Tafton
(570) 226-2772
www.poconopinesmotorinn.com

This lovely motel is right across from Lake Wallenpaupack and has a lakefront spot with a dock for guests. Twelve rooms, a lodge, and cottages with kitchens and fireplaces are available; cottages are not available in winter. A playground is available for children, and barbecue pits and picnic tables are scattered about for guests to use. The game room is also a favorite hangout for kids. Lawn games such as shuffleboard and badminton are available too. Children 11 and younger stay free, but an extra crib is $5.00.

Scottish Inn $
US 6 and US 209, Milford
(570) 491-4414, (800) 251-1962

The office at the Scottish Inn resembles a Swiss chalet with interesting gingerbread trim and huge baskets of fuchsias. Each recently renovated room has a little green arch over the door. Options include basic, clean motel rooms of varying sizes and one efficiency.

Shohola Falls Inn $
US 6, Shohola
(570) 296-7396

Shohola Falls Inn is on state game lands, just around the bend from Shohola Falls and Shohola Lake. From your cabin, you can walk to the lake and the falls. The inn itself, now a private home, was a stagecoach stop and later hosted cast members of D. W. Griffith's *The Informer* and *A Feud in the Kentucky Hills* while they were filming in the area. Although it is set in the Pennsylvania hills, during Prohibition, a Kentucky-style moonshine still was operated in the woods right near the inn.

The cabins are two-bedroom housekeeping units with kitchens, sitting rooms, and porches. They are furnished in typical Pocono rustic style—lots of wood and simple furniture, just what you would expect in a mountain cabin.

One cabin, a converted barn, has a fireplace and can sleep 12 people upstairs in dormitory-like bedrooms.

Guests can swim in the pool, use the grill and picnic tables, play shuffleboard, horseshoes, or walk off into the miles of trails that go through the state game land. Keep an eye out for the numerous hummingbirds that frequent the feeders around the office. Shohola Falls Inn closes after hunting season and opens again in April. Pets are welcome.

RV PARKS AND CAMPGROUNDS

The number of recreational vehicles on American highways is increasing in direct proportion to the number of Americans who are aging toward retirement—which means there are a lot of them. They range

Many RV parks across the nation permit the dumping of dish and bath water—collectively known as "grey water"—directly on the ground, but Pennsylvania has a law barring the practice. Therefore, if your RV unit does not have a storage tank, it is a good idea to pick one up at an RV supply store so that you can haul the soapy stuff to your park's public sewage dump.

from little two-bed tent-camper trailers that have to be cranked up and down, through Class C motor homes with cabover beds, to bus-size Class A land yachts complete with full baths and satellite dishes, or "fifth wheels" with rooms that slide out to make full-scale homes.

But regardless of class or cost, they all have one thing in common; they have to be parked somewhere when the people using them to cross the country wish to sleep or stop and see the sights. As a result, RV parks, ranging from the fairly primitive to the downright luxurious, are springing up all over the landscape. Some of them are so deeply embedded in the landscape that they are hard to find, and in this listing, we will go into excruciating detail where necessary to give you directions.

Some RV parks in the Poconos are open only in spring and summer, while others operate all year. Most offer spaces ranging from primitive, for tenting only, through water and electric to full hookups with sewer lines included. Most accept pets if they are kept leashed at all times, but some do not, and we will make a point of that fact where applicable. Prices fluctuate with the season and the number and variety of amenities offered, but in general, you should find nightly rates in summer ranging from $19 to a high of $44. Rates are based on double occupancy; in most places children and extra adults pay from $2.00 to $4.00 more. We can't begin to list all the RV parks in our area, but here are a few representative examples.

Delaware Water Gap/ Shawnee-on-Delaware

Ken's Woods
Mink Pond Road, Bushkill
(570) 588-6381

For urbanites who really want to get away from it all, this is the perfect campground. Ken's Woods is so deep in the woods that Daniel Boone might get lost trying to find it; but once there, he would feel right at home. There are 150 water and electric RV sites here and 50 tent sites. There is a recreation hall, a miniature golf course, and a limited supply store. There are 20 full hookups, and a dump station at the entrance.

Tent sites go for $22 a night, and RV sites are $25.

Otter Lake Camp Resort
Creek Road, Marshalls Creek
(570) 223-0123, (800) 345-1369
www.otterlake.com

This 250-acre sylvan spread girdling 60-acre Otter Lake is the Biltmore of RV parks. It boasts 300 sites adjacent to archery, soccer, softball, and tennis courts, large indoor and outdoor swimming pools, a fully equipped game room, and tons of space-age playground equipment for the kids. The lake offers fishing, swimming, paddleboating, and canoeing, and a long list of organized recreational programs and activities is available. The general store is fully equipped.

The park is open all year; summer site rates for two people are $38 for water, electric, and cable television hookups; and $41 for a full hookup ($47 on the lake). Winter rates go down to $31, $34, and $39 respectively.

Shady Acres Campground
Turkey Ridge Road, Off Highway 611
Portland
(570) 897-6230

Shady Acres offers 70 RV sites equipped with water, cable, and electric. Most of these sites are occupied by seasonal campers.

Very few are available for overnight, so call before you go. A central dump station is available for blackwater disposal. There are also about 30 primitive tent sites, and all sites are shaded on the perimeter of a 2-acre fishing lake. A swimming pool, a fully equipped playground, and a pavilion for bingo complete the amenities. Restrooms and showers are very clean, and the store is well stocked. Campers especially enjoy Shady Acres' miniature horses, pigmy goats, peacocks, pheasants, and a family of ducks that waddle through the campground in a straight line.

Shady Acres is open May through October. Rates are $23 for RV sites and $21 for tents.

Stroudsburg/East Stroudsburg

Cranberry Run Campground
Hallet Road, off Highway 191, Analomink
(570) 421-1462
www.poconocamping.com

This 65-acre campground has 75 full sewage, water, and electric hookups, and all go for $28 a night. Tent sites are $23 a day, and discounts are offered to weekly, monthly, and seasonal campers. There is no swimming pool, but a lovely sylvan lake provides fishing, boating, and swimming. Organized events range from karaoke nights and talent contests to pool tournaments and bingo. No weekend throughout the season, which lasts from April and runs through October, is without its activities, even though the site is only minutes away from some of the best shopping, restaurants, attractions, and nightlife in the Poconos.

To reach Cranberry Run, take I-80 Marshalls Creek exit to US 209 and immediately turn left onto Highway 447 north. Take Highway 447 through the dogleg at the first traffic light and follow it to Highway 191 south. Take a sharp right at the end of the bridge onto Hallet Road and follow it 0.5 mile to the campground.

Mountain Vista Campground
50 Taylor Drive, East Stroudsburg
(570) 223-0111
www.mtnvistacampground.com
Though as heavily wooded as most campsites in the Poconos, this one is far less remote; civilization, with all its attractions and diversions, is only minutes away.

Mountain Vista, which is open all year, offers 190 level RV sites, equipped both as full hookups and with water and electric only. Tent sites are also available, as are cabins and travel trailers for those who enjoy the woods but like their own bathrooms. The trailers have kitchens, as well. The scene is rustic, but amenities are plentiful, including tennis, shuffleboard, swimming, horseshoes, volleyball, badminton, basketball, fishing, hiking, and a host of planned activities ranging from Chinese Auction through craft classes to bingo. Kids can enjoy excellent playground equipment.

Summer rates are $31 for water and electric and $35 for full hookup with sewer. If you're running an air conditioner, that's $3.00 extra.

To get to Mountain Vista, take I-80 Marshalls Creek exit to US 209 north to Marshalls Creek, turn left at the light, and look for Craigs Meadow Road at the Country Kettle store. Turn right and proceed 1 mile, then go left on Taylor Drive for 500 feet.

West End

Don Laine Campground
790 57 Drive, Palmerton
(610) 381-3381, (800) 635-0152
www.donlaine.com
A total of 150 shaded sites—120 of them equipped with full hookups—rim an open field housing a spacious swimming pool, playground, and recreation hall. If you don't happen to own an RV but still want to take advantage of camp life, you can rent a trailer here. The recreation hall boasts a 36-by-66-foot dance floor, and weekends feature bands playing country-western and golden oldies. The camp store is fully equipped.

Don Laine is open from April to November. Full hookups are $23 a night; water-and-electric–only sites go for $22.

Milford/Lake Wallenpaupack Area

Countryside Family Campground
Highway 670, Honesdale
(570) 253-0424
www.countrysidefamilycampground.com
This immaculately clean RV park boasts 65 water and electric sites as well as an extensive tenting area, and unlike many of its rural competitors, it is easy to find. Just take US 191 north out of Honesdale, bear left on Highway 670 north, and drive for 6 miles until you see the sign. Countryside, formerly Rainbow Family Campground, has full toilet and shower facilities, a play area for the kids, a recreation hall, and a sizable pool, all in a parklike woodland setting. A fairly extensive general store is available. Rustic cabins and RVs are available to rent at this campground, which is open all year. During the summer, enjoy hayrides and bingo on Saturday nights.

Daily summer rates, for two adults and two children younger than 18, are $28 a night for water and electric hookups, and $22 for a primitive tent site. Weekly, monthly, and seasonal rates are available.

Cherry Ridge Campsites & Lodging
Cherry Ridge Camp Road, Honesdale
(570) 488-6654
www.cherryridgecampsites.com
This extensive park, which boasts 115 full-hookup RV sites and five with water and electric only in wooded, field, and shaded sections, has been in operation for three decades. But RV people are not the only campers welcomed here. There are primitive tenting facilities, and Cherry Ridge also has housekeeping cabins and rooms for rent to those unequipped for camping. (See this chapter's "Motels/Motor Inns,

When traveling in a recreational vehicle, never forget three important things: a heavy-duty outside extension cord, an extra length of potable water hose, and plenty of bug repellant and anti-itch medication. Your camper may be luxury on wheels, but you're still essentially living outdoors and will be greeted— eagerly—by gnats and mosquitoes almost wherever you go.

Cabins, and Cottages" section.) A sheltered, spring-fed private lake is available for swimming and boating, and the usual toilet, shower, and laundry facilities are available.

The campground is open from May through October. Rates are $27 a night for full hookups, $18 for tent sites and water and electric hookups only. Square, round, and country line dancing programs are held every weekend throughout the season.

To reach Cherry Ridge, take Highway 191 south out of Honesdale or Highway 296 from Waymart, in both cases to State Road 3028, and follow the signs.

Lake Wallenpaupack

There are four RV park and camping areas open to the public on the shores of Lake Wallenpaupack, and all four are owned by Pennsylvania Power & Light Company (PPL), which also owns the lake and the hydroelectric dam that created it. Though they vary in size, all four are beautifully situated on the lakeshore in the deep shade of hardwood and hemlock tree stands. All offer water and electric hookups, but none have individual sewage dumps, only a single dumping station for registered guests in self-contained units.

PPL owns the water in the lake, but because all of the property immediately adjoining the lake is privately owned, no swimming is permitted anywhere save at one public beach at Wilsonville on the

eastern shore. State and National Park Service regulations are in effect, which means no pets at any of the RV sites, and no alcohol is allowed in picnic areas on Epply, Kipp, Burns, and Cairns Islands, all of which are accessible by boat and all of which have grills and picnic tables.

Rates are the same at all four parks: $20.00 a night for one to four people and $3.00 extra for each additional person. Showers are an extra 25 cents, and boats may be launched for a fee of $7.00, which is good throughout your stay. Long-term seasonal rates are available. Advance reservations are recommended. The summer season runs from the last Saturday in April to the third Sunday in October; the winter season, during which no electricity, showers, or laundry facilities are available, runs from the third Sunday in October to the last Saturday in April. Winter rates are $10 per night for one to four campers. Find out more at www.pplweb.com.

Here are descriptions and locations of the four parks:

WILSONVILLE

This park is the largest of PPL's four, with 160 tent and trailer sites. It is just off US 6 on the extreme eastern shore of the lake, just a few miles south of Hawley. Slip docks are available for rent, and gasoline for boat and vehicles is sold. A public swimming beach—the only one on the lake—is nearby, operated by Palmyra Township, which charges admission. Hiking trails and a children's play area are nearby. For reservations, call (570) 226–4382.

LEDGEDALE

This is a serene campsite on the lake's southernmost tip. It offers 69 tent and RV sites, along with a toilet, shower, and laundry building. The site, on the extreme western point of the lake just off Interstate 84, adjoins an 80-acre natural area offering 2 miles of hiking tails. For reservations, call (570) 689–2181.

IRONWOOD POINT

This park offers 47 spots for tents and trailers as well as 13 scenic lakefront sites for walk-in camping. It is just down the beach from Ledgedale (see previous entry) off Highway 507 on a wooded hilltop overlooking the lake and Burns and Kipp Islands. This area also boasts a children's play area and a picnic pavilion. Boat slips are available for rent and gas for boats and vehicles is also available. For reservations, call (570) 857–0880.

CAFFREY

This is the smallest of the PPL parks, with only 29 sites in field and wood-lot settings. Still, it has all the amenities offered by the other three parks and is near a restaurant-lounge and marina. The area is popular for boating, with good prevailing westerly winds for those under sail. For reservations, call (570) 226–4608.

TIMESHARES

Like love and marriage, timeshares and resorts go together. Despite the fact that some timeshares are sold by high-pressure techniques, they have given many people with modest incomes the opportunity to stay at world-class resorts. If you attend a sales pitch at a resort, make sure everything is explained, and find out what your monthly payments and yearly maintenance fee will be before you sign. Don't go unless you're seriously considering the possibility of buying a timeshare; some of the salespersons use very high-pressure sales techniques.

Typically, when you buy a timeshare, you purchase one particular week's use of a property at the resort. For instance, you might purchase the rights to stay in a townhome next to the golf course at Shawnee every year for the first week in October. (Many timeshares have gone to defining what you are purchasing as a ⅕ 2nd ownership in a property, and there are some technical differences.) The purchase of the timeshare is handled somewhat like a mortgage, with most people paying on time. You also pay a yearly fee that covers repairs and maintenance on the unit. A timeshare owner gets to use the amenities of the resort, which can be considerable. The owner may, for a fee, trade his or her week for a week at another resort in the same network. (The largest resort network, RCI, has more than 3,700 affiliated resorts around the world.) Since you own the week in your timeshare, you can also lend the unit to friends during that week and pass your ownership on in your will. Timeshare units may also be rented out to vacationers.

Although there is a good deal of variation, the typical timeshare unit is a two-bedroom home or condominium apartment. Usually it will have two double beds in each bedroom plus a fold-out couch in the living room, and it will be nicely decorated. Many units are downright luxurious.

Timeshare, or "deeded fractional vacation ownership" as those in the business call it, has increased in popularity exponentially in the last two decades, currently boasting nearly three million owners in the United States and twice that worldwide.

Quite a few resorts in the Poconos have timeshare units. Since the amenities available to the owners are those of the resorts, our descriptions in our "Resorts" section will give you a good idea of what you're buying. If you are interested in purchasing a timeshare, you can call the resorts directly or buy a timeshare through a reseller. When people no longer want their timeshare, they go to a reseller, and though they pay an up-front fee for marketing, it's something like selling a property. The advantage of buying through a reseller is that you typically pay 50 to 60 percent less. A disadvantage is there may not be a share at the resort you're interested in for the week you want. Often, too, original owners get more benefits and privileges than do those who buy through a reseller. Your best bet is to inquire at the resort and through a reseller, then compare. A local reseller is

Affiliated Timeshare Resale Ltd., (570) 619-7646.

Timeshares affiliated with a Pocono resort (see the resorts' previous descriptions) are:

- Caesars Brookdale—Brookvillage
- Fernwood—Fairway Villas, Greenhouse Tree Tops
- Pocono Manor—Carriage House
- Shawnee—Depuy-Shawnee, Northslope at Shawnee, Ridgetop, Valley View, River Village I and II, Shawnee Village
- Split Rock—Westwood Villas and Galleria
- Tamiment—Eagle Village at Tamiment Resort (call the resort for information on timeshare sales)

A few timeshare resorts are not affiliated with another resort, these include:

Sciota Village at Big Valley
Kress Road, Sciota
(570) 992-5659

Sciota boasts a clubhouse with activities, tennis courts, playground, restaurant, nature trails, an outdoor pool, on-site fishing, whirlpool, sauna, and hot tub. Its units are three-bedroom—larger than the average timeshare. Sciota is just south of the Stroudsburgs and near many Pocono activities.

Tanglwood Resort
US 6 and Highway 507, Hawley
(570) 226-6161, (800) 228-2968
www.vrivacations.com

Tanglwood has villas next to Lake Wallenpaupack, around its George Fazio-designed golf course and slopeside at its own ski area. In addition, it offers indoor and outdoor pools, a health club, tennis, a playground, basketball, a restaurant, and a private beach on the lake. It is right in the center of the many activities available to tourists around the lake.

BED-AND-BREAKFASTS AND COUNTRY INNS

In Europe, bed-and-breakfasts are the cheap way to go. People fix up the extra room in their house, and you share a bathroom with the family. Often, in the evening you sit with your hosts in their living room and talk. It's kind of like visiting relatives, except you have no obligations to these people but to be polite—and to pay. Of course, staying in people's homes helps tear down the glass wall between you, the tourist, and the people of that country. You usually end up having wonderful conversations with the folks you meet—the other guests as well as your hosts. Staying in a bed-and-breakfast is a good way to get a glimpse into what life is really like on the other side of the big pond.

Here, the term bed-and-breakfast conjures up romantic images of gorgeous old homes, lovingly restored, and made into elegant retreats, complete with a gourmet breakfast. Add a sylvan setting, and you have the perfect description of most Pocono bed-and-breakfasts. While Pocono bed-and-breakfasts may not always be your cheapest option, they are quite reasonably priced compared to other types of accommodations, and they offer many advantages.

Most important is the atmosphere. Most bed-and-breakfasts are small, so you won't have to contend with crowds. Many are decorated with lovely antiques. Some are adults-only, which may be considered an advantage by people looking for respite. Most are in beautiful settings, and they may offer hiking trails, swimming, and other amenities. Recreational amenities are noted in this section, as are places that are adults-only. Never assume you'll have access to swimming pools, televisions, and private bathrooms. If those things are important to you, ask. Each bed-and-breakfast is the creation of its owner, and each is unique.

A country inn is a larger establishment that usually includes bigger rooms with private baths, often sumptuously decorated to reflect an era or style. Some offer fireplaces and/or Jacuzzis, others suites; some have extended facilities in cottages outside the main lodge. To be considered an inn by the Independent Innkeepers Association, dinner must be served, and the owners must be in-residence. Breakfast can be chosen as an option with the room, and most accommodations also have highly regarded restaurants that are open to the public. There are usually some other amenities, such as a pool, game room, tennis courts, or a great room for relaxing in front of a fireplace after a day of skiing or vigorous antiquing. Country inns, unlike bed-and-breakfast establishments, are more along the scale of small, grand hotels of the past, when a hotel was an enclosed environment offering a menu of on-site options as well as serving as a home base for guests who preferred browsing and wandering.

Many owners of both kinds of hostelries (in some cases, the line between them is thin) talk about hosting family reunions, weddings, conferences, retreats, and special parties. The idea of renting out an entire inn for your family or friends can be very appealing, and many establishments offer special rates for groups.

You may pick a bed-and-breakfast or a country inn for the antiques, for the incredible food, for the interesting-sounding owner, or strictly for the location. No matter what choice you make, you won't be staying in an anonymous motel room—you'll be surrounded by personality.

Before we take a journey through the towns and country roads to review the enticing array of inns, let's get some business out of the way:

Credit cards are generally accepted—exceptions will be noted. If you wish to know about a specific credit card's acceptability, check with an establishment about its policies.

Pets usually are not allowed, but in keeping with the individualistic nature of bed-and-breakfasts and country inns, some owners are happy to accommodate your animal. We mention the inns that welcome pets.

Many inns don't accept children younger than a certain age, and others not at all. We note the policies where guidelines are explicit. If you're planning on bringing your little ones, check before you make a reservation.

As a general rule, smoking is not permitted. Many establishments allow smoking on verandas or porches, and a small few allow smoking in a designated area. If smoking is a concern for you, talk to the innkeeper about her or his smoking policy.

Most of these inns are very old and may not be wheelchair accessible. We suggest you inquire in advance about accessibility if you or someone in your party has special needs.

You may stumble on a pretty inn that has a vacancy, but if you pick the wrong time, say NASCAR weekend at Pocono Raceway (see the related Close-up in our Attractions chapter), you might find every room in the area taken. Call ahead for a reservation to avoid being disappointed. Most inns are filled during the fall foliage season, ski season, summer, and general holiday seasons (Thanksgiving, Christmas, Easter, Presidents' Weekend, and the Fourth of July weekend). Reservations require a deposit, which is credited toward your bill. If you have to cancel, deposits may be refunded with enough advance notice. Check with the individual establishments for their reservations and deposit policies.

Costs for bed-and-breakfasts and country inns vary widely and can depend upon the type of accommodation, length of stay, and amenities. Some inns have suites or luxury rooms that cost more than their basic rooms, and sometimes for a few dollars more, you can get a lake view or a sitting room.

The following key is a general guideline of the average rate you would pay per room per night (double occupancy) during peak season. Many inns have simple rooms and luxury suites, which vary widely in their rates; we have tried to reflect both rates in our listings. Prices are subject to change.

PRICE-CODE KEY

$80 or less	$
$81 to $110	$$
$111 to $160	$$$
$161 or more	$$$$

DELAWARE WATER GAP/ SHAWNEE-ON-DELAWARE

Arrowheart Inn $-$$$
3021 Valley View Drive (Highway 191)
Bangor
(610) 588-0241
www.arrowheartinn.com
Arrowheart Inn is perched on the Kittatinny Ridge and has a breathtaking view of the wide valley leading down to the Delaware River, which is bordered by distant, misty hills. The house was built in the 1960s by John Oliver Nelson, founder of the nearby Kirkridge, a spiritual retreat center (see Camps and Conference Centers), and home to Columcille (See the Close-up in our Attractions chapter). Its simple, clean lines emphasize the incredible view. Owners David Palmer and Ed Hill had been going to Kirkridge for years, and when they decided to open a bed-and-breakfast, they were thrilled to be able to buy this property from the retreat center. The wooded spot offers lots of wildlife—a hawk circles right above the house, and a

bear has been spotted walking through the woods.

Arrowheart has white walls set off by fascinating art, much of it Native American–inspired. There are lots of windows with incredible views and beautifully restored hardwood floors. The four guest rooms have generous closets with white cotton robes for the guests' use and lots of extra blankets. Each is named for the animals inhabiting the artwork in the room. The Owl Room, with a private bath, has a striking, contemporary Ethan Allen bedroom set atop a beautiful Chinese rug that almost looks Navajo. The Bear Room has twin iron bedsteads and is decorated country-style with all kinds of beary touches. The Deer Room has an Amish star quilt on its mission-style bed, an antique blanket chest, and a rocker. Tall people like this bed because their feet can comfortably stick out past the footboard. The large Peacock Room, with a panoramic view, private bath, and private entrance, has a spectacular stained glass peacock fountain window.

The tiled bathrooms evince a '60s look with robin's egg blue tubs and flowery shower curtains made by Ed. "This isn't a Victorian house," Ed confessed. "There's no disguising it, so we're decorating to an upscale '60s theme." Both Ed and David are excellent needleworkers, and Ed's hand-crafted place mats, napkins, and quilt hangings are available for purchase.

Weekly yoga classes are available at the inn, you can book a session with a certified massage therapist ($60), and an enclosed outdoor Jacuzzi-style hot tub gives guests a chance to relax in warm, whirling water while contemplating the stars. A comfortable living room has lots of stuffed chairs and a resource table with information about attractions in the area. Make sure you look at the geological survey map of the spot you're standing upon. A set of shelves holds books for the guests to peruse—mysteries, self-improvement, Native American subjects, as well as gay and lesbian studies.

Guests at Arrowheart get a full gourmet breakfast with homemade breads, waffles, pancakes, and more. Afternoon tea with baked goodies is also available. The Kirkridge Retreat Center is only three minutes away over a footpath through the woods, with Columcille another three minutes beyond. Ed and David get many of their guests from retreats at the center—some people stay in the area a few more days—and from the gay community in nearby cities. There is no smoking anywhere at the Arrowheart Inn. As Arrowheart strives to provide a quiet retreat for its guests, Ed and David prefer that you leave your children at home, unless they're older than 12 and well behaved.

Buttermilk Falls Bed & Breakfast $–$$
5231 Buttermilk Falls Road
Shawnee-on-Delaware
(570) 426-7440
www.buttermilkfallsbnb.com

If it's location you want, you can't beat Buttermilk Falls Bed & Breakfast. You can sit on the wicker-filled front porch, contemplating the dramatic waterfall across the street, you can wander down the hill and enjoy the 3.5-acre property including falls that run under a bridge and make a final dash to a creek at the edge of the back yard, sit at a table and contemplate the creek that runs away from the falls, fish for trout right there (make sure you have a license; the township building is next door), or you can look out any window of the house and see water. You can even walk down the hill and shop at the

Don't book a bed-and-breakfast if you're a party person. Bed-and-breakfasts prefer quiet guests who will not disturb the others, rather than beer-guzzling, loud-music playing dance animals. On the other hand, If you want to party with a bunch of your friends or your family, it's great fun to book an entire bed-and-breakfast.

little craft shop on the property, which features handmade goodies for the kitchen, for brides, baby, home decoration, and holidays.

Buttermilk Falls was a popular boarding house in the early part of the 20th century, but had fallen into disrepair when Bill and Gail Scott bought it in the mid-'90s. They have been working hard to restore it, and today it's a comfortable, friendly bed-and-breakfast.

Start your day by telling Gail how you want your eggs, French toast, pancakes, or waffles. Then grab a cup of coffee and sit on that flower-decked porch, communing with the waterfall. Gail also has a full complement of board games and jigsaw puzzles for people who can't tear themselves away from the porch. When your hot breakfast is ready, Gail will peek out and invite you to the country-style tongue-in-groove pine-paneled breakfast room, where you'll get not only a hot entree, but juice, bacon or sausage, homemade cottage potatoes, fresh fruit, cereal, and muffins. Gail loves to redo the room every couple of months to reflect the season. "Repeat guests like to see that," she says. So tablecloths and linens, as well as the decorative chachkas around the room, celebrate the season or an upcoming holiday. Pick your seat carefully—there are windows on three sides of this room, and most of them have great water views.

All the guest rooms have individually controlled air conditioners. Four rooms share a bath, while one has its own. The Brookview has a Thomas Kincaid wallpaper border, white painted furniture, a double bed, and a fabulous view of the stream below. The Evergreen, in a wilderness theme, has a TV, a double bed, and soap and washcloths tucked into a tiny canoe. The Vintage offers two antique twin beds with the old-fashioned springs and all-cotton mattresses. "They're really comfy," says Gail. "Everybody raves over them." The Waterfall Room has prints of waterfalls on the walls, a queen bed, a private bath, sitting area, TV/VCR, and an incredible view of the backyard falls. Guests can share a TV sitting room with a VCR, books, lots of videos and a green velvet love seat.

Gail and Bill keep fishing poles in the barn, croquet in a side yard, a wonderful playhouse for children, bunnies in a hutch, and a friendly golden retriever named Duke. Birdhouses and feeders are everywhere.

Children are welcome at Buttermilk Falls, as are pets, but you must arrange ahead of time for either. Smoking is allowed only on the porch.

The Gatehouse Country Inn $$$
River Road, Shawnee-on-Delaware
(570) 420–4553
www.gatehousecountryinn.com

When Fred Waring, leader of Fred Waring and the Pennsylvanians and developer of the Waring Blendor, wanted a home for his family in his beloved Shawnee-on-Delaware, he redesigned a stable built at the end of the 19th century. Today Waring's house is a gorgeous, gabled bed-and-breakfast, surrounding a walled-and-flowered courtyard, with a distinctive round icehouse in one corner.

The folks who bought the house from Waring's widow redecorated, taking it from Hollywood-lavish to simply elegant. The current owners, Cindy and Gordon Way, have taken advantage of the renovations, done more of their own, and added their special touches to this fabulous bed-and-breakfast. You can hang out in comfy couches by the huge stone fireplace at one end of the Great Room and admire the beams crossing the ceiling and marching down the walls. High windows let in light and maintain privacy, and French doors lead out the to courtyard. This is a huge room, perfect for parties, and tales of the fetes hosted by Waring are sometimes heard in the village. Cindy and Gordon have added an antique apothecary chest from their hometown, Wayne, Pennsylvania, to one end of the room and filled it with crystal and silver, most of which was passed on to them by family members. Note the huge angel doll, dressed in lace, from Gordon's great-grandmother. Make sure you notice the wonderful 1844 school map of the world in the reception room, with "unexplored Africa, Alaska, and Russia" showing vast areas of unknown territory.

If the weather is good, start your breakfast with coffee in the courtyard. Then move to a table by the window in the great room for baked goods and a fruit plate, followed by a hot dish.

Every room has a private bath, and all but the Cabin Room have individually controlled air-conditioning, and all have wall-to-wall carpeting. The Carriage Room has a queen-size bed, a huge cedar closet, antiques, built-ins, and a small balcony overlooking the grounds and New Jersey's Kittatinny Ridge beyond. The Courtyard Room has gold walls, a king-size bed and a double bed (perfect for your children 12 and older, who are welcome here), and a deep green love seat. Note the crewel bird embroideries done by Cindy's grandmother. The cabin room has its own staircase, an Adirondack log full-size bed, and a balcony. Guests are invited to use an enormous game room full of drawers that held supplies to sew costumes for the Pennsylvanians. There's a pool table here, toys, and lots of board games. A charming Loft Room takes the overflow when the bed-and-breakfast fills up.

There are fascinating touches everywhere—Asian prints and Shawnee memorabilia. You can ditch your car and spend your time exploring the village and walking the trails nearby, or you can investigate all of the Poconos from this great location on the edge of the Delaware Water Gap National Recreation Area. If you're a golfer, be sure to get some tips from Gordon, who spent a summer on the European tour as a professional golfer. He's now chairman of the Shawnee Inn's new Tillinghast Golf Academy (see our Accommodations and Golf chapters). Smoking is allowed outside only.

If you want to stay at a bed-and-breakfast, it's wise to reserve a room ahead of time, particularly at the smaller inns. During summer, winter ski season, and fall foliage seasons, it's especially difficult to find a vacancy.

The Shepard House   **$$–$$$**
108 Shepard Avenue
Delaware Water Gap
(570) 424-9779
www.shepardhouse.com

The Shepard House was built in the early 1900s as a boarding house. It was called "The Fair View House" because of the beautiful valley view from its location at the top of the town of Delaware Water Gap. The present owners, Ruth and Wayne MacWilliams, bought it in 2000 and have been renovating the guest rooms in this lovingly restored, country Victorian guest house in the heart of historic Delaware Water Gap. (See our History, Arts and Culture, Overview, Attractions, and Annual Events chapters for related information about Delaware Water Gap.)

The beautiful veranda is a relaxing, romantic spot, colorfully accented with flowering plants and furnished with rockers and an old-fashioned wicker porch swing for two. Catch the breezes as you read, look at the surrounding mountains, watch for deer and hummingbirds, or just relax. You also can pack a lunch to munch in the picnic area.

The double-occupancy rooms, all with private baths, are accented with beautiful antiques and lace curtains. The house is fully air-conditioned, and guests can relax in the private living room with a large color TV.

Shepard House is just off the Appalachian Trail and a short walk to all the Delaware Water Gap events and activities, even the pool at Shull Park. (See our Kidstuff chapter.)

Breakfast and afternoon tea are served daily. Fresh-ground and brewed coffee and homemade muffins start your breakfast, followed by appetizers and a home-cooked special. Afternoon tea is served with a selection of sweet treats and other refreshments.

Children 12 and older are welcome.

Stony Brook Inn $$–$$$
River Road, Shawnee-on-Delaware
(570) 424–1100
www.stonybrookinn.com

Folks around Shawnee joke that Pete and Rose Ann Ferguson are collecting Waring houses, because for years they summered in a home they bought from one of Fred Waring's sons, and recently they bought this house, which belonged to another Waring son. Collecting is one of Rose Ann's passions, and she's crazy about Longaberger baskets, which you'll see all over the house used in both decorative and utilitarian ways. (She's a Longaberger dealer, too, so if you love the baskets, she can help.) Stony Brook Inn is the culmination of a dream Rose Ann has held. "I've been collecting stuff over 20 years, thinking that's going to be for my bed-and-breakfast," she says. "I just had to find the right house." Rose Ann taught home economics in a New Jersey school, and she gets to employ all of her skills running this gracious establishment.

You enter through a lovely screened porch overlooking the heated in-ground pool. The living room boasts a large stone fireplace, lots of comfortable seating, a TV, books, and magazines. Note the unusual coffee table. It was a hatch door for a sailboat and is so sturdy that Rose Ann has no problem if you put your feet up on it.

The house is fascinating, with rooms on uncountable different levels. Everywhere you look, there's a three-to-four-step staircase to take you to another

room. Four rooms, all with private baths and individually controlled air conditioners, make up Stony Brook Inn, and no guest room shares an adjoining wall with any other guest room. The Country Bear Room, on the first floor, features twin beds that can be converted into a king. Bears are everywhere in this room, and Rose Ann encourages you to pick them up and play. Some guests have even added to the collection. This room is on the first floor and has a terrific view of a small waterfall across the street. The Bridal Suite is the most lavish and private of the rooms. You turn a corner, go up a few steps, and you're in bridal heaven, with high windows for extra light, lots of lace, a king-size bed, and vintage bridal portraits. The sitting room has a table made from a primitive butter churn, a down-filled fainting couch, and a TV and VCR. The Oak Room, with a queen-size bed, boasts antique oak furniture and a wonderful view of the falls. An old-fashioned claw-foot bathtub sports a European-style showerhead, offering you the option of a handheld or regular shower. The Rose Room, in muted pinks, is in the back of the house overlooking the swimming pool and has a queen-size bed. This is the quietest room in the house, as it faces away from the road and the waterfall. All the fabrics and wallpaper borders in here are Longaberger. The bathroom has an unusual square tub with seats.

You can eat breakfast, served on Longaberger pottery, in Stony Brooks' lovely dining room or on the porch. Rose Ann enjoys cooking and offers a country breakfast including baked goods, bacon, juices, fresh fruit, and a hot dish. The entree might be sausage-and-cheese strata, a three-cheese casserole, or some other interesting concoction. If you have any dietary restrictions, Rose Ann is good at incorporating those into her morning menu. And if you like something, ask for the recipe. She's happy to help.

Stony Brook's location is terrific. It's right across the street from the Shawnee Playhouse and Shawnee Falls Studio (an

---

A bed-and-breakfast can be an elegant setting for a small wedding or a special party. Talk to the owners about what they can do for your special occasion.

art studio that also offers workshops, see our Arts and Culture chapter), and next to the Shawnee General Store. All of Shawnee, including the Delaware River, is within a short walk. A stream winds its way along the border of the property. You can cross the stream to the General Store, pick up fishing poles, bait, and a license, and try your luck right here. Rose Ann is an avid hiker, and is happy to recommend longer hikes, if you can tear yourself away from this pleasant spot.

STROUDSBURG/EAST STROUDSBURG

Stroudsmoor Country Inn   **$$-$$$$**
Stroudsmoor Road, Stroudsburg
(570) 421-6431, (800) 955-8663
www.stroudsmoor.com
Stroudsmoor's main building, built in sections during the 1840s and 1880s, houses half of the guest units. Two of the main rooms are suites, and there are two more suites in the Highlander cottage across Marketplace Commons, a green surrounded by cottages that evokes the commons of a country village. On the other side of the commons, directly across from the inn, you'll find one-, two- and three-bedroom cottages with private baths and color TVs. The Ledgemere suites are completely luxurious, right down to the Italian marble bathrooms. The main building's lobby, filled with lovely antiques, has wainscoting and a fieldstone fireplace.

The inn is situated on a 150-acre mountain overlooking Stroudsburg. The views are spectacular and take in the panorama of the Pocono Mountains. Part of the inn's charm is its family tradition; it has been operated for almost 20 years by the Pirone family—mother, father, daughters, sons-in-law, and grandchildren.

Guests awaken to a hearty country breakfast. The outdoor swimming pool, delightful indoor natatorium (with a fitness center and whirlpool spa), an Aveda spa, and the popular on-site restaurant all make

staying here a wonderful experience. Several large party rooms make this an excellent place for a wedding. Stroudsmoor guests have special privileges at the nearby Glen Brook Golf Club. Special golf, ski, and spa packages are available.

Rooms in the inn are cozy and decorated with period antiques. All have air-conditioning, private baths, and color TVs.

Bed-and-breakfast lodging includes a four-course breakfast each day. On Sunday a champagne brunch is served. Guests can also choose the Full American Plan.

MOUNT POCONO AREA

Brookview Manor B&B Inn   **$$$-$$$$**
Highway 447, Canadensis
(570) 595-2451, (800) 585-7974
www.thebrookviewmanor.com
The huge wraparound porch and stone-and-clapboard siding on this Victorian home are reminders of the heyday of summer homes in the Poconos. "Romantic" is the feeling innkeepers Gaile and Marty Horowitz have achieved here. The floors are highly polished hardwood graced with contrasting area rugs. In the library, a stone fireplace with inset bookshelves and benches provides a lovely contrast to the rounded corner-window area where a piano sits surrounded by the beauty of the woods. Just off this room is a smaller sitting room decorated for the hunt in plum and green plaids with woodsy-scene borders. Afternoon refreshments—part of the amenities at Brookview—can be enjoyed here.

The dining rooms are exquisite, and Gaile and Marty have added another dining room to accommodate fans of his cooking. Rich burgundy walls set off by white lace curtains make the center room a jewel. To its right is a lovely enclosed sun porch with curtains and cheery decorations. To the left is a raised formal dining area, set for dinner beneath a bank of windows with transoms of stained glass in oak leaf and acorn patterns. Brass, etched-glass and crystal lighting fixtures throughout the house are original, including the chandeliers in the dining room and wall sconces in each guest room and in the hallway.

Brookview Manor has 11 guest rooms and suites, including those in the carriage house across the lawn from the main house. "Each room is different," says Gaile. "Each has its own personality." All rooms have private baths, some have fireplaces, clawfoot tubs, or Jacuzzis, and each is furnished with beautiful antiques. The Fireplace Room, as elegant as any in this lovely home, has a fireplace and a dramatic four-poster bed. The Victorian suite, with windows looking out into the forest, has a separate sun porch sitting room overlooking the brook and a huge bathroom. The bed is queen-size, and the bathroom is made even more beautiful by its stained-glass windows.

Breakfast here is always a special treat. Marty was a chef in New York, working at places like the Lawrence Village Park House. When he worked at Colony Hill, he had the honor of serving President Reagan with meals from his original recipes. Recently, Marty was named sixth best bed-and-breakfast chef in the country by the magazine *Arlington's Inn Traveler*. Of course you'll get muffins, fruit, juices, banana nut bread and such, but Marty likes to have fun with his hot dish. If you're lucky, you'll get his Casserole Ali, an artful combination of soufflé, French toast, ham and eggs and cheese omelet. Or perhaps he'll be concocting a French toasted stuffed with strawberries. Whatever Marty makes, you'll be getting food fit for a president. He can also do a prix fixe gourmet dinner, if you wish ($50 per person). You don't have to stay at Brookview Manor to sample Marty's cuisine. Weekend breakfast and Saturday night dinner are open to the public, by reservation only. Afternoon refreshments, including more delicious homebaked specialties, are served in the sitting room, on the porch, or anywhere else you'd like to enjoy them. In nice weather, the little patio across from the house is an ideal spot to spend a

relaxing afternoon under the trees that tower over the gracious lawns.

There is quite a bit of property to roam here. For a real treat, cross the road toward the brook, and follow the path (about a mile) to a secluded waterfall. Gaile and Marty will be glad to direct you there and to any other spot you're interested in seeing, and they'll be happy to pack a picnic lunch for you, too.

Country Surrey Inn $$$$
Third Street, Gouldsboro
(570) 842-2081

When you round the bend in the road on the way to the Country Surrey Inn and first catch sight of Gouldsboro Lake, you'll have to catch your breath—the lake is gorgeous. That's why, as you approach the Country Surrey Inn, you'll see lots of chairs, all facing the lake. Country Surrey is practically surrounded by the lake and takes full advantage of it. The dining rooms have large lakefront windows, and in the good weather, you can eat on the terrace overlooking the water. You can swim and fish right from the front yard, or you can walk over to Gouldsboro State Park (see our Parks chapter) and partake of the many activities offered there. The Country Surrey also has bicycles for its guests. Thirty rooms, in three buildings, make up this inn. Many have king-size beds, and most of the couches pull out to make beds. Rooms sleep two to six people. All are furnished simply but comfortably. ("The only antique here is me," says Mary Kelly, the proprietor.) The Lakeside Suites are only a few steps from the lake and most have large picture windows with good views. The white-columned Lakeview suites are similar, though some have fireplaces, some have living rooms with a pull-out couch, and some have a small extra room with a single bed—perfect for a child. The Chalet's rooms are similar, but since it's behind the Lakeview Suites, not every room has a view of the lake. We recommend the second floor front rooms of the Chalet, because they are the most reasonably priced, and they still have a great view. There's also a small one-bedroom apartment that rents by the week or month. It's under the eaves with a fully equipped kitchen, living room, bedroom, and bathroom. Tall people might have to pad the tops of their heads in this apartment, but it's charming. The big news at Country Surrey is that a successful New York chef has taken over the dining room and opened La Terraza, a Northern Italian restaurant. You can come here for dinner, rent a bed-and-breakfast room, or stay on the Modified American Plan—breakfast and dinner. As a bed-and-breakfast guest, you'll get a full breakfast overlooking the lake. Mary prides herself on one-to-one attention, and even accompanies the bus groups that stay here when they go sightseeing, "Because," she says, "they laugh at my jokes." Children are welcome. There's no smoking in the dining room.

Crescent Lodge $$–$$$$
Highways 191 and 940, Paradise Valley
(570) 595-7486, (800) 392-9400
www.crescentlodge.com
This gracious country inn is at once elegant and homey. It has been owned by members of the Dunlop family for more than 50 years. Accommodations include rooms in the main inn and private cottages. Meals, including breakfast, are served in the exquisite dining room. The grounds contain a heated outdoor pool, tennis court, and hiking trails. The lodge is central to the towns and attractions accessed by Highway 191 in Paradise Valley.

Options include rooms with double or queen-size beds, deluxe rooms with a canopy bed, or a suite with living room. All cottages have private sun decks and vary by layout and amenities (Jacuzzis, fireplaces, canopy beds). One cottage includes a country kitchen, a TV with VCR, and sunken Jacuzzi.

All accommodations are beautifully decorated with matching draperies, lace, floral patterns, warm pastels, wall-to-wall carpeting and more.

The Crescent Lodge is in a delightful, elegant country setting. The grounds are lovely, expansive, and inviting. The restaurant is highly acclaimed and open to the public. (See our Restaurants chapter.)

Dreamy Acres $
Highway 447 and Seese Hill Road
Canadensis
(570) 595-7115
This little hideaway is across a bridge that traverses the creek running through Dreamy Acres. Bill and Esther Pickett have owned this old-time bed-and-breakfast since 1959—"before there were bed-and-breakfasts," as Mrs. Picket tells it.

The main house has two guest rooms with a shared bath, and the adjacent lodge has four rooms, two with private baths, and two with a shared bath. The decor in each is contemporary. The lodge has a main living room for all lodge guests and a screened porch with traditional green porch chairs. From May until October only, a continental breakfast—juice, coffee, sweet rolls, and muffins—is served in the dining room of the main house. Though breakfast is served only in-season, rooms are available all year. Families return to Dreamy Acres generation after generation with their children 12 and older. You can blow dreamy smoke rings here, as smoking is allowed in designated areas.

Farmhouse Bed & Breakfast $$–$$$
Grange Road, Mount Pocono
(570) 839-0796
www.thefarmhousebnb.com
This 1850 homestead, nestled beneath giant evergreens, offers four suites and a caretaker's cottage. Owners Nick and Fern Cannizzaro may be new to the Poconos, but they're not new to the business. Fern's family owns bed-and-breakfasts and inns in Vermont, while Nick and his father have owned restaurants in New York. Their experience helps them pamper their guests in this beautiful setting.

Each suite has a private bath, queen-size bed, refrigerator, color TV with VCR,

Most travelers today take two-to-four-day weekend vacations. To fill their rooms during the week, many bed-and-breakfasts and country inns offer lower rates Monday through Thursday. You can save a fair amount of money if you can swing a vacation on those days of the week.

and stereo. Each also has a fireplace for winter and air conditioning for summer; as well as an electric tea kettle with instant coffee, tea, herbal teas, and hot chocolate provided. There are two comfortable suites in the main house—the Parlor Suite and the Master Suite. Each suite has its own special feel. A wall of library shelves in the Parlor Suite adds a homey touch. The Master Suite has a wood stove instead of a fireplace. Each suite also has its own entrance from the lovely screened slate porch that guests are free to enjoy.

A short distance from the main house is the cozy Caretaker's Cottage. This welcoming suite is in the renovated icehouse of the original 1850 homestead. Downstairs is a lovely sitting room with fireplace. Upstairs is an adorable bedroom with bed and bath, all decorated in country comfort. This is a very private spot.

Also on the 6.5-acre property are two more suites—the Sundown and Sunup. Both have the same amenities as the Master and Parlor. The rooms are large, country-casual, and cozy. These two suites adjoin—perfect for two couples who want to spend a weekend together. Each suite has a separate entrance and fireplace. The Sunup has a kitchen, living room, and an extra bedroom with a daybed. The Sundown has a double-size tub and separate shower. A deck runs the full length of the lodging, and it looks out over the rustic beauty of the Farmhouse's wooded property.

And what about breakfast? Nick is an experienced chef and has developed 20 different styles of French toast, 10 different styles of pancakes, and lots of omelets with garden-fresh ingredients. Everything

is done fresh—"There are no microwaves on the property," says Nick. All the baked goods are also made on the premises. Breakfast includes coffee, tea, juice, fruit that's in-season, breakfast meats, and one of Nick's hot specialties, or you can have eggs any style. There are extra baked goods on the weekend.

Breakfast is served at a large, family-size table in the dining room with floor-to-ceiling windows that afford expansive views of the property. Nick says there's a bird show every morning at feeders just outside the window, and, if you're lucky, you may catch sight of some deer or other animals that call the Farmhouse's property home. The chef's delightful kitchen overlooks the dining area and the sitting room joined by a huge fireplace.

There is absolutely no smoking anywhere on the property, and, as this is a quiet, romantic bed-and-breakfast, children are not welcome here.

Frog Town Inn   **$$–$$$**
Highway 390, Canadensis
(570) 595-6282
www.frogtowninn.com
This inn has been a stopover for travelers since the 1890s. Stan and Carol Zimmer bought it in 1994 and have restored it. The Zimmers have developed a fine reputation for serving elegant "French Country" meals, and Frog Town Inn has become a well-respected dining spot in the Poconos. (See our Restaurants chapter.)

All 10 guest rooms have private baths and are decorated with beautiful antiques. Five suites have sitting areas, and all the rooms have color TVs. Each room or suite is decorated differently: one has a four-poster bed, one has a brass bed, and another has an antique maple bed; some have marble-top dressers or side tables; and all have different color schemes.

The inn has a cozy pub open to the public, with a fireplace and a TV for relaxing after a rough day of Poconos shopping, skiing, hiking, or swimming.

Stan prepares a full breakfast daily for guests of the inn. It generally consists of pancakes or French toast, a fresh-made omelette full of goodies such as shitake mushrooms, bacon or sausage, fresh muffins and popovers, fresh fruit, and juice.

The Merry Inn   **$$**
Highway 390, Canadensis
(800) 858-4182
**www.pbcomputerconsulting.com/
themerryinn**
This cozy home away from home is run by innkeepers Meredyth and Chris Huggard. It has central air-conditioning in six rooms, all with private baths and TVs. The decor is a mix of country-casual plaids and florals with Victorian accents. The large rooms are complemented by two outdoor decks, one of which has a hot tub overlooking the woods. There are two large common areas used as lounges and sitting areas.

Children are welcome here, since Huggard herself has an 10-year-old who helps keep the atmosphere homey. Pets are allowed on a limited basis. Check with Meredyth before you bring Rin-Tin-Tin.

Huggard serves a full breakfast every morning. It always includes three or four main choices with bacon or sausage and home fries. Choices include pancakes with apples, French toast stuffed with raspberries and cream cheese, orange French toast, or eggs any style.

Mountaintop Lodge   **$$-$$$$**
Highway 940, Pocono Pines
(570) 646-6636
www.mttoplodge.com
Merrily Baxter-MacKay is part of the history of Pocono Pines. Her great grandfather, Rufus Wilder Miller, built Lake Naomi for his Pocono Spring Water Company. In the winter he harvested ice to keep Philadelphia's iceboxes cool. Today Lake Naomi is the centerpiece of an exclusive development (see our Relocation chapter), and one of Miller's descendants runs a charming bed-and-breakfast a short walk away.

Merrily grew up in Mountaintop Lodge. It was built in the 1920s as a ladies' boarding house and once sat across the street from a train station. She has restored the building from floor to ceiling stenciling the walls and sewing the duvet covers, window treatments, and pillows. The inn has a light, airy feel, with white walls accented by floral fabrics. Beautiful antiques are combined with new pieces, giving the inn a lovely look while providing comfortable spots to sit and relax. The color schemes and fabrics give each of the 12 guest rooms an individual flavor that is mirrored in their private baths. Playful touches abound, such as a bedside table made from old suitcases and Merrily's grandmother's lace collar and cuffs, framed and hung on the wall. Every room has a queen- or king-size mattress and down comforter. Some suites have fireplaces and Jacuzzis. The house is shaded by tall trees, and every room has individually controlled air conditioning and heat. The Grand Suite has a king-size bed crowned with a drapery suggesting a canopy. An inviting sitting room, fireplace, and cedar-wrapped Jacuzzi complete that suite. Merrily has recently added a guest house that sleeps six. It's closer to Lake Naomi's beach and perfect for families.

A breakfast buffet with fresh orange juice, fruit, homemade granola, and a variety of hot breakfast dishes is usually served in the Great Room. Make sure you admire the beautiful silver service that belonged to Merrily's grandmother. On one end of the great room is a huge fireplace filled with birch logs. Overstuffed couches cry, "Sit on me!" On the wall above the couches, you can peruse photos depicting the early days of Pocono Pines. A series of small antique breakfast tables facing a wall of windows fills out the room.

Not all bed-and-breakfasts and country inns have air-conditioning, telephones, or TV in every room. If any of these things matter to you, check the listing or ask the innkeeper.

A huge porch wraps around two sides of the building, and you can sit at one of the many candlelit tables on the porch admiring the baskets of fuchsia or just contemplating the woods beyond.

Guests of the Mountaintop Lodge may take advantage of the amenities at Lake Naomi and the Pinecrest Lake Golf and Country Club. A pretty swimming beach is a five-minute walk from the Lodge. Guests can swim, fish, play tennis, golf, swim in a pool, use the snack bar, or eat at the gorgeous restaurant open only to Lake Naomi clubhouse members. Guests can also walk the trails in the woods behind the inn, go cross-country skiing on trails through a nearby development, and play croquet, horseshoes, and board games. A tented backyard makes a lovely settting for a wedding. Children 12 and older are welcome. Smoking is allowed on the porch only.

Pine Knob Inn   **$$-$$$$**
Highway 447, Canadensis
(800) 426-1460
www.pineknobinn.com
Pine Knob Inn dates from the Civil War. It has 18 guest rooms, all with private baths and decorated with antiques. Each room has its own character, though all are informal and cozy. The circular driveway leads to an expansive porch surrounding two sides of this comfortable country place. Two gazebos grace the lawns, and a white picket fence surrounds some of the flower-filled gardens.

A swimming pool, tennis courts, and an array of lawn games are available for relaxation and recreation. The Brodhead Creek runs by, and fishing is allowed with a valid Pennsylvania license.

Innkeepers John and Cheryl Garman pride themselves on their excellent food, so overnight accommodations can also

---

Many bed-and-breakfast owners pride themselves on their gourmet cooking, and many, for a fee, will pack a picnic lunch or make you dinner. Be sure to ask.

---

include a five-course gourmet dinner of continental cuisine. (See our Restaurants chapter.) Other options can include lodging only, bed-and-breakfast, or breakfast and dinner. With its romantic setting and fine chef, the Pine Knob specializes in weddings.

WEST END

Blueberry Mountain Inn   **$$-$$$**
Thomas Road, Blakeslee
(570) 646-7144
www.blueberrymountaininn.com
The Blueberry Mountain Inn takes you by surprise. Its salmon-colored exterior and white trim immediately catch your attention. Expansive verandas jut off into interesting architectural angles and accent this at-once modern and colonial Caribbean-style structure.

Blueberry Mountain Inn is proud that it has achieved a three-diamond rating from the American Automobile Association and three crowns from the Pennsylvania Travel Council. They are also members of the Ecotourism "Green" Hotels Association, which means that they try to keep the environment as chemical free as possible, using natural cleaners where they can. As they're a new building, they have installed a very sophisticated air filtering system, which can help people with allergies breath easier. Rather than chlorinate their indoor swimming pool, they use ozone to kill the bacteria, a system used widely overseas.

Built in 1994, the inn is filled with antiques that date back more than a century. There are six rooms (all with queen-size beds); one is a master suite sleeping up to six. The Great Room is beautifully accented with a potpourri of antiques including walnut tea carts, wing chairs, and a piano. The Violet Room has furniture brought from France by innkeeper Grace Hydrusko's grandmother's great-grandmother. Two sitting rooms are for guests, a great room with a wonderful stone fireplace and a library. You'll also find an indoor pool, outdoor spa, game room, and a shared kitchen. Special accommodations have been made for the physically challenged. There is a lake on the property for fishing (no license is required, but bring your own equipment) and canoeing.

Saturday's breakfast is varied and full, while Sunday brings a very special buffet. Special dietary needs can be accommodated with advance notice.

Business travelers can take advantage of fax service and telephones as well as corporate account options.

Chestnut Hill Bed & Breakfast $$-$$$
Highway 715, Brodheadsville
(570) 992-1257, (800) 992-1860
www.chestnuthillpoconos.com

Terry and Debbie Connelly have always wanted to run a bed-and-breakfast inn, so when Chestnut Hill Bed & Breakfast went on the market, they were thrilled to get it. Built between 1835 and 1860 by German immigrants, this homestead became known in the area as the Treehaven Estate. It stands beside McMichaels Creek.

Two cozy rooms and a suite upstairs, plus the bright, sunny Garden Suite, provide guest accommodations. The Garden Suite includes a queen bed, a comfy leather chair, and wall-to-wall carpeting as well as a private entrance, a kitchen, and a sitting room with fireplace, rocking chair, and daybed. The blue-trimmed kitchen has a freestanding wood stove/fireplace and all the accoutrements needed in a modern kitchen, including a microwave and coffeemaker. Debbie puts a little basket of extras in all the rooms, including bottles of Frangelico and her own soaps and shampoos. In the Garden Suite, the basket includes coffee, tea, and some extras for the kitchen. This suite also offers a cable TV, phone for local calls, a huge, mural-painted bathroom, and its own private patio with picnic table and grill. Children 12 and older are welcome in the Garden Suite only.

Each room upstairs is decorated to a theme. The Victorian room has an antique high-back, oak, queen-size canopy bed,

armoire, fancy chair, and porcelain doll in its own little rocking chair. You can see the pond from this room.

Lilacs and Lace has a lush, European style, four-poster, iron, queen-size bed hung with draperies, as well as an antique armoire, marble-topped nightstands, and a handpainted dressing table.

The Port Charleston Suite has a nautical theme with dark furnishings reminiscent of a sea captain's stateroom. A fascinating antique burlwood chest provides a place to hang your clothes and lots of drawers. The lovely sitting room has an easy chair and a blue wicker chair. You can sit and watch and listen to the babbling brook across the lane from this spot. The rooms have lots of special touches. They all have private baths with a sink separate from the bathroom—traditional European layout—and each sink area is set off as a little oasis, allowing two people to perform their morning ablutions at the same time. Ceiling fans, air-conditioning, a CD player, and fresh flowers are found in every room.

Shared spaces include two comfortable living rooms and a TV room with a comfy couch, cable TV, VCR, sound system, and beautiful grandfather clock. The adjoining sitting room includes comfortable seating facing the fireplace and a majestic carousel horse.

Debbie and Terry take pride in their breakfast specialties. The scent of fresh muffins and breads perfumes the house on weekends, and on weekends guests are offered homemade muffins, breads, fresh fruit bowls, a concoction of yogurt and fruit, and gourmet coffees and teas. In addition, guests can choose from six entrees, including peaches and cinnamon Belgian waffles, Denver scrambled eggs, or a decadent cinnamon French toast. Breakfast is in the Victorian, cathedral-ceiling dining room. In warm weather, breakfast can be enjoyed on the outdoor deck. During the week a continental breakfast is offered. You can also have a homemade snack in the afternoon.

Outside is a lovely pond with a miniature dock and boathouse. Lots of acres of woods beckon to the wanderer. Scattered across the property are benches, gliders, wicker sets, and picnic tables. You may not smoke inside the house, but outside, the deck and patios provide comfortable smoking spots.

Innkeepers at most child-free inns are more concerned with children's potential for disturbing other guests than they are about little people's entropic tendencies. In many cases, an inn that doesn't normally allow children will welcome them if a family rents the whole inn—on the theory that if the kids are your own, they won't "disturb" you.

Grassy Hill   **$$**
80 Carpenter Lane, Palmerton
(610) 826-2290
www.jimthorpe.com

Drive through farmland and into a patch of woods where you'll see Grassy Hill, a long white home decked with flower boxes and surrounded by lovely flowerbeds. Carole Cortazzo, one of the owners, loves to garden, and the results of her work—flower arrangements—are everywhere. When you arrive at Grassy Hill, Carole and her husband Ralph offer coffee, tea, or wine. If the weather's good, you can sit on the patio, get to know the Cortazzos, and gaze at the gardens a-flutter with butterflies and hummingbirds. Past the gardens, the land drops off and then rises in a tree-covered ridge. You could sit all day, watching toy-size cars and trucks move along a lane on the ridge. Beyond that ridge is the dramatic Lehigh Gap fading away in the mist. The Appalachian Trail runs along one of the ridges you can see, and hikers use Palmerton as a stop-off point. You can also see Blue Mountain's ski slope from this point. Deer often come by in the evening to eat the corn the Cortazzos leave out for them. The land goes down a large hill, and Ralph often builds a campfire at the bottom.

If you can tear yourself away from the patio and gardens, the inside is lovely, too. A dining room has lace-draped windows, a fireplace, and lovely wood floors accented by a Native American rug. One wall is entirely made up of bookshelves. A TV room has overstuffed couches. Upstairs, a pink room has a queen bed, private bath, flowery curtains, and a print of the Lehigh Gap. A beautiful antique oak dressing table and low window complete the room. A beige room has a double bed, a wicker rocker, and another antique dresser. The bed is placed so that you can lie in bed and see out the low window into the woods across the lane. The largest guest room is under the eaves. It has a queen bed, lots of antique furniture, and a pretty flowered rug. It opens into a bright room with morning glories Carole stenciled on the walls, skylights, two double beds, and a private bath. This is a perfect suite for people traveling together or for families with children 12 or older. Journals in every room carry the happy writings of former guests. A full breakfast is served with sausage or bacon, potatoes, fruit juices, and an entree like oatmeal pancakes or Grand Marnier French toast. In the good weather you can eat out on the patio.

Massage therapy administered by a certified therapist is available. Smoking is allowed outside the house only.

The Harry Packer Mansion   **$$$–$$$$**
Packer Hill, Jim Thorpe
(570) 325-8566
www.murdermansion.com

Your first reaction to this magnificent mansion is going to be "Oh, my God," and that's exactly what owners Pat and Bob Handwerk want to hear. "We've tried to make every room so exquisite that you open the door and say, 'Oh, my God,'" says Pat. Perched on a hill next to the Asa Packer Mansion, this castle was a wedding gift from father to son, and no expense was spared on the lavish interior. Today, it is one of two bed-and-breakfasts in Pennsylvania to be awarded four diamonds from the American Automobile Association. If the Harry Packer Mansion looks familiar, it was the model for Disney World's haunted mansion.

You will be awed by the stained and leaded glass, the 16-foot painted ceilings, the carved mahogany, the beautiful period antiques, and the elaborate carved and tiled fireplaces. But very few mansions of this caliber actually invite you to sit on the furniture, let alone put your feet up and sleep on it.

Six guest rooms in the mansion itself and six more in the carriage house are every bit as lavish as the magnificent rooms downstairs. Harry's Suite is our favorite, with a lovely sitting room, a bedroom with a fainting couch and a Minton-tiled fireplace surrounded by an elaborately carved built-in shelving unit. The bathroom is something out of a movie, full of wood paneling, marble fixtures, and the deepest tub we've ever seen.

Breakfast, set with linen, china, crystal, and silver, is a full gourmet buffet including fresh fruit, homemade breads, pastries, German eggs, or eggs l'orange, breakfast meat, and more. In good weather you can eat on the wisteria-covered veranda overlooking the valley—a nice spot to sit at night and sip a glass of wine while watching the stars. In colder weather, you'll have breakfast in a dining room so elegant you'll feel like you're a guest of Andrew Carnegie.

Leave your children at home; the mansion is too gorgeous for smudgy fingers tracing the wall up the stairs. When they grow up and get married, you can send them here for a honeymoon. It would be easy to become uptight around guests invading this incredible place, but the Handwerks are relaxed and friendly.

As if all this splendor isn't enough, the Handwerks put on a number of special events at the mansion. Murder mysteries entertain guests every weekend, and the Harry Packer Mansion has been chosen as hosting the Best Murder Mystery on the East Coast by *Condé Nast*. They have also been named the B&B/Inn with the Best Activities by the *Book of Lists*. Monthly

Victorian high teas give the public a chance to enjoy the ambiance of the veranda; and at Christmas the Handwerks put on a Victorian Ball. The balls feature live music, delectable food, guests in period costume, and dancing (Victorian-style, of course). The high teas and balls are open to the public by reservation.

Inn at Jim Thorpe $-$$$$
24 Broadway, Jim Thorpe
(570) 325-2599, (800) 329-2599
www.innjt.com

The exterior of this inn, in the heart of Jim Thorpe, bespeaks Victorian elegance, with wrought-iron porch railings and balconies. According to legend, many greats have come here—General Ulysses S. Grant, President William Howard Taft, Buffalo Bill Cody, Thomas Edison, and John D. Rockefeller.

The rooms are elegantly furnished in Victorian style. Lace abounds, as do ornate wooden headboards and period antiques. There are private baths in each room, with pedestal sinks and marble floors. The rooms have air-conditioning, cable TV, and telephones. The suites each have a fireplace, whirlpool, king-size bed, kitchen, stereo, TV, and VCR. The decor is absolutely elegant. The Inn at Jim Thorpe also offers conference facilities, including two fully equipped meeting rooms.

Morning brings a continental breakfast buffet with large selections of fresh muffins, pastries, and cereals to accompany your coffee and juice. The Emerald Pub is part of the inn and is a wonderful place to dine. (See our Restaurants chapter.)

Children 6 and younger stay for free.

Sweet Reflections $-$$
574 Oak Grove Drive, Lehighton
(570) 386-5406
www.jimthorpe.com

If Sweet Reflections looks familiar, take a look at the Currier & Ives print on the wall in the living room. The house in the print looks exactly like Sweet Reflections, a brick farmhouse built in 1857, down to the way the lane curves away toward a hill. It's possible the house was used as a model, say owners Al and Jan Naclerio, but they haven't confirmed it yet. At any rate, Sweet Reflections will take you back to an earlier, slower, more reflective time. Sit on the porch and rock on one of the antique wicker chairs. Inside the house, the floorboards are extra wide, and there are some unusual touches like the rare spindle wheel rocking chair. "The Pennsylvania Dutch were so frugal," says Jan, "that they reused everything." So when a spinning wheel was no longer usable, it was made into a chair.

A full country breakfast is served in the dining room, painted blue and white, Jan's favorite combination ("it's restful," she says) and filled with lace. Breakfast is an entree such as French toast made with homemade raisin bread, pancakes ("made from scratch, not from a box"), or scrambled eggs baked with cheese, bacon, and crumbs. You'll also be served homemade muffins made with Granny Smith apples, fresh fruit; sausage, bacon, or ham; and fresh bagels. Jan has an herb garden and likes to use mint and other herbs right from the garden.

Upstairs there's a library with lots of gardening books and more checkers sets. A country-style bathroom has lace curtains and an original claw-foot tub. A drawer full of goodies such as toothpaste, shampoos, and bandages are available to guests. All the rooms have queen beds, journals, air conditioning, and each is named. Romance is full of lace, white-painted furniture and wicker. A lace curtain decorates a four-poster bed. Flower Time has rag rugs and two beds, perfect for bringing your kids. Lace curtains and flowery bedspreads create the atmosphere in this room. Monet has a curtained four-poster, a Victorian fainting couch, and more lace. A variety of perfume bottles sit on a mirrored dressing table. Jan loves lace and doilies, and examples of her collection are strewn everywhere.

There's a garden with a picnic table and benches. A pond holds lots of goldfish, and if you listen carefully, you'll hear frogs. Water lilies add color to the pretty pond. Sweet Reflections is a relaxed, homey place, and children older than five are welcome. In the journals, guests write that they feel at home here and that the food is particularly good. Smoking is outdoors only.

VictoriAnn Bed and Breakfast $–$$$
68 Broadway, Jim Thorpe
(570) 325–8107, (888) 241–4460
www.thevictoriann.com
This town house inn is in the heart of Jim Thorpe on Broadway. The eight rooms are decorated in Victorian decor, and some have king-size beds. Three of the rooms open out onto the second-story veranda on the side of the house and overlook the appealing gardens. The veranda extends the length of the house, and guests are invited to have friends over to enjoy refreshments alfresco. VictoriAnn's is colorful, lacy, and flowery, with high ceilings, polished floors, nooks and crannies, and art all over the place. Classical music fills the air in the sitting room.

Hostess Louise Ogilvie serves up a full breakfast in the dining room or, weather permitting, in the garden, including fresh melon and grapefruit, cereal with bananas, hot porridge with white raisins, a choice of scrambled eggs with mushrooms or blueberry pancakes and either bacon or ham.

MILFORD/LAKE WALLENPAUPACK AREA

Academy Street Bed & Breakfast $$
528 Academy Street, Hawley
(570) 226–3430
www.academybb.com
Seven large, air-conditioned rooms make up this delightfully restored Victorian in the middle of Hawley, just five minutes from Lake Wallenpaupack. Four rooms have private baths, and two have half baths. Each room is decorated differently in a Victorian motif. There is the Elizabeth Barrett Browning Room, furnished entirely in antique wicker, and the Four-Poster Room, featuring a queen-size four-poster

bed. Every room has a TV, VCR, and CD player, and guests may borrow from the Academy Street's video and CD library. The dining room—the setting for breakfast—has a lovely fireplace, as do the sitting and main rooms. The porches, with antique seating arrangements, overlook the carefully planted and maintained Victorian gardens.

A full gourmet breakfast is prepared daily by owners Michele and Manuel Rojas. Amaretto French toast, omelettes, soufflés, eggs Benedict, fresh fruit, muffins, and other delicious items await you. More delights are served at late night dessert. Michele used to have a dessert catering business, so her baked goods are like nothing you've ever tasted. Make sure you try her gourmet brownies with five different chocolates and four different nuts.

Bischwind   **$$$-$$$$**
One Coach Road, Bear Creek
(570) 472-3820
www.bischwind.com

Bischwind is a Bavarian manor that is breathtaking in its Old World splendor. The original home was built in 1886 by Albert Lewis, an industrial magnate and contemporary of Asa Packer. The home has hosted Presidents Theodore Roosevelt and William Howard Taft as well as famed aeronautical engineer Igor Sikorsky. The estate is set among tiered gardens of baronial grandeur that lead from a magnificent slate terrace gracing two sides of this miniature castle.

The entrance hall features polished wood, Oriental rugs, and marvelous antiques from here and abroad. Off this hall is a cozy fireplace with comfortable seating for those who wish to warm up after a winter outing. Leading from the hall is the Bridal Salon, a spectacular room with Louis XIV furnishings amid pink, blue, and white valances, draperies, and carpets. A bank of leaded-glass windows graced with white lace comprises one wall of this delightfully airy salon. Under the windows are wide, comfortable window seats that face the center of the room and

> *If dietary concerns are an issue for you, discuss them with the innkeeper. Some are able to meet your needs better than others, but virtually all will help if they are able.*

the 100-year-old, white Steinway piano. A crystal chandelier crowns this breathtaking space, which is used for weddings and other grand occasions of up to 75 guests.

Opposite the salon is the Presidential Dining Room, with Tiffany transoms in the windows that top the French doors opening onto the terrace. The opposite wall of the dining room has a fireplace with a leaded-glass window above it that presents a view of the fenced grounds and woods surrounding this wondrous home.

The impressive suites here feature fireplaces, living rooms, private baths, and antiques. Four-posters, marble tops, armoires, and black lacquer add to the opulence. The Theodore Roosevelt Suite has a library, chaise, and leather wing-backed chairs. The headboard of the queen-size bed travels toward the ceiling in a design fit for royalty. Laces and beautiful hangings add a soft touch. This is a truly romantic and elegant place to start a new life or renew old vows.

Breakfast at Bischwind is a four-course gourmet-affair brunch that includes filet mignon or poached salmon. On their Web site, you will find recipes for some of the Bischwind specialties served at breakfast.

This estate is the home of the Von Drans, who have spent their lifetime restoring it to the splendiferous state it's in today. The romantic elegance of Bischwind is intensified by the presence of the delightful Mrs. Von Dran. If you have the opportunity, ask her to recite her excellent mock-Elizabethan poetry, full of wit and intelligence and enhanced by her professional delivery.

Children 12 and older are welcome here. Weddings are splendid here, and exclusivity is the keyword for executive meetings away from the office catered with exceptional delicacies and elegance.

Black Walnut Country Inn $$–$$$$
Firetower Road, Milford
(570) 296-6322
www.theblackwalnutinn.com

The Black Walnut Country Inn is a family affair, owned by Stewart Schneider and run by his son and daughter-in-law, Robin and William Schneider. This is a great bed-and-breakfast for families, too, with farm animals, a pond for fishing and swimming, and lots more.

Elizabeth Taylor and Malcom Forbes have stayed at Black Walnut, and many playwrights and theater-types come here to enjoy the solitude, especially in winter. A New York play-writing couple used the inn one weekend and spread their script all over the empty room floors as they worked themselves into a creative frenzy.

The inn has 12 rooms and a cabin that sleeps seven. Four of the rooms have full baths, four have half-baths, and four share baths. Some rooms have televisions, and all rooms are decorated with antiques. Victorian bureaus accent the flowered wallpaper, comforters, and curtains.

There's more to the Black Walnut than the cozy, antique-filled rooms. There are paddleboats and powerboats in the pond and a swimming dock. You can enjoy the animals in the petting zoo; hike (or cross-country ski in winter) the 160 acres of woods and trails; relax in the hot tub; or play a game of pool. The pond is stocked for catch-and-release fishing.

Breakfast, in a dining room full of glass that looks out over the lake, is served buffet-style and includes a variety of fruits, baked goods, juices, eggs, sausage, bacon, and other morning treats.

The folks at the Black Walnut are trilingual, speaking English, Spanish, and American Sign Language. Their phone is TTY capable. The Black Walnut also boards horses, making this the perfect retreat for the city-dwelling equestrian.

Cliff Park Inn & Golf Course $$$–$$$$
155 Cliff Park Road, Milford
(570) 296-6491, (800) 225-6535
www.cliffparkinn.com

Cliff Park Inn is a lovely old white house at the end of a road surrounded by a rolling nine-hole golf course (see our Golf chapter) that is bordered by a deep, piney wood. A wide porch with lots of green rockers, and some Adirondack chairs out on the lawn give guests a great excuse to sit and watch white-clad golfers play against the emerald-green fairways. The inn was built as a farm by George Buchanan in 1820. By 1900, Annie Buchanan had turned it into a small summer hotel. Recently the fifth generation of Buchanans turned the inn over to Yvonne and James Klausmann, who also run the lovely Pine Hill Farm Bed and Breakfast. Yvonne and James have been renovating and upgrading this wonderful property.

Each guest room is freshly painted and decorated in a comfortable Americana with reproductions of antique furniture; the pieces look classic but will take years of heavy use. All the rooms have a private bathroom and air-conditioning. Some have sitting porches—little rooms off the bedroom with windows on three sides. Smoking is allowed in the bar and outdoors only. Two parlors downstairs are warm and inviting. The smaller parlor has been made into a library, with built-in shelves, lots of books, and leather seating. The larger parlor has a game table and lots of comfortable seating.

In addition to playing golf and rocking on the porch, guests can hike the 7 miles of marked trails with, Yvonne says, "the best views in the park." The lovely town of Milford is just five minutes down the road, and a few more minutes will take you into Delaware Water Gap National Recreation Area with its many activities (see our Parks chapter).

Just beyond the parlors is the exquisite Cliff Park Inn Restaurant (see our Restaurant chapter). Breakfast in the restaurant is included in the price of the room. Cliff Park Inn has been awarded three stars by the Mobil Travel Guide, both as an inn and a restaurant, an honor given to fewer than 30 inns nationwide. Triple A has also awarded them three stars.

Call if you want to bring your children. At press time, Yvonne and James had not yet decided on their policy regarding children.

Dimmick Inn and Steakhouse $-$$$$
101 East Harford Street, Milford
(570) 296-4021
www.dimmickinn.com

The popular Dimmick Inn and Steakhouse, famous for its buffalo burgers and kazoo-toting waiters (don't tell them it's your birthday—see our Restaurant chapter) has opened 10 beautifully restored guest rooms upstairs. The spacious rooms boast antique furniture, handmade bedspreads, drapery, and canopies. Some have a private bath, and some share. Guests can take advantage of queen beds, cable television, and air-conditioning. Pets are welcome by pre-arrangement. While the Dimmick Inn is right in the heart of Milford, they also rent out a guest house "in the country" that holds up to four people with two bedrooms, a living room, dining room, and kitchen.

Double 'W' Ranch Bed and Breakfast $$$
Double 'W' Road, Hawley
(570) 226-3118
www.triplewstable.com

More than 40 years ago, Doris Waller's husband decided he wanted to leave Manhattan and become a dairy farmer. They found a property outside Hawley and started to buy cows. The Waller's friends from Manhattan kept visiting, and soon

Doris found herself feeding and boarding people on a regular basis. They bought some horses, and their guests wanted more. Eventually they had so many horses, they gave up the idea of a dairy farm, sold the cows, and turned their property into a ranch.

Today, the Double 'W' is a bed-and-breakfast where you can sit on the large deck and contemplate some of the 60 horses that comprise the Triple 'W' riding stable. The house, built about 140 years ago by an Italian stonemason, is paneled in dark wood and has some interesting wooden arches. It's furnished to evoke a ranch—an extremely comfortable ranch. The carpets are thick, and the couches in the common rooms are comfy. A few decorative touches here and there testify to Doris's Lenape ancestry. The rooms, most with private bath, are simple and clean.

Doris serves a full country breakfast with pancakes, waffles, French toast, meat, eggs, juice, pastry, fruit, coffee, and tea in a large airy dining room.

You can play horseshoes, volleyball, or badminton; sit in front of the large stone fireplace; watch the large-screen TV; go hiking on the grounds; fish and ice-skate or go tobogganing and cross-country skiing in winter; but the real draw is the horses. (See our Recreation chapter for a full description of the stables.) Guests can watch the horses all day, and they get a special discount on riding. The stable's hay rides are supposed to be so much fun that tourists have been known to ride them one night and come back the next. When there's snow on the ground, guests can ride in an antique sleigh. (See our Winter Sports chapter.) An especially interesting option at the 'W' establishments is an overnight horse ride with camping.

Children are welcome here, and they in turn will love the horses, cats, chickens, and pigs. Smoking is allowed only on the enclosed porch. If you take the Shortline bus from New York City to Hawley and call, the Wallers will come pick you up (by car, not horse), but make sure you have a reservation first.

The Falls Port Inn and Restaurant　$-$$$
330 Main Avenue, Hawley
(570) 226-2600
www.thefallsportinnandrestaurant.com

Perched on a corner of Hawley's Main Avenue, the Falls Port Inn and Restaurant was built by a Baron von Eckelberg in 1902. By the time Dorothy Fenn and her late husband got hold of it, the building looked more like a flophouse than a grand hotel. Together they created a remarkable restaurant (see our Restaurants chapter), and a gorgeous inn. The beautifully restored lobby has William Morris wallpaper that Fenn found in an antique shop. To complement the paper, the Fenns hired a plaster artist who could do relief work on the wall—the kind you see in very old, very beautiful homes. Fascinating antique pieces are placed throughout the inn.

The rooms upstairs are spacious, and most have private baths and beautiful matching period bedroom sets.

Stuffed toys at the top of the stairs are loaners for children who forgot their own and need a cuddle to take to bed. There's a television room for guests who don't have a TV in their own room.

Guests are served a continental breakfast of fresh orange juice, pastries, and excellent gourmet coffee. Small pets are welcome.

Many innkeepers will gladly accommodate your extended family for a reunion or a special occasion—often at discounted rates. It's fun to fill an entire bed-and-breakfast with your family.

The French Manor　$$$-$$$$
Huckleberry Road, South Sterling
(570) 676-3244, (800) 523-8200
www.thefrenchmanor.com

This French chateau, made of stone and lumber from the woods on-site, is owned by the same family that owns the Sterling Inn (see subsequent entry). It's rated by *Country Inns Magazine* as one of the top 10 country inns in America. You'll find six guest rooms and nine suites. Six of the suites, with fireplaces, Jacuzzis, and private wrought-iron balconies, are in the new Maisonneuve. The chateau was built in 1932 as a retreat for Joseph Hirschhorn. It is modeled after Hirschhorn's French manor in the south of France and is full of unique European touches that make outstanding elegance the keynote. All of the rooms have private bath, cable television, telephone and modem jack, air-conditioning, and bathrobes.

The roof of the French Manor is made of imported Spanish slate; the interior and great hall are cypress. Romanesque architecture dominates; vaulted ceilings in the dining room, a huge stone fireplace, and grand arches complete the picture. This is a top-notch place for small corporate conferences.

The grounds contain an indoor swimming pool, tennis court, and nine-hole putting course. There's also a private lake for swimming, boating, fishing, and ice-skating; a nature trail—marked and maintained—that leads to a waterfall; croquet, sledding, and cross-country skiing trails. The French Manor is truly a magnificent retreat.

The meals feature European cuisine, sumptuously prepared and elegantly served. No smoking is allowed in the guest rooms or the dining room. The inn is owned and operated by Ron and Mary Kay Logan, who maintain it as a getaway for the discriminating adult guest.

Pegasus Bed & Breakfast　$-$$
Woodtown Road, Shohola
(570) 296-4017
www.pegasus-inn.com

Pegasus, in Shohola, was built in 1923 as a country inn. While it has been modernized, it retains its original charm. The wraparound porch, formal dining room, and immense living room complement its rustic, natural setting.

Pegasus has a luxury suite plus eight rooms. Some have private baths, some share. Each room is furnished with an iron bed and antique dressers and is wallpapered in cozy floral patterns. Many of the guests are Europeans who, according to the innkeeper, seem to enjoy Pegasus' casual hominess.

The third floor features a shared kitchen equipped with microwave and refrigerator for guests who wish to cook for themselves. A VCR and large video library are available, as well as a stereo and player piano. This country-casual, old-fashioned inn offers a full breakfast including fresh-squeezed orange juice plus eggs from the innkeeper's own chickens, waffles, pancakes, or French toast—the items change every day.

Children are welcome here for no extra charge. The game room is full of games and toys; the film library features Disney classics; and a volleyball net, basketball hoop on the garage, and a rope swing in a big tree summon active young folks.

Groups come here for family reunions and old-fashioned weddings and to find comfy accommodations while visiting friends and family during the holidays.

Pine Hill Farm Bed & Breakfast $$$$
Pine Hill Farm Road, Milford
(570) 296-5261
www.pinehillfarm.com

This early 1900s hillside country farm is wonderful for folks seeking a quiet, well-mannered weekend getaway. The delightful farm is perched above the Delaware River north of the village of Milford. It seems to be miles away from the rest of the world, yet it's quite close to town and all of its attractions.

Yvonne and James Klausmann took over Pine Hill in 2000, and since the bed-and-breakfast was featured in a *New York* magazine piece, their phone has been ringing off the hook.

Accommodations include two rooms in the main house and four luxury suites in two outbuildings.

The Jack Rabbit and Mountain rooms in the Main House, have king-size beds, private bath, air conditioning, CD players,

and excellent views of the Delaware River Valley. The two cottage suites are charming with beamed ceilings, king-size beds, private baths, air conditioning, TV, CD players, refrigerators, and spacious living rooms. The newest deluxe suites in the recently renovated henhouse feature large stone fireplaces, two-person Jacuzzis, king-size beds, CD players, minifridges, satellite television, and private, outdoor sitting areas.

The decor is eclectic country with a few tasteful antiques.

Breakfast—a buffet of cereals, yogurt and fruit, plus a hot dish—is on the terrace, with views all the way to the Delaware River. If you prefer, Yvonne will deliver a basket of goodies to your door, and you can break your fast in the privacy of your room.

Pine Hill has 277 acres, including lots of private trails. Talk to Yvonne, and she will fix a picnic lunch and leave it for you beside their lovely waterfall.

Leave your young children at home; Pine Hill Farm accommodates children 12 and older only. Smoking is not permitted indoors.

Roebling Inn on the Delaware $-$$$
Scenic Drive, Lackawaxen
(570) 685-7900
www.roeblinginn.com

The Roebling Inn, a quaint yet stately Greek Revival home, was office and home to Judge Thomas J. Ridgway, superintendent and tallyman for the Delaware and Hudson Canal Company. The home has been fully restored by innkeepers JoAnn and Donald Jahn, and it is on the National Register of Historic Places. Lovely little gardens and paths lead to the various doorways around this white clapboard, shuttered jewel. One of the joys of this inn is its location on the Lackawaxen River (two doors down is the Zane Grey Museum); it is directly across the street from the river (actually, it's barely a street) and its lawn extends to the river's edge. On the riverside is a dock from which you can go boating. The front porch, complete with comfy chairs, offers a great view of the river.

The cozy rooms are furnished with country antiques and accented with cheerful matching comforters and curtains. One lovely room has a delightful raised sitting area with a daybed. Each room has a private bath, air conditioning, great beds (mostly queen-size), and cable TV. (Donald feels that while he and JoAnn have kept this home historically accurate for the sake of its place in history, guests should have a decision about watching TV in privacy in the evening.) There is also a private sitting room for guests. The breakfast room is decorated in cheery floral prints, and delicate white sheers grace the stately windows. The tables are set for two or four, and diners at each table are treated to a peaceful view of the river.

The Jahns provide a hearty, cold breakfast-buffet table, with homemade fruit cobbler, your choice of cereal, and fruit. They add to this tasty spread their own special turn at eggs and bacon; hearty omelettes; or hot, steamy pancakes; and coffee. In the evening guests are served hot tea and cookies. Donald was originally a restaurateur and country club manager, and he has focused all of his expertise on this little gem of an inn by the river.

In addition to the rooms at the inn, there is an adjacent one-bedroom cottage for two to four guests.

The Jahns are knowledgeable about local history and special places. They'll point out the many places to walk, play tennis, swim, canoe, fish, and sightsee (ask about the Roebling Aqueduct). Come to the Roebling Inn in the winter and walk across the street for prime eagle watching. On a good day, you should be able to see a dozen or more in the trees and swooping to the water for fish.

Smoking is limited to the cottage and outdoor porch areas; children younger than 12 can be accommodated in the cottage.

The Settlers Inn at Bingham Park $$$-$$$$
4 Main Avenue, Hawley
(570) 226-2993
www.thesettlersinn.com

The Settlers Inn in Hawley is a European-inspired Tudor manor. There are 20 rooms and suites full of antiques and decorated with wicker and soft, quilted, comforters. All rooms are air-conditioned and have private baths and telephones with modem ports. Several rooms have luxurious Jacuzzi-style jet tubs.

The dining room looks out over the lovely grounds. A hearty country breakfast featuring locally produced food constitutes your morning fare here. The restaurant at The Settlers Inn is well known for its wonderful presentation of fresh local vegetables, fruits, and herbs, and its menu is responsive to the seasons. (See our Restaurants chapter.) Guests and the general public can enjoy lunch and dinner and guests have the option of staying on the Modified American Plan.

Adjoining the inn is a gift shop and gardener's spot, the Potting Shed. The Settlers Inn is a great place to stay as you explore the historic delights of Honesdale and the beautiful Lake Wallenpaupack region (see our Attractions and In, On, and Around the Water chapters).

The Sterling Inn $$$$
Highway 191, South Sterling
(570) 676-3311, (800) 523-8200
www.thesterlinginn.com

The Sterling Inn is owned and operated by Ron and Mary Kay Logan, who also own the French Manor (see previous entry). This is the first of the Logan's inns, and it exudes relaxed country charm.

You'll find 65 rooms and suites, some in the main inn and others around the grounds in cottages and in the lodge. The Country Cottages, along the nature trail, have fireplaces, two-person Jacuzzis, antique furnishings, a front porch, refrigerator, microwave, and coffeemaker. The

Fireplace Suites have a living room, fireplace, cable TV, refrigerator, coffeemaker, and a private deck overlooking the Wallenpaupack Creek.

The amenities include an indoor pool and spa; a lake for swimming, boating, fishing, and ice skating; and acres of trails for hiking and nature programs, as well as badminton, snow tubing, tobogganing, and cross-country skiing. You'll also find tennis courts, shuffleboard, and volleyball. Enjoy a picnic along the creek that flows nearby or at any of the other great little areas that surround you.

Breakfast, lunch, and dinner are served in the Hearthstone Dining Room. Your room charge is based on the Modified American Plan—breakfast and dinner are included. All meals include hearty country fare, and gourmet picnics can be prepared for your afternoon jaunt into the woods.

Deep muscle massage and foot reflexology are available by appointment. If you

In the Poconos, most days are bearable, especially up the mountain (Mount Pocono, Canadensis, Cresco, Mountainhome, Skytop). When night falls, the temperature drops rapidly, and through most of the summer, we have cool evenings and pleasant mornings. Many Pocono people prefer to take advantage of nature's air conditioning and use ceiling fans and open windows rather than an air conditioner.

want to treat yourself to a therapeutic massage, ask about an appointment when you make your reservations. Entertainers amuse the guests on weekends, and special packages include romantic weekends, murder mystery weekends, family weekends, and more. Check the Web site, or call to find out what's coming up at the Sterling Inn.

RESTAURANTS

We admit it. When we started eating our way across the Poconos, we expected hearty portions of decently prepared American food, but nothing to wow the palates of New York and Philadelphia food snobs.

We were wrong.

We have fine traditional restaurants in the Poconos, but there are also top-quality gourmet bistros that can hold their own for skill of preparation and imaginative ingredients against any restaurants in any major city. We have ethnic restaurants though not enough. There are seafood restaurants, and there are restaurants tucked away in charming spots you'd never think of exploring.

What about local cuisine? We don't have too much that will mystify you, like Southern hush puppies or New England's shrub, but you may find a few remnants of Pennsylvania Dutch cooking at some of our restaurants. Apple dumplings—baked spiced whole apples, wrapped in dough and usually served with milk or cream—are a local delicacy. Shoofly pie is a must-try—you'll find it at local bakeries. The filling is made from molasses and brown sugar, and the pie comes as "wet bottom," with more molasses, or "dry bottom," like a regular pie. Potpie made Pennsylvania Dutch–style doesn't have a crust. Instead, meat, vegetables, and 2-inch square noodles all simmer together until done. Perversely, a "Dutch pot pie" means there's crust on the bottom and sides only. You might find fritters at a flea market—they're fruit or veggies mixed in an egg batter and deep fried. Pennsylvania Dutch bean soup often turns up at carnivals and fairs, baked by church ladies as a fund-raiser. Church ladies also make chow chow, a pickled relish of corn, green tomatoes, four kinds of beans, and other vegetables.

Only the brave of heart and the strong of stomach will appreciate our pickled pigs' feet, scrapple (meat scraps, combined with cornmeal and pressed into a loaf), and souse (the unwanted parts of the meat and pimento in gelatin). Cornmeal mush is our version of polenta, sliced and fried for breakfast. Our Pennsylvania sticky buns—like cinnamon buns, only yummier—are famous around the country. From the Polish/Russian side of our heritage, you might encounter pierogi (pronounced with a hard "g"), usually mashed potatoes inside a ravioli-like dough, sautéed with lots of onions; and halupki, cabbage leaves stuffed with ground beef and rice and simmered in a tomato broth. If you look, you'll find some of these foods in the Poconos, but if you really want to find Pennsylvania Dutch cuisine, head just outside of our region to the western Lehigh Valley between Allentown and Reading. The little country inns there still serve lots of good traditional food.

In this chapter we group our restaurants by region instead of by type. Most of the time you're not going to want to travel an hour to eat Chinese—unless it's great Chinese. Take a look through the other regions. You may find a good excuse to go exploring.

Don't forget to try the resorts. Many of them open their dining rooms to the public (call first if you're not sure), and resort diners typically demand top-quality food and service. Lingering over a meal at a resort is a reasonable way to treat yourself to a bit of the resort experience without diving into one of those Roman towers. (See our Accommodations chapter.) Whether you're a resident or a visitor, it's a lot of fun to sample the food and the atmosphere at different resorts.

Many people go into the bed-and-breakfast business especially because they want to run a small restaurant and serve gourmet food. By opening a bed-and-breakfast, they diversify their income and can give their restaurant a chance to find its customer base. Some of our best Pocono restaurants are part of a small lodging (see our Bed-and-Breakfasts and Country Inns chapter), so even if you don't stay there, try the food.

We have our share of fast food, and new chain restaurants are constantly being built in retail strips at the edge of our larger towns. We once traveled through Europe with a woman who wouldn't eat anywhere but McDonald's. It was a little odd passing up the local spaetzle in a walled Bavarian city to search out a Big Mac. Whenever we visit a region, we much prefer sampling the local food to eating at a predictable fast-food restaurant. Of course, we also have our favorite chains, but we try to do most of our eating out at local restaurants. We assume you're familiar with the major fast-food chains, so we don't deal with them in this book.

Good food is not overly expensive in the Poconos. If you're from a big city, you should be pleasantly surprised when you get the bill.

Many of our restaurants are small, and nonsmoking areas don't seem as important to people here as to urbanites. In fact, more people seem to smoke here than in the cities. We let you know if a restaurant requires smokers to indulge outside or if you might expect smoke rising from the next table while you dine. Since many of our restaurants are in older buildings, you can't assume wheelchair accessibility. If the restaurant is newer, you're more likely to be able to get in and get around on wheels. If accessibility matters to you, call ahead and check.

The following dollar-sign code is based on entrees for two without appetizer, drinks, dessert, or a tip. We have taken the lowest and highest-price entrees and added them together to estimate an average price for entrees for two. Of course, if you order appetizers, dessert, or drinks, your total will come to more. These are dinner prices. At most restaurants,

expect lunch to cost a little less. The dollar signs represent the following price ranges:

PRICE-CODE KEY

$20 or less	$
$21 to $30	$$
$31 to $45	$$$
$46 or more	$$$$

Unless noted, all restaurants accept major credit cards and serve alcoholic beverages. If you want to use a card that is not one of the big two (Visa and MasterCard), call ahead to make sure yours is accepted.

It's always a good idea to call ahead and make reservations; you not only guarantee a table for yourself, but also confirm that the restaurant is open. The restaurant business is volatile; restaurants open and close routinely, and in the Poconos some change their days of operation from year to year. All information in this chapter has been confirmed as of spring 2005, but by the time you read this, some of it has changed; so call ahead. We let you know when reservations are required or strongly recommended.

We've made a valiant effort to eat in as many restaurants as possible, but given time and stomach constraints, we know we missed some good ones. If you find a restaurant that should be in the book, drop us a line and let us know.

Happy eating!

DELAWARE WATER GAP/ SHAWNEE-ON-DELAWARE

Alaska Pete's Roadhouse Grill and Moondog Saloon $$$
U.S. Highway 209, Marshalls Creek
(570) 223–8575
www.alaskapetes.com
This fun-food restaurant may look like part of a chain, but there's only one Alaska Pete. Tiffany lamps, thick wooden paneling, and an interesting selection of antiques are complemented by very

RESTAURANTS

Call before you set out for a particular restaurant. Hours and days change, and if they're having trouble with something in the kitchen or if the air-conditioning's broken, they may close for the evening.

pleasant, well-trained servers. The food is a little expensive by local standards, and it's predictable. Fried mozzarella sticks, Buffalo Billy Wings, and a regional specialty—pierogies—are among the appetizers. Pastas, seafood, burgers, chicken, and steaks are just some of the entrees. Don't fill up on the excellent, fresh salad bar, because the entrees are enormous. Try the intriguing Dawson City Salmon in a cucumber dill sauce, the roast duck in an orange house sauce, or the super-meaty king crab legs. There's also a good by-the-glass wine list. Don't be misled by an overfull parking lot; there's plenty of room for a big crowd inside.

Complete separation between the smoking and nonsmoking sections is achieved by seating smokers in the bar, which has a huge stone fireplace merrily blazing away on a cool March evening and two big-screen TVs.

Built by local developer Frank Riccobono, who is responsible for the controversial Marshalls Creek Dairy Queen, the restaurant replaced his beloved Burgers and Company. Alaska Pete's is open for lunch and dinner seven days a week.

Antelao Restaurant $$$
84 Main Street, Delaware Water Gap
(570) 426-7226
www.delawarewatergap.com

There was once a bakery in Brodheadsville called Sassafras. This bakery was so fine that people from all over the Poconos found excuses to travel there and bring home exquisite breads and pastries. Owners Michael and Elvi De Lotto sold the bakery to a family that opened and closed Sassafras on Main Street in Stroudsburg. Meanwhile Michael and Elvi went on to

restore a lovely Victorian home on Main Street in Delaware Water Gap. They opened a perfect little restaurant there.

You enter Antelao through a lavender-and-sage-filled garden. The host greets you and points to a poster of a mountain peak called Antelao in Italy's Dolomites. It's there, he says, that the owner's family comes from. Then you're led into a light and lovely dining room with sparkling wood floors and understated white-and-green curtains.

Like the bakery once did, the food surpasses expectations. You start with some fabulous Sassafras-style rolls. We visited on St. Patrick's Day and were treated to Irish soda bread. The temptation is to fill up, but don't; there's such good food to come, and if there are any rolls left, the waitress will pack them for you to take home. Try an appetizer of artichoke hearts blended with homemade ricotta cheese wrapped in a crepe and served with dried mushroom and a splash of garlic oil. Crab cake lovers can have a small one for an appetizer, or a larger one, festooned with Antaleo's special mashed potato balls and sautéed vegetables for an entree. The menu changes seasonally, but when we were there, it included a light and lovely butternut squash cannelloni with sage butter, an autumn pork loin with prosciutto sautéed in an apple brandy with dried fruit, as well as several other sophisticated dishes. Service is friendly and swift.

Desserts are equally intriguing; their homemade chocolate truffles with raspberry syrup are the talk of the town.

Antelao's is a smoke-free, cell phone–free restaurant that's open for dinner Thursday through Sunday. Reservations are strongly suggested, as the dining room is small, and the restaurant is popular. They don't have a liquor license, but they're happy to provide wine service if you bring your own bottle. If you love Antelao, stop in at Dolcetto's (see our Shopping chapter) just down the street. It's a cooperative venture between Big Creek Winery and Antelao Restaurant, and here you'll find many of the exotic ingredients the chef uses in his cooking, as well as those chocolate truffles.

Brandli's Pizza, Pasta, and Vino $$
6A Foxmoor Village, US 209
Marshalls Creek
(570) 223-1600
www.brandlis.com

Brandli's is a pizza parlor that has been sectioned off and gussied up to present the chef's highly original Italian creations. Of course, there's pizza and subs, but you'll also find temptations like ravioli with sun-dried tomatoes and cheese in basil cream sauce and capellini in pink cream and wine sauce with prosciutto and artichoke hearts. The specials are artfully served on big, colorful Italian plates. Brandli's is open every day of the week for dinner. There's counter service daily for lunch.

The Deer Head Inn $$
5 Main Street, Delaware Water Gap
(570) 424-2000
www.deerheadinn.com

The Deer Head is legendary as a jazz club (see our Nightlife chapter), but the food here easily matches the quality of the music. You can choose from a low-priced regular menu with fare like crab cakes, chili, and pizza, or try one of the more ambitious specials like filet mignon topped with melted gorgonzola cheese and a red wine reduction, or poached fillet of salmon with a basil lime sauce. If you want wine by the glass, you're not at the mercy of the bar's choice—there's a good list.

The rooms are hung with lovely paintings by owner/chef Dona Solliday and noted local artist Sterling Strauser. Before you leave, take a peek in the men's room where the Deer Head is reputed to have the world's largest urinal. The Deer Head serves dinner Thursday through Sunday. If you stay for the music Friday or Saturday, expect to pay a $5.00 cover charge, and if you make reservations (advisable when there's music), there's a $10.00 per person food and drink minimum. Sunday's music, usually piano, is free.

Minisink Hotel $$
River Road, Minisink Hills
(570) 421-9787

The rustic porch and neon beer signs make this place look like a tavern. It is, but the food is excellent, the portions are generous, and children are welcome at mealtime. There are no menus; a cheerful sign over the bar lists the varied fare—terrific pizza and pasta, burgers with a loyal local following, and seafood. The linguine with red clam sauce is huge and fabulous. This is a friendly place. No wonder our neighbors all flock here. (See our Nightlife chapter for more about the nighttime ambience.) The Minisink Hotel serves lunch and dinner seven days a week.

Northeastern Pizzeria $
The Village Shopping Center, US 209
Marshalls Creek
(570) 223-7534

Northeastern Pizzeria will deliver your order to your home, resort room, or vacation retreat anywhere from Bushkill to Shawnee-on-Delaware, along US 209 or up to Spruce Run along Highway 402.

Specialties include a variety of pizzas, hot and cold subs, and some Italian entrees. If you crave mussels, calamari, veal, or eggplant—delivered, mind you—this is a good place to call seven days a week for lunch and dinner. You can eat at the restaurant (there are a few tables), but delivery is Northeastern's specialty. Not a bad idea after a full day of skiing, shopping, sightseeing, hiking, swimming, skating . . .

Petrizzo's Italian-American Restaurant $$
US 209 South, Bushkill
(570) 588-6414

John Petrizzo is the third generation of Petrizzos to run this casual Italian restaurant. Don't expect candles in Chianti bottles; the room is small and light, accented by stained glass lamps. The next room holds a full bar with beer on tap, a good selection of wines, and lots of locals sitting around and chatting. The food—from traditional Italian pastas to steak and seafood—is good, with large portions and very reasonable prices. Some of the herbs used in the dishes are grown right outside the back door. Try the homemade lasagna or the veal parmesan, dishes that always get raves from diners. John Petrizzo goes around to each table handing out brochures for his favorite Pocono attractions, and sometimes he grabs a guitar off the wall and sings Italian favorites. "If they don't have fun," he says, "they're not coming back to the Poconos." You can have fun at Petrizzo's daily at lunch and dinner. Smoking is allowed in all parts of the restaurant.

Saen Thai Cuisine $$
Shawnee Square, Buttermilk Falls Road
Shawnee-on-Delaware
(570) 476–4911
www.pinksafe.com

If you haven't tried Thai cuisine, head right over to Saen's where you'll find food that resembles Chinese but is cooked in curry sauces, chili sauces, ginger, and delicate basil sauces that you'll think about for days afterward. If you're familiar with Thai food, you'll be thrilled by Saen's, which can hold its own against any Thai restaurant from Boston to Washington, D.C. The food is so good here that other restaurant owners have told us they like to eat at Saen's on their day off. Try the delicious vegetarian spring rolls. If you like hot sauce and say so, Boon, one of the owners, will bring out progressively hotter sauces until you cry uncle. Another favorite appetizer is the satay—marinated chicken skewers grilled and served with a peanut sauce and cucumber salad. The peanut sauce, a house specialty, is delicious. Jasmine rice, which smells like popcorn, is brought out in a silvery tureen. Make sure you read the chalkboard, or you'll miss specials like "Evil Shrimps," a spicy shrimp and vegetable dish in red curry sauce. The regular menu includes seafood, chicken, beef, or vegetables. Make sure you try the sweet Thai coffee or the Singha Beer made in Thailand. The restaurant is small and is decorated with beautiful art objects from Thailand. The atmosphere is tastefully elegant. Saen's often fills up, so come early, come on a weeknight, or reserve a table ahead. Lunch and dinner are served every day but Monday.

Tom X Inn $$
Tom X Road, Marshalls Creek
(570) 223–8154
www.ccpbigridge.com

There are several explanations for Tom X's unusual name. One story says that a farmer named Tom and his family were slaughtered by Lenapes here. Since no one knew his last name, the grave marker said, "Here lies Tom X." Another story says that this historic inn was the site of the first local brothel, thus X as in X-rated. One more legend claims that Tom Mix, an early movie cowboy, spent time here and even owned the inn for a time. If this one is true, the X was boiled down from Mix. Tom X Inn is tucked away on a country lane, which makes it a neat place to take your out-of-town guests.

Continental cuisine is served at this historic inn, a favorite spot for Delmonico steak. Seafood specials include shrimp scampi with lots of lemon, garlic, and dry sherry. Burgers and chicken dishes round out the menu. There's a salad bar, and the bread basket has some particularly yummy sweet breads. We always end up taking something home for lunch the next day. The decor is rustic, with lots of wood, plants and windows overlooking the stream that runs past the property.

Tom X Inn is open for dinner Thursday through Sunday.

Trail's End Cafe $$$
Main Street, Delaware Water Gap
(570) 421–1928

Trail's End is best known for its breakfast and lunch, which is available Wednesday through Saturday, and for its marvelous Sunday Brunch, but make sure you catch the dinner on Friday nights only (reservations are strongly suggested). The Pierogies Poblano are delicate and lovely, with a topping of onions and tomatoes sautéed in a lightly vinegared sauce. The blackened rib eye beef will melt in your mouth. The ravioli du jour takes you to the top of ravioli's potential. For breakfast, try the homemade granola or house specialties such as Napoli eggs or breakfast burrito. The French toast is made with homemade bread. Pasta, sandwiches, salads, and pizzas made with Trail's End's own sauce on plain or whole-wheat crusts are featured for lunch. The pretty dining room has its original pressed tin ceiling, lovely flowery window treatments, a few nice country antique sideboards, and paintings of flower gardens that are so lush as to be fantastical. No alcoholic beverages are served, but the staff is happy to set up a bottle of wine brought by you. Smoking is not permitted, and they accept cash or personal checks only.

Valley View Inn & Restaurant $$$
794 Sunrise Boulevard, Mount Bethel
(570) 897-6969
www.valleyviewrestaurant.com

You'll have to know Valley View is here, because you're not likely to pass it on a casual trip to Mount Bethel. The way, through some rolling farmland, is well marked; just follow signs from the Mount Bethel crossroads. Make sure you look toward the east as you go—there's a spectacular view of the Delaware Water Gap along the way. The building rambles and has some interesting alpine touches that make it look like a medieval barn you'd encounter in the Black Forest. It used to be a German restaurant, but it has been taken over by new owners and is now concentrating on French cuisine. Inside are stone walls and heavily beamed ceilings that make you feel like you're in a castle. A large upstairs room is popular for weddings and banquets and you may hear a wedding band through the ceiling. The food is artfully presented; a pasta dish came with a charming bundle of asparagus tied with a scallion and standing upright. Try the pepper-crusted yellow fin tuna with mango corn salsa and red and

white butter emulsion or sample the veal medallions with langostinos, white asparagus, and mushroom cognac reduction. Another favorite is the New Zealand rack of lamb with zucchini ratatouille. The rich desserts are lovely too. Smoking is allowed in the bar only, and the smoking tables are grouped around a stone fireplace. Valley View Inn & Restaurant is open for dinner Friday through Sunday.

Water Gap Diner $$
55 Broad Street, Delaware Water Gap
(570) 476-0132

Italian and Greek dishes are offered here along with regular diner fare. The made-from-scratch soups have an incredible reputation. There are also lots of homemade desserts. You won't find chrome on this diner, but the interior is the height of '60s diner elegance. Water Gap Diner is open daily for breakfast, lunch, and dinner.

Whispering Pines Restaurant $$$
Country Club of the Poconos at Big Ridge, US 209, Marshalls Creek
(570) 223-7323
www.ccpbigridge.com

Although this is a private, gated community, the terrific restaurant is open to the public. Call for reservations, and they'll leave your name at the gate. The restaurant is in the clubhouse, and the high-ceilinged room is elegant, with huge windows overlooking the golf course and a stone fireplace at one end. The food is superb—we had the creamiest mashed potatoes we'd ever tasted, and when we asked for oil and vinegar for our salad,

The Entertainment Book, a discount coupon book is available with generous discounts at several of our restaurants and attractions. Most of the restaurants listed offer you two entrees for the price of one. The book is sold as a fund-raiser in the fall and winter. If you miss it then, you can get it direct by calling (800) 374-4464.

they gave us balsamic vinegar. Try the osso buco braised pork shank with a rich sage sauce or the half-grilled chicken with hunter sauce. Sunday brunch is always lovely. The restaurant is smoke free, but smokers may light up at the bar. Though the restaurant is casual, appropriate attire is required. Country Club of the Poconos offers lunch every day, dinner Thursday through Saturday, and Sunday brunch. Reservations are strongly suggested.

Wolf Hollow Restaurant $$$
Water Gap Country Club, Mountain Road, Delaware Water Gap
(570) 476-0300, ext. 20
www.watergapcountryclub.com
Wolf Hollow is the restaurant of the Water Gap Country Club, but it's open to the public. The accent here is on golf, and paintings on the simple white walls depict famous courses from around the globe. Diners can sink into very comfortable armchairs or sit outside on a lovely patio with a great view of the greens. Try the Chicken Chardonnay, a chicken breast sautéed with shallots, mushrooms, diced tomatoes, and white wine. Other interesting selections are the Maryland Crab Cakes with a classic remoulade and the Veal Fantasy, sautéed with artichokes, shrimp, sun-dried tomatoes, and shallots in a demi-glace sauce. Don't eat too much of the delicious loaf of hot bread, or you won't have room for your entree. The expected dress is "casual but proper" (meaning no jacket or tie required, but leave the blue jeans at home). Reservations are requested for dinner. There's a full bar at one end of the room, and smoking is allowed in the lounge and bar only. The dining room is smoke-free. A few rooms (see our Accommodations chapter) are available, and it's a great setup for golfers, as the course is excellent. (See our Golf chapter.) Wolf Hollow is open Memorial Day weekend to Labor Day weekend for lunch Tuesday through Sunday and dinner Wednesday through Saturday. It closes each year around Thanksgiving and reopens in early April for weekends only.

STROUDSBURG/EAST STROUDSBURG

Bamboo House $
US 209 Business, East Stroudsburg
(570) 424-2460
This traditional Chinese Restaurant has a variety of Szechuan, Hunan, Cantonese, and traditional Chinese favorites. It also offers an American selection of steaks for those in your party who are not inclined to Chinese, and a children's menu that is more American in choices, including hamburgers. It has two dining rooms decorated in an Oriental motif.

Dinner is served every day but Tuesday, and lunch is offered Wednesday through Saturday.

Besecker's Diner $
427 North Fifth Street, Stroudsburg
(570) 421-6193
The parking lot is always jammed at this very popular diner on the northern outskirts of Stroudsburg, as locals swarm in for such daily specials as the all-white meat turkey burger with garlic. Breakfast is available here at all times seven days a week, as are lunch and dinner. Morning specialties, to go with the eggs, are Pennsylvania Dutch scrapple and grilled cinnamon bread. No credit cards.

Brownie's in the Burg $$
Seventh and Main Streets, Stroudsburg
(570) 421-2200
www.browniesintheburg.com
A popular spot right in the heart of Downtown Stroudsburg, Brownie's in the Burg offers sandwiches, snacks, and dinners in a casual atmosphere. Start with Garlic 'Shrooms, garlic-infused mushrooms battered and deep fried, or a quesadilla with chicken breast. Then pick something from the sandwich menus. How about a French dip, with thinly sliced roast beef and Swiss cheese on a French roll, served "au jus" for dipping? Or, for dinner, have steak or chicken fajitas or flounder Florentine— flounder stuffed with spinach and feta, topped with lemon, butter, and white

wine. Brownies is open for lunch and dinner every day, and is part of the Best Western Pocono Inn (see Accommodations), which also offers the Café Pocono, open for breakfast, the Front Row (see Nightlife), open until 2:00 A.M., and the Hideaway, a small bar off the lobby.

China Buffet $$
24 Eagle's Glen Mall, US 209 Business East Stroudsburg
(570) 476-7658

This is a great place if you love all kinds of Chinese food and want some of everything. The buffet, which features piles of all-you-can-eat crab legs, is served every day at lunch and dinner, and there is also an a la carte menu. The food is constantly replenished, so it is always hot and fresh. Szechuan, Hunan, and Cantonese dishes such as General Tso's chicken, shrimp, and green beans (delicious—lots of fresh garlic), sweet and sour pork, dumplings, chicken, and broccoli, and wonton soup, and standbys such as egg foo young and fried rice, are at the buffet and on the menu. There is a reduced price for children.

Ciro's $$
728 Main Street, Stroudsburg
(570) 476-2476
www.cirosbistro.com

Downtown businessmen seeking an upscale lunch break are the mainstay of this family-friendly Italian bistro, which specializes in brick-oven pizza with crusts rolled in sesame or poppy seeds. All the pasta here is homemade, and many dishes are made from old family recipes. The "Bottomless Bowl" of pasta offers a choice of spaghetti, linguine, rigatoni, bowties, fettuccine, or penne with marinara, pesto, or oil and garlic sauce—all you can eat. For a real treat, try the Chicken con Basilico, chicken breasts in a pink cream sauce flavored with fresh basil over imported Italian pasta. And whatever you do, don't miss the basil and garlic salad dressing.

Ciro's is open for lunch and dinner seven days a week. The entire restaurant is nonsmoking.

Compton's Pancake House & Family Restaurant $
105 Park Avenue, Stroudsburg
(570) 424-6909
www.comptonspancakehouse.com

As the name implies, standard breakfast fare—eggs, pancakes, bacon, and sausage, etc.—is served here all day in an American diner atmosphere. Compton's also serves lunch and dinner. Compton's serves breakfast and lunch every day of the week, dinner every day but Monday and Tuesday. The clientele here consists mainly of local families and travelers since the restaurant is right next door to Days Inn (see our Accommodations chapter). Reservations are accepted only for large groups.

Dallas' Island Style Caribbean Cuisine $
246 North Cortland Street East Stroudsburg
(570) 424-9224

Dallas has a takeout counter, a tropical-theme dining room, and very friendly Jamaican proprietors. They offer the gamut of authentic Jamaican food—fried plantains, jerk chicken, pasties, ackee and saltfish, oxtail, and much, much more. If you're uncertain about a dish, ask Patsy Dallas for an explanation; she might even bring you a free sample. These people are very generous. There are plenty of selections for vegetarians, too, and if you ask, they will prepare something that works with your special diet. In addition to a full selection of Jamaican entrees and side dishes, try the special breads and the bottled beverages, including Irish Moss, coconut water, and Jamaican ginger beer. Dallas is open for lunch and dinner every day but Tuesday.

The Dansbury Depot $$$
50 Crystal Street, East Stroudsburg
(570) 476-0500

This depot was built as a railroad station and freight house in 1864 and saw many changes while serving as an important stop for those heading to summer camp in the mountains or coming to the Poconos

If you want to sample local cuisine, look for a fair or a festival. Funnel cake, dough that's dripped into hot oil with a funnel and then sugared, is a Pennsylvania favorite.

for vacation. It also served as a canteen for servicemen stationed at Tobyhanna Army Depot during World War II. Today the Dansbury Depot is one of the most popular restaurants in the area. The restaurant's recessed windows offer a view out over tracks that once hummed with activity. It is a bright and cheerful place.

Be careful when you order because they put the most wonderful breads on the table—the lemon poppy seed bread is famous—and it's tough to keep from filling up on them. (They are for sale as you leave, if you want to continue the experience at home.) There are lots of specials, such as the Station's Homemade Crabcakes with blue crabmeat; Chicken Elizabeth, chicken breasts sautéed with marinated tomatoes, onions, mushrooms, deglazed with sherry wine and finished with rich cream and melted Swiss cheese or Jack Ryan Shrimp; jumbo shrimp sautéed with tomatoes, mushrooms, and green onions in a gorgonzola cream sauce over pasta. Lunch and dinner are served every day of the week.

Evergreens Restaurant $$$
Clarion Hotel, 1220 West Main Street
Stroudsburg
(570) 424-1930, (800) 777-5453
This elegant restaurant is in-house at the Clarion Hotel. (See our Accommodations chapter.) Here diners relax in an eclectic contemporary atmosphere overlooking an atrium housing the hotel pool and gazebo. The menu boasts a wide range of chicken, veal, steaks, and chops as well as seafood ranging from deviled crab cakes and swordfish to grilled, baked, or blackened salmon filet. The Clarion recently added

an Indian menu, available Monday through Friday, and everybody in town who likes Indian food is raving. There are smoking and nonsmoking areas; reservations are accepted.

Everybody's Cafe $$$
905 Main Street, Stroudsburg
(570) 424-0896
This lovely restaurant is in a beautifully appointed, restored Victorian house on Upper Main Street. The decor is rich and warm, with deep greens, cane-backed chairs, and Victorian print wallpapers in each of the intimate dining rooms featuring fireplaces with blackboards above announcing the specials of the day. Outdoor dining on the front porch is a treat for those who love to enjoy the fresh air as they dine in elegance.

The menu is enormous, and in addition to a full range of international selections, it offers lots of exciting vegetarian and dairy-free items. Paella is a specialty of the house. There are also some great tastes in "pocket" foods: pitas, baguettes, and tapas, and dessert tortes are quite tempting.

The restaurant is open for lunch and dinner all week.

Fallano's at Cherry Valley $$$
Cherry Valley, Highway 191, South
Stroudsburg
(570) 992-5107
www.mountpocono.com/fallanos.htm
Italian cuisine is the specialty here, with such pricey but delicious entrees as lobster and shrimp in brandied tomato cream sauce with julienned garden vegetables and a capellini cake or Chicken Scarpariello with garlic, mushrooms, Italian sausage, and hot or mild peppers. A children's menu is available. There is no smoking, and reservations are strongly recommended. In fact, if you're planning to dine here on a holiday, make them well in advance. Fallano's is open for dinner every day but Monday.

Flood's $$
732 Main Street, Stroudsburg
(570) 424-5743

This Hibernian-style pub has a vast beer menu, with soups, salads, and sandwiches to match. If you're feeling more ambitious, try the Irish Whiskey Steak or Shrimp in a Basket. Lunch and dinner are served from 11:00 A.M. through 1:00 A.M. Monday through Saturday, with live entertainment some evenings (see our Nightlife chapter). The pace is slow here, so be sure you're not in a rush at lunchtime.

Hot Bagels $
704 Milford Road, East Stroudsburg
(570) 421-8340

This little vest pocket delicatessen serves much more than merely bagels, though bagels—especially the kind that come with lox and cream cheese—are the big item. A full line of sandwiches, heroes, and other goodies is also available for breakfast and lunch seven days a week.

J.R.'s Green Scene $$$
Budget Motel, off I-80 exit 308
East Stroudsburg
(570) 424-5451
www.jrsgreenscene.com

You might not expect to find one of the best restaurants in the Poconos at the Budget Motel, but that's how it is with the Green Scene. Here, diners feast high on a hill from an eclectic menu in front of bump-out bay windows overlooking a scenic valley. The room has a light, airy feeling. Three different seating areas are decorated with pink tablecloths and napkins.

JR's has a great, 35-item salad bar, terrific Friday night specials, fresh-baked breads, and lots of good choices. Garfield would kill for the spinach lasagna, and the full pound of king crab legs is a big favorite. There is even a vegetarian section on the menu. J.R.'s also claims no one beats its stuffed filet of flounder engorged with real crabmeat and topped with a gulf shrimp.

J.R.'s is open every day for breakfast and dinner all year, and it offers lunch Monday through Friday. The children's menu is reasonably priced.

La Pequeña Mexicana $
424 Main Street, Stroudsburg
(570) 421-6646

When José and Cristina Olivares emigrated to the United States, they brought a delicious slice of their homeland with them. Their little cafe on Lower Main, with its small sideline of Mexican groceries, serves the most (possibly the only) authentic Tex-Mex cuisine in the Poconos. Only at La Pequeña Mexicana can aficionados find spicy menudo—the tripe soup so prized south of the border—and just one of José's gigantic tacos would almost feed a family of four. Tortas, tamales, fajitas, chicken mole, carne asada, and other Latino delicacies round out the menu. José doesn't have a beer and wine license, but diners are free to bring their own.

Main Street Lounge $
418 Main Street, Stroudsburg
(570) 424-2431

This clean and cozy little tavern on Lower Main has been serving the community "since before the 1955 flood" (see our History chapter) with some of the lowest lunch and dinner prices in town. The highest price on the regular menu here is an eight-ounce Black Diamond steak for $6.50. Reservations are not necessary. The Lounge is open for lunch and dinner every day but Sunday. No credit cards.

Marita's Cantina $$
745 Main Street, Stroudsburg
(570) 424-8355

A little touch of Mexico as well as the American Southwest is found here in an atmosphere of blazing south-of-the-border color: coral, turquoise, navy blue, and red enclosing a room full of gaily painted jugs, chests, ponchos on the walls, and colorful tables and chairs. Portions are generous, and the bar offers a full range of Mexican beers as well as two-fisted Margaritas. Marita's is a favorite of young singles and families. After you have stuffed yourself with chili, chimichangas, burritos, fajitas, mango shrimp, and rellenos, try the fried ice cream for desert.

Marita's is open daily for lunch and dinner. Walk in for lunch; call for dinner reservations.

Mollie's $$
622 Main Street, Stroudsburg
(570) 476-4616
Mollie's is a legend in this area. Mollie started her restaurant during the Depression, across the bridge in East Stroudsburg. It was a place where no one left hungry whether they had money or not. Mollie knew what everyone wanted, and lunch boxes were brought in each morning and filled with food while folks sipped coffee.

Today Mollie's is a lovely restaurant on Main Street. Uncovered brick walls, clean (Mollie's hallmark) and polished hardwood floors, and a bright, airy dining area all make this one of the most popular stops for locals. Light lunches, gourmet treats, and satisfying desserts fill the menu. There are daily specials posted on the blackboard as you walk in. Mollie's serves breakfast and lunch every day but Tuesday, and liquor service is available.

Peppe's Ristorante $$$
Eagle Valley Mall, Highway 447 North
East Stroudsburg
(570) 421-4460
www.peppesonline.com
Fine Italian and American cuisine is served here in an earthy setting with brick walls,

arches, and bistro-style tables. All dishes are homemade and very tasty, lightly seasoned, and delicately flavored. The homemade pasta, espresso, and cappuccino are specialties as are the lasagna and seafood dishes such as lobster tails, shrimp scampi, fillet of sole fiorentina (stuffed with spinach and bleu cheese), and linguine with clams. Peppe's Caesar salad, one of the best in the Poconos, is prepared right at your table.

This restaurant is open for dinner every day. Reservations are a good idea.

Sarah Street Grill $$
550 Quaker Alley, Stroudsburg
(570) 424-9120
www.sarahstreetgrill.com
The menu is quite varied at this lovely spot in Stroudsburg. Its back-street location makes it quiet and accessible from Sarah Street and Quaker Alley. There are two dining rooms inside and two great bars—one at which to sit and one at which to stand. The outside, second-floor dining deck nestles among the trees and makes a great spot for lunch, dinner, or drinks and a snack.

Delmonico steaks—big 20-ounce Delmonico steaks—are the specialty. Other items include sandwiches, pasta, chicken, scampi with asparagus, and vegetarian meals such as artichoke and mushroom pesto with penne pasta. A sushi bar is now open Tuesday through Saturday evenings.

Check it out. Sarah Street Grill is open every day for lunch, dinner, or in-betweens. See our Nightlife chapter for more on the two bars here. There are 12 television sets to accommodate sports buffs.

Siamsa Irish Pub $$
636 Main Street, Stroudsburg
(570) 421-8434
www.siamsairishpub.com
This latest addition to the Poconos' vast array of restaurants is billed as an authentic Irish pub, hand-built in Ireland and shipped to Stroudsburg for assembly by Irish craftsmen. From its elegant oak bar

---

Many pizza places and some small restaurants do not accept credit cards. If you're not carrying enough cash, take a look at the door when you walk in. Usually decals of the credit cards they take will appear there or by the cash register.

---

to the cozy Victorian booths, stained glass, and stenciled ceiling, it fairly oozes ambience and, with evening entertainment from such *auld sod* groups as The McCabes and The Bogside Rogues, it lives up to it's name, pronounced "Sheemsah," which means "fun and music" in Gaelic.

The menu offers such obligatory Irish dishes as corned beef and cabbage, shepherds pie, and Dublin fish and chips (available with a sizable array of domestic and imported beers), but in a bow to globalization, you also can get Buffalo wings, nachos, and quesadillas. The pub, installed in a former bank building in July 2004, kept one artifact of the past—the heavy vault door, which now shields a cozy table for two. Service is good and the food is excellent.

Steak & Rib Inn $$$
US 209 North, East Stroudsburg
(570) 588-9466
www.steakandrib.com

Can you believe a 32-ounce Porterhouse steak? Well, they have them here, as well as other steaks cut to order. Want more choices? Try the delicious pasta dishes and fresh seafood.

Steak & Rib Inn, which has been serving the area for 16 years, is open all day and features a special sandwich menu as well as a children's menu, so everybody can enjoy. Also check out the Bullpen Lounge where you'll find 13 beers on tap as well as bottled imports and domestics. The environment is casual and cozy—a place for two or a whole family to dine at lunch or diner.

Stroudsmoor Country Inn $$$
Highway 191 and Stroudsmoor Road
Stroudsburg
(570) 421-6431, (800) 955-8663
www.stroudsmoor.com

For truly elegant dining in Italian-American country opulence, this is the place. The inn sits atop its own mountain, giving diners in the restaurant a breathtaking view of mountains and valleys while they select from a veritable cornucopia of a soup and salad bar or from a menu featuring such specialties as gnocchi and pesto ala genovese, or seafood scampi and salmon with strawberry sauce. The Sunday brunch is legendary. The inn has housed guests for more than a century (see our Bed-and-Breakfasts and Country Inns chapter). Reservations are requested. Stroudsmoor is open for breakfast and lunch every day (well, brunch on Sunday) and dinner every day but Sunday.

Sweet Creams $
429 Main Street, Stroudsburg
(570) 421-7929

This favorite luncheon spot of downtown store clerks and business people is an old-fashioned ice-cream parlor with gourmet sandwiches and cappuccino. Try the Highlander, a roast beef sandwich seasoned with French onion soup and stuffed with boursin and mozzarella cheeses, peppers, and tomatoes. Their gourmet stuffed potatoes are excellent, too. All 16 flavors of ice cream are homemade, as are the pies and other desserts that fill the menu. An added touch is the little art gallery on the wall. There is no bar here, and reservations are not necessary. Sweet Creams is open daily in the summer for lunch, Wednesday through Sunday for dinner. The rest of the year, it's open Wednesday through Sunday for lunch and dinner.

Vinny D's Catering and Deli $
Strawberry Fields Plaza
US 209 Business, East Stroudsburg
(570) 421-6868
www.vinnyds.com

Vinny D's may be the only bonafide New York–flavored delicatessen in the area. Its menu is huge, ranging from such deli-style breakfast treats as the Morning Monster, which is grilled pastrami and melted Swiss cheese with two eggs on a Kaiser roll, as well as a wide variety of hot and cold sandwiches. The grilled Portobello mushroom sandwich is a favorite, and shelves are well stocked with gourmet foodstuffs.

Sweet pastries are available as are espresso, cappuccino, and regular coffee to go with them. Any one of nine triple-decker sandwiches would fracture Dagwood Bumstead's jaw. All of this and much, much more is, of course, also available as catered meals for groups.

Check the local newspapers for advertisements on nightly restaurant specials and discount coupons. You might also find coupons in brochures available at all the Pocono Mountain Vacation Bureau offices and many other tourist spots.

Willow Tree Inn $$$
601 Ann Street, Stroudsburg
(570) 476-0211

What a lovely place to eat lunch or dinner, or as owner George K. Nunn puts it, "pass the time of day, be it in the parlor, the lounge, the restaurant, or the south yard veranda beneath the shade of the tree." This beautiful restaurant is in another restored Victorian house in Stroudsburg, right on McMichaels Creek. From the front, you see a lovely house. When you walk in, you see a cute parlor and bar area. Then in the dining room is a spectacular view of a giant willow tree by the creek, as seen through a wall of floor-to-ceiling windows. The dining room has two levels, both of which face the tree. Outside is the veranda, beneath the tree, for dining al fresco.

Just sitting here is a joy, but the food is top-quality gourmet fare. Pesto bowties with sun-dried tomatoes and mushrooms; Maryland blue crab sautéed with sherry, butter, mushrooms, and asparagus; sole amandine; chicken française; veal Oscar; tournedos au poivre, and salmon fillet are just some of the tempting menu items. Desserts are daily specials. The Willow Tree Inn is open Tuesday through Saturday for lunch and dinner, Sunday for dinner only. There's also a pleasant bar here.

MOUNT POCONO AREA

Bailey's Grille & Steakhouse $$$
Highway 611, Mount Pocono
(570) 839-9678
www.baileyssteakhouse.com

The Ultimate Onion, spicy hot barbecue wings, mesquite-grilled shrimp, baby back ribs, and crab cakes are just a few of the menu items at Baileys.

Baileys is owned by the same people who own Smuggler's Cove in Tannersville (see entry below). This bar/restaurant provides an enjoyable setting for casual meals. Lunch and dinner are served daily.

Barley Creek Brewing Company $$$
Sullivan Trail and Camelback Road
Tannersville
(570) 629-9399
www.barleycreek.com

This microbrewery, just off Highway 611, between the Crossings (see our Shopping chapter) and the Camelback Ski Area (see our Winter Sports chapter) serves a delicious selection of handmade beers—and even more delicious dishes to go with them. The atmosphere is a fusion of Colorado ski lodge and English pub, and it specializes in such hearty fare as the very English shepherd's pie, a wild game medley of elk, venison, and wild boar, and beer-battered onion rings. At the top of the menu is the one-pound center cut buffalo strip steak. The pub serves lunch and dinner seven days a week and features live entertainment Friday and Saturday. (See our Nightlife chapter.)

But beer is the centerpiece, and if you're at a loss as to which brew to try, order the Sampler—six four-ounce glasses, ranging from Creek Lite through the smoky Brown Antler to the yeasty and powerful Renovator. You can take your favorite brew home in 22-ounce bottles, a half-gallon jug called a "growler," quarter and half kegs, or in the "sixtle," a five-gallon keg. Barley Creek Beer is now available at more than 60 locations between Scranton and Philadelphia, including several eateries in the Poconos. The proprietors are especially proud of their rich, dark bitter bock brew, which they claim was named by no less personage than Arnold Schwartzenegger. It's called Alby Bock (think about it).

Cameltop $
Camelback Road, Tannersville
(570) 629-1661

This lodge at the summit of Camelback Mountain serves lunch from spring to fall every day. The mountainside deck provides a panoramic view of most of the Pocono Mountain area. The atmosphere is definitely casual. Camelbeach Water Park customers (see Attractions) can take the ski lift to the restaurant. If you're avoiding the water, but want the view, drive to the top of the mountain. Sandwiches and snacks are served cafeteria-style.

Cook's Touch $$$$
Highway 390, Mountainhome
(570) 595-3599
www.cookstouch.com

Cook's Touch, named for owners David and Cindy Cook, serves American cuisine made with high-quality ingredients in huge portions and at reasonable prices. The place was packed the night we went there.

The restaurant is housed in an old Victorian and has lots of windows. The ones in the smoking room overlook a pretty wooded lot. The walls are hung with paintings by a local artist, and the exhibit changes from time to time.

Service is excellent; when we were concerned that our daughter was too hungry to wait for a table, they brought a chicken basket for her to eat while we were waiting at the bar. When you sit down, look for a large basket of scones and rolls. Try the mozzarella cheese bread, which is essentially a grilled cheese sandwich breaded, fried, and served with marinara sauce for dipping. Don't each much, though, or you won't have room for your main course—this appetizer is larger than many entrees at other restaurants. Intriguing entrees include veal Italiano with sun-

dried tomatoes; Portobello mushrooms, sweet basil and garlic, topped with mozzarella; and seafood lasagna with layers of shrimp, scallops, and crab in a creamy marinara– parmesan sauce. The entrees are served on what look more like trays than dinner plates, and we went home with a veritable mountain of doggie boxes and bags. The chef, owner David Cook, is happy to prepare anything to meet the requirements of special diets, and if you call a few days in advance with a request that requires special ingredients, he's happy to prepare just about anything.

The Cook's Touch is open in the summer Monday through Friday for lunch and dinner every day. The rest of the year Cook's Touch is closed on Tuesday and Wednesday. Reservations are strongly suggested at this popular eatery. If you plan to eat here often, ask for the dinner club card and bring it every time. Once you've supped here eight times, your ninth meal is free.

Crescent Lodge $$$
Highway 191, Paradise Valley
(570) 595-7486
www.crescentlodge.com

A favorite in the region, Crescent Lodge serves more than 20 different entrees in a county inn atmosphere. The marinade of fresh vegetables served with each meal is delicious. House specialties include New York sirloin, roast crisp Long Island duckling, and Chateaubriand for two (which must be ordered in advance). The appetizers are worth a try too—oysters casino, smoked trout, and barbecued duck breast are a few of the choices. In the off-season the restaurant is open for dinner Tuesday through Sunday. Usually Monday is added during the summer, call to confirm. Reservations are suggested.

The Edelweiss $$$$
Highway 940, Pocono Lake
(570) 646-3938
www.theedelweiss.com

If you can't make a trip to Germany, this authentic Old World restaurant provides a

Many restaurants automatically add a tip if you are part of a party of six or more. Look to see if the tip has been added before you add any more.

convincing re-creation of a German dining experience. Generous portions of food emphasize the Black Forest region: weiner, jaeger, or veal schnitzel; and veal Edelweiss. You'll also find American dishes such as steak and seafood, or, if you're really adventurous, try something from the wild game menu, available November through March. You can try rabbit, venison, buffalo, gosling, alligator, or even ostrich. Waitresses complete the theme by wearing traditional dirndls. Lunch and dinner are served daily, with breakfast offered on the weekends.

The restaurant holds a huge Octoberfest Saturdays in October. The restaurant also offers a pastry shop and a gift shop filled with beer steins, cuckoo clocks, nutcrackers, smokers, and Christmas decorations.

The Forks at Buck Hill $$
Highway 390, Mountainhome
(570) 595-7335

Large portraits of unidentified ancestors remind patrons that this building has a history dating to 1878. The wooden tables and the understated green and red decor provide an elegant complement to an already beautiful building. Meals include pasta, chicken, seafood, veal, and steak. Consider the chicken stir-fry, Pocono Mountain brook trout, salmon béarnaise, and pork chops pizzaiola. In addition to the main dining area, there is a separate lounge and an outdoor deck.

The Forks at Buck Hill serves dinner Tuesday through Sunday and lunch on Saturday and Sunday.

Frog Town Inn $$$
Highway 390, Canadensis
(570) 595-6282
www.frogtowninn.com

Canadensis' original name lives on at the Frog Town Inn, an elegant yet comfortable restaurant and inn (see our Bed-and-Breakfasts and Country Inns chapter). The dark green walls of the dining room set off the lovely antiques and make the crystal and candles seem to sparkle all the more. There's a small library off the dining room with a single table where you can pretend you're lord of the manor giving a dinner party. At the back of the dining room is a greenhouse filled with plants and more tables.

The French Country cuisine is excellent. Make sure you try some of the fabulous appetizers such as shrimp and sea scallops with white wine, creme, and herbs and the, um, frog legs. (While the owners didn't have any frog fetishes when they bought the place in 1994, people keep giving them frog-theme items. They stopped counting the frogs that are scattered around the inn when they got to 100.) You'll be served a basket of homemade bread. Dinner can range from pasta with pan-seared shrimp and sea scallops, basil, grape tomatoes, and white wine to pork medallion served with caramelized onion and apple chutney. Everything is meticulously prepared and delicious.

You might notice a dummy sitting at the piano who looks a little out of place. She started life as a scarecrow for a Halloween contest and moved indoors when the weather got cold. Despite her lifeless personality, she has made quite an impression on some of Frog Town's diners and occasionally has left with a male guest, only to return with Skytop's bellboy the next morning. Too bad she can't tell us what she was doing.

Frog Town Inn is open for dinner Thursday through Saturday year-round. Smoking is allowed only in the bar, which has some tables for diners as well.

Hampton Court Inn $$$$
Highway 940 East, Mount Pocono
(570) 839-2119
www.mountpocono.com

The steaks are cut and trimmed in-house at Hampton Court, and they're all certified

Angus steaks. This gives some indication of the care that goes into preparing every meal. No artificial preservatives or flavor enhancers are used, and very little salt is added. Regulars know they can special-order variations of menu items. Grilling is done over lava rocks because of concerns regarding the healthiness of charcoal cooking. Entrees include beef, pasta, seafood, veal, and an excellent roast duckling served with Hampton Court Inn's own Grand Marnier cranberry sauce.

Three dining rooms are small, so reservations are a good idea. Dinner only is served every day except Tuesday.

Homestead Inn   **$$$**
Sand Spring Drive, Cresco
(570) 595-3171
www.thehomesteadinn.net
Tucked away on a country road just off the main road, the Homestead Inn is worth looking for (signs along Highway 390 in Mountainhome show the way). Philadelphia caterers Drew and Susan Price moved here in 1980 and camped in the basement while renovating the restaurant. Since that time they have built a loyal customer following and have received a great deal of recognition for their excellent food. Three lovely rooms, each one different, make up the inn. One, a small but elegant room with Wyeth prints, has a large window overlooking a working peat bog. Another has a fireplace that is popular in the winter.

Though the restaurant is beautiful, the food is the real draw. The menu changes twice a year, with lighter fare in the summer. Expect to see dishes such as Sweet Baby Cakes, crab cakes served with a roasted sweet red pepper sauce, or the Shrimp in the Deep Blue Sea, with bell peppers and plum tomatoes flamed with blue curacao sauce. Make sure you try the wild mushroom ravioli appetizer, prepared in a creamy pesto sauce. The signature dish of the Homestead Inn is a filet au poivre, filet mignon in a seasoned cognac pepper sauce. You'll be served a plate of crisp carrot and celery sticks as well as a basket of hot tea cakes and rolls, but save room for your dinner; the food is wonderful. The wine list is also extensive and features some unusual selections. The restaurant has deservedly won a number of awards, including a nine-years-running Silver Spoon Award, as well as three diamonds from the AAA Motor Club.

The Homestead Inn is open for dinner daily in summer and every day except Monday the rest of the year. It's a sophisticated city restaurant in a beautiful country setting. Eating out doesn't get much better than this.

Lee's Tokyo Hibachi Steakhouse $$$$
Highway 611, Bartonsville
(570) 421-1212
www.leesrestaurant.com
Join strangers around the hibachi for the circus that goes with the meal. Kids of all ages love it when the Japanese chef juggles sharp knives, spatulas, cups, and condiments—catching some of them in his hat—then challenges diners to catch bits of shrimp or beef in their mouths as he flicks them like peanuts through the air. Japanese and Chinese beers as well as hot sake are available to wash it all down. Lee's is open for lunch and dinner Monday through Friday, dinner only Saturday and Sunday. Make reservations; the place gets crowded.

Lopsided Inn   **$$**
Highway 196, Tobyhanna
(570) 839-8421
Outside the Lopsided Inn, you'll find Pocono kitsch—some wagon wheels and a couple of concrete bears. Inside, one half is a smoky neighborhood bar (see our Nightlife chapter), while the other half is a family restaurant, complete with friendly waitresses and pictures of the kids on the wall. The food is plentiful and good. You'll find chicken stuffed with crabmeat, Italian sausage and peppers, shrimp scampi, stuffed steak, veal, and other staples of American and Italian cooking.

So why is it called the Lopsided Inn? "The roof used to be lopsided until we fixed it," says Rosie, the owner. "Some customers say there's a little sag up there yet." The Lopsided Inn is open for lunch daily and dinner Thursday through Sunday. If you use any coupons for your meal, the balance must be paid in cash.

Mary Ann's Dairy Bar $
Highway 447, 2 miles north of Analomink
(570) 424-5698

This little soft ice cream, burger, and hot dog stand would barely qualify for listing as a diner were it not for what amounts to one of the most stunningly beautiful summer "dining rooms" in the Poconos. The area, surrounded by kitschy stone dogs, bunnies, owls, and little megalithic standing stones, consists of picnic tables in the deep shade of an ancient hemlock grove. Chipmunks join you for lunch, and there are teeter totters for the kids. When Ben and Jerry's Ben Cohen was asked for a list of his top 10 favorite ice-cream stands, he included Mary Ann's because of the generous amount of candy they put in their slurries.

Mountainhome Café/Deli $
Highway 390, Mountainhome
(570) 595-3839

Mountainhome is an old-fashioned cafe featuring gourmet coffee and a whole wall of hot sauces for sale. Lots of interesting antique bric-a-brac is scattered around the café, especially some antique coffee cans, a grinder, and an institutional clock stopped forever at 6:00. The atmosphere is informal, and lots of folks seem to know each other here. You can read a magazine while sipping a coffee or cappuccino in a giant teacup, eating a bagel, sandwich, or bowl of soup. Interesting sandwiches include the Ragin' Cajun, roast beef with roasted red peppers, melted cheese, and Cajun mayonnaise. Try the cracked peppermill smoked turkey or the chili with black beans and chipotle peppers. You can even sample a bit of coffee cake when you pay at the register. Mountainhome Café/Deli is open Monday through Saturday for lunch.

Mountainview Bar & Grille $$
Chateau at Camelback, 300 Camelback Tannersville
(570) 629-5900
www.chateauresort.com

This lovely alpine lodge seats diners at huge bay windows overlooking a sylvan lake into which a man-made waterfall, originating in the restaurant itself, plunges. The Mountainview, with such specialties as an awesome chicken Caesar salad as well as grilled New York steak Napoleon, lightly pounded and stuffed with Portabella mushrooms, sun-dried tomatoes, and mozzarella cheese, caters to skiers in the winter, vacationers in summer, and Chateau guests and locals at all times, serving breakfast, lunch, and dinner seven days a week. Reservations are a good idea.

Pine Knob Inn $$$$
Highway 447, Canadensis
(570) 595-2532, (800) 426-1460
www.pineknobinn.com

This lovely country inn, run by John and Cheryl Garman, serves dinner Wednesday through Sunday from mid-June through October and Friday through Sunday the rest of the year. Breakfast is available on weekends. The gourmet dining in the Brodhead Room includes such specialties as boneless breast of duck dressed with a fresh thyme bordelaise and served atop a pearl onion compote; pan-fried rainbow trout stuffed with crab and shitaki mushrooms and topped with a Dijon lime Bearnaise; and black-peppered linguine, dressed with wild mushrooms and artichoke hearts in a vegetable béchamel.

As you walk in the door, notice the "dynamic wine rack," designed by John Garman. More than 100 varieties of wine are displayed on the rack, many you can't buy at the state store. Garman buys two or three bottles of wine that look interesting to him and then moves on to another variety, so there are always new wines here for you to try.

The inn's long history dates back to 1847 when it was built as a house for tannery owner Dr. Gilbert Palen. He was responsible for renaming the town Canadensis (nee Frogtown and later Coveville) after *tsuga canadensis,* the botanical name for the hemlock trees so prevalent in the area. The house began accepting guests in 1886 (see our Bed-and-Breakfasts and Country Inns chapter).

Pocono Brewing Company $$
Highway 611, Swiftwater
(570) 839-3230
www.poconobrewingcompany.com

The first thing you notice about Pocono Brewing Company, or PBC, as they call themselves, is the large hexagonal tower with shiny brewing equipment. When PBC built this restaurant and sports pub, their intention was to brew beer, but they soon learned that Pennsylvania state law said that if they brew their own, they could only serve their own. Preferring to offer customers more than 100 beers from around the world (33 of them on tap), PBC decided to contract with a local brewing company to create PBC beers, and the brewing equipment today is simply decoration.

Don't be discouraged if the parking lot is full. There's plenty of room in this large, popular restaurant, and you'll probably get a table right away. You enter through the noisy, friendly 3rd Base Sports Pub, and unless you ask for a table in the smoking section, you go to the restaurant, a spacious room at the back. Cathedral ceilings, wood beams, green accents and a huge stage with a fireplace at the back make up this room.

Though PBC's raison d'être is beer, the food is surprisingly good. Start with a crab cake, an enormous macho nachos (too much for two people), a Portobella Napoleon (marinated Portobella mushrooms layered with roasted red peppers, eggplant, fresh mozzarella, and marinara sauce, finished with balsamic vinegar) or chicken wings with Thai peanut sauce, hot chipotle sauce, or one of eight other sauces.

Then move on to an entrée—chicken, fish, steak, or burgers—try a crab cake or a pork porterhouse topped with a sweet Granny Smith apple glaze. The veggie burger is two marinated Portobella caps with roasted red peppers, fresh mozzarella, pesto, and balsamic vinegar. Yum. Desserts are the usual excesses, including a brownie sundae, a towering Oreo cookie cake, and tiramisu. Plentiful waitresses offer excellent service. Weekends often bring live music to PBC (see our Nightlife chapter), and in good weather customers carouse at the outdoor Tsunami deck. A Starbucks kiosk provides Express Breakfast daily, and PBC is open for lunch and dinner every day.

Pocono Mountain Travel
Center Mega Buffet $$
Highway 611, Bartonsville
(570) 421-1770

Truck stops, which are growing up and becoming sophisticated, aren't being called truck stops any more. Now, as in the case of this one, where big rigs from all over the country congregate, they're being called travel centers, but the euphemism doesn't affect the menu. It still offers a lot of food at very affordable prices served up from the Mega Buffet of the name. This buffet consists of a salad and soup bar with Mexican and Italian dishes, homemade baked goods, carved meats, and a wide range of desserts. Breakfast is served at all times, and the buffet is open 24 hours a day, 7 days a week.

Pocono Pub $$
Highway 611, Bartonsville
(570) 421-2187
www.poconopub.com

A little family restaurant and tavern across from the Howard Johnsons, Pocono Pub serves all the expected pub sandwiches and appetizers. Burgers, Philly steak sandwiches, pizza, and chili are some of the favorites. Full dinner entrees from chicken scampi to New York strip steak are also available. The kids' menu is very, very reasonable. Pocono Pub is open every day. Visit Sunday afternoons in fall to watch pro football on the pub's TVs; there's also karaoke on Tuesday and Sunday and live entertainers on Saturday nights.

Smuggler's Cove $$
Highway 611, Tannersville
(570) 629-2277
www.smugglerscove.net

Seafood is the specialty in this nautically themed dining room, while burgers, wings, fajitas, and seafood are all available in the adjoining Castaways Lounge. Favorites on the seafood menu are lobster and shrimp paella, coconut shrimp, and beef and reef, with a choice of London broil or sirloin with baked stuffed shrimp with crabmeat or shrimp scampi. The Cove urges reservations and serves lunch and dinner seven days a week.

The Swiftwater Inn $$$
Highway 611, Swiftwater
(570) 839-7206

You'll feel like you're at grandma's house when you dine at the Swiftwater Inn. Like grandma's house, the dining room is furnished with an eclectic collection of old-fashioned furniture, down to the pictures of the kids on the bookshelf. the inn, sitting by a stream in Swiftwater, was built in 1778 and is listed on the National Register of Historic Places.

The food is old-fashioned too, but lobster tails, fresh Pocono trout in pecan butter, and filet mignon should satisfy most customers. Regular customers favor the prime rib. There's a crowded, hopping bar in the next room. (See our Nightlife chapter.) The Swiftwater Inn is open for dinner in the summer Thursday through Sunday and, in the off season, Friday through Sunday.

The Tannersville Inn $$
Highway 611, Tannersville
(570) 629-3131
www.tannersvilleinn.com

Tannersville Inn serves reasonably priced steaks and seafood. For late-night appetites, a bar menu, featuring tacos, shrimp, steamers, and an assortment of sandwiches, salads, and chicken dishes, is

served until 1:00 A.M. The restaurant menu has fancier seafood meals such as lobster tail and shrimp stuffed with crabmeat plus plenty of steak, chicken, and pasta offerings. The inn began serving the public as a stagecoach stop in 1825 and is a popular local gathering spot.

Lunch and dinner are available daily. Bands perform many nights. (See our Nightlife chapter.)

Tokyo Tea House $$$
Highway 940, Pocono Summit
(570) 839-8880

You'll have to look sharp to find Tokyo Tea House. It's in Pocono Summit in a strip mall opposite a lighted chiropractor's sign. It's worth looking for this restaurant because it serves excellent Japanese cuisine. The gorgeous, sizzling teriyaki is the best we've ever seen, and the owners claim that many of their New York City customers tell them that the sushi is the best they've had anywhere. Judging by the quality of the food at Tokyo Tea House, it's a credible claim.

Tokyo Tea House is open for lunch and dinner year-round every day but Tuesday.

Van Gilder's Jubilee Restaurant $$
Highway 940, Pocono Pines
(570) 646-2377
www.breakfastking.com

The Jubilee Restaurant strives to make sure no one leaves hungry. As the self-declared "breakfast king of the Poconos," they have been "expanding waistlines since 1968." Breakfast platters such as the Pocono Sampler and the Country Boy Breakfast are local legends. The Pocono Sampler, as described on the menu, begins with an appetizer; then the chef serves what is described as his creation. The menu proclaims: "You gotta have a big appetite for this one! This is where our chef takes over—just about everything on our menu . . . No sharing!"

More conventional, the Country Boy Breakfast features two stacks of pancakes, scrambled eggs, bacon, and sausage.

Breakfast, lunch, and dinner are served

daily. The on-site Pub in the Pines, open every evening, serves tavern food including, on Thursday only, six flavors of chicken wings.

WEST END

Andrew Moore's Stone Bar Inn $$$$
US 209 Business, Snydersville
(570) 992-6634
www.stonebar.com
A country tavern with fireside dining, intimate booths, and namesake stone bar, this restaurant serves outstanding classic American cuisine such as prime Angus beef and rack of lamb as well as native game such as venison and wild boar. The chef smokes his own trout and makes the sausage and ice cream himself. Vegetarians need not be intimidated. There's a separate section of the menu for them. The appetizers, including Baked Crabmeat Au Gratin with artichokes and horseradish as well as escargot with garlic and asparagus in puff pastry, are worth a taste. The Stone Bar Inn is open for dinner every day.

The Bagel Experience $
Ames Plaza, US 209, Brodheadsville
(610) 681-4703
As the name might imply, a huge line of bagels of all styles and flavors lives here, but they are not the only "experience" available. This little shop, in the heart of a thriving shopping center, also carries a full line of sandwiches and other breakfast and luncheon goodies, but do not delay because the Experience closes at 4:00 P.M., 2:00 P.M. on Sunday.

Beacon 443 Diner/Restaurant $$
35 Blakeslee Boulevard
Lehighton
(610) 377-1782
This popular amalgam of diner and restaurant serves breakfast, lunch, and dinner seven days a week. The menu is standard American, with a low-cholesterol menu for health-conscious patrons. Beer and wine are available; no reservations are necessary.

Black Bread Café & Catering Co. $$$
47 Race Street, Jim Thorpe
(570) 325-8957
www.blackbreadcafe.com
This charming little bistro, specializing in Northern Italian cuisine, is located in a Victorian home in the middle of one of the most interesting shopping areas in Jim Thorpe. Dine downstairs or in the upstairs lounge on homemade pasta and a host of seafood specialties, including a very popular orange roughy in white wine sauce. Black Bread serves lunch and dinner every day; reservations are advised.

Caruso's $$
99 East Bridge Street (Highway 443 and US 209), Lehighton
(610) 377-5666
An informal restaurant serving lunch and dinner daily, Caruso's features standard Italian pasta, chicken, and veal entrees. The pizza is very popular too. The wine list is surprisingly good for such a casual restaurant.

Chestnuthill Diner $
US 209 at Highway 115, Brodheadsville
(570) 992-3222
Breakfast, served all day, and homemade soups and pastries baked on the premises are favorites at this popular little diner in the heart of the West End. Daily seafood specials are a standard offering. The Chestnuthill is clean, shiny, always crowded, and open seven days a week from 5:00 A.M. until 11:00 P.M. Chestnuthill now has a liquor license. Owners of the Chestnuthill also operate the Mt. Bethel Diner (Highway 611, Mount Bethel; (570) 897-6409) and Billy's Pocono Diner (Highway 611, Tannersville; 570-629-1450).

Christine's Road House $$$
Highway 715 South, Reeders
(570) 629-1210
This onetime country tavern began its life in 1890 as a dance hall and, in 1958, evolved into the first Chinese restaurant in the Poconos. Today, it offers the richest menu of Southern, Texas, and Creole

Many restaurants do not have licenses to sell liquor, wine, or beer, but most of them will provide "setups" if you want to bring your own. If in doubt, call and ask.

cooking in the region as its owners travel the nation seeking such new recipes as chicken breast stuffed with corn bread and cooked in an apricot glaze, oven-baked catfish with pineapple salsa, Spicy Louisiana Meatloaf with five peppers, and a 14-ounce sirloin steak on a sizzle platter with Texas Longhorn Sauce. Dinner is served seven days a week.

Effort Diner $$
Highway 115, Effort
(610) 681-4212

This simple Yankee diner serves hearty fare at breakfast, lunch, and dinner seven days a week. Delicious homemade sticky buns, pies, and apple dumplings are specialties of the house.

The Emerald Restaurant $$$
24 Broadway, Jim Thorpe
(570) 325-8995
jimthorpedining.com

This Irish restaurant is the heart of the beautifully restored Inn at Jim Thorpe (see our Bed-and-Breakfast and Country Inns chapter), which was built in the 1840s. The Victorian dining room has a tin ceiling and paintings of old Mauch Chunk, the former name of Jim Thorpe. The combination of Irish hospitality and Victorian romance is unbeatable. Try such Irish offerings as shepherd's pie, bubble and squeak (roast turkey, ham, and vegetables with homemade mashed potato topping), chicken potpie, or Dublin-style fish and chips. After dinner, visit Molly Maguire's Pub downstairs, where the true spirit of Ireland and the dark history of the region (see our History chapter) really kicks in.

Lunch and dinner is served daily; reservations are in order.

The Hamilton $$$
Hamilton South Road, between Sciota and Saylorsburg
(570) 992-9108

Hardwood floors, spacious seating, quilts, assorted crafts, and antiques provide an informal yet gracious setting for diners at the Hamilton. Beef, veal, pork, chicken, and seafood entrees are offered. The liver is a local favorite. The Hamilton goes "from light bites to full dinners," and those less hungry can try a sandwich or a personal pizza. Dinner is served every day but Monday.

The Inn of William Stoddard $$$
Stage Coach Road, Stemiersville
(610) 377-3878

This historic inn predates the Civil War. It's not easy to find, so call for directions, but the owner says "once you find us, you won't forget us." You can picture folks relaxing on the large porches and socializing as they have for well more than 100 years. It is a casual gathering place that combines nostalgia with such specialties as quail, pork satay, whole lobsters, and Alaskan king crab. The inn is open Wednesday through Saturday for dinner only as well as Sunday dinners in the fall. The price scale given here represents the standard menu. Many seafood specialties fall under the classification "Catch of the Day" and are market priced. Reservations are appreciated but not required.

JT's All American Steak and Ale House $$$
5 Hazard Square, Jim Thorpe
(570) 325-4563
jimthorpedining.com

This elegant chop house, now owned and operated by the same folks who own The Emerald Restaurant (see previous entry), is housed in the oldest landmark in Jim Thorpe—the Hotel Switzerland, which has been serving guests since 1830. The top of the menu in this Victorian dining room is the "all-American" 24-ounce prime sirloin steak for only $12.95 (you can share it with a dinner companion for an extra-plate charge of $8.00). The rest of the menu covers steaks, chops, chicken, seafood, and pasta. It is worth a trip to the pub for lunch just for a look at the marble-columned, hand-carved back bar. (See our Arts and Culture chapter.)

Lunch and dinner are served seven days a week, and reservations are appreciated.

King Arthur Dining Room $
US 209 Business, Sciota
(570) 992-4969

The Camelot theme decor here is carried over to such menu items as brook trout Sir Galahad, pork medallions Sir Gawain, and duck Morgan Le Fay. Steak, lobster, and veal also are featured. Save room for a dessert such as baked Alaska meringue, three flavors of ice cream, and cake flambe at your table. Lunch and dinner are served daily with some tables at large windows overlooking a sylvan lake. Reservations are accepted.

McGinley's Pocono Trail Lodge $$
Highway 115, Blakeslee
(570) 646-3015

This rustic Irish restaurant has served the Blakeslee area for nearly 40 years with a standard hearty American menu topped by wings (which they claim are the best in the Poconos), hot turkey, crab cakes, and, of course, corned beef and cabbage on St. Patrick's Day. A generous soup and salad bar is included with all lunch and dinner entrees. Reservations are not necessary, and the lodge is open every day of the year save Christmas, for dinner and for lunch on Saturday and Sunday.

Murphy's Loft $$
Highway 115, Blakeslee
(570) 646-2813
www.murphysloft.com

Lunch and dinner are served daily at this little log cabin constructed in 1934 as a haven for hunters and outdoorsmen. Breakfast is available on Saturday and

Sunday. In addition to the restaurant, you may dine or have drinks on the deck or at the outdoor bar overlooking a waterfall, garden, and in-ground heated pool. Menu items include steaks, seafood, veal, sandwiches, chicken, and pasta. All frying is done with no-cholesterol shortening.

Old Schoolhouse Tavern $
4740 Long Run Road, Lehighton
(610) 377-5745
www.oldschoolhousetavern.com

We bet students in the late 1800s would never have expected their schoolhouse to become home to terrific chicken wings, steak, and seafood. The original building has been expanded to accommodate this successful business. Lunch and dinner are served daily.

Platz's Restaurant $$$
101 Harrity Road, Lehighton
(610) 377-1819

This restaurant/bar resembles an overgrown rec room. Old books, pictures of unidentified ancestors, old sports equipment, signs, and other random knickknacks fill every available space. The atmosphere is casual, stressing fun over formality. Sandwiches, seafood, pasta, and steaks are included on a menu packed with familiar favorites. Lunch and dinner are served daily. Reservations are recommended on weekends, as the combination of residents and day-trippers from nearby Beltzville State Park often make for standing-room only.

Robert Christian's $$$
Highway 940, Blakeslee
(570) 646-0433

This elegant restaurant, with its rustic early American decor, offers some of the most exquisite cuisine in the Poconos and arguably the best service anywhere. Robert Christian's serves lunch and dinner daily and is known for its specials. The specials menu is varied, including: early bird specials available 4:00 to 6:00 P.M. during the week and 1:00 to 6:00 P.M. on

Sunday, consisting of mostly Italian entrees with soup, salad, and bread; dinner for two on Tuesday and Wednesday, with some intriguing entrees such as tequila chicken or twin crab cakes, plus soup, salad, bread, vegetable of the day, choice of side dish, and a full carafe of house wine for $29.95; and midweek specials such as oven-roasted turkey (Sunday) or prime rib (Thursday) with soup, salad, bread, vegetable, and choice of side dish. The regular menu includes steak, seafood, and pasta selections. A favorite is veal Oscar—veal medallions prepared with crabmeat, asparagus, and béarnaise sauce. Other specialties of the house include duck in raspberry and Chambord sauce; and a Seafood House–Style consisting of scallops, shrimp, broccoli, crabmeat, and mushrooms on a bed of linguine. There is a special "Lite Fare" menu of sandwiches, and at dinner, a generous tureen of soup goes with every entrée. Reservations are advised.

Snydersville Diner $
US 209, Snydersville
(570) 992–4003
One of the most popular diners in the Poconos, the Snydersville features a rich menu of daily specials ranging from baked haddock and Salisbury steak through pork and sauerkraut to chicken and waffles. The baked goods are virtually worshipped here. Every Sunday, the line to enter stretches out the door and through the parking lot. Breakfast, lunch, and dinner are served.

Sunrise Diner $
3 Hazard Square, Jim Thorpe
(570) 325–4093
This is a classic diner with an art-deco stainless-steel back bar and a full dining deck outside. Sunrise is just off the historic square rimmed by the Carbon County courthouse and the train station. Daily specials, ranging from homemade pierogies and soups, roast turkey with homemade whipped potatoes, to meat loaf, are featured seven days a week. The

diner is open daily for breakfast, lunch, and dinner during the summer. During the winter, it is open for breakfast and lunch on weekdays, as well as dinner on Saturday and Sunday. It's always open 24 hours on weekends.

Trainer's Inn $$$
845 Interchange Road, Lehighton
(610) 377–4350
Eat at Trainer's on a Thursday night, and you can have surf and turf for $14.95, but call because specials change every week. Pasta, chicken, and veal also are offered. Another favorite light item is Buffalo shrimp, prepared Cajun-style and covered in the wings sauce. Burgers and cheese steaks are good as well. Lunch and dinner are served seven days a week. Reservations are suggested on weekends only.

Ye Olde Saylors Inn $$
Highway 115, Saylorsburg
(570) 992–5200
Area residents consider this restaurant one of the true bargains in the Poconos. Large portions of familiar American dishes such as ham, steaks, chicken, and fish are served in a friendly, family atmosphere. You will not find any exotic specials or pretentious decor, just simple, good food served in large dining rooms decorated with crafts created by local artists. Dress casual, and arrive hungry.

Dinner is served Thursday through Saturday and Sunday from noon to 7:00 P.M. Reservations are accepted.

MILFORD/LAKE WALLENPAUPACK AREA

A.J.'s Fireplace $$$
Highway 507, Tafton
(570) 226–2701
The fireplace in the name sits outside the building. It is a relic from an earlier structure. The bar and restaurant inside are handy for folks in a hurry who need a plain old good meal. Burgers, sandwiches, appetizers, and pizza are offered for lunch

and dinner every day. The dinner menu adds a few more entrees such as steaks and chicken. The restaurant stays open until 2:00 A.M., so it is great for late-night stops. Take-out service is available.

The Alpine Restaurant $$
U.S. Highway 6, Honesdale
(570) 253-5899
www.thealpineonline.com

Lovers of German foods need to visit The Alpine. In addition to the restaurant, there is a gift shop and butcher shop. Deli cases are filled with homemade wursts; fresh sausage; and cut-to-order beef, veal, and pork. The bakery offers everything from apple strudel to assorted European tortes. Gift items such as beer steins, crystal crafts, and even German newspapers, magazines, and compact discs are on sale.

Lunch and dinner are prepared Wednesday through Saturday, lunch only on Tuesday and Sunday. The cuisine, decor, music, and dress of the waitresses are straight out of the beer garden. Throughout the year, The Alpine hosts festivals and outdoor barbecues in its own pit. The biggest is an Octoberfest held in the middle of August. Call for information on the dates of other activities.

Apple Valley Restaurant $$
Apple Valley Village, 101 Pine Acres
Milford
(570) 296-6831
www.applevalleyrestaurant.com

Apple Valley serves fun-food favorites in large portions at reasonable prices. Barbecued ribs, steaks, burgers, Chicago-style pizza, and assorted chicken and pasta dishes are available. Especially popular are their barbecue ribs and their sizzle steak, which really sizzles. The restaurant offers lunch and dinner daily.

Alley Oop's Pub, a nightclub at Apple Valley, features bands or comedians on weekends and daily appetizer specials. (See our Nightlife chapter.) The restaurant and pub are part of the Apple Valley Village complex of gift shops. After you eat, you can shop, visit the Shocopee School-

house (see our Kidstuff chapter), or feed the ducks at the duck pond.

Cordaro's Restaurant & Lounge $$
186 Grandview Avenue, Honesdale
(570) 253-3713

Cordaro's boasts a banquet room and bar and lounge in the basement and caters outside events, but the decor is refreshingly American diner, with home-baked pastries in a display case and a jukebox in every booth. For more than 50 years, the Cordaro family has served food in Honesdale. In the 1950s, Phil Cordaro began providing coffee and doughnuts to the workers building Honesdale High School. Since the coffee often arrived too cold to drink, Phil started to deliver it in insulated stainless-steel containers. So began the "coffee run," which became a staple in Honesdale until the family gave it up, along with the old restaurant, to move to the current location in 1961. The dining room and C.C. Lounge nightclub were added in 1981.

Breakfast, lunch, and dinner are available daily. The menu offers sandwiches, seafood, pasta, salads, and burgers. A discounted menu is provided for seniors older than 55. Reservations are taken only for large parties.

Dimmick Inn & Steakhouse $$$
101 East Harford Street, Milford
(570) 296-4021
www.dimmickinn.com

The Dimmick has been entertaining guests since 1855. Original owner Frances Dimmick was one of the most colorful women in Pike County history. She was an accomplished violinist, horsewoman, fly-caster, and markswoman who preferred to wear men's clothing—highly unusual in the late 19th century. The Dimmick is on the busiest corner in Milford and has large porches where you can eat during good weather and, at the suggestion of the management, harass the passers-by. Inside, you can eat in green and white dining rooms with a garden-like atmosphere or in the wood-paneled bar. The extra-crisp salad is served family style from a big bowl. The entrees are enormous, and, if you ask your waiter nicely, maybe he'll pull up a chair and help you finish—or box it up for you to take home. The menu includes a couple of dishes made with buffalo meat, which is lower in cholesterol, fat, and sodium than beef, turkey, or chicken. The St. Louis-style barbecued ribs are made with the Dimmick's own sweet barbecue sauce. The twin sirloin fillets, charcoal grilled and served with bourbon-scallion demi-glace and grilled mushrooms are also popular. The serving staff is not only friendly, but downright funny. Don't mention it's your birthday, or you run the risk of being serenaded by the Dimmick Inn Marching Kazoo Band. The Dimmick has opened 10 beautiful guest rooms upstairs (see our Bed-and-Breakfasts and Country Inns chapter). Don't miss the Dimmick; it has a fun, casual atmosphere and excellent food. The Dimmick serves lunch and dinner daily.

Many of our restaurants are along twisty country roads. Be sure to allow ample driving time when making your reservation. Tell the restaurant staff where you're coming from, and they should be able to give you a good estimate of your driving time.

Ehrhardt's Lakeside Restaurant $$$
4 Highway 507, Hawley
(570) 226-2124
www.ehrhardts.com

The Ehrhardt family has been in the restaurant business for more than 50 years. Several generations now work at the restaurant which overlooks Lake Wallenpaupack and the family's adjacent inn. (See our Accommodations chapter.) The atmosphere is sunny and casual, and the view is spectacular.

Steaks, prepared in a variety of ways, come with a trip to the salad bar, garlic parsley mashed potatoes, and another vegetable. Especially interesting is the Hunter Sauce, a combination of Yuengling Lager demi-glace, rosemary, mushrooms, roasted red peppers, and tomatoes. Or you might want to try the Bailey's Chicken, a lightly seasoned and breaded chicken breast, pan-seared, broiled, topped with dusted fried shoestring onions, and smothered in a Bailey's Irish Cream sauce.

Ehrhardt's is open daily for lunch and dinner, and a lavish breakfast buffet is served Sunday. Take-out service is available. Slips are provided for customers who arrive by boat, and in July and August, the Upper Deck serves such bar food as wings, steamers, hot dogs, and hoagies. Look for monthly specials. Reservations are not necessary for lunch, but they are accepted for dinner.

The Falls Port Inn and Restaurant $$$$
330 Main Avenue, Hawley
(570) 226-2600

Set in a meticulously restored hotel, the Falls Port Inn and Restaurant is truly exceptional. You'll be treated to dishes like sirloin steak au poivre, a completely trimmed sirloin with cracked peppercorns in a cognac cream sauce, or Chicken Remi, boneless chicken breasts with shiitake mushrooms and sun-dried tomatoes in a cognac cream sauce over homemade pasta. It it's lobster you crave, Falls Port has twin rock lobster steamed or baked and stuffed, and somewhere in the recesses of the kitchen, those crustaceans are crawling around in their own 150-gallon tank until you make your request. The pasta dishes are fabulous and imaginative, and all the pasta is fresh made.

Ever since we ate here, we've been dreaming of the coffee. Whether it's excellent beans, which are purchased directly from a roaster and are never more than 48 hours from having been roasted, or the method of preparation (a French press plunged at your table), this is the creamiest coffee we've ever tasted—and we're not talking about the addition of milk.

Three gorgeously restored rooms make up the restaurant (upstairs rooms are also available for overnight guests—see Bed-and-Breakfasts and Country Inns chapter). The back rooms are perfect for special parties. If you're an Arts and Crafts–era enthusiast, note the genuine William Morris wallpaper that the owner discovered in an antique shop. Unusual antiques are placed strategically as focal points.

The Falls Port Inn and Restaurant is worth a special trip to Hawley. Look for an awning that says, "The Grand Cafe," on a corner of Main Avenue (we had a little trouble locating Falls Port until we saw the awning). This is one of the most sophisticated restaurants in the Poconos. It's open every day but Tuesday in the summer, for lunch and dinner, and for Sunday brunch. The rest of the year, Falls Port is open Wednesday through Sunday for lunch and dinner.

The French Manor $$$$
Huckleberry Mountain, Highway 191
South Sterling
(570) 676-3244, (800) 523-8200
www.thefrenchmanor.com
This elegant French restaurant was constructed as a private retreat in 1932. It is modeled after the original owner's estate in France. German and Italian masons were brought in to construct the stone chateau using stone and lumber from the surrounding mountains. Many children of these workers still live in the region. The manor boasts an imported Spanish slate roof, cypress interior, and a dining room with a Romanesque arched entry, thick-beamed ceiling, and a massive stone fireplace. (See our Bed-and-Breakfasts and Country Inns chapter for more information on overnight accommodations.)

The manor serves dinner Tuesday through Sunday and breakfast every day from one of the most exotic haute cuisine menus in the Poconos: Roasted wild Chilean sea bass in natural juices and syrup of white wine on a bed of fennel stewed with lemongrass, medallions of lamb sautéed with a sauce of burnt honey and dried apricot, sea scallops caramelized

Hours often change seasonally, and restaurants sometimes close in exceptionally bad weather or during the slow season. During winter, call ahead to confirm that the restaurant you want to try is open.

slowly in a savory puree of coconut and braised shallot, filet mignon stuffed with broiled lobster napped in mushroom cognac creme, and of course, classical escargot au Bourguignônne.

Inn at Woodloch Pines $$$
off Highway 590, Hawley
(570) 685-8002
www.woodloch.com
The entire Woodloch operation is top-shelf, offering friendly elegance in every phase of the resort complex. The meals available to the general public at the restaurant are no exception.

The Inn dining room serves a complete meal package including appetizer, entrée, dessert, salad, vegetable, potato of the evening, bread, and nonalcoholic beverages for a set price. There is a different menu every night, but a representative bill of fare would include lobster tails, grilled salmon or swordfish, veal Oscar, baked Virginia ham, or roast tenderloin of beef. A family-style meal also is offered—the food is served on platters, and everyone helps themselves.

Dinner is served daily but is available to those who are not staying at the resort only when there's room. Summer nights are often full, but the rest of the year is a good bet, especially Wednesday nights when, for only a little more, you can eat and then go over to the nightclub for a Broadway-style revue. (The revue is also available Saturday nights, but it's harder to get a reservation then.) Since reservations are required, call and see if there's room, and then you can have a couple of hours of the Woodloch Pines experience. After the meal, you can have drinks in the Oak Bar Lounge.

Le Gorille $$$$
Twin Lakes Road, Shohola
(570) 296-8094

As the name implies, primate memorabilia dominates the décor. The menu for the day is written on a blackboard; there is no set list of entrees. The owners prepare the food, purchase the produce locally, and smoke the fish in their own smokehouse. Two meals you might encounter here are grilled marinated hanger steak, a very tender French cut, with roast garlic mashed potatoes, or grilled tuna with guacamole and soba noodles in a ginger orange sauce.

Le Gorille is open for dinner only Wednesday through Sunday from April through December. From January through March, the restaurant is open only Friday, Saturday, and Sunday. Reservations are recommended, as the dining room accommodates fewer than 40. No credit cards.

Because of the rural nature of the region, few restaurants deliver. Finding a place that will bring food to you outside of the larger towns is difficult. Most places that deliver are pizza parlors. Even they usually deliver only within a few miles of their location.

Overboard Restaurant $$$
Highway 507, Greentown
(570) 857-0254

As the name might imply, Overboard carries a nautical theme from its tongue-in-groove cedar walls covered with little ships' wheels, netting, shells, and other seagoing knickknacks to the light blue tablecloths and curtains. The decor, however, does not limit the menu, which ranges from their most popular dish, Seafood Madison (consisting of shrimp and crab sautéed with tomatoes, broccoli, and garlic over angel hair pasta) to veal marsala in a rich demi-glace.

The dining room is very small and is often filled with locals who regularly dine

on the steak and seafood offerings. Reservations are encouraged. Dinner only is served daily in the summer and every day but Wednesday the rest of the year. Daily specials of seafood, veal, chicken, and steak are offered.

Paupack Hills Golf and Country Club $$$
Yacht Club Drive, off Highway 507
Greentown
(570) 857-0251

Although on the grounds of a private country club, the restaurant is open to the public. The view of the golf course and surrounding woods would make anyone want to leave the table and hit the links. Proper attire is required. Patrons do not need to wear jackets and ties, but wearing jeans and a T-shirt will likely leave you hungry. Dress for casual, leaning toward elegant, dining.

On the menu's high end, the twin lobster tails and rack of New Zealand lamb are excellent. Less costly and also tasty is the penne rigati, an old-world macaroni served with Neopolitan meat balls. Lunch is served daily; dinner Thursday through Sunday.

The Settlers Inn at Bingham Park $$$
4 Main Avenue, Hawley
(570) 226-2993, (800) 833-8527
www.thesettlersinn.com

The Settlers Inn's atmosphere of inviting elegance begins the minute you enter the lovely Tudor mansion. The large bluestone fireplace near the Tavern calls out for people to gather around it and chat. Stone patios and elaborate gardens, including a herb garden that supplies the kitchen, decorate the outside, while Gothic cathedral chairs and candles accent the dining room.

The owners have researched the culturally diverse early settlers of the Poconos and patterned the cuisine after theirs. As a result, you might find some Scandinavian, African, and Native American dishes on the menu. Whenever possible, Pennsylvania products are served, including wines, beers, mushrooms, and cheeses. Meats are smoked in-house, and maple syrup, meats, and fish are purchased from local farms and hatcheries. All breads and baked goods are prepared in the inn's kitchen.

Since most of the entrees use local products, the menu changes with each season. A personal favorite is pork osso buco au jus with mashed potato succotash. Or, if you're really hungry, Australian rack of lamb with Shiraz lamb jus, wild rice pilaf, and Merguez lamb sausages.

The restaurant is so popular in the Poconos that it keeps a mailing list to inform regulars of upcoming menu additions and special events with special menus. The Settlers' Victorian Christmas dinners sell out annually; people often make reservations months in advance.

Lunch and dinner are served daily. The dining room and guest rooms at the inn (see our Bed-and-Breakfast and Country Inns chapter) are strictly nonsmoking. Reservations are recommended.

Twin Rocks Restaurant $$
I-84 exit 5, Hamlin
(570) 689-9112

They appear to have blacktopped Kansas to create this enormous truck stop, and like truck stops everywhere, the restaurant aims its menu at hungry people. Breakfast, lunch, and dinner are served seven days a week in the sort of atmosphere in which waitresses banter with their customers, and guys comfortably sit down to eat without removing their baseball caps. No reservations are accepted, and there is no bar—just plenty of good, rib-sticking food, epitomized by that trucker's Breakfast of Champions, chicken-fried steak and eggs with country cream gravy. If that's too heavy for you, try the Fruits of the Forest pie—an amalgam of strawberries, rhubarb, apples, raspberries, and blackberries.

An easy way to figure a 15 percent tip is to take 10 percent of the total bill, and then half of 10%. Add them together, and you'll have 15. You're not expected to tip on the tax, so if you use the total figure, you'll be tipping a little above 15 percent, which should be perfect if the service has been good.

Water Wheel Cafe & Bakery $$$
150 Water Street, Milford
(570) 296-2383
www.waterwheelcafe.com

The food at the Water Wheel Cafe & Bakery has achieved a level of sophistication that holds its own with any big city restaurant. It's easy to see why the *Washington Post* called it "the most perfect luncheon spot in all the Poconos," but we especially like dinner here. Expect dishes like crispy hazelnut pork chops served with garlic-whipped potatoes and imported penne with artichoke hearts and cured olives in a pesto sauce.

Like the *Post* says, lunch is a lovely event here. If it's warm, you can sit on a deck overlooking the Sawkill Creek. The sandwiches are local legends. Favorites include melted open-faced brie with Granny Smith apples and toasted almonds on Swiss health bread and prosciutto, goat cheese, roasted peppers, and sun-dried tomatoes on Italian bread. Several vegetarian options are offered.

The Water Wheel is open daily for breakfast and lunch, Thursday through Sunday for dinner. Reservations are necessary because of limited seating. The Water Wheel has done a beautiful restoration on an attached bar. It's filled with antiques (check out the chair with a removable seat and guess what that was for), and it has compiled an excellent wine list. They often host live jazz and blues on Friday and Saturday in a lovely, intimate setting. Watch for their jazz jams on Sunday and blues jams on Thursday, when you're invited to participate.

NIGHTLIFE 🍸

Even though we are essentially rural, we have plenty of nightlife in the Poconos. Top jazz musicians play in a number of places, including one of the oldest jazz clubs in the country, the Deer Head Inn in Delaware Water Gap. Our acoustic, rock, and country performers deliver some great music too. If you're lucky you can spot a musician playing at a local club who backed up Bob Dylan, the Coasters, or another well-known band. Even the dreaded karaoke is worming its way into Pocono nightlife.

Our bars range from country honky tonks to fancy resort discos and everything in between. Some of the resorts bring in nationally known comedians and bands to perform in their lounges. While resort patrons might get preferential tickets, the general public is always welcome.

On a weekend evening you can cruise from club to club down Main Street in Stroudsburg. You'll be amazed at how many people are doing the Main Street strut and crowding into the bars. Though Stroudsburg is as close as we get to an urban center, you'll find a good number of nightspots in the smaller towns and along country roads too.

If bar hopping is not your cup of vodka, you can attend the many concerts and plays that are offered here. There's a good showing of groups devoted to classical music, and the Broadway-style musicals that are popular with local theaters are absolutely professional. (See our Arts and Culture chapter for information on venues presenting concerts and theater.) The Mountain Laurel Center for the Performing Arts in Bushkill plans to present world-class music and theater on a weekly basis and should draw even more cultural tourists to the area. When we moved here, we joked that all the area lacked was a good foreign-film house, but within a year, Pocono Cinema and Coffee Shop was bringing in movies the more commercial theaters won't show.

We're close enough to New York City, Bethlehem/Allentown, and Scranton/Wilkes-Barre that you might consider a trip into the city for some special event. Every Friday, the *Pocono Record*'s "Weekend" section runs a comprehensive list of nightspots and concert and theater performances happening both locally and in nearby cities. A look at that section will convince you that there's plenty to do in the Poconos after the sun sets.

BARS AND NIGHTCLUBS

The number of places offering live music is astounding and, contrary to trends in other parts of the country, much of the music is original. Make sure you get a chance to hear some of our terrific local musicians. Even if you're not a smoker, be prepared to suck in a little secondhand smoke. Although some clubs have good air filtration systems, most nightlife spots in the Poconos feature tobacco smoke as part of their atmosphere.

Delaware Water Gap/ Shawnee-on-Delaware

The Deer Head Inn
5 Main Street, Delaware Water Gap
(570) 424-2000
www.deerheadinn.com
This is an extraordinary club with excellent food and world-class jazz. (See our Close-up in this chapter for more information on the Deer Head Inn.)

Minisink Hotel
River Road, Minisink Hills
(570) 421-9787

Tucked next to a stream on twisty River Road, the Minisink Hotel looks like the quintessential rural tavern. Inside there's an excellent menu that's available until closing time (see our Restaurants chapter), a pool table, wood stove, old-fashioned steel-tip dartboard, and a great juke box stocked with lots of Bob Dylan and other favorites from the '60s. Some of the more interesting characters from around the area frequent this bar, and the crowd is friendly. Locals love the Minisink.

Stroudsburg/East Stroudsburg

The Hoop
745 Main Street, Stroudsburg
(570) 424-1950
www.hoopclubvogue.net

One of the largest nightclubs in the Poconos, the Hoop is an easily recognized landmark in downtown Stroudsburg. The complex consists of a 1950s-style diner attached to the front of a Victorian mansion like some kind of bizarre bay window. On the first floor, amid the chrome diner fixtures, live bands—with an emphasis on Jersey shore and Philly bands—perform Thursday through Saturday. Between sets, a DJ ensconced in a 1956 Buick 8 spins. Club Vogue, a New York–style dance club with black lights, and a strobe fills the second floor. If you get tired of the noise, head for the outdoor deck with a full bar, where you can talk or watch the street life below. On the third floor, the Play Pen offers TVs and a pool table. Most of the patrons of the Play Pen end up hanging over the rail, watching the dancers one floor down.

On a weekend night, this place is hopping, with a line out front and a no-nonsense bouncer who cards everyone. The Hoop is open Monday and Wednesday through Saturday, drawing a young

Many people get confused by our arcane liquor laws when they want to buy alcoholic beverages. You can buy a six-pack of beer at most bars and a case or more at a beer distributor. Some microbreweries also sell beer to go. Wine and hard liquor are available at a Pennsylvania State Store.

crowd of vacationers, locals, and college students from nearby East Stroudsburg University.

Lackawanna Hotel and Tavern
87 Crystal Street, East Stroudsburg
(570) 424-1441

Most nights the Lackawanna is your basic smoky drinker's bar, but Stan, the owner, is the local boom-bas guru, and if you can convince him to play, the place will be transformed.

For the uninitiated, a boom-bas is a person-size stick with a kind of pogo attachment at the bottom. Cymbals hung with sleigh bells, a tambourine, cowbell, and wooden block complete the get-up. The accomplished boom-bas player bounces the stick on the ground and then hits one of the attachments to the accompaniment of the Lackawanna's great juke box, whose selections range from "The Clarinet Polka" to "Orange Blossom Special." Stan encourages newcomers to try one of his boom-bas sticks and even has a young disciple who says, "Stan taught me everything I know." Although the boom-bas is trickier than it looks, Stan says, "As long as you have rhythm, you can play."

The drinks are cheap, and the folks are friendly, especially when the boom-bas bounce.

Sarah Street Grill
550 Quaker Alley, Stroudsburg
(570) 424-9120
www.sarahstreetgrill.com

Sarah Street Grill is the place to be, and all the cool people are here. Students from ESU, their professors, artists, real estate

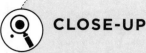

If You Like Jazz, You'll Love the Deer Head

Delaware Water Gap has a hot reputation as a jazz town, and the Deer Head Inn is the hub of the jazz community. Music is the main course every Friday and Saturday night and Sunday afternoon. Since the local musicians tour internationally, whether you see someone who lives up the block or someone who's just here for the weekend, you'll be watching world-class jazz in an intimate setting. The food is terrific too, so bring your appetite. (See our Restaurants chapter.) Half the room is designated as a no-smoking section, and the architecture of the club keeps the air mostly clear on that side.

One of two remaining hotels from the days when Delaware Water Gap was a top tourist town, the Deer Head has been presenting jazz since the '50s, making it one of the longest-running clubs in the country. If you're lucky, local musicians will stop by, and you'll be treated to an impromptu jam session. A $5.00 to $10.00 cover charge (Friday and Saturday only; Sunday there's no cover) will get you a seat close to some of the best jazz anywhere. If you reserve a spot here, be prepared to spend at least $10 on food.

Because of our proximity to New York City, our reasonable cost of living, and because the big resorts once provided steady work for top musicians, many performers known around the world live in the area, and the Deer Head books them as often as it can get them. Among the locals you might see here are:

- Phil Woods, who has been called the heir to Charlie Parker and the best living saxophone player.
- Bob Dorough, best known for writing and singing much of the cartoon series "Schoolhouse Rock," and one of the few vocalists to record with Miles Davis. Dorough is a witty, engaging performer.
- Dave Liebman, a prodigiously creative composer, revered around the world for his avant-garde work on saxophone. His master classes inspire the next generation of players.
- Urbie Green, a master trombone player who played with Benny Goodman, among others. His son Jesse, an up-and-coming pianist, plays the Deer Head frequently.
- Kim Parker, stepdaughter of both Charlie Parker and Phil Woods. Kim's whole life has been steeped in jazz. (A piece of her childhood was portrayed in Clint Eastwood's *Bird*.) She's a passionate vocalist and is revered in Europe.
- Howie Collins, known for his seven-string guitar playing. Howie played with many of the greats, including Peggy Lee, George Shearing, and Wynton Marsalis. One cut he's not so proud of playing on is "Corinna, Corinna" on Bob Dylan's first album (he wasn't impressed with Dylan). Howie doesn't lead a band, but you might catch him backing up the engaging vocalist and piano player Donna Antonow.

The Deer Head Inn is one of the longest running jazz clubs in the country. JANET BREGMAN-TANEY

Even if you're not able to catch one of our world-famous locals, you're bound to see great music here. Some of the "local" performers, such as Rick Chamberlain, Jerry Harris, Eric and Vicki Doney, Janet Lawson, Alex Watkins, Jesse Green, Mike Melillo, and Nelson Hill, have either studied with our better-known artists or have played with them frequently. Some of them are building careers and you can catch them on the upswing. With such high standards locally, when the Deer Head brings in out-of-towners, you can bet they'll be top-notch, too.

The Deer Head helped spawn Delaware Water Gap's Celebration of the Arts jazz festival, which runs the weekend after Labor Day right across the street. (See our Annual Events chapter for a complete description.)

agents, and attorneys pack into a long narrow room when one of the area's top acoustic singles or bands plays—and there's live music here most days. Many good business and romantic connections start in this room. If you don't like being a sardine, you can move into the room on the side or, in summer, onto the outdoor deck where you can still hear the live music over speakers.

Sarah Street has an excellent reputation for its food. (See our Restaurants chapter.) Wednesday's open-mike night has been known to attract some of the area's best performers. There's high-quality live, original music here every day of the week, except during football season, when live NFL games play for avid fans on a dozen TVs, including two big-screen boxes. Check out the sushi bar, too, open Tuesday through Saturday for dinner.

Mount Pocono Area

The Abbey at Swiftwater Inn
Highway 611, Swiftwater
(570) 839-7206
For a bar in a mammoth old inn, the Abbey is remarkably small. On Friday the room is packed for live bands. If you don't

get a seat, expect to stand along a wall. The lucky few snag one of the handful of tables in front of the band. If you want to play pool, you have to walk through the stage area, around the band's equipment and up a couple of steps. The cramped quarters only add to the festive atmosphere. The Abbey is popular with area residents, employees of Aventis Pasteur Laboratories (right across the highway), and guests of nearby resorts who are out for a night of local entertainment. There's karaoke here on Sunday, too. The Swiftwater Inn has been serving guests since 1778 and is on the National Register of Historic Places. (See our Restaurants chapter.)

Barley Creek Brewing Company
Sullivan Trail and Camelback Road
Tannersville
(570) 629-9399
www.barleycreek.com
You'll think you're in Colorado in this spacious après-ski–style room with beautiful wooden beams designed by Ted Benson, a frequent guest on public-television's This Old House. The customers, seated around long wooden tables, all look happy—probably because the beer's so good. Barley Creek is a microbrewery with an adventurous brewer. In the seven years it has been in operation, this establishment has put out just about any style of beer you can think of, plus some you would never imagine. Traditional beers range from American brown ale to a dark German lager. Some of the more adventurous selections include an oatmeal stout and a chocolate porter. The beers are especially yummy because the brewers use only the best malted barley, 150-year-old Ringwood yeast, and very pure water from Barley Creek's own artesian well. If you want to know what Ringwood yeast is, take the tour of the brewery, offered Monday through Friday at 12:30 P.M.

The restaurant offers an unusual menu including lots of English food (see our Restaurants chapter), but the place is

hopping on weekends. Friday and Saturday, acoustic singles, duos, and the occasional band help keep the hills alive with
the sound of music (Barley Creek is 2
miles shy of the Camelback Ski Area; see
our Winter Sports chapter). If you fall in
love with the place and want everybody
to know, visit the brewtique, featuring lots
of Barley Creek shirts and stuff.

During the summer you can sit at their
outdoor deck bar enjoying the magic of a
Pocono evening, and you can play wiffle
ball in Barley Creek's new stadium dedicated to the sport. Barley Creek sponsors
several special events including a Brew-
grass Festival and the Great Pocono Wing
Off. Even if you don't like beer, you'll like
Barley Creek.

Lopsided Inn
Highway 196, Tobyhanna
(570) 839-8421

The Lopsided Inn is your basic Pocono
working-class bar—smoky, friendly, and
fun. On Friday and Saturday nights, everyone gets lopsided and dances to tunes
spun by a DJ. (See our Restaurants chapter for more information.)

Memorytown Tavern
Grange Road, Mount Pocono
(570) 839-1680
www.memorytownusa.com

Part of a complex of shops, this tavern
features live music on the weekends, usually classic rock, sometimes country. The
decor might remind you of what would
happen if there were an explosion in your
grandparents' attic. Funhouse mirrors and
a vintage scale at the entrance give a hint
of the surprises inside. Shotguns, a sleigh,
a canoe, a large drum, mounted fish,
mounted animal heads of species
unknown, and vintage tools fill every available inch of wall and ceiling space. You
will enjoy sitting at a table and trying to
identify the odd accessories that surround
you—or at least making up uses for them.
The Tavern serves more than 70 beers
from around the world, and the view of

the lake is beautiful. In good weather, you
can sit on a lovely outdoor deck.

Pocono Brewing Company
Highway 611, Swiftwater
(570) 839-3230
www.poconobrewingcompany.com

This popular restaurant/night spot offers
an assorted menu of activities. On weekends, there's often live music or a DJ in
the restaurant, a spacious room with
cathedral ceilings, wooden beams, and a
huge stage. They favor blues at PBC, but
cover-bands also play here. Frequent special events, such as a Cinco de Mayo celebration and an all-male revue, notch up
the atmosphere.

You enter through the 3rd Base Sports
Pub sporting several large satellite TVs
pledged to live sporting events. The bar is
crowded, noisy, and happy with a mix of
folks just off work mingling with tourists.
A greenhouse room houses a pool table
and video games. You can get lunch or
dinner (see our Restaurant chapter) or
just snack and drink. More than 100 beers
from around the world, at least 33 of them
on draft, are offered here. There's a good
selection of "New Age Beverages," too,
including several hard ciders.

Although a large hexagonal room contains brewing equipment, after PBC built
their brewing room, they discovered that
Pennsylvania law says that if you brew
your own, that's the only beer you can
carry. Choosing to offer lots of beers, PBC
contracted with another brewery to produce a Pocono Brewing Company Ball
and Chain Lager as well as a Black Ghost
Porter. The still is strictly decoration, but
the beer is varied and delicious.

The Tannersville Inn
Highway 611, Tannersville
(570) 629-3131
www.tannersvilleinn.com

On Friday, you can take part in a hilarious murder-mystery dinner theater, but you must reserve a spot ahead of time. There's a buffet and two hours of interactive laughter. It's a tad risqué, so you must be 18 or older to join the fun. Catch the live bands—usually blues, rock, or bluegrass—and bar food specials here, Thursday through Sunday. The owner is a real character and loves to make sure everybody has a good time at this comfortable establishment. (See our Restaurant chapter for more information.)

Milford/Lake Wallenpaupack Area

Alley Oops Pub
Apple Valley Village, U.S. Highway 6
Milford
(570) 296-6831
www.newsfax.com

There's live entertainment here on Friday and Saturday. Alley Oops features acoustic musicians, blues bands, and eclectic music. There's no cover except on special comedy nights, which feature three comedians plus live music. Alley Oops features a different special on food and spirits every night of the week. The pub, attached to the Apple Valley Restaurant, is one of those fun places with lots of neat stuff on the walls.

Tom Quick Inn Sports Bar
411 Broad Street, Milford
(570) 296-6514
www.tomquickinn.com

At the back of the Tom Quick Inn (see our Restaurants and Accommodations chapters), this sports bar is much larger than it appears from the outside. The saloon has knotty pine walls and televisions all over. Watch out for the bar snacks—the portions are enormous. Games include air hockey, pool, pinball, and darts. There's an open mike on Tuesday, karaoke on Wednesday, and a DJ spinning music for dancing on Friday and Saturday nights. Being close to the courthouse, the saloon fills up on Friday when attorneys and government workers unwind after a long week. Make sure you try the Tom Quick root beer.

RESORT NIGHTLIFE

Resort entertainment takes many forms. Nearly every type of resort has at least a cocktail lounge. Many of the larger resorts have shows on weekends. Some book well-known comedians and musicians. If you're staying at the resort, you may receive complimentary tickets for the show with your room package.

Spend a few hours in a quiet bar, sipping brandy by a fire, or go for the noise and glitter of the big shows. Either way, you can have a taste of the resort experience, and you don't necessarily have to stay there. Of course, if you find you like the ambiance, you may end up booking your next vacation at a resort.

The four Caesars resorts (Cove Haven, Paradise Stream, Pocono Palace, and Brookdale) are famous for hosting comedians such as Jay Leno, Dennis Miller, Elayne Boosler, and Howie Mandel. Oldies acts are popular at most of the Pocono resorts; some devote entire weekends to them. In addition to big names, many resorts have local bands playing dance music in their lounges. These are usually open to the public, frequently without a cover charge. More detail on the resort facilities may be found in our Accommodations chapter. All the lounges mentioned here are open to the public.

Delaware Water Gap/ Shawnee-on-Delaware

Fernwood
U.S. Highway 209, Bushkill
(888) FERNWOOD
www.resortsusa.com

Fernwood offers cabaret nights in Mama Bella's, live music in the Trolley Stop Pub, and occasional nationally known comedians and musical acts in the Events Center. If you like fireworks, drop by on a Friday night in the summer. Fernwood's July 4th spectacular includes a fair, a band, and an excellent fireworks display. The resort regularly hosts professional wrestling, and it's a kick (not literally) to see those wrestlers walking around the grounds—they're not as big as they look on TV!

Shawnee Inn
River Road, Shawnee-on-Delaware
(800) SHAWNEE
www.shawneeinn.com

Riverdance, the Shawnee Inn's outdoor riverside restaurant, offers warm weather entertainment many evenings. It's a lovely spot to sit with a drink, listen to music, and watch the Delaware River's dark waters passing. Charlie's Lounge, too, hosts live music. The rest of the year you might find karaoke on Friday and live music on Saturday, but it depends on the crowd, so call first to see if something is scheduled. Charlie's Lounge offers light dinners, big-screen TV, and a pool table. Most nights, the patrons of Charlie's Lounge are denizens of the resort and go to bed early so they can greet the sunrise on the golf course.

Charlie's is a great place to go during the day, when you can sit near the window and watch egrets in the wetlands at the edge of the golf course. In winter, grab a hot toddy and sit in front of the fireplace just outside the bar. On a summer evening, take a glass of wine to the front porch of the Shawnee Inn and watch the stars come out over the Kittatinny Ridge.

You don't necessarily have to be a guest at a resort to take part in its nightlife. Call the resort that interests you to find out if members of the public are welcome in their nightclubs. ℹ

The inn has revived a tradition made popular by Fred Waring—summer evening concerts on the lawn. These take place on Tuesday nights and they're free, although you're encouraged to make a donation. Get there early, or bring your own lawn chair. Refreshments are available during intermission. During winter, the Tuesday night concerts are held in the lobby by the fireplace.

Stroudsburg/East Stroudsburg

Hillside Inn
Frutchey Drive, East Stroudsburg
(570) 223-8238
www.poconohillside.com

The club's name, the Walnut Room, originates from a large walnut tree that fell in the old outdoor swimming pool and was used to build the bar. Dancing and a disk jockey provide Friday's entertainment. Live music, often jazz, fills the club on many Saturdays.

Penn Hills Resort
Highway 447, Analomink
(570) 421-6464,(800) 233-8240
www.pennhillsresort.com

Any night of the week you'll find musicians, bands, magicians, comedians, and Penn Hill's own game shows, all in Reflections Night Club. Events are held nightly and begin at 8:00 P.M. with no cover or minimum drink charge. Penn Hills tries to vary the entertainment but emphasizes quality. The atmosphere is casual, and remember that this is a couples resort—so while lots of locals come here on a regular

Many of the local performers sell their tapes and CDs at their gigs. You won't find these recordings at your nearest Tower Records, so if you like the music, buy the tape. You'll be supporting the arts and bringing home a special souvenir.

basis, most people are attached. If you're looking for romance, you're not likely to find a new person here. Reservations are recommended on the weekends, when there's a show, but they're not required.

Mount Pocono Area

Caesars Brookdale on the Lake
Highway 611, Scotrun
(570) 839-8844
www.caesarspoconoresorts.com
One of four Caesars resorts in the Poconos, Brookdale features comedians and magicians, and bands in the Applause Night Club. Try a special drink called the Caesars Passion Potion and keep the glass. There is plenty of room for dancing. Away from the dance floor, the Rolls Royce Lounge, has a large-screen television. Since Brookdale is the one Caesars resort for families, they also have lots of entertainment geared to children—watch for clowns, jugglers, snake and animal shows, magicians, and Hawaiian dancers.

The Caesars resorts, especially Cove Haven, regularly book nationally known comedians and oldies music acts. Tickets are included with room packages or may be purchased by the general public.

The other Caesars resorts have similar lounges and clubs with dance music and live entertainment nightly. they are: Caesars Paradise Stream (Highway 940, Mount Pocono; 570-839-8881), Caesars Cove Haven (Highway 590, Lakeville [near Lake Wallenpaupack]; 570-226-4506), and Caesars Pocono Palace (US 209, Marshalls Creek; 570-588-6692).

Crescent Lodge
Highway 191, Paradise Valley
(570) 595-7486
www.crescentlodge.com
Every Friday, Saturday, and Sunday, this award-winning country inn features piano in the lounge.

West End

The Resort at Split Rock
Lake Drive, Lake Harmony
(570) 722-9111
www.splitrockresort.com
The Rock Bar at the Lodge has live bands Friday and Saturday. Check out the game room with billiards, darts, and some favorite games from your past. Open daily, weather permitting. The Galleria Night Club offers live music every night but Sunday. Saturday a comedian or magician trades sets with the band.

NEARBY LIVE-MUSIC VENUES

A number of venues within a one-hour drive of the Poconos feature nationally known bands, comedians, theatrical productions, and classical music performances.

F.M. Kirby Center for the Performing Arts
71 Public Square, Wilkes-Barre
(570) 826-1100
www.kirbycenter.org
F.M. Kirby Center is a beautiful old theater hosting concerts by the Northeastern Pennsylvania Philharmonic as well as dance, film, and theater performances. World-famous performers—including such diverse talents as Cyndi Lauper, Jerry Seinfeld, and Jewel—have appeared here too.

Godfrey Daniels
7 East Fourth Street, Bethlehem
(610) 867-2390
www.godfreydaniels.org
Godfrey's is a folk music club that has

been around so long it attracts big names despite its small size. John Gorka got his start here and returns regularly. Call or check the Web site for a schedule. If you're planning on going to Godfrey's, make reservations; the small room often sells out.

Montage Mountain Performing Arts Center
I-81 at exit 51, Scranton
(570) 961-9000
www.montage-mountain.com

During the summer, Montage hosts a concert series that usually begins in early June. Sting, the Allman Brothers Band, Bob Seger, Rod Stewart, and Ozzy Osbourne are just a few of the acts that have played this lovely outdoor arena. The stage is set at the bottom of a ski slope on top of a mountain overlooking the Wyoming Valley. Concertgoers may either purchase reserved seats at the base of the mountain or bring a blanket and choose a spot on the slope to relax under the stars. Tickets are available at the box office or through TicketMaster outlets. To charge by phone, call (570) 693-4100. (See our Day Trips chapter for additional information.)

Scranton Cultural Center
Masonic Temple, 420 North Washington Street, Scranton
(570) 344-1111, (888) 669-8966
www.scrantonculturalcenter.org

Scranton Cultural Center's home is in the Masonic Temple and Scottish Rite Cathedral—an excellent example of art deco architecture and part of the Lackawanna Heritage Valley (see our Day Trips chapter). They host performances by national and local touring companies, children's theater, and Scranton Community Concerts. Call or visit their Web site for the latest performance schedule and ticket prices. Tickets are available at the box office or through TicketMaster, (570) 693-4100.

Can't get enough of that jazz? Check out East Stroudsburg University's Jazz Master Series, with lectures by working jazz musicians twice a week during the fall or spring semesters. It's free and open to the public. Call the university for more information, or watch the paper for listings.

Stabler Arena
124 Goodman Drive, Bethlehem
(610) 758-6611
www.stablerarena.com

On the campus of Lehigh University in Bethlehem, Stabler Arena is used mainly as a basketball court, but well-known bands and other types of shows perform here too. Years ago, Billy Joel played a show here as a gesture to the fans he immortalized in his song "Allentown." More recently, Hootie and the Blowfish spent the day at the amusement park Dorney Park before spending the evening performing at Stabler. A few moments from that day were included in a video the band released in 1995. Concerts are held throughout the year. To purchase tickets, contact either the box office or TicketMaster outlets (215-336-2000).

The Stanhope House
Main and High Streets, Stanhope, NJ
(973) 347-0458
www.stanhopehouse.com

Living blues legends and the best young prospects regularly visit this club that's just east of the Poconos across the Delaware River. Its well-worn roadhouse character creates the best atmosphere for regional rock and blues musicians. Stanhope House has a three-song limit. If you

East Stroudsburg University often has special events and concerts that are open to the public. Check the Pocono Record's "Weekend" section for listings.

don't like the music, and you leave before the end of the third song, you can get your money back.

State Theatre
453 Northampton Street
(610) 252-3132, (800) 999-STATE
www.statetheatre.org
In Easton along the Lehigh River, this majestic theater has been fully restored to the ornate palace it was in 1920s. In addition to lavish stage production, the theater hosts big-name comedians, singers, jazz, and classical performers as well as children's theater. The State even has its own ghost whom they have named Fred and believe is the man who managed the theater company there between 1936 and 1965.

Wachovia Arena at Casey Plaza
255 Highland Boulevard, Wilkes-Barre
(570) 970-7600
www.wachoviaarena.com
A hockey rink, this concert hall is right off

exit 168 of Interstate 81. Big-name acts such as Sting, Brooks and Dunn, and Korn play here.

MOVIE THEATERS

Movies are perhaps the Poconos' weakest entertainment point. We do have a fair number of screens, and we get all the big movies, but many of the same films are shown from theater to theater, and we often have to turn to the video stores to catch up on the ones we miss.

Pocono Cinema & Coffee Shop does a lot toward bringing in the art movies and the ones the other theaters miss, but they have only three screens and can't catch everything. There's talk of building more theaters, but nothing solid, so far. Milford hosts the Black Bear Film Festival each year in October, bringing in independent films and film industry professionals (see Annual Events).

Sit-down Cinemas

The movie theaters in the Poconos include the following.

- Casino Theater (Pocono Boulevard [Highway 611], Mount Pocono; 570-839-7831, www.mountpocono.com) has only one screen, but there's a large ice cream parlor and sandwich shop in the lobby, a video game room to one side and a 19-hole miniature golf course outside. The theater is an old-fashioned 300-seater with a wide screen. They concentrate on family movies, although the R-rated ones are often shown later at night. They show movies that have been out a couple of weeks, so they can keep their prices very low. The Casino Theater is a great place for a birthday party.
- Cinema 6-Honesdale (Route 6 Plaza, Honesdale; 570-251-FILM, www.holly wood.com) has six screens, some with

digital sound and some with stereo surround sound. Waiting for the movie to start? You can pass the time at the theater's video arcade.

- Foxmoor Cinemas (Foxmoor Outlet Complex, US 209, Marshalls Creek; 570–223–7775, www.hollywood.com), has a video arcade and seven small theaters showing first-run, popular films.
- Loews (Stroud Mall, Highway 611, Stroudsburg; 570–421–5703, www.enjoytheshow.com) has seven screens offering the current movie hits in two mall locations. If you catch the early show, you can have dinner in the mall's food court.
- Mahoning Valley Cinema (Carbon Plaza Mall, Highway 443, Lehighton; 570–386–4406, www.mvcinema.com) with eight screens, offers first-run movies with digital surround sound.
- Pocono Cinema & Coffee Shop (88 South Courtland Street, East Stroudsburg; 570–421–FILM, www.pocono cinema.com). With three screens and lots of extras, Pocono Cinema & Coffee Shop offers foreign films and arthouse hits that don't run at the more commercial theaters, as well as films they think deserve more play than they get at the other local theaters. Leave a little extra time before the movie, because there's a coffee shop that sells cappuccino and lattes along with some excellent pas-

tries. There's an art gallery in the lobby that features the work of local artists. The theaters have incredible sound, with Dolby, full stereo surround, which fools you into thinking you're in the middle of the movie. If you're here on a date, look for a love seat in the third row from the back on the left in each theater. The green theater has a second love seat in the third row from the back on the right. Assisted listening devices are available.

- Tri-State Theatres (US 6 and US 209, Matamoras; 570–491–5000) has a drive-in screen in addition to its two indoor screens that offer at least one first-run film.

Drive-ins

Drive-in theaters evoke visions of ponytails, poodle skirts, and really bad movies. In most places they're extinct, but we have one in the Poconos. There aren't enough drive-ins to run specially made bad movies anymore, so these two carry first-run movies, though they get horror when they can. Drive-ins are fun for their own sake. Within our region are:

- Tri State Theatres (US 6 and US 209, Matamoras; 570–491–5000) also has an indoor cinema.

SHOPPING 🎁

or shoppers, the Poconos have it all, from the Crossings, where 106 heavily discounted factory outlets compete for your attention, to a raffish flea market on U.S. Highway 209 known to locals as "Little Baghdad," to American Candle where candles, though numbered in the thousands, constitute only a tiny fraction of the available merchandise. Meanwhile, merchants on our main streets do business in the charm of a Victorian ambiance unmatched anywhere. Best of all, Pennsylvania imposes no sales tax on clothing or groceries (food only), which probably is why cars bearing New York and New Jersey license plates flock to the area all year like weekend refugees.

Whatever your reason for shopping, you'll find plenty of choices here. Needless to say, we could not physically visit every wonderful shop, outlet, boutique, antique store, or jewelry showcase in the region. There simply are too many of them, and while we strove to take in as many as possible, what is discussed here represents only a fraction of the whole, so go out and explore for more on your own. You'll be glad you did.

In this chapter, we focus on the wide range of merchandise offered and provide a brief snapshot of the main streets down which your shopping foray will take you. But main streets are not the only places to hunt for bargains.

As we noted in our Getting Around chapter, the Poconos region is comprised primarily of country roads. To get from one place to another, you must travel a distance on at least one of these picturesque Pennsylvania byways—interstates and four-laners are only peripherally involved in our town-to-town travel. That means you constantly—almost every other mile—come upon a delightful shop that will cause you to blurt out, "Stop here! Stop there! I want to see what they have."

Most of the shops we have noted are on a secondary Pennsylvania highway, such as 940, 611, or 191; these establishments are not alone. As you head toward one, you're such to find 10 more shops along the way. So enjoy your tour of the Poconos; check out our Getting Around chapter to see where you'll end up; and experience the fun of discovering a special shop.

Of course, if you want to shop, you need money. In case you run out, there are plenty of banks around; or if you are shopping for loans, CDs, or IRAS, you'll certainly find a bank to help you out. Three area banks with offices all around the region are PNC Bank, Mellon Bank, and Nazareth National Bank. PNC is almost nationwide and has locations in every major area of the Poconos and on many of the routes we point out to you here and in our Getting Around chapter. For information about locations, call (800) 443-2347; you can even access your PNC accounts and do your checkbook balancing through this customer-service response line.

The central number for Mellon is (800) 635-5662. The Nazareth National Bank has branches in Stroudsburg, East Stroudsburg in the Wal-Mart superstore, and in Brodheadsville. Nazareth's central number is (800) 996-2062.

Most stores accept major credit cards, and a growing number of stores are equipped with systems that accept your ATM card for purchases, deducting the amount directly from your checking account. Some merchants take local checks from customers with enough identification (driver's license and credit card); in the very large complexes, some stores are more willing to accept an out-of-state check. Crossings Factory Outlets, Foxmoor, most shopping malls, and Wal-Mart all have ATMs on-site, so you can get cash if you need it. ATMs also are available at virtually every bank in the Poconos, and you'll find banks along every Pocono road.

OUTLETS AND MALLS

The Poconos are full of outlet complexes, some small and some large; this area also has stand-alone outlet stores, the Stroud Mall, and mainly minimalls. In this section we highlight representative stores in outlet complexes, independent outlets, and notable malls and minimalls. Some points of note before we jump into a shopping frenzy: First, store hours change depending on the day and season; we have included a main number for each outlet complex, so you can call ahead to verify hours before you go to shop. Second, please note that retail outlet stores come and go (another good reason to call ahead), so hurry up and shop—so many stores, so little time!

Delaware Water Gap/ Shawnee-on-Delaware

Foxmoor Village Outlet Center
U.S. Highway 209, Marshalls Creek
(570) 223-0165
Foxmoor is designed like a small village; there is even a little bridge to cross the stream that runs through the site. All paths lead inward to a central gazebo with benches, shrubbery, bright flowers in season, and a view of all directions in which your family members or friends might have wandered in search of bargains. You can sit here and let the children play, or eat an ice cream cone and enjoy the view. Brandli's Pizza, Pasta, and Vino (see our Restaurants chapter) and the Foxmoor Cinemas (see our Nightlife chapter) are also here; so when you're tired of shopping, you can catch a meal and a show.

Many inward-facing outdoor malls, like Foxmoor, face a challenge in reeling in customers. Foxmoor has never achieved its

potential customer-wise, but there are a few great stores you'll want to know about. The notable shops here are the Book Warehouse and Sneakers Unlimited. These stores are covered in their own categories, subsequently. Sangoma, an organic day spa, can also provide a good break from the shopping experience. The YMCA has a branch here, too, which we hope will bring in more shoppers and more success to the other stores at Foxmoor.

Odd-Lot Outlet
US 209, Marshalls Creek
(570) 476-1900
www.oddlotoutlet.com
Odd-Lot is aptly named; it has thousands of odd items including the things you've seen in those catalogs that stuff your mailbox. These items can't be sold in stores because they aren't appropriately packaged. Odd-Lot sells them for less than half the catalog price, without shipping and handling charges, and you can examine the merchandise and see if it's worth buying. Of course, with the magic of the Internet, Odd-Lot Outlet now makes many of those items available by cyber-order, still at enormous discounts.

Odd-Lot claims to be the largest seller of Poconos souvenirs—T-shirts, key chains, mugs, salt and pepper shakers, and so on. Odd-Lot Outlet has a free gift bar from which everyone in the store, even those who don't buy anything, are welcome to select a gift.

Stroudsburg/East Stroudsburg

Pocono Outlet Complex
South Ninth and Ann Streets
Stroudsburg
(570) 421-7470
www.americanribbon.com
This complex supports a group of outlets rimming the American Ribbon Store, which is housed in a historic textile mill

(the textiles industry was once strong in this region). There are new stores opening up all the time, and we focus on some here, while others will be placed in their own categorical sections of this chapter.

American Ribbon is loaded with ribbons for every need and an extensive selection of supplies for making bridal favors, decorations, and other wedding novelties. The sister store is American Ribbon Fabric, with fabric and needlework supplies as well as foam, batting, and other necessities for the serious seamstress, upholsterer, or crafter—all in one well-stocked location.

The already cavernous building recently has been expanded to house a fully equipped sewing center and a hobby shop with several model trains running through displays of every conceivable craft.

While Earthlight Natural Foods is not an outlet shop, it is an excellent, extensive collection of healthy foods, as well as bulk spices and grains, beauty products, and books.

Pro-Art carries professional art supplies and offers classes.

The Potting Shed has a huge selection of silk flowers, foliage, houseplants, and dried flowers.

At Gary's Meat Market, you'll find an old-fashioned butcher shop, and Keyco Warehouse sells bulk discount food to restaurants and to individuals.

Pocono Outlet Complex is open every day except Christmas, New Year's, and Thanksgiving.

Stroud Mall
North Ninth Street, Stroudsburg
(570) 424-2770
www.stroud-mall.com
This mall, anchored by Sears, JCPenney, and the Bon-Ton, has more than 65 specialty shops and smaller stores representing national, regional, and local merchants. All shops are on one level; the only second-floor is in the Sears section, which introduced the area's first escalator when it opened. Merchandise here, in what amounts to an air-conditioned indoor city, is as varied as any city's main street would offer. You'll find VCR tapes, dress shops, cut-rate shoes, countless gift items, and household accessories, some of which are sold throughout the year from little vendors' carts throughout the mall.

Needless to say, there is no room here to list all the shops in this complex. A few will be described where applicable under their own categories elsewhere in this chapter.

If you need a place to sit (other than the many benches that line the center of the mall), you can relax and grab a bite to eat at the Pavilion Food Court, a little oasis of fast-food outlets serving everything from hamburgers and ice cream to pizza.

Stroud Mall has an information desk next to Sears where wheelchairs are available for free for those who need them; strollers are available for rent. Multiplex movie theaters are in two parts of the mall.

Mount Pocono Area

Crossings Factory Stores
Highway 611, Tannersville
(570) 629–4650
www.thecrossings.com
By far the largest and most impressive factory outlet mall in the Poconos and, according to many sources, America's top factory store outlet, the Crossings Factory Stores in Tannersville is immediately off Interstate 80 exit 299. This beautiful complex of eight buildings, is literally at the crossroads of

I-80 and Highways 611 and 715. The complex has 100 stores and has been expanding ever since its opening in August 1991. An estimated 30,000 shoppers are in the Crossings whenever the parking lot is full, and it is full most of the time.

Stores in the complex offer prices that almost give you a license to steal on an expansive line of designer clothing, shoes, housewares, and other top-of-the-market merchandise. We do not attempt to list them all here, but there are a few specialty outlets, inclusion of which will be made under their specific sections elsewhere in this chapter.

The only downside to shopping at the Crossings—especially on summer weekends—is traffic gridlock. The traffic flow off I-80 and from Highway 611 south frequently is bumper-to-bumper. Avoid the crowds and traffic by arriving at 10:00 A.M. just as the stores open. Still, shopping at the Crossings is an adventure, especially at Christmas when the sales are incredible. You can pick up such wonderful stocking stuffers and gift items as silver, brass, afghans, table linens, framed art, clever toys, and puzzles from all over the world, along with T-shirts, caps, and trendy clothing.

If you need to replenish your strength to continue shopping this multilevel smorgasbord of designer and famous-brand shops, stop at the food court at the end of Building B where a fast-food menu ranging from pizza to Oriental favorites can be found.

West End

Pocono Sweater Mills
US 209, Brodheadsville
(570) 992-5111

Compared with the shopping metropolis at the Crossings, this little factory outlet is less than a village, but its prices are just as impressive. This is a great place for women's clothing, where skirts, jackets, and sweaters are priced at 30–60 percent less than retail.

The Crossings, at Tannersville, is the largest factory outlet complex in the Poconos, but another is on the way. Watch for it, in Minisink Hills, right where Highway 209 and I-80 intersect.

FARMERS MARKETS, FARM STANDS, AND ORCHARDS

The Pocono region is farm country, and throughout summer and autumn, a cornucopia of sun-ripened fruits and vegetables can be found along the side of area roads as family farms, orchards, and truck gardens offer their wares directly to the public. Most stands carry a wide assortment of flowers and culinary herbs.

As you drive along our many country roads (see our Getting Around chapter to get your bearings), you will spot little signs scrawled on oak tag with arrows pointing to a lush harvest of tomatoes, sweet corn, melons, peppers, summer squash, zucchinis, red potatoes, broccoli, cucumbers, pickle cucumbers, peaches, and more. In fall, you'll see signs for apples—Macs, Cortlands, red and golden delicious—by the basket, half-basket, peck, even pick-your-own (great fun and a cost-saver). In June you can pick your own strawberries; throughout summer, pick your own blueberries and peaches. Look in the Pocono Record's "Classified" section and throughout the paper for who's selling what, when, and where.

We include some well-known farmers markets for you, but it's also fun to discover your own special farmer or market. So don't forget to look for the signs as you drive along the country byways that crisscross the Pocono Mountains. Fresh-grown delights await at stands along virtually every road. Even if you don't see anyone tending the stand, stop and see what's available. Many farmers operate on the honor system: Weigh your tomatoes, peppers, or squash; count out your ears of corn; then drop what you owe into the

Look for fresh cider at the farm stand and farmers' markets as soon as you see apples coming up for sale. You can't beat fresh apple cider, hot or cold!

moneybox. In a heartwarming throwback to how things used to be, these folks trust you. It's a great reason to come here!

Delaware Water Gap/ Shawnee-on-Delaware

Pocono Bazaar Flea Market
US 209, Marshalls Creek
(570) 223-8640
www.poconobazaar.com
While most folks come for the fleas, the Pocono Bazaar Flea Market has a good selection of produce, spices, fresh mozzarella, and baked goods.

The Village Farmer & Bakery
13 Broad Street, Delaware Water Gap
(570) 476-0075
This great little farm market specializes in locally grown, in-season fruits and vegetables, including strawberries, apples, fresh cider, blueberries, tomatoes, broccoli, and our August delight—corn. Even more than produce, you'll find baked items here, especially their famous pies—more than 40 different varieties, including blueberry, blackberry, pumpkin, strawberry, rhubarb,

The Farmers' Market on Main Street in Stroudsburg is a great shopping experience. It's a good place to get organic produce, fresh cheese, handmade soap, and baked goods, and it's a social event. Folks take the time to visit with friends and neighbors they encounter at the market. Try Pocono garlic, the crop for which our region is best known.

red raspberry, apple, and shoo-fly. We suggest the "fruit of the forest," which contains apples, strawberries, rhubarb, red raspberries, and blackberries. You can buy any type of pie with a regular or a crumb crust. Other taste-teasers include apple-walnut and pumpkin-cream cheese pies—yum! Folks with special dietary needs can buy pies made with Equal instead of sugar.

In the spring, the Village Farmer offers a wide selection of plants for your garden. All year round you'll find some intriguing chachkas here as well.

Stroudsburg/East Stroudsburg

A&J Vegetables
US 209, Stroudsburg
(570) 424-2647

Highway 611, Stroudsburg
(570) 424-2647
A&J Vegetables farm stand has two locations in Stroudsburg. Both stands are open from the end of July, when the first tomatoes, cucumbers and corn start to ripen on the Chipperfield Drive farm, until November, when the last of the apples, pumpkins, and cider are gone.

Monroe Farmers Market
Main Street between Eighth and Ninth Streets, Stroudsburg
no phone
Every Saturday morning from mid-May through Thanksgiving, this market on the north side of Main Street becomes an old-fashioned farmers market as farmers from Stroudsburg to Nazareth bring their crops to town. From 8:00 A.M. until noon, vendors offer vine-ripened tomatoes and other fresh vegetables along with homemade pecan pie, meats, eggs, designer vinegars, flowers, and herbs. Garlic— the flavorful "hard-necked" variety for which the Pocono region is famous—is an especially big seller.

Mount Pocono Area

Pocono Farmstand and Nursery
Highway 611, Tannersville
(570) 629-4344

This stand is open daily year-round and features produce from local farmers such as corn, tomatoes, broccoli, strawberries, apples, beans, zucchinis, and more. It also has a great selection of bedding plants, annuals and perennials, shrubs, and trees as well as lawn ornaments, pottery planters, and other decorative garden items. While you are busy looking at the great buys, your children can enjoy the petting zoo (in the fall only; see our Kid-stuff chapter). You'll also find a great country bakeshop on the premises where fresh-baked pies and breads are sold; you can even order in advance—an especially helpful option around the holidays.

West End

Gould's Produce and Farm Market
Frable Road, just off U.S. Highway 20
Brodheadsville
(570) 992-5615

As with most farm markets in the Poconos, Gould's offers much more than just field-fresh produce. Flowers and herbs are a specialty as are Amish-style bulk condiments, spices, locally produced honey, and preserves. Gould's is open daily from May through Thanksgiving, and Thursday, Friday, and Saturday in winter.

Heckman's Orchards
Highway 115 North, Effort
(570) 629-1191

On Highway 115 North in Effort, between Brodheadsville and Long Pond, is a large farm market with a great selection of fresh fruits and vegetables: beans, lettuce, and strawberries in the early spring; great zucchini all summer long; tomatoes, corn, and spaghetti squash in late summer; and apples, pumpkins, and squash in fall. In June, Heckman's is a good spot for straw-berry picking (for anyone 10 and older); in fall, pick your own apples (bring some cheese and have a picnic when you're through). You can also pick your own sour cherries and pumpkins in season.

FLEA MARKETS

Delaware Water Gap/ Shawnee-on-Delaware

Pocono Bazaar and Flea Market
US 209, Marshalls Creek
(570) 223-8640
www.poconobazaar.com

We've been to flea markets around the country and never have seen a larger one than this. You'll find literally everything here—clothing of every description, "miracle" gadgets with barkers extolling their virtues, secondhand stuff, fine antiques, underwear, housewares, fresh produce, baked goods, and more. This is a fascinating place to browse, to listen to other people's conversations, and to graze—you'll find all kinds of food here too. If you have something to sell, you don't need a reservation; just get in line at 6:00 A.M., and the staff will find you an outdoor spot. The Pocono Bazaar and Flea Market is open all year on Saturday, Sunday, and some holidays.

GENERAL STORES

Delaware Water Gap/ Shawnee-on-Delaware

E.D. Huffman & Son
US 209, Marshalls Creek
(570) 223-8468

Huffman's, which was established in the early 1820s and has stayed in the family ever since, offers "a little bit of every-thing"—souvenirs, fishing and hunting equipment, groceries, hardware, toys, and more. There's a bar in the back that sells

For the truly bizarre in shopping, visit Country Junction, self-named "the world's largest general store." Among other one-of-a-kind items there, you'll find intricately detailed faux big game animal heads for your den, including an elephant head large enough to dominate a hotel lobby.

only beer ("it's a very old license," says one of the Huffman sons-in-law). That makes it a true taproom—one that has been in operation so long that veterans of all our wars could have conceivably hoisted a brew here. Parking looks a little tricky, but you can park between the gas station and the store, behind the store, or in the small lot across Highway 402.

Shawnee General Store
River Road, Shawnee-on-Delaware
(570) 421–0956
Shawnee has just about anything you need in the way of groceries, unless you're cooking something esoteric. Make sure you try their excellent smoked meats. Owners Bill and Theresa Rooth also carry T-shirts, fishing supplies and licenses, guidebooks, snow shovels, hats, gloves, magazines, newspapers from the surrounding metropolitan areas, and almost everything else you'll ever need. When every other store in the area has run out of snow shovels, check with Shawnee; they probably still have a couple. Half the store is a deli that serves breakfast and lunch (the deli is open until 6:30 P.M., so you can have a light dinner here too). It's a particularly pleasant place to sit and eat. The crowd is friendly (most of them know each other), and there's always a paper to read. The store is open seven days a week, every day but Christmas, Thanksgiving, and New Year's Day.

The Shawnee General Store was built in 1859 by John Depui Labar and his wife, Sarah. John was a descendant of Nicholas DePuis, the first European settler in the area. Shawnee looks almost the same on the outside as it did in their day and has been in operation continuously since that time.

West End

Country Junction
US 209, Forest Inn
(610) 377-5050
www.countryjunction.com
This Service Team Home Center bills itself as "the world's largest general store," but it is more than the name implies. Country Junction houses practically everything under the sun, from pet and garden supplies, to lumber and lawn equipment, to tools, fine country-style furniture, and gifts and collectibles. The whole thing is housed in a barn-like structure big enough to serve as the hanger for a couple of 747 passenger jets. A better motto might be, "If you want it, we've got it."

SPECIALTY SHOPS

Antiques

The Poconos are rich in history; therefore, there is little wonder that artifacts of that history abound. Antiques shops, ranging from the large and impressive to little out-of-the-way corners in villages barely on the map, have grown like dusty mushrooms all over the area. As a result, competitive pressures hold prices at levels unheard of in such metropolitan areas as New York and Philadelphia. So intensive is the trade, that Hawley and Honesdale have more antiques outlets than they do grocery stores or pharmacies.

Any "antiquing" venture here is a treasure hunt. Rare and valuable items sometimes show up at yard and garage sales, and even shop proprietors may not realize what they have tucked away on their shelves. With so many antiques outlets in our area, we are able to list only a few, so if you enjoy an occasional trip to yesteryear, take time out from your job, housework, or vacation and seek out the rest.

DELAWARE WATER GAP/ SHAWNEE-ON-DELAWARE

Delaware Water Gap Antique Outlet
Highway 611, Delaware Water Gap
(570) 420-1224

With 4,000 square feet in the building that once housed a popular club called the Blue Note (Jackie Gleason hustled pool here), Cindy Fodor sells a little bit of everything. You can pick up something here for under $20 or buy a fine antique bedroom set for thousands. The quality tends to be high, and the prices are exceedingly reasonable. Fodor carries furniture, glass, jewelry, silver, musical instruments, vintage clothing, old stoves, quilts, and lots more. Tags on each item explain what you're seeing. "There are no necessities here," says Fodor. "This is stuff for the fun part of life." This shop is open by appointment only.

Indian Trader Curios
Highway 611, Portland
no phone

While the back room has military antiques and a huge collection of framed autographs, the front room has whatever owner Joe Nasrallah says, "I can get my grubby hands on." There are lots of antiques as well as plenty of stuff that's just old and interesting.

Knott Necessarily Antiques
The Covered Bridge Shops
425 Delaware Avenue (Highway 611)
Portland
(570) 897-7140
www.slatebelt.org

Glass bottles, jewelry, furniture, dishes, tools, toys, and candles fill this enormous shop. Don't miss the basement, which features reproductions as well as antiques.

The Marketplace
Main Street (Highway 611)
Delaware Water Gap
no phone

This shop is a center for a number of dealers. It's hard to leave empty-handed. You'll find antique furniture, jewelry, dishes, toys, clothing, records, and lots more at reasonable prices. The Marketplace is open weekends year-round.

Portland Antiques and Collectibles
Highway 611, Portland
(570) 897-0129

Glassware, books, furniture, and lots of things from the '40s and '50s comprise the offerings at Portland Antiques and Collectibles.

STROUDSBURG/EAST STROUDSBURG

Eleanor's Antiques
809 Ann Street, Stroudsburg
(570) 424-7724

Two Eleanors hold forth here—Eleanor Buff and Eleanor Muncie—so you never can go wrong by calling out the name. The Eleanors feature a general line of antiques and collectibles with an impressive array of primitives, linens, glassware, and smalls. Eleanor's is closed Sunday.

Ibis
517 Main Street, Stroudsburg
(570) 424-8721
www.ibisantiques.com

This shop specializes in antiques and decorative arts of the 19th and early 20th

Yard sales, garage sales, porch sales, barn sales, rummage sales, church sales—all are ongoing shopping events in the Poconos. Look in the Pocono Record's "Classified" section Friday, Saturday, and Sunday to find them. Also, look for those oak-tag signs Insiders love to post; they will direct you to unadvertised sales.

centuries, including art deco, art nouveau, and Victorian. Paintings, mirrors, art pottery, Orientalia, unusual boxes, and costume jewelry from all of those periods are featured, and all are in mint condition. You'll find no reproductions here. Hours are 11:00 A.M. to 4:30 P.M. Ibis is closed Wednesday and Sunday.

The Poconos region is a great area for antiquing. You'll find fascinating furniture and other objects at affordable prices. Competition and customers' demands have kept antiques from becoming too expensive.

Lavender Place
350 Main Street, Stroudsburg
(570) 424-8791, (570) 424–7087
This charming antiques store on Lower Main presents a labyrinth of aisles, surprise side rooms, and nooks and crannies—all packed with the treasures of yesteryear. If you are partial to Victorian furniture, this is the place to shop for breakfronts, china cabinets, clocks, and other relics of the era. Glassware, gift quilts, jewelry, linens, paintings, and greeting cards themed to days of yore also clamor for attention. Lavender Place also buys antiques, but it no longer accepts them for sale on consignment.

Olde Engine Works Market Place
62 North Third Street, Stroudsburg
(570) 421-4340
www.oldengineworks.com
An unprepossessing exterior hides an absolutely huge, 23,000-square-foot interior with 125 dealers offering every conceivable category of antique and collectible. The line of mint-condition solid-oak furniture, from desks to vintage chests of drawers, is especially impressive. Collector dolls, estate jewelry, old toys, dolls, books, spice boxes, sheet music, model trains, antique firearms, and memorabilia from every era and category round out the collection. Col-

lectibles from the '50s and comic books are big sellers here as well.

The Olde Engine Works is a former factory that made winches for shrimp and fishing boats all along the Atlantic coast, and many of the accoutrements of that trade still hang from the high ceiling.

MOUNT POCONO AREA

Cotton Candy Country Store
Highway 390, Canadensis
(570) 595-3492
Don't be fooled by the flaking paint; inside Cotton Candy Country Store is a treasure of antiques, "junque," and new crafts. The owner, Helen, makes chenille bears, bunnies, decorated heart pillows, and clothing for dolls (including American Girl garb at affordable prices). The enormous store has fabric, old trims, and threads; antique kitchen tools; dishes of every description; costume jewelry; toys; vintage clothing; bottles; glass doorknobs; globes for broken light fixtures; Christmas decorations; and just about anything else you can imagine.

Marli's Arts and Antiques
Highway 447, Canadensis
(570) 595-3876
Marli specializes in country furniture, prints, and paintings. (After visiting dozens of antique shops, we actually bought something from Marli, and we're tempted to go back for more.) Marli's son and daughter-in-law also offer hand-carved, hand-painted fish. They take custom orders, so you can have them re-create the one that got away, and if they make it a little bigger than it was, who's to know? Marli, a gracious lady who has lived all over the Western Hemisphere, has been running this store since the early '60s and thinks she may have the oldest antiques shop up the mountain.

Pocono Peddlers' Village Antique & Flea Market
Highway 611 and Stadden Road
Tannersville
(570) 629-6366

More than 100 area antiques dealers offer their wares for sale under one roof at this popular three-building antiques mart and flea market. For a mass-market approach to antiques and collectibles, this is the place to come. Peddlers' Village is open Thursday through Monday.

WEST END

Added Touch Antiques
US 209 Business South
Snydersville
(570) 992-7070

The "added touch" of the title here is a fine collection of high-quality porcelain and glass as well as a wide line of furniture, jewelry, paintings, Orientalia, and collectibles. The basement is an antiquer's delight, full of what the proprietor calls "semiprecious junque." Antiques are bought as well as sold here, and consignments are considered.

Heritage Craft
Cherry Valley Road at Camera Drive
Saylorsburg
(570) 992-CANE

Heritage Craft is in the business of restoring antiques. Caning, rushing, and splinting are the central crafts here, both for furniture and baskets. The store also sells supplies associated with these skills. Owner John Skelton is a fourth-generation caner who, with his wife, Pat, does work for individuals, restaurants, resorts, and antique dealers. Skelton repairs cane rush, sea grass, wicker, round reed, and Shaker tape. But two of Skelton's most interesting repairs constituted none of the above. One of his special jobs was repair of a 300-year-old papier-mâché chair inlaid with mother-of-pearl; the other was restoration of a leg broken off an antique carousel horse by movers.

Rinker's Antiques
Village Edge Drive, off US 209 Business
South, Brodheadsville
(570) 992-6957

Oaken furniture, refinished or as is, is the specialty here; but furniture is by no means the only category you will find in this 2,400-square-foot store. Old lighting devices, primitives, and collectibles also are offered. Rinker's is open on weekends only.

Lots of professional craftspeople live in the Poconos, and some welcome you into their homes. The Pocono Arts Council puts out a brochure each year listing the "Arts in the Poconos." Check there for shops that you might otherwise miss. The brochures are widely available in shops as well as in racks of brochures.

Sciota Historic Crossing Antique Center
US 209 Business South at Bossardville
Road, Sciota
no phone

This West End crossroads is home to a cluster of four independent antiques shops, all presenting an eclectic inventory of treasures from days gone by. They are Whispers in Time (570-992-9387), Upstairs at Corner Antiques (570-992-4893), R&W Antiques (570-216-2849, 570-236-5247), and Yestertique (570-992-6576). Whispers in Time is open seven days a week; the rest are open only on Saturday and Sunday. Specialties include oaken and Victorian furniture and accessories, as well as antique lighting and such refinished kitchen artifacts as Hoosiers, step-back cupboards, and other country items. You'll also find fine china from Limoges, Transferware, and Flow Blue.

Wakefield Antiques
US 209 Business South at Rim Rock
Drive, Snydersvile
(570) 992-7226

This shop offers a general line of antiques, including a wide selection of bakers' racks, primitives, oak and pine furniture, kitchenware, china, glassware, jewelry, and textiles. A wide array of gifts also are on display.

CLOSE-UP

A Bluestone Castle Offers Many Treasures

Okay, here's your mission. Go out and find a 4-foot-tall art deco dancing girl cast in bronze, a mounted Samurai warrior, enough Tiffany lamps to light up a convention hall, a 10-foot porcelain Chinese temple jar, a life-size replica of an Italian organ grinder complete with monkey, and a whole band packed inside an $11,000 player piano.

No, this isn't a scavenger hunt; this is Castle Antiques & Reproductions Inc., a 25,000-square-foot warehouse outlet where authentic antiques mingle most democratically with reproductions of authentic antiques in a stunning array that ranges from breathtaking beauty to outrageous kitsch.

Inventory at this unique shopping wonderland—the largest of its kind in the Northeast and perhaps even in the nation—is in a constant flux as its proprietor, Ralph Losinno, logs some 200,000 frequent-flyer miles a year in a never-ending worldwide search for merchandise. Antiques, ranging from clocks to massive Victorian hardwood buffets and armoires, represent about 25 percent of Losinno's stock; the remaining 75 percent constitutes reproductions, primarily from Asia and the Pacific Rim, that are exquisite works of art. Exact replicas of early American firearms gleam from a glass case, while ersatz Tiffany and reverse-painted lamps that would fool an expert spread soft, colorful light down a center aisle of the massive showroom. Here, French Empire mingles with turn-of-the-century art nouveau and the art deco of the 1920s and 1930s, and pine and oak furniture reproductions in styles Federal, Victorian, and French exude an air of old-world opulence. And the buyer does not have to be an expert to know what is an antique and what is a reproduction. Blue price tags mark the former, while the latter bear white tags.

MILFORD/LAKE WALLENPAUPACK AREA

The Antique Exchange
209 Belmont, off US 6, Hawley
(570) 226-1711
www.haexchange.com
Twenty-five area dealers ply their trade under one big barn-like roof at this general outlet. Each occupies its own space, and some have telephone numbers other than the primary; they are specified here.

Primary vendors include Circa Antiques (570–226–9252), with a general antique line, and Lois' Berry Patch (570–346–1113), with antique prints and magazines in addition to a general line.

Needless to say, with all those participants, you are likely to find everything you're looking for in antiques—and a few things you didn't even know existed. The display of dinnerware and glass, ranging from Yellow Vaseline and Polychrome to Flow Blue and Blue Willow, is spectacular.

Forest Hall Antiques
214 Broad Street, Milford
(570) 296-4299
www.foresthallantiques.com

Outside the Castle, giant Foo dogs and lions hand-carved from marble guard the entryway, along with a wide selection of garden ornaments and cast-iron gates fit for the mansion of a billionaire. Happily, you don't have to be a billionaire to shop here.

Compared with prices at more urban antiques stores and smaller, less impressive reproduction outlets, these are quite reasonable. The aforementioned fully instrumented player piano "Nickelodeon" was the most expensive item we could find, and beautiful hardwood doors with exquisitely etched glass panels were offered for a mere $750 each.

The Castle, so named because that is what it most resembles with its dark façade and battlement, began its existence in 1880 as a water-powered gristmill built on the southern outskirts of Hawley. Eventually, the mill became a silk factory, and that evolved into what it is today—a showcase of fun, fable, and fantasy. And though its uses have changed over the years, it remains the largest bluestone building in North America and a must-see in the Poconos whether you're really into bronze dancing girls or not.

The entire downstairs portion of the Castle is open to the public, but the second floor is open only to "the trade." To view merchandise there, you must be a dealer and have the credentials to prove it. But whether you're shopping for a hotel chain, your own living room, or for nothing at all, don't miss this outlet. If you buy nothing at all, you'll still leave with the feeling that you have just visited one of the most marvelous museums you've ever encountered. And if you do buy, well . . . just think what the neighbors will say when they see it.

Castle Antiques & Reproductions Inc., just off US 6 at 515 Welwood Avenue in Hawley, (570) 226-8550 or (800) 345-1667, www.castleantiques.com, is open Monday through Saturday from 8:30 A.M. until 5:00 P.M.

Take the grand staircase up to the second and third floors of Forest Hall, once home to a forestry school associated with Yale University. On the second floor, it's hard to bring your eyes down from the magnificent ceiling to the antiques, but once you've caught your breath, you'll see the wares of a number of dealers offering fine furniture, dishes, dolls, clothing, musical instruments, art deco items, and much more. On the third floor, Peter Spielhagen offers European antiques from the 16th to the 19th centuries. Spielhagen's enormous andirons, chairs, stoves, and other items are unlike any you've seen unless you've spent some time in the fine houses of Europe.

Schoolhouse Gallery
Forest Hall, 202 Broad Street, Milford
(570) 296-2223
Cards and tags explain the fine art, pipes, glass, toys, period furniture, and Majolica pottery in the Schoolhouse Gallery. Occasionally, you'll also find some artifacts from area Lenape tribes here.

Timely Treasure
US 6, Hawley
(570) 226-2838
www.timelytreasures.com
Victorian and turn-of-the-century furniture—as is or completely refinished—is the
dominant category here, but in six rooms
of treasures, you'll also find some new gift
items. Timely Treasures also has an extensive line of glass work, much of it from the
turn of the century when glass making
was a thriving local business.

BOOKSTORES

Whether you're a resident or a visiting
tourist, nothing helps you kick back and
relax better than a good book. Read it at
home, read it poolside while on summer
vacation, or read it while curled up in front
of a crackling fireplace at the ski lodge.
You don't even have to pack your own.
There are plenty of good bookstores in
our area, and the following are a few of
our favorites.

Delaware Water Gap/ Shawnee-on-Delaware

Book Warehouse
Foxmoor Outlet Center, US 209
Marshalls Creek
(570) 223-1680
www.book-warehouse.com
Specializing in publishers' overstocks, Book
Warehouse offers some great bargains.
You can buy hardcover copies of popular
books for less than the retail price of the
softcover copies, and softcover copies
here are very cheap. Most books are 50 to
60 percent off retail price. Book Warehouse
carries a wide selection of books. Especially
notable are the audio books; the large
selection of children's books, some in Spanish; computer books; the assortment of
blank journals; and seasonal books, including lots of calendars.

Dingmans Falls Visitor's Center
Delaware Water Gap National
Recreation Area, US 209
Dingmans Ferry
(570) 828-2253
www.nps.gov
Among the maps, posters, and souvenirs,
there's an excellent bookstore. The Visitor's Center carries books on our national
parks, Americana, nature, children's books,
fishing, trail guides, and books on local
archaeology. The Kittatinny Visitor Center,
off I-80 just over the bridge in New Jersey, also has an excellent bookstore.

Pocono Bazaar and Flea Market
US 209, Marshalls Creek
(570) 223-8640
www.poconobazaar.com
We've seen two booksellers consistently
here over the years, and who knows who
else might pop up. Both of the regulars
have a good selection of publishers' overstocks. Children's books, mysteries, and
art books are especially well represented
at these booths.

Stroudsburg/East Stroudsburg

Carroll & Carroll Booksellers
740 Main Street, Stroudsburg
(570) 420-1516
This shop is a bibliophile's dream. The
selection, both in hardback and paper-
back, is huge and diverse. The science-
fiction section alone occupies a sizeable
chunk of wall space, as does one of the
finest collections of children's books in
any used book store in the region. Carroll
& Carroll also has an extensive array of
first and rare editions, and if in all this
bounty you still can't find the title you're
looking for, the proprietors will ferret it
out and let you know when it arrives in
the store.

Waldenbooks
Stroud Mall, Highway 611, Stroudsburg
(570) 421-6039
www.preferredreader.com
Waldenbooks is a national chain, and as a rule, we do not include chain stores in this guide. However, since this Waldenbooks is the biggest first-run bookstore in the Poconos, we felt its inclusion here is called for. This is the place to go for those top-of-the-critic-list best sellers as well as the newest paperbacks. The store also has the usual complete array of categorized offerings and a large children's section. Calendars, maps, atlases, and gift items abound.

Mount Pocono Area

Book Cellar
The Crossings Factory Outlets, Bldg. A
Highway 611, Tannersville
(570) 620-0511
This outlet offers a diverse collection of remaindered hardbacks at prices reduced by as much as 90 percent. A wide selection of paperbacks is also available, and special orders are taken.

Milford/Lake Wallenpaupack Area

Milford Book Cellar
201 West Harford Street, Milford
(877) 881-BOOK
www.themilfordbookcellar.com
In the basement of the historic 1904 Milford School, Milford Book Cellar offers 25,000 gently used and new books in a large range of categories. They also locate and sell books over the World Wide Web.

Mill Run Booksellers
Upper Mill, 150 Water Street, Milford
(570) 296-BOOK
www.yp.com

Mill Run carries a wide variety of books including a good selection of children's titles, gift books, fiction, mystery, nature, mood cassettes and CDs, and more. The proprietor is knowledgeable and can help you find books that suit you.

Mill Run Booksellers is in the Upper Mill, a 19th-century grist mill, and you can see the old water wheel at work from the back of the store.

CANDLE SHOPS

Candle shops are a real draw in the central Poconos. Some tour companies even bring busloads of shoppers here. Candle shops have mushroomed into emporiums that carry various styles and sizes of candles as well as lots of souvenirs and collectibles. They also specialize in custom-made candles for weddings, anniversaries, and other commemorative events.

Most shops make candles on-site—a curiosity draw and an integral part of the shopping experience. Candles are such a hot item, you'll find them in almost every gift and specialty shop in the Poconos. But the places we include offer incredible selections, workmanship, quality, and value.

Stroudsburg/East Stroudsburg

Pocono Candle Shop
US 209 Business
East Stroudsburg
(570) 421-1832
www.poconocandle.com
The shop is filled with candles of all types, and demonstrations of ribbon candle making are a specialty. The store, a large two-story country barn–style structure, also carries an extensive line of collectibles detailed in the subsequent "Souvenirs, Gifts, and Collectibles" section of this chapter. If you're hungry, snack on some homemade fudge. Bus tours are welcome.

Mount Pocono Area

The American Candle Shop
Highway 611, Bartonsville
(570) 629-3388
www.amcandlecollectible.com
This is the Poconos' largest candle shop, encompassing more than 40,000 square feet. The company has its own manufacturing facility in Wind Gap to supply this store. Specialties include carved candles. And check out the huge wedding department, including favor supplies and unity candles.

Scheduled carving demonstrations are a big hit with bus tourists; drop-in shoppers are free to watch whatever candle-making activity is going on at the moment. This candle shop also houses a country candy store (customers love the chance to buy by the piece) and a gourmet coffee shop (enjoy a cappuccino while you browse). The American Candle Shop also stocks several collectibles. (See this chapter's "Souvenirs, Gifts, and Collectibles" section.)

House of Candles
Highway 715, Henryville
(570) 629-1953, (888) 6CANDLE
www.houseofcandles.com
House of Candles has four levels packed with everything you could possibly imagine in a candle and then some. Make sure you go downstairs to see the 1,000-pound story candle (we're not saying it's pretty) and upstairs for the great bargains on candle closeouts. Downstairs, you can also watch candle making. House of Candles is known for its carved wedding candles and for excellent prices. Since House of Candles makes its own items, it can sell them to you wholesale. Candles by other manufacturers and collectibles fill out the shelves of the packed rooms. While parents browse, children can watch the garishly colored Chinese pheasants, sheep, goats, and miniature horses strutting around an enclosure next to the parking lot.

Memorytown Candle Crafter
Grange Road, Mount Pocono
(570) 839-1680
www.amcandlecollectible.com
Sister shop to American Candles, you'll find candles of every variety, souvenirs, and collectibles throughout this multi-room shop. Downstairs there's a print shop and museum with some very old printing machines. (See our Attractions chapter.)

CHRISTMAS SHOPS

Christmas items are sold in Poconos outlets and in specialty shops. Some candle shops (see previous section) stock extensive selections of Christmas collectibles. Most gift and collectibles shops (see "Souvenirs, Gifts, and Collectibles" in this chapter) also carry Christmas ornaments and decorations.

In this section we include shops that primarily sell theme trees; nativity scenes (wood, pewter, porcelain, ceramic, terra cotta); angels; and scads of lacy, bright, tinkly, sparkly, romantic, heavenly, adorable, cute, gorgeous, wonderful, eye-popping Christmas-season decorations for home, hearth, and tree.

Stroudsburg/East Stroudsburg

The Christmas Factory
US 209 Business, south of Marshalls Creek
(570) 223-0717
It's Christmas in July . . . and every other month of the year, at this cavernous Yule-tide outlet. Christmas trees decorated beyond mortal imagination fill the place like a glittering forest, and such collectibles as Snowbabies and Carolers crowd among Kurt Adler, Midwest and Roman ornaments, displayed on the trees that light up the store. Trees are deco-

rated in themes—all angels, all reds, all village pieces, and so forth. The Christmas Factory also sells garlands, wreaths, and bows that match and complement the trees and ornaments.

CLOTHING
Stroudsburg/East Stroudsburg

The Apple Tree
726 Main Street, Stroudsburg
(570) 421-2798
One would expect to find a store of this caliber on 5th Avenue in New York City. Women with discriminating taste will enjoy a sojourn to the Apple Tree, which carries a full range of women's apparel from sporty to dressy. Prices, like quality, are on the high end, and service is friendly, personal, and knowledgeable.

Dunkelberger's for Men
581 Main Street, Stroudsburg
(570) 421-7950
www.dunkelbergers.com
This men's haberdashery—right through a doorway from its women's equivalent—features top of the line brands in sportswear: Patagonia, Sorel, Columbia, North Face and Woolrich. Prices are on the high side, but so is quality. Like its sister shop, the men's store also serves as uniform and accessory headquarters for Boy Scouts and Cub Scouts. Its collection of Filson brand luggage and outerwear is especially impressive.

Dunkelberger's for Women
577 Main Street, Stroudsburg
(570) 421-7950
www.dunkelbergers.com
This upscale boutique, under the same roof as its parent company, Dunkelberger's Sports Outfitter, carries high-quality lines in women's attire, including

full ranges of Pendleton and Woolrich, as well as handbags, jewelry, and shoes by Brighton. The shop also is supply headquarters for Girl Scouts, carrying every needed item of uniform and accessories.

Yellow Moon
431 Main Street, Stroudsburg
(570) 420-1950
The watchwords here are "fun, funky, and functional," adjectives that apply to the jewelry as well as to a unique line of clothing. The jewelry features designs by world-renowned Thomas Mann, who started his career in Stroudsburg and Echo of the Dreamer, semiprecious stones in their natural state, in chunky silver settings, which are so popular they fly out the door. The clothing runs from the moderately priced Putumayo (yes, they stock the CDs from around the world, too) with a wide variety of styles in great prints and washable rayons to Babette, a San Francisco line of absolutely unique, hand-pleated, completely washable casual-to-dressy pieces. Yellow Moon also carries Dansko Shoes, which started as a clog company but has expanded their line while emphasizing a comfortable foot bed. Dansko is the only shoe approved by the American Podiatric Medical Association.

Mount Pocono Area

Lesh's Leather
Highway 611, Swiftwater
(570) 839-7349
www.leshleather.com
Living up to its name, Lesh's Leather has a terrific selection of leather hats, leather vests, leather jackets, leather chaps, and leather handbags in both Western and motorcycle styles. You'll also find good Native American jewelry, a large selection of Minnetonka moccasins, boots, Western hats, Outback coats, and bolo ties.

West End

The Treasure Shop
44 Broadway, Jim Thorpe
(570) 325-8380, (800) 833-1782
www.irishtreasureshop.com
The flavor of "the auld sod" is packed into
this little gift and clothing boutique where
some of the richest Irish woolens—hats,
scarves, caps, sweaters, jackets, and blankets—this side of Killarney can be found.
The shop also has a large inventory of
Celtic jewelry as well as imported condiments, teas, colognes, aftershaves, candles, plush toys, and gift items.

Marianne Monteleone
97 Broadway, Jim Thorpe
(570) 325-3540
www.shopmmdesign.com
The proprietor of this boutique designs
her own line, which includes many one-of-
a-kind articles in hand-woven silk. Muted
prints and colorful vests abound. Marianne
has done many new pieces for her "Travel
Collection" in microfiber. All of it is pricey,
but unique. In addition to Marianne's own
designs, she offers painted silks by Marcia
Ferris and Leni Hoch, fiber arts by Mary-
anne Kirchoff and hand-knitted items by
Claire Marcus.

FURNITURE (UNUSUAL)

Delaware Water Gap/
Shawnee-on-Delaware

Frederick Duckloe & Bros. Inc.
Highway 611, Portland
(570) 897-6172
www.duckloe.com
Frederick Duckloe opened a carriage shop
in Portland in 1859, but soon began to
specialize in making Windsor chairs and
benches. The tradition has been carried
on by his descendants, and today the
shop makes beautiful chairs, benches,
stools, and tables out of the finest woods,
using traditional woodworking techniques.

Approached by the Smithsonian, Mystic
Seaport, Independence Hall, and others,
Duckloe has reproduced significant colonial pieces down to the type of wood
originally used. Duckloe's two stores, on
Portland's main street, carry their own
furniture as well as pieces by other fine
makers including the Stickley Mission Collection. Watch for announcements in the
paper of occasional warehouse sales.

HEALTH FOOD

Stroudsburg/East
Stroudsburg

Earthlight
829A Ann Street, Stroudsburg
(570) 424-6760

US 209, Ames Plaza, Brodheadsville
(610) 681-8396

Highway 611, Fountain Springs
Tannersville
(570) 619-6592
This long-established health-food, dietary-
supplement, and vitamin store, with its huge
array of dried herbs and folksy general-store
atmosphere, sells organic produce, breads,
pastries, pasta, and healthy brands of
soda pop, in addition to culinary and
medicinal herbs offered in bulk from big
apothecary jars, plus lots of books.
  Earthlight has sister stores with the
same name, owned and operated by the
same proprietors, in three locations.

JEWELRY AND ROCK SHOPS

Stroudsburg/East
Stroudsburg

Findings Jewelry and Art Gallery
39 North 7th Street, Stroudsburg
(570) 426-1888
Findings is a small, but enchanting store in
a lovely brick building in Courthouse
Square. Daniel Varipapa offers his own

Michelangelo with a Chainsaw

"Michelangelo with a chainsaw" may conjure up an unlikely image, but no other description fits Raf Dionysius and dozens of his fellow practitioners throughout the Poconos. Dionysius is a sculptor, but a chainsaw is to him what a chisel was to Michelangelo, and whereas the great Renaissance artist worked in marble, Dionysius carves his images out of tree trunks. He works in many mediums but prefers white pine to the hardwoods common to northeastern Pennsylvania because "pine is easier to cut and it isn't as hard on the chainsaw."

Chainsaw sculptors now work all over the Poconos. You'll find them displaying their wares at flea markets, farm stands, and alongside many country roads. Some of the work is crude and some, magnificent. Dionysius said his passion for chainsaw sculpting has spread equally in the ranks of his own family.

"I actually have six people in my family who do this—including my 16-year-old son," he said. "We're spread out through the Poconos and go down as far as Lancaster. We teach one another; we learn from one another. We hang out with one another and we carve together."

Dionysius works with chainsaws equipped with "quarter" or "dime" tips, so named because the tips of their cutting bars end in circles the size of the coins in question. His creations are roughed out with the main blade, then detailed with the small tips, capable of creating the texture of a bear's coat or an eagle's feathers. Dionysius paints some of his sculptures and leaves some rustic, and his bears can be designed to hold everything from mailboxes to signs ranging from WELCOME to GO AWAY.

Dionysius sells his creations from a roadside stand on the grounds of Regina Farms garden supply at 5181 Milford Road in East Stroudsburg. They range in price from $29 for a small bear all the way up to $1,200 for a life-sized bruin or raptor.

gorgeous designs in gold and silver with precious and semiprecious gemstones. He also offers pieces by other unique jewelers and some carefully selected estate pieces. There's a small collection of work by some of the area's top artists for sale here, too.

14Kt. Outlet
616 Main Street, Stroudsburg
(570) 421-5081
Offering unusually low prices, Ron Siwiec, the owner of 14Kt. Outlet, who's also a skilled goldsmith, has loyal customers from here to Hawaii. Ron knows his pre-

cious and semiprecious stones, and makes jewelry with such unusual stones as tanzanite, apatite, watermelon tourmaline, drusy stones, and more. If you're a traditionalist, Ron also uses diamonds, opals, emeralds, and such. Ron also does custom work and repairs.

Liztech Jewelry
95 Crystal Street, East Stroudsburg
(570) 424-5681, (800) 531-9992
www.liztech.com
A wonderfully whimsical shop, Liztech's flagship offering is their own sparkly jew-

Because this is a tourist area, most stores that cater to visitors are open on the weekend. Other days of the week vary by store. Call ahead if you're heading to a specific shop.

elry. Each piece has a name like Wild Woman (a female with some kind of hula hoop), Kokopelli, or Hos-pi-tal-I-tea (a jeweled teacup). Each is made with antique beads (the creator, Jill Elizabeth, goes bead mining in some old warehouses in Providence, R.I.) and wired onto a mirror-like material. They're wildly popular in the area (just start looking for them, and you'll see lots of Liztechs being worn in the Poconos), and they're sold at craft shows all over the United States.

In addition to her own jewelry, Liztech offers other people's work, including jewelry by Ricky Boscarino of Luna Park, as well as interesting clocks, pens, lamps, children's toys and more. In the back of the shop, an unusual line of painted furniture and sticks is offered.

Mount Pocono Area

Planet Earth Gallery
Highway 611, Scotrun
(570) 620-9599
Jewelry and rocks are far from the only things you'll find here, but the rock collection has many museum-quality pieces for sale at reasonable prices. The fossils are especially impressive, and one piece from Morocco—its shell fossils polished and gorgeous—is as tall as a person. There are also beautiful crystals and lots of other rocks. The jewelry is imported from around the world, with especially impressive collections of amber, Asian, and Native American pieces. Planet Earth also carries incense and aromatherapy supplies, candles, interesting furniture, Indian bedspreads, clothes, several different types of tarot cards and other oracular

systems, books, pewter and crystal fantasy sculptures, designs featuring celestial objects, and Buddhist supplies.

West End

The Gem Shop
31 Broadway, Jim Thorpe
(570) 325-3007
A glittery treasure trove of jewelry styles reproduced from molds and castings made from the 1800s through 1940, and of restored antique pieces from the late 19th century, seize the eye as you walk into this elegant shop. Lacy sterling silver studded with garnet and peridot compete with Austrian leaded crystal and cut glass for attention amid a fine collection of artistic picture frames, wine racks, sculptures, and African wood carvings.

Milford/Lake Wallenpaupack Area

Doni-Jewelry Designs
105 West Harford Street, Milford
(570) 296-DONI
Doni, the designer and owner of Doni-Jewelry Designs, does all kinds of custom work in designing, fabricating, and redesigning gold and silver jewelry, but she's concentrating on fine jewelry with precious stones. Her pieces are unique and immediately recognizable.

Jewelry, Gems and Minerals of the World (Marliese Wells Enterprises)
209 East Harford Street, Milford
(570) 296-8188
Rocks and expertise are the fare in this tiny shop. Marliese Wells is an expert mineralogist, and all the rocks in the shop have been picked up by the Wells or members of their extended family, with the exception of a few that have been acquired through trading. You'll find pieces for your kid's rock collection as well as museum-quality specimens here. If

you're a senior citizen, bring some identification and you'll get a discount.

POTTERY AND GLASS

There are many potters in the Poconos. Shops crop up along the back roads between Bangor and Stroudsburg, Hawley and Mount Pocono, Jim Thorpe, and Blakeslee, and all around the mountain. Watch for them as you drive. Many also are listed in the Pocono Arts Council Directory (570) 476-4460. Call the council for the names of some potters or for a copy of the directory.

A number of fine artists in all media show and sell their work as well as teach their crafts here. And here are a few potters well worth visiting.

Mount Pocono Area

Holley Ross Pottery
Highway 191, La Anna (between Cresco and Newfoundland)
(570) 676-3248
www.pocono.org
The sales room at this factory features pottery at outlet prices. There is a huge selection of pottery, fiesta glass, and cranberry glass among the many types of wares. Free pottery-making demonstrations make this shopping stop a learning experience too. Visit the free woodland park after you shop. Holley Ross is open May 1 through mid-December.

Reece Pottery
Crestmont Drive, off Highways 191 and 507, Newfoundland
(570) 676-9140
www.reecepottery.com
Functional and sculptural stoneware are the specialties of Thomas Reece. Reece has been making pottery for more than 35 years and has sold pieces in galleries all over the country, especially throughout New York and New Jersey. His functional,

high-glaze pieces have been bought by entertainment stars such as Rita Moreno, Bill Murray, and Matt Le Blanc.

The Newfoundland shop (in a barn) has been expanding ever since it opened to the public. Many of Reece's pieces are one-of-a-kind; special-order work includes vases, serving ware and sculptures, which he can even personalize with photographs.

Reece Pottery is open daily except Tuesday May through December and weekends January through April. Hours vary seasonally; please call ahead.

Milford/Lake Wallenpaupack Area

Dorflinger-Suydam Sanctuary and Glass Museum
Long Ridge Road, White Mills
(570) 253-1185
www.dorflinger.com
This spot is a glassworks museum and gift shop, a wildlife sanctuary with nature trails, and a concert center for the summer Wildflower Festival. (See our Arts and Culture chapter.)

The museum displays hundreds of pieces of cut, engraved, and etched glass from Dorflinger glassworks. The gift shop sells fine contemporary glass pieces of every type—earrings, bowls, serving pieces, vases—as well as books about glass, wildlife, and art. There is also an art exhibit in this shop that's only open Wednesday through Sunday from May to November.

SOUVENIRS, GIFTS, AND COLLECTIBLES

Gifts, collectibles, and souvenirs—the gewgaws travelers love to take home to friends and family—constitute a major nationwide industry and they have quite a presence on shop shelves throughout the Poconos.

A Dazzling Shop on Crystal Street

If you're new to the Stroudsburg area, you've probably noticed quite a few women flashing shiny, mirror-like pins and earrings, cut into shapes like an angel, a sprite, or a mythological figure and wrapped with colorful wire and exotic glass beads. To an outsider it looks like there's some kind of secret organization around here, and these are the badges; but Insiders know that this is Liztech jewelry, made above a bank on Crystal Street in East Stroudsburg. Years ago, Jill Elizabeth, Liztech's founder, made, as she puts it, "really ugly" beaded necklaces and sold them at craft shows. In search of new materials at a trade show, she was handed some chromium architectural laminate samples used for making mirrored panels in hotel lobbies. She played with the shiny material a couple of times, but wasn't particularly inspired. Then one day, she tried cutting some Egyptian hieroglyphs out of the material and wrapping them with colorful magnet wire and beads she had lying around. When she took the results to a craft show, they were so unusual that only the other artists bought them, but as she showed them more and more, especially in New York's Central Park South and Washington Square craft bazaars, people began to respond and she gave up the beads to concentrate on these pins.

Today Liztech employs quite a few people and sells their jewelry at boutiques and craft fairs all over the United States and in some parts of the rest of the world. Liztech's back rooms have piles of the chromium panels and spindles of wire in all kinds of luminous colors, some quite rare. (As the wire is color coded for use in magnetic motors, it gives a whole new meaning to the term "electric blue.") There's also a "bead library." "I go to Providence, Rhode Island once a year," says Jill. "They have close-out houses with boxes of things from the '20s and '30s. I mine for old glass stones from Czechoslovakia, Bohemia, and Austria that were made between the wars. I dig through floor-to-ceiling shelves with a flashlight in one hand and a razor blade in the other. The boxes are so old, some of them crumble as I look through them." What she finds are luminous glass stones that simulate fire opals and star sapphires, others that are carved or engraved, stones that look like moons or deep blue eyes. All these are incorporated into Liztech designs that can be whimsical or spiritual but are always sparkly. While Jill brings in a prototype based on an idea and some

---

Most stores carry gift items and collectible lines of some type, including candle shops, gift shops, food shops, Christmas shops, and, of course, the major outlets mentioned earlier in this chapter. As for souvenirs, there is scarcely a store in the area that does not stock a line of them.

But there is one problem of definition here. The Poconos also offer a feeding frenzy for antique buffs, and many

stones, "All of our brains together work better than one alone. We have meetings and everybody has input." Although Liztech produces large numbers of pins, earrings, bracelets, and other shiny objects, each piece is cut, burnished, wrapped, and finished by hand.

Though Liztech has been a presence on Crystal Street for years, a couple years ago, Jill Elizabeth and her husband, Scott Maclaren, began building a gallery on the first floor of the same building. Using design ideas from Ricky Boscarino of Luna Park, they have created a shop that's as whimsical as the Liztech designs. The gallery features Liztech's entire line, but it also carries jewelry by other designers, as well as interesting toys, chachkas, and lighting. There's a case of Judaica, and the back room features Sticks' unusual line of furniture. Longtime Liztech fans like to stop by, see what's new, and plan their next acquisition. Twinkling Kokopellis, garden fairies, circus ponies, healing hands, and bear paws share display cases with Anasazi antelopes, curly-tongued chameleons, and trees of life.

Jill is always experimenting with new creative work. Inspired by the wonderful old glass she finds, she's learning to make glass beads. She has traveled to France and Venice to attend workshops and see glassmaking techniques, and she's having

The Tree of Life is one of Liztech's most popular creations. LIZTECH

lots of fun creating twisty rods, speckled rounds, and clear beads shot with gold. She claims she's just playing at beads and is still a novice, but we hope to see some original Liztech beads incorporated into the work someday. In the meantime, Jill Elizabeth exhorts her patrons to, "Go forth and sparkle!" Liztech, 95 Crystal Street, East Stroudsburg; (570) 424–5681, (800) 531–9992, www.liztech.com.

antique stores also carry items that could be classified as collectibles, just as shops emphasizing collectibles frequently have a few antiques on their shelves. Our rule of thumb, therefore, will be the percentage

of antiques against the percentage of gifts and collectibles offered. Where a store is predominately an antique outlet, it will be placed in the previous "Antiques" section, while those selling mostly gift and collectible items are detailed here. On your way to visit them, you're bound to pass others we haven't yet discovered, or new ones that have just jumped onto the bandwagon. So explore and enjoy.

Delaware Water Gap/ Shawnee-on-Delaware

Country Kettle
US 209 Business, Marshalls Creek
(570) 421-8970, (877) 553-8853
www.country-kettle.com
If Santa Claus ever decides to give up his North Pole workshop, all he'll have to do is buy into this eclectic gift-and-collectible outlet. It has something for everyone in every age group, including an eating orgy for the sweet tooth that we discuss in detail in the following "Sweets and Eats" section of this chapter. Collectibles include Rudolph and the Island of Misfit Toys, tons of wicker work, scented candles, a virtual garden of silk flowers, and porcelain treasures from Tom Clark, Precious Moments, Annalee, and many more. Bells and brass and glass and crystal and gift items abound, along with Pocono Mountain T-shirts, and sweat shirts.

Mary Stolz Doll Shop & Museum
McCole Road, Bushkill
(570) 588-7566
If you're a doll collector, this place is heaven. Collectible dolls from a number of different makers are available at reasonable prices. If you're a Barbie collector and missed a particular model, we can almost guarantee you'll find it here. You'll also find an extensive collection of doll-house furnishings and high-quality paper dolls.

We have a nice selection of teddy bears in Pocono shops, but we also have many black bears and deer that walk wherever they please. Be careful on country roads. Be aware of their potential presence, both day and night.

Upstairs at the Hobby Hut, you can buy trains, planes, models, and accessories.

Mary Stolz also has a doll museum (see our Attractions chapter). It is just across the street from the Pocono Indian Museum on US 209 in Bushkill.

Water Gap Gallery
Main Street, Delaware Water Gap
(570) 424-5002
www.delawarewatergap.com
Fine handcrafted pottery, leather, hand-painted glass, and wonderful wooden spoons share the shelves with some interesting jewelry made by a local silversmith.

Stroudsburg/East Stroudsburg

Beary Best Friends
763 Milford Road (US 209 Business)
East Stroudsburg
(570) 421-7050, (888) 827-2327
www.bearybestfriends.com
For a truly extensive selection of teddy bears, seek out Beary Best Friends. The collection here, as at other places, includes the famous Boyd's Bears, but this shop has the widest selection within a 50-mile radius. These bears are well cared for by proprietor Susan Paul, who brushes their hair and irons their clothing before they are ready to make your acquaintance.

Paul carries an extensive line of bears created by artists including Elizabeth Lloyd (Cupboard Bears), Crystal Smythe (Bookshelf Bears), and many others. You'll also find the Barbie of bears, Muffy Vanderbear, who has her own monogrammed towels, silver brush and mirror, beautiful furniture and, as Paul says, "enough clothes to make us all jealous!"

Designer Crafts
578 Main Street, Stroudsburg
(570) 420-1228
www.designercraftsonmain.com
Collectibles here are strictly on the high end, both in terms of price and quality.

This exquisite shop offers a wide range of carved utensils, metal sculpture, fabric art, and ceramics as well as jewelry, paintings, wooden toys, pottery, and stunning works from Philadelphia colorist Armond Scavo and woodworking wizard Nick Molignano. A picture-framing shop of high artistry also is on premises.

Floral Boutique
13 North Fifth Street, Stroudsburg
(570) 424-6662, (800) 688-6662
This little shop offers much more than flowers, though flowers are its main stock in trade. The Boutique also is a showcase of country crafts, gifts, collectibles, plush toys, peacock feathers, marvelous Victorian-style birdhouses, and exquisite dried-flower arrangements. All are arranged in the entry way, making the customer feel that he is entering a bower when he goes in to pick up that bouquet for Mother's Day or Valentine's Day.

The Green Caboose
Highway 611 and Terrance Drive
Stroudsburg
(570) 422-6550
As the name might imply, this is a train-themed toyshop with a full line of L.G.B. 5-gauge trains, Brio wooden railway systems, and Thomas the Tank Engine and Friends. The Green Caboose also deals in Armour die-cast collectibles, the Boyd's collection of plush animals, Breyer model horses, East African jewelry, model kits, and William Britain collectibles. A large selection of T-shirts, golf caps, sweatshirts, conductor's caps, and other souvenir apparel also is on display.

Pocono Candle Shop
US 209 Business, East Stroudsburg
(507) 421-1832
www.poconocandle.com
In addition to any candle you can imagine, there are lots of collectibles here. Lines include Precious Moments, Harbour Lights, Department 56, Snowbabies, and much more packed into the crowded rooms of this candle shop.

Something Special
Eighth and Main Streets, Stroudsburg
(570) 421-6860
This modern version of the Old Curiosity Shop presents a three-dimensional kaleidoscope of craft and gift items—chess sets, picture frames, desk sets, figurines, baskets, wind chimes, candles, games, puzzles, cards, T-shirts, and more. It is the perfect place to browse and find that one-of-a-kind gift or collector's item. So tempting to the touch is the colorful and frequently frangible array of merchandise that children younger than 16 are not allowed unless accompanied by their parents.

Stockade Miniatures Toy Soldier Store
4 North Sixth Street, Stroudsburg
(570) 424-8507
www.stockade-miniatures.com
Don't let the word "toy" in the title fool you; this little boutique just a half block off Main Street is for the very serious adult collector. Here "Soldiers of the World" hold forth in frozen poses of combat as they fight in virtually every war known to history. Napoleon is locked in battle with Wellington at Waterloo; Doughboys fight in the Ardenne; and GIs hit the beaches of Normandy and the Pacific Islands. There are even Mongol hordes, knights in armor, and a whole collection of cowboys and Indians, complete with forts and stockades. Antique metal and plastic figures are bought, sold and traded here, but kids aren't left completely out. There is a selection of toy soldiers for them too—just to get them started toward the collecting habit.

Total Home Health Care
437 Main Street, Stroudsburg
(570) 421-1110
If this store were a person, it would be diagnosed as one with a severe multiple personality disorder; and while that might be very bad for a person, it is very good for a store. Total Home Health Care specializes in a wide array of trusses, crutches, braces, walkers, and other orthopedic devices, but right next to that

array is a display of collectibles as eclectic and unique as the store itself. Here you'll find fashion dolls, clown dolls, sculptures, one-of-a-kind miniature porcelain carousels, Judaica, jewel boxes, and merry-go-round horses. They are displayed right beside designer belt buckles, holiday flags, and decorative eggs. And if all that were not enough for any one store, Total Home Health Care also sells books and magazines, offers homeopathic and herbal medications, and fills prescriptions.

Mount Pocono Area

American Candle
Highway 611, Bartonsville
(570) 629-3388
www.amcandlecollectible.com

"Candle" describes only a fraction of the goods offered in this cavernous outlet of gifts and collectibles. The place is jammed with just about every collectible line of ceramic figurine: Armani, Emmet Kelly Jr., Disney, Enchantica, Fenton, Boyd's Bears, Department 56, Pocket Dragons, and Annalee Dolls.

And if that's not enough, add the music boxes, plates, mugs, ornaments, crystal, and pewter. The store opened with 2,500 feet of retail space in 1978; today it boasts more than 40,000 square feet. Your only danger, apart from hypershopping, is getting lost.

The Arts and Crafters Paradise Bazaar
Highways 940 and 390, Paradise Valley
(570) 839-5730
www.bycrafters.com

If you've been to one of our local arts and crafts shows, you'll recognize the works of many of our local crafters among the handmade items from Pennsylvania, New York, and New Jersey here. The offerings are mostly country crafts, and you'll find some interesting furniture at decent prices. You'll also find beautiful North Country Wind Bells, wreaths and swags, iron work, painted bird houses, hand-crafted soap, seasonal items, bears, dolls, and jewelry. This is a very popular store.

Switzerland Old World Gifts
Highway 611, Tannersville
(570) 620-2003

This shop stocks all of the main collectibles, including Boyd's Bears and Bearstone Teddies, but it also carries an extensive collection of Ulbricht and Steinbach nutcrackers and smokers and Anton Schneider cuckoo clocks from Germany's Black Forest. As part of their promotion of the Steinbach and Ulbricht items, the folks at Switzerland Old World Gifts invite these two masters to visit every summer and sign their work. Interested customers who can't make it in to meet these crafters can pre-order a signed piece by credit card; call in advance. This shop also carries Budweiser steins, Department 56, Swarovski, and Harbour Lights as well as an extensive collection of Old World Christmas ornaments.

The Toy Soldier
Highway 191, Paradise Falls
(570) 629-7227
www.the-toy-soldier.com

Part of a toy soldier museum (see our Attractions chapter), this is the largest collection of miniature soldiers in the country as well as regimental "militariana" like drums and bugles. Collectors from all over the world come here to see the museum and buy things from the shop. The Toy Soldier is open by appointment only; you must call ahead.

The Old Village Trader
Highway 611, Mount Poconos
(570) 839-8030

The main floor of this 50-year-old store has tons of souvenirs, raccoon caps, and lots of other types of headgear. Upstairs is a bevy of baskets. Downstairs you'll find a huge selection of discount toys—just the thing to keep vacationing kids happy. Don't miss the incredible selection of lawn ornaments in the Old Village Trader's new Home and Garden annex.

West End

J.T. Hooven Mercantile Co.
42 Susquehanna Street, Jim Thorpe
(570) 325-2248
This gift shop, just off the town square in Jim Thorpe, retains the general-store atmosphere it has carried since it opened in that capacity in 1882. Today, it offers a wide array of estate jewelry, knickknacks, teddy bears, dolls, candles, potpourri, country crafts, old-fashioned kitchen collectibles, and anthracite coal sculptures. An H.O.-gauge model train collection is spread for rail buffs upstairs.

Milford/Lake Wallenpaupack Area

Giffard & White
Upper Mill, 150 Water Street, Milford
(570) 296-5151
www.giffardandwhite.net
At Giffard & White, you'll see high-quality pottery, picnic baskets, the largest collection of Judaica in the area, creative toys, stationery, jewelry, clocks, art glass, and other distinctive gifts and home accessories from all over the world.

Hare Hollow
322 Broad Street, Milford
(570) 296-5757
Many of Hare Hollow's customers come for the collections—Boyd's Bears, Lizzie High Dolls, Yankee Candles, and more—but you'll also find baskets, country primitives, pottery, stained glass, hand-crafted accessories, kitchen stuff, and prints in this crowded shop.

The Milford Craft Show
120 Harford Street, Milford
(570) 296-5662
www.poconovacations.com
Twig rockers, cypress garden furniture, fanciful painted country furniture, primitive paintings and prints, candles, pottery, herbal vinegars, jams, jellies, boxes,

Christmas ornaments, jewelry, stained glass, bird houses, clocks, decorated shirts, and collectibles are among the country crafts you will find in room after room of this popular shop.

Ursula's Barn
Highway 191 South, Hamlin
(570) 689-2649
You'll find a large collection of collectibles, folk art, and antiques in this cow barn. Ursula's unique collection includes folk art of Vaillancourt and Leo Smith, Boyd's Bears, Lizzie High Dolls, All God's Children, and June McKenna Collectibles, to name a handful. Christmas ornaments and collectibles also are abundant, including Department 56, Heritage Village, Byer's Choice Carolers, Christopher Radko ornaments, Old World Christmas ornaments, and lots of Santas. The selection here is enormous.

SPORTS OUTFITTERS

Delaware Water Gap/ Shawnee-on-Delaware

The Pack Shack
88 Broad Street, Delaware Water Gap
(570) 424-8533
www.packshack.com
Close to the Delaware Water Gap National Recreation Area, Pack Shack provides rentals and sales of just about any equipment you will need to enjoy the park. In the summer, Pack Shack rents canoes, rafts, tubes, and kayaks (see our In, On, and Around the Water chapter). They offer instruction and guides, or you can rent their equipment and take off on your own. They also run a rock climbing and

---

Auctions are not just great places to get a bargain, they're also immensely entertaining. Check the classifieds for listings of auctions. They usually include a detailed list of what's available.

---

rappelling school on cliffs in the park. In winter you can rent or buy cross-country skis and snowshoes. They will teach you how to use your new equipment and give you advice on the best trails for your level of experience. It's always wise to reserve your rental equipment in advance, but they can usually serve walk-ins too. Pack Shack also carries backpacking and camping equipment (Appalachian Trail hikers find this store's location convenient). The prices are excellent, and the advice and instruction are top notch.

Starting Gate
US 209, Bushkill
(570) 223-6215
www.startinggateonline.com
Starting Gate carries all the sportswear you need, summer and winter. In summer you'll find sports clothing, swimming gear, in-line skating and hockey equipment, skateboards and skateboard stuff, mountain climbing equipment, and a good line of sports shoes here. During the winter there's a great selection of warm clothing for skiers and other cold-weather people, skis, snowboards, sleds, and more. There's a rental shop for bikes, skateboards, and in-line skates in the summer, and skis and snowboards in the winter. You can skate or skateboard at their on-site skate park (see our Kidstuff chapter). The single-speed bicycles are suitable for use along the riverside McDade Trail in the Delaware Water Gap National Recreation Area.

Why rent skis here instead of at a mountain? The price may be better, you shouldn't have to wait in line, and packages can be arranged for multiple days. Often, the equipment is in excellent shape, because it doesn't get used heavily. During the off-season, you can buy last year's ski equipment at great prices—the big sale comes after Labor Day. Summer is when the Starting Gate also gets in next year's line of skis and clothing, so you can get a preview of what's coming up and outfit yourself while it's still broiling.

Stroudsburg/East Stroudsburg

Dunkelberger's Sports Outfitters
Sixth and Main Streets, Stroudsburg
(570) 421-7950
www.dunkelbergers.com
There are no outdoor sports this upscale store does not outfit. Canoes and kayaks hog the limelight on the showroom floor, along with hunting and fishing equipment, a wide array of archery equipment, including an indoor archery range, river gear, and camping equipment. A top-of-the-line inventory of sports clothing for men and women is offered in adjoining rooms. All major brands in sporting gear are carried here.

West End

Buck's Sporting Goods
47 Indian Hill Road, Lehighton
(610) 377-3779
www.bucksportinggoods.com
Buck's carries a general line of sporting goods, but archery is the specialty here. All brands of bows and related equipment, including PSE, Martin, Hoyt, High Country, Golden Eagle, Jennings, Diamond Mathews, and McPherson, are offered as are archery target systems. The store boasts an indoor archery range where a bowman can warm up for the hunting season.

Blue Mountain Sports and Wear
34 Susquehanna Street, Jim Thorpe
(570) 325-4421, (800) 599-4221
www.bikejimthorpe.com
This store carries the top lines in sporting equipment and clothing for hiking, biking, skiing, snowboarding, or just sitting around après-ski in front of the fireplace with a hot toddy at hand. The store deals heavily in mountain biking (see our Recreation chapter), carries just about everything an outdoorsman or woman would want,

except tents. There is no room for tents, but you'll find everything else, and if the prices seem a bit high, rest assured they only match the quality of the merchandise.

SWEETS AND EATS

The following is a taster's choice of special places that create delectable goodies. those who cater to our sweet teeth offer everything from fresh pretzels and "penny candy" to ice cream and funnel cake. We have chocolate here that runs beyond the ordinary to industrial-strength and even, in some cases, to weapons grade! Some of our Pocono purveyors offer tours and free tastes, and many will ship their products anywhere you want them to go. So get your blood-sugar up and running, and check them out to your stomach's content.

Delaware Water Gap/ Shawnee-on-Delaware

Country Kettle
US 209 Business, Marshalls Creek
(570) 421-8970, (877) 553-8853
www.country-kettle.com
Here is an oasis for the sweet tooth. In addition to its enormous and eclectic inventory of souvenirs, candles, sculptures, and collectibles, the Kettle also offers barrels and barrels of penny candy—Mexican hats, anise bears, jujubes, peanut butter logs, Reese's Pieces, M&Ms, chocolate-covered raisins and nuts, and the like. In addition you'll find shelf after shelf of jams, jellies, marmalades, cheeses, coffees, teas, designer mustards and vinegars, and all manner of other goodies for the gourmet. Fresh fudges and chocolates are made daily, and popcorn is popped right on the premises.

Dolcetto's
Delaware Street and Waring Drive
Delaware Water Gap
(570) 420-1198
www.delawarewatergap.com

A cooperative effort between Big Creek Vineyard and Antelao Restaurant, this lovely little store features a wine tasting counter and lots of interesting and exotic foodstuffs. Here you'll find Bulgarian vegetable spreads, cheeses, high-quality mustard, dark sesame oil, and that thin pickled ginger you get with sushi, among other fascinating items. They even sell Antelao's chocolate truffles. This is the ultimate pairing of wine and food.

Village Farmer & Bakery
13 Broad Street, Delaware Water Gap
(570) 476-0075
This great bakery specializes in pies—more than 40 different varieties, including blueberry, blackberry, pumpkin, strawberry, rhubarb, red raspberry, apple, and shoo-fly. We suggest the "fruit of the forest," which contains apples, strawberries, rhubarb, red raspberries, and blackberries. You can buy any type of pie with a regular or a crumb crust. Other taste-teasers include apple-walnut and pumpkin-cream cheese pies—yum! Folks with special dietary needs can buy pies made with Equal instead of sugar. There's also a great selection of gourmet foods—jellies and sauces, dip mixes, candles and more. Some foods, such as ice cream, pizza, chicken potpie, and hot dogs, can be eaten at outside tables or taken home. In the spring, The Village Farmer offers a wide selection of plants for your garden. During the summer and fall, there's a decent selection of local produce. All year-round you'll find some intriguing chachkas here as well.

Stroudsburg/East Stroudsburg

Sweet Creams
429 Main Street, Stroudsburg
(570) 421-7929
This old-fashioned ice cream parlor offers 19 flavors of ice cream—all homemade—as well as pies and other pastries to make a

dessert-lover's dream come true. See our Restaurants chapter for more details.

Truly Tasteful
730 Main Street, Stroudsburg
(570) 421-7226
www.trulytasteful.com
Truly Tasteful stocks gourmet food items, many of them locally made. You can find gourmet pastas, sauces, hors d'oeuvres, jams, crackers, scone mixes, all types of teas, instant cappuccino, and many varieties of gourmet coffee. All food items sold here, whether under the Truly Tasteful label or another, are personally taste-tested by all of the employees to determine if it is an item the store should carry. The shop also carries unique gift items and some antiques.

Truly Tasteful opened 14 years ago as a 300-square-foot shop specializing in gourmet items. Today the store has a solid presence on Main Street in Stroudsburg, and wholesales to more than 13,000 retail outlets around the country including Hallmark stores and Cracker Barrel.

Ironically, this shop's huge growth came as a result of the terrible winter of 1994. When the weather prevented shoppers from getting to the store, the owner decided to try her hand at wholesaling, and business boomed. Truly Tasteful ships gourmet gift baskets—choose a ready-made item from the basket menu or place a custom order—all over the world.

Upon entering, shoppers are offered one of the store's gourmet beverages. Every Saturday of a holiday weekend is an "Eat Your Way Through the Store Day," with free samples served all day long—steak in barbecue sauce, dips, pasta, muffins, jams, breads, mulled cider, and teas. Thanksgiving weekend is a three-day "Eat Your Way" event.

Weegee's
560 Main Street, Stroudsburg
(570) 424-8177
The rich aroma of 60 varieties of gourmet coffee fills this elegant little coffee shop in the heart of town. Colombian, Arabic, and other beans, flavored and straight, are served along with espresso and cappuccino. A wide array of specialty condiments and foods also are available.

Mount Pocono Area

American Candle
Highway 611, Bartonsville
(570) 629-3388
www.amcandlecollectible.com
There is more to this enormous bazaar than the candles, gifts, and collectibles mentioned elsewhere in this chapter. Though the penny candy of old costs a lot more than a penny now, everything you may remember from childhood is here, packed into 200 barrels. Grab a bag and fill it up with Gummi Bears, chocolate pretzels, malted milk balls, nonpareils, jelly beans, Willy Wonka Guppies, Jordan almonds, saltwater taffy, Mary Janes, sour balls, licorice, and dozens of other favorites from time gone by. You'll also find Pocono Mountain fudge, chocolates, fruit and nut mixes, and candy molds and chocolate melts to use in making your own candy at home. Now that your blood-sugar is looming at the Mount Everest level, stop at the old-fashioned ice-cream parlor and soda fountain and have a cup of gourmet Colombian coffee.

Callie's Candy Kitchen
Highway 390, Mountainhome
(570) 595-2280, (800) 252-7750
www.calliescandy.com
Make sure you're there for Mr. Callie's wonderful chocolate-making demonstration, which is offered several times a day. He not only gives you a lecture on chocolate and chocolate coating—passing around more samples than you can eat—embedded in this chocolate-coated event is an excellent lecture on marketing. The diversity of candy in the shop is astounding, and the staff make almost all of it themselves, including the all-day suckers. Pocono Mountain Bark is a favorite, with

its varieties of chocolate and nuts. Another specialty is chocolate-covered strawberries. The customers love the chocolate-covered pretzels and the Pocono crunch, a mix of Rice Krispies, butterscotch, and cashews. In-season, all different kinds of fruit are covered with chocolate including blueberries, peaches, and grapes. For a taste of something different, try the chocolate-covered cream cheese.

Callie's Pretzel Factory
Highways 390 and 191, Cresco
(570) 595-2280, (800) 252-7750
www.calliescandy.com
Handmade soft pretzels are baked and served right before your eyes—fresh and hot. Onion, garlic, cinnamon, pizza, and even hot dog pretzels are some of Callie's specialties. Get a hot dog wrapped in a crisp pretzel and a cinnamon pretzel for dessert, and you'll have a tasty, quick, and inexpensive lunch while you shop your way down Highway 390. Try to catch the demonstration of making hard candy and hard pretzels. These treats have become very popular with visitors. The Pretzel Factory also carries more than 25 varieties of gourmet popcorn. Don't miss Callie's Left-Handed Gift Shop with more than a hundred necessities and whimsical items for lefties.

Cooks Tour
Highway 191, Mountainhome
(570) 595-0370
Need a gadget to do some great cooking? You'll find it here. Cooks Tour has top-quality cooking tools and some hard-to-get ingredients. The best part of the store is the expertise. Logene Britton and Helene Zwerdling are experienced cooks and can help you select the best knife, the best pot, and the best peppercorns for your own cooking. Our personal gauge of the depth of a cooking store's gadgets is whether they have a spaetzle maker—a tool you won't find in your local department store. Cooks Tour has at least two different kinds of spaetzle makers, which puts them among the better cooking

stores. In addition to gadgets, they carry cookbooks, spices, pastas, sauces, flavored vinegars and mustards, chocolates, and lots more.

Cooks Tour has a lovely demonstration kitchen, and they offer hands-on classes and demonstrations of a variety of international cuisines and classic cooking techniques. On the weekends, you might get lucky and walk in when they offer samples of some of the foods they carry.

Just Desserts
The Crossings Factory Outlets
Building C, Tannersville
(570) 629-5120
Readjust your blood sugar level here with velvety chocolate concoctions, creamy rich cheesecakes, or if you need to justify the indulgence by touting the protein value of your dessert, nut-encrusted or nut-filled delicacies. Then you can shop a bit longer before you drop.

Pocono Cheesecake Factory
Highway 611, Swiftwater
(570) 839-6844
This constantly expanding slice of heaven began in the kitchen of owner Priscilla Moore. When the demand for her home-baked cheesecakes became too great to accommodate from her kitchen, she opened a small shop in Mountainhome, which she outgrew in five months. The current Pocono Cheesecake Factory has been expanded and renovated from a five-room house. Moore sells 'em home-made, right from the premises—huge, rich, creamy cheesecakes with a savory pastry crust. Amaretto, chocolate, chocolate chip, carrot cake, raspberry . . . the list goes on as the combinations evolve. You can also choose plain cheesecake and cap it with the fruit topping of your choice. Buy a slice of cheesecake, a whole cake, a half or a quarter. To please everyone, get a selection of different flavored quarters.

There are no tours of the "factory," but you can see them making the cheesecake during the week in the glassed-in kitchen behind the counter. The Pocono Cheesecake Factory ships cakes all over the country except in July and August, when the weather might spoil your lovely cake. They're a great gift idea, and you can order with your credit card.

Rocky Mountain Chocolate Factory
The Crossings Factory Outlets
Building B, Tannersville
(570) 688-4058
www.rmcf3.com
The big, fat plush bear who sits outside this factory outlet for the sweet tooth lures folks into a chocoholic heaven, with every shade, grade, and gradient of the delectable stuff at hand. The menu here also includes such goodies as frozen bananas and cheesecake—all dipped in chocolate, or course.

Milford/Lake Wallenpaupack Area

Gertrude Hawk
Route 6 Mall, US 6, Honesdale
(570) 253-5874

Pocono Plaza, 314 Lincoln Avenue
East Stroudsburg
(570) 424-2977

Stroud Mall, Highway 611, Stroudsburg
(570) 424-2170
www.gertrudehawkchocolates.com
Gertrude Hawk has become a chain, but no dissertation on Pocono chocolatiers can be complete without it. In addition to its regular menu of truffles, creams, and other wondrous goodies, the store in

Honesdale, tucked away inside a very large shopping center, also offers a huge section of "seconds"—chocolates deemed not quite right in appearance for the main candy case. There is absolutely no difference in taste or texture between these delectables and the ones at the front of the store—except that they are reduced in price by 50 percent. Gertrude Hawk also offers great gift baskets, boxed selections, and gourmet jelly beans with such out-of-sight flavors as tutti-frutti, cotton candy, and (believe it or not) buttered popcorn.

Village Coffee and Tea
East Harford Street, Apple Valley Village
Milford
(570) 296-8663
You can have coffee, to drink here or take home, in all of its varieties and other goodies. Sit at one of the tables, or order your coffee to go. There are also lots of teas and some distinctive teapots here.

TOYS

We don't have a Toys R Us or an F.A.O. Schwartz, but that doesn't mean we can't fill the Christmas stocking or supply the birthday party with the stuff of dreams for little ones. We have lots of toys, and here we include some of our favorite outlets for them. Be sure to check the previous "Souvenirs, Gifts, and Collectibles" section for details about where to find teddy bears, collectible dolls, and other specialty items.

Stroudsburg/East Stroudsburg

The Encounter
515 Main Street, Stroudsburg
(570) 424-6132
www.theencounter.com
Comic books, role-playing games, and collectible card games top the interest list here. Every day but Monday, children line the long tables in the back playing Poké-

If you're buying country furniture, make sure the drawers open and close easily, and give it a careful look, front and back. Some painted pieces of new furniture are crudely made to keep the price down. If you actually expect to use a piece, make sure it works.

mon, Magic, War Hammer, or some other game. Check in the store or on their Web site for a schedule. The Encounter also offers a wide range of action figures from Spiderman to Spawn (repeating their familiar masked faces on T-shirts), and a full line of *Star Wars* figures, toys, accessories, literature, as well as other collectors' items.

Kay-Bee Toy & Hobby Shop
Stroud Mall, Highway 611, Stroudsburg
(570) 476-0359
www.kbtoys.com
Kay-Bee is a chain store, but since it is the largest of its kind in the area, we felt it necessary to include it here. This mall outlet could sub for Santa's warehouse and never miss a nice child on his list. The store is packed floor to ceiling with plush toys, dolls, games, light sabers from *Star Wars*, battery-driven toys, and more delights than ever could be named here. Don't bring your kids here as a break from your other shopping unless you plan to leave with something. The temptations are just too many and too much for little eyes.

Mount Pocono Area

Toy Liquidators
The Crossings Factory Outlets
Building A, Tannersville
(570) 629-9566
www.kbtoys.com
Overstock from stores and warehouses, old lines of toys retired from regular retail outlets, and items rendered obsolete by a change of design fill the shelves at this jackpot of bargains, an affiliate of Kay-Bee Toys. Because stock is bought in bulk at cut-rate prices, you'll find some of the best buys around. You can find air-hockey games, in-line skates, die-cast cars, Barbie and baby dolls, and lots more. If you're making your toy-shopping trip any time in the vicinity of Christmas, come early because the place will be jammed.

UNIQUE STORES

We have some retail outlets that defy categorization. Here we find the magical and the mysterious, the eccentric and exotic—and the downright indefinable. We group them all together here. For the most part, you'll find them, as the section title states, unique.

Stroudsburg/East Stroudsburg

The Chocolate Spot and Pocono Teddy Bear Workshop
762 Main Street, Stroudsburg
(570) 420-9424
www.thechocolatespot.com
It's every child's dream (whatever the age of the child in question): spend an afternoon eating chocolate and making teddy bears. This sweet shop, specializing in a milk chocolate ranging from dark to ivory, with truffles and fudge on the side, boasts a veritable teddy bear factory in the back room, where counselors teach kids how to put a plush toy together, stuff it, stitch it, and take it home in a log cradle. There is no age limit for participants, and walk-ins, with their parents, are welcome. The Workshop also schedules parties in advance, starting at $15 per guest and going up to $25 for one at which every attendee gets decked out in a complete themed outfit.

Frazetta's Fantasy Corner
186 South Courtland Street
East Stroudsburg
(570) 421-9054
Frazetta's carries top-quality costumes for rent and sale. You'll also find wonderfully horrifying masks, props, wigs, stage makeup, and karate clothing here. Halloween is the big time of the year at Frazetta's; they get even more costumes for children and adults.

Local Color
427 Main Street, Stroudsburg
(570) 420–1530

Local Color is to the average print shop what the Starship *Enterprise* is to the Wright brothers' flying bicycle. Graphic designer Bob Barker does fliers, brochures, ads, invitations, announcements, and other necessities of the business world, but he does them with a state-of-the-art laser color copier that turns them into works of art. Barker creates greeting cards by laying flowers from his own garden in the copier's template. The resulting prints are in vivid color and so realistic that they appear almost three-dimensional. With a French twist, he call them "*fleur du jour,*" and sells them for $2.75 each. On other projects, he can take an original design straight from the computer to the copier; his specialty is "anything to do with the creative use of paper."

Seasons
615 Main Street, Stroudsburg
(570) 424–3160

This is as wild and wonderful a collection of funky jewelry, stained glass, silk-screened T-shirts, crazy ties, and other artifacts of the imagination as one will find anywhere. Seasons carries a unique line of hilarious greeting cards with messages ranging from double entendre through rude to downright crude. If ever you want to lay a major insult on some one, here's the place to find it.

Shooting for the Moon
5052 Milford Road, East Stroudsburg
(570) 223–0103
www.shootingforthemoon.com

Kathy Brown calls her eclectic little boutique of myth, magic, and mystery, "A different kind of store." That may be the understatement of the decade. The "difference" is palpable the minute one walks through the door. The atmosphere is warm and friendly and the air redolent of Brazilian bark, sandalwood, and handmade patchouli candles. Display cases glitter with a wide range of jewelry; soft wind chimes sing overhead, and runes, tarot decks, and astrological aids are in abundance. The store features a colorful collection of fun and funky fashions, including belly dancing outfits with all the accessories, and figurines of elves, fairies, unicorns, and dragons clamor for attention. Shooting for the Moon staff includes certified practitioners of Reiki and aromatherapy (see the "Health Care" entry in our chapter on Relocation). Services include readings, book sales, and classes covering an exotic array of metaphysical studies. Another branch of Shooting for the Moon recently opened in Brodheadsville in the West End.

Stroudsburg Foto Shop
724 Main Street, Stroudsburg
(570) 421–2830
www.stroudsburgfoto.com

There is nothing unique about the average camera store, but Stroudsburg Foto is far from average. You can buy film almost everywhere, and when you walk into a megastore in a megamall or in the heart of big metropolitan district, you can buy just about any sort of camera you desire; just plunk down your credit card and take it away. But when you do, don't ask about its use or special features because (a) the clerk doesn't know, (b) the clerk doesn't care, and (c) the clerk wouldn't want to talk to you even if (a) and (b) weren't in operation.

But this is Main Street, where if you're here for a while, you'll be called by your first name, and where if your new photo equipment doesn't work out, you can take it back. Buy a camera or equip your dark room at the Foto Shop, and when you walk out with the item, you'll know all there is to know about it, because the folks here will take you through it step by step—even if the stepping takes all afternoon. Stroudsburg Foto also offers the best developing in the area, a wide selection of telescopes, and lots of frames, and other photo accessories.

Mount Pocono Area

Theo B. Price Lumber
Highways 191 and 390, Cresco
(570) 595–2501, (888) 478–1236
www.theobprice.com

Don't be fooled by the name. Lumber is only a part of this historic shop started by Theordore Price in 1905 as a miner's supply store. The shop has gone through many phases, reflecting the changing times. It was a general store and a grocery store after the mines became mechanized and until the supermarkets blew away the competition. Then the store went into hardware, and under Marianne Miller, Price's granddaughter, the shop has expanded into a huge, rambling store filled with a little bit of everything.

One room has gourmet food including Vermont's Green Mountain Coffee and Grafton Cheese. Miller has a special interest in teas, and you'll find quite a variety of herbal and green teas here. Other rooms are filled with great gift items—original art, Williamsburg pottery, authentic Amish hats, hand-carved ducks and birds, Santas of all descriptions, toys, bears, quilts from Lancaster, fabric and quilting supplies, Limoges boxes, and more. Miller has a great eye for folk art, and some of the items here are museum-quality.

Look carefully around the store and you'll see an original scale, the original cash register that rang to $20 (the most amount of money anyone could imagine a customer spending), original counters, and some of the early merchandise arranged on a ledge near the ceiling. There's a pot-bellied stove with a chair in front of it that begs for a chessboard on a barrel, but the store is too packed with merchandise to leave room for a barrel. Two of their most popular lines are Burt's Bees products and Vera Bradley handbags.

Price is a popular spot for tourists, and you'll see why when you explore this fascinating store; just leave yourself plenty of time. Come on a Saturday and taste samples of cheese and crackers. During the rest of the week, there's usually free coffee until noon, iced tea in the summer, and hot cider in the winter.

West End

Emporium of Curious Goods
15 Broadway, Jim Thorpe
(570) 325–4038

The arcane and the occult reign supreme in this little boutique of mysteries. The Emporium carries a full line of New Age books, tarot decks, incense, crystal balls, rings and pendants of "magick," and all the artifacts necessary in the practice of Wicca (see our Worship chapter). Their line of Renaissance-style clothing has proved extremely popular, especially with brides-to-be. The collection of gargoyles—those demonic-looking creatures of Christianity placed atop Europeans churches as guardians against evil—and cunning sculpted trolls is the best we've seen anywhere.

Mauch Chunk 5 & 10
9 Broadway, Jim Thorpe
(570) 325–2341

With the demise of the once-giant J.J. Newberry and F.W. Woolworth chains, this is one of the last "five and dimes" left on the planet. It sells everything five and dimes of yesteryear ever sold, and the ambience of the good old days when a nickel or a dime actually bought something worth taking home is free.

The Red Sled
US 209 at 6200 Interchange Road
Lehighton
(610) 377–3535

This is as rich and eclectic a collection of country crafts, pottery, woodwork, primitives, fabrics, and candles as one will find anywhere. Gourmet teas and coffees share space with prints, slates, art supplies, dolls, and a whole family of Boyd's Bears. Rowe, Bennington, and clay pottery fill the shelves, and an entire back room is dedicated to Yankee Candles. If the Ghost of Christmas Present ever touched Grandma's attic, this is what it would look like.

Milford/Lake Wallenpaupack Area

Le Monde et Vous
Cottage at the Upper Mill, 150 Sawkill Avenue, Milford
(570) 296-4497
Packed into a tiny cottage is a whole world of imports. You'll find jewelry from Indonesia, China, India, and our own Southwest; Buddhist singing bowls and bells; African carvings; cloth from Indonesia and Ghana; rare carved dowry boxes from India; antiques directly from Tibet; and beautiful batik dresses from Indonesia. The owners travel all over the world to find interesting items made by indigenous people. Please call before you visit the shop to make sure they're open.

Phoenix Antiques, Crafts and Gifts
US 209, Dingmans Ferry
(570) 828-8870
Phoenix is in the carriage house of a former Dutch Reform Church built in 1850 and listed on the National Register of Historic Places. The shop has tons of great Southwestern stuff—very fine Native American pottery at excellent prices; Mexican fantasy sculptures; limited edition Southwestern prints by well known artists; the largest selection of Native American jewelry in the tri-state area, including a good selection of unusual turquoise from the Manassas mine, a turquoise that has beautiful brown matrix; and more. Every time you turn your head, you'll see fascinating things you desperately want. There are some unusual antiques here too. Huge cupboards made by Texas Mennonites and tables made with birch logs are some of the larger pieces for sale. Sprinkled among the Southwestern stuff are items from around the world. Because so much in this store is one-of-a-kind, you'll find different things in here all the time.

Phoenix is in the Delaware Water Gap National Recreation Area and is surrounded by gorgeous, Eden-like gardens full of tropical plants that have to be taken in each fall. The public is welcome to tread the paths through the gardens and admire the fabulous plantings. If you're lucky, you'll catch the prickly pear, which is actually native to some parts of this area, covered with yellow flowers in May and June.

OUR MAIN STREETS

In the final analysis, America is nothing more than Main Street. Sinclair Lewis knew it and wrote about it. Norman Rockwell knew it and immortalized it on posters and magazine covers in paintings that captured the soul of a nation. Whether we actually live in the hypertensive canyons of Manhattan, the cornfields of Iowa, the wilds of Wyoming, or in the glitz and glitter of California, we instinctively seek out Main Street because that is where the attitudes and the personalities and the living philosophies of our villages, towns, and cities are formed.

When the interstate highway system started bypassing those villages, towns, and cities in the 1950s, conventional wisdom said Main Street was finished—but it wasn't. When the first shopping malls came into being in the 1960s, Main Street again was said to be all washed up, but once again, it survived. And it survives today—the tough, resilient heart of America. You meet your own people on Main Street. The customer is always right there, and if you've been in the area any length of time, merchants on Main Street call you by your first name.

Not all main streets are called Main Street, of course, but it doesn't matter because Main Street isn't a place; it's a state of mind. So let's go out onto the main streets of the Poconos and meet the people who represent that state of mind. Here are a few snapshots of what you might expect to find when you get there.

Delaware Water Gap/ Shawnee-on-Delaware

DELAWARE WATER GAP

The Water Gap Resort anchors one end of Delaware Water Gap's Main Street. Traveling downhill from the resort, we come to the Water Gap Trolley Stop with the sightseeing trolley (see our Attractions chapter), a miniature golf course, snacks, and some friendly ducks. Main Street climbs back up another the hill from the trolley stop, passing intriguing private homes (one is a converted church) as well as some shops and restaurants. The first business you'll come to is Antelao Restaurant, which has a terrific reputation (see our Restaurants chapter). Farther on is the Marketplace (see the "Antiques" section of this chapter), an indoor antique and flea market. Higher still is the Antoine Dutot School and Museum (see our Attractions chapter). Next door to the museum is the Trails End Cafe (see our Restaurants chapter) with excellent food and some lovely pottery for sale. Across the street, at the crest of the hill is the Presbyterian Church of the Mountain, which offers free Sunday evening concerts in its gazebo during the summer and runs the Appalachian Trail Hiker's Center with a sign that declares Georgia is 1,100 miles to the south and Maine is 900 miles to the north. Hikers have said that the church is one of the best facilities for them along the trail. Going past the church, you come to the Deer Head Inn (see our Restaurants, Arts and Culture, and Nightlife chapters), a wonderful restaurant and one of the best places anywhere to see live jazz. Across from the Deer Head is Water Gap Gallery, where you can buy pottery, leather goods, art glass, jewelry, and the CDs of local jazz artists. Past the gallery is Dolcetto, a cooperative venture between Big Creek Vineyard and Winery and Antelao Restaurant. You can taste the wines and buy exotic ingredients for home cooking in this shop. Walk to the end of the street (now called Delaware Street) to see the Castle Inn, the resort Fred Waring used for his choral rehearsals and seminars. While one part of the inn still houses Shawnee Press, Waring's publishing arm and a major force in choral music nationally, the rest of the inn is unused. Over the years, various buyers and plans for the Castle Inn have been announced, but thus far, it remains vacant, except for the weekend after Labor Day, when the Delaware Water Gap Celebration of the Arts (see our Arts and Culture chapter) is held on the grounds of this lovely spot. Cross over to Mountain Road, which runs along one side of the Deer Head, and you can walk up a couple of blocks to catch the Appalachian Trail.

PORTLAND

If you want to park your car and spend all day antiquing, go to Portland. Its main street is lined with antique shops, the famous Duckloe Furniture company (see the previous "Furniture" section) and an outfitter that rents canoes, kayaks, and tubes. Some weekends, Portland puts on sidewalk events to encourage people to come and see its shops. When you need a break from antiquing, you can cross the walking bridge with a wonderful view of the Delaware Water Gap over the river to Columbus, New Jersey, and back. There's a great spot to get in the river right next to the bridge.

MARSHALLS CREEK

Every metropolitan area around the country has its strip: the area on the edge of town with lots of chain stores, fast-food places and motels. US 209 in Marshalls Creek is such a strip, and new business are constantly springing up here.

In fact, as the last few green spots get bought up and built up, controversy over development seems to center around US 209 and Marshalls Creek. Some of the hills have been stripped away to make nice flat parking lots for places like Dairy Queen. The highway can get horribly backed up on weekends. The Pocono Bazaar and

Flea Market (see "Flea Markets" in this section) is usually blamed for the back-ups, but there's a real problem with the intersection of US 209 and Highway 402. The Foxmoor Outlet Mall (see "Outlets and Malls") and Starting Gate (see "Sports Outfitters") are on US 209, as are a few hotels, including the Shannon Inn, and Werry's Cottages, Motels and Pub (see our Hotels, Motels, and Resorts chapter). A number of restaurants including Alaska Pete's and Petrizzo's (see our Restaurants chapter) are also along 209. Although Marshalls Creek addresses alternate with East Stroudsburg addresses with no visible logic, what feels like the end of the Marshalls Creek "strip" is the Fernwood Resort, which straddles the highway just before the entrance to the Delaware Water Gap National Recreation Area.

Stroudsburg/East Stroudsburg

STROUDSBURG

Stroudsburg's main street is divided into Upper Main and Lower Main, and both fairly glow with the patina of a rich and varied history.

Upper Main is anchored by the Stroud mansion (see our Attractions chapter), built in 1795 by Colonel Jacob Stroud, the town's founding father, as a gift for his son. It serves now as a museum and as headquarters for the Monroe County Historical Association, and it is surrounded by a stately host of Victorian mansions, most of which have long since been converted into elegant shops and restaurants.

Upper Main flows past 19th-century buildings on both sides of the street, housing an eclectic company of local merchants, art galleries, excellent restaurants, chic boutiques, banks, and a beautiful church. With one sharp turn at the Wallace Building, a onetime hardware store now housing a series of specialty shops, the street becomes Lower Main. The Wal-

lace Building's parapet still bears a sign announcing commerce in "wheels, spokes, shafts" and other necessities for horse-drawn wagons long since vanished in the mists of time.

On Lower Main, you will find the old Holland Thread Mill Factory, a touchstone of architectural excellence with its restored brick front, small gardens, and brick walkways. The old factory now houses several small shops, modern apartments, and office space.

The ambience of Stroudsburg's Main Street has been further enhanced by the work of the Jacob Stroud Corporation, an organization that was created to promote Main Street by running special events and working with the concerns and needs of the varied merchants to create a cohesive and thriving Main Street. The entire effect is that of a time machine taking a historic neighborhood back into the era in which it originally was designed.

EAST STROUDSBURG

Dansbury Depot is the centerpiece of Crystal Street, East Stroudsburg's "main street." Although a devastating fire in 1996 wiped out many of the stores on Crystal Street, it has recovered beautifully. This restored train depot houses a great restaurant by the same name (see our Restaurants chapter), and some small specialty shops.

Across the street is the whimsical Liztech Gallery, featuring fine crafts and art in an architecturally adventurous interior. Liztech's owner, Jill Elizabeth, has plans for Crystal Street, and if you start seeing whimsical mosaics around tree planters and into a park next to the Dansbury Depot, know that it's Jill's doing.

East Stroudsburg's main street continues around the corner to Courtland Street and the Pocono Cinema (see our Nightlife and Arts and Culture chapters) and the fantastic Frazetta costume shop. (See our "Unique Stores" section in this chapter as well as our Attractions chapter.)

Washington Street completes the "main drag" of East Stroudsburg, which originally was destined to be named Dansbury—hence the name of the old railroad depot.

Mount Pocono Area

MOUNT POCONO/ MOUNTAINHOME

Mount Pocono's Pocono Boulevard is a busy main street with ancient souvenir shops like the Old Village Trader (see "Souvenirs, Gifts, and Collectibles"), restaurants, and the Casino, and a truly great movie theater (see our Nightlife chapter). It's quaint and definitely old Poconos. Not too much of Mountainhome is walkable, since its main street is PA 390 and it's pretty spread out, but it has intriguing restaurants like Cooks Touch (see our Restaurants chapter), places to stay, especially the lovely Naomi Village; and some excellent stores including Price's fabulous hardware store (see "Unique Stores") and Cooks Tour (see "Sweets and Eats"). The Pocono Playhouse (see our Arts and Culture chapter) is just off the main drag. This is one of those streets where, walking or driving, you'll want to stop every block or two and check something out.

West End

JIM THORPE

Jim Thorpe actually has two main streets—Broadway and Race. Broadway starts at the railroad station and tourist information center beside the Lehigh River, passes Market Square and winds up the hill to West Broadway. Race Street branches off, forming a Y that leads down to US 209, which parallels the Lehigh River and is part of the street base of Jim Thorpe's shopping area. Take a walk up, down, and around these narrow, winding streets with squares, courts, and parks

and you may think you are in some picturesque Alpine village in Europe.

Shops and galleries line the streets, along with several quaint bed-and-breakfasts and country inns (see our Bed-and-Breakfast and Country Inns chapter). Art galleries and museums abound, and whatever you do, do not miss the Mauch Chunk Opera House, the Dimmick Memorial Library, and the Old Jail (see our History, Arts and Culture, Attractions, and Restaurants chapters).

Train rides leave from the historic station in town from May through October, and the Asa Packer mansion-cum-museum is a rich time-trip back into a history we now can only imagine. (See our History and Attractions chapters.)

But the real "trip" is Race Street—an atavistic reflection of the 1960s counterculture now re-emerging in love beads, sandals, and a wide panorama of New Age esoterica. All of this is growing vigorously amid little art galleries and boutiques of strange and wondrous things in the middle of the Stone Row built in the 1840s by coal baron Asa Packer to house his workers and artisans. St. Mark's Church (see our Attractions chapter), a treasure house of Tiffany windows, English Minton tile floors and stone carvings, and steep stone garden terraces blend with the new in a remarkably happy marriage of history and the future.

Milford/Lake Wallenpaupack Area

MILFORD

Milford is a Victorian town that would have made the perfect location for filming The Music Man. Broad and Harford Streets—US 6 and US 209, respectively—intersect in Milford, and you can walk along them both, sampling the restaurants, antique shops, and crafts galleries. Note especially Forest Hall, the beautiful bluestone building at the corner of Har-

ford and Broad. Stand about a block away and look at its stunning roof line. The original part of the structure, facing on Harford, was built for painters of the Hudson River School, who worked in one building in New York City. Milford's most prominent family, the Pinchots (see our History chapter), provided a studio so the painters could spend the summer in a cooler clime. Paths were cut in the nearby woodlands for them to wander and find good spots to immortalize on canvas. Take a good look at some of those Hudson River paintings, and you'll see Delaware River scenes. The rest of the building, facing on Broad Street was built to hold Gifford Pinchot's forestry school on the second and third floors, while providing retail space for Milford on the ground floor.

Keep your eyes open and peer down the side streets. Some of the most interesting shops are not on the main drag. In fact, the town is so lovely, you should walk the side streets and admire the architecture.

HAWLEY

Hawley doesn't have Main Street, but it does have Main Avenue, and what the heart of this little village may lack in sophisticated decor, it more than makes up for in the warmth and friendliness of its people. Main Avenue is home to one of the best country inns and restaurants in the Poconos—the Settlers Inn at Bingham Park (see our Restaurants and Bed-and-Breakfasts and Country Inns chapters). The history here is one of coal, canals, and railroads. The village was named for Irad Hawley, first president of the Pennsylvania Coal Company. The old railroad parallels the town, and off Main, some lovely Victorian manses still carry the color of days gone by.

HONESDALE

Another honest-to-geography Main Street dominates this historic old town where the first steam engine ever run in the United States made its debut. Built in England and transported to the United States, it was called the *Stourbridge Lion,* and it now rests on display in the Smithsonian Institution. A reproduction of the *Stourbridge Lion* is housed in the Wayne County Historical Society Museum, on Main. Stately Victorian homes line quiet streets on either side of Main, along with three churches that are architectural gems (see our Attractions chapter) and a charming city square. Honesdale once was nicknamed "Maple City" in honor of some 1,500 maple trees planted by city fathers to provide shade. Many of them still grace the landscape.

ATTRACTIONS

ttraction is a funny word, especially in a tourist area. The biggest
attraction here is the natural environment. The gateway to the Poconos,
the Delaware Water Gap, was once called
"the eighth wonder of the world." Its visual
power has been somewhat diluted by busy
Interstate 80 winding through, but it's still
breathtaking. We have the Delaware River,
designated a "wild and scenic river"; it gives
us paths for walking, beaches for sunning
and swimming, and a wonderful watery way
for canoeing, rafting, and tubing (see our
In, On, and Around the Water chapter for
details). We have numerous waterfalls (see
Our Natural World for directions to some of
these), babbling brooks, pristine lakes, deep
hemlock-covered gorges, and high spots
where we can see miles of beautiful land
spread out before us.

Because the Pocono region is a tourist
area, and has been for a long, long time, it
boasts lots of man-made attractions too.
These range from the deeply spiritual
Columcille (see this chapter's Close-up) to
kitschy miniature train layouts. We also
have numerous small museums with excellent exhibits. Most of these museums are
treated more extensively in the Arts and
Culture and Native Americans chapters,
but we mention them here too so you
won't forget them when you're leafing
through these pages looking for something to do.

This area is full of history. Events you
might have learned about in school, such
as the Walking Purchase, happened here.
There are lots of historical markers scattered around the Poconos; take the time
to stop and read them. It's fun to learn
that you're standing on the spot where the
first European settler built his home.

Attractions could easily include all the
items listed in Parks; Our Natural World;
Arts and Culture; Kidstuff; In, On, and
Around the Water; and Recreation. We

don't want to repeat ourselves too much,
but you should also look in these chapters
for interesting places to visit.

ADMISSION PRICE

The following is a price code for admission to attractions. The price listed is for
adults. Children and senior citizens' admissions are usually lower.

$5.00 or less	$
$5.01 to $10.00	$$
$10.01 to $15.00	$$$
$15.01 or more	$$$$

DELAWARE WATER GAP/ SHAWNEE-ON-DELAWARE

Antoine Dutot School & Museum $
Highway 611, Delaware Water Gap
(570) 476–4240
www.delawarewatergap.com
In 1793 Antoine Dutot purchased the land
that is now the town of Delaware Water
Gap. He designed a settlement and
named it Dutotsburg, setting aside some
property to be used for religious or educational purposes. Sometime later in that
century—no one knows exactly when—this
school was built on that land. Dutot would
be happy to know that, though its days as
a school ended in 1969, the building is
now a museum and still serves an educational purpose.

One classroom of the museum re-
creates a school of the 1920s. You can sit
at a school desk, complete with inkwell,
and watch a dramatic 11-minute slide presentation on the history of Delaware Water
Gap. The next room is filled with local
memorabilia—postcards and photos of the
town during its glory days as a resort
area, very young photos of Fred Astaire
and his sister Adele, who vacationed here,
a small collection of Native American

ATTRACTIONS

points and celts found around Lake Lenape on the Appalachian Trail, and Arnold Palmer's golf shoes. The first floor hosts a changing exhibit of local artists.

The museum is open Memorial Day through mid-October.

Bushkill Falls $$
Bushkill Falls Road, Bushkill
(570) 588-6682, (888) 628-7454
www.bushkillfalls.com

Billed as the "Niagara of Pennsylvania," Bushkill is one of the most impressive waterfalls in the region. (see Our Natural World chapter for more information and more falls). Surrounded by moss, ferns, and wildflowers, the Bushkill Creek plunges off a 100-foot cliff into a deep pool.

Four trails wander through the woods and by the falls. The green trail, the shortest and easiest, is a 15-minute walk to the main falls. The yellow and blue trails go farther into the woods—45 minutes and an hour respectively for a round trip. These trails take visitors to more falls and the beautiful Upper Canyon and Laurel Glen. If you like to hike, take the orange trail—the longest—covering nearly 2 miles of often steep, wooded terrain. You will need at least two hours to complete it. All the trails are well maintained and well marked. Benches are placed strategically at particularly scenic spots and at the top of steep sets of stairs. Although lots of people hike the green and yellow trails, the blue and orange trails, requiring a little more work on your part, will reward you with some quiet moments and lovely scenery.

Also on the property are gift shops; miniature golf; fishing; paddleboats; a large, gracious picnic pavilion complete with Adirondack chairs and a twig lounger; ice cream and fudge shops, and a

Native American exhibit that emphasizes the local Lenape ways. (See our Native American chapter.) The Native American Exhibit is wheelchair accessible; Bushkill Falls is not.

Cold Air Cave
Highway 611, south of Delaware Water Gap

Just south of Delaware Water Gap on Highway 611, between the Point of Gap and Arrow Island overlooks, look on the west side of the road; you'll see just enough room to park some cars. Pull in and you'll feel a surprising rush of cold air, no matter how warm the day. A short, rocky path leads to the cave. Bring a flashlight and peer inside. You can see the entire cave from the entrance; it used to be deeper, but parts of it have collapsed over the years. For this reason, we wouldn't recommend going inside. At one time, a cabin was built over this cave, and the owner chilled sodas in the cold air. He charged tourists a nickel to see the cave, but they could have a soda for free. Rangers speculate that there could be a cold mountain stream under the cave, and that its shape traps the cold generated by the stream.

Delaware Water Gap
Interstate 80, at the Pennsylvania/New Jersey border

This is the one sight we always take our out-of-town guests to see. The water gap was most likely formed by the Delaware River, butting its way through a mountain—it's an awesome sight. You can see the gap from I-80, 15 miles or more west of the border and from numerous other high spots throughout the eastern Poconos, but it's best viewed right up close.

If you travel Highway 611 south from the village of Delaware Water Gap, you will see a number of places to stop. The first, Resort Point Overlook, is on the site of one of Delaware Water Gap's most famous hotels, the Kittatinny House. Begun in 1829 by Antoine Dutot, the original resort could house 25 guests. By 1860 the Kittatinny House could hold 250–275 overnight visitors and was possibly the most prestigious place to stay in the country's second most popular inland resort town (No. 1 was Saratoga Springs, New York). Even though the kitchen was housed in a separate building, Kittatinny House eventually burned to the ground. You can see one of the ovens from the old kitchen by taking a short path just to the left of the stone wall at the overlook. The path is narrow and so full of poison ivy, however, that we would recommend looking for the ovens only before May, when the poison ivy hasn't taken over, or later in the year when the undergrowth is gone. Don't attempt it when the ground is slippery, either. You have to cross a stream via a narrow bridge with no sides, and you definitely wouldn't want to slide off. There's a beautiful hiking path that leads to the Appalachian Trail just across Highway 611 from this overlook.

Keep going south on Highway 611 to the overlook called Point of Gap. From there you can see the "Indian Head," a stone profile that reminded people of Chief Tammany, a 17th-century Lenape leader. The profile is somewhat eroded, but you can still make out the main features. Park in the lot and look at the right side of the mountain, where it's all stone. Follow the stone up to the tree line—that's Chief Tammany's hairline. Once you've located his forehead, look back down to find his nose, a piece of rock projecting from the mountain. You should also be able to spot his eye. On a nice day, you'll probably see rock climbers all over the chief's face. You'll almost always see hawks riding the updrafts from the mountain, and if you're lucky, you might spot a bald or golden eagle.

Mary Stolz Doll & Toy Museum $
McCole Road, Bushkill
(570) 588-7566

The Mary Stolz Museum (see our Kidstuff chapter) has a fascinating collection of antique dolls—among them an original Kewpie doll; fashion dolls from 1900; porcelain dolls from Limoges; ivory, wax,

and celluloid dolls; and a number of Kammer & Reinhardt dolls from Germany. More recent collections include some Danbury Mint dolls; a whole bunch of Barbies and Jems; some mechanical toys from the 1950s, including the monkey who claps a pair of cymbals; and a series of Hess gasoline trucks. There are some rooms in miniature, many assembled by Mary Stolz herself. The gift shop is as fascinating as the museum, with collectible dolls for sale at reasonable prices. You can buy that Barbie you missed when it was in Kmart, and you'll pay only a few dollars more. There's also a great collection of dollhouse furniture for those who like decorating in miniature. The museum is open daily. Days and hours vary with the season; call to make sure they're open. There's no admission to the shop, but if you bring your kid, you likely will have to buy something!

The Pocono Indian Museum $
U.S. Highway 209, Bushkill
(570) 588-9338
www.poconoindianmuseum.com

Artifacts and exhibits at this museum depict the history of Northeastern Pennsylvania from about 12,000 years ago through the arrival of European settlers prior to the American Revolution. You can see examples of bark houses, pottery, and weapons and learn how the Lenape were nearly eliminated by whites over a period of roughly 100 years. (See our Native Americans chapter for more information.)

The 30-minute, self-guided tour is accompanied by an audio recording.

A large gift shop sells Native American items, including clothing, toys, jewelry, pottery, and an excellent collection of books you won't find at other area bookstores.

The museum is open seven days a week.

There are lots of historical markers scattered around the Poconos; take the time to stop and read them. It's fun to learn that you're standing on the spot where the first European settler built his home.

Read up on our history; our History chapter is a good place to start. A familiarity with local history will give you a much greater appreciation for many spots around the Poconos.

Pocono Snake and Animal Farm $$
US 209, Marshalls Creek
(570) 223-8653
www.poconovacations.com/attractions/
zoo-animal-parks/poconosnakefarm

If you like to talk to the animals, Pocono Snake and Animal Farm has more than 100 species that will talk back to you. You can safely watch a rattlesnake rattle and make threatening displays at you—a scary enterprise, even though there's plenty of wire and glass between you and the reptile. Fred, the capuchin monkey, loves to throw himself at the glass to make the humans jump, while the other capuchins leap around and show off for you. If you're lucky, you'll get to see a wolf and a Pennsylvania black bear play together. The pot-bellied pig will show you where the food dispenser is, so bring some quarters. When you go into the petting enclosure, be careful; the goat likes to get out to see if anyone left food around another dispenser. Don't worry; you can lure her back with a handful of feed. If you're smart, you can even elude the goat and feed the beautiful deer in the enclosure. The snake and animal farm now sells bottles so that visitors may bottle feed the animals, something the visitors say they love.

Although the enclosures are traditional concrete and wire zoo cages, they are much larger than required by law. All of the mammals here were born in captivity and hand raised. Most of them are friendly and crave your attention. Some can even be fed and petted. The Pocono Snake and Animal Farm tries to breed many of their animals, so some may be off at their version of a honeymoon hotel (heart-shaped food dishes?) Some of the animals appear on New York–based talk shows, so if that

cougar looks familiar, you might have seen it on TV.

The snake and animal farm is open daily from the end of May through November and weekends, weather permitting, the rest of the year.

Shawnee Place Play & Water Park $$$
Hollow Road, Shawnee-on-Delaware
(570) 421-7231
www.shawneemt.com

Children love the water slides and play areas at Shawnee Place. They can splash around in the water or frolic in a large bin filled with small plastic balls. Magic shows and hands-on workshops are held throughout the day. (See our Kidstuff chapter for more information.) Most of the activities are ideal for children ages 2 through 12.

Shawnee Place is open daily from mid-June through Labor Day.

Thunder Creek Quarry $$$$
Creek Road, Marshalls Creek
(570) 223-7177
www.mountainmanor.com

Built to resemble an old mining building, the arcade room at Thunder Creek looks like a casino for kids. As in a casino, there are no clocks on the wall, and there's thick carpeting under foot. While some of the games resemble gambling machines (you can drop your token into a machine that will come maddeningly close to pushing other tokens through a slot and into your waiting hands), most are arcade games that award the kiddies tickets, redeemable for toys at the desk. Instead of luscious babes in scanty costumes dancing through, you may run into T.C., a costumed mascot that's supposed to be a friendly wolf. If you want babes, try the playroom where the little ones take off their shoes to cavort on a soft climbing element with a small ball pool where they can "swim" around.

There are snacks and light meals of the pizza/hot dog variety. You can eat in the air-conditioned arcade room or sit outside on a deck overlooking the bumper-boat pool. A really nice go-kart track has a bridge you drive over and under; rookie racers can use a simpler, oval track. A miniature golf course entertains miniature golfers as well as adults.

There's no admission to Thunder Creek; each attraction is a separate price, and discounts on multiple rides are available. There's also an all-day admission price. Thunder Creek is open every day during the summer. The outdoor elements stay open until it's too cold, while the indoor arcade is open year-round on the weekend.

Water Gap Trolley $$
Highway 611, Delaware Water Gap
(570) 476-9766
www.delawarewatergap.com

A nicely appointed trolley rides through the scenery and history of the Delaware Water Gap area. Your guide tells you about our history, from the time the Lenape were dominant to the present, while showing you sights like the Delaware Water Gap, the cold air cave, the Castle Inn, Historic Shawnee Church, and the homes of famous people who lived here.

The trolley has an excellent sound system so we could hear clearly, and our guide was wonderful. Unlike many tourist guides, he knew his history well and conveyed it in an entertaining manner. Whether you're a tourist or a longtime resident, this tour will give you some new insights into the area.

The Water Gap Trolley has been adding amenities to its trolley stop. While waiting for the next tour, you can play Pro-Am minigolf (see our Recreation chapter), eat snacks available at the stand, buy souvenirs, or feed the friendly ducks.

The tour schedule starts at the end of March and goes into November, weather permitting. Tours run about every 1.5 hours (call for the day's schedule as it varies seasonally), rain or shine. Groups are welcome, but reservations for every-one are strongly suggested. You can also charter a Water Gap Trolley for weddings and parades.

STROUDSBURG/EAST STROUDSBURG

The Frank Frazetta Museum $$
US 209, East Stroudsburg
(570) 424-5833

Resembling a small stucco castle, this museum presents the work of an artist who has drawn comics; book covers including the *Conan the Adventurer* series; posters for movies such as *What's New Pussycat?*, and much, much more. In fact, the minute you see some of Frazetta's paintings, you will recognize the influence he has had on George Lucas's *Star Wars*.

Here Frazetta's oils, watercolors, and incredibly detailed pencil drawings are presented framed and in a gallery, instead of in the commercial context in which you have seen his work before, and it's here that you realize just how masterful he is as an artist. Ellie Frazetta, Frank's wife, will show you a couple of the important paintings in the collection, and then she sets you loose to contemplate the rest. The oils are luminous, and though they depict fantasy scenes, the light and super-real detail reminds you of the Dutch masters. Devils, heroes, and barbarians are caught at the moment before a strike, weapons raised, and muscles straining. Mostly naked women, some vulnerable, some powerful, demonstrate Frazetta's mastery of the human body.

A gift shop offers books, posters, and some special Frazetta items.

The museum is open Saturday and Sunday only April to Christmas; call for hours. To find the museum, take the Marshalls Creek exit from I-80. Turn left onto Business 209 at the light in Marshalls Creek (a small shopping center will be on your right), and watch for a former florist, now Woodpecker Signs, but you'll see the moldering greenhouses, on the right. As soon as you see Woodpecker Signs, look for a driveway on the left with a square concrete column. Turn into the driveway, and bear left at the arrow pointing to "Museum." Drive carefully; lots of children live here. The museum will come up on your right. The only time you are allowed on this private road is when the museum is open. At all other times, you will be trespassing.

Quiet Valley Living Historical Farm $$
Quiet Valley Road, Stroudsburg
(570) 992-6161
www.quietvalley.org

Costumed in traditional clothing, guides and role players give you an idea of what life was like in the 18th and 19th centuries on this Pennsylvania Dutch farm. The complex contains more than a dozen buildings, some original and some newly built.

Typical daily activities include spinning, weaving, meat smoking, and vegetable drying. Depending on the time of year, you might also witness broom making, butter churning, and basket making. Your children can pet the farm animals and play on the hay jump in the barn. The farm is shown by guided tour except during the Harvest Fest and Farm Animal Frolic, when you can wander around on your own. (See our Arts and Culture chapter for more information. Also consult the Annual Events chapter for information about the Quiet Valley Harvest Festival held every October, the Old Time Christmas tours in December, and the Farm Animal Frolic in May.)

Quiet Valley is open late June through Labor Day, Tuesday through Sunday.

Stroud Mansion Museum $
900 Main Street, Stroudsburg
(570) 421-7703
www.mcha-pa.org

Stroud Mansion is the restored home of town founder Jacob Stroud. It serves as the Monroe County Historical Association's museum and repository for records, maps, and memorabilia including early photos, tools, and finished products highlighting area industries. There are furnished rooms with some wonderful antique pieces, fascinating toys, an excellent exhibit of Native American artifacts (see our Native Americans chapter for details), fine art, and a changing exhibit that highlights interesting aspects of Monroe County history.

Like other county historical museums in the Poconos, this is a good place to go for information on your family history.

The society also operates two small museums, the Driebe Freight Station and the Bell School. (See their listings in this chapter.)

Stroud Mansion is open Tuesday through Friday and most Sundays. Donations are accepted.

MOUNT POCONO AREA

Callie's Candy Kitchen
Highway 390, Mountainhome
(570) 595-2280, (800) 252-7750
www.calliescandy.com

Come to Callie's for the candy-making demonstration, in which Mr. Callie, the founder and owner of Callie's Candy Kitchen, gives a hilarious demonstration of chocolate making and marketing, passing out so many candy samples that you won't have room for the last few. The diversity of the candy is astounding, and the staff make almost all of it themselves, including the all-day suckers. Pocono Mountain Bark is a favorite, with its varieties of chocolate and nuts. Another specialty is chocolate-covered strawberries. The customers love the chocolate-covered pretzels and the Pocono crunch, a mix of Rice Krispies, butterscotch, and cashews. In-season, all different kinds of fruit are covered with chocolate including blueberries, peaches, and grapes. For a taste of something different, try the chocolate-covered cream cheese.

Callie's is open daily (weekends only in January). Bus tours are welcome. Call to find out when demonstrations are scheduled.

Callie's Pretzel Factory
Highways 390 and 191, Cresco
(570) 595-2280, (800) 252-7750
www.calliescandy.com
Handmade soft pretzels are baked and served right before your eyes—fresh and hot. Onion, garlic, cinnamon, pizza, and even hot dog pretzels are some of Callie's specialties. Get a hot dog wrapped in a crisp pretzel and a cinnamon pretzel for dessert, and you'll have a tasty, quick, and inexpensive lunch while you shop your way down Highway 390. The Pretzel Factory also carries more than 60 varieties of gourmet popcorn. Don't miss Callie's Left-Handed Gift Shop with more than a hundred necessities and whimsical items for lefties.

Callie's is open daily; weekends only in January.

Camelbeach Waterpark $$$$
Camelback Road, Tannersville
(570) 629-1661
www.camelbeach.com
Camelbeach is aiming to be the biggest, baddest water park in the East, and every year it adds some awesome new element toward that end. The newest attraction is the Checkered Flag, an eight-slide racing complex. Other notable rides are the Vortex and Spin Cycle, the only pair of bowl slides in the Northeastern United States. There's the Kahuna Lagoon Wave Pool, producing waves that range from gentle to 6 feet. At eight stories, the Titan is the tallest waterslide of its kind in the world. Are you beginning to get the picture? The park offers a total of 22 waterslides covering a wide range on the fear-factor scale from scary to unthinkable. For the less adventurous, Camel Cove is an interactive play pool that's only a foot deep, but has geysers, buckets, slides, and lots of other play elements. There's also a nice deck for weary parents. The Blue Nile, an adventure river ride, is absolutely relaxing after the tall stuff, at least until you hit a geyser. You can also swim in an Olympic-size swimming pool, ride in bumper boats, or play miniature golf. Guests can take a scenic chairlift to the top of Camelback

Mountain and enjoy the view. You can even get lunch at Cameltop.

Camelbeach also offers a day camp. (See our Camps and Conference Centers chapter.) The water park is open weekends and Memorial Day from mid-May through mid-June, daily through Labor Day. You can purchase general admission, spectator (they won't let you on the rides), evening only, or return tickets and season passes.

Cresco Station Museum
Just off Highway 191, Cresco
(570) 595-6157
Lovingly renovated and furnished by members of the Barrett Historical Society, this museum, in an old train station, has exhibits that change from year to year. Currently there's a country store, a depiction of a Civil War scene with toy soldiers, antique toys, early cooking utensils and early needlework, and a display of miniature lamps and early lighting. The museum is open Memorial Day through Columbus Day on Sunday afternoons; in July and August, Wednesday and Saturday afternoons are added, and the museum will also be open for some special-occasion tours in December—watch the papers for the announcement. Good signage points to the turnoff from Highway 191 to this fascinating museum. Donations are encouraged.

Holley Ross Pottery
Highway 191, LaAnna
(570) 676-3248
www.pocono.org
Holley Ross makes decorative pottery with gold and luster (mother-of-pearl) glazes. Monday through Friday, you can tour the pottery-making operation at 11:00

If you are traveling a great distance, call ahead to confirm that the attraction you plan to visit is open. Some places change hours or simply close in bad weather.

> *Make sure you check the "Weekend" section of the* Pocono Record *every Friday. There you'll find information on costumed re-enactments at historic villages, new age ceremonies at Columcille, report-card days at Shawnee Place (a discount for every "A" you can show on a report card), and lots more special events at area attractions.*

A.M. At other times, peer through the windows to see casting and decorating rooms in operation. Half the attraction here, though, is the astonishing variety and incredibly low prices on pottery. (See our Shopping chapter.) The Fiesta dinnerware collection is especially impressive. After you see the operation and make your irresistible purchases, take a walk across a swinging bridge and over the soft pine needle-and-woodchip trails of Holley Ross' enchanted forest. The paths through this quiet hemlock grove take you along a pretty stream to a small lake lined with picnic tables for a quintessential Pocono experience. Holley Ross is open May 1 through mid-December.

Memorytown
Grange Road, Mount Pocono
(570) 839-1680
www.memorytownusa.com
The complex includes a lake, paddleboats, a playground, picnic tables, friendly ducks, a print shop museum, a game room, a museum of the American patriot, a covered bridge, a tavern with music on the weekends, and some shops (see Shopping). Some of the buildings here are more than 150 years old. The tavern holds several theme weekends including Dixieland and German music weekends. Memorytown also presents a Civil War re-enactment every August.

The Toy Soldier
Highway 191, Paradise Falls
(570) 629-7227
www.the-toy-soldier.com

Tiny soldiers lay in wait for an enemy on a rock outside this astonishing private museum. Inside you'll be treated to miniature marching bands, regiments of turbaned Indians, a diorama of the Ashanti campaign, miniature elephants sporting incredibly detailed carpets, doughboys in a trench behind barbed wire facing bayonet-brandishing enemies, the Kennedy funeral cortege, a scene of Grosvenor Square in London (make sure you look in the windows), the streets of Hong Kong, 850 figures depicting an elaborate Durbar coronation in India, and even a scene with Queen Victoria at her diamond jubilee being presented with a box of—toy soldiers! Many of the scenes are built around real military artifacts—uniforms, pointy Prince Albert helmets, military drums, and an O.B.E. medal. Note some tins of chocolate sent by Queen Victoria to British soldiers in the Boer War.

This collection may be the largest display of toy soldiers in the country. It has been assembled by Jim Hillestad, who also runs a mail-order business for toy-soldier collectors. Hillestad is happy to show off his museum to those interested in history or toy soldiers, but it is open only by appointment. Absolutely no children younger than 12 will be admitted. Hillestad also maintains displays of his toy soldiers at Skytop (see our Accommodations chapter), Crescent Lodge, Cresco Station Museum, and Theo B. Price Hardware. (See our Shopping chapter.)

WEST END

Asa Packer Mansion $$
Packer Hill, Jim Thorpe
(570) 325-3229
www.asapackermansionmuseum
.homestead.com
Industrialist Asa Packer had interests in mining, canal boats, and the Lehigh Railroad. He founded Lehigh University and ran for President of the United States in 1868. And he lived a lavish existence in this mansion.

Built in 1860 by European craftsmen, the mansion and its contents are the same as they were in 1878 when Packer and his wife celebrated their golden wedding anniversary. The library contains a desk, chair, and bookcase from General Robert E. Lee. A replica of the crystal chandelier in the drawing room was used in the movie "Gone with the Wind." Throughout the house you'll find hand-carved furniture, paintings, sculptures, china, and gold-leaf walls. Take special note of the huge Victorian music box that Packer's daughter loved so much, she had it dismantled and packed in trunks to accompany her wherever she traveled.

The mansion is open 11:00 A.M. to 4:15 P.M. daily from June 1 through October 31 and on weekends throughout April and May, November, and the first half of December.

The Bell School
Cherry Valley Road, Stormsville
(570) 421-7703
www.mcha-pa.org
Classes were taught at the Bell School from the 1870s to 1953. Now you can see exhibits on the history of Monroe County schools. It's open Sunday afternoons in July and August and by special appointment at other times. Admission is free, but donations are welcomed.

Mauch Chunk Museum and Cultural Center $
41 Broadway, Jim Thorpe
(570) 325-9190
www.mauchchunkmuseum.com
The original stone structure, built in 1843, housed St. Paul's Methodist Church until 1978. Today, the museum tells the story of the town's early history (Jim Thorpe was once called Mauch Chunk), including a 30-foot replica of its Switchback Railroad. (See our History chapter's Close-up for the story of this colorful mode of transportation.)

Other exhibits explain the importance of the region's early industries, teach visitors how a canal lock worked, discuss the presence of the Lenape Indians, and reveal how the town came to renamed for a legendary Olympic athlete. (See our Arts and Culture and Native Americans chapters for more information.)

The museum is open every day except Monday.

The Old Jail Museum $
West Broadway, Jim Thorpe
(570) 325-5259
www.experiencepa.com
Built in 1871, this jail executed seven members of the Molly Maguires, a secret society founded in Ireland, by hanging. These anthracite miners used terrorism to force the mine owners to improve working conditions, and they were hated by the mine owners and bosses. Many members of the Molly Maguires were accused of murder, though some considered these accusations unfounded. On the eve of his execution, one of the men placed his hand against the wall of his cell, claiming that the handprint would remain there forever as a symbol of his innocence. The print is still visible in Cell 17, although the wall has been washed, painted, plastered over, and dug out. (See our History chapter to read more about the saga of the Molly Maguires.)

The 72-room structure includes 29 cells, a warden's apartment, and a 16-cell dungeon. It served as the county jail until 1995. Guided and self-guided tours are available.

The jail is open the weekend before Memorial Day through Labor Day every day except Wednesday. The jail will open for group tours in May, just call ahead to arrange one. It is open weekends only in September and October.

Old Mauch Chunk H.O. Scale Model Train Display $
Hooven Building, US 209, next to the railroad depot, Jim Thorpe
(570) 386-2297, (570) 325-4371
www.geocities.com/omchotd
On the second floor of the old Hooven Mercantile Company building, this

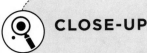

NASCAR Fans from Everywhere
Flock to Pocono Raceway

It used to be a spinach farm.

Walking around Pocono Raceway, one has a hard time imagining this land being home to anything but racing. Excitement surrounds the track, even on non-race days. A stroll down the main straightaway, even when it resembles an abandoned parking lot, is a privileged experience—something like standing at home plate in Yankee Stadium.

A ride around the track in an ordinary street truck is exhilarating. Trees fly by as the vehicle climbs the curves and accelerates coming out of them. Somehow, mere driving becomes racing—though the speedometer says 55 mph, it feels more like 200.

Over two weekends every summer, NASCAR racing's finest drivers come to the mountains to do battle on this strip of macadam. There are only four 2.5-mile tracks in the country, and the most unusual is Pocono Raceway's at Long Pond.

Almost as colorful as the races at Pocono is the track's history. In the early 1960s, a group of area businessmen, including Dr. Joseph Mattioli, purchased 1,025 acres of woods and spinach fields to build a track. By working through winters, the contractors had Pocono ready for the first event on its 0.75 mile oval in 1969; the initial 500-mile race on the 2.5-mile oval, the Shaefer 500, ran in 1971.

Today, of the original visionaries, only "Doc" Mattioli remains involved. His son, Joseph III, supervises the day-to-day operation of the track.

"Our first event was rained out, snowed out, and fogged out," said Joseph Mattioli about the super-modified race that was rescheduled three times from October 1968 to May 1969. "We had a streak of the worst weather imaginable." The frequently uncooperative weather in the Poconos still can play havoc with the race schedule. Wildlife is a factor too—races have been delayed by a stray deer or even a bear wandering onto the track, reminding everyone that, in spite of the crowds and all the exhaust, they are still in the country.

During the track's second year of operation, Hurricane Agnes devastated the facility. After rebuilding, the Mattiolis went on to face financial difficulties that almost closed Pocono on two occasions. High mortgage rates and the energy crisis in the 1970s threatened the raceway. While several other major tracks closed at that time—including Ontario, Trenton, and Langhorne—Pocono managed to survive.

Part of the reason for the raceway's success is its easy accessibility to New York, Philadelphia, and all of New Jersey. "We can draw from 60 million people who live within a 200-mile radius of the Poconos," Mattioli said. Indeed, the raceway has become so popular that lots of people from far beyond 200 miles come for the weekend.

Designed by two-time Indianapolis 500 winner Roger Ward, the raceway is a true tri-oval because it features only three curves instead of the usual four, and each is banked differently—a high-banked curve for stock cars and NASCAR, a flat one for Indy cars, and a mid-banked curve with a pitch that falls between the other two.

Because of the nature of the countryside, Pocono Raceway lacks symmetry, making each turn an entirely different adventure. Adding to drivers' headaches are three straightaways of varied lengths. The track's investors originally were hoping for a design similar to Daytona's or Indianapolis' Motor Speedway. That goal proved impossible, but they actually got a better track. Pocono provides an unmatched test of equipment and driver skill because the race cars cannot be set up for any one set of conditions; Pocono has them all. Many racers consider Pocono the toughest track in the country.

A big difference between auto racing and many other professional sports is that participants risk their lives every time they suit up. Mistakes are potentially deadly, and constant quick thinking is essential.

All this activity brings tens of thousands of people to the Pocono Mountains. Naturally, the money they leave behind gives the area's economy much-needed revenue and creates many jobs for residents. Based on an average annual attendance figure of more than 100,000, the Pocono Mountains Chamber of Commerce estimates Pocono Raceway's economic impact on Pennsylvania at more than $158,000,000 each year. The majority of race fans, more than 60 percent, come from out of state and stay in the Poconos for several days, filling hotels, restaurants, and shops for the entire weekend. Even if you're oblivious to the races, you can't miss the "Welcome Race Fans" banners hung by businesses throughout the area.

Pocono races are televised nationally, giving the region millions of dollars worth of media exposure. Watching at home, however, is not the proper way to experience a race. Like many other great sporting events, racing must be seen firsthand to be fully appreciated. Those who view a race on television miss the carnival-like atmosphere that precedes the nail-biting excitement. They miss the opportunity for a picnic or a tailgate party. At Pocono, both are possible within the huge infield, which could hold 200 football fields and offers fans the chance to celebrate within the event rather than outside it.

To understand that NASCAR racing is more than a start, a finish, and a couple of accidents in between, attend one of the races. Develop an appreciation for the subtleties of driving strategy, such as when to pass and when to pit for fuel. Watch pit crews change four tires and fill a gas tank in approximately 20 seconds. See a burst of every imaginable color as cars roar by, only to be replaced by a completely different rainbow a few seconds later. Second-guess the drivers as they second-guess each other. Pick a car and imagine yourself behind the wheel. NASCAR racing, more than anything else, offers spectators an opportunity to fantasize about driving in a way that defies traffic laws and common sense. We can't drive bumper-to-bumper at 200 miles per hour on I–80, but we can dream about it at Pocono Raceway.

The traffic jams before the races at Pocono Raceway are legendary. Leave plenty of time to get there on race day, adding even more time if it is raining.

two-level display boasts 13 separate main lines, with some trains pulling as many as 50 cars along nearly 1,100 feet of track. The elaborate re-creation contains more than 200 miniature buildings, 100 bridges, and a burning building with fire trucks.

The display is open daily mid-June through Labor Day. The first two weeks in June and the day after Labor Day through October, it's open Wednesday through Sunday. The rest of the year it's open weekends and holidays only.

Rail Tours $$-$$$
US 209, Jim Thorpe
(570) 325-4606, (610) 250-0968
www.railtours-inc.com

Relive the days when as many as nine trains per hour passed through Jim Thorpe. This steam engine pulls out of the town's train depot early April through Labor Day, Saturday, Sunday, and holidays for a 40-minute, 8-mile excursion through the Lehigh River Gorge and around the mountains. Beginning July 4 through Labor Day, the train's last run is the Lake Hauto Special, which goes 20 miles in just less than two hours.

Throughout October, you can ride on the Flaming Foliage Ramble. The 34-mile trip takes just under three hours. A 40-minute Santa Claus ride in early December puts families in a holiday mood. These

trips often sell out prior to departure, so call ahead for schedule and reservation information.

MILFORD/LAKE WALLENPAUPACK AREA

Carousel Water & Fun Park $$$
Highway 652, Beach Lake
(570) 729-7532
www.carousel-park.com

This complex has water slides, bumper boats, go-karts, miniature golf, a batting cage, game room, kiddie cars, a snack bar, and picnic area.

The park is open weekends May through mid-June, daily mid-June through August, and one more weekend through Labor Day. Admission is free; you pay for rides on an individual basis. A pay-one-price option, good daytime only, is available.

Claws 'N' Paws Wild Animal Park $$$
Highway 590, Hamlin
(570) 698-6154
www.clawsnpaws.com

Claws 'N' Paws is a private zoo that is surprisingly large. More than 120 species are housed in wire and wood cages scattered along wooded paths. The lion paces by a glass window where you can stand so close you'll see the saliva on his teeth. A sign warns you to back off if Punjab, the male tiger, turns his back end toward you and lifts his tail. Tigers spray just like kitty cats do. You'll see a gorgeous white tiger, a rare Asian binturong, and an adorable porcupine that has a rolling walk like a drunken sailor. Someone with a twisted sense of humor put the wolf cage right next to the deer.

Keepers give informative talks at various pens throughout the day, and shows are presented in an outdoor theater. We saw a parrot show that was hilarious. The birds rode parrot-size tricycles and roller skates and beat our daughter at poker. At other times, you can go into a lory parrot cage and get covered with gentle birds

Don't forget to stop by the Pocono Mountains Vacation Bureau visitors information centers for brochures on area attractions. See our Getting Around chapter for a list of visitors centers throughout the Poconos. You can also visit their excellent Web site at www.800poconos.com.

that peck at the apples you hold. You can also feed carrots to Twiga, the giraffe who will slobber all over you. There's a petting zoo, a baby-animal enclosure, a "Wild West Territory," where you can mine for gem stones, and a barnyard. Especially popular is the Dino Dig, where children can dig in the sand for "dinosaur bones." Just watch out for the llamas—their spitting distance is really impressive. Also, don't be taken in by the sweet-looking pony at the barnyard that comes over for affection—he bites.

Claws 'N' Paws is open May through October seven days a week, weather permitting.

The Columns $
608 Broad Street, Milford
(570) 296-8126
www.pikehistory.org

This distinctive building houses the museum of the Pike County Historical Society. The Columns received national attention when tests confirmed that the blood-stained flag in its collection was used to cradle President Abraham Lincoln's head after he was shot at Ford's Theater in 1865.

A significant exhibit is devoted to Charles S. Peirce—philosopher, logician, scientist, and founder of pragmatism—who lived near Milford from 1887 until his death in 1914. There's also a good exhibit of Native American artifacts that were found nearby.

The Columns is open Wednesday through Sunday in July and August, and Wednesday, Saturday, and Sunday April through June and September through November. (See our Arts and Culture and Native Americans chapters for more information.)

Costa's Family Fun Park $-$$$$
U.S. Highway 6, Lords Valley
(570) 226-8585, (800) 928-4FUN
www.costasfamilyfunpark.com

Costa's specializes in finding something fun to do for every member of the family. Little guys can pedal non-motorized go-

karts, or use the toys in a climbing and slide area. Older kids can take a few swings in the batting cages or race the Leopard-, IROC-, and Jaguar-style go-karts. You'll find plenty of arcade favorites in the game room. For golf types there's an 18-hole miniature golf course and a driving range. An air-conditioned restaurant and outdoor porch provide food. The little ones will be delighted to find kids' meals with surprises in them, just like at the burger chains.

The park is open weekends in May, every day from Memorial Day through Labor Day and then weekends through Columbus Day. Admission is free; you pay between 50 cents and $8.00 for each activity.

Dorflinger Glass Museum $
Long Ridge Road, White Mills
(570) 253-1185
www.dorflinger.org

More than 600 pieces of Dorflinger glass are displayed here. The company, established in White Mills in 1862, was known as one of the best glass makers in the world. Presidents Lincoln and Wilson both used Dorflinger glassware. Twenty-eight companies once produced glass in Wayne County, lured here by the fine sand that is essential to the glass-making process.

On a bright day, the sun shines through the museum windows, and the glassware is magically illuminated, painting a colorful rainbow around the museum. The exhibit contains examples of cut, enameled, etched, gilded, and engraved glass.

The museum is part of the Dorflinger–Suydam Wildlife Sanctuary, a 600-acre conservation area that hosts a series of concerts during the summer. (See our Parks, Annual Events, Shopping, and Arts and Culture chapters for more information.)

The gift shop contains glass souvenirs, Christmas ornaments, and an extensive collection of books on glassware.

The museum is open mid-May through the beginning of November, Wednesday through Sunday.

Golf Park Plus   **$-$$$$**
Golf Park Drive, Hamlin
(570) 689-4996, (570) 689-0560
www.golfparkplus.com

Two miniature golf courses contain unexpected hazards such as roughs, sand traps, water, islands, and bridges. Other facilities include bumper boats, go-karts, a scenic train ride, a driving range, and paintball (reservations recommended). A snack bar, a kiddieland, and an arcade complete the park.

Golf Park Plus is open daily May through October and Monday through Friday the rest of the year. Attractions are priced individually. (See our Golf chapter for information on the driving range.)

Grey Towers   **$**
US 6, Milford
(570) 296-9630
www.na.fs.fed.us

Grey Towers is the former home of two-term Pennsylvania governor Gifford Pinchot. He also founded the United States Department of Agriculture Forest Service. In 1963, just before his assassination, President John F. Kennedy visited Milford to acknowledge Pinchot's conservation efforts.

This magnificent French-style chateau provides panoramic views of Milford and the Delaware River Valley. Its rooms are fully furnished, and memorabilia is exhibited throughout. Allow at least an hour to tour the building and the grounds. The property is maintained by the USDA Forest Service.

Grey Towers is open daily Memorial Day through October, and tours are given on the hour. (See our Arts and Culture chapter for additional information.)

i

One of the best sources for information about area attractions—besides this book, of course—is the free magazine This Week in the Poconos. *You can find it among the tourist brochures in lobbies of restaurants and hotels.*

The Pennsylvania Fishing Museum
Pecks Pond Store, Highway 402
Pecks Pond
(570) 733-2555
www.peckspond.com

The Fishing Museum features exhibits of vintage fishing equipment including creels, rods, reels, and lures. Also on display are early fly- and ice-fishing tools, motors, decoys, and folk art. Anglers will enjoy comparing their equipment to that used decades ago.

The museum is in the Pecks Pond Store near Pecks Pond. Look for the large wooden fisherman outside.

The museum is open daily spring through fall; call for winter hours.

Stourbridge Rail Excursion   **$$$-$$$$**
303 Commercial Street, Honesdale
(570) 253-1960
www.waynecountycc.com

This diesel engine train, which leaves from downtown Honesdale, takes scenic excursions throughout the year. In spring, ride the rails on the two-hour trip with the Easter Bunny. Theme trips in summer include Great Train Robbery Runs, Dinner Theater, and a Bavarian Festival. Fall brings the popular foliage outings, such as a four-hour trip along the Lackawaxen River with stops at the Zane Grey Museum and Roebling Bridge. Ghosts haunt the train for Halloween. And Santa and Mrs. Claus bring treats for children on the Santa Express held several times in early December. A Winterfest train takes you on a four-hour excursion to Hawley, where you can see the Victorian town dressed in its Christmas best.

Call for the specific dates and reservations.

Wayne County Historical
Society Museum   **$**
810 Main Street, Honesdale
(570) 253-3240
www.waynehistorypa.org

A replica of the Stourbridge Lion, the first commercial locomotive to run in the United States, is housed at this museum.

The Lion made its historic trip near Honesdale. The original train is part of the collection at the Smithsonian Institution in Washington, D.C. Next to the Stourbridge Lion is the Eclipse, a passenger gravity car, with a hand-stenciled ceiling and carved wood interior.

The museum has an outstanding collection of canal photos and other memorabilia. The city of Honesdale was founded as a port for trains hauling coal from the Lackawanna County anthracite regions to New York City. The coal was transferred to canal boats here. Possibly the largest piece of anthracite ever mined sits in the museum's newest gallery. Don't miss the Vernon Leslie exhibit with artifacts of the Lenape Indians; it's astonishing in its quantity and variety. (See the Native Americans chapter for a full description.)

The museum's Torrey Gallery, named after the original Honesdale surveyor, offers changing exhibits emphasizing local artists, and when they don't have an art exhibit, they plan to show Torrey's surveying tools. The gift shop has some good books, including a self-guided walking tour of Main Street.

The museum is open Saturday January through March and Wednesday through Saturday from April to December. Ask for a brochure on the changing exhibits.

Zane Grey Museum
Scenic Drive, Lackawaxen
(570) 685-4871
www.nps.gov
Regarded as the "Father of the Western Novel," Zane Grey lived in Lackawaxen from 1905 to 1918. The museum, operated by the National Park Service, is in Grey's former house.

The office and study now house Grey's memorabilia, exhibits, photographs, and books. Original artwork and manuscripts are among the collection.

While Grey lived in New York City around the turn of the century, he regularly visited the Lackawaxen area to fish.

Museums, even the small ones, usually have wonderful gift shops. You can buy hard-to-get books on subjects related to their exhibits. Gifts for children, jewelry, and unique crafts are often available, too. One more advantage—gift shops help support the museum, so a portion of your purchase price is going for a very good cause.

On one of these trips he met his future wife, Lina Elise Roth, whom he affectionately called Dolly. With her encouragement, he overcame early professional rejection and became a successful writer. Roth helped finance Grey's first novel *Betty Zane,* which was published in 1903.

By 1905, Grey gave up his New York dental practice, and the couple moved to Lackawaxen. Grey's first western novel, *The Heritage of the Desert* (1910), and his most famous, *Riders of the Purple Sage* (1912), were published while he lived here.

The Park Service staff conducts guided tours, which take a minimum of 30 minutes. Souvenirs and copies of Grey's books still in print are available for sale.

The museum is open Memorial Day through Labor Day, Friday through Sunday. After Labor Day and through the third week in October, the museum is open weekends only. It's closed the rest of the year. The schedule changes yearly, so call or check the Web site before you go. (See our Arts and Culture chapter for more information.)

ARCHITECTURAL GEMS

Churches often carry the hopes and dreams of their communities. Some have been elaborately or interestingly built as vessels for these dreams and for people's religious convictions. In this section, we point out five churches of interest because of their architectural and historical significance.

Columcille: A Playground for the Spirit

Columcille is one of the most astonishing sites in the Poconos. Stone megaliths, scattered across a rolling park, recall Stonehenge, Avebury, the chapel of Iona off the coast of Scotland, and other Celtic monuments.

You can enter the park through Thor's Gate, a trilithon every bit as impressive as the ones at Stonehenge. Walk along an avenue of standing stones and you come to St. Columba chapel, a small stone building with benches for meditation and a large rock in the middle that some people feel has special energy. The rock was raised from the site, and when it was placed in the chapel, a snapping turtle stood by the stone for three days. A bell tower lies beyond the chapel, and on the spring day we visited, a maypole with colorful ribbons stood in the middle of the tower. Other standing stones and circles are placed throughout the site. There's even a rock-chasing dog named Duke, who will try to interest you in a game of toss the stone.

While this is a deeply spiritual place, a sense of humor is also evident. Maps of the site show sea monsters beyond "the hills of New Jersey." Here and there you might even encounter some elf-size trilithons, dolmens, and stone circles.

The grounds of Columcille, south of the Stroudsburgs on the side of Blue Mountain, have been surveyed and cataloged by the Smithsonian National Museum of Art as a megalith park and Celtic art center and it has been designated as a National Heritage Site. The keeper of Columcille, Rev. William H.

Cohea Jr., an ordained minister, refers to his park as "a sacred earth space and place of myth and mystery."

Columcille is named in honor of Colum Cille, the 6th-century Irish monk who founded a monastic community on the island of Iona off the coast of Scotland. St. Columba traveled there in A.D. 536 with a group of monks to study and celebrate their Celtic Christianity. When Europe entered the Dark Ages, Iona remained a center of "culture, faith, and hope. Art flourished: nature was celebrated."

"From early times people have been setting stones," Cohea said. "Our Celtic ancestors raised stones throughout France, especially in Brittany, 8,000 years ago. In France, 5,000 stones were set in a straight line, and 2,300 are still standing. There is even evidence of stones being set in Wales 16,000 years ago by men living in caves." Today, there are more than 50,000 stones still standing around the world.

Many years ago on a trip to Iona, Cohea became aware that he, too, needed to set up stones. From that time on, he moved toward that vision. In 1979, he and his partner, Fred Lindkvist, erected the first stone structure at Columcille—the St. Columba Chapel. There's no formal religion in the chapel or out among the circles. Although Cohea is a minister, he avoids imposing any one religion on the place. He prefers, instead, to let each individual invest it with his or her own spirituality.

After the chapel was built, construction of the St. Oran Bell Tower followed. It was patterned on 8th-century Irish bell

Thor's Gate guards one entrance to Columcille. JANET BREGMAN-TANEY

towers. The Circle of Stones followed the bell tower; then a pond was added. The Megalith Park was the next stage, and stones continue to sprout up all over the property. Two wooded sites are set aside for men and women who wish to meditate separately. You may see crystals, evocative roots, and a Venus of Willendorf placed on the stones in the women's circle.

The huge stones are from this site and from nearby rock quarries. Some weigh at least 30 tons and had to be lifted by cranes and backhoes. All are set in the ancient tradition: The foundations are dug deeply and filled with many smaller stones. Then the megaliths are placed on this base.

Why did Cohea put these stones here? What motivated him?

"For me the stones seem to draw energy from the land—healing energy," he explained.

Cohea says he meditates on how long stones have inhabited the earth compared to humankind—a thought he describes as "a very humbling experience."

Columcille is a place for quiet meditation. It draws people to sit and rest

The entire property at Columcille is scattered with standing stones, large and small, but there's only one trilithon. JANET BREGMAN-TANEY

against the rocks warmed by the afternoon sun; to stand on the rocks to see as far as they can; to inspect the rocks to see what fossils lay hidden in their recesses. There is a feeling here of peacefulness, of oneness with the earth. As you wander in Columcille, notice the hushed reverence people observe when they enter the circles. Conversations are whispered; visitors search for places to sit in solitude.

As a work of art, Columcille is astounding. As a place of the spirit, it is awe-inspiring. If you have problems with expressions of religious feeling that may be different from your own, you should pass on this site; but if you find expressions of spirituality exciting in their many forms, Columcille will inspire you.

You'll probably be frustrated the first time you try to find Columcille; we missed it, and nearly everybody we know who's been there has had a difficult time finding it at first. Even the people who live and work nearby don't seem to know it's there. But persist—this is an extraordinary, magical spot, and it's worth a protracted quest.

Columcille (2155 Fox Gap Road, Bangor, 610–588–1174, www.columcille.org) is just off the Appalachian Trail. From Stroudsburg, take Pennsylvania Highway

West End

St. Mark's Episcopal Church $
21 Race Street, Jim Thorpe
(570) 325–2241
www.stmarkandjohn.org
St. Mark's Episcopal is at the bottom of Race Street, and its spires reach up toward the mountains that encircle it. This Gothic Revival stone church was built in 1869. It features Tiffany windows, a wrought-iron passenger elevator, and the original Minton tile floor made in England. The design of the French Caen stone reredos (decorative screens above the rear altar) is a copy of the one in St. George's Chapel, Windsor Castle, England. St. Mark's is still in use and is the site for concerts presented by The Bach and Handel Chorale. (See our Arts and Culture chapter.)

The church is open for tours daily by appointment.

The bell tower and stone circle at Columcille. JANET BREGMAN-TANEY

191 South toward Bangor. You'll see two signs on the left-hand side of the road for Kirkridge. At the second sign, turn left onto Fox Gap Road. Again, you'll see signs for various Kirkridge buildings. Go past "The Farmhouse," turn left on Quaker Plane Road, and park in the small lot. You'll soon find yourself among the stones of Columcille.

Milford/Lake Wallenpaupack Area

Bethany Presbyterian Church
Highway 670, north of Honesdale
(570) 253-6316

Bethany Presbyterian still serves a congregation founded in 1813. Bethany is a carbon copy of a church designed by the great British architect Sir Christopher Wren, but his original, in England, doubtless went up with more alacrity. Construction began on Bethany Presbyterian in 1823, but, hampered by an ongoing lack of funds, it was not completed until 1836.

The Dutch Reform Church
US 209, north of Dingmans Ferry

The Dutch Reform Church was built in Greek revival style in 1850. It has four massive, wooden columns, heavily fluted in the style of ancient Greece. The church is now a private home, and its carriage house is now a southwestern shop called Phoenix (see our Shopping chapter). It was acquired through the Historic Property Leasing Program authorized by the National Historic Preservation Act of 1966, which identifies guidelines for appropriate use of historic structures. The property is owned by the National Park Service, and the leaseholders must comply with park regulations for maintaining the integrity of the building and its setting and demonstrate its compatibility with recreation-area activities.

Good Shepherd Church
Highway 402, Blooming Grove
(570) 775-6791
Good Shepherd was built in the mid-1800s. It's an exact replica of a Gothic country church in England. It is built of all native stones and has stained-glass windows imported from Italy.

Grace Episcopal Church
Just off Courthouse Square, Honesdale
(570) 253-2760
Grace Episcopal was built in 1854 from hand-hewn native sandstone laid all the way to the steeple top with a craftsmanship that is all but forgotten today. It is home to the congregation of Grace Episcopal, which was founded in 1831. The dark luster of the sandstone, aged for nearly 150 years, is accented by stunning stained-glass windows.

NATIVE AMERICANS

Drive along U.S. Highway 209 north of Bushkill in the Delaware Water Gap National Recreation Area, and you will see why people have inhabited this region for at least 12,000 years. A long, fertile floodplain leads to the Delaware River, once so full of fish that William Penn complained that the numerous sturgeon leaping into the air endangered small boats. The river provided abundant food, clear water, and a ready road—one that people could easily traverse in canoes to trade with other villages and seek out game. The floodplains end in wooded ridges that, even today, are full of deer, bears, and wild turkeys. There was fertile land for gardens, a river stocked with food, and it was an easy place to hunt. The cold winters kept the Poconos from being the Garden of Eden, but it was close. Nearly every open field along the Delaware River has given us evidence of prehistoric human occupation.

The glaciers moved out of the region between 15,000 and 13,000 B.C., and between 12,000 and 10,000 B.C., people moved in. The first inhabitants knew a much different place from that we know today. The climate was colder, and the vegetation was tundra—mossy with short, scrubby bushes, and evergreens. Mammoths, mastodons, and caribou roamed the countryside. Small bands of hunters and their families followed the large game animals moving along the river valley. An archaeological site near Shawnee-on-Delaware has produced tools, points, fish bones, a hearth, and wild hawthorn pits that were carbon dated to around 8800 B.C. The artifacts indicate that by then the hunters were beginning to gather plants for food too.

As the climate warmed, the forests arose, and the large animals headed out. They were succeeded by deer, bears, moose, foxes, elk, rabbits, wolves, cougars, and many other small species. Without the large animals, the natives turned to fish and to the plant food they could gather. People began using baskets and soapstone cooking pots, and they developed more stone tools. Eventually they added pottery and dugout canoes to their raft of implements.

Between A.D. 1000 and 1600 the Natives epitomized the Eastern Woodland culture. Some lived in bark-covered long houses, or wigwams, with dividers making separate compartments for individual families. Others lived in smaller, single-family wigwams. They raised corn, beans, sunflowers, and squash in gardens near their homes. They gathered nuts and produced maple syrup from the trees around them. They hunted small game, netted the abundant fish, and used freshwater mussels for flavoring. Their villages were not fortified, suggesting that their relationships with other groups were peaceful. They took to carving faces in their pottery vessels, clay pipes, and pendants. These pendants, carved from rock, were worn so the face would appear upside down to others, but the wearer could look down and see the face correctly.

These woodland people called themselves Lenape, "the people" or "the original people," and their language is part of the Algonquian family. They lived along the Delaware River, which they called the Lenape Wihittuck, or "the river is beautiful." Other Algonquian-speaking tribes referred to the Lenape as "grandfathers," a term of great respect, because they were thought to be the original Algonquian-speaking people. Lenape originally lived along the Atlantic Coast from Manhattan Island to Delaware Bay. These were the people who sold Manhattan, the "island of hills," to the Dutch for the equivalent of $24 in trade goods. They spread across New Jersey and occupied the land

It is against federal law to remove any artifact or piece of a historic site you might view or visit. In fact, it's a felony. Don't even pick up any arrowheads, as you may disturb valuable archaeological sites. If you do spot any artifacts in the park, please notify park personnel so the park archaeologist can investigate.

surrounding the Delaware River. As European settlement pushed westward, more Lenape moved out of New York and New Jersey and joined their cousins in the mountainous regions around the Delaware. One of the most important settlements was in our region, just north of Delaware Water Gap, a settlement occupied by a group of Lenape called the Minsi or Munsee. Today, the land along the river from the Water Gap north to Port Jervis, New York, is called the Minisink, after the Minsi.

The European settlers, naming the river after Lord de la Warr, called the Lenape the Delaware Indians. The way the Lenape tell it on their Web site is a little different, though. They say that the first European who tried to pronounce their name had a great deal of trouble saying Lenape. When he finally got it right, the Lenape said, *"Nal de ndeluwén! Nal ne ndeluwén!"* Which meant, "That's what I said! That's what I said!" When the settler heard "ndeluwér," he said, "So that's your name—Delaware!"

Although there were some exceptions, most early encounters with European settlers in the Minisink were peaceful. But relations ran into trouble over land, most notably in 1737, when the Lenape were cheated by the way an agreement called the Walking Purchase was carried out. (See our History chapter for a detailed account of the Walking Purchase.) The Lenape asked the governor of the colony to give them back the Minisink, which they felt had been unfairly included in the Walking Purchase. When he refused to

help, the Minsi went on a rampage, massacring every settler they could find. The settlers called on the Iroquois Confederacy to help them expel the Minsi from their land. The Minsi were subject to the Iroquois. Apparently, the Iroquois were annoyed that the Minsi had, supposedly, signed a treaty without consulting them, and they insulted the Minsi, calling the Minsi warriors "women," a fierce insult at the time. The Minsi were forced to move west to Wyoming, Pennsylvania. The tribe kept moving for 130 years until it settled in Oklahoma and Ontario, Canada.

Today, the largest part of the Lenape nation—nearly 10,000 people—lives around Bartlesville, Oklahoma, with a smaller group of about 1,000 in Anadarko, Oklahoma, and two small reservations in Munsee and Moraviantown, Ontario with a combined population of about 2,000. Another 1,500 Lenape live in northern Wisconsin, and a group of mixed Ojibwe/Lenape live near Ottawa, Kansas. Groups of Lenape also live in different parts of New Jersey.

After a legal review of treaties going back to 1866, the United States Department of the Interior granted federal recognition to the tribe in 1996. Before that, any government-to-government relations (tribal recognition means that the United States sees the tribe as a separate government) were conducted through the Cherokee Nation. Recently the Lenape nation made the news when a group of Oklahoma Lenape brought claim to some acreage in Easton, which they claimed was never legally transferred. The land they have asked for includes the Crayola Factory (see Day Trips). The tribal representatives expressed the wish to put a gambling facility there or swap their claim for some other land in Pennsylvania. The claim will be decided in federal court.

The tribe has a strong presence on the Internet. A Lenape who was raised traditionally became a successful computer and communications engineer in California. He returned to Oklahoma and re-involved himself with the tribe. He established the Lenape Information System Association to provide affordable information-technology access to every citizen in his community. As a result, Native Americans—especially the Lenape—have a vibrant presence in cyberspace. Visit the Lenape homepage at www.delawaretribeofindians.nsn.us. You can read about the traditional Lenape way of life, their history in the Poconos, and issues that are important to the tribe today, and you can learn key phrases in the Lenape language. Don't miss the fascinating page that describes the tribal sense of humor.

You will find some Lenape in the Poconos. Their ancestors managed to avoid the march west by moving out of the disputed lands but they stayed close and kept a low profile. Some intermarried with Europeans. Some of these Lenape now have resettled in their ancestral homeland and are proud to reclaim their tribal heritage.

While the Lenape were the dominant tribe here, some Pocono businesses are named after the Shawnee. That's because a group of Shawnee lived briefly on the site of what is now Shawnee-on-Delaware. Like the Lenape, the Shawnee are in the Algonquian language group and share many cultural traits with their "grandfathers." Their homeland was southern Ohio, West Virginia, and western Pennsylvania. In the 1660s, the Shawnee were driven from their homeland by the Iroquois, who wanted to use the land for hunting. One band of Shawnee found refuge with the Lenape, who allowed them to settle in several places, including Shawnee-on-Delaware just upriver from an important Lenape settlement. They left about the time of the Walking Purchase, returned to their Ohio homeland and were pushed out again, this time by American settlement. They moved southward and eventually settling in Oklahoma. The most famous Shawnee was Tecumseh, who with his brother organized a multitribal movement to resist white expansion. They were defeated by William Henry Harrison at the Battle of Tippicanoe. Today most Shawnee live in Oklahoma.

EXHIBITS

Delaware Water Gap/ Shawnee-on-Delaware

Bushkill Falls Native American Exhibit
U.S. Highway 209, Bushkill
(570) 588–6682
www.bushkillfalls.com
Bushkill Falls Native American exhibit was built as an accurate recreation of daily life among the Lenape. Its centerpiece is an 18-by-10-foot wigwam built expressly for the exhibit from the fallen trees on this property. A full-size dugout canoe and several display cases line the walls. The cases show very high quality Lenape artifacts, including some you don't see in most of other exhibits, such as paint pots and soapstone cooking pots. Good explanatory material above each display demonstrates how people used these artifacts. While the exhibit was built with an eye for accuracy, the day we visited, Peruvian flute music was playing on the sound system and some cowry shells (a Pacific and Indian Ocean shell) were scattered among the porcupine quills and other materials the Lenape used for making things. We hope that someone will make sure no more cultural anomalies intrude in this otherwise excellent presentation. Gift shops outside the exhibit include an assortment of Native American crafts.

The Native American Exhibit is just one part of Bushkill Falls. (See the Attrac-

Interested in discovering your Native American roots? Write to Northeastern Native American Association and Adopted Tribal Peoples (NENAA), P.O. Box 266, Jamaica, NY 11423, an agency that serves as a clearinghouse for such information.

Say it in Lenape:

- *"Hi" or "Hello"—hè (pronounced heh)*
- *"Goodbye" or "I will see you again"—Làpich knewël (pronounced luh-peech knay-wahl)*
- *"Give me some coffee"—mili kàpi (mee-lee kuh-pee)*

tions and Our Natural World chapters.) You can also hike the paths to the falls, eat in a picnic grove, take paddleboat rides, play miniature golf, and shop for souvenirs.

Bushkill Falls is open April through November. The price of admission includes the exhibit and the falls. The rates are subject to change, and you are advised to call. The Native American Exhibit is wheelchair accessible; Bushkill Falls is not.

The Pocono Indian Museum and Gift Shop
US 209, Bushkill
(570) 588-9338
www.poconoindianmuseum.com
Housed in a large, white-columned mansion, the museum is comprised of a carefully arranged series of six rooms. The rooms contain artifacts—many from Delaware River site excavations nearby—and examples of Lenape lifestyles. Additional exhibits feature objects from other Native American nations. Your self-guided tour includes a recorded narration explaining the displays. One room contains pictures of herbs used by the Lenape and includes clear explanations of how and why they were used. While most museums simply present ancient artifacts, here arrows, atlals (throwing sticks), bolas, scrapers, awls, and axes have been rebuilt so you can see how the stone artifacts worked on wooden handles and shafts. A full-size wigwam gives you a good sense of what it was like to be inside a Lenape home.

The rest of the building is a gift shop with some fine jewelry, drums and shakers, an extensive selection of moccasins, audio cassettes of contemporary Native American musicians, an intimidating collection of Indian-themed T-shirts, and a variety of related souvenirs. Upstairs you'll find the most comprehensive selection of books on Native American subjects in the Poconos, including a good number of books on Pennsylvania tribes. The gift shop is worth a trip all by itself, and you can shop without paying admission to the museum.

The museum opens seven days a week.

Stroudsburg/East Stroudsburg

Monroe County Historical Association
900 Main Street, Stroudsburg
(570) 421-7703
www.mcha-pa.org
The basement of the Monroe County Historical Association houses an incredible collection of Native American artifacts. Arrowheads, tomahawks, hafted axes, hammerstones, knife blades, adzes, atlals, and weights are joined by rope-decorated pottery, effigy pipes, gorgets, and beads. Some of these were picked up by collectors in the mid-1800s, and although most of the artifacts were found locally, 19th-century collectors wouldn't think twice about mixing in artifacts from other areas, so some of the more interesting pieces may be from out west. Charts in the display date the arrowheads by type, demonstrating that some of the finest pieces are the oldest. Any Insiders who have pulled arrowheads out of their flowerbeds will be fascinated by these charts.

The Historical Association also has a fine selection of books and vertical files on Native American history and traditions in the Poconos. (See our Arts and Culture and Attractions chapters for related information about the museum.) The museum is open Tuesday through Friday and most Sundays.

West End

Mauch Chunk Museum and Cultural Center
41 West Broadway, Jim Thorpe
(570) 325-9190
www.mauchchunkmuseum.com

The museum focuses on Jim Thorpe, the Native American Olympian and professional football great. Rare photos of Thorpe's life are featured. The exhibit includes a photo display from his youth and late adulthood as well as a famous photo of Jim Thorpe and King Gustav of Sweden in 1912 after the Olympics. At that time the king told Thorpe, "Sir, you are the greatest athlete in the world," to which Thorpe replied, "Thanks, King!"

The Native American exhibit here spotlights the Lenape people and artifacts from their daily life. Other items include artifacts of the Bear Clan as well as a reproduction of a painting of Lappawinzo, the Lenape sachem who signed the release for the Walking Purchase and was one of the first Native Americans to have his portrait painted.

The museum is open every day except Monday. (See our Attractions and Arts and Culture chapters for more information about Mauch Chunk Museum and Cultural Center.)

Milford/Lake Wallenpaupack Area

The Columns Museum of the Pike County Historical Society
608 Broad Street, Milford
(570) 296-8126
www.pikehistory.org

The Native American Exhibit on the second floor of this museum contains artifacts of the Lenape, including weapons and tools used in everyday life, such as scrapers, bowls, tomahawks, and arrowheads. Documentation is provided for some items.

The Columns is open Wednesday through Sunday in July and August and Wednesday, Saturday, and Sunday April through June and September through November. (See our Arts and Culture chapter for more information about the Columns.)

The Wayne County Historical Society Museum & Research Library
810 Main Street, Honesdale
(570) 253-3240
www.waynecountyhistoricalsociety.com

The Wayne County Historical Society runs a museum and research library that has more than 4,600 Native American artifacts gathered from the Upper Delaware River and its environs. These pieces represent finds from the four major periods of inhabitation: Paleo, Archaic, Woodland, and Contact. They are part of a much larger collection that was the lifetime work of late county historian Vernon Leslie, who willed them to the historical society with exact plans for how they should be displayed.

The exhibit is called "Faces in Clay," which also is the name of one of nine books written by Leslie. A local high school teacher and amateur archaeologist, he began collecting artifacts at age 14—a process he continued until his death at age 83 in 1994. The collection includes the very first artifact he found as well as the last, which was left on his desk when he died. All artifacts are cataloged according to archaeological documentation standards on 3-by-5-inch index cards and are available for reference to the serious collector.

The exhibit is housed in a setting meant to represent the dark, quiet green of the forest. A dugout canoe,

An archaeological site near Shawnee-on-Delaware has produced tools, points, fish bones, a hearth, and wild hawthorn pits that were carbon dated to around 8800 B.C.

Attend a powwow, a festival in which people from different tribes get together to dance and celebrate their culture. Everyone is welcome to come and observe, and there's usually a chance to buy Native American crafts and eat traditional cuisine. Be as respectful as you would if you were visiting a cathedral. You are among contemporary people celebrating their spirituality.

carbon-dated A.D. 1650, is backed by a lush forest scene. The clay-colored floor has bear paw prints to lead you around the display. As you walk through the exhibit and read the information provided, you are surrounded by the sounds of forest and river, even the sounds of someone paddling a canoe. Along one side, artifacts are arranged in sites as you would have found them along the Delaware River from northern Wayne County through

Monroe County. The artifacts on the opposite wall are arranged chronologically according to periods of habitation. They present important features of Native American life, including hunting and gathering techniques and social customs.

The museum also features an exhibit on the Delaware and Hudson Canal, a replica of America's first steam engine, and other exhibits that change on a yearly basis. (See our Attractions and Arts and Culture chapters for related information.) For scholars, the museum includes an extensive research library of books, a vertical file of surnames for genealogists, a file of historical subjects, newspapers on microfiche dating back to the 1840s, catalogs, and maps. Library staff will assist with research for people who are unable to visit.

The museum is open Wednesday through Saturday April through December and on Saturday January through March. Guided tours are accommodated with advance reservations.

WINERIES

Spend a day in the gorgeous countryside cruising from winery to winery, discussing grapes with the head winemakers, and tasting until you can taste no more. You might be getting images of California's Napa Valley, but we're describing Pennsylvania. With 61 wineries—some of world-class quality—Pennsylvania is a major player in East Coast winemaking. That's fitting since we have a 300-year history of fermenting grapes. In fact, one of the first vineyards in the country was planted by William Penn, the Commonwealth's namesake.

Penn intended to make his wine from French grapes, not the "foxy" varieties he found growing wild here. Unfortunately, a disease called phylloxera attacked all of the European grapes planted in the United States and eventually spread to Europe, decimating grape crops everywhere. Grape growers here and overseas found that if they wanted to grow European grapes, they had to graft the vines to American rootstock in order to grow a vine resistant to phylloxera.

Pennsylvania wine growers today produce wine from four sources: Vinifera, or European varieties of grapes; Labrusca, or native grape varieties; hybrid varieties; and other fruits.

Wine tasting in the Poconos gives you a chance to explore country roads, try surprisingly good wines, and enjoy conversation with interesting people. We've tasted a lot of wines in a lot of places, and we're impressed with our local winemakers. Not one of them makes the Vin de Old Socks we've tasted so many times elsewhere.

Four wineries operate in or right outside the Pocono Mountains, all in the southern part of the region. Farther north in Pennsylvania, early-season frost and harsh winter weather make growing grapes nearly impossible. Unlike the great wine-producing areas of Upstate New York, our region lacks the large bodies of water that help regulate the temperature of the surrounding countryside and prevent early frosts. Grape-eating critters, too, make growing difficult here. Because this is a wet region, our grapevines are subject to more fungal attacks than the grapes in California.

Any way you look at it, Pocono-area grape growers work hard for their crops. Most northern growers will tell you that the farther north you grow a grape, the more flavorful and full of character it becomes. And research from Cornell University's Cooperative Extension has shown that the more northern-grown grapes have significantly more reserveratrol, an antioxidant that can help prevent heart disease and also shows promise in preventing and fighting cancer. So in a cosmic act of fairness, our Pocono wineries have to work harder to grow their grapes, but they get more back for their work.

The wineries near the Poconos are close enough to each other that, if you are ambitious and have a hollow leg, you can visit them all in a single day. In fact, the wineries have put together a tour brochure to help you find our four regional wineries and five more in the Lehigh Valley, south of Allentown. Look for the "Lehigh Valley Wine Trail" brochure at each winery as well as at tourist information centers.

The Poconos is home to one of the most highly regarded wine authors in the northeastern United States. John J. Baxevanis, a geography professor at East Stroudsburg University, writes extensively on viticulture and enology. In addition to his books on French wines, look for his outstanding book The Wine Regions of America, *published in 1992.*

With 61 wineries—some of world-class quality—Pennsylvania is a major player in East Coast winemaking.

Each winery sells its own products and offers free tastings. All can produce personalized labels for special events like weddings and anniversaries. Alcohol sales in Pennsylvania are heavily regulated, so if you want to purchase any other wines, you must go to a state-operated Wine and Spirits Shop. Regional stores can be found at the following locations:

- Pocono Plaza, Lincoln Avenue, East Stroudsburg
- 1060 North Ninth Street, Stroudsburg
- 761 Main Street, Stroudsburg
- 551 Belmont Avenue, Mount Pocono
- Highway 390, Cresco
- Ames Plaza, U.S. Highway 209, Brodheadsville
- Tannersville Plaza, Tannersville
- 1215 North Street, Jim Thorpe
- 221 Delaware Avenue, Palmerton
- 143 South Street, Lehighton
- Village Center at Lords Valley, Highway 739, Hawley
- Blakeslee Village Center, Highway 940, Blakeslee
- 106 West Harford Street, Milford

The observant among you will notice that we cover one winery from outside our official Pocono borders. This one is so nearby—and its wine is so good—that we decided to bend our own rules a little and include it for your tasting pleasure.

 American grapes you might encounter in Pennsylvania wines include Concord, Delaware, Niagara, and Catawba. Most winemakers make sweet wines from these grapes, and many Pennsylvania residents prefer sweet wines, though that may be changing.

WEST END

Big Creek Vineyard and Winery
Keller Road, Kresgeville
(610) 681-3959
www.bigcreekvineyard.com

Outlets at:
BCV Wine Sales and Tasting, Race Street, Jim Thorpe
(570) 325-8138

Dolcetto, Delaware Street and Waring Drive, Delaware Water Gap
(570) 420-1198
Big Creek gets the prize for the most beautiful wine tasting room. The winery is in a huge, airy building with a high wooden ceiling. The white stucco walls are accented with paintings and sculpture by local artists. Look out a window, and you'll see the vineyard sloping down toward the building. Look over a rail, and you can watch the winemaking process a floor below.

Big Creek is the youngest of the four regional wineries, open to the public in 1996. Even before it opened, however, Big Creek won a bronze medal from the Pennsylvania state competition for its Chambourcin, a dry red wine. Among its other reds are a buttery, mellow Cabernet Franc, and a rosé-style Vin di Pasqualina, named after a great aunt of winemaker Dominic Strohlein, who runs the business with his mother and brother. Their whites include a smoky, flinty Carmé, made from Chardonnay grapes, and a sweeter Dulcinea, named after the Man of La Mancha's elusive lady love. "The whole operation is a quixotic adventure," notes Strohlein.

The vineyard currently produces around 6,000 gallons a year, and Strohlein is expanding both the amount and the varieties of wine he produces. He's justifiably happy with the current selection. "Our wines are very approachable," he says. "Although they have good longevity, they can be drunk immediately." Big Creek's wines sold out in the first year of production and have been selling so briskly that Strolhein says, "We'll always be out of something." Strolhein is concentrating more on dry wines because, he says, that's what his family drinks, and he is now producing a wine from Italian grapes, something that's relatively rare in Pennsylvania. That wine "almost gets sold before it makes it to the tasting room," he says.

A few wine-related items are available in the tasting room, including wine baskets you can fill for gift giving. The wines are also available at some local restaurants.

Big Creek Vineyard is open afternoons, seven days a week. If you're visiting in fall or winter and want to taste, call ahead to make sure the stock isn't sold out.

To find Big Creek, follow US 209 to Highway 534 W. Then following signs for the vineyard, go 0.1 mile to Beltzville Road, then 1.3 miles to Keller Road. Turn left onto Keller Road and go 0.3 mile to the second driveway on the left.

Cherry Valley Vineyards
Lower Cherry Valley Road, Saylorsburg
(570) 992-2255
www.cherryvalleyvineyards.com

You can see Cherry Valley's winery from Highway 33. The tasting room and shop is housed in a beautiful purple and green farmhouse that was once owned by John Saylor, for whom Saylorsburg is named. The farmhouse is surrounded by intriguing gardens, a gazebo and springhouse. A pavilion next to a pond hosts musical afternoons, weddings, and other special events. In the vineyard is an old one-room schoolhouse that is said to be haunted.

Cherry Valley is the largest local vineyard, producing 30,000 gallons and 32 varieties of wine. Winemaker Nicholas Sorrenti presides over the pressing. His father, Dominic, established the vineyard and is still a strong presence there, always adding some nice touch to the gardens and a little sparkle to the atmosphere. Dominic learned to make wine in his family. Nicholas has learned from his father, and from winemakers in France. Cherry Valley wines can be surprisingly sophisticated, and their champagne could easily go head-to-head with any French champagne.

At the end of June each year, Split Rock Resort in Lake Harmony hosts the Great Tastes of Pennsylvania Wine & Food Festival. More than 20 Pennsylvania wineries participate. (See our Annual Events and Festivals chapter for details.) This is a great chance to sample a lot of different wineries' products in a festive atmosphere.

Cherry Valley's wines have won lots of medals both nationally and internationally. This winery markets its award-winning, premier wines under the Sorrenti label. Cherry Valley Vineyards received the Pennsylvania State Governor's Cup in 2001. That's the highest award a vineyard can receive in the state, and it was given to them when they won a gold medal for their Raspberry Spumante at the Pennsylvania Farm show. In fact, the blueberry, blush, and strawberry spumantes have all done incredibly well in competitions.

The Sorrentis are especially proud of their showing in the 1996 Amenti del Vino International competition where their 1995 Ravat won a gold medal; their 1994 Riesling, 1994 Foch, and 1994 Burgundy won silver; and their 1995 Chardonnay and 1995 Chablis won bronze.

Mary Sorrenti, wife of Dominic and mother of Nicholas, loves their champagne. "It's like magic," she says. "If you take some to a party, it feels like someone sprinkled glitter in the air. It gives you a good buzz with no hangover." Like most small wineries, the Sorrentis keep chemicals out of the process as much as possible, both in growing the grapes and in making the wines. This is as natural as

When you taste wine, don't forget to look at the color, swirl the wine around, stick your nose in the glass (not the wine), and take a big sniff. Sight and smell add a lot to the wine-tasting experience.

you're going to get and still get a good wine. Mary says they can't make enough premium red for their customers. We suggest that you try some of their six varieties of fruit wines too. We've tasted fruit wines in other states that taste more like cough syrup than wine, but Cherry Valley's natural fruit wines are light and fun. You can practically taste the fuzz in the peach wine.

You can access the Appalachian Trail from Cherry Valley's property, and Cherry Valley offers hot lunch buffets plus a hike several weekends a year.

Cherry Valley is open for tastings daily throughout the year. The shop also carries some wine-related items, the Sorrenti's own vinegar and gift baskets stocked with wines and food.

To reach Cherry Valley Vineyards, take Highway 33 south to the Saylorsburg exit. Turn left, and proceed to Lower Cherry Valley Road. Turn left; the winery entrance will be on your right.

CLOSE ENOUGH ...

This vineyard is technically in a region called the Slate Belt, just south of the Poconos. However, since it's just outside our area and very close to the other vineyards, we thought you might like to visit this one, too.

Franklin Hill Vineyards
7833 Franklin Hill Road, Bangor
(610) 588–8708, (888) 887–2839
www.franklinhillvineyards.com

Pocono Outlet:
The Wine Shop, Fountain Springs West
Highway 611, Tannersville
(570) 619–7260

Franklin Hill may be the only woman-run vineyard in Pennsylvania. Owner Elaine Austen and head winemaker Bonnie Pysher have kids (now grown) and know how hard it is to work around them, so when the kids get off the school bus, the

harvest stops for Franklin Hill's staff of working moms. In fact, Austin's son works for the winery, too.

Set amid high rolling hills with an awesome view of the Kittatinny Ridge, the vineyard has a modest tasting room that shares space with oak wine barrels and fermentation tanks. Franklin Hill produces 17,000 gallons a year.

The wines are so good that, the first year out, the Country White won a gold medal in the Pennsylvania state competition. The Country Apple, with a Granny Smith-like bite, won a gold medal in 1997's state competition, while in 2002, the Seyval Blanc won silver and the Simple Red won bronze.

We don't normally like pink wine but found Franklin Hills' Country Rosé to be excellent. Pysher says that a lot of her customers say the same and that she uses a different recipe for her rosés than most other wineries. The Country Red is a particularly interesting wine because, though it's 100 percent concord grapes, it has none of the sharp edges we associate with other concord wines, like Manischewitz. It's a light, friendly wine that would be perfect on a picnic or as a base for Sangria.

The reason the wines are so good, Pysher claims, is that Franklin Hill starts the winemaking process "with really nice grapes. You can only make a wine as good as the grapes, so we try to be excellent grape growers." Pysher recommends harvest time, throughout September and early October, as the best time to visit the winery. In fact, if you're interested, you could find yourself in the vineyard picking grapes.

Franklin Hill emphasizes customer service. Once during a snowstorm, when the road was impassable, Pysher hopped on a snowmobile to take samples of their custom labels to a bride-to-be who had to make her plans that day. If you want to bring a group for a tour, or if you want to have a wine-and-cheese party at the winery, just call, and the folks at Franklin Hill will make the arrangements.

The winery is open for free tastings and sales Monday through Saturday year-round. Its 20 varieties are also for sale at outlet stores in Bethlehem and Easton.

To find Franklin Hill Vineyards, take Highway 611 south to the stoplight in Martins Creek. Proceed straight through the light onto Front Street (611 turns to the left). At the top of the hill, make a right onto Franklin Hill Road and proceed 1.7 miles. Franklin Hill Vineyards will be on your right. Turn in, drive to a fork in the road, and bear left. The winery is a low building built into a bank at the end of the road.

With a few exceptions, wine offered by Pocono wineries sell for between $5.00 and $15.00 per bottle. Most wineries give discounts on purchases by the case. You can usually mix varieties in a single case.

KIDSTUFF

Left to their own devices, many kids will vegetate in front of the TV or disappear into a video game. After several hours of this kind of activity, they'll walk by a room full of toys, past a window disclosing a perfect day, come to you and say, "There's nothing to do."

There's plenty to do in the Poconos. Outside your door there's a natural paradise waiting to be explored, skated on, bicycled over, swum around, and fished. In this chapter you'll find lots of good places to take your children. Don't stop here, though. There are activities for kids in other chapters too: Winter Sports; Recreation; Camps and Conference Centers; Arts and Culture; Attractions; and In, On, and Around the Water. Also keep an eye out for special events like the ones in our Annual Events and Festivals chapter. Many festivals now include children's areas with entertainers and hands-on activities. If you have a little extra time, our Day Trips chapter has some ideas for great forays a little farther afield.

There's so much to do in the Pocono region that your children will probably grow up before you've exhausted all the possibilities.

ADMISSION PRICE

The following is a price code for admission to attractions. The price listed is for adults.

Children and senior citizens' admissions are usually lower.

$5.00 or less	$
$5.01 to $10.00	$$
$10.01 to $15.00	$$$
$15.01 or more	$$$$

LET'S PLAY

We have play parks with waterslides, bumper boats, climbing equipment, go-karts, miniature golf, and more. New ones are springing up every year, but these should get you started.

Delaware Water Gap/ Shawnee-on-Delaware

Pocono Mountain Go-Karts $$–$$$$
U.S. Highway 209, Marshalls Creek
(570) 223-6299
www.poconogokarts.com
"Go-karts is all we have here," says the man who answers the phone at this location. Pocono Mountain Go-Karts is open weekends from April through Memorial Day and then daily from then until Labor Day. From Labor Day until Thanksgiving it's open on weekends only.

Shawnee Place Play & Water Park $$$
Hollow Road, Shawnee-on-Delaware
(570) 421-7231
www.shawneemt.com
Besides the water slides, this play park has hands-on workshops, games, and net climbs. If you get too hot outside, go into the air-conditioned buildings to see one of the magic shows. It is a great place for summer birthday parties too. For families with a mix of kids up to 12 years old and toddlers, there is a dry toddler area that's fun for the little ones, while the bigger

---

i

Check out **The Miracle Shopper, This Week in the Poconos,** *and* **Yankee Clipper** *for discount coupons to many of the places mentioned in this chapter, including skating rinks, animal parks, and playlands. The Pocono Mountain Vacation Bureau has recently issued a book of coupons, and many area businesses also offer terrific coupons on the Web.*

kids enjoy the more active play elements. One of the best parts of Shawnee Place is the bridge over the wetlands, leading to the park. If you peer into the water, you'll see turtles, catfish, and a host of other wetland denizens.

Special festivals throughout the summer bring food, music, crafts, and chairlift rides to Shawnee Place. (See our Annual Events chapter). Watch the papers for report card day, right after the end of school. Kids get a dollar off for every "A" they've earned. Shawnee Place is open daily from mid-June through Labor Day.

Thunder Creek Quarry $$$$
Creek Road, Marshalls Creek
(570) 223-7177
www.mountainmanor.com
A kiddie casino—whoops, we mean arcade!—and soft-play area indoors complement the outdoor bumper boats, playing field, miniature golf course, and go-karts, including a special track for minidrivers. Birthday party packages are available. (See Attractions for more information.)

Stroudsburg/East Stroudsburg

Camelbeach Water Park $$$$
Camelback Road, Tannersville
(570) 629-1661
www.camelbeach.com
This is an awesome water park with 22 of the baddest, scariest waterslides in the East and a serious wave pool—great fun for the teens. There's also an interactive play pool that's only a foot deep but has lots of play elements, a few more sedate rides, and a nice, comfortable deck where Mom and Dad can hang out. (See our Attractions chapter for more information.)

Pocono Mountain Go-Karts
& Play Park $$-$$$$
Highway 611, Bartonsville
(570) 620-0820
www.poconogocarts.com

You'll find two great go-kart tracks here, one for kids shorter than 54 inches and one for the bigger kids and their parents. The parks also have collision carts (a cross between bumper cars and bumper boats), an 18-hole miniature golf course, batting cages, an indoor arcade, a balloon fighting game called "water wars," and a snack bar. And in case you get bored, they've also added a full-size skate park for boards, bikes, and blades, with a half-pipe, full pyramid, half pyramids, beef box, quarter pipe, drop-ins, and lots of movable boxes and rails. Catch your breath—there's paint ball on four fields of play, a climbing wall, a trampoline, archery, bankshot basketball, and a scrambler. They've added pony carts and a carnival park that should entertain kids 12 and younger and includes a chain swing, a kiddie roller coaster, a whip, bumper boats, and an antique car ride.

The park is open daily Memorial Day through Labor Day and weekends in April and May and September through November. Pocono Mountain Go-Karts is a great place for a birthday party.

West End

Imagination Zone $
Monroe Plaza, US 209
Brodheadsville
(570) 992-5035
A large store space has been turned into an imaginative indoor playground here with a huge custom-designed play system including tunnels, climbing nets, a ball pit, slides, and a moon bounce. A separate toddler area gives the little ones a chance to play safely away from the enthusiastic excesses of their bigger counterparts. Arcade games that give tickets you trade for prizes line a back wall.

Upstairs in a separate area, kids can play laser tag. This is a mom-and-dad-friendly place, and there's even a big-screen TV so you can catch the game while keeping an eye on the kids. A kid-

ℹ️ *Monroe County Recreation, (570) 992–4343 or (570) 421–2871, has lots of programs for kids and adults. The offerings change each season, but they include swimming lessons, tennis lessons, dance lessons, trips, and so on. Call for a brochure or to be put on the mailing list.*

friendly pizzeria also offers ice cream. There's no admission charge, but if your child wants to scramble around on the play system or play laser tag, it will set you back $2.50—some people just want to play the arcade games or eat. Birthday party packages run from $5.99 to $11.99 per child, but they take walk-in parties, too; call to make sure there's room. The Imagination Zone is also a licensed day-care center and runs a summer camp. Imagination Zone is open all year, every day except Christmas, Thanksgiving, and New Year's Day.

Milford/Lake Wallenpaupack Area

Carousel Water & Fun Park $$$
Highway 652, Beach Lake
(570) 729-7532
www.carousel-park.com
Carousel has two giant waterslides, bumper boats, kiddie and adult go-karts, an arcade, batting cages, and miniature golf. A snack bar is available for treats, or you can bring your own food and enjoy it in the picnic area. (See our Attractions chapter for more information.)

Costa's Family Fun Park $-$$$$
U.S. Highway 6, Lords Valley
(570) 226-8585, (800) 928-4FUN
www.costasfamilyfunpark.com
Costa's, east of Lake Wallenpaupack, features a game room, a batting cage, miniature golf, go-karts, a driving range, and a kiddieland with tube mazes, crawling

webs, a web ladder, and a sea of balls. The restaurant has an outdoor porch for dining and offers kids' meals. Birthday party packages are available.

Admission is free; you pay per ride. (See our Attractions chapter for details.)

LET'S MAKE SOMETHING

There are lots of ongoing arts and crafts classes for kids. (See our Arts and Culture chapter.) The following are some places that offer special workshops. Keep an eye on the listings in the *Pocono Record* for workshops offered by local museums, environmental centers, and other cultural institutions. You might also call a favorite museum and ask what's coming up for the little ones. Many such places print a calendar or newsletter that they'll be happy to send you.

Stroudsburg/East Stroudsburg

Quiet Valley Living Historical Farm $$
Quiet Valley Road, Stroudsburg
(570) 992-6161
www.quietvalley.org
Learn to make a corn-shuck doll and then make a broom to sweep up the mess. Quiet Valley offers a variety of workshops in traditional crafts for all ages. Its newsletter lists upcoming workshops. During the Harvest Fest, children can try their hand at various crafts in sessions offered right on the spot. (See our Attractions, Arts and Culture, and Annual Events for more information.)

West End

Mauch Chunk Museum and
Cultural Center $
41 West Broadway, Jim Thorpe
(570) 325-9190
www.mauchchunkmuseum.com

Mauch Chunk runs an annual children's art show in cooperation with the Carbon County School System. The show has been held in March as part of the National Youth Arts Month. Check with them for details.

IN OLDEN DAYS...

Delaware Water Gap/ Shawnee-on-Delaware

Antoine Dutot School & Museum $
Highway 611, Delaware Water Gap
(570) 476-4240
www.delawarewatergap.com
Let your kids explore the 1920s-style classroom in this museum. You can lecture them while they sit at the desks and play with the inkwells. (See our Attractions chapter for more details.)

Mary Stolz Doll & Toy Museum $
McCole Road, Bushkill
(570) 588-7566
Girls will be fascinated with the antique dolls in this museum, but the old Barbies and Jems may get an even bigger response. Watch out, Ma, there's an incredible gift shop that's bigger than the museum. Don't come looking for books by the three-time Newberry Honor-winning children's author; this is a different Mary Stolz. (See our Attractions chapter for details.)

The Pocono Indian Museum $
US 209, Bushkill
(570) 588-9338
www.poconoindianmuseum.com
Do you know where the term "sitting Indian-style" comes from? Learn about this and other fascinating facts, sit in a wigwam, and peruse one of the most extensive collections of artifacts of the local Lenape tribe. Again, watch out—to a kid, the gift shop is the most important room in a museum, and this one is big.

(See our Attractions and Native Americans chapters for more information.)

Quiet Valley Living Historical Farm $$
Quiet Valley Road, Stroudsburg
(570) 992-6161
www.quietvalley.org
You can spend the day down on the farm exploring, petting, and playing. Harvest Fest and the Farm Animal Frolic are especially fun for kids. Our daughter always wants to dress 18th-century style to go here. (See our Attractions and Annual Events chapters for more information and special events at Quiet Valley.)

West End

The Bell School
Cherry Valley Road, Stormsville
(570) 421-7703
www.mcha-pa.org
Here's another re-creation of your kids' favorite pastime—school. This is a one-room schoolhouse. (See our Attractions chapter for details.)

The Old Jail Museum $
128 West Broadway, Jim Thorpe
(570) 325-5259
www.experiencepa.com
If your kids are Goosebumps fans, take them here to see the mysterious handprint on the wall. (See our Attractions chapter for more information.) You can also point out that if they're not good, they could end up in a place like this!

Old Mauch Chunk H.O. Scale
Model Train Display $
Hooven Building, US 209, Jim Thorpe
(570) 386-2297, (570) 325-4371
www.geocities.com/omchotd
When you're tired of riding the real thing in Jim Thorpe, pop in next door to see this miniature version. The model train display is in the Hooven Building, next to the railroad depot. (See our Attractions chapter for more information.)

Many libraries and schools offer a story hour, and some libraries have reading and writing clubs during the summer. Call your local elementary school or library and ask if they have story hours or any other programs for children.

Rail Tours Inc. $$-$$$
Train Depot, US 209, Jim Thorpe
(570) 325-4606, (610) 250-0968
www.railtours-inc.com
If your kids have echoed the folk song and asked "Daddy, what's a train?" take them on this old-fashioned steam-powered excursion. (See our Attractions chapter for information.)

Milford/Lake Wallenpaupack Area

Schocopee Schoolhouse
Apple Valley Village, US 6, Milford
no phone
www.pikehistory.org
A restored schoolhouse from the 1820s gives your children the chance to experience a school from stricter times. Schocopee Schoolhouse is open weekends from Memorial Day to Labor Day.

Stourbridge Rail Excursions $$$-$$$$
303 Commercial Street, Honesdale
(570) 253-1960
www.waynecountycc.com
Besides the usual scenic excursions, this diesel train runs several theme trips including an Easter Bunny ride, a Great

Rangers' talks at the Delaware Water Gap National Recreation Area as well as at our state parks and environmental centers are often geared to kids. Call the park of your choice and ask what special programs they're offering that are appropriate for your child's age.

Train Robbery, a haunted Halloween ride, and a Santa Express. (See our Attractions chapter for more information.)

LET'S EXPLORE NATURE

Children have an inexhaustible desire to learn about the natural world. Since the Poconos is set in the middle of a series of parks, many with knowledgeable naturalists on staff, there are lots of opportunities for kids to learn.

Delaware Water Gap/ Shawnee-on-Delaware

Delaware Water Gap National Recreation Area
US 209, Bushkill
(570) 588-2452
www.nps.gov
Two self-guiding programs are available for kids. Children ages 6 through 12 can borrow the Junior Naturalist Discovery Pack. The backpack contains spades, bottles, and other necessary implements to complete three of six suggested activities. The activities are meant to orient children to the park and its natural offerings. When a child completes the required activities, he or she receives a Junior Naturalist patch and is eligible to do the self-guided Junior Ranger Program.

The Junior Ranger Program involves a booklet of activities that kids age seven and older can complete at their own pace during a visit to the park. One activity requires children to speak to a park ranger and attend a presentation about how rangers interpret the park for visitors. The emphasis is on understanding a ranger's daily responsibilities. Backpacks and program packets also are available at the Kittatinny Visitor Center, off Interstate 80, just over the state line in New Jersey, (906) 496-4458.

There are also programs that allow teachers to use the park as a classroom.

Teacher-led geology classes, hikes on a portion of the Appalachian Trail, and the Junior Naturalist Discovery Packs are great educational opportunities. The Pocono Environment Education Center (PEEC), (570) 828–2319, in Dingmans Ferry is a wonderful place for teachers to take their classes for an overnight and attend a program on some aspect of the natural world. (See the related Close-up in our Parks chapter.) Student workshops are offered in nature studies, canoeing, problem-solving activities, and other nature-related subjects. The facilities here are excellent, and the experience is one that makes a deep impact on the children and their teachers. Many Pocono school systems take advantage of these pro-grams. Weekend seminars and workshops on a variety of subjects are available to the public including some with an empha-sis on kids' activities. Watch the *Pocono Record* for information, call PEEC for a calendar of events, or go to that Web site www.peec.org.

Stroudsburg/East Stroudsburg

Monroe County Environmental Education Center
8050 Running Valley Road, Bartonsville
(570) 629–3061
www.mcconservation.org
The Monroe County Environmental Educa-tion Center offers programs for children during the week and on weekends year-round. Many homeschooling parents (see our Education chapter) take advantage of these programs to enhance the science portion of their home-based curriculum. Programs are offered for children as young as four years. There are summer opportunities here for kids ages 4 through 18 (see our Camps and Conference Cen-ters chapter for summer camp programs). Single sessions cover topics such as "Insects," "Animal Tracks," "Trees and Paper," "Worms," and other nature-related

subjects of interest to kids. The center also takes children on a series of field trips to important nature sites. Birthday parties are a specialty here, with a group activity on a chosen topic such as wildlife, predator/prey, trees, birds, a scavenger hunt, and other fun, nature-oriented themes.

If you're canoeing, kayaking, or even tubing, make sure your child wears a life jacket (you should, too). Even strong swimmers can encounter conditions that they can't handle. On the river, you'll get a ticket if you child is younger than 12, in some kind of flotation device, and without a life jacket.

LET'S GO TO THE FAIR

A trip to the fair is always fun. See our Annual Events and Festivals chapter for some of the local fairs. Look in the papers for schedules and discount coupons. Many fairs, carnivals, and circuses are sponsored by community-service organizations such as Kiwanis or volunteer fire departments. Going to a fair is a great way to support important work while having family fun. Ticket prices vary, but there are usually family nights that offer a set price ticket for the whole evening. If you have moved into the area recently, consider volunteer-ing at one of the stands. It's hard work, but it's a good way to meet your neighbors.

LET'S GO TO THE PARK

Parks in the Poconos range from munici-pal facilities offering playgrounds, swim-ming pools, and picnic tables to state parks and national recreation areas featur-ing hiking, swimming, and camping opportunities as well as interpretive pro-grams and restored villages. Many of these places have programs for children. For additional information and options,

CLOSE-UP

The Fine Arts Discovery Series (FADS): Concerts for Children

Some of the most exciting performance work done today is in children's music and theater. That's why we're so lucky to have the Fine Arts Discovery Series (FADS), which presents internationally recognized children's performers in the Poconos. This is a series all parents should attend with their children, but even if you don't have kids, these performances are well worth catching.

The list of performers includes local well-known professional musicians, but performers from around the world have also become part of the Fine Arts Discovery Series. Local performances have spotlighted the Pocono Youth Chamber Orchestra, the Poconos Saxophone Quartet, Janet Lawson, Ballet Guild of Lehigh Valley, Caliope, the Ballet Theatre of Scranton, the Touchstone Theatre, the Mock Turtle Marionette Theatre, and others. Favorites from farther afield include the Little Theatre of the Deaf, David Holt, Spotlite on Opera, the Nai-Ni Chen Dance Company, the Jose Greco II Flamenco Dance Company, the Ishangi Family Dancers, and Soh Daiko, a Japanese Taiko drumming company.

The 2003–2004 series included John McCutcheon, Lehigh University Sym-

check out some other chapters: Recreation; In, On, and Around the Water; Winter Sports; and Parks. In particular, check out Beltzville State Park, in Lehighton, and Promised Land State Park. These two sites have an abundance of programs for children that are noted in the aforementioned chapters. Promised Land runs free nature-based programs all summer long. Beltsville offers day camps, day programs, weekend programs for families, and other activities throughout the summer season.

Some of the play parks hold a report card day the week school ends. The price of admission is reduced for children with "A"s on their report cards. Watch the papers for ads for report card days.

If you want to enjoy a day at the playground with your children, there are lots of neighborhood parks for you to explore.

Delaware Water Gap/ Shawnee-on-Delaware

Shull Park
Oak Street, Delaware Water Gap
(570) 476-0331
This lovely little park has a swimming pool, a basketball court, and a playground. You can sit at a picnic table and lunch with your friends while the little ones play. The pool, which is well kept, opens when school is out and closes when school begins. Rates vary, but seniors older than 55 and children younger than 4 get in

phony Orchestra, Little Theater of the Deaf, and Road to the Isles. Most of the performances are preceded by a workshop, giving children a chance to interact with the performers and deepen their understanding of the music they are about to experience in concert. Study guides, suggesting appropriate activities, are also available.

FADS has tried to maintain its policy of affordable fine-arts programs for the family. They have developed strong corporate backing that helps offset costs for the programs. In the past, grants from the Monroe County Arts Council have helped, as have grants from The Pennsylvania Council on the Arts. These efforts have kept ticket prices low; season reserved seat tickets are $25.00 per person; general admission seating prices are

$8.00. Workshops cost $5.00 per child.

As Susan Stillo-Wilkins, one of the founders of the series, reiterates in press releases and conversations, she and the people who now are the backbone of the Fine Arts Discovery Series for Children feel that, "In these times when children are constantly bombarded with artificial stimulation from TV, video games, and the like, there's a need for family-oriented entertainment where young children can discover and experience the thrills and joys of live performances." And they do, thanks to the Fine Arts Discovery Series.

For more information about the Fine Arts Discovery Series (FADS) of Concerts for Children, call (570) 476–FADS, write to P.O. Box 1126, Stroudsburg, PA 18360, or go to www.fineartsdiscoveryseries.org.

free. Seasonal, resident, and nonresident rates apply. Shull Park has changing rooms and restrooms. It is a great family spot, and many folks who grew up swimming here now bring children of their own.

Stroudsburg/East Stroudsburg

Dansbury Park
Day Street, East Stroudsburg
(570) 421–6591

This park has a busy swimming pool and swimming lessons in the morning for residents and nonresidents of all ages. Resident and nonresident rates are available for daily and season passes. The pool is open daily from the end of the school

year to the beginning of the next. Recently renovated, the pool includes three waterslides and a zero-depth entry, which makes it easier for senior citizens and disabled people to get into the water. A snack bar, changing rooms, and restrooms are on site. This pool is well maintained, and people from all around the county enjoy using it. Dansbury also has a playground, basketball courts, ball fields, barbecue grills, and a picnic pavilion. There are lots of trees to enjoy and benches to sit on and relax while the children play. A new, popular skateboard park in Dansbury attracts the street surfers.

Gregory's Park/Pond
Highway 447, East Stroudsburg

In this pretty little park along the banks of a pond, you'll find benches, picnic tables, ducks, and geese. Throughout fishing season, you'll almost always see someone with a pole plying the pond here.

Stroudsburg Municipal Pool
West Main Street, Stroudsburg
(570) 421-5444
Available to residents and nonresidents alike, this pool opens tentatively June 5 through August 29. Changing rooms, showers, restrooms, picnic tables, and a snack concession stand are by the pool. There are resident and nonresident rates for swimming. The pool is open every day of the week. Call for information about hours and swimming lessons.

This town park also offers a playground, tennis court, basketball courts, a baseball field, and picnic tables.

Waterfront Park
Twin Falls Road, East Stroudsburg
Twin Falls Road makes a loop off of US 209, starting at the pretty Twin Falls, and winding up about a quarter of a mile farther along on 209. Just beyond the falls is Waterfront Park, with baseball diamonds, soccer fields, a basketball court, a small picnic pavilion, play equipment for the little ones, and a gazebo. The waterfront is the pond that courses over the falls, and it's filled with ducks and geese. Kids love to feed the birds, and fish in the pond. An old farmhouse is used for Boy Scout meetings and such. You can walk along the road to a bench, where you can view the falls. Drive slowly and very carefully on this road. It's narrow and twisty, and there are children and aggressive geese right around the next bend.

Zacharia's Pond
Third Street East, East Stroudsburg
The park, surrounding a pretty pond with ducks, includes a picnic pavilion, play equipment, playing fields, a grill, a wheelchair-accessible fishing dock, Porta-johns, and a wooded jogging path around the pond with the moldering remains of a parcourse. The American Legion hall is up the hill, and if you're lucky, you'll find a party in the

pavilion with a good band filling the whole park with music. Residents fish in the pond in summer and ice skate on it in winter.

West End

Mauch Chunk Lake Park
625 Lentz Trail Highway, Jim Thorpe
(570) 325-3669
Mauch Chunk Lake Park is discussed in other chapters (Parks; Recreation; Winter Sports; and In, On, and Around the Water). It is an especially nice family park in the summer, with swimming, boating, and court games available. Biking trails make it a fun spot for family bike treks.

Milford/Lake Wallenpaupack Area

Ann Street Park
Fifth Street, between West Catherine and Ann Streets, Milford
In the spring, you'll find fabulous lilacs in this park, dedicated to the Milford High School, which merged with Matamoras and is now Delaware Valley High School. There's lots of play space here, a large traditional playground, picnic tables, a basketball court, and a baseball diamond.

Bingham Park
US 6, Hawley
Bingham Park has a playground, baseball diamonds, a lovely old-fashioned bandstand, and basketball and tennis courts.

LET'S GO SKATING

If your kids like to skate, they have the option of ice-skating or roller-skating all year round at various facilities. Most of these rinks offer birthday party packages that are especially popular with area children.

Mountain Manor, (570) 223-8098, is open for ice-skating in the winter. These and other places to ice-skate are noted in our Winter Sports chapter, including Mauch Chunk Lake Park and some of the state parks. Many of the resorts also have ice-skating and/or roller-skating, so be sure to check for these activities when you review our Accommodations chapter.

For roller-skating try the following places.

Delaware Water Gap/ Shawnee-on-Delaware

The Starting Gate   **$$**
US 209, Marshalls
(570) 223-6215
www.startinggateonline.com
If your kids are heavily into in-line skating and skateboarding take them to the Starting Gate, about 0.25 mile north of Foxmoor Village. Children younger than 18 must have a signed release form to use the facility. It has miniramps, a fun box, slant ramps, a wall ride, other ramps, and neat things for kids to jump on and off with their skates or skateboards. (BMX bikes are allowed here on weekdays.) There are no restrictions on types of in-line skates; however pads, wrist guards, and helmets must be worn. (See our Recreation chapter for details.)

Stroudsburg/East Stroudsburg

Big Wheel   **$$**
Highway 191, Stroudsburg
(570) 424-5499
www.bigwheelskating.com
Wednesday and Friday afternoons are for families at Big Wheel. The Hokey-Pokey and the Chicken Dance on skates are highlights of the afternoon. Programs for toddlers are held Wednesday mornings and Fridays at lunchtime. Children can use their kiddie skates or ride their plastic rid-

All the commercial skate parks in the area require a helmet, elbow and kneepads, wrist guards, and a signed release form from a parent. If you don't have pads, check with the skate park; they may rent some.

ing toys, and parents can skate with them. Open skating is Friday evenings as well as Saturday and Sunday afternoons. (See our Recreation chapter for details.)

Parties are fun here in the party room. There is always lots of activity on the weekends, but a separate smaller skating area in the party room makes the parties manageable.

West End

LaRose's Skating Rink   **$**
US 209, Lehighton
(610) 377-1859
www.larosesskatingrink.com
This skating rink has been family-owned for more than 75 years, so families are important here. Public skating is on Friday and Saturday evenings. The rink accepts private parties every day. You may use your own skates, but they must be rink safe (no protruding axles, etc.), and they must be clean. LaRose's inspects your skates before you can roll. Rentals are also available. LaRose's is the oldest continuously family-owned and operated roller-skating rink in the country. (See our Recreation chapter for more information.)

LET'S GO SKIING AND SNOWBOARDING

You will find some very good programs for children at Pocono-area ski resorts. (See our Winter Sports chapter.) Kids can start learning to ski at four, and the sooner you get them onto the slopes, the more natural it will be for them. It's downright embarrassing for those of us who started skiing in our 40s to see these little ones whizzing gracefully past us. Many programs take your kids for a half-day, leaving Mom and Dad free to fall without the embarrassment of being laughed at by their kids. The programs at most mountains insist that snowboarding lessons start when the kids are a year or two older.

Most of the mountains offer full- and half-day programs for children's instruction. Most of them also offer racing for older kids. Check the listings in Winter Sports for more details.

Snow tubing is great fun for kids, and most of the ski mountains now offer a separate snow tubing area (see our Winter Sports chapter).

Many area schools sponsor after-school ski programs. Students ski or snowboard once a week for six weeks at a price that's way below what you'd pay for individual sessions. The base fee is for a lift ticket, and the prices go up depending on the child's needs for lessons or equipment. Whatever part of the package you need, the programs are reasonably priced (less than $100). Some schools bus their students to the mountains, while others require parents to deliver their children. In late October, start looking for ski information in the bottom of your kid's school bag, under the crushed Twinkies.

LET'S GO TRICK-OR-TREATING

Trick-or-treating is a time-honored, if strongly regulated tradition in the Poconos. Each town decides which day is trick-or-treating day (not always on Halloween), and the hours during which children may go begging are published in the paper. Since some Pocono residents live far from other homes, many parents take their children into a town to trick-or-treat. The prettiest streets in Stroudsburg and East Stroudsburg as well as the village of Shawnee are especially popular, but any village or development where the houses

are close together works. The best places, of course, are those where you know the people who answer the door. We would be very leery of taking our child to a neighborhood where we knew no one. Be sure to check the newspaper for locally assigned dates and times.

Not all of the schools in the Poconos celebrate Halloween during school hours. Some have bowed to pressure from the religious right, and if they have any celebration at all, they hold it on the weekend when attendance is optional. If Halloween falls on a school day, you might see some depressed kids in these schools. Other schools hold costume parades at the end of the day their municipalities designate as trick-or-treating day. The children dress up and parade around the school grounds, while the parents watch and applaud each class' efforts. Even the teachers get into the fun and wear some outrageous outfits. If your school celebrates Halloween, they'll send a note home with details.

Haunted barns, houses, and hayrides seem to pop up out of nowhere at this time of year. You'll see signs along the roads and advertisements in the newspaper. Generally, they are run by local community-service organizations as fund-raising efforts.

Stroudsburg/East Stroudsburg

Main Street—Stroudsburg
The Jacob Stroud Corporation sponsors a Halloween Parade in Stroudsburg each year. Children and adults dress up and march down Main Street, where merchants give away candy. The costumes are judged for prizes. Long after the parade is over, costumed people of all ages march up and down examining the crafts booths, food, and games that line the street.

Stroud Mall
Highway 611, Stroudsburg
(570) 424-2770

The Stroud Mall has a trick-or-treating night, usually the night before Stroudsburg's official trick-or-treating night. Merchants stand outside their stores and hand out goodies, sometimes coupons, to an endless stream of children who seem to do a Halloween dance around the mall. Check the *Pocono Record* during Halloween week for particulars.

Mount Pocono Area

Barrett Township
Highway 191, Mountainhome
(570) 595–2602
www.barrett.Monroe.pa.us
In Barrett Township, the local business folk dress up and parade with costumed children down Highway 191, distributing candy to all the parade watchers who scramble after the treats. The Pocono Mountain High School Marching Band provides some haunting music for this event. The parade is usually held the Sunday before the Halloween. Check the *Pocono Record* for the date and time.

Many individuals and businesses create Halloween tableaus in their front yards, and you can cruise the township, enjoying these scenes from "Scarecrow Town," another area tradition.

West End

Broadway/West Broadway—Jim Thorpe
In Jim Thorpe, the main street (Broadway and West Broadway) is dressed up for theatrically inspired events, spearheaded by the group at the Mauch Chunk Opera House.

LET'S TALK TO THE ANIMALS

Give a kid a chance to commune with other species and you can almost guarantee a happy kid. Of course, our Poconos have lots of wild animals that live close to us. Skunks wander through our yards at night. Deer dot the landscape at twilight. A black bear occasionally ambles down the street. Eagles, hawks, and vultures soar in circles overhead. Woodpeckers, hummingbirds, golden finches, ducks, and geese fill the skies, trees, and riverbanks. Wild turkeys sometimes cross in front of our cars, and flattened groundhogs decorate our roads.

Still, it's fun to be able to look a bear right in the eye—safely. Feeding and petting deer is more thrilling because we see them in the wild on an almost daily basis. The Poconos has many places where kids can pet farm animals as well as gape at more exotic species.

Delaware Water Gap/ Shawnee-on-Delaware

Pocono Snake and Animal Farm $$
US 209, Marshalls Creek
(570) 223–8653
www.poconovacations.com/attractions/ zoo-animal-parks/poconosnakefarm
The Snake and Animal Farm has more than 100 reptiles and live animals. Besides monkeys, alligators, and really huge snakes, it has a petting zoo with some gentle deer. (See our Attractions chapter for more information.)

Stroudsburg/East Stroudsburg

Pocono Farmstand and Nursery
Highway 611, Tannersville
(570) 629–4344
Pocono Farmstand and Nursery features a petting zoo with goats, sheep, donkeys, and other farm animals from late August until sometime in November.

Quiet Valley Living Historical Farm $$
Quiet Valley Road, Stroudsburg
(570) 992-6161
www.quietvalley.org

Farm animals are part of Quiet Valley's regular tour. In the spring the annual Farm Animal Folic lets the children—and you—delight in seeing the newborn lambs and other baby animals and interact with their parents. Your children can also participate in a number of activities such as butter churning that will give them a sense of what life was like in the 18th and 19th centuries. (See our Attractions, Arts and Culture, and Annual Events chapters for more information about this living museum.)

Mount Pocono Area

House of Candles
Highway 715, Henryville
(570) 629-1953
www.houseofcandles.com

While mommy is inside buying a lifetime's worth of candles, the children can visit with the Chinese pheasants, sheep, goats, miniature horses, and ducks outside. There's also a candle-shaped fishpond full of koi. If they're too young to be outside when you're in, promise them that if they're good and don't break anything, you'll take them out to see the animals when you're done shopping.

The shop is closed on Sunday and major holidays.

Bethlehem, only 45 minutes south of the Poconos, is a terrific place to catch children's performers all year round. Bethlehem Musikfest, (610) 861-0678, which runs for 10 days in mid- to late August, has one stage devoted solely to children's music, featuring nationally known performers, and has children's activities throughout the festival.

West End

Country Junction
US 209, Lehighton
(610) 377-8400
www.countryjunction.com

Country Junction, which bills itself as "the world's largest general store" (see our Shopping chapter), has a year-round petting farm. Llamas, goats, chickens, ducks, and sheep await your child's eager hands. Admission is free, but cups of food, which make the animals friendlier, can be bought. Country Junction is open daily.

Milford Area/Lake Wallenpaupack Area

Claws 'N' Paws Wild Animal Park $$$
Highway 590, Hamlin
(570) 698-6154
www.clawsnpaws.com

This is another great place to talk to the animals. (See our Attractions chapter.) For those who love tigers, Claws 'n' Paws has a rare white Siberian tiger as well as the more common orange kind. There's plenty to do and see—special programs are performed on almost every half-hour. There are also farm animal exhibits, animal feedings, and petting zoos. If you have younger children, don't miss the Dino Dig, where they get to play paleontologist, digging in the sand for "dinosaur bones."

Malibu Ranch
Seventh Street, Milford
(570) 296-7281, (800) 8-MALIBU
www.malibududeranch.com

For a real change of pace, you might consider this dude ranch, which features rodeos, hayrides, and other special horse events throughout the year. You can make a weekend of the ranch. For $80 per day per adult (ages 6 to 16 are half-price, and children younger than 5 are free) you get to stay at this ranch. The price includes meals, a rodeo or hayride, and all horse rides and ranch facilities. This family place offers trail rides, a rifle range, an arcade, an indoor pool, a petting zoo, and other great stuff to do. (See our Accommodations chapter for more information on staying here.)

WHAT ABOUT TEENS?

Teens in the Poconos have plenty of opportunities for activity. There are lots of programs for them at the schools—sports teams, bands, theater groups, activity clubs, yearbooks, literary magazines, school newspapers, and so on. There are also youth groups for teens at churches and synagogues. We have noted several opportunities throughout the book: The Pocono Youth Orchestra (see our Arts and Culture chapter) is an excellent outlet for young musicians; some teens get involved in the many theatrical productions put on here, not only as performers, but also as techies (see our Arts and Culture chapter); skiing and snowboarding are popular teen activities. In our Winter Sports chapter, we note programs for teenage sliders. In Recreation, we point out different opportunities for your family's teenagers, especially if they are into mountain biking. In this chapter we note the area skating rinks and education-based programs that also offer teens some great choices for their leisure time. See our Camps and Conference Centers chapter for specialized programs that cater to your teen's sports and arts interests.

Main Street Stroudsburg has become a vibrant teen hangout, with Over the Edge, a punkish clothing shop; the Sanctuary, a performance space downstairs from Over the Edge; Games 3, a video

If you have bored teenagers in your family, suggest they consider volunteering at the local hospital. Many area hospitals (see our Relocation chapter) are grateful for the help of teenage volunteers. Their presence cheers up those who are ill, and proves to be a real asset in the pediatrics wards.

game store set up for great game play; and the Encounter, a comic book and collectible cards shop that features tournaments on certain nights of the week.

The arcades at the Stroud Mall in Stroudsburg, Thunder Creek Quarry in Marshalls Creek, and Pocono Go-Carts in Bartonsville (see the "Let's Play" section in this chapter) are places teens frequent. Coffeehouses and clubs that cater to teens offer an alcohol-free environment with poetry, contemporary singer-songwriters, open mikes, and even techno dance parties—all activities that draw significant numbers of teens. Many of these clubs come and go, but if you talk to some local teens, they can recommend some good places.

If your teen is a budding guitarist, check out the Martin Guitar Company, in Nazareth. The place is a guitar player's mecca. (See the Close-up in our Day Trips chapter.)

If you're an Insider, don't forget volunteer opportunities to keep your teens happy. Libraries are always looking for volunteers. There are also lots of summer camps, retail businesses, and resorts that hire teenage workers. In Pennsylvania you can get your working papers at age 14. Many teenagers here start working as soon as they can.

ANNUAL EVENTS AND FESTIVALS

The Poconos don't have everything. There is one element that is in short supply all year. It's called boredom. This book contains separate chapters dedicated exclusively to winter sports, recreation, and a host of regional attractions, but they still don't cover everything there is to do. There are so many annual events, festivals, and occasions for celebration and merrymaking in the Poconos that one could make a full-time job of attending them.

Church groups hold craft shows and bake sales. Fire departments and ski resorts host carnivals in summer and special events during ski season. Communities have flea markets; resorts and school districts present musical spectaculars; and agricultural fairs have provided family fun for decades. Watch for small circuses that come to towns throughout the area in the summer.

The following entries describe some of the larger annual activities held in the Poconos. They are arranged by geographic region and approximate chronological order by month. Most admission fees cited are for 2003 events, and while every effort has been made to pinpoint 2004 scheduling dates, both fees and dates are subject to change. Call the numbers with each listing for cost and calendar updates.

ADMISSION PRICE

The following is a price code for admission to annual events and festivals. The price listed is for adults. Children and senior citizens' admissions are usually lower. Because most of these events take place only once a year, price often changes from year-to-year, usually in an upward direction.

$10.00 or less	$
$10.01 to $15.00	$$
$15.01 to $20.00	$$$
$20.01 or more	$$$$

JANUARY

Pennsylvania Learn to Ski Day $$
Various locations throughout the Poconos
(570) 421-5791, (800) 762-6667
www.800poconos.com
One day during the first week in January, folks who have never skied get the chance to learn for a small fee—usually around $10. Participating ski areas in the Poconos have included Alpine Mountain, Camelback, Big Boulder, Blue Mountain, Jack Frost, and Shawnee. Reservations are required at most mountains. Call the individual ski areas (see our Winter Sports chapter for details) for restrictions and reservations. Or call the listed toll-free number to speak with a representative of the Pocono Mountains Vacation Bureau about this program.

FEBRUARY

Milford/Lake Wallenpaupack Area

Ice Tee Golf Tournament $$$
Lake Wallenpaupack, U.S. Highway 6
Hawley
(570) 226-3191
Golfers play nine holes on frozen Lake Wallenpaupack in late February. The fairways are line with Christmas trees. A driving contest awards prizes to the golfer who hits a ball closest to a replica of mas-

cot Wally Paupack. Refreshments are available. Admission is free for spectators.

MARCH

Stroudsburg/East Stroudsburg

Beach Party Weekend $$$$
Camelback Ski Area, Camelback Road
Tannersville
(570) 639-1661
www.skicamelback.com
The second weekend in March is Beach Party Weekend at this winter resort—a weekend in which the bar is converted to a tropical isle, complete with sand, exotic drinks, Limbo dancing, and seashells redeemable for prizes hidden all over the mountain.

Maple Sugaring Program $
Monroe County Environmental Education Center, 8050 Running Valley Road
Bartonsville
(570) 629-3061
www.mcconservation.org
On the second weekend in March, this environmental center conducts public tours that discuss the history of maple sugaring as well as early Native American and pioneer methods of collecting it. Observe demonstrations of the methods of collecting and cooking maple sugar. There's no charge to members of the environmental center.

Luck o' the Irish Weekend $$$$
Camelback Ski Area, Camelback Road
Tannersville
(570) 629-1661
www.skicamelback.com
That's right, in honor of St. Patrick's Day, on the weekend closest to St. Patrick's Day, shamrocks are hidden throughout the mountain. Find them and win a pot of gold (well, at least a prize).

St. Patrick's Day Celebration
Alpine Mountain Ski Area, Highway 447
Analomink
(570) 595-2150
www.alpinemountain.com
Here's another chance for leprechauns to ski for free (if dressed in green). Hidden shamrock tokens yield prizes for lucky finders. Even the beer is green on St. Patrick's Day weekend.

St. Patrick's Day Parade
Stroudsburg High School (Main Street Stroudsburg) to Dansbury Depot (Crystal Street East Stroudsburg)
(570) 424-9131
The Sunday after St. Patrick's Day, both Burgs go crazy for St. Patty. Most of our high school marching bands perform, volunteer fire departments parade their machinery, pipe and drum corps perform, politicians wave, and almost everybody hands out candy.

There are more events and festivals in the Poconos than we can begin to list here. For more information, go to www .poconosbest.com/festivals.htm or www .poconosbest.com/eventsoct00.htm.

Pocono Mountains Chamber of Commerce Business Expo $
Koehler Field House, Normal Street
East Stroudsburg
(570) 421-4433
www.poconochamber.net
Toward the end of March, local businesses gather in Koehler Field House to showcase their services and products. Of course, their job is to persuade you to switch to their bank, listen to their radio station, buy their windows, and so on, but in the process they give away lots of pens and other small goodies. There are bands that play and serious door prizes as well.

Mount Pocono Area

Annual Chili Cook-Off   **$**
Daniels Family Resort, Highway 447
Canadensis
(570) 595-7531, (800) 755-0300
The Pocono region's finest inns, restaurants, and chili enthusiasts serve up their best for you to sample in early March. The East Stroudsburg University Hotel School Culinary Arts Department adjudicates. Prizes are awarded, and country bands perform.

West End

March Madness   **$$$$**
Various locations
The nine vineyards on the Lehigh Valley Wine Trail, including the four Pocono Vineyards, offer pairings of wine and food every weekend in March. You buy a passport entitling you to go to these eating and drinking events. Call any of our local vineyards for details (see our Wineries chapter), but call early. The passports sell out.

Milford/Lake Wallenpaupack Area

Pike County Builders Show   **$**
Best Western at Hunt's Landing
U.S. Highway 209, Matamoras
(570) 296-5500
This show, held over a three-day weekend in late March or early April, attracts all the leading commercial and residential builders and the lending institutions. If you are looking to build or remodel your home, you will get a lot of ideas here.

Easter Craft Show   **$**
Hamlin Elementary School, Highway 191
Hamlin
(570) 689-4199
More than 40 crafters from New York, New Jersey, and Pennsylvania exhibit their wares at this show the weekend before Palm Sunday.

APRIL

Stroudsburg/East Stroudsburg

WVPO Health and Fitness Fair
Clarion Hotel, 1200 West Main Street
Stroudsburg
(570) 421-2100
www.935wsbg.com
This day-long, mid-April event is organized to familiarize people with the health and fitness options available in the Poconos. Free screenings and blood pressure tests are offered.

Pocono Train Show   **$**
Stroudsburg High School, West Main Street, Stroudsburg
(570) 834-7465
The Pocono Mountains Chapter of the National Railway Historical Society sponsors this model-train exhibit on the last Sunday in April. A running layout and test tracks are provided. You also may purchase trains at this event.

West End

Easter Bunny Train Rides   **$$**
Rail Tours Inc. Train Depot, US 209
Jim Thorpe
(570) 325-3673
The Easter Bunny hosts a 40-minute train ride on the second weekend of April. There is an Easter egg hunt at the end of the trip for children 8 and younger.

April Showers Concert   **$**
Mauch Chunk Historical Society, 41 West Broadway, Jim Thorpe
(570) 325-4439
Local performers and members of Studio Kids, a group of young performers, collab-

orate in a variety show including classics, show tunes, ballads, and popular music on the last weekend in April.

Great Brews Around the World International Beer Fest $$$$
Split Rock Resort, Highway 903
Lake Harmony
(570) 722-0111, (800) 244-7625
www.splitrockresort.com
Breweries from all over the world put the best of their brews on display at this event, which also features seminars, international foods, crafts, and music. The event is held on the first weekend in April. Nobody younger than 21 is admitted.

Milford/Lake Wallenpaupack Area

Bunny Run $$$
Stourbridge Line Rail Excursions
742 Main Street, Honesdale
(570) 253-1960
www.waynecountycc.com
The Easter Bunny and Mr. Mouse collaborate on the 2-hour, 26-mile rail run for little ones. It runs Saturday and Sunday, the weekend preceding Easter.

MAY

Stroudsburg/East Stroudsburg

Evening on Main
Downtown Stroudsburg
(570) 476-4460
www.poconoarts.org
An enhanced First Saturday, performers are on the street and in the galleries, and the art galleries host openings and special events. Many of the stores that remain open offer special discounts. This is like a progressive party throughout downtown Stroudsburg.

A Culinary Celebration of the Poconos $$$
Keystone Room, East Stroudsburg University, East Stroudsburg
(570) 421-4433, (570) 422-3511
Enjoy local wines and brews, culinary demonstrations and samples, music and raffle drawings at this edible event in mid-May. Proceeds benefit the ESU scholarship fund.

No longer is the Pocono region simply a place to vacation or honeymoon; it now literally is exploding with theater, dance, crafts, photography, painting, sculpture, prose, poetry, and an eclectic menu of music.

Farm Animal Frolic $
Quiet Valley Historical Farm,
1000 Turkey Hill Road, Stroudsburg
(570) 992-6161
www.quietvalley.org
This event, held the last weekend in May, presents a special chance for parents and grandparents to educate children about the animals on a farm. Costumed guides provide information about baby animals and eggs hatching in an incubator. Children enjoy petting the farm animals, riding ponies, and jumping into the haystack.

Greek Festival
Holy Cross Greek Orthodox Church
135 Stokes Avenue, Stroudsburg
(570) 421-5734
There's no admission fee to listen to the Greek music, watch the dancing, or enjoy the exhibits and church tours through Memorial Day weekend, but we challenge you to leave without buying some outstanding homemade Greek cuisine. Eat under the tent outdoors or in the basement of the church, but either way, you'll enjoy home-cooked Greek food in a festive atmosphere. The pastries are so good that you will be glad take-out packages

are available. If you miss this one, you can catch it again when it is repeated on Columbus Day weekend.

Memorial Day Parade
Main Street, Stroudsburg
(570) 424-9131
High school marching bands, fire companies, and other community organizations put on a display of patriotism in this old-fashioned Memorial Day parade.

West End

Jim Thorpe's Birthday Celebration
Asa Packer Park, Jim Thorpe
(570) 325-9281
This annual event includes a torch run, live music, vendors, Native American folklore, food, and a cakewalk.

Pocono Irish and Celtic Festival Jack
Frost Ski Area   **$$**
Highway 940, Blakeslee
(570) 443-8425
www.jackfrostbigboulder.com
There will be a "Wearin o' the Green" in late May when this popular ski resort celebrates the Irish cultural background of the area with Gaelic song and dance, a Punch & Judy puppet show, children's crafts, and even a Holy Mass at the lodge on Sunday.

JUNE

Stroudsburg/East Stroudsburg

Cranberry Bog Nature Walks   **$**
Monroe County Environmental Education
Center, 8050 Running Valley Road
Bartonsville
(570) 629-3061
www.mcconservation.org
These Wednesday guided tours, which start in June and last all summer, are the only way to experience the unique natural

wonder of the Tannersville Cranberry Bog. You will see orchids and insect-eating plants among other rare flora. (See Our Natural World and Parks chapters for more information on the bog.) Numbers of tour participants are limited; pre-registration is a must.

West End

The Pocono 500 NASCAR Nextel
Cup Race   **$$$$**
Pocono International Raceway
Highway 114, Long Pond
(570) 646-2300, (800) RACEWAY
www.poconoraceway.com
Twice a year—the first weekend in June and the third weekend in July—the stars of NASCAR come to the Poconos to compete at Pocono Raceway. More than 100,000 fans fill the raceway to watch NASCAR racing's superstars battle on this 2.4-mile tri-oval. Every race sells out, so order tickets early. (See our Attractions chapter for a Close-up on the colorful history of Pocono Raceway.)

Annual Heritage Day
Palmerton Borough Park, Palmerton
(610) 826-6572
www.palmerton.k12.pa.us/histsoc/lehigh
_gap_intro.html
The Lehigh Gap Historical Society recalls the past with free demonstrations and exhibits of old-time crafts, snack and ethnic foods, a cakewalk, and live entertainment in early June.

Great Tastes of Pennsylvania Wine
and Food Festival   **$$$$**
Split Rock Resort, Highway 903
Lake Harmony
(570) 722-9111, (800) 255-7625
www.splitrockresort.com
Winemakers from throughout Pennsylvania offer their products for sampling at this event. Food, music, and more than 50 arts and crafts dealers provide other entertainment when you need to take a

break from the wine at this late June festival.

Mountain Bike Weekend $$$
Mauch Chunk Lake Park
625 Lentz Trail, Jim Thorpe
(570) 325-3669
This event, held in mid-June, is the oldest and largest non-competitive mountain bike gathering in the eastern United States. One thousand biking enthusiasts enjoy the numerous trails surrounding Jim Thorpe. Clinics, organized rides, and various activities are included. Admission is by invitation only, and there is no e-mail or phone number for this event (the number published above is for the park where it is held). To receive an invitation, you must write to 634 South Spruce Street, Lititz, PA 17543, and send a self-addressed, stamped envelope; or go to www.soeast.com.

Milford/Lake Wallenpaupack Area

Annual Arts and Crafts Fair
Bingham Park, Hawley
(570) 226-3191
www.hawleywallenpaupackcc.com
The Hawley/Lake Wallenpaupack Chamber of Commerce brings more than 140 artists and crafters to Bingham Park. Some of the artisans travel from a great distance to come to this festival.

Wildflower Music Festival $$$-$$$$
Dorflinger-Suydam Wildlife Sanctuary
off US 6, White Mills
(570) 253-1185
www.dorflinger.org
Beginning in late June and continuing into July and August, this festival presents open-air performances of classical, jazz, folk, and popular music. Patrons may order gourmet picnic lunches from the Settlers Inn. Musicians who have played in the past include Jay Ungar and Milly Mason (whose music was the theme for Ken Burns' *Civil War* series on PBS), the

Check the Weekend section of the **Pocono Record** *every Friday for a listing of upcoming events. Don't forget to look in the Concerts, Onstage, and Nightspots sections for entertainment. You'll find listings for the Poconos, the Lehigh Valley, Scranton/Wilkes-Barre, and some close-by areas of northern New Jersey.*

Shanghai String Quartet, and the Kingston Trio, who made "Tom Dooley" the hit of the '50s.

JULY

Delaware Water Gap/ Shawnee-on-Delaware

Independence Day Celebration $$
Shawnee Mountain Ski Area, Hollow Road
Shawnee-on-Delaware
(570) 421-7231
Special games and activities and a barbecue lead up to traditional fireworks at dusk on the Friday closest to the Fourth of July. It's one price per carload.

Stroudsburg/East Stroudsburg

Independence Weekend Fireworks $$$
Camelbeach Waterpark, Camelback Road
Tannersville
(570) 629-1661
www.camelbeach.com
Fireworks explode over Camelback Mountain as Camelbeach Waterpark celebrates the Saturday of Independence weekend. If you're coming just for the evening, you pay a $10 parking fee. You can watch from your car, or go into the waterpark on the twilight ticket, which is $14.95 for adults, $12.95 for children ages 3 to 11.

Mount Pocono Area

Annual Antique Show and Sale   **$**
Mountainhome United Methodist
Church, Highway 191, Mountainhome
(570) 595-7282
Each year a different theme is selected for
this well-attended annual show in mid-July.

West End

The Pennsylvania 500 NASCAR
Nextel Cup Race   **$$$$**
Pocono Raceway, Highway 115, Long Pond
(570) 646-2300
www.poconoraceway.com
The best NASCAR drivers in the world
return to Pocono Raceway during the
third weekend of July for another battle.
Buy your tickets early; they sell out at
least a month ahead. See this chapter's
"June" listing and our Attractions chapter
Close-up for more information.

Milford/Lake Wallenpaupack Area

Lake Wallenpaupack Fireworks
Wallenpaupack High School, US 6
Hawley
(570) 226-3191
Gather at the high school to enjoy a fire-
works spectacular over the lake.

---

*What do beer, wine, maple sugar,
chili, gyros and spanakopita, garlic,
corned beef and cabbage, jambalaya,
pumpkin pie, and wurst and weiner-
schnitzel have in common? In the
Poconos, every one of them is celebrated at some point in the year at its
own festival—and that doesn't include
the tons of other ethnic comestibles
served at various country fairs.*

Great Delaware River Raft Race
U.S. Highway 209, Matamoras
(570) 296-5264
This 2-mile mid- to late-July race begins in
Matamoras and ends at the Best Western
Inn at Hunt's Landing. (See our Accommodations chapter.) The entry free is $50
per team (usually one to four people,
depending on the capacity of the raft)
and includes raft rentals for the race. The
short distance means that even inexperienced paddlers can compete and have
fun. Cash prizes are awarded to the first-,
second-, and third-place finishers. Proceeds benefit Help Our Kids, Inc. Spectators watch this event free of charge.

Annual Wayne County Antiques
Show and Sale   **$**
Wayne Highlands Middle School
474 Grove Street, Honesdale
(570) 253-2492
This normally great area for antiquing gets
even better in mid-July, when more than
50 dealers converge on the school to
show you their wares.

Audubon Arts & Crafts Festival   **$**
Wallenpaupack Elementary and Middle
Schools, US 6, Hawley
(570) 226-8847
Almost 100 professional, juried crafters
and nature artists from across the country
exhibit and sell their work at this show
held the third weekend in July. Demonstrations, nature films, free environmental
materials, and homemade refreshments
are available.

Annual Pocono Blues Festival   **$$$$**
Big Boulder, Highway 903, Lake Harmony
(570) 629-3131, (800) 468-2442
www.jfbb.com
Every summer, the biggest names in contemporary and traditional blues music
congregate at this sylvan lodge for an
outdoor weekend of food, frolic, and fine
performances by 21 national acts. Headlin-
ers in 2004 included the Blind Boys of
Alabama, Bobby "Blue" Bland, Mavis Sta-

ples, and many more. Dates vary from year to year, so call for scheduling and ticket information.

AUGUST

Delaware Water Gap/ Shawnee-on-Shawnee

Pocono State Craft Festival $
Sun Mountain Recreation Area, Hollow Road, Shawnee-on-Delaware
(570) 476-4460
www.poconocrafts.com
More than 100 juried designer craftsmen from Pennsylvania Guild of Craftsmen sell their work here during a weekend in late August. Craft demonstrations, musical entertainment, and an interactive children's play area are among the activities held under tents at this lakeside center.

West End

Carbon County Fair $
Palmerton
(610) 826-1862
www.carboncountyfair.com
The folks in Carbon County decided in 1999 that they wanted to re-establish an agricultural fair to showcase the hard work of local 4-H kids. This fair is smaller and has a more hometown atmosphere than most of the other area fairs, but there's still lots of entertainment and activities here, including games, such as Jell-O eating and a rolling pin toss, in which the fairgoers can participate. The fair is growing at an impressive rate. By 2001 they had 1,900 exhibits.

Annual Pocono Classic Rock
Biker's Rally $$$$
Big Boulder Ski Area, off Highway 903
Lake Harmony
(570) 722-0100, (800) 468-2442
www.jfbb.com
Motorcycles and rock 'n' roll capture, as

the publicity says, "the easy rider in your soul." A bikers' bazaar, chairlift rides, food, and beer are here along with such acts as the Marshall Tucker Band, Rick Derringer, and Joan Jett.

West End Fair $
West End Fairgrounds, US 209
Gilbert
(610) 681-4293
www.westendfairgilbertpa.com
For 83 years, people from throughout northeastern Pennsylvania have been visiting the Went End in Late August for this agricultural fair. Antique farm machinery is displayed, and prizes are awarded in many craft and cooking categories. Local businesses set up booths to promote themselves. A full midway with lots of serious rides sits at one end of the fair. The food—everything from carnival snacks to full dinners homemade by representatives of local nonprofit organizations—is outstanding. In addition to the free music, nationally famous country stars (Jeni Hackett and the Cramer Brothers in 2004) perform at the grandstand for a separate charge. The demolition derbies are always packed with folks who enjoy watching their friends destroy unwanted automobiles.

Milford/Lake Wallenpaupack Area

Annual Antiques Show and Sale $$
Wallenpaupack Area High School
US 6, Hawley
(570) 226-7513
The Antique Dealers Association of Wayne, Pike, and Sullivan Counties brings 70 dealers to this high school for a weekend in early August for the 35th annual staging of the event. There's food, too.

Pike County Agricultural Fair $$
Winona Falls Road, Bushkill
(570) 296-8790
Agricultural exhibits, entertainment, contests, rides, demolition derby, food, and

The Farmers' Market runs May through November, depending on the weather and the crops, on Main Street every Saturday morning 8:00 A.M. to noon. The early bird gets the best pick of the crops.

more are part of this fair that began in 1970, and moved to its present location in a wooded valley in 1999. This is a smaller, more manageable fair than some and takes place around the second week of August.

Summer Craft Fair $
Hamlin Elementary School
Highway 191, Hamlin
(570) 689-4199
One of three craft fairs sponsored by the Wayne County Chamber of Commerce, this show attracts craftspeople from New York, New Jersey, and Pennsylvania. It's always held two weeks before Labor Day.

Wayne County Fair $$
Wayne County Fairground
Highway 191, Honesdale
(570) 253-1108
www.waynecountyfair.com
One price pays for all at this early August gala of carnival rides, agricultural exhibits, and shows. Tractor pulls, horse pulls, and livestock shows are featured daily. Big-name country and polka singers, a demolition derby, and harness races are scheduled throughout the week. The fair began in 1862 and currently attracts nearly 100,000 people annually. You can also find some delicious food at this country fair. The admission fee includes most shows except the demolition derby.

Greene-Dreher-Sterling Fair $$
Highways 191 and 507, Newfoundland
(570) 646-4047
www.gdsfair.com
This agricultural fair, held from late August through early September, includes live farm animal exhibits, arts and crafts, a firemen's contest, live music, great food, pup-

pet shows, polka and country music, and demolition derbies. Some events, such as rodeos, demolition derbies, as well as motorcycle thrill shows, have a separate admission charge.

SEPTEMBER

Delaware Water Gap/ Shawnee-on-Delaware

Celebration of the Arts $$$$
Throughout Delaware Water Gap
(570) 424-2210
www.cotajazz.org
This nationally known outdoor festival brings together talented artists, chefs, and jazz musicians for the weekend after Labor Day. Most of the events are staged at the Castle Inn. Food concessions and artist booths supplement the terrific music on stage. Big names such as Phil Woods, Bob Dorough, and Dave Liebman share the spotlight with promising students and other area performers.

Scottish & Irish Festival $$$
Shawnee Mountain Ski Area, Hollow Road
Shawnee-on-Delaware
(570) 421-7231
www.shawneemt.com
Enjoy Highland athletics, bagpipe bands and parade, working sheep dogs, fiddlers, Irish and Scottish bands, Irish step dancing, Scottish exhibitions, whiskey tastings, and other vendors at the two-day mid-September festival.

Rodeo $$$
Shawnee Mountain, Hollow Road
Shawnee-on-Delaware
(570) 421-7231
www.shawneemt.com
Professional cowboys compete in five PRCA events including saddle bronco riding, bull riding, bareback bronco riding, calf roping, bull dogging, and more. Women will also compete in a sanctioned

Whitewater Release Days

Releases from the Frances E. Walter Dam make the Lehigh River an exciting white-water river over a couple of weekends in June. Call any of the whitewater rafting companies in the West End (see our Recreation chapter) and they'll get you set up to ride the waves.

barrel race. A country band plays prior to and after the rodeo and there is country line dancing.

Stroudsburg/East Stroudsburg

Pocono Garlic Festival
Courthouse Square, Stroudsburg
(610) 381-3303
The Poconos celebrates the crop it's known best for—garlic. Local growers grow hard-neck, big-cloved garlic in a number of vari-eties, and because there are so many microclimates in the Poconos, each grower's garlic is distinctly different. At this festival, you'll find garlic, garlic-laced food (even chocolate-covered garlic cloves), gar-lic art, garlic music, and garlic dance. Don't miss the Garlic-Eating Tuba Troubadours, christened "America's Smelliest Band" by *Disney Adventures* magazine. Some of the top tuba players in the Northeast munch garlic and then play, spreading their odor-ous music across the square.

Mount Pocono Area

Octoberfest   **$$$**
The Edelweiss, Highway 940, Pocono Lake
(570) 646-3938
www.theedelweiss.com
Three large tents are filled each Labor Day weekend with German music, danc-ing, food, and drinks. Children enjoy the clowns and the petting zoo. Arts and crafts are sold. The main attraction is the food—wienerschnitzel, bratwurst, knockwurst, pretzels, pastries, and much more. See our Restaurants chapter for more information on dining at the Edelweiss.

Milford/Lake Wallenpaupack Area

Annual Fall Arts and Crafts Fair
Bingham Park, Hawley
(570) 226-3191
www.hawleywallenpaupackcc.com
Join the Hawley/Lake Wallenpaupack Chamber of Commerce and more than 140 talented artists and crafters displaying their fine wares in Bingham Park in mid-September. These accomplished mer-chants travel from near and far to offer their work here.

OCTOBER
Delaware Water Gap/ Shawnee-on-Delaware

Lumberjack Festival   **$$**
Shawnee Mountain Ski Area, Hollow Road
Shawnee-on-Delaware
(570) 421-7231
www.shawneemt.com

Don't forget to head for Main Street in Stroudsburg between 6:00 and 9:00 P.M. on the first Saturday of every month. The galleries all run openings and there's often music outdoors. It's a big party with some of the most interesting folks in the area, and you're invited.

Contests, part of the Eastern U.S. Ironjack Competition, include log rolling, pole climbing, ax and chain saw competitions, buck sawing, chain saw carving, and pig racing. Arts, crafts, foods, live music, chairlift rides, and Paul Bunyan barbecue are available at this mid-October festival enhanced by autumn foliage at its peak.

Shawnee's Pocono Mountains Balloon Festival   **$$$**
Shawnee Inn, River Road
Shawnee-on-Delaware
(570) 421-4433, 800-SHAWNEE
www.poconoballoonfestival.org
In mid-October, the skies over the Delaware River are filled with more than 25 hot-air balloons. On Friday night the balloons are inflated on the ground where the glow of their propane burners creates a magical fairyland effect. Launches are scheduled for approximately 7:30 A.M. and 4:30 P.M. on Saturday and Sunday with rides available to the public. If the price of that adventure is too steep, tethered rides are also offered, in which the balloon goes up, giving a magnificent view of the Poconos in full autumn dress, but it does not wander with the wind. (Weather conditions affect launching times, and launches are cancelled if the weather is not right.)

On-the-ground activities include food and crafts vendors, live music, carnival rides, face painting, balloon sculptures, clowns, and more.

Shawnee Mountain Ski Area
Ski Swap
Hollow Road, Shawnee-on-Delaware
(570) 421-7231
www.shawneemt.com
Shawnee Mountain offers a huge number of used skis, boots, and ski clothing at very low prices. If you need anything to complete your ski-bunny look, and you don't mind used, this is the place to go for one weekend in late October.

Stroudsburg/ East Stroudsburg

Harvest Festival   **$**
Quiet Valley Historical Farm
1000 Turkey Hill Road, Stroudsburg
(570) 992-6161
www.quietvalley.org
Costumed interpreters carry out the typical routine of early Pennsylvania Dutch farm life, including demonstrations of beekeeping, needlecraft, candle dipping, blacksmithing, woodcarving, bread baking, spinning, dyeing, basketmaking, hewing, quilting, horseplowing, and hearth cooking. You may sample food and drink, including cider and breads, and enjoy children's games, folk entertainment, and pumpkin-decorating contests. The Harvest Festival is held in mid-October.

Stroudsburg Halloween Parade
Main Street, Stroudsburg
(570) 424-9131
On the Saturday closest to Halloween, Stroudsburg goes Halloween-crazy with a huge costume parade. This is not just for kids—lots of adults join the fun and march, too. Even some dogs get dressed up and parade. After the parade there are games, crafts, and food around Courthouse Square. Many downtown merchants run special sales, too.

West End

**The Great Pocono Pumpkin
Patch Festival**
Country Junction, US 209, Forest Inn
(610) 377-5050, ext. 541
www.countryjunction.com
A month-long celebration of autumn, this
festival features thousands of pumpkins,
fall decorations, Halloween costumes, carnival rides, carnival food, hayrides, a
haunted barn, and a petting zoo. Admission is free, but there is a separate charge
for some activities.

**Pumpkin Patch and Homecoming
Festival**
Old Homestead Tree Farm, US 209
Kunkletown
(610) 381-3582
www.oldhomestead.com
Every weekend in October, Old Homestead offers hayrides, a petting zoo, paddleboat rides, a corn maze, and pumpkin
picking. The farm is decorated for the season, and cider, jams, and cookies are sold.
Admission is free.

Fall Foliage Festival
Jim Thorpe
(570) 325-9190
Four hundred craftsmen offer their wares.
There are also a variety of exhibits, an
antique car parade, festival food, and
entertainment right in the center of Jim
Thorpe. This festival occurs around the
middle of October. Whitewater enthusiasts can take advantage of a dam release
along the Lehigh River during the day and
end in Jim Thorpe at the festival.

Milford/Lake
Wallenpaupack Area

Hawley Harvest Hoedown
Main Avenue and Keystone Street, Hawley
(570) 226-3191
www.hawleywallenpaupackcc.com
The fun at this community celebration in
early October includes hayrides, square

*To taste something new, turn to some-
thing very ancient by visiting the megalith park Columcille (see the Close-up in
our Attractions chapter) on one of the
old Celtic pagan holidays. From Beltaine
(May Day) to Sahmain (Halloween), the
festivals are celebrated among the
standing stones with ceremonies as old
as Stonehenge.*

and line dancing, pumpkin-decorating
contests, and an antique and collectibles
market.

Black Bear Film Festival $$-$$$$
Various locations around Milford
(570) 409-0909
www.blackbearfilm.com
Around the second week of October the
folks in Milford manage to snag independ-
ent films, children's films, and even special
drive-in features for their Black Bear Film
Festival. Along with these films, they offer
discussions, sometimes with the directors
or stars of the films, and they stage other
fun events. The festival was conceived, in
part, to promote the celebration of Pike
County's heritage as a film location. Many
early silent movies were shot there, and
even today, many people in the film indus-
try have summer homes in Pike County.

NOVEMBER

Stroudsburg/East
Stroudsburg

Pocono Train Show $
Stroudsburg High School, West Main
Street, Stroudsburg
(570) 834-7465
Like its April counterpart, this show, put
on by the Pocono Mountains Chapter of
the National Railway Historical Society,
offers model-train exhibits and vendors. It
always takes place on the third Sunday of
November.

West End

**Great Brews of America Classic
Beer Festival** $$$$
The Resort at Split Rock
Highway 903, Lake Harmony
(570) 722-9111, (800) 722-9111, ext. 800
www.splitrockresort.com
You must be at least 21 years old to sample the lagers, ales, and stouts from more than 20 North American Breweries. Two stages of music plus food and seminars are offered at this late November weekend event.

Milford/Lake Wallenpaupack Area

Christmas Craft Show $
Hamlin Elementary School
Highway 191, Hamlin
(570) 689-4199
The Wayne County Chamber of Commerce helps you with your holiday shopping by bringing in more than 40 craftspeople from New York, New Jersey, and Pennsylvania. Although this is not a juried show, they require that all items here be handmade.

DECEMBER

Delaware Water Gap/ Shawnee-on-Delaware

Messiah Sing-In $
Shawnee Playhouse, River Road
Shawnee-on-Delaware
(570) 421-5093
www.shawneeplayhouse.net
Every December you're invited to sing in Handel's "Messiah." The playhouse brings in a live orchestra and some wonderful soloists, and the audience sings the part of the chorus. There's also hot cider and a fire in the fireplace.

Stroudsburg/East Stroudsburg

An Old Time Christmas $$
Quiet Valley Living Historical Farm
1000 Turkey Hill Road, Stroudsburg
(570) 992-6161
www.quietvalley.org
Christmas is celebrated here the first and second weekends in December as it was in the 19th century. Costumed guides lead you past candlelit windows, and a living barnyard Nativity. Homemade gifts are available. Watch out for the Belschnickle! He definitely knows who's naughty and nice.

Musicfest
Stroudsburg High School, Main Street
Stroudsburg
(570) 421-1990
This crafts fair/music festival supports the Stroudsburg District's music program. The halls of the high school fill with lots of crafters offering seasonal goodies, whereas the various school bands and choruses perform in the auditorium. Sometimes different combinations of Stroudsburg students perform in the halls, as well. There are baked goodies in the cafeteria.

West End

Olde Time Christmas
Throughout Jim Thorpe
(570) 325-3673
The most beautiful event in this charming Victorian town is its Christmas celebration, held weekends in early December. Santa arrives on a lighted, horse-drawn trolley. A tree-lighting ceremony, children's theater productions, concerts, caroling, horse-drawn trolley rides, and decorated shops fill the town with holiday cheer.

Santa Claus Train Rides $$
Rail Tours Inc. Train Depot, US 209
Jim Thorpe
(570) 325-3673
When not on the Santa Express in Honesdale in mid-December (see subsequent entry), Santa takes folks on an 8-mile train ride along the Lehigh River.

Milford/Lake Wallenpaupack Area

Santa Express $$
Stourbridge Rail Excursion
303 Commercial Street, Honesdale
(570) 253-1960
www.waynecountycc.com
Weekends in mid-December, Santa and Mrs. Claus host an hour-long-plus holiday excursion. Children receive a special gift.

If you attend one of the Wildflower Music Festival's concerts, take along a folding chair. They're held in an open amphitheater, and the only natural seating is on the grass or among the pine needles. Also, feel free either to bring a picnic dinner or have one of gourmet caliber catered by the Settlers Inn. (See our Restaurants chapter.)

Winterfest Celebration
Downtown Hawley
(570) 226-3191
www.hawleywinterfest.com
A Victorian parade and train excursions from Honesdale to Hawley, caroling, concerts, a bonfire, a costume gala, and ice carving all evoke a Victorian Christmas in mid-December. Admission to some events is free.

ARTS AND CULTURE

Where can you walk among deer and wild turkey in a deep green forest or in the silver mist of a waterfall and, an hour later, admire jewelry handcrafted at Liztech Gallery, one of the most sophisticated and creative designers in the Northeast?

Where can you stroll down a main street converted once every month into an enormous art gallery, or find yourself dragooned into an interactive play, then cap the day with an opera concert, a bluegrass festival, a jazz performance with nationally known artists or an off-Broadway play, followed by dinner in a 170-year-old restaurant where the oaken back bar is a work of art fit for display in a museum? (See JT's All American Steak & Ale House in the "West End" section of our Restaurants chapter.)

Such a mix can be found only in the Poconos, where metropolitan levels of art and culture thrive in a rich historical setting of rural serenity. No longer is the Pocono region simply a place to vacation or honeymoon; it is now virtually exploding with theater, dance, crafts, photography, painting, sculpture, prose, poetry, and an eclectic menu of music.

As the renaissance, increasingly fueled by discovery of the region on the part of artists weary of the big-city scene, has grown, so have arts councils designed to coordinate and publicize it. Of these, the Pocono Arts Council is the most developed and organized. The organization is funded by the Pennsylvania Council for the Arts, local businesses, and memberships. Only through its help and cooperation have we been able to present much of the information about the arts scene in the Poconos.

While the Pocono Arts Council is the most centralized and far-reaching umbrella organization, other areas of the Poconos are developing their own in response to incoming artists who want to make this area home and in response to commuting city folks accustomed to diverse arts scenes. Artists are delighted by the Poconos' combination of country air, mountains, water, and proximity to New York City. They are moving to places like Jim Thorpe, where building after building is occupied by galleries, artisan shops, and studios of all types. They are moving into Pike Country, where the galleries are opening up in little spots all along the winding roads. And with the proliferation of arts and crafts, businesses are springing up as institutions of direct support.

The arts are changing the tempo of the Poconos. Gallery openings have become as attractive a Saturday evening event as hanging out in local bars. The arts scene truly has arrived, but with that arrival comes the biggest suspense thriller of the decade. Will the $36.6 million Mountain Laurel Center for the Performing Arts at Bushkill survive, or will it perish under the weight of massive debt?

The center, with its 2,500-seat concert pavilion, 1,100-seat Broadway-style theater, and 400-seat cabaret on the lakefront, opened with fanfare in midsummer 2003, after the state came up with $31 million in funding. But from the start, the center's envisioned bright future vanished in a welter of squabbling among members of the board of directors, the firing of its first artistic director, canceled concerts, broken promises, and mounting debt.

A new board, reduced from 30 volunteers to about 10, took over, vowing to turn the project around. By Labor Day weekend 2004, the new directors had managed to raise $100,000 in private donations and book concerts by the Blue Oyster Cult, B. B. King, country stars Don Williams and Ray Price, and the Beach Boys. At press time, we could only hope that the effort would pay off. If it does, we expect the beautiful woodland venue to profoundly enhance the arts scene in the Poconos.

In this chapter we point out the major arts organizations and representatives from each genre of the arts in the Poconos. We strongly encourage you, however, to contact the local arts organizations for directories or calendars of events. There are treasures in every art form waiting to be found. Local historical museums and libraries also are part of the cultural picture because they provide a backdrop of the region's past.

Note: We have not included any price codes in the chapter because we believe that to price Arts and Culture is to compare apples to bananas, or maybe even coconuts. The price code chart would have to run from under $20 to more than $1,000!

ART ORGANIZATIONS

Stroudsburg/East Stroudsburg

Music Study Club of the Stroudsburgs
RR 1, Box 257, Effort, PA 18330
(570) 629-0363
The music club has been around since 1912. Its mission is educational and performance-based. It provides concerts October through May showcasing established and up-and-coming young performers. It offers two scholarships to Monroe County students and sponsors Pocono Mountain young musicians and

adults, supporting them in the National Federation of Music Clubs Junior Festival held annually at East Stroudsburg University. We've attended concerts spotlighting young musicians and were impressed by the caliber of performance we heard. The program contained vocalists, violinists, and cellists, and all were very impressive. Adult members of the group play at music club concerts and other arts events. Members do not have to be musicians; they can just love music and be interested in supporting it in the Poconos.

Pocono Arts Council
18 North 7th Street, Stroudsburg
(570) 476-4460
www.poconoarts.org
The Pocono Arts Council is a nonprofit organization formed in 1975 by area residents to develop, foster, and support cultural awareness and artistic excellence in the Monroe County region. It publishes a monthly newsletter of cultural events and opportunities, and a countywide calendar of cultural events. Through its relationship with the county government and the business community, the council sponsors rotating art exhibitions in public buildings, awards Arts Community Support Grants to local artists and art organizations, provides an Arts-in-Education Regional Residency program to local school districts, awards Youth in Music Scholarships to young musicians, and provides grants from the Pennsylvania Council on the Arts to emerging arts groups. The council also sponsors First Saturday, a monthly celebration of the arts in Downtown Stroudsburg with art openings, street music, and lots of fun, and it co-sponsors an annual event showcasing the

For three days each summer, you can view brilliant work by local artists in Wayne County and visit them in their home studios as well. For more information, see the Wayne County Arts Alliance Web site, www.waynecountyarts alliance.org.

work of more than 100 members of the Pennsylvania Guild of Craftsmen. (See our Annual Events chapter for details.)

Pocono Chapter of the Pennsylvania Guild of Craftsmen
RD2, Box 2062, Stroudsburg, PA 18360
(570) 476-1849
www.poconoarts.com
The Pennsylvania Guild of Craftsmen is an association of professional craftspeople who create high-quality crafts. The Pocono chapter promotes its members and puts on the annual Pocono State Crafts Festival in August. (See our Annual Events and Festivals chapter.)

Mount Pocono Area

Arts on the Mountain
Trinity Church, Trinity Hill Road
Mount Pocono
(570) 629-0644
This group started in 1988 with the objective of presenting area artists in a series of events combining visual and performing arts. It presents four events a year that always include an art exhibition and a vocal or instrumental music concert or dramatic or poetry-based performance. The group always comes up with interesting combinations and is supported by quite a few notable area artists, including painters Peter Salmon and Penny Ross, and performers such as the Dixie Gents.

Buck Hill Art Association
Buck Hill Falls
(570) 595-7511
This group's central mission is to provide

culture and art for the Buck Hill Falls community and the environs and to help those who pursue a career in the arts. To this end, they sponsor an annual July art show at the Buck Hill Falls Tennis Club at which members exhibit their works competitively in a fund-raiser to provide scholarships for local art students. They also co-sponsor a yearly concert. They offer summer art classes and support the Kirby Library, a Buck Hill community center where they keep a collection of Buck Hill historical memorabilia. The association has been active since 1933.

West End

Carbon County Art League
77 Broadway, Jim Thorpe
(570) 325-9196
The Carbon County Art League meets every second Wednesday, and at each meeting a different artist demonstrates a technique. They sponsor trips to museums, and offer workshops and classes. They also sponsor art exhibits around the county during special events. The league has recently begun raising money for scholarships for Carbon County art students.

CULTURAL SOCIETIES AND MUSEUMS

Here, we focus on cultural societies and museums that reflect the history of the Poconos—and often are part of it. Other museums are included in our Attractions chapter. While we acknowledge that they also represent our culture, such operations are essentially businesses that survive on more than a nominal entrance fee and donations.

If you are looking for volunteer opportunities, museums and historical societies are always looking for helping hands. There are quite a few of them, and keeping them open to the public requires a reservoir of helpers. Since most operate on relatively small budgets and donations from visitors, volunteers are eagerly sought and highly esteemed. We've encountered a number of volunteers, mostly retired citizens; their knowledge about the exhibits is impressive, their excitement contagious. They, of course, know all the rumors and tales attached to the artifacts, and they sometimes share personal histories—often just as interesting—as they lead folks around on tours. Hours vary, so be sure to check with the museum before you go.

Stroudsburg/East Stroudsburg

The Gallery at Auradell
Stroudsmoor Country Inn
Highway 191 and Stroudsmoor Road
(570) 421-6431, (800) 955-8663
www.stroudsmoor.com

This charming country inn, the grounds of which almost constitute a small village, recently added this fine arts gallery featuring the work of local artists. Each artist featured is on exhibit for anywhere from three days to two weeks, and each gets a special artist's reception. In the course of a year, up to 75 local artists will be invited to display their work. The venue is perfect, since the view from this 200-acre facility high atop a mountain is so spectacular it ranks as a work of art all by itself.

Monroe County Historical Association
900 Main Street, Stroudsburg
(570) 421-7703
http://mcha-pa.org

This historical society is housed in the Stroud Mansion on Main Street in Stroudsburg. It promotes the preservation and protection of the county's history through exhibits, lectures, workshops, educational programs, outreach programs, and special events. Within it are many artifacts relating to the history of this area. (See our Native Americans chapter.) Changing exhibits on many aspects of the county's

history and an excellent historical and genealogical library make this a great place to visit over and over. The mansion is used throughout the year as a place for meetings and exhibits. The Driebe Freight Station, on Ann Street in Stroudsburg, and the Bell School, a one-room schoolhouse in Stormsville, are also part of the Monroe County Historical Association. The Driebe Freight Station, originally a railway station, is full of items representing life in the Victorian era, including a general store and blacksmith shop. The Bell School is a restored structure representing the Golden Age of one-room schoolhouses. (See our Education chapter for a related Close-up.) Both are open for tours. Stroud Mansion is open Tuesday through Friday and Sunday (except the first and third Sunday in November through April). Driebe Freight Station is open afternoons Wednesday through Saturday May through October. The Bell School is open Sunday afternoons in July and August.

Quiet Valley Living Historical Farm
1000 Turkey Hill Road, Stroudsburg
(570) 992-6161
www.quietvalley.org

The farm is open late June until Labor Day for guided tours Tuesday through Sunday. But summer tours are only part of what this living museum has going for it. There is a great Harvest Festival every Columbus Day weekend, with old-fashioned food, games, and craft demonstrations. Programs are provided for school children at different times of the year, allowing practical experience in arts and crafts, animal husbandry and early ways of life. Kids really seem to enjoy field trips there—especially the chance to jump into a haystack! (See our Kidstuff and Camps and Conference Centers chapters.)

Two other events are on everyone's list for a delightful step back into the past. The Farm Animal Frolic is a major event on the last two weekends in May. The farm is open to visitors to see livestock born that spring. The Old Time Christmas is scheduled the first two weekends in

December. Besides seeing the lovely decorations and a live Nativity scene, visitors are entertained by various local choirs, and children are delighted by tales of the Belschnickel, a Pennsylvania Dutch elfin creature who keeps track of children's behavior at Christmastime and brings candy to the good ones. Hot cider helps keep the winter chill at bay. (See our Attractions and Annual Events chapter for more information.)

West End

Mauch Chunk Museum and Cultural Center
41 West Broadway, Jim Thorpe
(570) 325-9190
www.mauchchunkmuseum.org

This museum is housed in the former St. Paul's Methodist Church—itself an excellent example of Victorian Ecclesiastical architecture. It features artifacts and photos of the history of Jim Thorpe, which embrace coal mining, canals, Lenape Indians, and the town's namesake, the famous Native American football hero and Olympian. (See our Native Americans chapter.) The museum features working models of a canal lock and the famous Switchback Gravity Railroad. (See the related Close-up in our History chapter.) The very large exhibit demonstrates how the railroad car ascended Mount Pisgah (in its earliest days, pulled by mules), then used the force of gravity to return cars laden with coal. An interesting side note to the switchback design: It became the basis for that staple of all modern amusements parks—the roller coaster.

Milford/Lake Wallenpaupack Area

The Columns
608 Broad Street, Milford
(570) 296-8126
www.pikehistory.org

This museum, owned by and housed in the Pike County Historical Society building in Milford, boasts one of the most priceless relics of American history—a flag stained by the blood of Abraham Lincoln. The blood stains, finally authenticated in 1996 by the Lincoln Scholars of America, are believed to have been deposited on the flag when it was placed beneath the head of the assassinated president shortly after he was shot by John Wilkes Booth. The flag, taken from bunting on the presidential box at Ford Theater, became the property of the theater's manager, who passed it on to his descendants who moved to the Milford area shortly after Lincoln's death. The family kept the artifact in secret, occasionally taking it out in hushed reverence to show to visitors, then returning it to its hiding place. But the flag is not the only artifact of interest at the Columns. Others, ranging from the grand to the simple, include gowns and antique furniture, an original restored railway stage and Native American artifacts (see our Native Americans chapter) including tomahawks and arrowheads (children like this section best). The Columns is open Wednesday through Sunday in July and August, and Wednesday, Saturday, and Sunday the rest of the year.

Dorflinger Glass Museum
Long Ridge Road, White Mills
(570) 253-1185
www.dorflinger.org

Guided tours of the glass museum are provided. This museum contains a collection of antique crystal glassware, a gift shop, a wildlife sanctuary, and the Wayne Area Sports Hall of Fame. Besides these attractions, the Wildflower Music Festival is held every summer in the open-air amphitheater. Past performers include Tom Chapin, Jane Olivor, and the River City Brass Band. Bring your own chairs and blankets for the performances. The rain site is the Wallenpaupack Area High School. The museum is open mid-May through October, Wednesday through Saturday.

Grey Towers
Highway 6 North, Milford
(570) 296–9630
www.pinchot.org
The former estate of the late governor and conservationist Gifford Pinchot, Grey Towers is a museum operated by the U.S. Forest Service. It is named for the towers that make up the façade of this French château-style mansion. It is filled with memorabilia from Pinchot's career in the Forest Service under President Theodore Roosevelt and his lifelong dedication to conservation.

One outstanding artifact on the museum grounds is the Finger Bowl, a huge laid bluestone table on a terrace under an arbor. The stone's hollowed-out center creates a shelf all around, and a pool of water fills the middle. The pool was used by guests to pass food items to one another. Wooden bowls were used as little boats to ferry salt, pepper, marmalade, and other condiments across the table at the request of a dinner partner. Though not the originals, the bowls still are there for you to try. Not surprisingly, children consider this the best aspect of the mansion. Grey Towers is open daily from Memorial Day through Veterans Day. Although admission is free, donations are encouraged.

Wayne County Historical Society Museum
810 Main Street, Honesdale
(570) 253–3240
www.waynecountyhistoricalsociety.com
The main attraction here is the replica of the Stourbridge Lion, the first steam engine to run in the United States. A model of the 1880 Delaware and Hudson gravity passenger car that carried riders up the gravity railroad track used by miners, and other items that link Wayne County to its place in history—between railroads and canals—are housed in this museum. New exhibits include the works of painter Howard Becker and the Marjorie Smith Gallery. The museum is open Saturday in January and February and Wednesday through Saturday, March through December. (See our Attractions and Native Americans chapters for more information.)

Zane Grey Museum
Scenic Drive, Lackawaxen
(570) 685–4871
www.nps.gov
Not many people know that the author of *Riders of the Purple Sage* and other Western classics was born Pearl Zane Gray in Zanesville, Ohio, or that the spelling of the ancestral surname was changed from Gray to Grey some 20 years later. Nor will many of Grey's fans know that he was a dentist before he became a writer and a big-league baseball player before he became a dentist. Visitors learn all those things at this little museum, overseen by the National Park Service. Once the homestead of Grey, it consists of a vestibule and four rooms, two of which contain memorabilia relating to his trips out West, his championship of Native American civil rights, his baseball career, and his passionate hobby—fishing. Even his dental tools are on display, though it generally is believed that he did not care for the profession. In any case, he never returned to it after becoming a successful author. A frieze of beaverboard, decorated by original artwork done by a cousin of Grey's sister-in-law, circles one wall at ceiling level. Grey's wife Dolly was also a noted fine artist. Grey's home is right on the Delaware River—a place he loved and in view of which he wanted to be buried. And he is; his grave is on the grounds of St. Mark's Church near his home. The museum is open Friday through Sunday from Memorial Day through Labor Day and weekends only throughout September and October.

FINE ART AND CRAFTS GALLERIES

Artists' receptions are one of the more festive events sponsored by many area galleries and arts organizations. Most

Downtown Stroudsburg openings are held on First Saturday, when the galleries all open in the evening, offering new shows, food, and a lovely party atmosphere. Other galleries have openings at other times. Watch the listings in the cultural calendar of the *Pocono Record* each week. Also, all galleries and organizations maintain mailing lists, which they use to inform members of openings. They are always delighted to add your name to their lists if you are interested in being notified of upcoming events. The Pocono Arts Council also publishes a monthly newsletter for its members that lists all upcoming cultural events. Artists sometimes open their studios for tours and exhibits. They have found these tours and exhibits very profitable, gaining commissions for future projects and selling exhibited works. Many of our galleries show both fine art and fine crafts. We're not talking about country crafts or folk arts—you'll find those in our Shopping chapter under Souvenirs, Gifts, and Collectibles. Here we're looking at the fine crafts pieces that could end up in museums, or at least in the museum shops. The crafts galleries we include here carry fine art as well, and are really galleries more than gift shops.

Delaware Water Gap/ Shawnee-on-Delaware

Antoine Dutot School and Museum
Highway 611, Delaware Water Gap
(570) 421-5809

This museum is in the town's original school (ca. 1860). It features art exhibits presented in showcases through the summer (with an opening-night reception). There's also a show over two weekends in December by some of the finest area craftsmen, just in time to help you with your holiday shopping. Upstairs is an exhibit of artifacts from the town's history back to its beginning in 1793. It also presents an audiovisual show of the development of the Water Gap (the geological formation) from its earliest history to the present. Dutot Museum is situated in the town of Delaware Water Gap, where winding streets and lanes climb up the mountainside. There are some lovely little cafes in the area where you can stop after your visit to the museum and before heading on to other attractions in the quaint turn-of-the-century resort town. The museum is open weekends only Memorial Day through mid-October. (See our Attractions chapter for details.)

Shawnee Falls Studio
River and Hollow Roads
Shawnee-on-Delaware
(570) 421-0952
www.shawneefallsstudio.com

In one of the oldest stone structures in the area, Shawnee Falls Studio features watercolor landscapes and other work by Gwendolyn Evans Caldwell. If you're lucky, you'll be there when she has her fresh-baked bread and scones for sale next to the paintings. Gwendolyn offers six-week courses and four-day workshops in watercolor, drawing, writing, and portfolio prep. She also offers a course called Herstory 9-Piece, which works to help women unlock their creativity and achieve their potential, as well as a course called Making Home Work, which looks at the home as a spiritual center. Gwendolyn also consults in interior design and offers a "Five-day Visitation" in which she travels to your home and takes care of your children while you vacation, all the while observing and setting rules. When you get home she makes recommendations to help you make your home work more smoothly. Shawnee Falls runs an open house in the evening on the first Friday of every month. Gwendolyn usually demonstrates an artistic technique, while her husband Bill Caldwell sings and plays guitar.

Stroudsburg/East Stroudsburg

Andrei Art Gallery
7 North 6th Street, Stroudsburg
(570) 476-4407
www.andreiart.com

Andrei Art Gallery represents some world-famous artists, mostly from the former Soviet Union. Among Andrei Protsouk's artists are Yuri Gorbachev, Alexandra Nichita, and Eugeni Gordiets. Many of these painters are represented in museums in Europe and the United States. Andrei features his own fascinating work most prominently in the gallery, and offers giclee prints, high-quality reproductions that look like original oils.

ARTSPACE
18 North 7th Street, Stroudsburg
(570) 476-4460
www.poconoarts.org

ARTSPACE is a cooperative of artists who rent a gallery that's in the front of the building the Pocono Arts Council occupies. They run monthly shows, sometimes featuring members, sometimes based on a particular theme, and once a year they rent the gallery to the arts council for an annual show. Show openings take place on the first Saturday of every month in conjunction with the First Saturday celebrations. To become a member of ART-SPACE, call and ask for information.

Designer Crafts on Main
578 Main Street, Stroudsburg
(570) 420-1228
www.designercraftsonmain.com

Designer Crafts celebrates "the American Crafts Movement," and features a wide range of baskets; carved toys and utensils ranging from cunning chopsticks to spoons, ladles, and cutting boards; sculpture in metal, fabrics, wood, and ceramics; and hand-crafted jewelry. Featured works by nationally known craftsmen include those of photo-art "colorist" Armond

Most historical societies offer classes in crafts that were practiced during bygone eras. For instance, the Stroud Mansion, in Stroudsburg, offers ornament-making classes around Christmas, and Driebe Station, also in Stroudsburg, offers Victorian crafts-making classes for children. Call your local museum or historical society and inquire about planned learning experiences for the whole family.

Scavo and Nick Molignano, who works with exotic woods. Although some of the top craftsmen from around the country are represented here, there is also a strong showing of local work.

Foxglove Gallery
805 Scott Street, Stroudsburg
(570) 424-3220
www.foxglovegallery.com

Foxglove gallery is like two galleries—one houses their collection of folk, country, and decorative arts, while the other houses antiques. The crafts side of the gallery features some of the area's top craftswomen.

Liztech
95 Crystal Street, East Stroudsburg
(570) 424-5681, (800) 531-9992
www.liztech.com

Although the front rooms of this whimsical shop are devoted to Liztech's own designs and other fine and fun crafts objects, there's a very demanding fine arts gallery in the back. Some of the area's top artists do shows here regularly, including Penny Ross, Dan Boldman, Ricky Boscarino, and Gary Kresge. Openings are always an event here.

Madelon Powers Gallery
East Stroudsburg University Fine Arts
Building, Normal and Marguerite Streets
East Stroudsburg
(570) 422-3483

To stay up to date on the artistic events and exhibitions constantly underway in the Poconos, subscribe to the Pocono Arts Council newsletter online at www.poconoarts.org. Then sign up for any of the many painting, sculpture, crafts, and music classes and workshops sponsored by PAC. Instructors are working artists with appropriate scholastic degrees.

Named for a long-time art professor at ESU, it's not easy to get your work into this gallery, so the shows tend to be of very high quality. Most shows feature a single artist, some local, some national. The gallery, run by the fine arts department at ESU, concentrates on fields that are taught there—mostly painting, graphics, and some ceramics. Occasionally a faculty member will put on a show, and once a year there's a show for the senior art majors. Some shows run an opening in conjunction with a concert at the Cecilia S. Cohen Recital Hall across the hall. The gallery is free and open to the public Monday through Friday in the afternoon.

Pocono Mountain Art Group
1817 Wallace Street, Stroudsburg
(570) 223-2381

This group has been in existence since 1935. Today it has more than 100 members and sponsors art shows, exhibitions, and demonstrations. For almost 20 years, the group has sponsored the annual Courthouse Square Art Show on 7th Street in Stroudsburg. It is open to all visual artists.

Richard E. Phillips Gallery
300 Main Street, Stroudsburg
(570) 421-7872

This gallery presents wood and bronze sculpture, mostly the work of Richard E. Phillips. Phillips is a local artist whose work has gained him an international reputation, including exhibitions in New York City.

School of Visual and Performing Arts
554 Main Street, Stroudsburg
(570) 424-5285

This combines a little of everything. It's a collaboration of dancer Kathy Kroll and shaolin master/painter Marilyn Cooper. On First Saturday there are always art exhibits and often performances. The rest of the time there are dance classes, tai chi and shaolin classes, as well as life drawing and other visual arts classes. In the summer they offer themed weeks for kids to explore their artistic sides.

Take Two Gallery
515 Main Street, Stroudsburg
(570) 476-4483
www.taketwogallery.com

Two artists travel the world and offer their finds, as well as their own art. You'll find African carvings, Asian fabrics, some unforgettable works in charcoal by three Thai artists, as well as Haitian owner Sylvestre Pierre's unusual paintings and his partner Nyrvah Richard's photographs and wearable art. This gallery is packed with treasures. At the time of printing, Take Two Galleries was closed.

West End

Artisan Picture Framing and Gallery
204 Main Avenue, Hawley
(570) 226-2700
www.artisanpictureframing.com

Picture-framer Peter Daniel's work is as much fine art as the oils and watercolors he embellishes with hand-milled precious woods and hand-rubbed stains designed to pick up tones of the paintings he frames. Area artists often display their works here.

David Watkins Price, Artist Studio
29 Race Street, Jim Thorpe
(570) 325-4544

This studio is operated by owner/artist

David Price, who is nationally known for his watercolors, prints, and graphic designs. He is also involved in the evolution of Jim Thorpe's historic and artistic center.

The Faulty Beagle
499A Lower Smith Gap Road, Kunkletown
(610) 381-2108
www.faultybeagle.com
This gallery exhibits contemporary paintings and sculptures by recognized local, national, and international artists, David Palmer, Eric Watts, and Valerie Mann. The gallery is open by appointment.

Hazard House Gallery
38 West Broadway, Jim Thorpe
(570) 325-8778
www.lebowartist.com
The gallery exclusively features the acrylics and watercolors of Joel Le Bow, whose studio also is here. The gallery is open weekends from noon until 5:00 P.M. during festivals and Jim Thorpe Art Walks. Other hours are by appointment only.

Shozo Nagano, Open Studio
39 Race Street, Jim Thorpe
(570) 325-3988
This gallery presents acrylic paintings on shaped canvas by internationally known artist Shozo Nagano. The works are three-dimensional and present painting in a way that stretches both the art form and what Shozo calls "metaphysical imagination."

THEATER

Theatrical performances in the Poconos include full-time professionals, part-time professionals, and amateurs, though even most of those who do not play for paychecks are of truly professional caliber. Plays and performances happen all the time, so the chance to audition and perform always is available. Auditions are announced in the *Pocono Record* or the *Pike County Gazette*. Sometimes auditions are posted on community bulletin boards in supermarkets or post offices. Call if you are interested in joining any theater groups or finding out about audition or performance schedules; troupes are always looking for new members.

Delaware Water Gap/ Shawnee-on-Delaware

Shawnee Playhouse
River Road, Shawnee-on-Delaware
(570) 421-5093, (800) 742-9633
www.shawneeplayhouse.com
The Shawnee Playhouse is housed in the former Worthington Hall, a onetime community center and library, in the picturesque town of Shawnee-on-Delaware. Smallness is part of the charm of this summer theater. It produces high-quality musicals all season long with energetic young casts imported from New York. Children's theater is also a component of the Shawnee Playhouse. They offer three Broadway-style musicals between the spring and the fall, a Christmas musical, and a "Messiah" sing-along around Christmas (see our Annual Events chapter). Other local groups sometimes use the 230-seat theater in the off-season.

Children 4 to 8 can learn all about live music, dance, theater, and world culture through enrollment in the Fine Arts and Discovery Series, featuring various artists in hour-long concerts, and in special preconcert workshops. Call (570) 476-3237 for registration, at $5.00 per child per workshop, or see the FADS Web site, www.fineartsdiscoverseries.org.

Area schools are another source of wonderful concerts and theatrical productions. Our area schools put on especially elaborate musicals, and the concerts by students are often excellent. Watch for East Stroudsburg School District's Music Department concert in March. They often bring in a composer and commission a piece. One of the school bands premieres the piece that night.

Stroudsburg/East Stroudsburg

Center Stage Players
3 Phyllis Court, Stroudsburg
(570) 476-8470
www.centerstageplayers.org
A nonprofit community theater organization, this group has been staging comedies, dramas, and mysteries since 1990. Their goal is to make participation in quality community theater available to community members at all levels of experience. Auditions are open and are always advertised in the *Pocono Record*. Center Stage Players presents a minimum of two plays in the spring at Shawnee Playhouse.

North East Theatrical Alliance
161 Third Street, Nazareth
(610) 365-8117
North East Theatrical Alliance is a community-based nonprofit theater organization. Under the direction of Sue Raesly, they produce a Broadway musical each year, and put it on at Bangor Middle School in Bangor. Partial proceeds go to fight child abuse. The musical they put on typically uses a lot of children, and many area children get a chance to perform with this group.

Pennsylvania Repertory Company
8 Wilderness Acres, East Stroudsburg
(570) 223-7034
Pennsylvania Repertory Company produces classic plays taught in school for students who are studying them. They have put on plays such as *Death of a Salesman, The Crucible,* and several of Shakespeare's plays. Pennsylvania Repertory Company is the brainchild of Michael Harron, who directs all the productions. Harron has done many projects in the area, and is highly respected as a director and an actor. Harron is reviving an area tradition, his musical reinterpretation of "A Christmas Carol," called "Tiny Tim's Christmas Carol." Those who are interested in being part of any of the productions are welcome to audition. Contact Harron or watch the local papers for audition announcements.

Pocono Lively Arts Inc.
P.O. Box 11, Stroudsburg, PA 18360
(570) 421-0936
This nonprofit, volunteer theatrical group was established in 1977 to offer opportunities to young performers. It produces professional-level musicals in July and November with orchestra accompaniment. Children always take part in the November production. And the talent in the area is so good, the performances sell out, so get your tickets in advance. They also offer a Young Artist Showcase in June to present the work of young men and women from the area who are pursuing the arts in college. On Christmas Eve, Pocono Lively Arts brings area singers together with community members to usher the holiday in with carols, and they have just instituted A Merry Tuba Christmas, in which Christmas music is played on the tuba. There are children's workshops in June and a children's production in early August, and a new "exploring theater" workshop now is available for teens. The group has open auditions, to which all members of the community are invited.

Mount Pocono Area

Pocono Playhouse
Highway 390, Mountainhome
(570) 595-7456
www.poconoplayhouse.com
During her World War II tour, USO show manager Rowena Stevens learned that many young soldiers never before had seen live performers. So after the war, she found a suitable field in Mountainhome, constructed a 500-seat theater similar to the ones used by the army for the USO shows and opened Pocono Playhouse in 1947 as the Poconos' first summer theater. Its opening production was *Dear Ruth,* starring Richard Kiley. Stars at the Playhouse have been a tradition for many years; some top performers who have played here include Larry Hagman, Hal Linden, Eddie Mekka, and Gloria Vanderbilt. The group holds auditions and rehearsals for its productions in New York City and performs here and in its sister theater to the south, Bucks County Playhouse in New Hope. Pocono Playhouse features a hefty season of seven musicals between June and October. The productions are Broadway-scale—suitable for the size of the theater. It also sponsors children's theater on weekends.

The on-again-off-again Mountain Laurel Center for the Performing Arts at Bushkill is on again. The controversial center, designed to bring world-class jazz, rock, classical and Broadway musical productions to the Poconos, was born in 2003 with a $15 million state grant for construction of a 10,000-seat concert pavilion. Construction was completed, but the venture wound up millions of dollars in debt with no operating money to book acts for the first season. The entire project appeared headed for failure, but at press time, an additional $375,000 state grant, coupled with a projected $750,000 windfall from the Pike County hotel tax, put Mountain Laurel back on track—at least for the 2005 season. The fresh infusion of cash was expected to put about 30 shows on the marquee.

West End

Mauch Chunk Opera House
Opera House Square, 41 West Broadway
Jim Thorpe
(570) 325-4439
www.mauchchunkopera.com
The Opera House is home for its own resident troupe and many groups that produce plays in the area. If you are interested in getting involved in any local theatrical productions, call the Opera House for audition and performance information. The Opera House has hired an artistic director and is eagerly promoting its theatrical troupe. You also can call for a schedule of what programs are being presented. The Opera House serves as a base for many artistic and cultural events in Jim Thorpe. It has been through various stages of use and is now coming back to its place as the center of the arts in Jim Thorpe.

MUSIC ENSEMBLES AND ORCHESTRAS

There are a number of instrumental and orchestral groups in the Poconos. Some are open to new members; others are professional groups that perform in this area and around the world. For instance, the Phil Woods Quintet, led by renowned jazz alto saxophonist Phil Woods, performs all over the country and at area events, including the Delaware Water Gap Jazz Festival. The Dixie Gents are headed by nationally known trombonist Rick Chamberlain. A summer concert series is held Sunday evenings at the Delaware Water Gap Presbyterian Church of the Mountain, on Main Street. It features free concerts,

Want music lessons for your kid but can't afford them? Most area schools offer class lessons on a band or orchestra instrument. Some will even lend you the instrument. Ask your school's music teacher how your child can participate.

both instrumental and vocal, by well-known area performers. Seats are not supplied—you have to bring your own chairs and blankets. (If it rains the concerts are held inside the church.) The Shawnee Inn holds a series of Tuesday evening lawn concerts throughout the summer, in a pavilion by the river. If it rains, the stage is turned around and the audience can sit under the pavilion. In the winter, Tuesday evening concerts are held by the inn's fireplace. Concert schedules are listed in the Friday weekend section of the *Pocono Record*. In this section, we look at community ensembles that perform in the area and are open, usually by audition, to members of the community.

Stroudsburg/East Stroudsburg

East Stroudsburg University/Community Concert Band
East Stroudsburg University, Fine Arts Center, Normal Street, East Stroudsburg
(570) 422-3759
The ESU/Community Concert Band was founded in 1987. Half of the members are ESU students, while the other half are a mixture of faculty, staff, alumni, and community members (a number of band directors from the local schools enjoy playing in this band). The band plays a formal concert and ESU graduation exercises each semester. They rehearse on Monday nights.

Pocono Youth Orchestra
P.O. Box 1101, Stroudsburg, PA 18360
(610) 965-0268
www.pocono-youth-orchestra.org
This group is responsible for two youth orchestras, the Junior String Orchestra and the Pocono Youth Orchestra. The Pocono Youth Orchestra is the only symphonic orchestra in Monroe County. Students in senior high are accepted based on auditions for string, woodwind, brass, and percussion. The junior String Orchestra is the associate group that serves as a training ground for young string players who have taken lessons. The orchestra plays two formal concerts a year at East Stroudsburg University in winter and spring. They also perform in schools throughout the region.

Trinity Centennial Band
RR. 1, Box 1343, Stroudsburg, PA 18360
(570) 421-4636
The Trinity Centennial Band was founded in 1991 by the late Russ Speicher to mark the 100th anniversary of Trinity Episcopal Church in Mount Pocono. The group, consisting of 45 local musicians ranging in age from the teens to over 80, plays traditional concert band music at various venues throughout the year across the Poconos, which means, says director/conductor Ralph S. Harrison, "we play a lot of John Phillip Sousa."

CHORUSES

There are several choral societies available for those who are interested in voicing their best notes. The groups usually require an audition of some type but emphasize that it is not meant to be threatening. Further notes about these groups: They are talented, and their performances are generally well attended. A highlight of the Monroe County vocal music scene is the annual Messiah Sing, held at the Shawnee Playhouse. Members of local vocal music organizations and anyone else who likes to sing get together to raise their collective voices in beautiful song. It is quite an event and one that always draws a crowd.

Stroudsburg/East Stroudsburg

Pocono Choral Society
P.O. Box 5, Stroudsburg, PA 18360
(570) 992-0160

This group performs three major concerts a year in Stroudsburg. Besides those main events, the chorus performs 40–50 additional concerts a year at various sites including East Stroudsburg University, New York, even Europe. In 1996 the group went on an 18-day tour of the British Isles where they sang in 10 concerts and participated in festivals, including one at Westminster Abbey and the International Eistedfodd in Llangollen, Wales. Pocono Choral Society usually tours some other part of the globe every four years, with most of the members participating. The group has been singing since 1981 under the direction of conductor Jerrold Fisher, who also conducts the Pocono Pops, the ancillary orchestra that performs with the Choral Society on a need basis. Pocono Choral Society is an audition-only group. Call to find out about auditions or to obtain schedule information.

Pocono Vocal Arts Society
5510 Concord Drive, Stroudsburg
(570) 476-4126

P.V.A.S. focuses on opera, art song, and musical theater repertoire. From Mozart, Bizet and Verdi to Romberg, Hammerstein and Porter, Pocono Vocal Arts Society performs locally at many events and also stages its own concerts four times a year. Watch for them also at the annual tree lighting ceremony in Downtown Stroudsburg and at Quiet Valley during the Har-

Many Pocono resorts provide weekend arts and culture events throughout the year. Weekends devoted to national music or dance are big draws. Showcases for Big Band or jazz concerts are presented. So, when considering a place to stay on your vacation or weekend getaway, ask if any such events are planned.

vest Festival. (See our Annual Events chapter.) A not-for-profit organization formed in 1995, P.V.A.S. is always on the lookout for talented individuals of all ages who want to work hard and learn a lot. Rehearsals are held every week, and vocal coaching is available. Call the group for the schedule of auditions.

Mount Pocono Area

Chorus of the Poconos
RR 1, Box 62C, Henryville, PA 18332
(570) 620-9529

This group is dedicated to barbershop harmony and is a member of the Barbershop Harmony Society. This group is open to new members, and its current members range from young adults to senior citizens still in their prime. Under director Tom Salmon, the chorus performs several concerts a year and plays civic organizations' banquets.

West End

The Bach and Handel Chorale Inc.
810 Carbon Street, Jim Thorpe
(570) 325-9440
home.ptd.net/~mmzjr/bhc

This group has been in existence since 1984 when it was founded to celebrate the births of Bach and Handel. It's conducted by Randall D. Perry. The chorale has performed with orchestras in Philadelphia. The group also presents four major concerts annually—a Palm Sunday Cantata, two Christmas concerts and one in spring. Its intensive schedule doesn't seem to daunt its members who come from all over the area, even New Jersey, to perform. Interested singers are invited to make an appointment for an audition.

Pleasant Valley Choral Society
P.O. Box 238, Effort, PA 18330
(570) 688-9067
www.geocities.com/pleasantvalleychoral
This group has been singing since 1983 and presents two concerts a year at Pleasant Valley High School. The society is dedicated to bringing musical enjoyment to the community both from the standpoint of the singers and their audiences. The group's repertoire includes pop tunes, show tunes, operettas, and light classics. A non-threatening audition is standard.

DANCE

A number of dancers and dance instructors in the Poconos teach everything from Scottish Highland through line dancing to modern dance and ballet. Area professionals perform as choreographers and at in-school programs.

Stroudsburg/East Stroudsburg

ESU University Dance Co.
Koehler Field House
East Stroudsburg University
East Stroudsburg
(570) 442-3761, (570) 422-3331
Under supervision of East Stroudsburg University's dance faculty, students in the department offer classes to the community. Saturday mornings are classes for children up to age 13, combining creative

dance, ballet, tap, modern, and jazz dance. The classes are separated into age groups among children 4 to 15. Friday evenings are for adult ballroom dance classes and yoga.

Kathy Kroll Dance and Paper Theater/ School of Visual and Performing Arts
554 Main Street, Stroudsburg
(570) 424-5285
Modern dancer Kathy Kroll is influenced by Nikolai, Limon, and ballet styles, but she has added her own twist—the coolest props anywhere. Because her husband is an origami artist, many of her dance works include giant origami figures, and sometimes the dancers actually fold the figure as part of the dance. Performances are given around the area and in New York City. Watch for her Garlic Breathing Dragon, at local festivals.

Kroll's School of Visual and Performing Arts offers classes in modern dance, ballet, pointe, acting, martial arts, and visual arts. The dance and martial arts classes are in a spacious sky-lit studio on a state-of-the-art dance floor. The studio is open on First Saturday and often presents mini performances during that event. (See "Fine Art and Crafts Galleries.")

Notara School of Dance and Acting
700 Phillips Street, Stroudsburg
(570) 421-1718
The Notara Dance Company specializes in classical ballet and presents other artistic dance/theater ventures. It produces two programs a year—in winter and spring. The winter holiday season is always set off by the Notara production of *The Nutcracker*. Students of the Notara studio perform with dance professionals for a weekend of sold-out performances. The spring production is a recital. Classes taught in this professional school of dance, include ballet, tap, jazz, pointe, modern dance, and acting. The spacious studio has a floating floor, which prevents injuries.

PA Dance Network
35 Dansbury Terrace, East Stroudsburg
(570) 426-6855
www.padance.com
Maria Triano-Boehning is the founder and director of PA Dance Network. She and her staff teach ballet and pointe, tap, jazz, modern, and lyrical dance as well as dance fitness, dance twirl (jazz dance and baton twirling), yoga, stretch, and a parent–child creative class. The studio is new and features a floating dance floor and a huge glass observation wall. PA Dance Network sponsors three concerts a year. An Evening of Lyrical Dance at the studio serves as a fund-raiser for the PA Dance Vision Repertory Ensemble. The second event, the Mountain Dance Concert at East Stroudsburg University, in which area choreographers are invited to perform along with the Dance Vision Ensemble, serves as a fund-raiser for the ensemble and the Pocono Arts Council. Art Beat, their third yearly presentation, is a concert of dance and music at Stroudsburg High School, which raises funds to help those undergoing treatment at Pocono Medical Center's Hughes Cancer Center.

PA Dance Vision
35 Dansbury Terrace, East Stroudsburg
(570) 426-6855
www.padance.com
The mission of this group is the promotion of dance awareness in the Poconos. Accordingly PA Dance Vision stages day-long seminars four times a year at East Stroudsburg University for students 11 through adult who are sufficiently advanced to study in master classes with noted professional dancers. At the end of each seminar, students involved stage mini performances illustrating what they have learned. PA Dance Vision also runs an outreach program, sending their touring company into preschools to expose them to dance. The PA Dance Network Touring Ensemble does 20–30 shows a year in regional school districts.

Pocono Dance Center
115 Seven Bridges Road, East Stroudsburg
(570) 424-6883
This studio has been operating for 20 years under the direction of owner Carrie Evers, a former Rockette and resort performer. The school teaches ballet, tap, and jazz. The dance company, the Pocono Dance Ensemble, performs throughout the area.

FILM

Stroudsburg/East Stroudsburg

Black Mariah Film Festival
Pocono Cinema and Coffee Shop, 88
South Courtland Street, East Stroudsburg
(570) 421-FILM
www.poconocinema.com
Jointly sponsored by the local Unitarian Universalist Church and the Pocono Arts Council, this is a festival of short films. Call the arts council, (570) 476–4460, for more information.

Pocono Cinema and Coffee Shop
88 South Courtland Street
East Stroudsburg
(570) 421-FILM
www.poconocinema.com
This art theater opened in 1996 to show films that do not make it to the mall theaters, and those for which the cineplexes are slow to compete with three screens. Pocono Cinema and Coffee Shop boasts a cineplex of its own. What makes this place even more fun is the coffee shop right inside that facilitates before-and-after treats and talk time. In the lobby, you can continue to enjoy your immersion in the arts because the walls provide a miniature art gallery for local artists to exhibit their work. You can become a member for a family membership fee of $20 a year. Membership entitles you to the monthly

preview newsletter and discounted ticket prices for your family and as many friends as you want to bring along.

Milford/Lake Wallenpaupack Area

Black Bear Film Festival
115 Seventh Street, Milford
(570) 409-0909
www.blackbearfilm.com

Emphasizing independent and innovative filmmakers that explore human conditions and the natural world, this festival takes place over the Columbus Day weekend. Films are shown at the old Milford Theater and a drive-in, whereas the borough hall is turned into a film salon where directors, actors, and others involved in the process of making the films can discuss how they do it. Three levels of tickets may be purchased: a gold pass gets you into all the films and events, including an opening gala and dinner, or you may purchase tickets just to the gala and opening night. Tickets for individual films are also available. The Milford area played a prominent role as a backdrop for silent films, and today the jewel-like small town is making a comeback as the perfect setting for a film festival.

LITERARY ARTS

Stroudsburg/East Stroudsburg

The Forwardian Society
2132 Wallace Street, Stroudsburg
(570) 476-4357
www.geocities.com/pauladam

The Forwardian Society is a fellowship of people who love the arts. Currently they run film nights, play readings, salons, and open readings for poets and writers.

Great Books
Eastern Monroe Public Library, 9 North Ninth Street, Stroudsburg
(570) 421-3819

Though the local Great Books club uses the Great Books company's reading list, they also branch out into other literature. They also use Great Books' discussion techniques, which make the discussion of literature available to people who would never dream of majoring in English. They meet the first Thursday of the month at the Eastern Monroe Public Library at 7:00 P.M. and the third Thursday of the month in a restaurant of their choice, October to June, and usually read one book every two weeks. Listings of the books to be read are available by calling the number above, or you can look on the calendar page of *Dignity,* the *Pocono Record*'s monthly magazine for people who are 50 and older. All ages are welcome to come for any number of sessions; you don't have to attend every one.

The New Book Group
Eastern Monroe Public Library, 9 North Ninth Street, Stroudsburg
(570) 894-4323

Meeting at the library on the first and third Tuesday of the month, The New Book Group reads and discusses 20th-century literature, mostly fiction and a small number of memoirs. You can usually find a flyer posted at the library listing the books this group will discuss. The group is on hiatus from late November until March.

Pocono Writers
P.O. Box 755
Stroudsburg, PA 18360-0755
(570) 421-6405
www.geocities.com/poconowriters

This group of writers meets the fourth Thursday of the month at the Eastern Monroe Public Library in Stroudsburg. They meet on the third Thursday in November and December so as not to interfere with the holidays. They come from all fields and all levels of ability, from just starting out to published authors. They are essayists, short-story writers, poets, novelists, and playwrights. Works are read aloud and passed around. It is open to anyone who is interested. No previous notification is required other than to show up and be prepared to enjoy the interaction and support.

SYLP-H
P.O. Box 804, Stroudsburg, PA 18360
(570) 421-3819
SYLP-H, which means Support Your Local Poet—Hooray, was founded in 2000 to promote poetry as a creative process and as a performance medium. The organization strives to be a venue where poets meet and exchange ideas. SYLP-H runs the Pocono Poetry Invitational—a performance in April (National Poetry Month) featuring five poets. The poets who perform one year pick the poets to perform the next year. SYLP-H holds regular open meetings and discussions on the fourth Friday of the month at Weegees Coffee Shop at 560 Main Street in Downtown Stroudsburg.

LIBRARIES

It hardly matters anymore whether your closest library is tiny or huge. Most libraries belong to Access Pennsylvania, which makes any library in the state available to Pennsylvania library cardholders. With Access Pennsylvania and interlibrary loans, you can get just about any book that's in print. Just be sure, if you order a book from another library, to pick it up when it comes into yours. The service is free, but most libraries charge hefty fees if you ask them to order a book and then don't use it.

Most libraries are computerized, and if you don't have access to the Internet, check out your local library. If they're not online yet, they probably will be soon. Many libraries also offer computers for reference research and word processing.

No computer? No Internet? No computer savvy? Your library is good for all three. Most libraries offer word processing and other programs as well as a hookup to the Internet. If the librarian isn't too busy, he or she will show you how to use the machine, too. If the librarian is busy, just ask a passing kid.

Delaware Water Gap/ Shawnee-on-Delaware

Eastern Monroe Public Library— Smithfield Branch
Route 209 at Foxmoor Village
Marshalls Creek
(570) 223-1881
www.monroepl.org
A small branch of the Eastern Monroe Public Library, you'll find current books and books on tape here.

Stroudsburg/East Stroudsburg

Eastern Monroe Public Library— Hughes Library
1002 North Ninth Street, Stroudsburg
(570) 421-0800
www.monroepl.org
Hughes moved into spacious new quarters about five years ago and is valiantly working to fill the building up with books and services. Books, videos, books on tape, a large children's library, a good reference and local history section, CDs and computer software, magazines, newspapers, and Internet connections are among the services offered here. There are concerts for children and the BookHouse, a monthly series of music and poetry for adults. Many area organizations make use of the community room, including a couple of book clubs that are open to the public. The yearly book sale in August, put on by the Friends of the Library, is a big event.

Eastern Monroe Public Library—
Pocono Township Branch
Municipal Building, Highway 611
Tannersville
(570) 629-5858
www.monroepl.org
This is another small branch of the Eastern Monroe Public Library offering books and tapes to Tannersville-area patrons.

Mount Pocono Area

Barrett Friendly Library
Highway 191, Mountainhome
(570) 595-7171
www.barrettlibrary.org
Called Barrett Friendly because the Quaker wife of one of the original managers of Buck Hill Inn established this library, it's still a friendly place. In addition to books, Barrett has audio books, music CDs, CD-ROMs for computers, periodicals, an Internet connection, computers for word processing, story hours for toddlers and preschoolers, summer reading programs, separate book discussion groups for adults and young adults, workshops, lectures, and an art show.

Clymer Library
Firehouse Road, Pocono Pines
(570) 646-0826
The collection at Clymer is fairly large, with audio books, children's books on tape, a story hour for children, a summer reading program, videos, an Internet connection, a word processing computer, and CD-ROM reference materials as well as plain old ordinary books. There are fre-

On vacation and want to check your e-mail? Go to the library. Nearly every library has at least one Internet connection, and it's free. You may have to wait for a little bit, but it's a pleasant wait—there's always something to do in a library.

quent lectures here and a multipurpose room available for community events.

Pocono Mountain Public Library
Coolbaugh Township Municipal Center
5540 Memorial Boulevard, Highway 611
Tobyhanna
(570) 894-8860
www.poconomountpl.org
In addition to books, the Pocono Mountain Public Library offers videos, CD-ROMs, books on tape, music CDs, an Internet connection, and story hours for toddlers. They offer free yoga classes on Tuesday and lots of kids' programs in the summer, including a summer reading program for preschoolers through teens with prizes for reading.

West End

Dimmick Memorial Library
54 Broadway, Jim Thorpe
(570) 325-2131
www.dimmicklibrary.org
Dimmick Memorial Library is reminiscent of an earlier day when, with radio, film, and television still far in the future, books were the only vehicles one might employ to explore the worlds of history, letters, and the human imagination. Opened in 1890, Dimmick retains its air of Victorian opulence despite a catastrophic fire that nearly destroyed it on December 13, 1979. Books not lost to the fire were waterlogged and, in the bitter winter, actually found frozen into blocks of ice after firemen doused the blaze and shored up the building for restoration. Thanks to a company called Air Products in Allentown, irreplaceable local history books were saved. Some of them had been stored in a vault, and others were stashed beneath a desk in the basement where, though never threatened by flames, they were soaked by the fire hoses. Air Products collected and freeze-dried them, and they are available to historians and nostalgia buffs

today, little the worse for wear.

Despite its old-fashioned look, Dimmick is an active, contemporary library. In addition to an ever-growing collection of books, Dimmick offers many up-to-date services, including books on tape, videos, children's books, large-print books for people who may have difficulty reading small letters, a local newspaper on microfilm that goes back to 1829, a fax machine, books on local history, family biographies, Census microfilm for Carbon County from 1790 to 1920, various cultural programs, twice yearly book sales, a children's reading program for preschoolers, a summer reading program for kids, and book signings.

Lehighton Area Memorial Library
124 North Street, Lehighton
(610) 377-2750
www.library.cpals.com
Like the community it serves, Lehighton is a tiny library. In addition to books, they carry audio books, an Internet connection, and computers for reference. Lehighton organizations run summer reading programs and other occasional children's programs there.

Western Pocono Community Library
2000 Pilgrim Way, Brodheadsville
(570) 992-7934
www.wpcl.lib.pa.us
The Western Pocono Library is in new quarters and has expanded its collection and added a full reference section with reference librarians. In addition to books, here you'll find audio books and several computers with an Internet connection. Computer courses are offered as well. Make sure you look at the 34 shadow boxes by Phoebe Conrad on permanent exhibit; each one depicts a children's story or poem. There's no way to describe them, but they're exquisite. Western Pocono runs the Monroe County Literacy Council and offers GED and ESL courses as well as adult literacy classes. Programs and discussions for the entire community are offered through the Pennsylvania Humanities Council. There are children's

story hours two days a week here as well as a summer reading program. Back Door Books, in the old library building, offers a fantastic collection of new and used books and records, with sales benefiting the library. The Friends of the Library is very active, offering year-round activities including fund-raising tournaments, fairs, and parties.

Milford/Lake Wallenpaupack Area

Hawley Public Library
103 Main Avenue, Hawley
(570) 226-4620
www.plowc.org
Hawley renovated their building a few years ago and nearly doubled their size. They're especially pleased that the children's library was able to expand. In addition to books, Hawley carries audio books; music CDs; videos; a good local history collection; lots of computers for the Internet; a pamphlet file with odds and ends like maps, interesting trip brochures, and medical information; a large print collection; a special collection for young adults, and a good assortment of magazines. Hawley also offers programs for children, a summer reading program, a story time for preschoolers, baby and me story times, lectures, presentations, art classes, and craft classes for kids.

Hemlock Farms Library
1976 Hemlock Farms, Hawley
(570) 775-6466
In addition to books, Hemlock Farms Library has audios, videos, and story hours.

Don't forget to check your local library for upcoming events. Libraries often bring in lecturers, poets, and musicians, and these varied cultural programs are usually free to the libraries' patrons.

Newfoundland Area Public Library
Main Street, Newfoundland
(570) 676–4518
www.plowc.com
Newfoundland is a very small library, but it's part of the Wayne County Library system with access to all of Wayne County's resources. In addition to books, they have audio books, videos, CDs, magazines, and four computers with Internet access. They offer a Saturday morning children's program with story and crafts and a summer reading program.

Pike County Public Library
201 Broad Street, Milford
(570) 296–8211
www.pcpl.org
The Pike County Public Library has an active interlibrary loan program—patrons regularly order books from almost any library in the country. They also issue cassette players and talking book machines to blind patrons. During the summer, they run a six-week themed children's program. The library sponsors book discussion groups for adults. They also have Internet connections, books on tape, and videos.

Pike County Public Library—Dingman
Delaware Elementary School Branch
Highway 739, Dingman Township
(570) 686–7045
This branch of the Pike County Public library offers, in addition to books and periodicals, a summer program for children. Call for details.

Pike County Public Library—Lackawaxen
Township at Greeley Branch
Highway 590, Greeley
(570) 685–3100
A branch of the Pike County Public Library, Greeley offers books, audio books, an Internet connection, and a children's summer program. They also offer a preschool program during the school year.

DAY TRIPS 🚗

Frankly, there's so much to do within walking distance of where we live, it's hard to get the family into the car to go anywhere. Still, whether you're in the Poconos for a week's vacation or whether you live here, you eventually will want to explore the larger area. Since Philadelphia and New York are within two hours of the heart of the Poconos, there are enough day trips to fill several guidebooks, enough attractions to fill a small country. Traveling only two hours from the Poconos, you can go to the heart of a city and hit major cultural institutions, or you can find yourself in countryside where people work the soil much as they did 100 years ago.

Don't neglect the possibility of day trips within the Poconos. If you are in Stroudsburg, a trip to Jim Thorpe, Lake Wallenpaupack, or Milford would constitute a day trip, and each area is well worth the time. In nearly every chapter of this book, we tell you about neat stuff to see, do, buy, and eat in every part of the Poconos. No matter where you are, there's something you shouldn't miss on the other side.

It would be impossible to tell you about all the day trips from our area, but here are some suggestions to get you started.

NEARBY DESTINATIONS

Some of these day trips are just beyond our regional borders.

Have Balloon Will Travel
Phillipsburg, NJ
(800) 60-TOFLY
www.haveballoonwilltravel.com
Right over the Delaware Bridge from Easton, you will find Have Balloon Will Travel. You'll spend about one hour in the air, but the whole adventure takes 3 to 4 hours.

Bring a camera and expect to see some beautiful views of the countryside. Balloon flights cost $450 per couple, and reservations are required.

Old Mine Road
Start at the Kittatinny Point Ranger's Station on the New Jersey side of the Delaware Water Gap (open daily 9:00 A.M. to 5:00 P.M. in the summer, weekends the rest of the year; call 908-496-4458). Pick up some maps, ask the rangers for suggestions, take along a picnic lunch, and spend the day exploring. Old Mine Road meanders along the river with lots of good places to stop and relax or to hike, swim, camp, and canoe. Local legend has it that Old Mine Road was used by 17th-century Dutch traders to transport copper from mines along one of the trails you can hike, to what is now Kingston, New York—making the road the oldest highway in the country. Though recent research shows that the road was built in the 19th century, and the copper could not be extracted in any quantity using 17th-century technology, it's a good story—and the road is lovely.

Along the road, Millbrook Village (12 miles north of Interstate 80, 908-841-9531) is a restored 19th-century rural community. Some of the buildings are open 9:00 A.M. to 5:00 P.M. weekends, Memorial Day through August, and craftsmen demonstrate traditional blacksmithing, woodworking, and other skills of the period. The first full weekend of October is a special Millbrook Days celebration with people in period dress recreating the daily life of the 19th century. If the village is closed, you can still get an interpretive brochure and walk the quiet lanes. A couple of the historic buildings have buttons you can punch to activate a taped voice that tells you about the site. Walk along the old village road that follows a babbling stream. About a half-mile past the schoolhouse, you'll come to Watergate, a grassy picnic area surrounding a pretty lake. Watergate was once an elaborate estate. All that's left of the original buildings are a couple of fairy-tale castle towers topping a small dam.

Continuing north on Old Mine Road, follow signs for Peters Valley, and you'll come to Peters Valley Craft Education Center, another restored village with a fabulous craft gallery and several studios with artists-in-residence. The center offers workshops in traditional and contemporary crafts with nationally recognized artists. Late in September, Peters Valley holds a juried crafts fair. The gallery has variable hours depending on the season and the work they have to accomplish, but it's usually open six days a week in the summer. Call (973) 948–5802 to see if the gallery will be open when you pass by and to request a catalog of Peters Valley's many interesting workshops.

To get to Old Mine Road, cross the river on Interstate 80 and take the first exit, which is for the Kittatinny Point Visitor Center. The center is to the left. If you're not going there first, turn right off the ramp and cross under I-80, following signs for the Worthington State Forest, which will put you on Old Mine Road. Peters Valley is near the Dingmans Ferry Toll Bridge (see the Close-up in our Getting Around chapter), which you can take back over to the Pennsylvania side.

Weona Park
Highway 512, Pen Argyl
(610) 863-9249
If you're a fan of carousels, you must visit Pen Argyl's Weona Park, which has a beautiful Dentzel carousel. The carousel, built in Germantown in 1917 and brought

here in 1923, is in a round wooden building and is open Friday from 6:00 to 9:00 P.M. and Saturday and Sunday from noon to 9:00 P.M. weather permitting. You'll pay $1.00 for the ride, and you can try to catch the brass ring for a free ride. Weona is a charming old-fashioned town park, with some kiddie rides, a miniature golf course, an Olympic-size swimming pool, a picnic grove, playing fields, basketball and tennis courts, a playground, and an awesome new skate park. The name is not a Lenape word; the citizens of Pen Argyl decided to make it very clear that "We own a park."

Take Highway 512 into Pen Argyl (the easy way is from Highway 33 South, but you can find more scenic routes on your map). The park surrounds Highway 512, so you can't miss it.

METRO DESTINATIONS
Allentown/Bethlehem/ Easton Area

Allentown, Bethlehem, and Easton are about 45 minutes south of the Poconos.

Bethlehem
Bethlehem has a beautiful old Main Street that runs above the Lehigh River and is anchored by Moravian College. Visit Bethlehem during Musikfest in mid-August when the city is transformed by a series of stages presenting more than 1,000 free musical performances over 10 days and nights. You can stroll through the old part of the city serenaded by medieval minstrels, polka all day under a tent, or sit in a beer garden, sampling good food and listening to some of the top folk musicians in the country. Each evening, a performance is given by a nationally known act such as Queen Ida, the Temptations, the Artie Shaw Orchestra, or Mitch Ryder. You can buy tickets for a seat up close or sit on the grass a little farther from the stage for free. Another great time to visit Beth-

lehem, also called the Christmas City, is during the Christkindlmarkt, held late November through mid-December. It's a family holiday market with craft, entertainment, and children's activities. The city features lots of Christmas-themed displays. You can call the visitor center at (610) 868-1513 or (800) 360-8687 for details and a brochure.

Allentown

Visit Allentown during Mayfair at the end of May, when a large city park becomes a focus of music, art, and regional food for five days. Dorney Park and Wildwater Kingdom, 3830 Dorney Park Road, Allentown, (610) 395-3724, an amusement/water park with five fabled roller coasters, is another popular Allentown destination. Daily admission is $35.75. Hours vary; call ahead to see if the park is open.

Easton

Easton, just east of Allentown/Bethlehem has the flashy Two Rivers Landing and the older Hugh Moore Park. At Two Rivers Landing, (610) 515-8000, you'll find The Crayola Factory, where families can see how crayons and markers are made and then participate in interactive projects that encourage you to think "outside the lines." Your admission to the Crayola Factory also gets you into the National Canal Museum, where you can see a replica of a canal boat and learn about life on the canals in the 1800s. Two Rivers Landing is open September through March, Tuesday through Saturday; April through June, Monday through Saturday; and July through Labor Day, every day. Admission to both attractions is $9.00. Children 2 and younger are admitted free. Admission, however, is not guaranteed, and reservations are strongly suggested. To get to Two Rivers Landing, take Highway 611 south to Easton, and follow the signs for the Crayola Factory (it's off Third Street, two blocks after you pass U.S. Highway 22). At Hugh Moore Park, (610) 250-6700, you can picnic, hike on park trails and rent a boat or canoe. Visit the Locktender's

House Museum or the Archives and Library, or take a canal boat ride. The ride is mule-powered, lasts about 45 minutes, and includes a costumed interpreter. You can catch a canal boat seven days a week late June to Labor Day and every day but Monday May through late June. Admission is $9.00 for adults and children 2 and younger are free. From US 22, take 25th Street south 1.6 miles to Lehigh Drive, turn right, and go 0.5 mile to a stop sign. Turn right at the entrance bridge to Hugh Moore Park.

Metro New Jersey

Metropolitan New Jersey has a number of attractions that might interest you. The Statue of Liberty and Liberty Park are a not-to-be-missed duo in Jersey City; although the statue is closed at press time, it's still an impressive sight (about 1½-hour drive). Take I-80 east to the New Jersey Turnpike and head south to exit 14; proceed to Liberty Park. From the park, you can take a boat to the Statue of Liberty. The Meadowlands sports complex is another close-by drive (less than two hours). Here you will find concerts, the pro football Giants, the New York Jets, the New Jersey Nets, the New Jersey Devils, the Metrostars (soccer), the New Jersey Gladiators, the New Jersey Storm (pro lacrosse), horse racing, and flea markets. Take I-80 east to U.S. Highway 3 in New Jersey. There are plenty of signs to keep you from getting lost.

Philadelphia

Philadelphia is two hours away by car from the central Poconos. Philadelphia would fill an Insiders' Guide all by itself, so there's plenty to do. Visit Society Hill, a colonial neighborhood so architecturally intact you'll feel like you're in Williamsburg. Historic houses and museums are sprinkled throughout this neighborhood.

Cruise the Internet for information about your day trip destination. Many area tourist agencies have terrific sites that will give you all kinds of information and even detailed directions to a place. However, call before you go. Sometimes changes are made, and the Web page is not updated. It's awful to drive two hours to reach a place that has closed.

The Liberty Bell and Independence Hall are at the northern edge of Society Hill. At Independence Hall you can stand in the room where our forefathers hatched our Revolution and later hammered out our Constitution. It's humbling to realize how much happened in one room. Across the street from Independence Hall to the southwest is the Curtis Building. There's a Maxfield Parrish mosaic in the lobby called "Dream Garden." It's made with Tiffany's Favrile glass in 260 shimmering colors. It's one of two mosaics done by Tiffany and the only work by Parrish in glass. Make sure you stop in to see it—you won't be sorry. The waterfront at the eastern edge of Society Hill boasts the Independence Seaport Museum with lots of interactive exhibits, a World War II submarine, and an 1898 flagship you can explore. The southern edge of Society Hill is South Street, the fabled place where "all the hippies meet." Visit the art galleries and shops or just watch the people. Make sure you try a Philadelphia cheese steak before you leave!

Another good Philadelphia trip would be to the Benjamin Franklin Parkway. Many of the major museums are here, all within walking distance of each other. You can visit the Franklin Institute Science Museum; the Academy of Natural Sciences, with dinosaur skeletons and a room you can walk into that's full of live butterflies; the Rodin Museum, with the greatest collection of Rodin sculptures outside of Paris; the Please Touch Museum for children 7 and younger; and the Philadelphia

Museum of Art, America's third-largest art museum. The Philadelphia Zoo is just across the river.

There's much more to do in Philadelphia. Stop at the visitors center at 16th Street and JFK Boulevard, (800) 537-7676, for some ideas.

To get to Philadelphia from the Poconos, take Highway 33 south to US 22 west, to the Northeast Extension of the Pennsylvania Turnpike (Interstate 476, also marked as Highway 9 on older maps). If you're in the western part of the Poconos, you can get on I-476 where it crosses I-80, near Lake Harmony. Take I-476 south. You'll go to the end of the Northeast Extension, go through a tollbooth, and continue to follow I-476 until you see signs for the Schuylkill Expressway, Interstate 76. Take the Expressway into Philadelphia to see the sights there or out to Valley Forge for another good day trip. There are signs all along the way to the major attractions, but get directions or a map ahead of time, so you won't get confused and wind up somewhere in Camden.

If you do end up in Camden, the popular New Jersey State Aquarium is on the waterfront.

New York City

New York City is close enough (it's about 1.5 hours to the George Washington Bridge) that you could go in just to see a show, visit a museum, see the sights, or do some shopping.

Just south of the George Washington Bridge, you can eat and shop your way through the West Side, stopping at the American Museum of Natural History and the New York Historical Society to view the exhibits. Catch a snack under the whale in the Natural History museum; it's one of the world's greatest places for a cafe. Go north of the bridge on the Henry Hudson Parkway to see the medieval art and gardens of the Cloisters and explore beautiful Fort Tryon Park.

Fifth Avenue is called Museum Mile, boasting the Metropolitan Museum of Art (catch the summer sunset from the roof of this museum), the Solomon R. Guggenheim Museum, the Museum of the City of New York, and a number of ethnic museums celebrating the culture of different immigrants. Central Park is always lively, with lots of people skating, a carousel, playgrounds, a restaurant, bike rentals, interesting sculptures, and beautiful landscaping creating all sorts of environments.

You can take a Martz Trailways bus (see our Getting Around chapter) to the Big Apple, leaving from Mount Pocono or Delaware Water Gap. Or, you can drive straight into New York City on I-80. Take I-80 east to the George Washington Bridge and proceed downtown on the West Side Highway, from which you can turn off on almost any street between 125th and the Fulton Fish Market. You can also take I-80 to the New Jersey Turnpike. If you continue south, the turnpike will take you to the Lincoln Tunnel for uptown and midtown locations, or you can go to the Holland Tunnel for downtown, Greenwich Village, Wall Street, Chinatown, and Little Italy.

For listing of events in New York City, *The New York Times* is available at most local newsstands.

Scranton/Wilkes-Barre Area

Scranton and Wilkes-Barre are towns in the Lackawanna Valley, which played an important part in the American Industrial Revolution. At one time this region was responsible for supplying more than 80 percent of the nation's anthracite coal. Around the coal industry grew the manufacturing (especially silk) and rail-transportation industries—part of the historical basis for many day trips in this region. These towns were built in the heyday of the Industrial Revolution, and the architecture as well as the ethnic makeup

Consider going "down the shore" for the day. New Jersey has an enormous coastline a couple hours east of the Poconos, and a trip to the ocean is fun any time of year.

of the towns reflect this influence. Whether you lunch in the art deco beauty of the Lackawanna Train Station (with burnished wood, brass, and skylights), walk through one of the ethnic neighborhoods where Old World languages and traditions are still honored, or stop at a beautiful Gothic-style church, you'll find plenty of fascinating sights.

The region has been undergoing a major revival, in part due to the Lackawanna Heritage Valley Authority (LHVA), which is a partnership of government, business, and community organizations and some individuals. Through Lackawanna Heritage Valley, Pennsylvania's first Heritage Park, the story of the region's role in the Industrial Revolution is told in museums, historic sites, and tours.

The information clearinghouse for the Scranton/Wilkes-Barre area is the Pennsylvania Northeast Territory Visitors Bureau, which is responsible for the daily coordination of the region's tourist activities. For information about Lackawanna County, call the bureau at (800) 22-WELCOME.

You can get to Scranton and Wilkes-Barre via I-81 or Interstate 380, depending on what part of the Poconos you're in. Both roads are accessible from I-80 from the south and Interstate 84 from the north.

Carriage Barn Antiques
1550 Fairview Road, Clarks Summit
(570) 587-5405
www.carriagebarnantiques.com
If you shopped all the antiques places in the Poconos, consider this day trip to the Carriage Barn, with more than 6,000 square feet of shopping space housed in a 100-year-old Pennsylvania bank barn (a

C.F. Martin & Co. Inc.: Guitar Mecca

If you're a guitar player, you know Martin guitars, you probably love Martin guitars, and unless you already have one, you've probably always wanted a Martin guitar. In an age when superb luthiers have sprung up all over the country, Martin has retained its reputation for outstanding instruments. From Willie Nelson's nylon-string guitar with a huge hole worn in the top to Eric Clapton's pearl-inlaid beauty, Martins are played by most of the top guitarists. A tiny Martin Backpacker guitar went over the top when astronauts took it aboard the space shuttle *Columbia* in 1993.

The C.F. Martin guitar factory gives free tours every weekday except holidays at 1:15 P.M., and you'll be surprised at the size of the crowd that gathers. Backwoods pickers, record company executives, serious guitarists and just plain folks wait for their tour guides in the museum, ogling the ukulele that went on the Byrd expedition to the North Pole as well as several older, unusual Martin instruments. (C.F. Martin founded the company in 1833, fleeing a restrictive guild system in his native Germany. The Violin Makers' Guild tried to keep the Cabinet Makers from building musical instruments. Martin was a member of the Cabinet Makers.) Several brand-new guitars sit on the wall below a sign that says, "Please play, but use care," and a few skilled players unhook the guitars and fill the air with resonant chords.

When you finally step through the doors onto the factory floor, you'll experience an unexpected thrill. You'll see guitar pieces everywhere, stacks of beautiful rosewood, maple and mahogany sides, unfinished guitars hanging on dollies waiting for their next coat of lacquer.

We expected all the factory workers to be little old German men with mustaches and thick glasses who trained at the feet of master luthiers; but the workers look like the lady next door with the nice flower garden, the young man down the street with the tattoos, and your second grade teacher. Martin likes to train its employees from the bottom up. Most people start in the string-making department and move into luthery as jobs become available. No one gets stuck sanding guitar tops for 20 years, either. Martin likes to cross-train its employees

barn built into the side of a hill so there are two ground-level entrances, one at the hill's bottom and one at it top). This particular shop was featured twice in *Country Living* magazine.

The Carriage Barn has an extensive collection of antique furniture, memorabilia, and collectibles. You can find furniture from the most elegant periods (17th, 18th, and 19th century) to primitives and more modern pieces such as pool tables, juke boxes, and entertainment centers. The Carriage Barn also features a sign collection that has been acquired over 25 years, with original advertising signs for Sinclair Gasoline and Breyer's Ice Cream.

Restoration is a major part of the services here too; there's a full-time staff to

so they can do most of the stations in the factory. While some of the work, like inlaying the mother-of-pearl in the neck and front, is highly skilled, most of the jobs simply take time and practice to master. The process has been broken into a series of reasonable tasks that look like even we could perform them. It's fascinating to watch people gluing on the X-bracing that gives Martins their distinctive sound, scraping the excess glue off the necks and all the other painstakingly minute jobs that go into making a big guitar. Martin has about 750 employees who turn out about 250 guitars and thousands of strings every day.

The most thrilling moment of the tour is near the end when you come to a guitar that is being strung for the first time. You're there to hear the first chords of a brand-new instrument. It's something like being present at the birth of a baby.

To get to the Martin Guitar Factory, take Highway 33 south to the Nazareth exit, Highway 191. As you enter Nazareth, look sharp for a 7-Eleven coming up on the left. Just before the 7-Eleven is Willowdale, a small residential street that you'll probably miss. Make a right onto Willowdale. At the stop sign, turn left on

Bill Mitchem final polishes a custom-built Martin Guitar. C. F. MARTIN & CO.

St. Elmo's Street, then right onto Sycamore by an unmarked swimsuit factory. The Martin Factory, 510 Sycamore Street, Nazareth, is three blocks up on your right. Tours leave promptly at 1:00 P.M. Monday through Friday, except holidays; 10:00 A.M. tours for groups of 10 or more ($3.00 per person) may be arranged by calling (610) 759–2837.

return furniture to its original condition. People come from across the United States to shop here, and the Carriage Barn will ship anywhere in the world.

To reach Carriage Barn Antiques, take I-81 exit 59 to Waverly. Take a right off the exit, another right at the Mr. Z's Supermarket, and one more right onto Fairview Road.

Everhart Museum
Nay Aug Park, Mulberry and Arthur Avenues Scranton
(570) 346–7186
www.everhart-museum.org
This museum of natural science and art is in Nay Aug Park, a city facility popular with Scranton residents. There is a gallery for 19th- and 20th-century European and

American art works and one for American Folk Art. There are ethnic galleries exhibiting work from Native American, African, and South Pacific Oceanic societies. Other galleries house exhibits of prehistoric fossils, Dorflinger glass (see our Attractions, Arts and Culture, and Shopping chapters), regional and European paintings, mounted birds in dioramas of wilderness setting, and minerals of the region. Everhart Museum is open Wednesday through Sunday year-round. This stop is a big school field-trip destination.

Greystone Gardens
829 Old State Road, Clarks Summit
(570) 586-5493
www.greystoneg.com

Greystone Gardens sells plants and flowers, runs a series of horticultural lectures (call for a schedule), and features a cafe (570-587-3215) in the midst of its planted perennial gardens, ponds, and fountains. Floor-to-ceiling windows allow you to immerse yourself in nature while you sip a cappuccino or a glass of wine with your light lunch. In good weather, you can eat outdoors in the terrace garden. Menu items include pasta, soup, salads, and sandwiches. All the herbs used are fresh from the garden. Afternoon "Tea for Two" is served after 2:30 P.M. in the cooler months and includes a three-tier tray of finger sandwiches, scones, miniature pastries, and desserts. Reservations are needed for tea.

Of course, you'll find plants for sale: annuals, perennials, shrubs, trees, and houseplants. Take the Clarks Summit exit from I-80 to Highway 611 north. Go through the commercial section of Clarks Summit, cross the concrete railroad bridge, and turn onto Old State Road. It's worth the trip.

Houdini Tour & Show
1433 North Main Avenue, Scranton
(570) 342-5555
www.houdini.org

If you're a fan of Harry Houdini and magic, come here to learn about his history and secrets. The hour-long tour features exhibits of his memorabilia and films with some of his amazing feats. The museum is open Memorial Day weekend and every weekend in June. They're open daily in July and August. Other times of the year, the tour schedule changes so you are advised to call.

Columbus Day weekend through October 31, a "Halloween Spooktacular" includes a magic show. Reservations are required for this event. The exhibits are not open at this time.

Lackawanna Coal Mine
51 McDade Park, Scranton
(570) 963-MINE, (800) 238-7245
www.thevisitorscenter.com/mine

This exciting trip is in McDade Park, site of the Pennsylvania Anthracite Museum (see subsequent entry). Your tour takes place 300 feet underground. Guides are either retired miners or specialists (teachers and guides familiar with the industry) who give details about what life was like for the miners of "black diamonds" back in the days when the coal industry was king. The tour is a neat history lesson for kids and adults. Of course, the tour guides like to remind you that the roof could fall in at any moment, like it did on the miners from time to time . . . or poison gas could rise up and kill everyone . . . but no tourists have been lost yet, so we think the tour is pretty safe.

The entrance is through the original "shifting shanty" where miners changed clothing at the beginning and end of their shifts. It now houses the Company Store Gift Shoppe. The museum is open seven days a week April through November.

Montage Mountain
Montage Mountain Road (exit 51 off I-81), Scranton
(570) 961-9000
www.montage-mountain.com

In winter, Montage Mountain is a formidable ski resort with 21 trails, seven lifts, and the most challenging black diamond trail in the area. In summer, a 15,000-seat amphitheater hosts the likes of the Moody Blues, Aerosmith, Britney Spears, Fleetwood Mac, and other top-selling acts.

Bring a picnic supper and enjoy it before the show, or stop at one of the concession stands and buy anything from hot dogs to sausage with peppers and onions. Beverages, including beer, are on sale to quench your thirst.

For concert tickets, contact Ticket-Master, (570) 693-4100, or the box office, (570) 961-9000.

Pennsylvania Anthracite Heritage Museum
McDade Park, Scranton
(570) 963-4804
www.phmc.state.pa.us
Like the Lackawanna Coal Mine (see previous entry), this museum is part of the Heritage Valley complex. Through images, sounds and video, visitors learn how immigrant miners lived. Immigrants were of major importance to the area, and this museum traces their influence on the coal industry, the silk industry, and community life. Exhibits include a reproduction of a mining tunnel, a silk-threading machine, and reproductions of a kitchen, church, and saloon from the immigrant era, which began around 1820 and hit its peak during the coal boom years from the late 1800s to the 1920s.

The museum is open seven days a week.

Scranton Iron Furnaces
159 Cedar Avenue, Scranton
(570) 963-3208
www.phmc.state.pa.us
The remnants of four massive stone blast-furnace stacks from the old Scranton Steel Company, the second largest iron producer in the United States in the late 1800s, are the basis for this historic site. They were built between 1848 and 1857. The exhibit tells the story of how this important industry grew—and how Scranton grew up around it. The Steamtown train runs to this site as part of its excursion (in-season). The furnaces are within walking distance of Steamtown National

Historic Site in downtown Scranton (see the subsequent entry). They are open daily April through October. No admission fee is charged.

Scranton/Wilkes-Barre Red Barons
Lackawanna County Stadium
235 Montage Mountain Road, Moosic
(570)969-BALL
www.redbarons.com
The Red Barons are the triple-A baseball affiliate of the Philadelphia Phillies. Going to see them in action is a great family activity, and the players you see here this week could be playing in the majors the next. Throughout the season there are all kinds of giveaway games and special events such as umbrella giveaway night, free camera day, caps, fireworks, and so on. Special family nights are also great bargains. This is a small stadium, and watching a game here gives you a taste of the good old days of baseball.

The Red Barons' season runs from April to September. Games may be played any day of the week, and starting times vary, so call the box office to see if the team is in town. Prices range from $5.00 for the bleachers to $7.50 for the lower box seats; talk about a bargain! Group rates are available. There's a Stadium Club Restaurant, (570) 963-6441, if you want to eat dinner here, but you can always rely on the hot dog man for a real hometown experience.

To reach the stadium, take exit 51 off I-81.

Steamtown National Historic Site
150 South Washington Avenue, Scranton
(570) 340-5204, (888) 693-9391
www.nps.gov
This national historic site is the place to climb aboard an old-fashioned train and discover the joys of rail travel as experienced during the last century. The trains run from their home in the Scranton Yard of the Delaware, Lackawanna & Western Railroad (maintained by the National Park Service) to Moscow, Pennsylvania, and back, with a stop at the Scranton Iron Fur-

A number of churches, senior citizen clubs, and other organizations sponsor day trips to different locations in the New York, New Jersey, and Pennsylvania areas. Check the **Pocono Record, Dignity,** and other local newspapers for information on these trips.

naces (see previous entry). The $15 ride includes a program presented by a park ranger that explains the history of the area's railroad and the rail yard. The site also includes the Steamtown Museum, open daily year-round except Thanksgiving, Christmas, and New Year's Day. Learn about the history of railroading in the History Museum, a restored roundhouse. Also check out the Technology Museum, with a program explaining how the trains operate. For a schedule of Steamtown excursions, check the Web site or call. Since seating on the train is limited, reservations are suggested. If you want to travel during the fall foliage season, your seats must be reserved well in advance.

FARTHER AFIELD

Crystal Cave
Highway 222, Kutztown
(610) 683–6765
www.crystalcavepa.com
A guide takes you on a 45-minute tour through the underground caverns and explains the many formations in this popular cave. There are concrete walkways and railings to keep you safe. Outside the cave are a gift shop, restaurant, miniature golf course (so the claustrophobic members of

The Delaware is considered an easy river for boaters because it is broad and flows slowly, and thousands take to the water in canoes, inner tubes, rafts, and kayaks every summer.

the group can stay occupied), nature trail, and museum about caves and their development. It's a cool alternative in summer—bring a sweater—and still not too cool in the fall and spring. The cave is closed December, January, and February; open seven days a week the rest of the year.

Hawk Mountain Sanctuary
Hawk Mountain Road, Kempton
(610) 756–6961
www.hawkmountain.org
Atop the Kittatinny Ridge overlooking the Appalachian Mountains, the views from the lookout areas at this sanctuary are breathtaking. But the real draw is the annual migration of hawks, eagles, ospreys and more than 10 other species of birds of prey that begins in September. The greatest number of birds arrive in October and move on in November. Migrations of bird-watchers from all over the Northeast accompany the migrations of birds. Hawk Mountain has three trails, one of which connects to the Appalachian Trail. The trails lead to north and south lookouts and the River of Rocks. The trail to the south lookout is now wheelchair-accessible. The other two are not easy trails to hike. Even the shortest trail to the north lookout has some rough spots to negotiate. The 3.5-mile loop trail from the south lookout to the River of Rocks is very, very steep—almost gorge-like. If you are not in good shape, avoid the longer trails and take the short trail to the first lookout; it will still be worth the trip. Spotters at this lookout are college students studying the birds of prey for the Hawk Mountain Sanctuary Association and are very helpful in identifying the birds flying by or circling overhead. There is a wonderful gift shop and museum at the entrance.

Take Highway 33 to US 22 west and proceed to Interstate 78 westbound. From I-78, take exit 11 to Lenhartsville and go north on Highway 143 about 5 miles to the parking lot. You can also reach I-78 via I-80 to I-476 southbound (a.k.a. Northeast Extension of the Pennsylvania Turnpike).

Knoebels
Highway 487, Elysburg
(570) 672-2572, (800) 487-4386
www.knoebels.com

Although this family amusement park is 1.5 hours from the heart of the Poconos—almost twice as far as Dorney Park—most Pocono people go here. Knoebels is an old-fashioned amusement park—lots of rides and great fantasy architecture in a series of shaded groves. The bumper cars—because of their shape, speed, and the kind of rubber bumper they sport—are supposed to be the best in America (as rated by USA Weekend). The Phoenix, a vintage wooden roller coaster, was rescued from an amusement park in San Antonio, Texas, and reassembled here. A magazine that specializes in roller coasters rated it fifth-best in the United States. The newest roller coaster, the Twister, has also been rated among the top 20 in the country. The 1912 Carmel Carousel is gorgeous. You can sit on the stationary outer horses and grab for the brass ring or you can ride the galloping inner horses. The Knoebel family has a thing for carousels. They have assembled a museum with some beautiful carousel critters, and wonderfully out-of-tune pipe organs play all over the park. Live bands perform every weekend in May and September and every day during June, July, and August. There's also an anthracite museum with some interesting artifacts from the coal mines. If you like to get wet, bring your bathing suit. There's a pool and different water slides.

You can camp in your own tent or vehicle at Knoebels, or you can rent a cabin in their campground. Take a walk through the campground to see cabins built to resemble: a one-room schoolhouse; little log cabins; and a cross between a Conestoga wagon and a gypsy caravan. There's a good variety of food available at the park, and also lots of picnic pavilions. If you're visiting Knoebels with a group, you can reserve a pavilion ahead of time. They come complete with electricity (you'll see people carrying around electric pans) and grills.

Tourist bureaus offer all kinds of help. Call and you can get reservations, brochures, and even coupons sent to your home. If you can't locate a tourist bureau in the area where you're going, call the local Chamber of Commerce for information.

There's no admission charge to Knoebels; you pay by the ride. There are one-price options and bargain days, as well. Take I-80 west to exit 34, which leads to Highway 487 south (at Bloomsburg). Follow Highway 487 through Catawissa; you'll see signs for Knoebels.

Pennsylvania Dutch Country

A drive of about two hours from the heart of the Poconos takes you to another century. You'll see the Amish people in their black buggies, hex signs on barns, and wonderful produce stands. The people here farm with animals instead of machines, so the countryside is a patchwork of small farms, the likes of which you won't see anywhere else in this country, except in other Amish settlements. There are exhibits and interpretive centers. A particularly good one, the People's Place, 3513 Old Philadelphia Pike, Intercourse, (570) 768-7171, is at the entrance to Kitchen Kettle Village. When you're in Intercourse (that really is the name), notice the general store at the center of town with the phone booth in front of it. That's the storefront featured in the movie *Witness*. If you're in the market for furniture, the Amish make beautiful country oak pieces at reasonable prices. Ask for directions to the nearest Amish furniture barn. Make sure you try a family-style restaurant like Good'n Plenty in Smoketown. Call the Pennsylvania Dutch Convention and Visitors' Bureau, (570) 299-8901, (800) PADUTCH, for a free map and visitors guide.

To find Amish country, take Highway 33 or I-476 (the Northeast Extension of the Pennsylvania Turnpike) to US 22. Head

The Monroe Country Recreation Depart-
ment sponsors day trips throughout the
year. They also offer discount tickets to
ski mountains, amusement parks, and
some museums. For a list of trips and
discounts or to find out what's going on
that week, call (570) 992-4343.

west on US 22 from Highway 33 or, from
Interstate 476, take US 22 one exit east.
Grab Highway 309 south from US 22 and
go about 3 miles to U.S. Highway 222
west. US 222 will take you to the Lancaster area. You can get off on the country roads and wander, or you can take U.S.
Highway 30 east to Highway 340 east,
which takes you through Bird-in-Hand and
Intercourse (yeah . . . we know).

The Hudson Valley

Here's another area close to the Poconos
that would make an enormous Insiders'
Guide all by itself. A trip on the Internet
will reveal lots of good, detailed tourist
information on Hudson Valley sites. As you
enter New York State, look for information
booths that are waiting to pile tons of
tourist brochures into your eager hands.

Hudson Valley options are many. Less
than 45 minutes from Milford, near Warwick, NY, is Sugar Loaf, a crafts village
that claims an unbroken 250-year tradition of crafts. (Sugar Loaf insiders admit
that crafts were revived in the village during the 1960s.) The village has more than
50 shops, most of them featuring locally
produced, high-quality crafts. There's also
a lovely theater that offers professional
productions throughout the summer. Special events bring in even more crafts people. For more information on Sugar Loaf,
call (914) 469–9181. Nearby Warwick, NY
has specialty shops, historic sites, and
good restaurants. During late July through
mid-September, you can attend the New
York Renaissance Faire in Sterling Forest,
Tuxedo, NY, (914) 351–5171.

There are lots of astonishing mansions
and homes to visit along the Hudson
Valley. Sunnyside, West Sunnyside Lane,
Tarrytown, NY, (914) 638–8200, was
Washington Irving's storybook cottage.
Lindhurst, 635 South Broadway, Tarrytown,
(914) 631–4481, is a 19th-century gothic
revival mansion that overlooks the Hudson
River. At Philipsburg Manor, U.S. Highway
9, Sleepy Hollow, NY, (800) 448–4007,
you'll visit a working farm and gristmill
from the 18th-century. Kykuit, US 9, North
Tarrytown, NY, (914) 631–9491, was the
home to four generations of Rockefellers.
An extraordinary collection of 20th-century
sculpture by Henry Moore, Alexander
Calder, Louise Nevelson, and others graces
the gardens. Visits to Kykuit are primarily
by reservation, visitors without reservations are accommodated on a space-
available basis, so make reservations if you
want to be sure to get in. Van Cortlandt
Manor, South Riverside Avenue, Croton-on-
Hudson, NY, (914) 271–8981, is an 18th-
century estate with a fantastic kitchen and
a reconstructed 18th-century tavern. The
collection of vernacular Hudson Valley
furnishings is especially interesting. Montgomery Place, River Road, Annandale-on-
Hudson, (914) 758–5461, a 434-acre estate
and mansion, was once called the most
beautiful mansion in the nation. Vanderbilt
Mansion National Historic Site, US 9, Hyde
Park, NY, (914) 229–9115, is an impressive
Gilded Age home to one of America's
most prominent families. Just 2 miles
down the road, the Franklin Delano Roosevelt National Historic site, US 9, Hyde
Park, NY, (914) 229–9115, has Roosevelt's
home and a museum devoted to Franklin
and his wife, Eleanor.

If you're willing to go a little farther,
visit Old Rhinebeck Aerodrome, where
you can see antique and reproduction aircraft—in the air! Airshows run every weekend from mid-June to mid-October from
2:00 to 4:00 P.M. You'll see barnstorming
tricks on biplanes from the 1930s, a "dog-
fight" between a 1917 Fokker tri-plane and

a Sopwith Camel (pay attention to the rotary motor—the only speed control the pilot had was to turn it on and off). And, if you're lucky and conditions are right, they'll try to lift the oldest working aircraft in the country, a 1909 Bleriot, a few feet off the ground. This is one of two places in the world (the other's in England) where you can see so many pioneer airplanes flying, and it's an awesome show.

The museum and aerodrome are open daily May 15 through October 31. Take I-84 out of Milford, and in New York, catch I-87 going north. Get off at exit 19, and follow the signs to the Rhinecliff-Kingston Bridge. Catch New York Highway 199 over the bridge and follow signs for the aerodrome. Call (914) 758-8610 for more information. Woodstock and New Paltz are also nearby and worth a visit.

PARKS 🌳

Rush in a raft down a raging river or just picnic beside it while eagles, hawks, and vultures soar overhead. Hike around the top of Camelback Mountain or stand atop the cliffs that wall in the Delaware Water Gap and view horizons that will take your breath away. Or, simply commune with nature at the level of the forest floor amid hardwood trees, ferns, rhododendron, blackberry, blueberry, and a teeming population of bird and animal life.

Such is the pastoral side of the Poconos, where enormous acreage, preserved and protected from development, has been set aside for public use in state and federal parklands. Here, you can do all the things covered in some of our chapters: Fishing and Hunting; Recreation; In, On, and Around the Water; Our Natural World; and a few more not yet touched upon.

So come on in, take a hike, catch a fish, pick some berries, pitch your tent, feed a chipmunk, and enjoy the land.

NATIONAL RECREATION AREAS

Delaware Water Gap National Recreation Area
Park Headquarters, River Road, off U.S. Highway 209, just south of Bushkill
(570) 588-2452
www.nps.gov

The most recognizable of all the parks in the Poconos, this national recreation area has the advantage of the Delaware Water Gap as its calling card. It comprises almost 70,000 acres along a 40-mile stretch of the Delaware River from Interstate 84 to the Gap and includes land in both Pennsylvania and New Jersey.

To fully understand the park, guests should begin their day at one of the visitor centers. These are at Kittatinny Point off Interstate 80 on the Jersey side of the

river, in the Delaware Water Gap, (908) 496-4458, and on US 209 at Bushkill, (570) 588-7044.

The Kittatinny Point Visitor Center is open daily from 9:00 A.M. to 5:00 P.M. in late spring, summer, and early fall. The rangers give educational programs there in the summer. It's open 9:00 A.M. to 5:00 P.M., weekends only, late fall, winter, and early spring. Bushkill Visitor Center is open from 9:00 A.M. to 5:00 P.M. Memorial Day to Labor Day. The center could close earlier than expected, depending on the weather. Call before you go if there's any doubt. Park headquarters, on River Road in Bushkill, is open Monday through Friday 8:00 A.M. to 4:30 P.M., excluding federal holidays.

Sightseers can explore the many back roads throughout the park and be rewarded with waterfalls (see the Our Natural World chapter), lush woodlands, and beautiful fauna. Also watch for hawks and bald eagles, which winter here during January and February, but maintain a smaller presence throughout the year.

US 209 follows a close path along the river from Bushkill to Milford. Be sure to stop at Childs Recreation Area near Dingmans Ferry to view the waterfalls (see the Our Natural World chapter); they are a short, easy hike from the parking lot. The trail winds through a gorge filled with varied vegetation, deer, and birds. Being in a gorge surrounded by waterfalls and thick tree cover is a great way to beat the summer heat. Enjoy the scenic drive along the river, but be warned: The National Park Service enforces the 45-mph speed limit. So take your time, and enjoy the scenery.

The Delaware is considered an easy river for boaters because it is broad and flows slowly in most places. Thousands take to the water in canoes, inner tubes, rafts, and kayaks. Lifejackets must be available for all adults on anything that floats—even a tube. Children 12 and younger must wear lifejackets at all times. The rangers are vigilant about this, because they are very concerned about drownings. You'll get a ticket if they catch you in a canoe, on a raft, or in a tube without a lifejacket. Access points are located every 8 to 10 miles to accommodate daytrippers. More than 20 independent companies are licensed to rent equipment to boaters. Information on them and a map of all the access points can be obtained at either visitors' center or at the park headquarters. Also see our In, On, and Around the Water and Recreation chapters for details about some of these companies.

Two beaches are recommended for swimming: Smithfield Beach, at the south end of the park north of Shawnee-on-Delaware, and Milford Beach, right before Milford at the northern end. Both have lifeguards on duty every day, picnic areas, and plenty of parking. They are open from mid-June to Labor Day.

Recreation fees are charged at Smithfield Beach, Milford Beach, and Bushkill Access in Pennsylvania as well as at Depew Recreation Site in New Jersey. The fees are:

- Private vehicle (up to seven occupants), $5.00 per vehicle on weekdays
- Private vehicle (up to seven occupants), $7.00 per vehicle on weekends and holidays
- Vehicles with eight or more occupants, $1.00 per person per day
- Pedestrian or bicycle riders, $1.00 per person per day
- Annual Pass, $40 per vehicle (A second annual pass for a vehicle registered to the same name and address costs $20.)
- Annual Walk-in Pass, $10 per person
- Golden Age/Access Passport 50 percent discount

The beaches are beautiful, but a cozier spot for swimming is Hidden Lake, which is surrounded by trees and tucked away in the mountains near Smithfield Beach. To

The Delaware River may be shallow and slow, but it can also be treacherous. Swim only where there are lifeguards, and never try to swim across the river. If you get caught in a current, don't fight it; go with it and let it carry you to a calmer spot.

get there, take River Road to Hollow Road, and follow the signs to Shawnee Mountain. North of Shawnee, take a right on Hidden Lake Road and look for the signs for Hidden Lake (it's another mile or two). From US 209, take Hollow Road, and turn left on Hidden Lake Road just before reaching Shawnee Mountain. There is no charge for the use of this lovely lake. While swimming is permitted in the Delaware River, strong currents and sharp drop-offs make it unsafe in many areas. Never swim across the river; your best bet is to swim in the lifeguard-protected areas. You may splash in most of the creeks in the park; however, you're not allowed within 50 feet of the top of any waterfall. Swimming is also prohibited at Dingmans Falls, Childs Recreation Site, and Van Campens Glen.

Even model airplane buffs will find a user-friendly field where they can fly their motorized toys. It's called Hialeah Air Park, an open tract of land just north of Smithfield Beach that's leased from the National Park Service by the Roxbury Area Model Airplane Club.

Hunting and fishing also are permitted in the recreation area. (See our Fishing and Hunting chapter for details.)

There are extensive trails for hikers; maps are available at visitors centers. Approximately 25 miles of the Appalachian Trail are within the recreation area, mostly on the New Jersey side. A trail originating at the Dunnfield parking area off I–80 in New Jersey takes hikers to the top of Mount Tammany where they are rewarded with a breathtaking panorama of the Stroudsburgs and most of the Poconos. What better treat after a long walk than the opportunity to relax on cliffs at the top of the Delaware Water Gap! (See the "Hiking" section of our Recreation chapter.) Mountain bikes are permitted on roads and on the McDade Trail in the park. Five miles of the trail have been completed, between Hialeah Picnic Area and the Turn Farm. The McDade Trail will eventually cover more than 40 miles, from the Appalachian Trail in Delaware Water Gap to Milford. (See our Recreation chapter for details.)

Other sites of note within the recreation area are Peters Valley Craft Village (New Jersey), where craftspeople live, teach their art, and sell their wares; Milbrook Village (New Jersey), a re-creation of a late 19th-century rural community; and the Pocono Environmental Education Center (see this chapter's Close-up).

In winter, lakes and ponds are ideal for ice fishing. And several trails are open to cross-country skiers. Snowmobiles are not permitted in the park. (See our Winter Sports chapter for details.) Of course, these winter activities depend on the weather, especially the ice fishing, and we have had some warm winters lately. Call ahead if your heart is set on ice fishing or cross-country skiing.

Upper Delaware Scenic and Recreational River
NY Highway 97 between Port Jervis, NY and Hancock, NY
(570) 685-4871
April–October: (845) 252-7100
(24-hour river conditions)
www.nps.gov

Beginning at the northern boundary of the Delaware Water Gap National Recreation Area, this stretch of the Delaware River runs north to Hancock, New York. If offers some of the best boating opportunities in the Poconos.

The river runs through more than 73 miles of widely changing scenery and past historic buildings, including the remains of the canal system that once was the main means of transporting goods.

The fishing is outstanding. The most popular game fish are brown trout, rainbow trout, smallmouth bass, walleyes, shad (in spring), and American eels. Large stone walls resembling ski jumps in the middle of the river are eel weirs used by residents to trap the snake-like fish that many consider a delicacy. (See our Fishing and Hunting chapter.)

While most of the river is considered tame, with very little whitewater, there are a few places where rapids present challenges to boaters. The most difficult is Skinners Falls, just south of Milanville. This section of the river is classified Class I in terms of difficulty, meaning there are few riffles, small waves, and few obstructions. However, be careful around Skinners Falls—the rapids here can be very dangerous. The National Park Service recommends scouting them from land before attempting passage.

Lucky visitors who carefully watch might catch a glimpse of a bald eagle, osprey, great blue heron, or egret. More common sights are hawks, owls, and turkey buzzards. Your best time to watch for eagles is in January, when large numbers of them feed in the Upper Delaware.

On land, keep a sharp eye out for minks, muskrats, beavers, deer, bears, skunks, porcupines, snapping turtles, and raccoons, the latter of which are notorious camp thieves that will steal any food they can find, usually in their forays by night.

Two historic sites of note are Roebling's Aqueduct, the oldest existing wire suspension bridge in the United States, and the Zane Grey Museum, housed in the celebrated Western novelist's former residence. (See our Arts and Culture and Attractions chapters for more information.)

Almost all the land along the river is private property. Permission from the owners is necessary before camping overnight. Several companies operate campgrounds and rent canoes, rafts, and tubes. Because so much of the land is private, there is virtually no hiking on federal lands within the park. In 1999, the Park Service entered into an agreement with the Boy Scouts of America to permit limited public access to one of their trails at Ten Mile River Scout Camps. You may enjoy a strenuous 3-mile round trip on the Tusten Mountain Trail (Yellow Dot), accessible from the Ten Mile River public access. Hours are restricted (8:30 A.M. to 6:00 P.M.) and no fires or camping allowed.

The National Park Service headquarters for the Upper Delaware Scenic and Recreational River is at approximately the area's midpoint in Narrowsburg, New York. Other towns in the Upper Delaware are Matamoras, Lackawaxen, and Shohola in Pennsylvania and Port Jervis, Barryville, and Callicoon in New York.

Car travelers can best enjoy the views by driving on New York Highway 97, which closely follows the river and is a gorgeous road.

STATE PARKS

There are seven state parks in the Poconos, covering more than 35,000 acres. All but one are open to the public throughout the year, and all are equipped to accommodate disabled visitors with special parking and picnicking facilities. There are, however, a few prohibitions applicable to all visitors. Pets are allowed in some state parks; call ahead if you're traveling with Rover. They must be kept on a leash at all times, and they are never allowed in swimming or camping areas. Alcoholic beverages are prohibited, and no glass containers are allowed on rivers, at beaches, or near swimming areas. Open fires are allowed only in designated areas, but hunting and fishing during state-designated seasons are permitted if you have a license.

Day-use areas such as beaches and trails, are open from 8:00 A.M. to sunset. Swimming in the river and lakes is permitted from 11:00 A.M. to 7:00 P.M. from Memorial Day weekend to Labor Day weekend only where and when lifeguards are on duty. (See our In, On, and Around the Water chapter for more about swimming.)

Although the Upper Delaware Scenic and Recreational River Park encompasses 73 miles of river, only 30 acres are federally owned. The rest of the land along the river is privately owned. If you're planning to camp, make reservations in advance at campgrounds or lodging along the way. The parks' Web site, www.nps.gov, has a listing of campgrounds and lodging.

Given the size of Pocono parks, camping facilities cover a wide range, from modern cabins to primitive tenting sites. Fees range from $123 a night for nonresidents and $104 for state residents for a modern cabin sleeping up to 12 people all the way down to a nonresident fee of $13 to $11 for residents—for a rustic campsite devoid of electricity or running water. Some sites provide huts, tents, and yurts for those who arrive without tents of their own. Reduced weekly fees also are available.

The Poconos constitute a hiker's paradise, with wild trains inside and outside of its extensive park system. All seven state parks have designated trails, and rather than detail them here, we have created a special "Hiking" section in our Recreation chapter to outline hikes.

Check with state park ranger offices at the entrances of all seven areas for maps and information as well as fees and availability of sites you desire in the list that follows.

Stroudsburg/East Stroudsburg

Big Pocono State Park
Camelback Road, Tannersville
(570) 894-8336
www.dcnr.state.pa.us
From the summit of 1,306-acre Big Pocono State Park you can see much of northeastern Pennsylvania as well as parts of New Jersey and New York. On the top

CLOSE-UP

Pocono Environmental Education Center: The 200,000-acre Classroom

The typical high school nature class takes place in a room with gray concrete walls covered with maps and pictures of assorted wildlife. If students are lucky, there may be a stuffed squirrel or a fish tank in one corner. Textbooks attempt to convey nature's wonders through pictures and drawings.

Then there's the Pocono Environmental Education Center, the largest residential center of environmental education in the Western Hemisphere.

At PEEC, students and the general public learn firsthand about natural systems and develop a better appreciation for the beauty that surrounds us every day.

Once a resort named Honeymoon Haven, PEEC was created after the National Park Service acquired the land through the Tocks Island project. Started as a joint venture between the Park Service and Keystone Junior College in 1972, the facility became privately owned and nonprofit in 1986.

PEEC covers 38 acres, including 13 miles of hiking trails. Classes and workshops are conducted on the public land controlled by the federal government.

During the week, students—usually grades seven to nine—come to PEEC on field trips lasting two to three days. Teachers receive a list of available activities to choose from. Scheduled events usually include pond study, plant and animal study, and canoeing. Efforts are made to keep classroom work to a minimum and let the kids have fun while they learn.

The students, most of whom come from New York City and urban New Jersey, sleep in the 47 guest cabins that, years ago, housed young newlyweds.

The trip down River Road in the Delaware Water Gap National Recreation area is particularly scenic. You'll find many beautiful spots to view the river along this wooded, rural road. Just be careful of deer and wild turkeys crossing in front of you.

of interconnecting trails, ranging from smooth and flat to rugged and steep, wind through the woods. The mountaintop is encircled by a paved Rim Road, so you do not even need to leave your car to admire the countryside. Fifty picnic tables are available. The South Trail is open to horseback riders. Approximately 800 acres of the park may be used by hunters, including an area that is accessible for hunters with disabilities.

of Camelback Mountain, Big Pocono is accessible to both hikers who enjoy rugged terrain and passing motorists who simply want to enjoy the view. Seven miles

The land for the park was owned by Henry Cattell around the turn of the century. He so loved the view from his prop-

Because of their past use, the cabins are much better equipped than might be expected and feature huge, tiled bathrooms that cry out for heart-shaped tubs.

The focus of the experience at PEEC is nature, and the center offers a variety of natural places to explore and study: shady hemlock gorges, the Delaware River, ponds teaming with insect and amphibian life, upland and lowland forests, the unique flora and fauna found in boreal bogs, a fossil quarry, and so much more.

On weekends, year round, PEEC offers workshops for anyone interested in learning more about nature. Teachers also can earn credit for participating in programs at the center. Among the many workshops available are programs devoted to nature study, photography, environmental issues, bird watching, and family camping.

PEEC's staff maintains the grounds and buildings, leads the workshops, and runs the day-to-day operation of what is essentially a hotel devoted to nature. Guests register in the main building, which houses the library, bookstore, offices, a swimming pool, and classrooms (formerly the bowling alleys in the honeymoon days).

The countryside surrounding the buildings is perfect for nature study because so much flora, fauna, and landscape is represented: farmland, forests, ponds, a river, and waterfalls.

A beautiful resort that could easily have been destroyed or abandoned has been reclaimed as a unique center for nature study. Twenty-five thousand people come to PEEC every year to learn more about their environment and how to protect it. PEEC has worked so well, the National Park Service is considering replicating the system in parks across the country, and people from other countries, especially Russia, have come to participate in PEEC's international classroom.

For more information, call PEEC at (570) 828–2319 or go to www.peec.org.

erty that he wanted to share it. Cattell constructed a stone cabin at the summit that, for years, remained unlocked and open to anyone as shelter. In 1928, 12 years after Cattell's death, the Pennsylvania Game Commission purchased the land. It became a state park in 1954. Cattell might be satisfied to know that his land is now enjoyed by even more people than he could have imagined.

The road leading to the park is very steep and winding. Vehicles with trailers in tow should not attempt it. The park, which is open daily until sunset, closed in December and reopens in spring as weather permits.

Mount Pocono Area

Gouldsboro State Park
Highway 507, 1.5 miles south of Gouldsboro
(570) 894–8336
www.dcnr.state.pa.us
Most people visit Gouldsboro for the hunting, trapping, dog training, and fishing. Its 2,800 acres of land and 250-acre

lake are a sportsman's paradise. (See our Fishing and Hunting chapter for more information.) There are 10 miles of trails, including a sometimes demanding 5.8-mile loop.

The park has a designated swimming area with lifeguards that is open from Memorial Day weekend to Labor Day as well as plenty of wooded picnic groves. Boating is permitted in non-powered and electric-powered craft.

Promised Land State Park
Highway 390, 10 miles north of Canadensis
(570) 676-3428
www.dcnr.state.pa.us

Two lakes add to the beauty of this 2,971-acre park. Promised Lake is large, with an island in the middle, accessible by a bridge. The nature trail around the island is a lovely place to walk in the summer and a great cross-country ski trail in the winter. From the island, the lake looks mysterious, with coves and branches reaching spots you can't see. Four campgrounds provide more than 500 campsites for tents and trailers. In addition, 12 rustic cabins, one wheelchair accessible, equipped with electricity and private bath are available for rent. All are near recreational opportunities.

Swimming and picnicking are popular ways to spend an afternoon at Promised Land. The guarded beach area is open from Memorial Day weekend to Labor Day.

During summer, the park staff offers environmental education programs on topics such as plant and animal study. The park has a small museum containing arti-

facts, depictions of the natural features of the area, and the history of the Civilian Conservation Corps, the organization responsible for building many of the state park facilities.

Boating, hiking, and fishing are permitted on Promised Lake. Ice fishing is allowed, weather permitting, on both lakes, and again, in the right conditions you may ice-skate on Promised Lake. With 50 miles of trails, there's more than you can hike, and there will always be one more trail that you'll have to hike next time you visit. The terrain is varied and goes through rhododendron thickets and blazing forests. In early fall, the mushrooms are spectacular. Hikes can take you to waterfalls and a glacial lake. Come in mid-July when the high-bush blueberries are ripe, and don't be surprised if you see a bear. Hunting is permitted in one section of the park. Egypt Meadows Lake, a man-made body of water was constructed in 1935. Before the lake was built, the entire area was covered with hollow, soft meadow grass. The famed Dorflinger Glass Works in White Mills harvested the grass and used it to pack glass to be shipped.

Snowmobiles are permitted only on designated trails. Selected trails are open to visitors on horseback. No rentals are available. Bicyclists can enjoy a hardy 6.5-mile ride around the lake on Promised Land Road, but no bikes are allowed on hiking trails. See the "Mountain Biking" section of our Recreation chapter and our Winter Sports chapter for details about these and other related activities.

Tobyhanna State Park
Highway 423, 2.1 miles north of Tobyhanna
(570) 894-8336
www.dcnr.state.pa.us

From early April to December, this park's 140-site campground caters to outdoor lovers. There are no flush toilets or showers, so be prepared to rough it. There are playgrounds for the kids and a swimming area with lifeguards. A beach is open Memorial Day weekend to Labor Day. Dress for cold

Hikers on the Appalachian Trail in the Delaware Water Gap National Recreation Area can expect to see predominantly small trees, mostly chestnut oaks. The rocky landscape combined with the steep slopes causes most of the soil to wash away. Also, the ridge is exposed to all the extremes nature has to offer.

nights because of the high elevation—nearly 2,000 feet above sea level.

Four picnic areas—three wooded and one open—provide 300 tables. There also is a picnic pavilion.

Ice-skating and snowmobiling are permitted in winter.

Fishing, hunting, and boating are featured activities at Tobyhanna. Electric-powered boats are permitted on the lake, and many of the park's 5,440 acres are open to hunters during all recognized hunting seasons. Hunting is not permitted in some areas—generally those close to recreation facilities. Rowboats and canoes can be rented on an hourly, half-day, or full-day basis. (See our In, On, and Around the Water chapter for more information.)

The land encompassing Tobyhanna State Park was once used as an artillery firing range, and a few years ago, old, unexploded artillery shells were found. The entire park was closed and an extensive cleanup was undertaken, but you will still find signs warning you about unexploded artillery shells. Though it is unlikely, if you see a rusty metal pointed cylinder, 10 inches to 2 feet long, **DO NOT TOUCH OR DISTURB IT.** Report it to the park rangers as quickly as possible, so they can dispose of it safely.

West End

Beltzville State Park
Off US 209, 5 miles east of Lehighton
(610) 377-0045
www.dcnr.state.pa.us
When the U.S. Army Corps of Engineers created a flood-control project in Carbon County called Beltzville Dam, it also gave birth to this huge recreation center that provides popular weekend getaways for residents and tourists alike (nearly 500,000 people visit annually).

The park is among farms, orchards, and forested areas along Pohopoco Creek. Most recreation is centered around the 7-mile-long lake, which is stocked for fishing and open to most types of recreational

Hikes with the Poconos' most popular naturalist, John Serrao, are a great way to learn about the area's flora and fauna. He runs a series in spring and fall through the Monroe Career and Technical Institute. Skytop's guests walk with John weekly, and the state parks sponsor walks in the summer—watch the Pocono Record for dates and times.

boating. Waterskiing is permitted in a designated area. Docks and launch ramps are provided.

Hunters are allowed access to 1,707 acres of the park's land during authorized hunting seasons. Trapping and dog training are allowed in season.

Most people visit Beltzville to swim near the 525-foot sand beach open and guarded from 11:00 A.M. to 7:00 P.M. daily from Memorial Day weekend to Labor Day. Showers, food concessions, and first aid are available. One thing that makes Beltzville State Park unique is that there's an area of the lakeshore where fossils are fairly abundant. You're allowed to hunt them there and take some home.

An interpreter leads environmental education programs from March through November at the visitor center and amphitheater. Other activities include hiking on 15 miles of trails, snowmobiling, cross-country skiing on fields within the park and on the 9-mile Trinity Gorge ski trail, ice boating (see our Winter Sports chapter), sightseeing from Overlook Rotunda off Pohopoco Drive, and visiting the old covered bridge, which was relocated to the park and provides access to the beach from the picnic areas. Nearly all the park's facilities, except the trails, are wheelchair accessible.

Hickory Run State Park
Highway 534, near Hickory Run
(570) 443-0400
www.dcnr.state.pa.us
In the southwestern corner of the Pocono Mountains, Hickory Run has an unusual

feature—a striking boulder field that has been designated a National Natural Landmark. Part of the park was once glaciated and features sphagnum moss bogs and different flora and fauna from the unglaciated part. A remote mountain stream here offers a viable population of native brook trout. The 15,500-acre park has 43 miles of trails for hiking, as well as facilities for camping, hunting, fishing, and nearly every other outdoor recreation activity imaginable.

The campground's 381 sites for tents and trailers are equipped with modern facilities such as toilets, showers, and electricity. A camp store sells groceries and gear.

A guarded, sand beach is open to swimmers from Memorial Day to Labor Day. A concession stand provides sandwiches and snacks, which can be enjoyed in the large (475 tables) picnic area.

This enormous park has a special historical feature in the remains of sawmills and dams that early residents relied upon for power and basic building materials. Lumbering was a major industry here in the 19th century. Prior to the Civil War, the area was known as "Shades of Death" because of the thick forests of hemlock and white pine. According to local history, many early settlers died in these woods when, in the course of fleeing Indian war parties, they became disoriented in the trees and swamps and starved. (See our History chapter for more details about that perilous time.)

Many lumber camps and villages were created in the mid-1800s to handle the demand for wood from this area. The hemlock bark was used for tanning, the white pine for building material. All of the original trees were cut down by 1880. The park office and chapel are buildings that were part of the village of Hickory Run in the lumbering days.

Most of the park is open to hunters and anglers, except for those areas that are close to swimming, hiking, or other recreation areas.

Winter options are snowmobiling, cross-country skiing, ice-skating, sledding, and tobogganing.

To access the park, take I-80 to exit 274 and proceed 6 miles on Highway 534 toward Hickory Run.

Lehigh Gorge State Park
White Haven Entrance: off Highway 940, through the Thriftway parking lot
Rockport Entrance: Rockport Road
Glen Onoko Entrance: off Highway 903
(570) 443-0400
www.dcnr.state.pa.us
As the name implies, this park is filled with steep cliffs and rock outcrops as well as thick vegetation. Its northern end is accessible in White Haven; the southern point of entry is in Rockport, where you'll find the park administration office.

The Lehigh River is considered one of the most scenic in America, and this park's major draw is whitewater rafting. This is the most challenging area in the Poconos for boaters, canoeists, rafters, and kayakers, because it contains the roughest water in the region. Inexperienced rafters are discouraged from taking this section of the Lehigh River without expert guides. Entry to the river is confined mostly to designated areas—White Haven, Rockport, and Jim Thorpe.

Late March through June is the best period for the whitewater experience because of scheduled dam releases. The flow of water into the river is controlled by the U.S. Army Corps of Engineers at Francis E. Walter Dam. Flow rate information is available from the U.S. Army Corps of Engineers' Web site, www.nap-wc.usace.army.mil. It can range from 250 to 5,000 cubic feet per second; the higher the rate, the more dangerous the water.

Licensed commercial outfitters approved to operate in Lehigh Gorge State Park are: Whitewater Challenger, (800) 443-8554; Pocono Whitewater, (800) WHITEWATER; Jim Thorpe River Adventures, (800) 424-7238; and Whitewater Rafting and Paintball Adventures,

(800) 876-0285. (See our In, On, and Around the Water and Recreation chapters for additional information.)

Hunting and fishing are permitted throughout Lehigh Gorge's 4,548 acres, as are trapping and training dogs. Whitewater rafting between the Francis E. Walter Dam and White Haven is discouraged in order to promote fishing here. This area is stocked with trout and is very popular with anglers. (Check out our Fishing and Hunting chapter for details.)

Twenty-six miles of abandoned railroad grade are available for hiking, bicycling, and sightseeing (see the "Mountain Biking" and "Hiking" sections in our Recreation chapter); no motorized vehicles are allowed. The scenery is a memorable combination of cliffs, dense vegetation, and the weathered remains of the region's extensive canal system. The railroad grade is a well-known spot for mountain biking, and people come from all over to roll over it. Hiking in the gorge is allowed, but perilous. Be aware that an accident here could be life threatening. Interpretive programs and guided walks are offered April through September.

In winter, the railroad grade is ideal for cross-country skiing. A 15-mile stretch from White Haven to Penn Haven Junction is open to snowmobiles.

NATURAL AREAS AND ENVIRONMENTAL CENTERS

Stroudsburg/East Stroudsburg

Monroe County Environmental Education Center
8050 Running Valley Road, Stroudsburg
(570) 629-3061
www.mcconservation.org
Founded in 1976, the center presents a diverse group of nature programs and promotes environmental awareness through hands-on study of the natural environment of the Poconos. Programs include bird

If you're traveling along New York Highway 97 in Upper Delaware Scenic and Recreational River Park and the road seems familiar, there's a reason. It's a popular road to shoot for car commercials. When the camera tightens up on the shot, it looks like a dramatic, twisty road along a cliff we always presumed ran along the ocean.

walks, school visits, maple sugaring, and nature walks. Visit the Web site for information on upcoming events, or become a member of the organization. An individual membership costs $10, and you will receive a quarterly newsletter that details the center's activities.

The facility's Education Center is open Monday through Friday and the second and fourth Saturday of the month throughout the year and houses a library, gift shop, classroom, observation deck, and numerous exhibits. The building is on the grounds of the Kettle Creek Sanctuary, a 120-acre preserve with 2.5 miles of well-marked trails that are open every day.

From Highway 611 near Bartonsville, turn east onto Rim Rock Drive, right on North Easton-Belmont Pike and bear right onto Running Valley Road. The center is 0.7 mile on your left.

Tannersville Cranberry Bog
Bog Road, Tannersville
(570) 629-3061
www.mcconservation.org
Tannersville Cranberry Bog is a unique natural attraction in the Pocono Mountains. Visitors to the bog are struck by how different it is from the surrounding countryside. The flora more resembles the Canadian wilderness than northeastern Pennsylvania.

The Tannersville bog is the southernmost low-altitude boreal bog along the Eastern Seaboard. Some of the rarest plants in the state grow here. Two of these—the pitcher plant and the sundew plant—are insectivores; that's right, they feast on bugs. The bog's orchids are quite colorful, as are the dwarf mistletoe, yellow-eyed grass, yellow lady slipper, and rose pogonia. The skunk cabbage lives up to its name, as you will quickly smell.

The Nature Conservancy maintains the bog. Two nature trails are open to the public for hiking and cross-country skiing throughout the year. The trailheads are located along Bog Road near Cranberry Creek. Maps may be obtained at the Monroe County Environmental Education Center.

However, to enter the bog itself, you must be part of a scheduled bog walk or obtain a tour guide and special permission. Guided walks, open to the public, are held weekly from June to Labor Day. The requested donation is $3.00 per person. During the two-hour tour, you will learn about the bog's formation, the unique plant and animal life here and some handy general environmental knowledge. Call for more information. Do not go expecting to pick or buy cranberries.

From the intersection of Highways 611 and 715, take Highway 611 south and turn left on Cherry Lane, then turn right on Bog Road.

West End

The Nature Conservancy
in Northeastern Pennsylvania
Long Pond Road, near Pocono Raceway
Long Pond
(570) 643-7922
www.nature.org
For anyone wishing to learn all about black bears, ospreys, white-tailed deer, and a host of other fauna, and then take

up woodcarving, blueberry picking, and the exhaustive study of birds, this 24,000-acre land-conservation district is the place to go. The center is part of the Pennsylvania Chapter of the nonprofit Nature Conservancy, which has listed the Pocono region as one of the world's "Last Great Places." It offers a varied menu of programs in summer for adults and children. Preregistration is required, and most of the programs, if not specified for children, welcome everybody 10 and older. The Conservancy also sponsors periodic treks through the Tannersville Cranberry Bog, Lost Lakes, Thomas Darling Preserve, and other Nature Conservancy preserves.

Mauch Chunk Lake Park
Lentz Trail Highway, between Summit Hill and Jim Thorpe
(570) 325-3669
207.21.252.76/park/
The park's 2,500 acres offer campers and daily visitors all the expected activities—hiking, jogging, swimming, fishing, boating, softball, volleyball, horseshoes, and cross-country skiing, to name a handful.

The campground here is open from mid-April through late October (see the "Camping" section of our Recreation chapter). Site reservations are required.

The park is near four outstanding hiking trails, and maps are available. The 6-mile Shoreline Trail is favored by school groups because of the varieties of plants and animals that can be seen along it.

Milford/Lake Wallenpaupack Area

Lacawac Sanctuary
Lacawac Road, north shore of Lake Wallenpaupack
(570) 689-9494
www.lacawac.org
Named after the Lenape Indian word for "fork" (Minisink Path, a significant Indian trail, passed through here), Lacawac Sanctuary is a nature preserve. Within its 500

acres alongside Lake Wallenpaupack are a unique 52-acre glacial lake, Lake Lacawac, and mixed forest ecosystem.

Among the programs offered here are history tours, environmental education classes, guided nature walks, and a nature shop.

A mile-long public hiking trail, the Maurice Braun Nature Trail, loops through the property to overlook Lake Wallenpaupack. This leisurely one-hour walk begins in the sanctuary parking lot.

The sanctuary is maintained as a wildlife refuge. Lacawac Sanctuary Foundation is a nonprofit corporation dedicated to protecting Lake Lacawac and promoting the property's use for research and education. It is funded largely by the annual contributions of members.

The sanctuary is available (by appointment) for field trips by school groups. Under adult supervision provided by the school, students study flora, fauna, and geology.

From I–84 take exit 20 north toward Lake Wallenpaupack.

Lake Wallenpaupack
US 6 and Highway 590
southeast of Hawley
(800) 354–8383
www.pplweb.com
Since this 13-mile long, 5,700-acre lake was created in 1926 by the Pennsylvania Power & Light Company, it technically does not qualify as a "natural area," but don't tell that to the fishermen and boat enthusiasts who use it year round.

There are family camping sites along the lake, maintained by PPL. (See the "RV Parks" section in our Accommodations chapter.) Boat accesses are available. Three natural areas provide trails for hiking and cross-country skiing, and four islands have picnic facilities. See our In, On, and Around the Water chapter for information on boating, swimming, and camping at Lake Wallenpaupack.

RECREATION

Remember when you were a kid and your mother told you to go out and play? Past puberty, most of us have forgotten how to do that. Only in the vague memory that haunts our stressed-out, survival-oriented lives do we remember sandlot baseball, pom-pom-pullaway, and kick the can on warm summer evenings, or skating and building snowmen with carrot noses and black-coal eyes when the world was white with winter—all of which constitutes the best of all possible reasons to live in, or at least visit, the Poconos.

Here, you'll hear your mother's voice again, loud and clear, 12 months of the year, whatever your age or lifestyle. Water activities, winter sports, golf, hunting and fishing, attractions, and festivals and events all are covered in their own chapters. But that only scratches the surface. What follows here is a catalog of rest and recreation that often comes through vigorous physical activity. Either way, it all translates into sheer, unalloyed fun.

So do it: Go out and play. You'll never have a better opportunity.

ADMISSION PRICE

The following is a price code for admission to the businesses listed in this chapter. The price listed is for adults. Children and senior citizens' admissions are usually lower. In cases where you may want to play more than one game or take more than one ride, please be advised that the price listed is for one game or ride only.

$10.00 or less	$
$10.01 to $15.00	$$
$15.01 to $20.00	$$$
$20.01 or more	$$$$

Bicycles and all-terrain vehicles are barred from hiking trails in all state parks.

BOWLING

A family sport for generations, bowling appeals to everyone because it requires no particular physical abilities to participate. You do not have to be on a conditioning program to have a good time knocking down pins.

Bowling alleys have all the equipment you need. To choose the correct bowling ball from the house selection, pick a comfortable weight. Bowling balls generally weigh between 8 and 16 pounds. Your thumb should fit loosely in the thumbhole, enough to rotate freely. With your thumb in place, stretch your fingers over the finger holes. The big knuckle of each finger should be a quarter-inch past the near side of the holes. Always check for nicks in the holes that might cut your fingers.

The ideal bowling approach takes four steps. You should end leading with the foot opposite your throwing hand. If not, you stand a good chance of hitting your knee or foot with the ball, a potentially embarrassing and certainly painful accident.

Experienced bowlers use the marks on the lanes to determine where to throw the ball. It is much easier to aim for a mark closer to you that to just throw at the pins.

During the week, bowling alleys have leagues that use most of the lanes from approximately 6:00 to 9:00 P.M. Call ahead to make sure a lane is available.

Stroudsburg/East Stroudsburg

Skylanes $
Eagle Valley Mall, Highway 447
East Stroudsburg
(570) 421-7680
With 24 lanes, several pool tables, and arcade games, Skylanes has something to

entertain everyone. Computers keep score for you, giving you more time to kick back with a beer, which is sold at the counter. A pro shop sells bowling accessories.

Skylanes is open every day. Call for hours and reservations.

Mount Pocono Area

Mountain Lanes $
Highway 390, Mountainhome
(570) 595-2518
www.mountainlanes.com
With a cozy eight lanes, Mountain Lanes is small yet perfect for families. The kids will not get out of sight. Arcade games and a full-service snack bar are available. You don't have to know how to keep score; the alley's scoreboard will do it for you.

Mountain Lanes is open every day except Sunday. Call ahead to make sure it's open. On Saturday, designated Glow-bowl Night, bowlers, dressed in white, take their shots in the eerie glow of black lights with a fog machine adding atmosphere.

Alcoholic beverages are not served, but beer or wine may be brought in. Call ahead for group reservations for parties of more than 10.

Summit Lanes $
3 Park Drive East, Pocono Summit
(570) 839-9635
Summit Lanes, which opened in 1998, claims to be the newest state-of-the-art bowling center within 300 miles, with 36 New Brunswick Synthetic Anvil high scoring lanes and an automatic scoring system. They also have six billiard tables, an arcade with a redemption center, a pro shop, a children's playroom, a meeting room, food court, and lounge. They offer "cosmic bowling" on Saturday afternoons, which is glow bowling under another name, with black lights making your whites and various Dayglo painted items

glow cosmically. Summit Lanes offers open bowling every day of the week; call for specific hours.

West End

Haja Lanes $
Delaware Avenue, Palmerton
(610) 826-2450
Automatic scoring is available on all 12 lanes at Haja. A small snack bar sells hot dogs, sodas, and pizza. Other diversions include a few pinball machines, arcade games, and a jukebox.

Alcoholic beverages are not sold and may not be consumed in the building. Lanes are open to the public at varied hours Thursday through Sunday. Call for specific hours.

Fritz's Lanes $
Second and South Streets, Lehighton
(610) 377-5022
Fritz's Lanes offers computerized scoring, a snack bar, arcade games, a pro shop, and a jukebox.

The lanes are open to the public every day but Thursday. However, leagues occupy many lanes from approximately 6:00 to 9:00 P.M. every day during the week and on Saturday morning. Call for reservations.

Cypress Lanes $
Fourth and Cypress Streets, Lehighton
(610) 377-4570
A throwback to bowling's golden days, Cypress still uses the old-fashioned paper score sheets to keep track of the action on its six lanes. You can bring beer with you. A snack bar sells refreshments, and a small game room has pinball and arcade machines. Cypress offers open bowling every day but Thursday and Sunday. Call for hours—with only six lanes, you want to be sure there's one available for you.

Milford/Lake Wallenpaupack Area

Wallenpaupack Bowling Center $
U.S. Highway 6, east of Hawley
(570) 226-8499
Twelve lanes equipped with automatic scoring await bowlers at Wallenpaupack. An arcade and a snack bar are provided. Smoking and alcoholic beverages are not permitted. On Friday and Saturday nights, this alley goes cosmic for Ultra Bowl, with black lights and a fog machine.

Wallenpaupack Bowling Center is open to the public every day, but call for lane availability during the week owing to league play.

FITNESS CENTERS

Even though some fitness centers are for members only, others have a daily rate, so you can go there once, twice, or however many times you want. If the fitness center has a daily rate, the dollar signs in the listing indicate the price range to expect. No dollar signs are used on facilities you have to join to use. Some centers are part of national networks and allow members of that network to use their facilities free or at reduced rates. Those are noted. Most fitness centers will allow you to come in and try their facilities if you're thinking of becoming a member; call for information.

Delaware Water Gap/ Shawnee-on-Delaware

Pocmont Resort Fitness Center
Bushkill Falls Road, Bushkill
(570) 588-4733
www.pocmont.com
As part of a resort, Pocmont's newly built fitness center is geared toward pampering as well as toning. The center is open to monthly and yearly memberships from the public, and they urge you to grab your sneakers and a bathing suit and try it for

the day, free. Membership includes use of their beautiful indoor and outdoor pools, dry and steam saunas, towel service, and a very good selection of brand-new exercise equipment, including a Paramount equipment circuit, free weights, and an exceptional cardiovascular theater with treadmills, recumbent and upright stationary bikes, and lots more. The staff includes personal trainers, exercise physiologists, as well as post-rehab and sports management specialists.

Stroudsburg/East Stroudsburg

Pocono Family YMCA
809 Main Street, Stroudsburg
(570) 421-2525
Highway 191, Cresco
(570) 595-2730
Foxmoor Village
Highway 209, Marshalls Creek
(570) 223-9622
www.poconoymca.org
This very active community Y serves 6,000 members and program participants with swimming lessons, child care, day camps, sports, CPR, first aid, dog obedience classes, exercise classes, and much more. Membership is by the year and includes use of the facilities and lots of free classes. The Y also participates in the AWAY (Always Welcome at the Y) program, so if you're a member elsewhere, you're welcome to use this friendly facility. Y members rave especially about the excellent staff here, and members are very loyal. The Y plans to expand programs into the West End.

Pocono Wellness & Sport Center $$$
Eagle Valley Mall, U.S. Highway 209
business at Highway 447, East Stroudsburg
(570) 424-2333
www.wellfit.com
This is a full-service gym with indoor regulation-size basketball, tennis, and rac-

quetball courts, along with boxing work-out equipment. The center also boasts 33 Body Masters and Cybex muscle-building machines and 28 aerobic Exercycles, treadmills, rowing machines, ski machines, and stair-steppers. Bodybuilding is further enhanced by a fully equipped free-weight area. Men's and women's locker rooms have their own saunas. Members swim free at indoor and outdoor pools at Shawnee Inn and Golf Resort. (See our Accommodations and Golf chapters.)

The center offers a fully supervised 12-week program of exercise and nutrition, physical therapy and rehabilitative services, group exercise classes, yoga, and a personal fitness system including hands-on orientation to the exercise machines for new members. A chiropractor is on staff, and Swedish, reflexology, and sports massages are available. Monthly and yearly memberships are available. All facilities are open to nonmembers at a guest fee of $15 a day, but the center honors the Passport Program of the International Health Racquet and Sportslife Association, which has participating clubs all over the world. Visiting passport holders get in for $7.50 a day. A special on-site nursery is available for babysitting services, and the center offers a junior development program for teens ages 13–15. The center is open 16 hours a day, seven days a week, all year.

Mount Pocono Area

Elevations Health Club   **$$**
Highway 611, Scotrun
(570) 620–1990
www.elevationshealthclub.com
Elevations offers members unlimited, low-impact aerobics, Pilates, sculpture and tone, core training, kickboxing, cardio pump, step, power yoga, power zen, abs, and meditation. The gym is thoroughly equipped with a full range of Nautilus equipment as well as treadmills, Lifecycles, Stairmasters, Olympic free weights, and other aerobic and bodybuilding

machinery. The club offers nutritional counseling, massage, and personal training and runs a child-care service for members. All facilities are open to the public at a daily rate of $10. Elevations is open seven days a week.

West End

Blakeslee Fitness Center   **$$**
Blakeslee Village Shopping Center
Highways 115 and 940, Blakeslee
(570) 646–1050
Blakeslee Fitness Center is a full fitness facility with a large selection of free weights and cardio-circuit training machines. There are two to three machines of every type, and they're all conveniently grouped together, so there's no waiting and no cool down while you go from one room to another in search of the right machine. They also offer step, aerobic, yoga, toning, and stretching classes, and personal trainers are there to help you. Walk-ins are welcome at a daily rate, and memberships are available at monthly, quarterly, six-month, and yearly rates.

Health Works   **$$$**
Carbon Plaza Mall, 1241 Blakeslee
Boulevard Drive East, Lehighton
(570) 386–8080
www.ghmh.org
Gnaden Huetten Hospital's health and wellness center offers a complete fitness facility, including state-of-the-art exercise equipment, a large free weight room, a supervised playroom for children, and health and wellness education sessions.

West End Health and Fitness Club   **$$**
Liberty Mall, Shafer Drive, off US 209
Brodheadsville
(570) 992–3022
www.westendgym.com
This fully equipped gym offers 30 aerobics classes a week as well as a 35-machine array of Streamline bodybuilding and aerobic equipment in 10,000 square

feet of workout space. For those into weight lifting, there is a free-weight room with 20 benches and dumbbells ranging from 5 to 195 pounds, along with related bench-press equipment. Racquetball, tanning, and free babysitting are available seven days a week. New owners recently acquired the club, and they have added yoga classes, massage therapy, and elliptical machines. They hope to restore the pool, too. The guest rate is $10 a day for access to all facilities.

GO-KARTS

The Pocono region is famous for, among many other things, its racetracks, but you don't have to confine yourself in the spectator category to enjoy the sport. Go-kart tracks are popular throughout the area, with cars both for kids and teens as well as adults. So start your engines and hit the oval at any one of the following parks.

Delaware Water Gap/ Shawnee-on-Delaware

Pocono Mountain Go-Karts and Paintball $
US 209, Marshalls Creek
(570) 223-6299
www.poconogokarts.com
This go-kart fun park has two tracks, a Super for grownups and a Junior for folks shorter than 54 inches. Both oval tracks run over and under a bridge, covering 800 feet in all. There's also an indoor arcade and paintball. The park is open weekends only April through Memorial Day, daily through Labor Day, and then weekends only again until Thanksgiving.

Thunder Creek Quarry $
Creek Road, Marshalls Creek
(570) 223-7177
www.mountainmanor.com
This go-kart raceway boasts a 1,048-foot spiral track that crosses over and under a

bridge. Drivers must be at least 54 inches in height to take the wheel. A special kiddie track is adjacent to the main layout. This track is part of a family-fun complex with an arcade, bumper boats, minigolf, and other amenities. (See our Attractions and Kidstuff chapters for details.)

Thunder Creek is open every day during the summer. The indoor arcade is open on weekends year-round.

Stroudsburg/East Stroudsburg

Pocono Mountain Go-Karts & Play Park $
Highway 611, Bartonsville
(570) 620-0820
www.poconogokarts.com
Like its sister park in Marshalls Creek, two 800-foot go-kart tracks are featured here, one for kids shorter than 54 inches and one for the bigger kids and their parents. But this park also has a miniature Ferris wheel, a skateboard park, big bounce, a family tram train, turtle scooters, paintball on four fields of play, a climbing wall, a trampoline, archery, bankshot basketball, a scrambler, batting cages, an indoor arcade, and a snack bar. (See our Attractions chapter for details.) The park is open daily April through November.

Milford/Lake Wallenpaupack Area

Costa's Family Fun Park $
US 6, 3 miles east of Lake Wallenpaupack
(570) 226-8585, (800) 928-4FUN
www.costasfamilyfunpark.com
This winding 1,200-foot track, with long straight-aways and tight turns, supports both adult-size Leopard Karts and IROC models for kids 54 inches and taller. Part of a large recreational complex (see our Attractions chapter), it is open weekends

in May, daily Memorial Day through Labor Day, and then weekends through Columbus Day.

HIKING

The Poconos have almost as many perspectives as they do visitors. You can see the region from high in a hot-air balloon or from down in a river valley in a welter of whitewater. You can view the Poconos from the window of a train drawn by a 19th-century steam engine or through the time tunnel of sites where history is preserved as a living metaphor. But to really see the Poconos, you have to get right down onto the trails and into the woods where you can go one-on-one with the trees and the wildlife that call the region home. In short, nothing gets you closer to the essence of our mountains than a good old-fashioned hike. Here are a few of the places where hiking is at its best. For a more detailed rundown, check Web sites for trail maps, pick up maps and advice at parks' headquarters, or buy one of the books that detail hiking trails in the area.

Delaware Water Gap/ Shawnee-on-Delaware

Delaware Water Gap National Recreation Area Headquarters, River Road, off US 209 Bushkill (570) 588-2451 www.nps.gov
There are more than 60 hiking trails in this sprawling federal wildwood, including 25 miles of the famed Appalachian Trail, which runs through Delaware Water Gap and into New Jersey. Here you can hike in gorges, along the river, in loops through blueberry fields, to points where the view stretches out for miles and much more. For an extra treat, take a trail that runs adjacent to the Pocono Environmental Education Center. (See the related Close-up in our Parks

chapter.) Some trails listed as prime by the Appalachian Mountain Club include a moderate grade 8 miles up Dunnfield Creek to Sunfish Pond; a tougher 7-mile trek from Mine Road in Delaware Water Gap up Kaiser Trail, usually ending in a swim in the Delaware River; and a moderate 9-mile walk from the Gap to Camp Mohican and Catfish Pond.

Guidebooks and detailed maps can be picked up at National Recreation Area headquarters in Bushkill or at the Kittatinny Point Visitor Center off Interstate 80 in New Jersey.

STATE PARKS

There are a lot of natural hiking areas in the Poconos, but many of them are privately owned and posted. Seek the owners' permission before you intrude there. There also are small nature trails in such areas as Mauch Chunk Lake Park and Lake Wallenpaupack (see our Parks chapter), but most major hiking trails will be found in the region's six state parks. Here are a few of the best parks, detailed maps of which that are available at each of the park offices.

Stroudsburg/East Stroudsburg

Big Pocono State Park Camelback Mountain, Highway 715, off I-80 exit 45, Tannersville (570) 894-8336 www.dcnr.state.pa.us
Seven miles of trails, four of them interconnecting, traverse this marvelous sylvan park atop Camelback Mountain, which also is one of the prime ski areas of the Poconos. (See our Winter Sports chapter.) The South Trail and the Old Trail Road Trail, which follows a fairly level railroad grade, are easy walks for beginners, while North Trail and Indian Trail are steep, rugged, and recommended for experts in

top physical condition. The panoramic view from the top of Camelback is magnificent, encompassing part of Pennsylvania, New York, and New Jersey.

Mount Pocono Area

Gouldsboro State Park
Highway 507, 11.5 miles south of Gouldsboro
(570) 894-8336
www.dcnr.state.pa.us
This sylvan 2,800 acres in Monroe and Wayne Counties, with its 250-acre lake, offers Prospect Rock Trail, an 8.5-mile path circling the northern end of the park by way of the old entrance road. Portions are physically demanding and should not be attempted without proper footwear or by people who are not in good physical condition.

Promised Land State Park
Highway 390, Greentown
(570) 676-3428
www.dcnr.state.pa.us
Just 10 miles north of Canadensis, this sprawling 2,971-acre park of heavy forest surrounding four lakes is a treasure trove of more than a dozen short but very scenic hiking paths and nature trails. The longest, at 10 miles round trip, is Bruce Lake Trail, which starts a half-mile from the Big Inlet trailhead and ends on the north side of Bruce Lake. It crosses over several other trails and, after 4 miles, splits into the east and west branches, both of which are swampy and support beaver activity.

Bruce Lake Loop is an 8-mile walk beginning at the Rock Oak Ridge trailhead and winding around the lake. Other, shorter trails of interest include the Conservation Island Nature Trail, home to a wide variety of flora and fauna on the named island in Promised Land Lake, and the 1800 Trail, so named because it follows the park's 1,800-foot contour line through a varied hardwood forest. Both trails are just a mile long. Whittaker Trail is

a 1.5-mile round-trip showcase of rhododendron, mountain laurel, low-bush blueberry, and a mixed bag of hardwood forest. It ends at the junction of Telephone Trail where you will see a glacial depression, often filled with water in spring.

Tobyhanna State Park
Highway 423, north of Tobyhanna
(570) 894-8336
www.dcnr.state.pa.us
This 5,440-acre park is in Monroe and Wayne counties and boasts its own 170-acre lake. The entrance is 2 miles north of Tobyhanna on Highway 423. Here, hikers are offered a beautiful 5-mile woodland stroll around Tobyhanna Lake. An additional 7 miles of trails also are available, most of them ranging from flat to gently sloped. One killer pathway is the 3.3-mile Frank Gantz Trail, which connects the Tobyhanna trail system with those in nearby Gouldsboro. Do not try the Frank Gantz unless you are a fully equipped first-class hiker. And even if you are, don't try it alone.

The Lakeside Trail is marked in blue, the Frank Gantz in red.

West End

Beltzville State Park
US 209, 5 miles east of Lehighton
(610) 377-0045
www.dcnr.state.pa.us
This popular park offers hikers 15 miles of hiking through history. One of the most-walked pathways, the Saw Mill Trail, winds past the remains of a gristmill and a slate quarry from the 1770s. The western portion of the trail is easy hiking; the eastern portion is moderate to difficult.

Hickory Run State Park
Highway 534, White Haven
(570) 443-0400
www.dcnr.state.pa.us
This huge, 15,000-acre park boasts 20 designated hiking trails totaling 37 miles through a varied countryside full of deer,

turkey, squirrel, bear, snowshoe hare, and other wildlife. Several trails lead to scenic waterfalls, and one, the Boulder Field Trail, ends at a glacial deposit of large stones dumped there 20,000 years ago by a retreating glacier. The trail is 2.75 miles long and includes a steep uphill walk. This hike will take four to five hours. Easier trails include the Manor House, which follows a grassy old logging road with no hills or stones but plenty of trees and birds, and Stage Trail, which, at 4.5 miles, is wide and easy and bisects the park. The Stage Trail once was a major stage route between Philadelphia and Wilkes-Barre. A beautifully detailed map of the system is available at the park office.

HORSEBACK RIDING

Horseback riding provides a leisurely trip into the woods without a lot of effort (on the rider's part, at least). It is particularly popular during the fall foliage season when riders receive plenty of scenery in return for very little perspiration.

Always wear long pants to protect your legs from pinching or rubbing on the saddle. Shoes that tie on (not sandals) are best. In winter, long underwear might be a good idea, but definitely bring a hat and gloves. Make reservations ahead of time if you want to be sure of getting a horse. Most stables try to accommodate walk-ins, but since there are limited horses and limited guides, they prefer reservations.

Mount Pocono Area

Carson's Riding Stables Inc.   **$$$$**
Highway 611, 1 mile south of Mount Pocono
(570) 839-9841
www.poconos.org
For more than 45 years, Carson's has thrilled riders year round with guided trail rides. Cool off during summer with a ride down a shady lane. In spring, enjoy the aroma of fresh flowers. The brilliantly col-

ored foliage in fall and the peaceful, snow-laden hush in winter make for popular rides as well. Rides can be tailored to all abilities, and the staff always provides free instruction. Rides leave every hour on the hour; arrive at least 15 minutes ahead. Reservations are appreciated.

Mountain Creek Stables   **$$$$**
Highway 940, 3 miles east of Mount Pocono
(570) 839-8725
www.mtcreekstable.com
Mountain Creek specializes in easy western rides through wooded areas and streams. Guides equipped with radios accompany every trip. The rides last 45 to 50 minutes, and a two-hour ride is available by advance reservation. Rides depart every hour on the hour. Reservations are suggested. For safety's sake, helmets are provided for all young riders (optional for adults), and suitable footwear is available if needed. Pony rides also are available, or very young children can follow their parents (on horseback) in a horse-drawn wagon. You'll also find a Western gift shop on the grounds.

Pocono Adventures   **$$$$**
Highway 611, 1 mile south of Mount Pocono
(570) 839-6333
www.microserve.net/~magicusa
Rides range from a gentle 45-minute ride along nature trails to a four-hour trek across varied terrain. On the latter adventure, be prepared to walk, trot, canter, and gallop—and bring lunch. There is also a condensed two-hour version of the same ride. Trips are held rain or shine; rainwear is supplied. Guides and instruction before and during the ride are provided. Call for reservations. Pocono Adventures is open every day.

Pocono Manor Stables   **$$$$**
Off Highway 314, Pocono Manor
(570) 839-0925
www.poconos.org
With more than 3,000 acres, Pocono Manor has enough trails to keep even seri-

ous riders occupied. Beginners enjoy leisurely rides through forests of white birch, rhododendron, and mountain laurel. More advanced riders can canter along wooded trails to visit a stream or waterfall. Rides from one to three hours are available.

Their sleigh rides are winter traditions for many families. (See our Winter Sports chapter for details.)

Milford/Lake Wallenpaupack Area

Triple W Riding Stable Inc. $$$$
US 6, 4.5 miles north of Hawley
(570) 226-2620, (800) 540-2620
www.triplewstable.com
Riders are interviewed about past experience, evaluated, and assigned an appropriate horse from among the 60 or so at this 171-acre ranch. There are four trails graded by level of experience. Hayrides, sleigh rides, and overnight camping trips, complete with cookout and country breakfast, are available.

MINIATURE GOLF

You don't have to be able to hit the long drives or blast out of a bunker to enjoy golf in the Poconos. Miniature golf courses abound throughout the area, and they range from simple and easy to downright maddening. Some of them are attached to major attractions; others are independent entities; and nearly all Pocono resorts number them among amenities offered to their guests. There are too many miniature

---

Unlike other spheroids of sport, golf balls have dimples because dimples cut drag as the ball flies. Hit solidly, a dimpled ball can go up to 300 yards. A smooth ball, hit with the same force, would go only about 70 yards.

---

golf courses to give each one an individual listing, but here, by region, is a sampling.

Delaware Water Gap/ Shawnee-on-Delaware

Adventure Golf $
US 209, Marshalls Creek
(570) 223-9227
This complex 18-holer is one of the most colorful courses in the area. In keeping with its adventure theme, giant lizards, a great white shark, and a couple of haunted castles guard a collection of very tricky holes in rolling, convoluted surfaces. There are plenty of water hazards in the form of ponds, waterfalls, and a stream that curves through the course, which is as close to the championship links aficionados find in Florida or Myrtle Beach as any in the Northeast.

The signature shot comes on the 18th hole where one raps the ball up a steep ramp in pursuit of a hole-in-one that wins a free game. The course has a sizable picnic area and a snack bar. It is open April through May on weekends only, then daily throughout the summer. It takes an average of two hours to play this course. Group rates and children's parties are available.

Bushkill Falls Miniature Golf $
US 209 off Bushkill Falls Road, Bushkill
(570) 588-6682
www.bushkillfalls.com
This is a fairly simple and very old 18-hole course laid out on the forest floor at scenic Bushkill Falls. (See the Attractions and Our Natural World chapters.) In addition to miniature golf, this place rents paddleboats for a combination golf-boat package, and permits children to fish in the adjacent lake. There are plenty of birds in this sylvan setting—some of them of the barnyard variety. Don't be surprised if a gaggle of geese or a waddling duck or two show up to block your shots. The

course is open daily from April through November.

Water Gap Rolling Green ProAm Minigolf $
Highway 611 at Main Street
Delaware Water Gap
(570) 476-9766

This 10-hole course looks easy because it is relatively flat and completely devoid of the windmills, waterfalls, and other gewgaws that mark the average miniature golf course. Looks, however, are deceptive. In fact playing here is very much like playing a full golf course because the rolling AstroTurf, with beige areas designated as bunkers and blue ones as water hazards, closely imitates the real thing; hit your ball into sand or pond, and you take a one-stroke penalty. To complicate matters, the cup at each hole can be moved from place to place to make the course easier or more difficult so that you can play it one day and not even recognize it if you try again the next. Theoretically, this design system can be made to mimic in miniature any famous regular golf course on earth.

The course is connected to the famed Delaware Water Gap Trolley (see our Attractions chapter), so you can spend time waiting for the trolley to leave by shooting a few holes. The course is open the same hours as the trolley ride, from the first hint of spring until winter closes it down. And for those who can't get enough miniature golf, Water Gap Rolling Green has a unique solution—you pay for one game here, and you can play all day.

West End

Golf Plantation $
US 209, Kresgeville
(610) 681-5959

This moderately difficult course is a scenic one with a stream connecting several ponds throughout 18 holes of undulating greens with roughs and bunkers built in. It

is beautifully landscaped with a gazebo, a stone deer, and artfully placed flowers and ornamental trees and bushes flanked by red and white gravel and river stones. There is no particular signature hole, but the course does feature a small putting green so that you can warm up before you start to play. This miniature golf course is connected to a golf school with a pro shop and a driving range. (See our Golf chapter for additional details.)

This miniature golf course is open every day from April 1 until it gets too cold—usually the end of October, or the beginning of November.

Milford/Lake Wallenpaupack Area

Costa's Family Fun Park $
US 6, 3 miles east of Lake Wallenpaupack
(570) 226-8585, (800) 928-4FUN
www.costasfamilyfunpark.com

Play two minicourses as part of a full recreational complex. (See our Attractions chapter.) The unramped kids' course is nursery rhyme-themed, and the only signature hole is No. 11, where the putter must roll the ball through the blades of a turning wheel. The low score in any foursome gets a free game. The course is open on weekends only from May 1 through Memorial Day, then 7 days per week through Labor Day, and weekends again from Labor Day through Columbus Day.

MOUNTAIN BIKING

Mountain biking offers a vigorous physical and aerobic workout as well as some of the most spectacular scenery in the Poconos, but it also can pose plenty of peril to the unwary. There are trails for experts only that are capable of putting a tyro in traction, so know where you are and where you are going before you start pedaling. Beginners are advised to stick to less demanding trails, such as converted rail beds and deserted roads. Single-track trails (only one way through) over rough terrain can be very dangerous.

Use maps to select a trail best suited to your abilities. Always take a helmet, drinking water, snacks, an assortment of wrenches, screwdrivers, and an air pump in case of a breakdown.

Sometimes bikers share trails with hikers and horseback riders. Always yield the right of way to these other trail visitors.

Two Victorian towns—Milford and Jim Thorpe—are the destinations of choice for mountain bikers, though there are other good areas in Stroudsburg and at Camelback ski area, for instance. State and federal parks generally prohibit mountain biking on hiking trails, limiting them to specific trails or roads.

Jim Thorpe boasts some of the best trails on the East Coast, with Colorado-style paths scattered all around the town. In fact, *Cycling* magazine rated Jim Thorpe as one of the three top mountain bike destinations in the country. Jim Thorpe and Milford, together, offer the greatest trail diversity and the best accommodations in the Poconos. The scenery is spectacular whenever you elect to go.

Upon arriving in Jim Thorpe, visit Blue Mountain Sports & Wear. The staff knows all the surrounding trails and can recommend some to suit your taste and ability. Tell them you want a three-hour, gentle ride with views of the valley, and they will point you in the right direction. And, if you're an expert seeking some real action-adventure, they can accommodate that too. You also can rent or buy any equipment you might need and find maps of

any trail you might ride at Blue Mountain, or at other outfitters you will find listed at the end of this section. We suggest that you pick up a copy of *A Guide to Mountain Biking in Jim Thorpe & the Western Poconos* by David Matsinko.

A rundown of available trails in all four regions follows.

Stroudsburg/East Stroudsburg

Glen Park Trails
Glen Park, which most Stroudsburg residents know only as the location of a ball field, offers a surprising network of trails just beyond the field between Brodhead Creek and Highway 611, off I-80. Some 20 miles of varied terrain for intermediate to advanced cyclists run through a forest full of wildlife and awesome grades, with rocks, roots, and ruts to challenge the expert. Coyote, bear, and deer have been spotted here, but don't tackle them or the terrain unless you really know what you're doing.

Mount Pocono Area

Camelback
Bike paths here consist of jeep trails and fire roads, and because they pass through protected wildlife habitat, the Pennsylvania Game Commission will not allow them to be marked with signage. Maps, however, along with detailed instructions can be obtained at The Loft, an outfitter that sells and rents out mountain bikes and other outdoor sports equipment. The Loft is on Sullivan Trail, the road leading to the ski area, and while its maps do not spell out mileage, the staff there knows the area and can get you started toward terrain to match your skills.

Access to the trails is a parking lot about a mile past the entrance of the Camelback ski area. Unlike trails, the parking area is marked with signs designating it as in State Gameland #38. Terrain here is varied, with paths winding past two beautiful mountain lakes. Scenery from the mountaintop is spectacular.

West End

Jim Thorpe

There are three trails with starting points accessible only via cars or a shuttle run conducted at $15 per person by Blue Mountain Sports & Wear. It takes about 40 minutes to reach the trailheads, and all of them end in Jim Thorpe:

- Lehigh Gorge Trail No. 2, ranked for beginner through intermediate cyclists, runs from Rockport/White Haven and takes anywhere from one to four hours, depending upon where one decides to quit along its 15.5- to 24-mile run.
- Switchback Trail No. 2 runs from 9 to 18 miles, depending on the stamina of the rider, on a fairly easy railroad downgrade for beginners from Summit Hill. Expect to be on it for one to two hours.
- The Uranium Road is one of the more popular trails for advanced bikers. It runs for 18 miles from Broad Mountain as a rugged single-track descent of the scenic Lehigh Gorge. It can be ridden in two to four hours.

Other trails that begin and end in Jim Thorpe include the following:

- Lehigh Gorge Trail No. 1 is just about whatever you want it to be. Its skill-levels are ranked all the way from beginner to expert, and it can run as long as 60 miles. The average self-guided tour covering it all takes roughly eight hours.
- Switch back Trail No. 1 is an 11- to 18-mile stretch recommended for beginners since it is mostly level, with an optional steep rocky descent. Expect to be on it from 1½ to 3 hours.
- Flagstaff Mountain is one long 9-mile grade for the "energetic beginner." Expect to cover it in one to two hours. It is possibly the most scenic of all, with its

stop on top of the mountain for an unforgettable panorama of the surrounding countryside.

- Psycho Betty's Revenge is the one ride that begins and ends on Flagstaff Mountain, but don't let the name intimidate you. This 11-mile rolling single-track and fire road stretch, named for a rock band that frequently plays at the nightclub atop Flagstaff Mountain, is ranked as an intermediate, not a killer, grade.
- Mount Pisgah, which can range anywhere from 3.5 to 12 miles, is an intermediate trail offering a steep rock climb and descent with overlooks. Ride it in one to three hours.
- Mauch Chunk Ridge is a 10-mile stretch for experts only. It is hilly, rolling terrain with a tricky single-track descent that takes about two hours.
- Twin Peaks is another advanced trail climbing Flagstaff Mountain, Mauch Chunk Ridge, and Mount Pisgah for 20 rugged miles. Expect to be on it from 2½ to 4 hours.

Milford/Lake Wallenpaupack Area

Milford

The maple-lined streets of Milford are tailor-made for casual bikers cruising through this historic town filled with some of the most delicious Victorian architecture in the land. Ride over to former Governor Pinchot's estate or visit the waterfalls right outside of town. Take Mott Street to savor the neighborhood, then ride east of Broad Street, down to the Delaware River for a scenic tour of River Road to Grey Towers. (See our Arts and Culture and Attractions chapters.) Many of these quiet, cycle-friendly streets continue out into the countryside, but for the more adventuresome, there are some wildwood trails to challenge.

- The Mill Rift-Pond Eddy Loop offers a choice of runs ranging from 15 to 25 miles. The shorter run is a round trip from Mill Rift, 5 miles north of Milford, through deep woods along an old railroad track bed to Firetower Road. The Railroad was active until it was inundated in the great flood of 1955, and since it never was reactivated, it now serves as one of the finest bike trails in the county. Those seeking a more ambitious ride can leave the track bed and venture up Cummins Road to old Pond Eddy Road, then cross the river into New York State to return on NY Highway 97. Parts of this route have rugged off-road terrain with steep climbs.

- An easier ride is offered in Shohola Falls Recreation Area on US 6, 12 miles west of Milford, where a good flat dirt and gravel road parallels the western shore of a lake for 5 miles to a secluded swimming hole in Shohola Brook. There are more difficult paths along the way, but many of them are "boondockers," heavily overgrown with brush. These are state game lands, and eagles and osprey abound.
- In the Lackawaxen area, a 13-mile ride on Highway 590 and along the former towpath of the Delaware & Hudson Canal takes you past the old village of Lackawaxen and the oldest suspension bridge in the nation. You'll also pass the onetime home of Western author Zane Grey. (See our Attractions and Arts and Culture chapters.) Longer loops and spur rides are available along the way. Traffic generally is light.
- Mongaup Valley in New York State and Stokes State Forest in New Jersey are not technically part of the Poconos. They are in the Catskills and the Kittatinnys, respectively, but they are right across the river from Poconos bike trails, and they have some notable trails of their own. Mongaup Valley offers an old woods road beginning at a pull-off on NY Highway 97 north of Port Jervis. It follows the Mongaup River for 3 miles to a powerhouse, passing a picturesque old cemetery and several swimming holes along the way. This is state conservation

land, and eagles are plentiful. This trail is for mountain bikes only.

- Another New York ride worth visiting runs from NY Highway 97 at Pond Eddy to NY Highway 41, then north to Glen Spey, west to NY Highway 32 to Eldred, then south to Barryville where one picks up NY Highway 97 south back to the starting point. This 20-mile loop offers a nice variety of terrain from fairly steep roads and flat stretches along the Delaware River through small villages and past the onion domes of the Ukrainian Cultural Center.
- In New Jersey, low-traffic roads wind upward from the High Point State Park office 5 miles from Port Jervis to the highest point in the state, at 1,900 feet, then to nearby Sunrise Mountain along the Kittatinny Ridge. The view is spectacular, and several lakes offer swimming along the way. In Stokes State Forest, 12 miles from Milford on US 206, several rides of various distances are available. They consist of good low-use roads to mountain and valley vistas, with lakes offering swimming and fishing. Maps of the region are available at the park office in Branchville.

State and National Parks

Biking in the Lehigh Gorge is covered in the Jim Thorpe section, above. Tobyhanna State Park, the entrance of which is 2 miles north of Tobyhanna on Highway 423, is a 5,440-acre track of woodland straddling Monroe and Wayne counties. It boasts a 170-acre lake rimmed by a 5-mile loop of flat, well-maintained cinder path dubbed Lakeside Trail where the whole family can go cycling. Beginners will find this ride an easy one through green forests teeming with wildlife. In nearby Gouldsboro State Park, bikers are allowed only on old Highway 611. In Promised Land State Park, bikers are allowed only on the 6.5-mile paved road around the lake. Riders in the Delaware Water Gap National Recreation Area have a few options. You are welcome to ride along Old Mine Road, along the New Jersey side of the Delaware River. This is a scenic, somewhat hilly road you share with cars, running the entire length of the park. You'll pass many of the park's interesting features along this road, and there are many points of access to the river. Mountain bikers are invited to try Big Egypt Road, between Highway 209 and Milford Road in the Toms Creek Picnic Area. Big Egypt is a 2.5-mile hard-packed dirt road. You'll share it with some cars, though traffic is light here, and it's moderately steep. Freeman Tract Road runs from River Road about three quarters of a mile south of park headquarters to a dead end at the Delaware River. It's 3.5 miles of mostly hard-packed dirt road, few cars, and a couple of hills. Zion Church Road, also mostly hard-packed dirt with some rocky sections, has some steep spots and runs 1.5 miles between Hidden Lake Road and River Road. There's very little traffic on Zion Church Road. The newest trail, open to mountain bikes, hikers and cross-country skiers, is the MacDade trail, a gravel path along the river that eventually will run the full length of the Delaware Water Gap Recreation Area. At this writing, a few miles of it are open and access is from Smithfield Beach as well as another parking lot a few miles north of Smithfield, along River Road. In New Jersey, you'll find Blue Mountain Lake Mountain Bike Trail, for novice to intermediate riders. You'll leave Old Mine Road about 1.5 miles north of Millbrook Village to catch this trail. Beginners can ride around Blue Mountain Lake, while intermediate riders can take the 5-mile loop to Hemlock Pond.

In all other parks—state and federal—bikes are forbidden on hiking trails. (See this chapter's "Hiking" section for details.) It is a good idea to check at each park's individual headquarters for regulations.

Delaware State Forest

The state forestlands are scattered around the Poconos and have 27.5 miles of trails specifically for mountain biking as well as joint use trails where mountain bikes can share the road with ATVs and snowmobiles. Try the Pohopoco Trail, off Highway 115 near the Pocono Raceway, with areas for beginner to expert mountain bikers. Another trail, off of Highway 390 near Promised Land State Park, offers trails that are intermediate to expert. Some of the rangers are enthusiastic about mountain biking, so call for advice and more specific information, (570) 895-4000, or stop by the office they share with the Pennsylvania Department of Environmental Protection at HC1, Box 95A, Highway 611, Swiftwater for maps and advice. There are also map boxes at the trailheads. You can find out more about the Delaware State Forest by going to www.dcnr.state.pa.us.

Rentals, Supplies, and Advice

Because of the popularity of mountain biking, bike rental and support shops are common throughout the area. Here are a few that not only rent bikes, but also supply local trail information and maps, and in some cases, conduct shuttle services to put bikers at trailheads.

MOUNT POCONO AREA

The Loft
Camelback Road and Sullivan Trail
Tannersville
(570) 629-2627
www.loftsports.com
The Loft has performance mountain bikes for rent ($23 daily), along with skateboards, skates, and skis in winter, and while the shop maintains no shuttle, it will allow you to rent a portable bike rack so you can carry your wheels to whatever trails you want to ride. Most will want to ride trails atop the Camelback ski slopes, the base of which is only a short hop from the store. Helmets and water bottles come with rented bicycles.

WEST END

Blue Mountain Sports & Wear
34 Susquehanna Street, Jim Thorpe
(570) 325-4421, (800) 599-4221
www.bikejimthorpe.com

This upscale store caters to all outdoor sports, both with equipment and clothing, and offers a sizeable fleet of top brand-name mountain bikes, along with helmets, water bottles, and accessories for rent. Bikes rent for $27 per day; $15 per half day. Renting is a good way to try out a bike over an extended period of time before you purchase a new one. If the kids are along, rent Tagalong bikes, which are assisted on easy trails by an occasional tow from parents' bikes. Even toddlers can go along in children's buggies, also towed behind grownups' bikes. Blue Mountain supplies full trail information along with maps and runs a shuttle service to out-of-town trailheads.

Jim Thorpe River Adventures
1 Adventure Lane, Jim Thorpe
(800) 424-RAFT

This whitewater raft river guide service also offers mountain bike rentals that include a helmet, map, and a hot shower. Advance shuttle-service reservations are required. Rental rates are $5.00 per hour or $25.00 per day. Special group-rental rates for 15 or more bikers are available.

Peterson Ski & Cycle
Highways 115 and 940, Blakeslee
(570) 646-9223

This shop has a dozen bikes for rent. Bikes, with helmet included, rent for $20.00 per day, $6.00 per hour, and $15.00 for four hours. The staff knows all the local trails and can supply maps.

P.W. Mountain Bike Center
Highway 903, Jim Thorpe
(570) 325-3655
www.poconowhitewater.com

P.W. offers guided four-hour biking tours for beginning and experienced riders.

Shuttle service and rentals also are available. The shuttle costs $15 per person. Shuttle ride and bike rental are $37 per person per day. Half-day rates are also available. Reservations are recommended for the shuttle.

PAINTBALL

Those who want more of a workout with their time in the woods, along with a little combat action, should consider paintball. Dressed in camouflage, two teams attempt to capture each other's flag and return it to their base. Along the way, they "shoot" opponents with CO_2-powered guns loaded with paint pellets. The weapons and safety equipment have become high-tech in recent years. As a result serious injuries are rare, and the action is frantic.

West End

Skirmish U.S.A. $$$$
Highway 903, Jim Thorpe
(570) 325-8430, (800) SKIRMISH
www.skirmish.com

With varied playing fields on 700 acres, Skirmish has a setting for every paintball taste. Thick vegetation, fieldstone wall, and simulated villages provide cover. Fort Skirmish, Circle City, Black Hawk Down, Hood in the Woods, a castle, and the 23-building village are alternatives to the conventional "run though the woods" game.

Groups of 20 or more may play on private fields. All equipment and "ammunition" is provided. Skirmish U.S.A. is open every day throughout the year, but reservations are very strongly recommended. Skirmish is nationally recognized for its playing fields and is very, very popular. Rates include field judges, gun rentals, goggles, a face mask, and an ammo belt. If you desire, you may rent camouflage clothing.

Splatter $$$$
Jack Frost Ski Area, I-80 exit 43
Blakeslee
(570) 443-8425, (800) 468-2442
www.jfbb.com

Splatter features the first speedball arena in Pennsylvania. In "The Eliminator," shots fly by quickly as music pulsates all around the competitors. It is more intense than the conventional paintball game.

Other fields include Tunnel Town, a maze of trenches; Bunker Hill, filled with sandbag bunkers; and Hostile Takeover.

All equipment is available for rent. Daily rates include guns and all other necessary implements. The 2,500-acre complex is open every day April through November, and the fields change with the seasons. Reservations are recommended.

Milford/Lake Wallenpaupack Area

Kittatinny Paintball $$$$
NY Highway 97, Barryville, NY
(570) 828-2338
(800) 356-2852 (Float KC)
www.kittatinny.com

This mountaintop combat zone lies right across the Delaware River in New York State but it still ranks as a prime Pocono-area center. Veteran players say the rugged terrain on top of a heavily wooded mountain is unique, giving cover well beyond a maze of man-made bunkers for such games as Capture the Flag, Attack and Defend, Total Elimination, and Bounty Hunter. A favorite area of ambush, dubbed "Stonehenge," consists of a great pile of boulders full of places to hide.

Combatants are taken into the field in a big Army "deuce and a half" truck. The fee covers 50 paintballs, free CO_2, guns, and facemasks for players 18 and older. Younger soldiers, ages 13 to 17, play with parental permission. Extras include a Paddle & Battle special including a raft or canoe trip with paintball the next day for $5.00 off per person. All-night camping is

Paintballs are round, thin-skinned gelatin capsules filled with a colored, non-toxic, non-caustic, water-soluble, and biodegradable liquid. They do not cause permanent stains and pose no threat to the environment.

available on the premises. Kittatinny is open from May through October or November, depending on the snow. They're on the top of a mountain, so snowfall can occur earlier than down in the valley. Reservations are recommended.

ROCK CLIMBING

They call themselves "wall rats"; the rest of the world calls them crazy. They are people who get their kicks by dangling, either from a climbing harness or by their fingernails, to the sides of sheer rock walls as they forge their way to the top, often with nothing between them and death but a few hundred feet of empty space. There may be better ways to get a view, but don't tell that to the human flies. If you're one of them, here are a couple of places where you can practice the art.

Delaware Water Gap/ Shawnee-on-Delaware

Delaware Water Gap National Recreation Area
Headquarters, River Road, off US 209
Bushkill
(570) 588-2451
www.nps.gov

After practice at Cathedral Rock (see following entry), climbers will find the real thing in the heart of the Delaware Water Gap where the Delaware River slices a natural boundary between New Jersey and Pennsylvania. The sheer face of Mount Tamanny, which looms on the New Jersey side of the river, offers a real challenge both in rock climbing and rappelling. The base of the climb is accessible only by the very steep Red Dot Trail, and the scenery from the top is breathtaking.

The National Park Service, which has no regulations against rock climbing, requires neither sign-in nor registration of practitioners of the sport in any of the areas it administers, but it is a good idea to check in with them all the same—before and after you make your climb. A climbing guide may be purchased at the Kittatinny Visitor's Center, off Interstate 80 on the New Jersey side of the Delaware River, (908) 496-4458. The park service strongly recommends you wear a helmet and be trained and use proper equipment. Tell a friend or relative exactly where you plan to climb, where your car will be parked, and give him or her the national park's 24-hour emergency number: (800) 543–HAWK, which he or she may call if you are overdue.

West End

Cathedral Rock Climbing Gym   **$$$**
226 South First Street, Lehighton
(610) 377-8822
www.lehightonals.org
Practice or take lessons from the experts at this former church, built around 1843, where 8,500 vertical square feet of corners, cracks, slabs, overhangs, mantels, caves, chimneys, and all the rest of the topography so cherished by climbers has been installed. For the price of admission you can climb all day, practicing 22 specific approaches. Shoes and harness rent for an additional $2.50 each, and group rates are available. Cathedral Rock is open Friday, Saturday, and Sunday.

ROLLER-SKATING/ SKATEBOARDING

If you and your kids like to skate or surf the sidewalk or get airborne on a skateboard, you have plenty of opportunities to hot-dog in the Poconos. Here are a few of the spots where you can rent wheels (or in some cases, bring your own) and rock and roll. In addition to what is listed here, many of our resorts also have roller-skating, so be sure to check for these activities when you review our Accommodations chapter.

Delaware Water Gap/ Shawnee-on-Delaware

The Starting Gate   **$$**
US 209, Marshalls Creek
(570) 223-6215
www.startinggateonline.com
If your kids are heavily into in-line skating and skateboarding, take them to The Starting Gate, about a quarter-mile north of Foxmoor Village. Children younger than 18 must have a signed release form to use the facility. It has a 6-foot miniramp, fun box, pyramid, slant ramp, wall ride, other ramps, and neat things for kids to jump on and off with their skates or skateboards. There are no restrictions on types of in-line skates; however, pads and helmets must be worn. If you don't have them, you can rent skates and all the protective gear. BMX bikes may use the facility on weekdays. The Starting Gate is open every day as long as the weather holds out and there's no snow.

Stroudsburg/East Stroudsburg

Big Wheel Family
Roller Skating Center   **$$**
Highway 191, East Stroudsburg
(570) 424-5499
www.bigwheelskating.com
Big Wheel can host your birthday or other private party, doing it all so that you and your friends can have a ball. Looking for fall activities? The folks at this huge roller rink offer roller hockey and disco on wheels for all ages. Skate rentals are available, and hours of operation and prices

are variable, so visit their Web site or call and ask.

Pocono Mountain Go-Karts
& Play Park $-$$
Highway 611, Bartonsville
(570) 620-0820
www.poconogokarts.com
Although skating is just a small part of the enormous and varied park, skaters will appreciate the full-size park for boards, bikes, and blades, with a half-pipe, full pyramid, half pyramids, beef box, quarter pipe, drop-ins, and lots of movable boxes and rails.

West End

LaRose's Skating Rink $-$$
US 209, Lehighton
(610) 377-1859
www.larosesskatingrink.com
This skating rink has been family owned for more than 75 years, so families are a big concentration here. You can rent in-line skates at LaRose's. This rink accepts private parties every day. General rink hours are 7:00 to 10:00 P.M. Friday and Saturday and 1:00 to 5:00 P.M. on Sunday.

SHOOTING RANGES

Stroudsburg/East Stroudsburg

Sunset Hill Shooting Range $$
Highway 314, off Highway 611
Tannersville
(570) 629-3981
www.sunsethillrange.com
If you're a gun enthusiast, sharpen your skills here with a wide variety of handguns, ranging from .22 Colt to .44 Magnum, and with rifles ranging from the hunting variety to the M-16, the AK-47, and the Israeli Uzi. Bring your own weapon, or rent one here. Rental and ammunition prices on pistol and rifle ranges vary with caliber. Sunset Hill also offers trap shooting for shotgun enthusiasts as well as NRA instructors to advise veterans and teach beginners. The on-site store offers Western, military, and police displays and a wide range of ammunition, factory and re-loads alike. You must be 13 years old or older to participate, and hearing protection, also available for rent, is required for everyone. Sunset Hill is open every day except Tuesday and Wednesday year round.

Mount Pocono Area

Paradise Shooting Center
Merry Hill Road, Cresco
(570) 595-3660
www.anjrpc.org
Paradise Shooting Center specializes in working with tourists who have never shot a gun before. If you're a beginner or a relatively inexperienced shooter, an instructor works with you the entire time. You can rent a gun or bring your own. Rifles for rent include an AK-47, whereas pistols include .38s, .45s, Glocks, and more. You pay for the ammunition and, if needed, gun rental, rather than paying a set fee for time. The center has trap and skeet fields as well as a pistol and rifle range. In fact, this is the only skeet shooting facility in 70 miles. Paradise is open Friday through Monday, November through May. They're open every day the rest of the year.

FISHING AND HUNTING

For anglers, here's the roll call of lake, stream, and river in the Poconos: small mouth bass, largemouth bass, striped bass, rock bass, walleye, muskellunge, pickerel, rainbow trout, brown trout, brook trout, salmon, shad, sunfish, catfish, eel, crappie, bluegill, and turtles, of which you may have two per day.

And for hunters, here's the roll call of field and forest: black bear, beaver, white-tailed deer, coyote, doves, ducks, geese, ruffed grouse, wild turkey, fox, raccoon, rabbit, bobcat, pheasant, squirrel, mink, muskrat, quail, crow, and woodchuck, the last of which there is neither a closed season nor a daily limit.

All are present, accounted for, and awaiting spinner, bait, dry fly, rifle, shotgun, muzzleloader, or bow in a great outdoors that has been fished and hunted for at least 12,000 years.

One might think that after some 12 millennia of predation, there would be nothing left to hook, trap, or shoot in the four counties that comprise the Poconos, but that is not the case. The Poconos are teeming with fish and game. In fact despite an annual harvest by hunters of 480,000 to 500,000 white-tailed deer, and the loss of about 45,000 more to traffic—which is known to be only a fraction of the actual road kill—there are more deer now by about 10 to 25 per square mile in the Poconos than there were in 1982, when the Pennsylvania Game Commission started keeping census statistics. And as for fishing, the annual shad run on the Delaware River draws anglers hungry for shad roe—the caviar of the Poconos—from all over the nation.

This chapter is separated into sections for hunting and fishing. Each will describe the most popular game and fish in a given area, along with tips on how best to pursue them. Each section also will identify the best areas open to the public—and since a huge acreage is owned by state and federal governments, that's a lot—and discuss the wildlife you can expect to find there. But many private lakes, streams and woods are owned by rod and gun clubs whose members do not appreciate non-members invading their turf; so before you enter private land, always seek permission.

Licenses are required both for hunting and fishing. Information on where to purchase them and on license fees in various categories is presented in each section.

FISHING

Anglers can visit the Poconos and fish for several species, on more than one body of water, in the same day. In the four counties that comprise the Poconos, more than 12,000 surface acres of water and 300 miles of streams are open to public fishing. In addition, the Delaware River flows for 140 miles along the eastern edge of the region.

Fishing is a year-round activity in the Poconos.

Every March, more than a million shad begin their migration up the Delaware River; muskie and walleye fishing on the river is excellent as well, and because so many competing sites are here to lure the sportsman, the river actually tends to be underfished—especially from Milford north.

On large lakes, such as Lake Wallenpaupack and Beltzville Lake, the striped bass start biting in March, and streams in the region become flanked by anglers in mid-April when trout season opens. Also, popular panfish such as sunfish and perch become active in shallower lakes. Trout, shad, and panfish continue to be caught regularly through May. On the first Saturday of May, muskie, pickerel, and walleye seasons open on inland lakes. Fishing for these species is allowed all year on most of the Delaware River. By June, shad start to spawn and die, and walleye and muskie are harder to find, but even as they fade, bass season opens in the middle of the month.

Trout, bass, and panfish are plentiful through the fall. In winter, ice-fishing enthusiasts can cut a hole in a frozen lake and try for perch and pickerel.

To keep things really interesting, a number of fishing contests are held throughout the year. Pickerel and bass competitions are staged at Wallenpaupack in May and June; the Knights of Columbus always kicks off the trout season with a children's trout-fishing contest in Monroe County; and "Shadfests" are run at various times on the upper Delaware and on the Lehigh River at Jim Thorpe. In Monroe County, Pocono Creek and Tobyhanna Creek have been set aside for exclusive use of anglers 12 and younger, or those with physical disabilities.

Licenses must be signed in ink and displayed on an outer garment while fishing, and you must be prepared to furnish positive proof of identification. The trout/salmon stamp is required for fishing in waters where such species are known to dwell.

Whatever the category of your license, it allows you to fish all public waters, including the Delaware River and the Pennsylvania, New York, and New Jersey shores where the river separates the states. Minimum size requirements and daily limits are established for most species. Consult the fishing regulations you will receive with your license for information.

The most famous fish in the Poconos is the **trout.** In the late 1800s and early 1900s, resorts were opened to cater to the fly fishermen who came to play Brodhead Creek. Flies such as the artificial fly, the Henryville Special, the Analomink, the Hamlin, the Paradise, the Swiftwater, the Cresco, and the Canadens were created in the Poconos.

Standard flies such as mayflies, caddisflies, stoneflies, Drakes, nymphs, streamers, Wulff flies, Coachmans, and Compara Duns will attract trout in the Poconos. Rods should be 7 to 9 feet in length. You will need a strong reel and line bearing 4- to 8-pound test.

Brook trout are native to the Poconos. Browns and rainbows are stocked. In addition to artificial lures, trout will go after worms, flies, and insect larvae. While they are smaller than rainbows and browns, brook trout are regarded as prize catches because they are far more rare. If that's what you're searching for, visit one of the small spring-fed brooks in the Poconos, and use an ultra-light spinning rod and your lightest line with a very small lure or bait. Fly fishing for brookies is difficult, because the waters usually are very narrow and have overgrown banks.

Fishing Licenses

All anglers 16 and older need Pennsylvania licenses to try their luck in our waters. Licenses are available at more than 1,500 stores and bait and tackle outlets throughout the state. While fees are subject to change by will of the legislature, here's what they were in 2002:

RESIDENTS

Annual (ages 16 to 64)	$17.00
Annual (65 and older)	$4.00
Senior lifetime license	$16.00

(Available only at Pennsylvania Fish and Boat Commission and local county treasurer offices.)

NONRESIDENTS

Annual (16 and older)	$35.00
Seven-day (16and older)	$30.00
Three-day (16 and older)	$15.00

TROUT/SALMON PERMIT

Annual (all anglers) $5.50

Children 15 and younger fish free.

Stream fishing for trout is easier because many waterways are stocked by the state with thousands of browns and rainbows each year. Larger rods and lures can be used on these bigger waters, and there's more elbowroom for fly fishing. Nymphs and streamers work best when fishing early in the season in cold water. Other than opening day, fall is the best time to land trout, as they are more active when the water temperature is 50 degrees. The largest brown trout feed at night.

The Lackawaxen River and the Brodhead Creek are considered to be among the best trout-fishing spots in the country. Because they are so well regarded and publicized, they are very crowded, particularly early in the season. You might be lucky to find a choice spot on the shoreline. Wading in these deeper, faster waters is not easy.

To catch the larger browns and rainbows, use a medium-heavy 6.5-foot spinning rod with a 0.25- to 0.5-ounce lure weight and 6- to 8-pound test line. Fly fishermen will want a 9-foot rod with 7- to 9-foot leaders to accommodate the longer casts required on the larger bodies of water.

Many local anglers enjoy trying for trout later in the season, when the fresh-stocked "easier" catches have been taken, and the craftier, difficult fish still are around.

Smallmouth bass, which many fly fishermen consider to be just as much fun as trout, are at their peak in fall. They are actively feeding to fatten up for winter and will attack lures, plugs, and live bait

such as earthworms, minnows, hellgrammites, and leeches. In afternoons, bass can be found lurking in deep pools. Early mornings and late evenings, they head for riffles in search of food. **Largemouth bass** prefer thick vegetation and submerged logs. They hide in these areas and wait to feast on passing frogs and bait fish. Cast into shallow areas with thick cover using weedless jigs.

Bass can be caught from a boat or by wading into shallow areas. On the Delaware River, smallmouth fishing is excellent after a summer shower. The rain lowers the temperature of the water and adds oxygen to it, which stimulates the fish to feed.

Equally fabled as sport fish are **American shad,** which migrate up the Delaware River from the lower Delaware Bay to spawn. These silvery fish with deeply forked tails begin migration in mid-March and arrive near Bushkill by mid-April. At the same time, a small tree with white flowers blooms along the slopes of the river. Called serviceberry in other parts of the country, it is known as shad bush in these parts because its blooming coincides with the shad run.

The spring spawning run includes an estimated one million or more fish. The shad have the only naturally spawning population in Pennsylvania.

Shad travel in schools and average three to six pounds. They may be caught from a boat or from land. Light equipment—4- to 6-pound line and a lure known as a "shad dart"—is all you will need. Cast into slow-moving holes or eddies, and use a slight jiggling motion to slowly reel the dart back. Also keep an eye on the anglers downstream from you. If they start catching shad, a school is headed toward you.

Opinions differ widely as to what you should do with a shad once you have landed it. Some swear that smoked or baked fillets of the oily fish are great delicacies, while others just swear at the thought. One veteran outfitter at the Wacky Worm Bait and Tackle Shop in

Boat docks are great summertime hotspots for anglers to drop a line in and try their luck at bringing home some dinner. Docks provide fish with comfortable shade and food.

Gilbert (see our listing in the subsequent "Outfitters/Bait and Tackle Shops" section) offers this recipe: Skin and fillet the shad; dredge it liberally in cracker crumbs and Tabasco sauce; place fillets on an oak board; place the board in an open fire, and cook until well-blackened; then scrape off the shad and eat the board.

But on the subject of shad roe—the eggs of the female fish—there are few dissenters. It is the roe that most shad fishermen have in mind when they set their darts to dancing in the Delaware or the Lehigh. Breaded and battered—and every aficionado has his or her own recipe for this—then pan-fried, the roe makes a rare and delectable treat.

Unlike shad, **Northern pike, pickerel, walleye,** and **muskellunge** travel alone, stalking other fish from beneath logs and other underwater spots of ambush. The best fishing for them is in still water in weed beds. Look for water about 5 feet deep and a lot of vegetation. Pike and pickerel action is strong in fall. Walleyes as large as 14 pounds are taken from Lake Wallenpaupack, although average fish are 18 to 22 inches and weigh 7 to 10 pounds. Muskellunge can grow to be more than 40 pounds and run 50 inches in length. They average 40 inches and about 20 pounds. Pickerel more than 2 feet long are common in many lakes. Muskellunge must be at least 30 inches long to be legally kept; pickerel at least 12 inches; walleye at least 18 inches; and pike at least 24 inches. These are the largest game fish in the Poconos. Their strikes are strong and dramatic, and they put up a great fight. You must use strong gear to land them successfully. Spoon-shaped lures work well, because they move and glitter like living prey. Minnows also are effective as bait.

Pickerels, muskies, and pike are popular with ice fishermen. In winter the water at the bottom of a lake is warmer than that on the surface. Early in the season, before snow covers the ice is the best time to fish because more light filters through the ice and keeps the fish active.

Most ice fishermen use tip-ups, small wooden structures with a reel, line, and hook attached. A flag on the pole is tripped by the reel to indicate a bite. Minnows make the best bait. Tip-ups are scattered across a lake approximately 15 to 50 feet apart. Placement is a matter of guesswork and depends on how many holes you are willing to carve in the ice. If you start getting strikes in one area, move some of your other tip-ups closer to the ones that are producing. Because your tip-ups may cover a large area, be prepared to get plenty of exercise checking them, and take along an extra minnow bucket so bait is easily accessible. To keep your hands dry, use a dip net to get minnows out of the bucket. Wet hands chill quickly. In fact, in winter or early spring when lake and stream waters run near the freezing point, take extra precautions not to fall in. Hypothermia strikes swiftly and can be deadly. Experts say shivering and a powerful sensation of cold set in when body temperature reaches 97 degrees. At 93 degrees, amnesia sets in, followed by unconsciousness at 86 and death at 79. But hypothermia is not the only hazard. The shock of suddenly being plunged into icy water can produce an instant heart attack.

In ice-fishing, your minnows should be set as close to the bottom of the lake as possible, ideally near underwater debris such as logs.

Since you will be outside on a cold day, dress warmly in layers, and wear gloves. Make sure the ice is thick enough to support your weight. Over the last decade winters have been warmer, and only for brief periods has the ice been thick enough for fishing. Bring extra clothing in case you do fall through the ice.

Perch, bluegill, sunfish, and **crappie**—collectively known as panfish—are favorites of youngsters because they are plentiful and easy to catch. They enjoy quiet ponds, but are also found in larger bodies of water such as Lake Wallenpaupack and the Delaware River. Most are small, weighing less than a pound. You can fish for them throughout the year and keep as many as 50 of these combined species each day. There is no minimum size requirement.

Sometimes mistaken for a snake, the **American eel** is actually a long, slender fish. It is the only fish in North America to move downstream to the ocean to breed after living most of its life, usually around eight years, in fresh water. Females can be up to 48 inches long; males are usually about half that length. They leave our Delaware River to spawn in the subtropical waters of the Sargasso Sea southwest of Bermuda. Each female produces as many as 20 million eggs. After mating, the adults die. Only the females make the trek from the sea to inland rivers, streams, and, by squirming through mud or wet grass, ponds. Males stay close to the sea.

Some residents along the Delaware River consider eels a delicacy. Traps, called weirs, are constructed to capture them. Anglers often catch them by accident while trying for other fish.

Channel catfish can weigh as much as 30 pounds. Typically, the ones you will catch will be of the 3- to 5-pound variety. They are most likely found in the deeper parts of the Delaware River. By the end of June they have spawned and want to feed to regain lost weight. The best baits are natural foods such as crayfish and minnows. One well-regarded local fisherman successfully uses fresh chicken livers. Fish for catfish in the evenings. They can easily be identified by their keenly forked tails and the four to eight whiskers, called barbels, around their mouths. The whiskers help the fish find food. When handling a catfish, be especially careful of its dorsal fin, which is razor-sharp and can render a nasty wound upon the hand of an unsuspecting angler.

Pennsylvania's waters are among the cleanest in the country, but the Pennsylvania Department of Environmental Protection (DEP) has found a very small amount of mercury in certain waters and in certain fish. They have issued advisories on these fish in these waters, suggesting that people limit their consumption of these specific fish. On a national level, the EPA has suggested that sport fishermen eat no more than one meal per week of sport fish, to avoid a buildup of any contaminants. The Pennsylvania DEP concurs with that recommendation and the table below provides specific recommendations.

Following are some of the best public fishing waters in the Poconos and the fish you will find in them.

Delaware Water Gap/ Shawnee-on-Delaware

About 40 miles of the **Delaware River** are within the Delaware Water Gap National Recreation Area, which runs from Delaware Water Gap to Milford. Boat launches are off U.S. Highway 209. Beginning at the Kittatinny Point visitor center on the New Jersey side of the river opposite Delaware Water Gap and traveling north, the launches in Pennsylvania are Smithfield Beach Access, north of Shawnee; Bushkill Access, north of Bushkill; Eshback Access, south of the Pocono Environmental Education Center; Dingmans Ferry Access, at Dingmans Ferry; and Milford Beach Access, south of Milford.

Anglers can either take to the water or stay on dry ground. River game fish include American shad, smallmouth bass, muskellunge, sunfish, catfish, American eels, pickerel, and walleye.

All waters within the recreation area are open to sport fishing unless otherwise posted. Areas closed to fishing are the George W. Childs Recreation Site at footbridges and observation platforms, Dingmans Falls, from the top of the falls to the east end of the parking lot during the day, and the pool at the bottom of Silver Thread Falls. Fishing from a boat is prohibited on Hidden Lake.

Stocked waters within the recreation area are **Hidden Lake, Bushkill Creek, Lower Blue Mountain Lake, Flatbrook,** and **Dingmans Creek.** These are the spots to try for trout, bass, and sunfish. The National Park Service provides free maps showing the location of all of these bodies of water.

In winter, do not try to ice-fish on the river, as the ice is rarely (if ever) thick enough to support a person's weight. Given the river's current, falling through its ice could be deadly.

Stroudsburg/East Stroudsburg

While the big lakes and the rivers are in the mountain areas, you'll find some great fly fishing in the streams closer to these towns.

The best places for trout are the **Brodhead Creek** and **McMichaels Creek.** A 9-mile stretch of the Brodhead runs through the Stroudsburgs to the Delaware River. For McMichaels, try the area of the creek near Sciota.

In East Stroudsburg on Highway 447, **Gregory Pond** is a great place to fish for bass, sunfish, and perch.

Mount Pocono Area

North of Canadensis on Highway 390, two lakes in Promised Land State Park, the 422-acre **Promised Land Lake** and the 173-acre **Lower Lake,** are good places to try for bass, pickerel, muskellunge, and panfish throughout the year. Boat Launches are provided at both lakes.

The 250-acre **Gouldsboro Lake,** at Gouldsboro State Park on Highway 507 in Gouldsboro, contains fish similar to those Promised Land lakes. A boat launch is available on the southwestern shore.

Tobyhanna State Park's 170-acre **Tobyhanna Lake** is considered by many locals the best fishing hole in the Mount Pocono area. Bass, brook trout, catfish, yellow perch, and bluegill are common. In the winter, try the lake for pickerel, perch, and bass. Launch your boat from the eastern shore.

East of Blakeslee on Highway 940, 229-acre **Brady's Lake** is popular for bass, muskellunge, panfish, and pickerel. The lake, forged by a deteriorating 89-year-old dam, recently was slated for draining. But Gov. Ed Rendell filed a stay of execution in the form of $2 million in state funding for its rehabilitation.

For trout, try **Tobyhanna Creek** (Highway 611 near Tobyhanna), **Devil's Hole Creek** (Highway 940 near Mount Pocono), and **Pocono Creek** (Highway 611 near Tannersville).

West End

Beltzville Lake near Lehighton off US 209 is stocked with trout, some of which will run to a trophy size of 17 pounds. The lake also is home to some monstrous striped bass. Lunkers tipping the scales at 25 pounds have been taken. Panfish (sunfish, perch, etc.), pickerel, bass, muskellunge, and walleye also can be found on the large man-made lake.

Boat-launching ramps are at Pine Run East on the northern shore and Preacher's Camp on the south shore. Ice fishing is popular here.

The **Pohopoco Creek** below the dam is stocked with trout.

Other popular trout spots in the region are **Aquashicola Creek** (Highway 248, Palmertown), **Buckwa Creek** (Highway 903, Little Gap), **Big Bear Creek** (Highway 90d, Jim Thorpe), **Lizzard Creek** (Highway 248, Bowmanstown), and **Mahoning Creek** (Highway 443, Lehighton).

Hickory Run State Park, off Highway 534 near Hickory Run, has two stocked trout streams, the **Fourth Run** and the

The Lenape, who were native to this area, named the stream that, when it was dammed in 1928, became Lake Wallenpaupack. Wallenpaupack means "the stream of swift and slow water."

Sand Spring. **Mud Run** is also stocked with trout but is only open for fly fishing. The **Lehigh River** flows along the western edge of the park and contains some nice bass and trout. The 90-acre **Francis E. Walters Reservoir** is about 20 minutes away but is worth the trip for bass, panfish, trout, and walleye.

The largest lake in this area is the 330-acre **Mauch Chunk Lake,** near Jim Thorpe off US 209. Most of the game fish of the Poconos—bass, panfish, pickerel, trout, and walleye—are found here. A boat launch is near the western end of the lake. Fishing is not permitted on the east end.

Milford/Lake Wallenpaupack Area

The most famous fishing here is at **Pecks Pond,** west of Milford on Highway 402 north of Marshalls Creek. It provides a 315-acre, very shallow home for bass, panfish, and pickerel. The area around the lake is particularly scenic. Many trophy fish have been pulled from the thick vegetation in Pecks Pond. In winter, don't be afraid to bundle up and try some ice-fishing; it's worth the effort. While here, visit the Pennsylvania Fishing Museum (see our Attractions chapter) in the Pecks Pond Store on the edge of the lake.

Join the bald eagles and fish the 1,100-acre **Shohola Lake,** near Shohola Falls, which is renowned for its supply of bass, pickerel, trout, and panfish. Avoid the posted restricted area where bald eagles nest.

Like the Delaware Water Gap National Recreation Area, the **Upper Delaware River** is filled with bass, pickerel, eel, and American shad. The best river-access point for boats, and a great fishing spot as well, is in Lackawaxen. Western writer Zane Grey settled in this little town largely because of the great fishing nearby. (See our Arts and Culture chapter.)

The **Lackawaxen River** is nationally celebrated as a trout lover's paradise. On opening day, its shores are jammed with anglers. However, the river is very large and abundantly stocked, so by all means make some room for yourself and enjoy. Savvy anglers pay attention to the water-release schedule of the dam at nearby Lake Wallenpaupack, which empties into the Lackawaxen. The fishing is much better after rushing water from the dam enters the river and stirs up the fish. But a note of caution also is called for; the fluctuating water level can also stir up a boat, and the people in it, if they fail to see it coming.

Other less famous but productive trout waters are **Little Bushkill Creek** (near Bushkill), **Saw Creek** (near Dingmans Ferry), **Middle Branch Lake** (near Dingmans Ferry), and **Shohola Creek** (near Lords Valley).

Some lakes worth a look for bass, panfish, and pickerel are **Billings Pond** (near Lords Valley), **Lake Minisink** (near Dingmans Ferry), and **Little Mud Pond** (near Dingmans Ferry).

Fishing is a year-round activity at **Lake Wallenpaupack.** While the peak seasons are spring and summer, ice-fishing is prevalent throughout winter.

Anglers hope to catch bass, muskellunge, walleye, pike, trout, pickerel, perch, bluegill, and crappies. In recent years the lake has developed large weed beds that provide cover for young bass and panfish that sometimes grow to trophy size. The lake record for a brown trout is more than 17 pounds. The striped bass record is 35 pounds. The best places to look for trout around opening day are in shallow, rocky shoals. They like to hang out at the mouths of creeks that run warmer than the main lake. The best time to catch stripers at night is around the first full moon in June. By July, the lake can become very crowded

Pennsylvania DEP Recommendations Regarding Sportfish Consumption

WATER BODY	AREA UNDER ADVISORY	SPECIES	MEAL FREQUENCY
Lake Wallenpaupack	Entire lake	Walleye	One meal/month
Beltzville Lake	Entire lake	Walleye	Two meals/month
Tobyhanna Creek	Pocono Lake dam to mouth	Smallmouth bass	Two meals/month
Bushkill	Confluence of Saw Creek to mouth	American eel	Two meals/month
Promised Land Lake	Entire lake	Largemouth bass	One meal/month
Prompton Reservoir (W. branch of the Lackawaxen)	Entire lake	Largemouth bass	One meal/month
		Walleye	Two meals/month
West Branch Delaware River (Wayne County)	Entire section	Brown trout	Two meals/month

with pleasure boats, making it more difficult to find a quiet spot. Labor Day signals the end of the main tourist season, and anglers again dominate the lake. Fall is the best time to catch smallmouth bass. The best baits are spinner bait or crank bait. If you are looking for muskies, try fishing on a stormy day in November.

Encompassing 5,700 acres, Lake Wallenpaupack has plenty of room for everyone. Experienced anglers as well as novices will enjoy a day here. Even if you go home empty handed, the scenery is entertainment enough.

Boat launches are provided. (See our In, On, and Around the Water chapter for more information on the facilities at the lake.) The shoreline is filled with marinas, sports shops, boat rental stores, bait shops, and supply stores. You can hire a guide to lead you to secret spots.

Other lakes of choice for bass and pickerel are **Belmont Lake** (Highway 371 in Pleasant Mount), **Prompton Reservoir** (Highway 170 in Honesdale), **White Deer Lake** (Highway 590 in Hawley), and **Fairview Lake** (Highway 390 in Paupack).

Upper Woods Pond (Highway 371 in Cold Springs) is one of the few glacial trout lakes in Pennsylvania. The waters stay cold and are 90 feet deep. The lake is stocked with trout and Kikanee salmon. It also is stocked in winter for ice-fishing. The use of bait fish is prohibited.

Streams to try for trout are **Butternut Creek** (Newfoundland), **Dyberry Creek** (Honesdale), **Equinunk Creek** (Equinunk), and **Wallenpaupack Creek** (Newfoundland).

Finally, if all else fails and, being an angler prone to mendacity, you do not want to admit failure at home, stop off either at the **Paradise Trout Preserve,** (570) 629-0422, in Cresco or at **Big Brown Fish and Pay Lake,** (570) 629-0427, just outside of Effort, and buy your catch. Trout at the Paradise hatchery go for $3.95

a pound, with an added charge of $2.00 if you want to catch them yourself. The fishing fee is $2.50 at Big Brown, but you pay $4.25 a pound for trout and $5.50 a pound for bass. There is no charge at either place for the one that got away.

HUNTING

White-tailed deer delight visitors to the Poconos with sweet pastoral images of Bambi and his woodland friends, but many a resident sees a different picture. To folks trying to keep their sylvan yards landscaped, Bambi and his buddies are nothing more than a greedy gang of ornamental shrub-, tree-, and garden-munching vermin.

The problem lies less in the deer's natural appetite for yew, rhododendron, garden vegetables, and the tender bark of fruit trees than in the fact that there are so many of them. The total deer population in Pennsylvania approaches 1.3 million. Hunters harvest more deer in Pennsylvania than in any other state except Texas, which has six times as much land. And Pennsylvania usually sells more hunting licenses than any other state.

All of this, of course, is great news for hunters who come to the Poconos from all over the eastern United States to hunt in fall and winter seasons. Our diverse public game lands include high mountain meadows, thick wooded forests, and flat farmlands. Habitats similar to those found in the Midwestern United States, and even Canada, are also found in the Poconos. Throughout Pennsylvania, more than 1.2 million acres have been set aside as state forests, parks, and game lands.

Deer travel in small groups typically consisting of a doe, her fawns, and young female offspring. Bucks tend to go their own way at an early age. They travel together from summer through fall. Leadership is determined by antler tests, which sometimes become full-scale fights resulting in injury or death. Deer have been known to live as long as 18 years, although in Pennsylvania, most bucks are harvested before their fourth birthday, which is why it's rare to see a buck with a full rack of antlers.

The average range for a deer is 500 to 3,000 acres. However, they might travel as many as 50 miles in winter in search of food.

Lawns and gardens are not the only green areas that suffer when too many deer are on the land. Left uncontrolled, deer populations can overwhelm a forest, eating all vegetation within reach. Deer are also a real menace to drivers, and dead deer littering Pocono highways have become a front-page issue. In fact, a couple of years ago, Monroe County hired someone to remove roadkill. In the first seven months of his job, "Roadkill Rick" removed more than 1,000 dead animals, mostly deer, from the county's roadsides.

Since mankind long since has eradicated the natural predators that once held deer populations in check, they now have only humans to hunt them, and when not enough are taken, orchards, nurseries, and farms suffer heavy losses from deer that have nowhere else to feed. This affects the lives of both other wildlife species and human residents. In winter, young deer can starve because of a lack of food. As a result, deer management through hunting is essential, but hunting is carefully monitored to maintain a stable deer population.

But deer make crafty prey. They have pupils that open much wider than those of humans, allowing up to nine times more light to enter their eyes. This gives deer much better night vision than ours. Their antlers are among the fastest growing of the living tissues; and a buck's rack can grow 0.25 inch a day.

Some common sense tips for hunters include not using scented shaving lotions, soaps, hair tonic, or cologne before heading into the woods. Deer have a keen sense of smell and will quickly notice the unfamiliar odor. Hunters should start at first light when game is feeding. Deer move into the wind. You should find an appropriate blind against the wind and let the game come to you. At dark and before sunrise, deer move toward water.

If you spot tracks and want to tell if they are fresh, look for frost crystals. If they are there, the track was made the night before. When the sun dries the morning frost, the edges of the track tend to crumble. If the track is clean and there is no frost, then it probably is fresh.

Health-conscious hunters should know that deer meat, or venison, is one of the most wholesome red meats. It has one-fifth the fat content of beef or pork, and fewer calories and more protein than lamb, veal, beef, or pork.

After deer, the most popular target for hunters is Pennsylvania's largest game animal, the **black bear.** Pennsylvania bears tend to grow faster, attain larger-than-average weights, and breed earlier and more regularly than bears in other states. By age three, Pennsylvania bears average 258 pounds. Adults range in size from 380 to 480 pounds. The larger sizes of Pennsylvania bears can be partially explained by the presence of many parks, campgrounds, picnic areas, and landfills. They receive more contact with humans, and as a result, more calorie-rich food than bears in more isolated areas.

Pennsylvania black bear litters average three cubs, but dens with four and five cubs are not uncommon. Few other states have recorded a bear litter of four. Cubs are born during winter in the den the female has chosen for her period of hibernation.

Bears are much harder to take down than deer. They are also much harder to find. Pike County has the largest bear population in the state, estimated between 4,000 and 6,000. Should you find one, you had better be armed with a powerful rifle. A bear's dense muscles, fat, and bones can deflect shots from underpowered weapons. The average target area on a bear for a clean kill shot is less than one foot square.

Wounded bears head for the thickest cover available. If there is no snow on the ground, you must track the bear using a blood trail, so consider a bullet with enough power to pass through the animal and create a double blood trail. A total of 2,995 black bears were harvested statewide in the 2003 hunting season; 149 of which were taken in the Poconos.

Wild turkey season conveniently arrives just before Thanksgiving. Because there is danger of being accidentally shot, hunters must wear florescent-orange clothing when moving through the woods in search of turkey. Also, when stationary and calling, tie an orange band around the nearest tree so other hunters will not be fooled by your call and open fire on you. Every year the incidence of people being shot—and dying—when they are mistaken for turkeys is much higher than during any other hunting season. With implementation of broader blaze-orange regulations—100 square inches, visible 360 degrees when moving, must be worn—the incidence rates have dropped, but the danger remains, so be cautious.

Proper clothing is essential. Wear good camouflage, a facemask, and gloves. Another popular item is a turkey vest, which has a foam seat to make those calling positions more comfortable. The better vests have a pouch in the back to store your kill. Since a turkey can weigh more than 20 pounds, packing it there

The aqueduct originally constructed to carry water from the Lake Wallenpaupack dam to the power plant 3.5 miles away was made of 5 million board feet of Douglas fir shipped from the State of Washington. The wooden line—14 feet in diameter—was replaced with steel in the 1950s.

sure beats carrying over your shoulder. Make sure the turkey is in a comfortable shooting range, usually no more than 40 yards away, before you take your shot.

Popular small game in the Poconos include **squirrels,** which are active just after sunrise and in late afternoon; **ruffed grouse,** which begin drinking and feeding just after sunup; **pheasants,** which are found along roadsides in the morning and in farm fields later in the day; **rabbits,** which feed heavily at night; and **groundhogs.** Duck hunters can go after migrating **Canada geese, mallards, pintails, wood ducks,** and several other species.

Amid much controversy, a very limited number of permits to harvest bobcats was approved in 2000, and the state continues this program. A random drawing for these permits takes place in Harrisburg in September. Applications, available from the Pennsylvania Game Commission, www.pgc .state.pa.us, are accepted through July and the first two weeks of August.

Trappers try to outwit **mink, muskrats, beavers, raccoons, foxes, coyotes, opossums, skunks,** and **weasels.**

Following are some of the better public game lands in the Poconos.

Delaware Water Gap/ Shawnee-on-Delaware

Most of the land of the **Delaware Water Gap National Recreation Area** (see our Parks chapter) is open to hunters except for areas within 450 feet of any structures or trails. For a list of other areas of the park that are closed to hunters, go to their Web site, www.nps.gov, or drop by one of the Visitor's Centers for a map. (See our Parks chapter.). Hunters also are asked to be wary of hikers and others using the park's facilities. No hunting is permitted in fields with unharvested crops. Artificial or natural bait is prohibited. No hunting is allowed by any motorized vehicle or on any public road. Tree

stands must be freestanding and removable so they do not damage trees. No trapping is allowed.

Mount Pocono Area

Promised Land State Park, Tobyhanna State Park, Gouldsboro State Park, and **Big Pocono State Park** (see our Parks chapter) all have public hunting areas and are good locations to pursue deer, black bear, turkey, and small game. Trapping is permitted in designated areas.

This region is heavily forested with rugged mountain peaks and numerous glacial lakes. Many hunters consider these woods to be the most productive in the Poconos.

Two of the more popular state game lands are the 8,600-acre **Delaware State Forest,** near Canadensis and Tannersville, and the 25,500-acre **SGL** (State Game Land) **#127** near Tannersville.

West End

Hunting and trapping are permitted on 1,707 acres of land in **Beltzville State Park,** near Lehighton. Game species include pheasants, rabbits, ruffed grouse, waterfowl, and deer.

Hickory Run State Park, east of White Haven, is open to hunters from the end of September through March. Look for deer, turkey, black bear, squirrels, and snowshoe hare, a rarity in the Poconos.

State Game Lands #141, #129, and **#40** are near White Haven and north and west of Jim Thorpe.

Milford/Lake Wallenpaupack Area

The Milford area is dominated by private residential communities and hunting/ fishing clubs. Public lands are scarcer than in other parts of the Poconos. However, the wetlands and forests available hold many deer and black bear.

Northwest of Milford off U.S. Highway 6 are **State Game Lands #209, #180, #116,** and **#183.** These game lands total 21,564 acres.

North of Lake Wallenpaupack, hunters enjoy open stretches of land in northern Wayne County, near the New York border. **State Game Lands #70** and **#299** are at the far northern edge of the county. Northeast of Honesdale is **Prompton State Park** with 850 acres of public land. It is the only state-owned parkland in Wayne County. **State Game Land #159** is north of Honesdale on Highway 191 at Lookout. It covers 9,367 acres. Deer and small game are plentiful on these lands.

This region also is home to 14,000 acres of private farmlands that are great places to hunt pheasants and turkeys. Try talking to the landowner of a choice site for permission to hunt.

And never forget this: There is no open season on fishers, Hungarian partridges, otters, pine martens, and sharp-tailed grouse. These species are off-limits to all hunters at all times.

Hunting Licenses

All hunters are required to carry a Pennsylvania hunting license.

RESIDENT

Annual junior (ages 12 to 16)	$6.00
Annual adult (ages 17 to 64)	$20.00
Annual senior (65 and older)	$13.00

NONRESIDENT

Annual adult (17 or older)	$101.00
Seven-day small game (12 and older)	$31.00

Please note the following:

- Muzzleloader licenses are $11, whereas archery licenses are $16. Both may be used without purchasing muzzleloader and archery licenses during regular hunting seasons.
- Bear licenses are $16 for residents and $36 for nonresidents.
- The fees for fur-taker licenses to trap are identical to the ones for hunters.
- To hunt waterfowl, residents older than 16 must purchase a special duck stamp that costs $3.00. Nonresidents pay $6.00.

OUTFITTERS/BAIT AND TACKLE SHOPS

Because of the popularity of unparalleled hunting and fishing opportunities 12 months of the year in the Poconos, the region boasts almost as many general sports outfitters and bait and tackle shops as it does gas stations. They range from little mom-and-pop operations to super-stores, but all have one thing in common: Their proprietors are steeped in the lore of the area and know exactly where hunting and fishing action is best and what equipment is needed to partake of it. Most of them are eager to share the information with their customers.

Bait and tackle shops generally stock worms and minnows, along with a wide array of artificial lures. Most shops carry an assortment of line, hooks, swivels, bobbers, rods, reels, and accessories. Most outfitters also stock fly-fishing gear, and some smaller ones specialize exclusively in the sport.

Hunters can find ammunition of all sizes and guns of all gauges—including 18th-century style muzzleloaders—in which to load it. Cleaning kits, oils, lubricants, scopes, and grips are popular accessories usually in stock. Many outfitters also carry scents and calls as well as practice targets. And most sell an assortment of knives, binoculars, and hunting apparel as well.

There are so many outlets we can list only a few of them here, by region. Most of them sell hunting and fishing licenses as well as equipment, and you should find yourself in good hands wherever you go.

Delaware Water Gap/ Shawnee-on-Delaware

E.D. Huffman and Sons
Highway 209 at Highway 402
Marshalls Creek
(570) 223–8468

This general store, with its tap room and bait and tackle shop, has been in continuous operation in the village of Marshalls Creek since 1820. Live bait is sold from a vending machine on the front porch, giving fishermen access to worms and minnows 24 hours a day. Huffman's carries a fair inventory of rods, reels, lures, and accessories plus camping supplies and a basic line of groceries. No rifles or shotguns are sold, but fishing licenses are available. The store is open year-round.

Stroudsburg/East Stroudsburg

Dunkelberger's Sports Outfitter
585 Main Street, Stroudsburg
(570) 421–7950
www.dunkelbergers.com

This is an upscale superstore covering all aspects of outdoor sports and recreation. It stocks all the top brands in rods and reels, a full array of lures, wet and dry flies, and a full line of men's and women's clothing and footwear. Kayaks and canoes occupy a central display space, and on the hunting side, Dunkelberger's offers an arsenal of rifles, shotguns, and pistols as well as a full range of camping and archery equipment, including bows, in stock. The experts in the archery department will not only sell you bows and arrows, but they'll also tune them so they work together optimally, and you can practice at their state-of-the-art archery range. Dunkelberger's sells hunting and fishing licenses and is open all year.

Family Bait & Tackle Shop
624 North Courtland Street
East Stroudsburg
(570) 421–6918

This little shop, dedicated only to fishing, sells all varieties of live bait and maintains an inventory of more than 1,000 lures as well as a wide variety of rods and reels. It offers fishing licenses and is open from March through October.

Mount Pocono Area

Pop's Sports Spot
Highway 940, Pocono Lake
(570) 643–7677
ww.sportspotonline.com

This shop carries live bait—available inside during operating hours and 24 hours a day by vending machine—and archery gear out of all proportion to its size. Wet and dry flies are tied in-house, and at least two dozen top-brand bows are kept in stock at all times. Arrows are custom made, and gear can be tried out on a six-acre walkthrough "3-D" archery range. Pop's sells shot, guns, and rifles, as well as muzzleloaders, black powder, and ball ammunition. Some hunting and fishing apparel is in stock, and boat and canoe rentals are available. Pop's has grown tremendously recently with the addition of a 5,000-square-foot boat showroom. They offer rowboats, ski boats, bass boats, pontoons, and more, as well as Mercury engines, which they service, too. They will register your boat, and they even carry trailers to haul the boats you buy here. The shop sells hunting and fishing licenses and is open all year.

West End

A.A. Outfitters
Highway 534 at Hickory Run Road
White Haven
(570) 643–8000, (800) 443–8119
www.aaoutfitters.com

Highway 115, Blakeslee
(570) 643–8000

This operation, started by an entrepreneur working out of his home, now publishes catalogs and sells its wares worldwide. A.A. Outfitters, which maintains a sister store in Blakeslee, is exclusively devoted to fly fishing and runs an Angler's Academy to teach the fine art of fly casting to beginners who want to learn it and to experts who seek to hone their skills. The two shops carry one of the largest inventories of fly-tying equipment—feathers, hooks, jigs, and thread—in the Northeast plus top-of-the-line fly rods and reels. Custom-built rods are also available. The shop carries no hunting equipment, sells no licenses, and shuns spinning and bait-casting gear, but it does offer a high-end line of hunting and fishing clothing. Both shops are open all year.

Alpha Sporting 'N' Gun Shop
Highway 209 Business, Sciota
(570) 992–7026

Alpha sits between two prime trout streams—the McMichaels and the Old Mill—and carries a full selection of live bait, rods, and reels. For the hunter there's a full arsenal of firearms along with ammunition and reloading systems. Alpha Sporting 'N' Gun Shop recently expanded and now carries a full line of camping equipment. Fishing licenses are available, and the store is open seven days a week all year.

Wacky Worm & Tackle Shop
Highway 209, Gilbert
(610) 681–6226
www.wackyworm.com

This cavernous sporting goods superstore claims to have the largest fishing inventory in the northeastern United States, more than one million plastic lures on its walls and more than 800 rods and reels in stock at all times. The store also offers a wide selection of live bait, fishing and camping accessories, and an extensive array of archery gear. No shotguns or rifles are available in over-the-counter sales, but they can be ordered through a catalog. Wacky Worm offers fishing seminars throughout the summer months, and the proprietor, who will custom-make any lure desired, loves to dispense outdoor lore to his customers. Fishing licenses are available, and the store is open all year.

Milford/Lake Wallenpaupack Area

Angler's Roost & Hunter's Rest
106 Scenic Drive, Suite 1A, Lackawaxen
(570) 685–2010

This sports center, in the heart of a mini-mall, carries enough weaponry to start a small war. In addition to a wide selection of shotguns, rifles, and handguns plus ammunition for all of them, the Roost offers slingshots, blowguns, and air guns. They specialize in black powder. The fisherman will find an extensive inventory of lures and flies (both wet and dry) and rods and reels (mainly by Courtland), along with plenty of live bait. Camping gear and a host of other recreation items, including snowshoes, are offered. And as if that were not enough, the Roost books float trips (see In, On, and Around the Water) both for fishing and recreation, down the Delaware and Lackawaxen rivers. Fishing licenses are sold here year-round.

Herberling's Sport Shop
Off Highway 6, Prompton
(570) 253-1801
This little shop has been in business—primarily as a supplier to the hunter—since 1907. It carries a wide arsenal of shotguns, rifles, and handguns as well as black powder and ball, muzzleloaders, and reloading equipment for modern weapons. The shop boasts an indoor firing range for handguns and rimfire rifles. Fishing equipment is restricted to some light tackle and ice-fishing gear. Heberling's also carries Easy Go Utility Hunting Vehicles. Their extensive Web site offers a wide selection of goods, some directly from the manufacturer. Neither hunting nor fishing licenses are sold here, but the store is open all year.

Hunter's Gallery
Highway 590 at Highway 348, Hamlin
(570) 689-7898
Despite the name, this shop caters to the fisherman as much as to the hunter, with a wide selection of lures and flies and a full range of live bait. The store also carries a substantial inventory of firearms, ammunition, and archery gear, with about 20 bows kept in stock at all times. Hunting and fishing licenses are available, and the store is open year-round.

Ironwood Point Sport Shop
Highway 590, Greentown
(570) 857-0677
A very extensive range of lures and flies is available here, along with all the live bait a fisherman could desire. Rods and reels range in price from $10 all the way up to $555. Fishing licenses are available, and the store is open year-round.

Pickerel Inn
Highway 402 and Silver Lake Road
Dingmans Ferry
(570) 775-7737
This is a rural one-stop shopping center for the sportsman, with a delicatessen, a convenience store, and a gasoline and propane service station in addition to the

sports shop. The shop offers a full range of live bait and carries an extensive inventory of flies and lures, along with rods, reels, and accessories. For the hunter, they carry firearms along with ammunition for all calibers and gauges of guns. The store is open seven days a week, 14 hours a day, all year. Both hunting and fishing licenses are sold here.

Sportsman's Rendezvous
113 Harford Street, Milford
(570) 296-6113
This full-service hunting and fishing shop has been in business for almost 50 years. It offers a full line of lures and major brand flies and some of the sport's top brands of rods and reels, ranging in price from $30 for a full rig to more than $200 for a reel alone. The hunter will find a full inventory of firearms, along with a few bows and archery accessories. Hunting and fishing licenses are sold, and the store is open year-round.

FISHING AND HUNTING SEASONS

Actual dates for hunting and fishing in the Poconos are subject to change, but here are the dates that were observed in 2003.

Fishing

DELAWARE RIVER

Trout (all species)—April 13 to September 30.
  Largemouth and smallmouth bass, muskellunge and hybrids, striped bass and hybrids, pickerel, shad, and herring—open year-round.
  Walleye—open year round on the river between New Jersey and Pennsylvania; January 1 to March 14 and May 4 to December 31 on the river between New York and Pennsylvania.
  Sturgeon—an endangered species, cannot be taken at any time.

COMMONWEALTH INLAND WATERS, INCLUDING THE POCONOS

All species of trout and salmon—April 13 to September 1. Extended season—all approved trout streams and their downstream areas and all lakes and ponds, January 1 through February 28 and September 3 through December 31.

Largemouth, smallmouth, and spotted bass—All year except April 16 through June 17, when catch and immediate release only is permitted.

Muskellunge and hybrids, pickerel, pike, walleye and hybrids, sauger—January 1 through March 14 and May 14 to December 31.

American shad, herring, gizzard shad, striped bass, white bass and hybrids, sunfish, yellow perch, crappies, catfish, rock bass, suckers, eels, carp, white bass—open year round.

Hickory shad and paddlefish—closed; unlawful to catch or kill these fish.

Hunting

DEER

Archery—either sex—September 29 to November 10 and December 26 to January 12.

Firearms—either sex—November 26 to December 8.

Firearms—antlerless—October 18 to 20 for junior and senior license holders, disabled person permit (with vehicle), and Pennsylvania residents serving on active duty in the U.S. Armed Forces.

Flintlock—antlerless—October 13 to 20.

Regular flintlock muzzleloader—either sex—December 26 to January 12.

Bear—November 19 to 21.

Bobcat (by special license, only)—October 13 to February 23.

Turkey—October 27 to November 17 and, for bearded birds only, April 27 to May 25.

The Game Commission estimates that more than 45,000 to 60,000 deer are killed on roadways in Pennsylvania annually. Always keep an eye out for them while traveling on back roads. This is especially important during November and December, when icy roads combined with deer fleeing from hunters often cause traffic accidents.

SMALL GAME

Squirrel—youth hunt for junior license holders only, October 6 and 8; all hunters October 13 to November 25, December 10 to 24, and December 26 to February 9.

Ruffed grouse—October 13 to November 24, December 10 to 24, December 26 to January 12.

Cottontail rabbit—October 27 to November 24, December 10 to 24, December 26 to February 9.

Pheasant—October 27 to November 24; cocks and hens—October 27 to November 24, December 10 to 24, December 26 to February 9.

Bobwhite quail—October 27 to November 24.

Snowshoe hare—December 26 to January.

Crow—July 1 to November 25, December 28 to April 7 (Friday, Saturday, and Sunday only).

Woodchucks, coyotes, opossums, skunk, weasels—open season at all times.

Seasons and bag limits on ducks, geese, doves, woodcock, and other migratory game birds must conform to laws established by the U.S. Fish and Wildlife Service. Because this requires a lengthy federal process, these laws cannot be set until late summer in any year. Check at local post offices, or call the Pennsylvania Game Commission, (570) 675-1144 or (877) 877-9357.

WINTER SPORTS

When we moved to the Poconos, we decided we had to make friends with winter. We bought sleds, a toboggan, and cross-country skis. Going against our natural instincts, we got out in the snow every chance we could, and guess what? We had fun.

Probably the most important thing we learned in our attempt to winterize ourselves is how to dress for the cold. Wear layers—long underwear, shirts, and sweaters. If you alternate loosely woven layers like sweaters, with tightly woven layers, you'll trap the warm air inside your clothing, which is where you want it to be. Look for socks, boots, gloves, and hats that use special fibers like insulite, Polartec, and Gore-tex to keep you extra warm and dry. Gore-tex fabric is especially good, because it's waterproof. If your feet are cold, your whole body will be cold, so be sure to get high-quality socks and boots. Don't neglect a hat; you can lose a great deal of heat through your head. You can get wet from sweating (yes, you can get that hot in the snow) and from falling from sleds, skis, and ice skates. In fact, if you bring some extra clothing when you go out for an activity that might involve falling, you can change out of the wet garb and prolong your time outdoors. If you're skiing, consider tinted goggles that will protect your eyes from the blinding sun and blowing snow—and prevent them from tearing up when you're going really fast. If you wear glasses, use an anti-fogging agent so that when you heat up, your glasses don't steam up; and don't forget to put sunblock on your face when you spend a brilliant day on the slopes.

Pocono ski mountains all make snow, so as long as it's cold enough, you'll be able to ski, snowboard, or tube. The other sports, however, depend on the weather. One winter we'll have so much cold and snow you'll think we're in the Yukon; the next year, we'll get so little snow that you might as well be in Florida while your sleds and cross-country skis gather cobwebs in the garage. In the same month we can have spring one week and major winter storms the next. If you're determined to get out, and Mother Nature is not cooperating, remember that it often snows up the mountain when it rains down around the Stroudsburgs. Call Promised Land State Park for conditions up there, and you may get in a few extra days of winter fun you don't find down by the river.

The latest entry on the winter sports scene is snow tubing. Snow tubing is like sledding, except the trails are part of a ski mountain, and there's a tow that takes you to the top. All of the ski mountains now offer snow tubing.

Winter sports are not without their dangers. Most of the sports involve hurtling down hills or across frozen surfaces at thrilling speeds, which means that you're a likely candidate to break something. It's best to go with another person in case you get hurt and need help, even if you're going out to do something as staid as cross-country skiing. Whatever sport you choose, learn and observe the safety rules, and be considerate of others.

Even though most people greet emerging crocuses and daffodils with joy, winter sports enthusiasts feel a certain sense of sadness when they see the purples and yellows of spring, because they'll

---

Don't forget sunblock; the snow reflects the sun and you can get a bad burn on your face, even in the dead of winter. So pick up a good sunblock that's made for faces and use it!

have to wait another eight months before they can again experience that dazzling combination of snow, sun, and speed.

DOWNHILL SKIING

The glamour sport and the one that brings the most people to the Poconos is downhill, or alpine, skiing. We have six major ski mountains offering a variety of services. Some of the resorts and private communities have ski slopes too. All of the mountains allow snowboarding as well as skiing, and many now have separate snow tubing areas for those who like to take their winter sports sitting down.

Skiing may seem like a rich man's sport, but there are many ways to cut the costs. If you plan to ski regularly, there are season passes and books of tickets that will save you lots of money. These options must be bought preseason, so if an area interests you, call or write for rates and package deals before the season starts. If you live here, look for a ski club. These clubs typically offer a series of lessons, equipment, and lift tickets for a deep discount. The catch is that they take place at the same time every week, so you must be able to ski or snowboard at that time. Of course, you'll make friends in a ski club, and most are held at times when the slopes are not too crowded. If you can't find a club, talk to a ski mountain about forming your own. Most give discounts to groups, and if you organize a ski club, you may even find yourself skiing for free. Many ski areas look for volunteers to patrol the slopes or help in some other way. In return, volunteers get to ski for free; so if you have a little time to give, call your favorite mountain, and see if there's a service you can trade for free skiing. Another trick locals use is to work for the mountain in some capacity; even part-time jobs entitle skiers to lift privileges.

Skiing has many variables when it comes to price. If you have your own equipment, all you'll need is a lift ticket.

The "vertical" is the height of the hill, but different hills have different slopes or pitch. A hill with a short vertical could have very steep trails, while a hill with a long vertical could have gentle ones, and vice versa. "Getting vertical" means the hill has a difficult pitch, so it feels like you're going straight down.

Lift ticket prices are governed by factors such as time of day, day of the week, and holidays. Age is a determining factor in price too. Each area has its own bargain days—Ladies Day, Civil Service Day, Family Night, and specialty days.

Rates for lift tickets range from $30 to $46 for an adult, depending on the time of day, whether you plan to ski all day or night only, and what day of the week it is. Junior lift-tickets range from $26 to $45 depending on the day and whether the ticket is for a full day or night time only. Children 12 and younger are considered juniors at most ski areas, but there are some exceptions. Youngsters participating in learn-to-ski programs for children, such as SKIwee, receive lift tickets as part of the package. Senior-citizen discounts (the age varies but starts between 60 and 65) are available at all ski areas. Seniors older than 70 ski free anytime at Shawnee and for vastly reduced rates at some other mountains.

Of course, prices are subject to change without notice.

You can also purchase a package that gives you a discount on your lift ticket for a certain number of days. The packages are many and so varied that providing rates and options here would be formidable.

Snowboarders are allowed on all Pocono ski mountains; many even have special facilities for them.

Most ski areas have half- or quarter-pipes and snowboard parks enjoyed by snowboarders and a few daredevil skiers. The pipes look like half- and quarter-sections of those giant drainage pipes

> *Respect the slopes on a ski mountain, and don't try ones you're not ready to ski. Despite the fact that so many people do it, skiing can be a dangerous sport. Ski safely and respectfully—you'll be less likely to get hurt.*

many of us crawled through as children. They provide an area where snowboarders can ride up and down, jump, spin, slide, and generally have a good time.

While the sport looks easy, it requires a lot of skill and practice. Since snowboarding has become popular, accidents on snowboards have far outnumbered skiing accidents and, unfortunately, they tend to be more severe.

If you have never skied or used a snowboard before, please, please, please, take a lesson. Most mountains offer a reasonable first-time-on-skis package, which includes equipment rental, a lesson, and a lift ticket, usually limited to the bunny slope, which will be all you can handle at your first session. While skiing is not hard (if we can do it, anyone can) there are a few tricks you'll need to learn. Falling is not a problem; most first-timers do a fair amount. It's getting up that presents difficulties, especially when you're on a steep slope and feel crippled by those long things on your feet that keep wanting to slide out from under you. Make sure to ask your instructor to show you how to get up. If you fall getting off the lift, roll out of the way, so the next lift riders will not fall on top of you.

Ski areas also rent ski and snowboarding equipment. Rental packages are available for more than one day. Complete ski sets—skis, boots, and poles—rent for $20 to $28. Snowboard sets, which include the boards and boots, average $30 for a rental. Many mountains now rent helmets, too, for less than $10. We highly recommend this optional piece of equipment.

In every ski shop, you'll find skilled technicians who can make repairs on your equipment as well as make sure that the equipment you rent suits your needs. Lockers are available at all areas. Parking is free, but the parking lots are large; be prepared to walk a distance, carrying your gear.

All ski areas have restrooms and cafeterias. You can buy food or bring your own and eat in the open dining areas.

We don't have to have snow from the sky to make good skiing or snowboarding. (See this chapter's Close-up.) Most of the mountains begin making snow around Thanksgiving—earlier if the weather cooperates. If temperatures stay below freezing at night, snowmakers can provide a solid base before Christmas. Soon after the snowmakers begin their work, the skiers can begin their fun. The season is considered at its peak from Christmas through St. Patrick's Day, if cold conditions hold.

Nighttime temperatures need to be 28 degrees or below for good snowmaking. If we have rain or a warm spell of temperatures in the high 30s and low 40s for several days in a row, the snowmakers will push the snow around to keep as many trails open as possible. You'll probably find most of the mountains open during a warm spell, but call or check their Web site to find out about conditions. During warmer weather, the ski areas "up the mountain," Jack Frost and Big Boulder, will have slightly colder conditions and a possibility of more snow.

The major ski resorts usually offer special events throughout the season—races, carnivals, Torchlight Parades . . . the list goes on. Each mountain puts out a brochure listing winter events as well as seasonal specials on lift tickets, so call for a brochure.

Skiers' Responsibility Code

Most ski areas post the Skiers' Responsibility Code. Regardless of how you decide to enjoy the slopes, always show courtesy to others and be aware that there are elements of risk in skiing that common sense and personal awareness can help reduce. The following is a partial list officially endorsed by National Ski Areas Association (NSAA).

- Always stay in control, and be able to stop or avoid other people or objects.
- People ahead of you have the right of way. It is your responsibility to avoid them.
- You must not stop where you obstruct a trail or are not visible from above.
- Whenever starting downhill or merging into a trail, look uphill and yield to others.
- Always use devices to help prevent runaway equipment.
- Observe all posted signs and warnings. Keep off closed trails and out of closed areas.
- Prior to using any lift, you must have the knowledge and ability to load, ride, and unload safely.

Delaware Water Gap/ Shawnee-on-Delaware

Shawnee Mountain
Hollow Road, Shawnee-on-Delaware
(570) 421–7231
(800) 233–4218 (snow report)
www.shawneemt.com
Shawnee has 23 trails served by seven double chairlifts, one triple, and one quad lift. Its vertical is 700 feet. The staff starts making snow around Thanksgiving, weather permitting, and the trails open as soon as they're adequately covered. All trails are generally snow-covered from mid-December to St. Patrick's Day weekend. Night skiing is one of the attractions at Shawnee. After the mountain closes each night, Shawnee grooms every trail, so each morning they're perfect.

Shawnee is a friendly mountain. The top of the bunny slope will seem steep to beginners, but it doesn't take long to conquer it, and once you can do the bunny slope, there are lengthy trails down the

mountain that are no harder, just longer. Try the Pennsylvania first, and when that feels comfortable, try the Minisink. If you can get down the Minisink without mishap, you're ready for the intermediate trails. The lodge is large, with many different seating areas, and it has an outdoor deck overlooking the bunny slope. It's fun to sit in the window at the base of the mountain and watch the skiers come down the last leg of the trail. You can sip a cappuccino and see the beginners madly plowing down the slope while experts bounce between moguls on a black diamond trail.

Many ski packages are available with special daily rates: Monday is Men's Day, Tuesday is Ladies' Day, business people on Wednesday, civil servants on Thursday, and college students on Friday, all get a significant amount off the price of a lift ticket. Children 46 inches and smaller get a free lift ticket when accompanied by a paying adult. Seniors between 60 and 69 get a discount, and those 70 and older get a free lift ticket. Watch for special events like the costume carnival where costumed skiers get a free lift ticket.

The ski school is expert, and there are two lifts devoted to the beginner's area. Don't hesitate to get lessons if you're not a beginner. You can always use a little more technique, and the instructors are happy to take on more advanced students. Weekend training programs are available for the whole family, including a developmental race program for juniors.

Shawnee offers many programs for children based on the nationally ranked SKIwee curriculum. They start with Pre-SKIwee (ages 4 to 5) and continue up through Mountain Cruisers (ages 10 to 15). Babysitting service is available for children 18 months and older.

A terrain park and half-pipe area is available to snowboarders and adventurous skiers. A pipe dragon groomer ensures that the half-pipe is perfect, and a megawatt sound system with a CD jukebox provides just the right vibes for the snowboard park. Shawnee has a snow

> *If you're skiing a little too fast and feeling out of control, just turn and head up the mountain. You can use gravity to slow you down or to help you stop.*

tubing park, as well. (See our "Snow Tubing" section for more details.)

Shawnee maintains a very large stock of high-quality rental equipment. In fact, the rental shop, with more than 4,000 sets of ski equipment and 200 snowboards, claims to be the largest in the country.

Many area hotels and motels offer ski packages at Shawnee. Some offer good discounts, while others give you free skiing for the length of your stay. For details, see our Accommodations chapter or call Shawnee for suggestions. Packages change from year to year.

Shawnee is the first ski area you pass as you come into the Poconos from points east on I-80. The mountain is near Delaware Water Gap, Marshalls Creek, Bushkill, Stroudsburg, and East Stroudsburg.

Mount Pocono Area

Alpine Mountain Ski Area
Highway 447, Analomink
(570) 595-2150
www.alpinemountain.com
Alpine Mountain has 21 trails, 5 lifts, and a vertical of 500 feet. Its use of snowmaking equipment keeps snow on all of the trails. Alpine is a small, family-oriented mountain. Lift lines are rare, and the scenic slopes range from gentle to challenging. Because of its size, this is the perfect mountain if you're a worried mom or dad with kids who love to ski. You can sit in the lodge and see everything but the very top of the slopes, so you can keep an eye on your kids without having to ride the backs of their skis. Nighttime skiing is available most days.

You can take advantage of a variety of learn-to-ski packages and season-pass

rates. Watch for special events throughout the season including races on weekends.

Bargain lift rates are offered to Pocono residents on Monday, ladies on Tuesday, couples on Wednesday, college students and civil servants on Thursday, and senior citizens on Friday. A children's program Just For Kids, is available for four Saturdays or Sundays. Alpine also offers four- and six-week clinics to improve children's technique and teach them to race.

Alpine offers a half-pipe and terrain park as well as six chutes for tubing. Rental equipment is available for both skiing and snowboarding.

Alpine Mountain is centrally located, and the closest accommodations are in Analomink, Henryville, Stroudsburg, and East Stroudsburg.

Camelback Ski Area
Camelback Road, Tannersville
(570) 629-1661
(800) 233-8100 (snow report)
www.skicamelback.com
Camelback has 33 trails and 13 lifts, including two high-speed quad chairs. Its longest trail is a mile; its vertical is 800 feet. Camelback's snowmaking facility is the biggest in the Northeast and covers 100 percent of its area, ensuring plenty of snow throughout the season. Night skiing is available on all trails. Camelback is the largest ski area in the Poconos, and its trails are long. It has lots of easy and intermediate trails, but only eight expert trails; however, one is a double black diamond, so there's lots of terrain to explore for skiers at all levels. In addition to three lodges serving food at the base of the mountain, there's a restaurant at the top.

Camelback has many different ski programs and packages; call for information on the current specials. Seniors 65 and older ski at reduced rates. Children shorter than 46 inches ski free when accompanied by a paying adult. Monday, everyone gets a reduced lift ticket, while Wednesday offers specials to civil servants.

The children's ski school, offering kids' ski and snowboard programs, offers full-day programs. Children enrolled here receive instruction, a complimentary helmet rental, and continuous supervision as they try out their newfound skills.

Childcare is available in the nursery for children 12 months through 4 years old. Advanced programs and challenge racing are available for juniors and adults.

Snowboarders have two special terrain parks and a half-pipe for their tricks and tumbles. The half-pipe is groomed with a Pipe Dragon groomer, and both parks are lighted at night. Snow tubing is on nine trails. Single and family tubes are available.

Equipment rentals are available for one to three days as a package. In addition to skis and snowboards, you can rent high performance skis and helmets here.

At Camelback there are a variety of sponsored seasonal events based on holiday weekends, special tribute days, festivals, and races. Call for a brochure, check the website, or watch the papers to keep apprised of events here.

Accommodations are available at the base of the mountain at the Chateau at Cambelback. You'll find other lodgings nearby in Tannersville, Swiftwater, Henryville, Bartonsville, and Stroudsburg.

West End

Big Boulder Ski Area
Highway 903, Blakeslee
(570) 722-0100, (800) 468-2442
www.jackfrostbigboulder.com

Big Boulder has 7 lifts, 13 trails from beginner to expert, and a vertical of 475 feet. Big Boulder was the first commercial resort in Pennsylvania to make snow, and snowmaking keeps its trails open throughout the winter. Night skiing is available on all the trails, the half-pipe (for snowboarding), and even the snow tubing trails.

Big Boulder is a pretty ski mountain, perched at one end of Big Boulder Lake. This is a great area for beginners, as the easy trails are basically bunny slopes, while the intermediate trails are no harder than some mountains' easy slopes, with a

few dips thrown in for fun. Even the black diamond (the hardest) trails don't look too bad, although we haven't seen them all the way down.

A really nice feature that Big Boulder shares with Jack Frost is that the lift tickets are interchangeable. You can spend part of a day skiing at one resort and then move on to the other. Most people start at Jack Frost, because Big Boulder is open into the night, while Jack Frost closes at 4:00 P.M. You can take your rental equipment from one mountain to the other (talk to the rental shop before you do this), but snowboards must stay at the mountain from which you rent them. Snow tubing is also on the menu at both mountains. Lessons are available for skiing and snowboarding. There are discounted rates for lift tickets, late-season specials, and advance tickets. Of course, with this ski area as with all the other areas, deals change each season as the management finds new ways to serve the skiers. There are lots of special events and Saturday night entertainment, so call for a brochure or visit the Web site.

Family commitment is the watchword here, and to that end, both mountains offer a variety of lesson programs, depending on children's age, desire to ski or snowboard, and their abilities. The folks at the mountain will help you choose the program that is right for your child.

Youth tickets are available for ages 6 through 21, and children 5 and younger ski or snowboard free with a paying adult. Seniors 62 and older receive a discount. Competitive and noncompetitive junior racing programs are available for children ages 4 to 18. Babysitting is provided full day, half-day, and evenings.

An interesting program at Big Boulder is the Discovery Program, which allows beginning skiers and boarders to move at their own pace through a series of teaching stations that they can revisit as often as needed to learn a skill. The Discover Program includes a lesson, equipment rental, and lift ticket for limited terrain reserved for other "discoverers." Other learn-to-ski programs include group and private lessons.

Snowboarders will be delighted to find the perfectly groomed half-pipe off Trail 5. A beginner's terrain park, with smaller rails and jumps, is great for novice snowboarders and little folks.

Equipment for adults and children can be rented for all activities.

Accommodations nearby have package deals with Big Boulder, and some provide lift tickets valid for as long as you are here. For on-site lodging information, call (800) 468-2442, or see our Accommodations chapter.

Big Boulder is one of the Big Two Resorts: Jack Frost (see subsequent entry) is the other. The same Big Boulder information—applies at Jack Frost. Jack Frost does have some differences, as you will see.

Blue Mountain Ski Area
Blue Mountain Drive, Palmerton
(610) 826-7700
www.skibluemt.com

Blue Mountain has seven lifts (including a high-speed detachable quad), 30 trails (several are more than a mile long), and a vertical of 1,082 feet—the highest in Pennsylvania. The varied terrain includes a mile-long beginners' trail for those who want to take their time going down as they learn. The snowmaking equipment here keeps the trails covered all winter long. There are learn-to-ski packages and ski lessons. Special workshops are held for women and seniors. Senior citizens 65 and older receive a 20 percent discount every day, and children 6 and under ski free when accompanied by a paying adult.

Children's lessons are available full day and half-day for ages 4 to 12. Babysitting is available for youngsters 6 weeks to 5 years who don't want to ski; it's free Monday through Friday, but costs $2.00/hour weekends and holidays.

The racing program at Blue Mountain is available for youths and adults.

Snowboarders will appreciate two terrain parks with a half-pipe, quarter-pipe,

rail slides, tabletops, and big jumps. Snow tubers will find 11 slides and 3 tow lifts. Snow tubers can choose from single tubes or scream down the slides with friends or family in Blue Mountain's "Quadzilla" tubes.

Equipment rentals—individual pieces or complete packages—are available for adults, juniors, and children.

Blue Mountain is the Poconos' southernmost ski area and is closest to Jim Thorpe and Lehighton. You can find ski packages at nearby accommodations. (See our Accommodations chapter and call the individual inns, resorts, and motels for information on the latest deals.) Package deals are also specified on the Web site.

Jack Frost Ski Area
Highway 940, Blakeslee
(570) 443-8425, (800) 468-2442
www.jackfrostbigboulder.com

Jack Frost has 9 lifts, 27 trails, and a vertical of 600 feet. Its terrain is much more challenging than its sister mountain, Big Boulder, (see previous entry), which means that expert skiers can be accommodated right next to those looking for an easier pace. You'll find all levels of terrain at Jack Frost, though. The ski and snowboard schools and beginners packages are the same at both areas. Both mountains have programs that provide solid beginner preparation, and both offer the Discovery Program. (See the previous Big Boulder entry for details.) Jack Frost also has a 15-kilometer cross-country ski trail (dependent on natural snow) and an awesome tubing area. (See our "Snow Tubing" section.)

Because of the challenging terrain at Jack Frost, its racing programs (junior and adult) are renowned and have produced members of the U.S. Ski Team.

If you buy a lift ticket here, you can use it on the same day at Big Boulder. This is especially convenient, because night skiing is not available at Jack Frost, but you can move over to Big Boulder and keep on sliding. You can take your rental equipment with you to Big Boulder (talk to the rental shop before you do this). One unusual aspect of Jack Frost is that you drive in at the top of the mountain, so you can't see the slopes until you're on them.

The terrain at Jack Frost is diverse, with a terrain park, The Badlands, adding to the snowboarding and expert skiing fun.

Jack Frost runs the exciting "Adaptive Ski Program" for disabled people. Skilled instructors make the experience of skiing available to everyone who wants to take part. Special Ski Olympics are held here.

Milford/Lake Wallenpaupack Area

Big Bear at Masthope
18 West Colang Road, Lackawaxen
(570) 685–1400
www.ski-bigbear.com

Big Bear at Masthope has 18 trails with three lifts and a J-bar. The vertical is 650 feet. There's also a snowtubing tow and slope. One hundred percent snowmaking has the slopes open all winter, and the trails are lighted for night skiing. A terrain park keeps snowboarders happy.

Big Bear offers a ski school, a program for children, and equipment rentals. Some accommodations in the area offer special packages; call Big Bear for details.

Big Bear was built as part of a community development but is open to the public. It has a less commercial feel than many other ski mountains and caters especially to families and groups. Check the Web site for special events throughout the season.

Tanglwood Ski Area
Highway 390, Tafton
(570) 226–SNOW, (888) 226–SNOW
www.tanglwood.com

Tanglwood has two lifts, a tow, and seven trails of varying skill levels and a vertical of 415 feet. The longest trail runs for 1 mile. Downhill skiers and snowboarders

It's easy to find used ski equipment for sale in the Poconos. Watch for garage sales and ski area swaps held in the fall. After the ski season, many retail shops that sell ski equipment slash prices drastically to get rid of the current year's stock.

can enjoy the snowmaking on all of Tanglwood's trails. For those who don't mind the chill, Tanglwood is lighted at night for skiing under the stars. A snowboarding park provides extra fun for boarders. If you're a beginning skier, study the trail map carefully. There's a nice long beginning trail, Deer Run, but it can dump you into an expert trail if you're not careful. Talk to the other skiers at Tanglwood, and hold off taking Deer Run until you think you're ready.

A multilane tubing park provides some fun for those who would rather ride and slide. A rental shop can provide all your equipment needs.

A professional ski school offers private and group lessons for beginners and those who need to improve their skills. SKIwee programs are available in full- and half-day sessions for skiers ages 5 to 12.

Special packages are available. Juniors (12 and younger) and seniors (62 to 69) receive discounts. Children 5 and younger and seniors 70 and older ski free—though the children must be accompanied by a paying adult. Tanglwood is closed on Tuesday, except holidays.

Tanglwood is near Hawley and Lake Wallenpaupack. Accommodations packages are available at some nearby lodgings.

CROSS-COUNTRY SKIING

Glide through the quiet, snow-covered countryside, watching the river and sneaking up on the animals. Ski across a field with the light coming down in shafts, and the scenery will make you feel like you're

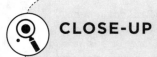

But Is It Really Snow?

It's white and cold and looks like snow, but if it's man-made is it really snow? You betcha. Snow is crystallized water that forms when the air temperature drops below 32 degrees, and any moisture in the air freezes into hexagonal crystals. Manufactured snow is made by pumping water into the atmosphere. The below-freezing air freezes the water, and voila—you get snow!

The ingenious process of snowmaking at a ski mountain requires a tremendous amount of equipment: huge air compressors; giant water pumps; miles and miles of piping for the air and water; enormous and complex microprocessor-driven, turbocharged generators; and hundreds of spray guns and nozzles to disperse the water into the air. All work together with Mother Nature and the snowmaking crew to ensure that when you arrive to ski, snow is covering your favorite slopes.

Snowmaking was invented in 1950 by three aeronautical engineers from Connecticut. Arthur R. Hunt, Wayne Pierce, and Dave Richey had worked together to create a unique design for skis, which they manufactured and sold. All was going well until a winter when the snowfall was negligible—and sales dropped drastically.

Pierce had an idea. In the backyard of the company, he set up a spray-gun nozzle, an air compressor, and a garden hose. Pierce, with the help of his partners, put the equipment inside a box on a stand and started to spray the water into the cold air. The next morning they had a 20-inch-deep pile of snow covering an area

20 feet in diameter. The partners got a basic-process patent and began snow-making at Grossinger's in New York and Big Boulder (Split Rock Lodge at the time) in Pennsylvania. A new era in skiing had begun!

The partners sold the company and patents and have not made anything from the profits their invention has generated since. But as Hunt remarked, he "still skis and [he is] glad the machine-made snow is there."

A great many others are glad too. With the advent of snowmaking, ski enthusiasts are no longer dependent upon nature's whim; they can ski wherever there is a mountain with temperatures cold enough to manufacture snow. The industry has boomed, and resorts that invested in the process have flourished.

One of the first to take complete advantage of the snowmaking system was Camelback Ski Area in Tannersville. Camelback was built on the premise that it would exist entirely on man-made snow if necessary. As its trails were cut out of the landscape, miles of pipelines for air and water were simultaneously laid out to ensure that every trail could be covered with man-made snow. In November, as soon as the temperatures drop, the snow engineers begin the process. Snowmakers provide a 3-to-5-foot base of snow with 2–10 inches of surface powder. Every night during the season (weather conditions permitting), the process is repeated to ensure maximum coverage, so all the slopes can be open every day. But snow-

There's no need to worry about whether it has snowed. As long as it's cold enough, every Pocono ski mountain makes plenty of the white stuff to cover their trails. POCONO MOUNTAINS VACATION BUREAU

making has become a two-step procedure. Once producing snow was perfected, keeping it nice and neat became a concern. Thus, the procedure called "grooming" evolved. Grooming smoothes out the snow, eliminating the moguls that develop during the day as well as the piles of snow alongside the trails. Grooming restores the powdery surface of the trails eliminating most of the granularity that can occur due to weather conditions, excessive use, or erratic snowmaking.

And grooming has definitely evolved.

In the beginning, people tried everything to restore the surface of the snow. They used tractors to drag chains, Ski-Doos to pull chain-link fencing, and tractors to pull harrows. Today, there are grooming machines. Crews of trained technicians use huge tractors with 2-foot-wide treads running on tracks more than 3 feet high, to push, rake, smooth, and crunch the snow into beautiful trails while skiers sleep.

But is it really snow, you ask? Will I ski well on it? Wouldn't it be better to go to a place where the snow is real?

Yes, it's still snow in its shape, density, and formation. Yes, you will ski well on it—you may ski better, because manufactured snow is smoother, a little more slippery, and stands up to skiers and weather conditions better than the natural stuff. Every major ski area in America uses snowmaking to augment its seasonal snowfall, to get the season started sooner and to extend it a little longer. From Mammoth in California, to Vail and Aspen in Colorado, to Killington in Vermont—some of the snow is "real," and some is manufactured.

So, if you are in the city, and temperatures are in the 40s, don't think you've missed out on your ski weekend or midweek escape. On the mountains it's always colder at night than at lower elevations, so the snowmakers can do their work. Whether your destination is Camelback, Big Boulder, Jack Frost, Shawnee, Alpine, Blue Mountain, Tanglwood, Big Bear, or another snowmaker-based ski area, relax. While you are sleeping or making an after-work, late-night drive to the Poconos, the snowmakers are diligently working with Mother Nature, manufacturing snow, and grooming the slopes for you and your family.

And it is real!

in one of those Hudson Valley paintings from the last century. Cross-country, or Nordic, skiing doesn't have the speed and glitter of downhill skiing, but there are no lift lines, no crowds, and no expensive tickets to purchase. Cross-country is skiing without the commercialization.

Some Pocono resorts have cross-country trails and provide equipment rentals for those interested in this vigorous workout.

When tied to a resort stay, cross-country skiing is free, except for equipment rental (see our Accommodations chapter). Most resorts allow non-guests to ski on their property for a fee. Jack Frost ski area offers cross-country ski trails, weather permitting. They do not make snow on cross-country trails. (See previous listing for details.) Other cross-country areas can be found in state parks and state forests.

Of course, many folks have a lot of land around here, and they ski off into their own woods. Others have friends who let them ski on their trails. You can ski almost anywhere there's snow, but we have some parks that pay special attention to cross-country skiers.

Delaware Water Gap/ Shawnee-on-Delaware

Delaware Water Gap National Recreation Area
U.S. Highway 209, Bushkill
(570) 588-2451
www.nps.gov
There are three official trails for cross-country skiing in the Delaware Water Gap National Recreation Area and lots of other trails you can ski. You can get a map of the trails on the Web or at the Kittatinny Visitor's Center, (908-496-4458), just over the New Jersey border off I-80.

One area, with 10 miles of trails, trail markers, and mounted maps, is in New Jersey around Blue Mountain Lakes (follow the signs off Old Mine Road, just 1.6 miles north of Millbrook, turn right on New Jersey Highway 624 and go another 1.5 miles to the parking lot). The skiing, with trails for beginning and intermediate cross-country skiers, is around a lake and through the woods. Interpretive signs will help you identify the tracks of animals that inhabit this area.

The second cross-country ski area is at Slateford Farm, south of the town of

Delaware Water Gap on Highway 611. Slateford Farm is on part of the Appalachian Trail and has ski trails of varying degrees of difficulty. There are some nice flat areas for beginners and some up and downhill areas. Right at the beginning of the trail is a small hill that feels like a steep mountain to a beginning skier. Many just take off their skis to nego- tiate the tiny slope. If you're a novice and don't feel like taking off your skis, watch out for the trees. There aren't any fees to use the trails, which are ungroomed.

The third official cross-country trail is the new McDade Trail which, when fin- ished, will stretch 40 miles along the Delaware River on the Pennsylvania side from Shawnee-on-Delaware to Milford. At press time, the first five miles of the trail have been finished, stretching north from Smithfield Beach. The entire trail should be done by 2005.

There are no rental facilities or equip- ment in the park, but the Pack Shack (see our Shopping and In, On, and Around the Water chapters for details) in Delaware Water Gap, (570–424–8533) is an excel- lent place nearby to rent equipment and get information on the state of the trails.

Mount Pocono Area

Gouldsboro State Park
Highway 507, 1.5 miles south of Gouldsboro
(570) 894–8336
www.dcnr.state.pa.us
Gouldsboro's 8 miles of easy skiing along an abandoned highway and park road is snow-covered much of the winter, as Gouldsboro State Park is "up the mountain."

Tobyhanna State Park
Highway 423, 2.1 miles north of Tobyhanna
(570) 894–8336
www.dcnr.state.pa.us
Tobyhanna's lovely Lakeside Trail winds in and out of a forest alongside a lake. The

Check ski mountains' Web sites. They offer up-to-the-minute snow condition reports, news of any special events, and coupons you can print for significant savings on a lift ticket or equipment rental.

i

5-mile trail is easy, with a few moderate dips. It's also open to snowmobiles, but it's not a great trail for them (too twisty), so it gets light snowmobile use.

Promised Land State Park
Highway 390, Promised Land Village
(570) 676–3428
www.dcnr.state.pa.us
Promised Land State Park has more than 30 miles of hiking trails that crisscross between Promised Land and the Delaware State Forest. These trails are good for cross-country skiers. A mile-long trail that rings Conservation Island is reserved exclusively for cross-country skiing. The trail has lovely views of the lake and benches for weary skiers. Trails are neither groomed nor maintained and, of course, are weather dependent. The park office in Promised Land is open Monday through Friday during the winter from 8:00 A.M. to 4:00 P.M. The office is not open on week- ends, but you'll find brochures in a rack outside the door.

If you want to know if trails are snow- covered, call the park or check their Web site. (See our Parks chapter for more information on the park.)

West End

Beltzville State Park
US 209, 5 miles east of Lehighton
(610) 377–0045
www.dcnr.state.pa.us
Beltzville has lots of open and rolling fields as well as 9 miles of ungroomed trails open to cross-country skiers. Park staff especially recommend the 4-mile-

long Trinity Gorge Trail, also open to snowmobiles, which follows an old road past fields and forests. Most trails in Beltzville State Park are fairly level and suitable to skiers of all ages and abilities. If you're looking for a little more challenge, try the Wild Creek Trail, which runs over hillier terrain.

Hickory Run State Park
Highway 534, near I-80 exit 41
(570) 443-0400
www.dcnr.state.pa.us
Thirteen miles of cross-country trails marked with blue blazes run past streams, springs, an old water tower, and the ruins of abandoned villages. The terrain varies from flat to steep.

Lehigh Gorge State Park
South Entrance, I-80 exit 40, White Haven
(570) 443-0400
www.dcnr.state.pa.us
An abandoned railroad grade, from Port Jenkins to Penn Haven junction, provides 26 miles of trail, which skiers share with snowmobiles. You can access the trail from three areas. In White Haven, take the road behind the Thriftway Supermarket off Highway 940. In Rockport the access is off Lehigh Gorge Drive. In Glen Onoko just outside of Jim Thorpe, enter the trail off Highway 903.

Mauch Chunk Lake Park
625 Lentz Trail, Jim Thorpe
(570) 325-3669
207.21.252.76/park/
The cross-country ski trail here is the switchback rail line. Don't be intimidated by the incline. While there are small sections of the trail that are steep and diffi-

---

ℹ️ *Pennsylvania Ski Area Operators' Learn to Ski Day usually during the first full week in January, gives folks who have never skied a chance to learn for free or for a small fee. To participate, call any ski mountain listed in this chapter and make reservations, which are necessary.*

---

cult, there's lots of flat, easy terrain for novice skiers. (See the Close-up in our History chapter for information on the Switchback Railroad.) Equipment rentals are available on a first-come, first-served basis and quantities are limited. You can rent a whole set or just the pieces you need. The price for the set is $20 per day (plus tax), or $10 after 2:00 P.M. (you must return the skis by 4:30 P.M.). You can also rent just the pieces you need.

Rates are subject to change, so check with the office.

Milford/Lake Wallenpaupack

Delaware State Forest
Highway 390, 3 miles south of I-80
(570) 895-4000
www.experiencepa.com
Bruce Lake Natural Area in Delaware State Forest has 4 miles of mostly flat trails passing through oak forests, wooded swamps, and beaver ponds. Expect to see wildlife. You can ski anywhere within the state forest, but these trails are marked for skiing.

SNOW TUBING

This sport has really caught on, and all of the ski mountains have built separate snow tubing areas with snowmaking for the days Mother Nature does not cooperate. Many tubing areas have their own warming huts or snack bars as well as a bonfire for warming frozen fingers and toasting marshmallows.

A ticket for tubing runs about $11 to $23 for two or more hours of fun. Some ski areas sell "combo" tickets, where you add about $10 more to the price of your lift ticket and you can tube, too. Tubing is a great excuse for a party, and many areas offer group discounts.

Snow tubing is run in two- to four-hour sessions, so call ahead for the schedule. Otherwise, you may be caught short or have to kill time waiting for the next session to start.

Delaware Water Gap/ Shawnee-on-Delaware

Fernwood
US 209, Bushkill
(570) 588-9500, (888) FERNWOOD
resortsusa.com
Two tows and single and family tube chutes on this hill on the grounds of the Fernwood resort make this a fun run. This is the one tubing park that is not part of a ski mountain.

Shawnee Mountain
Hollow Road, Shawnee-on-Delaware
(570) 421-7231, (800) 233-4218 (snow report)
www.shawneemt.com
Shawnee's "Pocono Plunge" has six chutes and two tows. Shawnee limits the number of tickets they sell per session to maximize the safety and enjoyment of their tubers.

Mount Pocono Area

Alpine Mountain Ski Area
Highway 447, Analomink
(570) 595-2150
www.alpinemountain.com
Six chutes are serviced by two tows. Tubes include individual and two-person sizes. The chutes have some "whoop-de-dos," bumps to make the slide more interesting. Some chutes are faster than others are. An indoor concession area provides a place where people can warm up and get a snack.

Camelback Ski Area
Camelback Road, Tannersville
(570) 629-1661
(800) 233-8100 (snow report)
www.skicamelback.com
Camelback has nine runs and four tows. Where many mountains send you straight down, some of Camelback's runs offer interesting loops off to the side. A pleasant snack bar offers vending machines, grilled food, and restrooms. A large fire pit is surrounded by benches.

West End

Big Boulder Ski Area
Highway 903, Blakeslee
(570) 722-0100, (800) 468-2442
www.jackfrostbigboulder.com
Big Boulder and Jack Frost, "The Big Two," were the first ski areas to bring tubing to the Poconos. Big Boulder's 13 tubing chutes include The Yukon Rapids, for individual tubes, and Klondike Kanyon, for family-size tubes that seat up to six. Five tows serve these areas. The North Pole is especially nice for little guys because the slopes are gentle. A fire pit surrounded by benches and some picnic tables provide the amenities here.

Blue Mountain Ski Area
Blue Mountain Drive, Palmerton
(610) 826-7700
www.skibluemt.com
Blue Mountain's 100-foot vertical tubing slope features "three levels of excitement" in their 11 chutes serviced by three tows. Their 1,000 tubes include "Quadzilla" family tubes and tubes for solo sliding. The terrain here is varied and really wild. A warming hut offers snacks, and there's also an outdoor picnic area

Jack Frost Ski Area
Highway 940, Blakeslee
(570) 443-8425
www.jackfrostbigboulder.com
The big news at Jack Frost is "The Avalanche," a six-sided family-size tube. Round family tubes and individual tubes also ply Jack Frost's eight chutes serviced by four lifts. The tubing "mountain" is 12-stories high. One of the chutes, "The Launch Pad," is purported to be for experts only. Picnic tables offer seats for

Go with the Snow

You stand in front of the snowy mountain you're about to conquer. You take a deep breath and grab the weapon that's going to help you conquer it—an enormous soft rubber tube. You and your fellow mountain sliders drag the tube to a tow line where a trained attendant hooks it up, and you're off, sliding slowly up the mountain, savoring the view and a quiet moment before the thrill begins. As you near the top, each adventurer rolls out and walks the last few steps to where another trained attendant unhooks your chariot. You and your fellows select a slope, and one more trained attendant gives you a push, telling you to bounce if you want to make it go faster. Suddenly you're sliding uncontrollably down the chute, up almost to the edge of the side and down again. You can bounce and lean into the descent or you can sit in the bottom, vainly trying to brake; but there's no steering a big, round, rubber tube. Your only choice is to

go with the snow. At the bottom, your brave fellows decide to try another chute, and up you go again.

Snow tubing invaded Pennsylvania eight years ago, and today all of the ski areas have separate tubing facilities, plus there are a few spots, former resort beginner ski areas, that are now excellent tubing slopes. Traditionalists may sniff at a sport that requires almost no skill (although getting out of the tube with finesse takes some practice) and does all the hard work for you; but the slopes are much steeper than most sledding hills, and they're often shaped to enhance your ride. Tubing chutes may have bumps and curves added to speed up and slow down the tube as it makes its screaming descent to the bottom. The slopes are generally the equivalent of a skier's advanced beginner's slope (a brave descent for a tuber), but the tubing parks are trying to outdo each other, and they're getting steeper. One area boasts a slope the equivalent of 12 stories high. If you're foolhardy, you can push the tube off the top, jumping into it as it starts to slide; just try to avoid jumping on top of your screaming companions. The four- to six-person family tubes go faster, and often their chutes are more elaborate, but when you tire of them, you can try an individual tube. Just big enough to fit your bottom, you can slide down the mountain in one of these sitting or lying on your front or back. Once you and your friends have tried all the individual chutes, try hooking up (holding onto each other's tubes) a move that increases the weight and thus

Careening down a hill in a tube, you will have to "go with the snow." POCONO MOUNTAINS VACATION BUREAU

You'll be laughing and screaming when you shoot down the mountain in a snow tube.
CAMELBACK SKI CORPORATION AND JERRY LEBLOND/POCONO MOUNTAINS VACATION BUREAU

the speed of your slide. Just position yourself so you're not screaming down the slope with your friend's feet in your face. You'll have plenty of contact with the snow, and if it's a warm day, there's a good chance you'll get wet. Wear waterproof clothes if you have them, or bring an extra set of dry clothes. If you're skiing, too, don't plan on wearing ski boots in the tubes; tubing parks will not allow them. Another good tubing accessory is a bag of marshmallows and some sticks. Many of the tubing parks have a friendly bonfire with benches all around.

The sport feels dangerous, but your most likely place to get bonked is at the bottom of the chute. People tend to stand around laughing and talking when their ride is over, forgetting that the next tubers could be zooming straight for them and about to knock everybody over. So move out of the way quickly, and your tubing adventure should not cause any, um, skiing injuries (it would be ignominious to admit you were hurt tubing). Some tubing areas, wisely, place height restrictions on small children. If you're thinking of taking your toddlers, call first, and find out if they can tube, too. One more thing you need for tubing is a pair of strong lungs—you're going to be doing a lot of screaming and laughing.

> Get to a ski or tubing area as early as you can. The slopes will be uncrowded, there will be no lines, and, if they groom their trails, the snow will be perfect. On a weekday, the crowds start gathering soon after school lets out. On a weekend, you'll have the mountain to yourself until about 10:30 A.M.

weary tubers, and Jack Frost's ski lodge is nearby.

Milford/Lake Wallenpaupack Area

Big Bear at Masthope
Colang Road, Lackawaxen
(570) 685–1400
www.ski-bigbear.com
There's only one tubing chute here for individual tubes, but it's 600 feet long and has some fun moguls (bumps). A towrope services this chute.

Tanglwood Ski Area
Highway 390, Tafton
(570) 226–SNOW, (888) 226–SNOW
www.tanglwood.com
Two 400-foot chutes for individual tubes and a tow make up Tanglwood's snow tubing area. A fire pit and picnic tables provide some warmth and a place to rest.

SNOWMOBILING

Some Pocono resorts and ski areas offer snowmobiling as a winter attraction. This sport is offered at an extra cost and on groomed trails. You can rent a single or double snowmobile for a half-hour or an hour.

All four Caesars resorts offer snowmobiling. Go to www.cpresorts.com or call (877) 822–3333 for more information.

If you're not staying at a Caesars, look in the Yellow Pages for businesses that rent them and take you to their own course, usually on-site. Some parks allow snowmobiling, but in these areas you must use your own snowmobile, as rentals are not available.

If you plan to use your snowmobile on public land, it must be registered. Download a registration form at www .dcnr.state.pa.us/snowmobile/index.htm. If you are from out of state, and your snowmobile is registered in your state, you should check to see if the registration is reciprocal. Pennsylvania registration is not reciprocal with New York, but it is reciprocal with New Jersey. You do not need to register your snowmobile if you use it on your own private property. However, if you go beyond your boundaries and end up on land or roads that you do not own, you are driving an unregistered vehicle and can be fined. The registration issue is not a concern when you're buying time at a ski area or renting from a snowmobile shop.

Please use only designated snowmobile trails in the parks. If you ride on unauthorized trails, you may destroy delicate ecosystems, and if you are caught, you will be fined. Snowmobiles are prohibited from operating on frozen lakes and shorelines. Snowmobile trails are open, weather permitting, from the third Sunday in January (see our Fishing and Hunting chapter) until April 1, as long as there is enough snow. To find out about trails throughout the state, go to www.dcnr.state.pa.us/forestry11404/snowmobile. For snow conditions call (877) SNO–MBLE.

Mount Pocono Area

Promised Land State Park
Highway 390, Promised Land Village
(570) 676–3428
www.dcnr.state.pa.us
The 23 miles of snowmobiling trails that traverse the state park and the Delaware State Forest lands are designated by orange diamond symbols. Maps are avail-

able at the park office in Promised Land and at the district office in Swiftwater (570-895-4000). There aren't any facilities for your snowmobile, so make sure you bring what you need. The maps indicate the parking areas where you can leave cars and enter the trails.

Tobyhanna State Park
Highway 423, 2.1 miles north of
Tobyhanna
(570) 894-8336
www.dcnr.state.pa.us
Tobyhanna's 5½-mile Lakeside Trail is open to snowmobiles, but it's not great because it's fairly narrow and very twisty.

West End

Lehigh Gorge
Access road behind the Thriftway
Supermarket off Highway 940
White Haven
(570) 443-0400
www.dcnr.state.pa.us
An abandoned railroad grade, from Penn Haven to White Haven, provides 15 miles of trail that snowmobiles share with cross-country skiers.

Milford/Lake Wallenpaupack Area

Delaware State Forest
Highway 390, 3 miles south of I-80
(570) 895-4000
www.dncr.state.pa.us
One hundred and twelve miles of noncontiguous trails in different areas of the forest are available to snowmobiles. The most popular trails are in the Peck's Pond area. Trailheads may be found at Burnt Mills, off Highway 402 south of Peck's Pond, off Highway 402 just north of Peck's Pond. The Snow Hill Snowmobile Trail can be found off Highway 447 south of Canadensis, the White Deer Trail is off

The Monroe County Parks and Recreation office in Snydersville has discount tickets for most of the area mountains. Call (570) 421-2871 for information on buying lift tickets for about $10 to $15 off the regular price.

Highway 402 north of Interstate 84, and the Owego Trail is near the intersection of Highway 739 and U.S. Highway 6. The extensive Pimple Hill Trails are accessed off Highway 115, 4 miles south of exit 43 of I-80. Turn south at the Pohopoco Tract sign. Call to request a map of more trails available from the Delaware State Forest. You may also find maps on the Internet and on the rack outside the office at Promised Land State Park.

ICE-SKATING

Most resorts offer indoor or outdoor ice-skating on their grounds. But you don't have to stay at a resort to skate. Try slipping and sliding on one of the following rinks.

Delaware Water Gap/ Shawnee-on-Delaware

Mountain Manor
Creek Road, Marshalls Creek
(570) 223-8098
www.mountainmanor.com
Mountain Manor's rink is open from Thanksgiving to Easter, weather permitting. The times of operation are 10:30 A.M. to 5:00 P.M. and 7:00 A.M. to 10:00 P.M. Admission to the rink for the general public is $6.00 for adults and teens and $4.00 for children 12 and younger (guests skate free, but pay to rent skates). Skate rental is $4.00. Hockey and figure skates are allowed here.

There's no organized ice hockey here, but popular pickup games take place on

> *Before you ski, board, or tube, call the mountain and find out their schedule. Some offer morning, afternoon, or nighttime sessions for a lower rate. It would be a shame to arrive an hour or two before the end of a session and have to buy an all-day ticket or kill an hour until the next session starts.*

Tuesday nights from 7:00 to 10:00 P.M., when the rink is reserved for these impromptu games. Anyone who wants to play can show up and join a team.

Mount Pocono Area

Promised Land State Park
Highway 390, Promised Land Village
(570) 676-3428
www.dcnr.state.pa.us
Ice-skating is allowed on a reserved section of Promised Land Lake, weather permitting. The area is maintained only insofar as the snow is pushed aside for skaters. No rentals, refreshments, or accommodations of any kind are available, except a Porta-potty nearby. Since conditions change on a daily basis, call ahead to see if the ice is thick enough for skating or check the winter activity report on the Web site. (During winter months, there aren't any running-water facilities available.)

SLEDDING AND TOBOGGANING

Sledding is generally offered at resorts and other accommodations to guests only. The resorts often have a sledding hill, which is neither groomed nor maintained. It's just a good hill that works when the snow falls. Sleds are usually free for guests. Dress warmly, and be sure to cushion all your tender areas.

Insiders generally have to scout out a good hillside. If you want to sled, find out where your neighbors go, and tag along. Soon you'll know the good spots too. If you're from out of town, keep your eyes open for good hills as you drive around. There are a few unofficial spots where many people congregate, but we can't list them here. Some landowners have had to forbid sledding on their hills because of insurance considerations, and we wouldn't want to push the ones who look the other way into posting NO SLEDDING signs.

There are two exceptions. Stroud Township has leased and assumed liability for sledding on a hill at Fifth and Avenue B in Stroudsburg, next to the Stroudsburg Wesleyan Church. It's a pretty good run, and there are signs up with proper sledding etiquette. Please observe the rules, so that the township will continue to make that hill available. Hickory Run State Park also makes areas of the park available for sledding and tobogganing when there's sufficient snow on the ground.

Good luck spotting the perfect sledding hill, and if you have trouble tracking one down, consider snow tubing (see the "Snow Tubing" section above).

HORSE-DRAWN SLEIGH RIDES

"Dashing through the snow, in a one-horse open sleigh, O'er the fields we go, laughing all the way." Sounds like a thing of the past? Quite a few of the local stables offer a "Jingle Bells" experience, weather permitting. You'll sit in an antique sleigh with toasty blankets to keep you incredibly warm. One or two giant horses will pull you through the snowy woods into a Currier & Ives print with you as the focal point. As you whoosh through the countryside, you are sure to spot a few deer and pheasants that are enjoying the day. Rates for rides in large sleighs generally run from $12 to $15 per person, while rates in a smaller sleigh can be around $60 per couple. Rates, as always, are subject to change.

Many of the following stables also offer winter horseback trail riding, which is quite an adventure. Make sure you call ahead for reservations. (See the "Horseback Riding" section of the Recreation chapter for related options.)

Stroudsburg/East Stroudsburg

Pocono Country Carriages Inc.
517 Hallet Road, East Stroudsburg
(570) 424-6248
www.poconocountrycarriagesinc.com
Drawn by two horses, Mikey and Blossom, that are managed by their driver/owner Eileen Pasquin, the sleighs are beautiful antiques from the early 1900s that have been lovingly restored. Sleigh bells jingle, and crushed-velvet sleigh blankets keep you incredibly warm. Eileen and her sleighs take you along a wooded trail. Watch for wildlife.

Mount Pocono Area

Mountain Creek Stables
Highway 940, 3 miles east of Mount Pocono
(570) 839-8725
www.mtcreekstable.com
You can ride in a beautifully restored antique sleigh that holds only two people or in a larger one that holds up to a dozen and is pulled by two huge, 2,200-pound Belgians. These sleigh rides go through wooded trails where you're likely to see all kinds of wildlife—deer, black bears, and wild turkeys, to name a few.

Mountain Creek prides itself on its spic-and-span stables and friendly horses.

Pocono Manor Stables
Off Highway 314, Pocono Manor
(570) 839-0925
www.poconos.org/members/pocono manorstables/

The Pocono Clydesdales take groups on sleigh rides across Pocono Manor's Golf Course. These rides are winter traditions for many families. There are three sizes of antique sleighs here: a very small one that holds two people, a larger one that holds 12; and a huge one that can carry 24.

Milford/Lake Wallenpaupack Area

Triple W Riding Stable Inc.
US 6, 4.5 miles north of Hawley
(570) 226-2620
www.triplewstable.com
Triple W takes their jingle-belled sleighs across their 185 acres of land. You'll go through the woods, over some roads (if the snow pack is good enough) and into a 20-acre field on top of the mountain, where you can see for 20 miles. The larger antique sleighs—one holds 15 people, and another carries 12—were originally logging sleighs. Triple W lines their flat beds with hay and gives you blankets to wrap around yourself. These are fun rides; people often bring champagne to enhance the experience. There's also a two-seat sleigh for a romantic ride. Triple W uses Belgians and Percherons to pull their sleighs.

ICE-FISHING

Another winter activity you'll see here is ice-fishing. You can ice fish at Promised Land State Park (570-676-3428), Beltzville State Park (610-377-0045), and Mauch Chunk Lake Park (570-325-3669). These lakes are open to the public, but are not maintained in any way. You must check with Promised Land and Beltzville state parks daily to find out if it is safe to ice-fish, just as you must do to ice-skate (see previous section). Mauch Chunk Lake Park is no longer allowed to monitor the ice (insurance company rules) so you fish here at your own risk. If you want to ice-fish, you must have a Pennsylvania State Fishing License (see our Fishing and Hunting chapter for where to obtain yours). Pennsylvania fishing licenses are available as of December 1 of the year prior to the license year. They are good for that December plus the entire following year—13 months. You can purchase a license online at sites.state.pa.us/Fish/licapp.htm or you can get one at many state offices, sports shops, resorts, and general stores. A list of the places you can purchase a fishing license in Monroe County can be found at sites.state.pa.us/Fish/flage/monr.htm. Those who live in some of the lake communities can ice-fish on their own lakes, weather permitting. Streams and ponds that are open to anglers, as noted in the Fishing and Hunting chapter, are possibilities for ice fishing, provided you check with the authorities in charge for accessibility.

ICE-BOATING

An unscientific survey of lifelong Easterners has revealed that hardly anyone around here has heard of ice-boating. It's fascinating to watch the beautiful sail-boats gliding swiftly across the ice like skaters. These "hardwater boats" range from skate sails, which allow an ice skater to wear a sail, to large sailboats on runners. Most of the lake at Beltzville State Park (610–377–0045), is available for this speedy sport, weather permitting. If you're of the ice-boating persuasion, call the park office in advance to see if the ice and snow conditions are suitable. It takes a very cold winter to freeze the lake, so the opportunity to pursue this sport comes only occasionally. Ice boaters must display a state park launching permit. Permits are available in the park's office, which is open 8:00 A.M. to 4:00 P.M., Monday through Friday through the winter. Pennsylvania residents pay $10, while nonresidents pay $15. (Closed for lunch 12:00 to 12:30 P.M., also closed holidays.)

IN, ON, AND AROUND THE WATER

The Poconos boast 11,373 acres of lakes stocked with fish and uncounted miles of flowing rivers and streams bejeweled by waterfalls. The fish are dealt with in our Fishing and Hunting chapter, and the waterfalls are covered in Our Natural World. The purpose of this chapter is to explore the other things you might do in, on, and around all this water.

The water referred to in this chapter, however, will be the kind over which nature, not mankind, presides. Accordingly, we will not include municipal swimming pools, all of which are dealt with in detail in Kidstuff, or water parks, which are covered in Attractions. Some might argue that such an exclusion would rule out such man-made lakes as Lake Wallenpaupack, which is the crown jewel of Pocono water sports, but Mother Nature took over that franchise almost from the moment it started to fill behind its man-made hydro-electric dam. In fact, of the 501 lakes that sparkle across the Poconos, 461 of them are man-made—the remaining 40 having been born of glaciers. But if you think the man-made variety are beyond nature's grasp, take it up with the trout, bass, walleye, pickerel, muskellunge, and other finny folk that have made those bodies of water home. There are no fish in municipal swimming pools, or tadpoles at the bottom of a water slide.

Options, then, in Mother Nature's waters include swimming, boating, water-skiing and jet skiing on her lakes and rafting and canoeing down rivers ranging from the rambunctious Lehigh to the lazy old Delaware.

In this chapter we focus on the water-worthy opportunities that await you on rivers and lakes throughout the national and state park systems and National For-est preserves. (See our Parks and Recreation chapters for a detailed presentation of what facilities and recreational opportunities, including hiking and camping, each park contains.)

This chapter does not discuss the available options at the many lake communities that contain a large percentage of residential and vacation homes. (See our Relocation chapter for information about vacation rentals.) It does, however, lead you to water sports havens in different regions of the Poconos (note each section's geographic subheads). "National Parks and Recreation Areas" is not divided geographically, as both representative entries encompass more than one region.

Before you use park areas or any waterways with a boat or other water craft, be sure to check with the respective park office or governing agency for a map and list of regulations (see our Parks chapter for contact numbers and other information about individual parks). Brochures are always available at the visitor center on U.S. Highway 209 in Bushkill and, in New Jersey, at Kittatinny Point Visitor Center on Interstate 80.

Be aware that your motorized boat must be registered. Canoes, kayaks and tubes do not have to be, but if they are registered, you don't have to pay launch fees at state parks. Registration for non-motorized water craft is $10 for two years. In all craft, even tubes, you must have U.S. Coast Guard-approved, wearable personal flotation devices (PFDs) or life jackets for each person on board. Be sure you know the Pennsylvania regulations for PFDs and boat (watercraft) registration; go to the Pennsylvania Fish and Boating Commission, Bureau of Boating Web site, www.fish.state.pa.us.

In general, alcohol and pets are not permitted in public park areas; alcohol also is prohibited on any boat trip booked through an outfitter, including whitewater trips. We point out areas and outfitters that allow pets.

Whether you are boating, water-skiing or swimming, in most places you will be surrounded by the beauty of mountains rising around you, often encircling you in what seems to be a cradle of green leafy boughs, blanketed with clear bright blue skies and rocked by sparkling, fresh water. Basking on a beach along the Delaware (whether one chosen for its lifeguard protection or one you discovered on your canoeing or boating sojourn), lounging by a pool nestled at the foot of a hill, watching your children play in a hidden lake near your campsite, or careening through the rapids at the bottom of the steep Lehigh River gorge, the mountains are always there—caressing, protecting, reaching, inspiring, invigorating, calming. And water rests contentedly—or courses wildly through gaps and gorges. Water and mountains together—beautiful, peaceful, wild—characterize the Poconos.

NATIONAL PARKS AND RECREATION AREAS

Renting a River Craft

You can rent a canoe, kayak, raft, or tubes for any number of on-the-water options, whether for a half-day of play, lessons on a new type of craft, or an overnight camping experience. Rates depend on what you want to do, how many of you want to do it, and how long you want to do it. Offers and coupon specials abound in this area, so keep an eye on local publications. Many concessionaires have family rates that allow a child (usually younger than 12) to go free as a third or fourth person in a group. Seasons also affect rates.

Group rates are an option for your camp, church, school, office, reunion, or even neighborhood outing, so don't be shy about asking.

Since rates also are subject to change, we only list a range for options here. To rent a canoe or raft, expect to pay around $29 per person midweek and $32 per person weekends (based on two people per canoe and four people per raft) for a day. Rates are usually $2.00 higher without reservations.

Tubing is less expensive—between $18 and $20 per day. Kayaking and solo canoeing are more expensive because there's only one person per craft. The minimum cost is about $34. Besides craft rental and paddles, rates usually include life jackets; shuttle transportation for people, luggage, and boats; river maps; and an orientation session. Again, group rates and specials are usually available. Credit cards and personal checks (restricted at some locations, so ask) are generally accepted.

Other costs include advance reservations and deposits (about $10 per person as a general rule), damage releases and security deposits (from $1.50 to $5.00 depending on options), and state sales tax (6 percent if you rent on the Pennsylvania side of the Delaware River, 7 percent if you rent on the New York side, where some upper Delaware companies are located). Guided trips are more expensive, and rates are subject to all the same considerations of day of week, number of persons, number of days, and so on. Cancellations are penalized according to certain advance-notice guidelines, which usually consist of the per-person deposit. So, plan your event carefully to avoid cancellations.

Many provisioners also offer lessons and other specials along with rentals. Some of the outfitters licensed for use in the National Recreation Area by the National Park Service follow in the subsequent "Outfitters" sections.

Delaware Water Gap National Recreation Area

This 40-mile stretch along the Delaware River allows swimming and boating (gas- or electric-powered, canoeing, rafting, tubing, and kayaking). The river is designated "wild and scenic," which means there are no dams, and the shoreline and adjacent lands are maintained in their natural state. Smithfield Beach and Milford Beach are the two guarded sand beaches open to the public for a fee of $5.00 on weekdays, $7.00 on weekends for vehicles with up to seven passengers. For a vehicle with more than seven passengers, the rate is $1.00 per head; thus, a bus carrying 40 people would pay $40.00. Those who walk, bicycle, or canoe in pay $1.00 each. A vehicle dropping off or picking up passengers pays no fee so long as it does not exceed a stay of one hour. There is a senior citizen discount, and annual passes are available to all for $40. Aside from swimming, these beaches also offer free (as long as you don't park here, otherwise you must pay the aforementioned fee) boat launching areas. Hidden Lake, just off Hollow Road near Shawnee Mountain, within the park's confines, is open to swimmers but is not guarded.

With few exceptions, swimming is allowed almost anywhere in the park area where you can reach the river from a picnic area, boat launch, or campsite. Swimming is not allowed at Dingmans Falls, George W. Childs Recreation Site, Van Campens Glen, or within 50 feet of the top of any waterfall.

The Hialeah Picnic Area, on River Road, north of Swawnee-on-Delaware and south of Smithfield Beach, flanks the river, though it's high above the water at most spots. Picnickers do swim here, but the climb down to the river can be treacherous. There's a steep path on the north end of Hialeah that's not too bad. Those who do climb down, sometimes with the aid of their own homemade rope guides, say the climb is worth it. You can walk out almost midway into the water, relax and talk with your friends as the river gently (unless we've just had a lot of rain) flows by. Always be aware of weather conditions, not only where you are but also at points upriver; heavy rains on the river or its tributaries can greatly increase the flow rate in a short period of time. There are no guarded beaches in this picnic area; in fact, the size and presence of a beach depends on the rainfall, which, when heavy, can raise the water level enough to cover any of the beaches—an unusual occurrence. You also can picnic at Toms Creek north of Bushkill.

Some words of caution are in order. The Delaware River in the park area generally is calm, with a lazy current and small, whirling eddies. But it is a river, and there are strong currents and sudden drop-offs at points. Always watch your step, whether swimming or boating. Don't take the river for granted. In the spring and after a heavy rain, usually placid spots can be swift and treacherous. If you discover an unexpected current keeps you from landing where you planned, don't fight it. Use the current to take you to a safe spot. And never try to swim across the river. You will only be putting yourself in great danger. At some points it seems narrow enough to swim across to the Jersey side, and it is tempting to take the risk. However, the currents change without warning, and there are deep areas that you might not see in the excitement of assessing whether you can make it. So, please don't try; people do drown here, including swimmers, boaters, and anglers. And don't drink if you're planning to swim,

The Delaware usually resembles the "Lazy River" of the song, but looks can be deceiving. Our great river hides treacherous currents and holes deep enough to swallow a freight train. Never venture on the river without a life vest and never, ever, attempt to swim across it.

tube, or boat. The majority of those who drown—and we get a few every year—have been drinking. Just remember you're not in an amusement park. This is a wild and scenic river, with the emphasis on wild. You are responsible for your own safety, so act responsibly!

While swimmers can get into the river almost at whim, boaters should use the boat launches. There are several on the Pennsylvania side of the park, and all have parking areas for your vehicles. (See "Additional Boat Launches" in this section.)

Note: Pets on leashes no longer than 6 feet are welcome at most locations. However, they are not allowed at Milford Beach, Smithfield Beach, Hidden Lake Beach, or on the mowed areas of Kittatinny Point Visitors' Center, Watergate Recreation Site, or Hialeah Picnic Area.

The park headquarters are east of US 209 just south of Bushkill. Call (570) 588-2451 for more information.

SMITHFIELD BEACH

To reach this beach, take US 209 to River Road at Bushkill if you're coming from the north. From the south, turn from 209 onto Buttermilk Falls Road following the signs to Shawnee, then turn left on River Road and go about 4 miles.

Swimming

Swimming is allowed at this beach while a lifeguard is present. There are very clean restrooms and bathhouses (all of the park's facilities are well maintained), a large parking lot, picnic tables on the grassy slopes above the river and in the woods alongside, and a sandy beach. If you picnic here, you can bring a grill as long as it has legs; a fire box may not touch the ground. Alcoholic beverages and pets are not allowed. There is no snack bar here, but drinking water is available.

Boating, Rafting, and Tubing

There are two boat launch areas at this site. The north end above the beach area

is for personal boat and raft launching. The launch below the south end of the beach is for boat, raft, and tube concessionaires to drop off and pick up rentals. You can use this beach area as the beginning, middle, or end of a trip on the river, depending on where you start and where you want to go.

Gas and electric power boats are allowed on the entire river, but the speed is restricted to 10 mph from April 1 through September 30.

MILFORD BEACH

Just before Milford, at the north end of the park, you'll find signs on US 209 directing you to this area.

Swimming

As at Smithfield Beach, swimming is allowed here while a lifeguard is present. This well-maintained area has very clean restrooms and bathhouses, a large parking lot, picnic tables on the grassy areas and in the woods alongside, and a sandy beach. If you picnic here, you can bring in a grill as long as it is on legs with a fire box that does not touch the ground. Pets are banned, and while there is no snack bar, drinking water is available.

Boating, Rafting, and Tubing

There are two boat launch areas at this site, one for personal boats and one for rentals picked up and dropped off by provisioners.

HIDDEN LAKE

From points south, take the Delaware Water Gap exit off I–80 and follow the signs to Shawnee, which put you on River Road. At the Shawnee Playhouse, turn left onto Hollow Road, and proceed past the Shawnee ski mountain. Turn right onto Hidden Lake Drive, and look for signs for the recreation area. If you're coming from the north, you can catch Hollow Road just south of the Foxmoor Village Outlets on US 209 (follow the sign for Shawnee).

Just before the ski mountain, turn left on Hidden Lake Drive, and continue until you see signs for the recreation area. You can also catch Hidden Lake near Bushkill by turning off US 209 onto River Road (at Fernwood) and turning right on Hidden Lake Drive.

Swimming, Picnicking, and Fishing

Hidden Lake is nestled in a hollow in the Minisink Hills, hence its name. Swimmers will find an unguarded sandy beach. A grassy picnic area sloping toward this small area attracts families for casual swimming, picnicking, and fishing. All activities can be done within about 20 yards of each other. The picnic area adjoins the beach and is close enough at points to hand treats from your table to a waiting child on the beach. For the anglers in your group, the area outside the mutually agreed-upon swimming area provides a fishing spot where you can keep an eye on your swimming companions. The only amenity at this area is a portapotty.

Boating

You'll find a boating access area on the lake about an eighth-mile before the beach parking area on the left. Electric-motor boats are allowed here as well as any non-motorized watercraft. This is a small lake (you can see both ends from the swimming beach), so large boats are not appropriate here. And while you are free to launch a boat, fishing from that boat is forbidden.

OTHER RIVER OPTIONS

You can canoe, kayak, power boat, or raft down the Delaware River at points between Milford and Delaware Water Gap, putting in at park-owned campsites (these campsites and boat accesses are free) along the river. All campsites are clearly identified in the *Delaware Water Gap River Guide,* available at the Park Service

Prepare for your boating experience by taking a boating-safety course. The Coast Guard Hotline will tell you where to register for a course offered in your area. The course includes "rules of the road," equipment requirements, boat handling, boat loading, weather notes, a float plan, emergency tips, and more. Call (800) 368–5647.

offices, US 209, Bushkill, (570) 588–2451. Campsites flank the shore from Milford south at Dingmans Campground; Hornbeck, north of Eshback Access, at Toms Creek (also a picnic site); Valley View, south of Bushkill; and south of Smithfield Beach. There also are several sites on the New Jersey side of the river—Sandyston, Buck Bar, Quinn, Peters, Hamilton, and Worthington State Forest—some of which have as many as 14 camp sites and include bathrooms. You can also camp overnight on the following islands in the river: Quicks, Minisink, Namanock, Shapnack, Sambo, Depew, and Shellenberger. There are only a few campsites at most locations (from single sites at Smithfield Beach and Bushkill to as many as 14 sites at Peters and Hamilton), and the rules are first-come, first-served, with a maximum stay of one night. In fact, there are guidelines as to how many days it should take you to go from one location to another, governing how many nights you are allowed on the river; check with the Park Office for details.

Some campsite guidelines include: fires in the steel grates provided at each campsite must only be fueled with wood from dead, fallen trees (a camp stove is preferred); you must dig your own latrine; and water for washing must be used away from the river. The Park Office provides a map and guidelines for all needs, including quiet hours, so be sure to check with park staff before you begin any overnight river journey.

Scuba Diving

Scuba diving nearly 100 miles from the nearest ocean? With the Delaware River, which has holes as deep as 100 feet, and with hundreds of lakes in parks throughout the Poconos in which to practice, why not? Two area diving schools teach the art of plunging into the depths with oxygen tanks in tow, and while it is illegal to spear fish in Pennsylvania, one at least can look at them in their native habitat. Also high on the river-diver's itinerary are a spot near Roebling Bridge, where musket balls fired in the Battle of Minisink in colonial times frequently are found and the site of a 1942 train wreck that left a boxcar and a flat car, with the remains of its cargo, some 60 feet down in the Water Gap, just downstream from the bridge to New Jersey. Should you wish to visit either scene, here are the places to start.

Mountain Recreational Scuba
195 Main Street, Tobyhanna
(570) 894-5759
www.mountainrecreationalscuba
.bizland.com
This school breaks the course work down into "modules," or classrooms—some of which are taken out of the water at an academic level, and some of which are taken under controlled conditions in a swimming pool—before students start free-diving in the Delaware or in various lakes of the region. The cost is $300, and certification is $15 more. The course usually lasts six weeks, but if students need extra instruction, classes will be extended. Mountain Recreational Scuba also sells, rents, and services diving equipment and kayaks and organizes diving trips to other parts of the world.

Pisces Divers
222 Willow Avenue, Honesdale
(570) 253-0552
www.piscesdiversonline.com
Pisces trains more than 100 new divers every year and, for real enthusiasts, arranges tour to Atlantic coastal waters, the Caribbean, and the South Pacific. But there is plenty of room to practice locally, not only in the Delaware, but also in a myriad of lakes and quarries throughout the Poconos. Pisces trains divers from raw beginner to instructor and guarantees certification for beginners. The rate for the full course is $359, which includes books and certification. It includes six classroom sessions and a like number of confined water dives in a pool or placid lake before taking to open water. Students in need of further instruction get it. Pisces maintains a boat on Lake Wallenpaupack for training and for taking divers out. They say that although the lake covered over some towns when it was made, contrary to popular belief, there are no towns to see under the waters.

Outfitters

Adventure Sports Canoe and Raft Trips
US 209, Marshalls Creek
(570) 223-0505, (800) 487-BOAT
www.adventuresport.com
This outfitter offers kayaks, canoes, or rafts or one, two-, or three-day trips (consistent with park trip-length guidelines) beginning at any boat launch between Milford and Delaware Water Gap. This company will transport you, the canoes, and rafts to a launch site and pick you up down river at a predetermined destination. Those who rent and transport the canoes or rafts themselves pay a cheaper rate that includes paddles and life jackets. The minimum age is 2 years old; all participants must be able to swim.

For overnight camping trips, Adventure Sports rents coolers, tents, and anything else you'll need. Free campsites in the park are noted in the Delaware Water Gap River Guide, available at the National Recreation Area's park office, US 209, Bushkill, (570) 588-2451. Remember, there are no reservations, even when going through a licensed outfitter.

Special arrangements can be made for groups of 10 or more for two-day trips. All necessary supplies can be rented too, but you must make reservations at least a day in advance.

Adventure Sports is open seven days a week from mid-April through mid-October. Take the Marshalls Creek exit off I-80, then proceed 2 miles to US 209 north.

Chamberlain Canoes
Minisink Acres, River Road, Minisink Hills
(570) 421-0180, (800) 422-6631
www.chamberlaincanoes.com

This outfitter has been on the Delaware 35 years. It offers canoes, kayaks, rafts, and tubes for day or overnight trips. Chamberlain Canoes offers trips from Port Jervis, N.Y. (east of Milford), southward to Slateford and Portland and any stops in between at any of the Park's boat launches. Transportation to and from the river is provided.

The age minimums for this outfitter are six years old for canoes and tubes and three years old for rafts.

Specials are available for senior citizens, children, and groups.

Chamberlain is open every day from mid-May to mid-October, depending on the weather. Take I-80 to the Delaware Water Gap exit. Follow the signs for Shawnee, which put you on River Road for a mile to Minisink Acres on the right.

Kittatinny Canoes
Dingmans Ferry Base, Highway 739 South
Dingmans Ferry
(570) 828-2338, (800) FLOAT KC

Milford-River Beach Base
Off US 209, 3.5 miles north of Milford
(570) 828-2338, (800) FLOAT KC

Matamoras Base, Delaware Drive, off US 209, just before Silver Bridge, Matamoras
(800) FLOAT KC
www.kittatinny.com

Kittatinny offers canoes, tubes, rafts, and kayaks. It has been around since 1941 (the grandmother, Ruth, is a legend on the river). Besides renting crafts, it also maintains two excellent campsites on the river for those who desire an overnight excur-

Whitewater classifications for rivers in the Poconos region are: Class I, easiest; Class II, moderate; Class III, difficult: Class III+ (noted during seasonal high-flow periods), for the very experienced only.

sion. They even have paintball, for those who would rather battle than paddle. Children must be at least four years old, must be able to swim, and must weigh more than 40 pounds to be properly fitted with a life vest.

Daily canoe trips and two-day trips for experienced canoeists and beginners are available, as are daily rafting and tubing trips. Whitewater trips depart from the Matamoras Base (about 8 miles east of Milford) and put in at an upper Delaware River location; trips range from 7 to 18 miles and last anywhere from three to seven hours. Easy, relaxed trips depart from Matamoras, River Beach, and Dingmans Ferry southward. The best choice for novices, these trips last from two to five hours and cover 5 to 12 miles. Daily tube trips run from the River Beach Base or a drop-off point in Barryville, NY, accessed from the Matamoras Base. Trip lengths vary according to water level, weather, wind, paddler's ability, and type of craft. You can count on a canoe doing about 2.5 miles per hour; rafts, 2 miles per hour; and tubes, a mile per hour. Of course, you also should factor in time for swimming, picnicking, fishing, and just enjoying the river and its environs.

Some specialty offerings include: Learn to Canoe days; basic kayaking; free mother or father paddlers on their special holidays; summer wildflower and wildlife tours (see eagles, ospreys, and great blue herons); and a fall foliage tour (waterfowl and birds of prey often are spotted on this trip too).

At least one of the campgrounds usually opens in mid-March, while the river trips begin in mid-April, depending on the weather. Both run through October, and if the weather is good, into November. Call for early-and late-season hours and to see which bases are staffed.

The Pack Shack
88 Broad Street, Delaware Water Gap
(570) 424-8533
www.packshack.com
The Pack Shack not only rents rafts, tubes, canoes, and kayaks, but also stocks all the camping gear needed for a foray down the river. They also rent duckies—two-person inflatable kayaks. Rental includes paddles, lifejackets, and a shuttle to and from river access points. Although this is a friendly river, Pack Shack offers tours with knowledgeable guides, too. They specialize in overnight guided trips for groups.

Shawnee Canoe Trips
Shawnee Inn, River Road
Shawnee-on-Delaware
(570) 424-4000
www.shawneeinn.com
This outfitter is at Shawnee Inn but is licensed to operate in the park and rents to the general public. It offers canoes, rafts, kayaks, and tubes for 3-, 6-, 9- or 13-mile unguided trips beginning at Smithfield Beach and ending at Shawnee, Delaware Water Gap, or Portland. Shawnee Canoes is open every day in season. You must be off the water by 5:00 P.M., however.

Age and height minimums to ride are: 42 inches tall for a canoe; 10 years old for a tube; and walking age for a raft.

Additional Boat Launches

Launching areas on the Delaware River in the recreation area are between Smithfield and Dingmans Ferry on US 209. Sites other than at Milford Beach, Smithfield Beach, or those managed by outfitters include Dingmans Ferry Access, Eshback Access, and Bushkill Access.

All launching areas are clearly marked as you head north or south on US 209.

There are parking areas for your vehicles and trailers and direct access to the Delaware River. There is no fee to launch a boat at any of these sites; parking at Milford or Smithfield is $5.00 to $7.00 per vehicle, depending on the day of the week.

UPPER DELAWARE SCENIC AND RECREATIONAL RIVER

This section of the Delaware River, between New York Highway 97 and Interstate 84 from Hancock, New York to Milford, provides moderate whitewater canoeing and rafting, manageable for beginners or the less experienced paddlers. While there are whitewater areas to challenge you on this stretch of the Delaware, there are also enough placid pools to allow you to relax and enjoy the landscape as you float or paddle. Along either side of the river from Skinners Falls in the north to River Beach at Milford, you might see—depending on the season—waterfowl, birds of prey, wildflowers, and the beautiful colors of nature, especially in spring, summer, and fall.

Land along the river is almost all privately owned, so check with the outfitter you use about spots on the New York side where it's permissible to stop, swim, picnic, and rest. There are no places to picnic or camp on the Pennsylvania side of the river. Campsites for overnight trips can be arranged through the licensed outfitters listed in this section.

Trips on the river are arranged through the several licensed outfitters along the river, mostly on the New York side except for Kittatinny Canoes (see the previous entry), which has three bases in Pennsylvania and two in New York. Kittatinny's northernmost Pennsylvania base, at Matamoras, provides transportation to the northern access points upriver from Milford; its two New York bases are in Barryville (21 miles northwest of Port Jervis) and Pond Eddy (14 miles northwest of Port Jervis). Kittatinny also has campgrounds in the New York section of the Upper Delaware.

Rates for rentals, overnights, guides, groups, and so on are the same as apply in the Delaware Water Gap park area. Reservations for these trips are always a good idea, but a spur-of-the-moment indulgence often can be accommodated. Remember sales tax: 7 percent in New York, 6 percent in Pennsylvania. Another expense sometimes associated with whitewater is a wet suit—a good option if the water is cold.

To obtain a list of available campsites and campgrounds not accessible through outfitters, contact the Park Service in Milford, (570) 685–4871, or go to their Web site www.nps.gov for a listing. Staff will advise arranging access to this section of the river through an outfitter that can transport you to one of its bases. Public access to the Upper Delaware is available every 5–10 miles, with access points scattered along both shores. Some access points offer public restrooms and boat launches. A detailed list is available on the park's Web site.

The following are some of the major outfitters in the Upper Delaware Scenic and Recreational River area.

Outfitters

Lander's River Trips
NY 97, Narrowsburg, NY
(914) 252-3925, (800) 252-3925
www.landersrivertrips.com

This outfitter rents canoes, rafts, kayaks, and tubes. Children must be five years old and weigh 50 pounds to fit into life jackets. Getaway packages are available for four or more adults for one- or two-day overnights, which are spent either camping or at the Ten Mile River Lodge with dormitory-style accommodations.

Unguided trips originate from as far north as Hankins, NY, and end at the base near Port Jervis. Tubing trips can cover as many as 5 miles, or you can stay at Skinner's Falls for the day. You can float around or through the falls, then portage your tube upriver along the path beside

the falls. You can spend a whole day here—transportation to and from included.

Lander's has campgrounds along the river at Skinner's Falls, Narrowsburg, Minisink, and Knight's Eddy for campers using Lander's or privately owned river craft. Campgrounds contain hot showers, snack bars, and camp stores. Campsites and lean-tos are available. Rates vary from $12 to $14 per adult or teenager; children ages 7 to 12 are half-price, and kids six and younger are free. Weekend stays include two nights; holiday weekends, three nights.

Lander's also maintains the Ten Mile River Lodge, an aptly named motel 10 miles down river from Skinner's Falls. Standard rooms for two people are $70 per night. Efficiencies for $89 are also available.

Two River Junction
106 Scenic Drive, Lackawaxen
(570) 685-2010

Part of a minimall including a restaurant and Angler's Roost & Hunter's Rest, Two River Junction offers canoes, rafts, kayak, and tube rentals on both the Delaware and Lackawaxen rivers. They'll drop you off and pick you up. If you need any fishing equipment, camping equipment, or anything else to make your river trip more pleasant, you can find it at Angler's Roost & Hunter's Rest. (See our Fishing and Hunting chapter.)

Wild and Scenic River Tours and Rentals
166 NY 97, Barryville, NY
(914) 557-8783, (800) 836-0366
www.laudersrivertrips.com

This outfitter, now part of Lander's River Trips, has proudly served the Orthodox Jewish community for more than two decades. They are well versed in Orthodox customs and send boys and girls out to separate parts of the river. They provide canoes, rafts, kayaks, and tubes. Self-guided trips are available from one of three river-access sites.

Discounts are provided for groups of 10 adults or more. Other group rates are offered, depending on the size of the

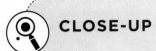

Pocono Rivers Offer a Wild, Wet, Wonderful Ride

You're in the middle of a raging torrent, heading at flank speed for a boulder the size of a Lincoln Towncar. The guy who is supposed to be steering your bouncy little rubber raft was thrown overboard five minutes ago, and the paddle they gave you back at the launch site seems to function in your hands as little more now than an oversize flyswatter. Meanwhile, high over the vertical cliffs that rise on either side of you, a dozen turkey vultures circle, waiting, perhaps, to see how your little excursion turns out.

No, you are not in the middle of a bad dream. You are wide-awake and drowning in adrenaline in the mighty grip of the Lehigh River, which has more whitewater than an Alka-Seltzer factory at flood time. You are wet; you are cold; you are terrified; and you are feeling that you never really have lived before this moment.

Forget roller coasters. Forget bungee jumping and skydiving; they're over in minutes. This is river rafting—a pulse-pounding, muscle-burning, Oh-my-gawd-we're-gonna-die adventure that will keep you hanging between terror and exhilaration for three and a half to six hours a trip. Only the bold go here! But, having said that, I must add that, past age 5, you're never too young or too old to be bold. If there is any wilder water in the Rockies, then, and then alone, will I stay ashore.

We took our baptism of water (forget fire; you couldn't light a cigar with a blowtorch out there) on a gray and dreary day in early spring shortly after arriving at the base camp of Jim Thorpe River Adventures on the west bank of the Lehigh River. River Adventures is one of many companies that put thrill-seekers in rafts, canoes, and kayaks both on the Lehigh and on the less turbulent Delaware that marks the eastern terminus of the Poconos. All of them are staffed by people who know their waterways better than the fish who live there.

River Adventures also rents mountain bikes and wet suits and sells baseball caps and T-shirts with such saucy sayings as "Bones Heal; Chicks Dig Scars" and "Pain is Temporary; Glory is Forever." Thus encouraged we were told to pack our lunches in waterproof containers, pour any beverages we may have brought along from glass bottles into plastic, since glass is not allowed on the river, and prepare for on-the-job training in the fine art of steering a raft with four-to-six people all flailing away in contrary directions with their paddles.

After a brief lecture in which we were told never to try to stand up in the river—"foot-traps" can grab you and pull you under—and always, should we fall overboard, to float downstream, bottom first with feet up, until rescued. We were issued life jackets and paddles, loaded onto buses, and carted 17 miles upriver to begin our journey.

A word of advice: If you do this early in the year, or on an overcast day at any time, rent a wetsuit, because before the

Whitewater rafting along the Lehigh River gives adventurers the thrill of battling the water, plus incredible scenery. MARTY GINTER/POCONO MOUNTAINS VACATION BUREAU

day is five minutes old, you will be wetter than you ever have been in your life. And, since "wet" quickly translates into "cold," a full wetsuit will keep your teeth from chattering (see our Fishing and Hunting chapter for a dissertation on hypothermia). We know this because we did not rent wetsuits, and all that dental activity really inhibited our need to scream from time to time.

Once at the launch point, we were loaded into our rafts, cast into the river among a dozen or so River Adventures personnel in nimble little kayaks—the motorcycles of river life—and told to please, whatever we did, try to stay together. We promptly strung ourselves out all over the river where we managed to hit and become hung up several times on all but maybe three of the rocks that stud this riverbed like teeth in a crocodile's gumline.

Our "captain"—the crew member assigned to sit in the back of the raft and man the tiller—wasn't the only "man overboard." About a quarter of the rafters fell in at one time or another and had to be fished out by kayak or passing raft. The day was not over for five marvelous, exhausting, jubilant, never-to-be-forgotten hours.

But it's not all thrills, chills, and close encounters with that old Mafia thing about sleeping with the fishes. There are placid moments, and to float through them down the Lehigh is to cruise the Garden of Eden. Cliffs draped in greenery laced with tiny waterfalls rise to some 300 feet above you most of the way. They reveal the occasional dark maw of a cave where a bear may or may not spend the winter, or stretches of weathered stonework remaining like some ancient artifact from the days when the river was dredged and shored up as a canal for coal-bearing barges. Along the shoreline, where you will stop occasionally for lunch or much-needed rest, the great iron river dredges left from the 19th-century rust, half-buried, in shoals of wildflowers.

As your raft clears a set of rapids and drifts momentarily into deeper, calmer water, great fish occasionally can be glimpsed floating in holes and eddies, and the skies are filled with hunting hawks, eagles and ospreys. And yes, they occasionally are filled with vultures too.

The thrill of the river lies in the fact that nowhere else can you be so close to it while it is happening—Ken Clark.

group; be sure to inquire. Reservations are recommended.

From points in Pennsylvania, take U.S. Highway 6 east from Hawley or west from Milford to Twin Lakes Road. Follow Twin Lakes Road across the Shohola Bridge into New York. Make a left onto NY 97 north and proceed about 0.75 mile. Or, from points in New York, take NY 97 north from Port Jervis or south from Narrowsburg. The outfitter is 0.75 mile from the Shohola Bridge on NY 97 north.

STATE PARKS

Mount Pocono Area

Gouldsboro State Park
Highway 507, 1.5 miles south of Gouldsboro
(570) 894-8336
www.dcnr.state.pa.us
Swimming, boating, picnicking, and fishing are water-related options here. The 250-acre lake is right past the park entrance on Highway 507, 1.5 miles south of Gouldsboro; follow signs for boat rentals and the dock—just past the swimming

area. The boat dock and beach of this 2,800-acre park are wheelchair accessible from Parking Lot 1. There are restrooms and bathhouses but no showers. Bring your own picnic—there is no snack bar.

Beaches are open for swimming daily from Memorial Day to Labor Day when lifeguards are on duty. There is no fee for swimming.

If you have your own boat, you can use the docks right past the beach 24 hours a day. Night fishing is permitted. Your boat must be registered in Pennsylvania to use it on the lake. You can rent canoes and rowboats at the dock. All boat users must have an approved life vest on board for each occupant; it is the law. Rentals come equipped with approved life vests.

Call the park office for more information.

Promised Land State Park
Highway 390, 10 miles north of Candensis
(570) 676-3428
www.dcnr.state.pa.us
This state park offers a large lake for swimming, two lakes for fishing and boating, picnic areas, and four campgrounds with facilities ranging from Class A to

primitive. Access to all areas is free. Costs are only for rentals, supplies, campsites, and launch fees for non-registered boats.

The park covers 3,000 acres. The upper lake is 450 acres; the lower lake, 150 acres. Offices are on Highway 390 west past the Village of Promised Land in the park. The office is open Monday through Friday in January, February and March. It's open every day the rest of the year. Wheelchair-accessible areas including ramps and walkways, are available; call the park office or stop in for daily information. Improvements and additions are always being made.

Swimming

The main beach is on the north shore of Promised Land Lake in the picnic area. It's open and attended by lifeguards (weather permitting) from Memorial Day through Labor Day. The sandy beach includes roped-off areas for swimming. There is a snack bar at the main beach, and tables and fire rings for your picnic and for guests at nearby campgrounds. Restrooms are available, as is a bathhouse with a hot-water shower that you feed with quarters (50 cents to start). The shower is open for campers staying at the primitive sites as well as swimmers at the lake.

On weekends this lake is always crowded. If you want to come for the day, plan on arriving before the beach opens. The parking lot fills rapidly—remember campers are close by. By noon the parking lots usually are full, and you'll have to park on the access roads and walk in.

Pickerel Point has a sandy, unguarded beach where you can swim at your own risk. The park asks that you read a list of posted regulations before you swim.

Boating

You can go boating or fishing on the upper and lower Promised Land lakes and on Bruce Lake (a glacial lake as is the park's very small Egypt Meadow Lake). Electric-powered motor boats—no gas-powered craft—are allowed on Promised

Land Lake. Powerboats must have a Pennsylvania registration. If your boat is registered out of state, or if you have an unregistered non-powered boat, you must purchase a launch permit. Temporary permits are $5.00 for seven days. Yearly permits, good at other Pennsylvania state parks, are $10 for Pennsylvania residents and $15 for nonresidents. You can rent boats at the boat concession by the hour or day, or for several days. Rates vary according to the type of boat (paddleboat, canoe, kayak, rowboat), starting at $13.50 per hour and ranging up to $55.00 for a full day.

Bruce Lake and Egypt Meadow Lake are not recreation areas; overnight camping and recreational vehicles are not allowed.

Bruce Lake is a 48-acre lake that is a 2.5-mile hike from the trailhead originating on Highway 390. If you bring your boat, you will have to carry it. This area is part of the Delaware National Forest, and no motor vehicles are allowed; park at the trailhead.

The hike to 60-acre Egypt Meadow Lake is only a half-mile or so from the trailhead on Highway 390. This lake is very weedy, and the fishing here is not very good. Swimming is not allowed in Bruce Lake or Egypt Meadow Lake. Maps available at the park office show all the trails, lakes, and campsites.

Other Opportunities

Many events and educational opportunities are available during the summer season at this park. There are naturalist walks

---

The American Red Cross says boaters always should carry a two-way radio or cellular phone, a compressed air horn, and a paddle, even if they are driving a motorized boat. A paddle not only can be vital in the event of motor failure, but also can be used as a rescue device if someone falls overboard.

Always wear a life jacket when you're in a boat. Even though the lake or river may seem placid and easy, if, somehow you upset, and the boat hits you on the head, the jacket will keep you afloat. Children 12 and younger must wear a jacket at all times. Older folks must have a flotation device in the boat.

and guided ecotours by canoe and on foot. There are nature crafts and talks for the children. In the park you'll find a naturalist museum and a Civilian Conservation Corps Museum (CCC alumnae met here in 1995 for a reunion). The scheduled offerings vary, and most are free. Call the park for a definite schedule each week.

Tobyhanna State Park
Highway 423, 2.1 miles north of
Tobyhanna
(570) 894–8336
www.dcnr.state.pa.us
Swimming, boating, picnicking, fishing, and camping are options near the water at 5,440-acre Tobyhanna State Park. The 175-acre lake is cradled on three sides by forest and hills; a sandy beach encircles the fourth. The lake is past the park entrance, and parking lots parallel the lake. The boat dock and beach are wheelchair accessible from any parking lot; the terrain is flat here, and there are paths to the water. There are restrooms and bathhouses but no showers. Bring your own picnic Memorial Day to Labor Day because a snack bar is not available.

Swimming

Beaches are open for swimming when lifeguards are on duty Memorial Day to Labor Day. There is no fee for swimming. Grassy picnic areas, wooded picnic areas, and a small playground adjoin the beach. There are 300 picnic tables and grilling facilities (bring your own charcoal) throughout the lake area (the detailed map at the park

office can help you find the one you prefer, other than those directly by the beach).

Boating

If you have your own boat, you can use the docks to launch. The docks are past the park office, which is just past the beach area on the same road. Docks are open 24 hours a day. Night fishing is permitted. Your boat must be registered in Pennsylvania to use it on the lake. If your boat is not registered in Pennsylvania, you can purchase a permit. Temporary launch permits are $5.00 for seven days. Yearly permits, good at other Pennsylvania state parks, are $10 for Pennsylvania residents and $15 for nonresidents.

You can rent canoes and rowboats. By law, boats must have approved life vests on board for all occupants; all rentals come equipped with approved life vests.

West End

Beltzville State Park
US 209, 5 miles east of Lehighton
(610) 377–0045
www.dcnr.state.pa.us
Swimming, boating, picnicking, fishing, and hiking are available at Beltzville State Park, US 209, 5 miles east of Lehighton, (610) 377–0045. The lake at Beltzville is the largest in this part of the Poconos (Lake Wallenpaupack has that distinction on the other side of the coverage area), so motorized boats are allowed here. The lake is 949 acres, comprising a large chunk of the park's total 2,972 acres.

Camping is not permitted. Admission to the park is free. Boat launching is free for Pennsylvania residents with a valid boat registration. Temporary launch permits are $5.00 for seven days. Yearly permits, good at other Pennsylvania state parks, are $10 for Pennsylvania residents and $15 for nonresidents. Boat rentals, available Memorial Day weekend through Labor Day, range from $10 an hour for a paddleboat to $75 an hour for a pontoon. Also available are rowboats, motor boats and canoes. The park office is open daily from Memorial Day to Labor Day, and Monday through Friday the rest of the year. Beaches, boat launches, and public areas are wheelchair accessible; call the park for details.

Swimming

The beach here is the largest in any of the park areas. Lifeguards are on duty from Memorial Day through Labor Day. There is a snack bar at the roped-off swimming area, picnic areas with grills, restrooms, and bathhouses with showers. Pavilions for picnicking are available for free on a first-come, first-served basis; if you want to reserve one, call (888) PAPARKS. Fees range from $36 to $72, depending on whether you're a Pennsylvania resident or not and whether you want the pavilion during the week or on a weekend.

Boating

Unlimited horsepower is allowed on this lake. The speed limit is 45 mph. Water skiing and Jet Skiing are allowed here. (This is the only public lake beach to allow this activity besides Lake Wallenpaupack.) Non-powered boats must be registered in Pennsylvania, or you must purchase a launch permit; powerboats must display current registration. Boat launches are open 24 hours a day, so fishing is allowed 24 hours a day as well. No fishing is allowed in the swimming area, but you may fish offshore.

Other Opportunities

This park offers day camps for children throughout the summer. Crafts, nature hikes, swimming lessons, week-long programs, day-long programs, and even family programs are available for free. Contact the park office in May to see what opportunities are planned for the summer season (local newspapers list them in summer-specials sections).

Hickory Run State Park
Highway 534, near Hickory Run
(570) 443-0400
www.dcnr.state.pa.us
This 15,500-acre park has a small, 40-acre lake. Swimming, picnicking, fishing, camping, and hiking are allowed at this state park. The office is open daily from Memorial Day to Labor Day, Monday through Friday during the rest of the year. The campgrounds are 1.5 miles from the office. The beach area is a mile past the office along a service road. A wheelchair-accessible ramp leads to the beach and picnic areas; park personnel suggest you contact the office for details. There are no daily fees for fishing (you must have a valid Pennsylvania fishing license if you are older than 16) or swimming. Fishing is only available from the shore, since there is no boating on this lake.

To find out about programs and recreational opportunities as you drive through the Delaware Water Gap National Recreation Area, tune your radio to 1610 AM when you reach Bushkill or the Dingmans Fall Visitor Center, both on US 209.

Swimming

There is a small, sandy beach, which is open mid-May through mid-September. Lifeguards are on duty Memorial Day through Labor Day. There are more than 400 picnic tables scattered around the beach on the grass, under trees, along the grassy rim of the knoll behind the beach, and in the woods farther removed from the beach area. Grills are provided at some table sites. To reach the beach from the parking lot, you have to walk up a hill on paths. A snack bar, restrooms, bathhouses, and showers are here.

Lehigh Gorge State Park
North Entrance, I-80 Exit 273
White Haven
(570) 427-5000
www.dcnr.state.pa.us

This park is primarily known for whitewater rafting. Hiking trails here become snowmobiling and cross-country skiing trails in winter. Camping and swimming are not allowed in this park, but Mauch Chunk Lake, a county-owned area, is adjacent to Lehigh Gorge at the Jim Thorpe end, and both activities are available there. (See our Parks and Fishing and Hunting chapters for information about other recreational opportunities.)

To tackle the whitewater in the turbulent Lehigh River and its canal, you must have an approved raft or canoe. Aluminum canoes are not recommended because they are easily dented. Regulation life vests or PFDs (we recommend Type II or V, designed for whitewater) are a must. Experienced paddlers can attempt this challenge without a guide; the inexperienced should not. Licensed concessionaires are allowed to operate in the park (see the outfitters listed below), and they can provide or suggest guide services.

There are no fees to enter the gorge area, but you should check with the park office before running the river. Water levels are controlled by dam releases in the spring and fall and at various times in summer. The releases greatly increase the flow, and thus have a marked effect on the danger of the river. The U.S. Army Corps of Engineers provides release information, www.nap-wc.usace.army.mil, as does the park office. Also, very low water levels make for a different but similarly dangerous situation, so access to the river is con-

---

If you're planning a river trip and a picnic, make sure that all the containers you take along are plastic. Glass containers are forbidden on the river in the park.

---

trolled by the park rangers during low-flow periods; the inexperienced are not allowed on the river when the water is very low or turbulent. Also, the number of people allowed on the river is controlled to ensure safety. One way the numbers are monitored is through the licensed concessionaires; the other is through the park office.

Enter the park at the White Haven (north) entrance. Other access areas are in Rockport and Glen Onoko. Pick up a map, check the Web site, or call the park office if you are planning a trip here. Parking is only available at Rockport, so make arrangements to be picked up if you are paddling on your own. The water down river from Jim Thorpe is not as difficult; by contrast, the upper waters are Class III (difficult) whitewater. Spring and fall are the most turbulent water times. If you want to try a whitewater adventure with your family, the summer is quieter, and local outfitters can turn you on to more low-key paddling opportunities.

One local outfitter, Lehigh Rafting Rentals, 242 Main Street, White Haven (570) 443-4441, or (800) 291-7238, rents rafts for self-guided tours only; call for reservations. Rates vary by season and day of the week, but you're looking at a minimum of $31.00 per person per raft plus wet suit ($10.00), mittens ($3.00), and booties ($5.00) if necessary (depending on the weather).

Following are approved concessionaires (outfitters) that offer guided whitewater experiences as well as rentals for the experienced whitewater enthusiast. Rates and methods of payment for trips vary, depending on day of week, time of year, guided or unguided, dam-release specials, summer events and other options. Peak-season (whitewater spring and fall) rates range from $33 to $50 per adult (children are about half-price or, with some specials, free with two paying adults). Wet suit rentals ($10 to $13) also might be necessary and are mandatory between March 1 and May 1. Don't forget to add in Pennsylvania sales tax (6 percent) on trips. Each outfitter has its own specials, which change every year, so contact the ones that interest you for their latest brochure of offerings. Reservations are recommended. Trips usually run rain or shine. All trips include transportation to and from the river and your vehicle. All outfitters recommend you bring a change of clothing. Alcoholic beverages are not permitted!

Outfitters also offer picnics and barbeques, group rates, breakfast specials, kayaking opportunities, and additional options too varied to list here. Contact any of the following for up-to-date offering.

A little note to help save you money: The outfitters often have coupons in their brochures or on their Web sites, so sending for one or picking up a brochure from a rack, is a good idea. In local grocery stores, diners, fast-food stands, and tourist attractions, you'll find racks with local magazines that also might include outfitter coupons. If you are in the area, check out these publications before you pay full price.

Jim Thorpe River Adventures
1 Adventure Lane, Jim Thorpe
(800) 424-RAFT
www.jtraft.com

The season for this outfitter is March through October. Staff encourage early reservations with a deposit of $20 per person. They offer specials for dam releases and summer rafting, so call to confirm dates. This outfitter offers several family options (children must be 5 or older). You can also rent mountain bikes here for the non-whitewater enthusiasts in your party.

Pocono Whitewater Adventures
Highway 903, Jim Thorpe
(800) WHITEWATER
www.whitewaterrafting.com

Kayaks and bikes are also available from this group, in case some of you want to whitewater raft, and some of you don't.

Call the 24-hour Emergency hotline, (800) 543-HAWK, to report emergencies or violations of the laws protecting the Delaware Water Gap National Recreation Area in the Delaware Water Gap National Park.

This outfitter also offers family-style float trips and Skirmish, a paintball war game (see our Recreation chapter). Some raft trips include a free barbecue lunch in a meadow. There is a snack bar, sports shop, and miniature golf at this facility. Advance reservations are highly recommended.

Whitewater Challenges
Stagecoach Road, White Haven
(570) 443-9532, (800) 443-8554
(800) 443-RAFT
www.wc-rafting.com

Whitewater Challengers offers discounts and specials for youth groups—scouts, weekends, summer rafting, and college days—as well as weekend trips, ice breakers, rafting/ camping, rafting/hosteling, and so on. Call for a brochure; the specials are always changing and growing. Age requirements vary, based on the trip; the youngest age allowed is 5 for summer rafting. Biking is also offered as are kayaking, canoeing, ecotouring, orienteering, and a soccer tournament.

Whitewater Rafting Adventures
Highway 534, Albrightsville
(800) 876-0285

Trips are offered at discounted prices in the summer when the water is less turbulent. Discounts apply to children, groups, scouts, and families. Group specials also are available for whitewater high times (Class III+ experiences). Kayak clinics, mountain biking, and paintball are available too. A complimentary cookout is part of this outfitter's package.

NATURAL AREAS

West End

Mauch Chunk Lake Park
Lentz Trail Highway, between Summit
Hill and Jim Thorpe
(570) 325-3669
www.dcnr.state.pa.us
This park has an absolutely beautiful, clear, mountain-surrounded lake. It is part of the county system and is administered by the Carbon County Parks and Recreation Commission. Swimming is available on a guarded beach. Campsites are available within walking distance to the lake; picnic tables are in a pavilion area above the lake and in the woods around the lake; and a snack bar adjoins the lake and pavilion area. Restrooms, bathhouses, and showers are here too. Parking is available directly in front of the lake. This facility is wheelchair accessible at all main areas.

Swimming

The sandy, guarded beach is open daily from the close of school through Labor Day. Fees for beach use differ for Carbon County residents and nonresidents (between $2.00 and $4.00 per person per day) and are subject to change. Physically disabled, children younger than three years, and senior citizens are admitted free. There is a tot-lot play area in the wooded picnic area near the beach. Across from the beach you'll find volleyball courts.

Boating

There is a camp store that rents boats by the hour and the day. Paddleboats, canoes, kayaks (single and two-person), and elec-

When you're in a boat, always wear your life jacket. More than 800 people are killed nationwide every year in boating accidents, and 9 out of 10 of the victims are not wearing life jackets.

tric motor boats are available for rent. A valid driver's license and a major credit card are required to rent. Boat launches are open year round, 24 hours a day. Restrooms are available at the boat launch.

Milford/Lake Wallenpaupack Area

Lake Wallenpaupack
US 6 and Highway 507, southeast
of Hawley
(570) 226-3702
www.pplweb.com
The Lake Wallenpaupack area has four Pennsylvania Power & Light-owned recreation centers that provide camping areas and boat launches managed by private concerns. There is a whopping 52 miles of shoreline in this natural area. PPL also maintains two hiking trails around the lake, picnic areas on the four islands in the lake, and public-access boat launches.

The sole public swimming beach is operated by Palmyra Township. Around the lake there are privately-owned marinas and boat-concessionaires that use the lake. Water skiing, Jet Skiing, fishing, canoeing, rafting, and rowing are all allowed on this large lake, whether from a campsite, a public launch area, the public beach, or your own vacation home. Check out the "Campgrounds and RV" section of our Accommodations chapter for write-ups on camping facilities at these individual recreation areas.

Lake Wallenpaupack is a popular boating lake. Large boats are allowed here, so water skiing is a major attraction.

Swimming

You can swim at the one public-access beach area on the lake—Palmyra Township Bathing Beach, (570) 226-9290, managed by Palmyra Township. It is across from the Pocono Mountains Vacation Bureau on Highway 590. The beach is open July 1 through Labor Day, when lifeguards are

on duty. The cost is $2.50 for adults, $1.00 for children younger than 12. There is a picnic area with two grills, a snack bar, bathrooms, changing rooms, and a shower. Pets and alcohol are not allowed.

Boating

The launching access at the four recreation areas is open to the public for $7.00 (no pets). One other public-access launch site is available for free. Needless to say it is very crowded on weekends, so we suggest paying the nominal charge at the fee areas for the convenience and elbow room. The free-access boat launch is run by the Pennsylvania Boat Commission, (570) 477–5717, for the Lake Wallenpaupack area. It is at the north end of the lake near the dam off Highway 590, a quarter-mile west of the US 6 intersection. The launch is open 24 hours a day, every day, all year long. Parking is available. To launch from this site, your boat must have a valid registration. Pennsylvania registration is not required on this lake. (Please note this is not the case at any lake in the state park system. Boating requirements for each lake area differ.)

You can picnic at the four recreation areas on the grass around the docks for free or pay $2.00 for a table. The four islands in the lake—Epply, Kipp, Burns, and Cairns—all have picnic areas with tables. Burns does not have restrooms, but the others do. You cannot camp on these islands and can only picnic during daylight hours; alcohol and pets are not permitted. These areas are accessible by boat only.

Boat Rentals

There are a number of places to rent boats, Jet Skis, water skis, and related water sports gear while in the Lake Wallenpaupack area. Here's one:

If you're canoeing, kayaking, rafting, tubing, or even swimming in the Delaware or Lehigh Rivers, wear water shoes or canvas boat shoes; the river bottoms are quite rocky, and you won't be able to stand without shoes.

Pine Crest Yacht Club Inc.
On Lake Wallenpaupack, Highway 507
Greentown
(570) 857–1136

This shop is part of the Pinecrest Resort. It is open to the public for powerboats, pontoon boats, sail boats, canoes, rowboats, water skis, Jet Skis, and other rentals. Rates start at $26.00 per half-hour for an aluminum fishing boat with outboard motor and $8.00 for water skis. The Pine Crest is open daily from May to mid-October.

Recreation Areas

The recreation areas for Pennsylvania Power & Light all operate under the same basic guidelines. They provide camp areas with boat launch facilities for a day- or short-term use and slips that can be rented for a short stay or the season (April to October). Campsites are $16.00 per night for one to four persons and $2.00 per night for each additional person. Reservations are strongly suggested, and a deposit is required (credit-card deposits usually are not accepted). Campsites include a tent site and electricity. Swimming is not allowed at the campsites or launch areas; however, there is a public swimming area, and swimming from a boat is allowed. Daily launch fees are $5.00, whether you are camping or just want to boat for the day. If you are camping, the $5.00 fee applies for the length of your stay. Seasonal sites are $900, electricity extra (prices are subject to change).

GOLF

Mark Twain once described the game of golf as "a good walk spoiled," but then, as now, he walked alone. For the millions who view golf and God in the same holy light, the only good walk is one that follows the bouncing ball. For them, the Poconos are heaven.

More than 35 golf courses are spread across the Poconos, giving players of all experience levels, from tyro to pro, access to links commensurate with their abilities. Families and beginners might try one of the many short, nine-hole facilities that have few hazards and generous greens and fairways. More serious golfers may chose from a number of professional-caliber courses. Highly regarded designers such as A.W. Tillinghast, Robert Trent Jones, Donald Ross, Jack Nicklaus, and Jim Fazio are represented. The best courses utilize the existing natural features to create trouble spots. Golf course architects love to taunt Poconos golfers with woods, streams, lakes, hills, cliffs, stone rows, and wetlands. Side-hill lies and undulating greens bordered by streams, woods and a few bunkers are common.

All total course yardage measurements offered here are taken from the men's tees. Resort courses are accessible to guests of the facility, who usually receive preferred tee times. Through a cooperative effort among 10 of the resort courses, visitors staying at one of the accommodations may book tee times at any of the others as well. Private courses, which may be played only by club members or their guests, are not included. Of necessity, public greens fees cited throughout this chapter are a year behind since courses intending to raise their fees from 2004 levels will do so after this book is in print. To be sure of costs, call ahead.

GOLF COURSES

Delaware Water Gap/ Shawnee-on-Delaware

Caesars Pocono Palace Golf Course
U.S. Highway 209 at Echo Lake
Marshalls Creek
(570) 588-6692
www.caesarspoconoresorts.com
Trees lining the fairways make this a tougher-than-average nine-hole par 34. The course is relatively flat (especially by Pocono standards), and the greens are fast. At 2,809 yards Caesars is longer than most nine-hole courses in the Poconos. The signature hole is the par 5 No. 7, which confronts the golfer with a tree-lined 550-yard drive that doglegs to the left.

Lessons, a practice area, a pro shop, a restaurant and bar, and a driving range are among the amenities at this resort course. Greens fees are $15 during the week, $20 on the weekend, for 18 holes for outside players; guests of the resort play for free. Guests of the resort pay $15 for a cart for nine holes, $25 for 18, while outside players pay $20 for a cart for nine holes and $35 for 18 holes. Walking is permitted unless the course is crowded, at which times carts are required. There are no tee times, but outside players are encouraged to call first and see if the course is busy. If it's busy, the guests of the resort receive preference.

Fernwood Resort & Country Club
US 209, Bushkill
(570) 588-9500
www.resortsusa.com
This resort course is user-friendly but still holds a few surprises. It is 18 holes, par 71, and 6,300 yards long. The most challeng-

ing hole is No. 13; woods encase the sloped fairway of this 348-yard par 4. The entire course is hillier than average for the Poconos.

Lessons, showers, a pro shop, clubhouse, snack bar, a practice area, lockers, and a restaurant and bar are among the facilities at Fernwood. Weekday greens fees are $39, and weekends are $48. The afternoon discount begins at 2:00 P.M. and is $25 midweek, $29 on weekends. Walking is not permitted.

Mountain Manor Inn & Golf Course
Golf Course Drive, off US 209
Marshalls Creek
(570) 223-1290
www.mountainmanor.com

Of the five nine-hole courses here, the Orange and the Silver provide the best 18-hole combination at 6,407 yards. The views of the Delaware Water Gap from the Orange course are exceptionally picturesque. The Silver boasts a 678-yard par 6 monster. Those looking for an easy walk over flat open land should try the Blue and Yellow courses, which measure 6,233 yards combined. They are shorter and easier to play.

Mountain Manor has both a PGA and a LPGA pro who offer lessons. Facilities include a pro shop, practice area, showers, lockers, a snack bar, a clubhouse, and a restaurant/bar. To best understand the subtleties of playing here, pick up a copy of a book written by the course pros that gives hole-by-hole tips on how to approach each shot. The book costs $7.00 and is available in the pro shop. Weekday greens fees are $22, weekend fees are $32. Cart rentals are $23 for nine holes, $36 for 18 holes, $54 for 27 holes, and $72 for 36 holes. Twilight rates after 3:00 P.M. weekdays and 4:00 P.M. weekends are $15.

Shawnee Inn & Golf Resort
River Road, Shawnee-on-Delaware
(570) 424-4000
www.shawneeinn.com

The original 18-hole course here was designed by A.W. Tillinghast in 1907.

Golfers will find 27 holes of championship golf at Shawnee, just 2 miles off Interstate 80 at the Delaware Water Gap exit. On two holes, golfers must shoot across the Delaware River. The 177-yard 7th on the Blue Course goes from the island back to the inn. The green is almost completely surrounded by woods. On the 159-yard 2nd hole of the Red Course, the destination is an elevated, heavily bunkered green on the island. Golfers hit their tee shots from the edge of the river, with the mountains in New Jersey as a backdrop. Both holes are par 3s. The pretty par 5 No. 2 on the Blue Course runs parallel to the Delaware River. The three nine-hole courses range in distance from 3,227 yards for the Blue Course to 3,023 yards for the White and 3,063 yards for the Red. Each course is par 36.

In addition to the bar and restaurant facilities at the inn, the course offers a driving range, lessons, a practice area, lockers, showers, a pro shop, and a clubhouse. Greens fees, including cart, are $50 during the week, $75 on weekends. Guests of the time-sharing facilities pay $50 and $60, respectively. If you're planning a stay at the inn and want to play the course, ask them to include a discounted rate in your package. After 4:30 P.M., unlimited golf costs $32. Golfers may walk the course, but they are still required to pay the full cart rate.

Tamiment Resort & Conference Center
Bushkill Falls Road, Tamiment
(570) 588-6652
www.taminent.com

Robert Trent Jones designed this 18-hole, par 72 resort course, which was completed in 1951. A comfortable balance is achieved between long and short holes. That said, everything else about the course is big. The total yardage, 6,599, is filled out by huge bunkers, generous greens, and football field-size fairways. The prettiest hole is the 580-yard, par 5 No. 17, which provides golfers with panoramic views of the surrounding countryside. Perhaps the toughest hole is No.

6, which is walled in by trees, leaving a narrow path to a green guarded by four bunkers.

The course features lessons, showers, a practice area, a pro shop, a clubhouse, a snack bar, lockers, and a restaurant and bar. Club rentals are available. Greens fees are $42 weekdays and $52 weekends, including cart. Twilight rates are $25 including a cart. Tamiment often runs special coupons in the Pocono Record; watch for them. Although not absolutely required, use of carts is strongly encouraged, as the course is unusually long.

Water Gap Country Club
Mountain Road, off Highway 611
Delaware Water Gap
(570) 476-0300
www.watergapcountryclub.com
Built in 1922, this 18-hole, par 72 roller coaster originally was called Wolf Hollow Country Club and was the birthplace of the Eastern Open. Dramatic elevation changes produce tricky rolls and can turn seemingly great shots into nightmares. Bunkers are plentiful; fairways, narrow; and greens, small. First-time players, even scratch golfers, will have difficulty making par here. Holes No. 5 and No. 14 present completely blind shots, and No. 12 is a tricky par 3 that travels 201 yards from an elevated tee, across a pond to an elevated green fronted by a 60-by-40-foot bunker. The total yardage of 6,187 gives little indication of the difficulty of play at Water Gap.

The restaurant at this country club is a local favorite for both golfers and non-golfers and is reviewed in our Restaurants chapter. Also available are a pro shop, lessons, lockers, showers, and a practice

area. Rates for nonmember and guests are weekdays, $39 until 1:00 P.M.; $30 from 1:00 to 3:00 P.M.; $29 after 3:00 P.M. Saturday and Sunday $39 until 7:00 A.M. (early bird special); $58 from 7:00 A.M. until noon; $39 from noon until 2:00 P.M.; $29 after 2:00 P.M. The fee includes a cart. Use of carts is not absolutely required, but strongly recommended, as the course is hilly, and walking adds a great deal of time to the play. There's no discount if you elect to walk. Various membership programs are available.

Stroudsburg/East Stroudsburg

Cherry Valley Golf Course
Cherry Valley Road, R.D. 1, Box 1341
Stroudsburg, PA 18360
(570) 421-1350
www.cherryvalleygolfcourse.com
A typically hilly, wooded Poconos track with plenty of water, this 18-hole public course begins with its longest holes, a 470-yard par 5. However, most holes after it are in the 200 to 300 yard range for a total yardage of 5,074 at par 71. A pro shop, snack bar, restaurant, and bar are on the grounds of the course. Weekday greens fees for 18 holes are $16 ($21 with cart) for seniors and $20 and $25, respectively, for others. Twilight rates (after 1:00 P.M.) are $17 and $22. Weekend fees are $25 ($35 with cart) until noon; $20 and $30 after noon. Nine-hole rates are $11 ($16 with cart) during the week and $15 and $20 on weekends.

Evergreen Park Golf Course
Cherry Lane, Analomink
(570) 421-7721
Part of the Penn Hills resort complex, this par 35 is considered by local players to be one of the Poconos' best nine-hole courses. Eight holes have sand traps, and four have water hazards. The signature hole is the 1st—a lakefront green at par 5. Irons receive a workout here. The greens

are typically in very good condition, and pin placements change daily, alternating course yardage between 2,535 and 2,578.

Evergreen offers lessons, a pro shop, a practice area, a clubhouse, a snack bar, and a restaurant. During the week, greens fees are $17; weekend and holiday fees are $20. After 1:00 P.M. Monday through Thursday, the twilight rate is $14; on weekends and holidays, twilight comes a little later—3:00 P.M.—and the rate is $17. Otherwise, carts rent at $25 for two people. However, for the golfers who enjoy the exercise, the course is relatively flat and easy to walk. Handcarts are available for rent at $4.00.

Glen Brook Country Club
Glen Brook Road, Stroudsburg
(570) 421-3680
www.glenbrookgolfclub.com

This 18-hole par 72 course was built in 1924. Glen Brook is tucked away in the woods west of Stroudsburg. It is a challenging 6,536-yard scenic beauty, accessible to the public. Noteworthy holes include No. 7, referred to as the "airplane hole" because it plays from one plateau to another, and No. 5, which features a difficult confrontation with a creek. Twelve guest suites on the property overlook a trout stream and are a two-minute walk from the first tee.

Facilities here include a driving range, showers, a practice area, a pro shop, clubhouse, lockers, a snack bar, and a restaurant with a bar. Lessons are also available. Greens fees are $24 on weekdays and $31 on weekends. Carts cost $16 per person. Walking is permitted prior to 3:00 P.M. every day, however after that time, carts are required. Reduced twilight rates are $14 on weekdays, $17 on weekends.

Terra Greens Golf Course
5006 Poole Road, East Stroudsburg
(570) 421-0120

A nine-hole par 36, Terra Greens has seven holes that are at least 350 yards long. The total yardage is 3,130, and this course is trickier than the average nine-

holer. Greens are long and hard, and natural hazard such as trees and water that encase the greens and fairways are used effectively. Hole No. 2, a 480-yard par 5, runs parallel to a beautiful lake.

A small pro shop and a practice area are provided. Greens fees are $15 weekdays and $22 weekends. After 3:00 P.M., fees are $12 on weekdays, $15 on weekends. Carts are $15 for nine holes and $20 for 18 holes. Club rentals, at $5.00, and pull-cart rentals, at $2.00, are available. Walking is permitted at all times.

Mount Pocono Area

Buck Hill Golf Club
Golf Drive, Buck Hill Falls
(570) 595-7730
www.buckhillfalls.com

This sylvan course is one of the oldest in the Poconos. Designer Robert White created the original 18 holes at Buck Hill in 1907. Then, in 1922, the venerable Donald Ross built a new 18-hole course on the old course's back nine. The three nine-hole courses are now designated the Red, the White, and the Blue.

The course once was part of a spacious luxurious resort that has since closed, but an active community surrounds the old resort, and the course has remained in operation and open to the public.

The Blue/White combination is the toughest, while the Blue and Red played together provide the best scenery. The course is heavily wooded, with rolling terrain and a creek providing natural hazards. The total yardage ranges from 6,048 to 6,327, depending on which combination is played. No. 5 on the Red Course is considered by many locals to be the most difficult par 4 in the Poconos. It plays 470 yards. Shots must be long and accurate. The green is frighteningly small. On the Blue Course, No. 7 is a tough par 3 set on a hillside and featuring a significant gully between the tee and the green.

Lessons, a driving range, showers, a practice area, pro shop, lockers, and a

The Pocono Mountains Vacation Bureau publishes a golf brochure that provides a detailed map of locations and other information about some of the region's top courses. Call (800) 762-6667 to have a free copy mailed to you. There's also detailed information in the Vacation Bureau's "Pocono Mountains Visitors' Guide" and on the Web (www.800 poconos.com), where you'll find links to the links.

restaurant/bar are accessible to golfers. The semiprivate course costs $40 to $55 on weekdays and $55 to $75 on weekends. Discount rates apply after 3:00 P.M. on weekdays ($25 to $35) and after 4:00 P.M. weekends ($35 to $45). Cart fees are included and required, though members can walk the courses after 3:00 P.M. Memberships and group rates are available.

Mount Airy Golf Club "The 18 Best"
Woodland Road, off Highway 611
Mount Pocono
(570) 839-8816

Although Mount Airy Lodge has closed, the golf club remains open. As the name implies, this course re-creates the best 18 holes in golf from around the country, including such fabled facilities as Pebble Beach and Augusta. Mount Airy is a public course designed for experienced players. The 6,426-yard par 72 course boasts 96 sand traps, and water comes into play on 10 holes. One of the best holes in the Poconos is the 555-yard, par 5 No. 16, which has bunkers on both sides of the fairway and a green surrounded by water and bunkers.

On the grounds of the course, golfers may utilize lessons, a driving range, a practice area, a putting green, a pro shop, and a snack area. Greens fees are $45 Monday through Friday, $55 weekends and holidays. Carts are included; there is no walking at any time. The twilight special, after 3:00 P.M., is $20 on weekdays

and $30 on weekends, including cart. Club rentals are available for $20 for 18 holes and $15 for nine holes. Advance tees times are required.

Mount Pocono Golf Course
Highways 940 and 611, Mount Pocono
(570) 839-6061
www.mountpocono.com

This nine-hole course in the heart of the Poconos is perfect for young people and senior citizens. It is short (2,400 yards) and easy to walk. Some holes are wooded; some have water. Weekday greens fees are $11; weekends $13. Though the course is nine holes, you may play it a second time for the same price. Twilight play, after 3:00 P.M., costs $8.00 on weekdays, $9.00 on weekends. Cart rental is $16 for nine holes and $22 for 18 holes. Club rentals are $4.00 and pull carts are $2.00. The facility has a pro shop. Discounts are available for senior citizens, and walking is permitted at all times.

Pocono Manor Inn & Golf Resort
Highway 314, Pocono Manor
(570) 839-7111
www.poconomanor.com

Of the two 18-hole par 72 courses at this resort, the East is shorter (6,310 yards) but more difficult—hilly, with small greens. Grass bunkers add a Scottish-links flavor. It is preferred by seasoned players. The West Course, at 6,675 yards, is newer, flatter, and more wide open. The Senior Pro Am was held on the East Course, which was built in 1912. The par 3 No. 7 on the East Course runs 77 yards down over a cliff. The layout on No. 7 is typical of the physical characteristics of this course, which is set in the wooded mountains.

Pocono Manor offers golfers a driving range, practice area, lessons, a pro shop, clubhouse, snack bar, lockers, and a restaurant/bar. Greens fees, including cart, are $40 weekdays and $50 weekends. Twilight play after 3:00 P.M. is $22. Advance tee times are necessary.

Skytop Lodge
Highway 390, Skytop
(570) 595-7401
www.skytop.com

Everything about this elegant resort is first-class, including the golf course. It is an 18-hole, par 71, 6,256-yard excursion across a wooded mountaintop. Shot-makers will enjoy playing here because placement is always crucial. The course is short, with tight fairways and small greens. Golfers face the toughest challenge on the last hole, a 352-yard par 4 with an elevated green bordered by a creek in front, a bunker on the right and a lake on the left. Many golf balls have tried to find the pin, never to be heard from again.

While at Skytop, golfers have access to lessons (through the Brian Boyle School of Golf), showers, a practice area, a pro shop, clubhouse, lockers, and a restaurant/bar. Guests of the resort and club members receive preferred tee times. Greens fees for resort guests are $47 per person, plus $21 per person for a cart. Nonguests pay $65. Carts are required until 3:00 P.M. after which time you may walk. Call to reserve a tee time.

West End

Hideaway Hills Golf Club
Carny Road, off US 209, Kresgeville
(610) 681-6000
www.hideawaygolf.com

Completed in 1994, this public 18-hole, par 72 has become very popular with area golfers. Two sets of middle tees give the well-kept course a variable yardage of 6,402 to 6,209. Golfers encounter a little bit of everything here, including elevated greens, 84 bunkers, and five lakes. After a comfortable start, holes No. 7 through No.16 provide some interesting challenges. The par 3 No. 7 already is a local legend. Its green sits 160 feet below the tee. For extra fun, the green is undulating; and a stream awaits those who hit short. No. 15, a par 4, features an island green in a three-acre lake. Complementing the course are a driving range, practice area, pro shop, clubhouse, and restaurant and bar. Lessons are offered. Greens fees and cart are $44 weekdays and $57 weekends. At twilight, you can play for $30 on any day. No walking is permitted.

Indian Mountain Golf Course
Highway 534, Kresgeville
(610) 681-4534

The fairways are open and the greens large at this 3,203-yard, par 35 nine-holer. One of the toughest holes is the par 3 No. 8, which has an elevated tee. Greens fees are $15 for nine holes and $17 for 18 holes on weekdays, $17 for nine holes and $19 for 18 holes on weekends. With a cart, fees are $22 for nine holes and $27 for 18 on weekdays, $24 for nine holes and $29 for 18 on weekends. Walking is permitted at all times. You'll find a full pro shop, club rentals, a picnic area under a roof, lessons, and a luncheonette. The facility also has a nine-hole, par 27 pitch-and-putt course, which is 971 yards long. The cost for it is $6.00 for 18 holes.

Mountain Laurel Resort & Golf Club
Highway 534, White Haven
(570) 443-7424
www.gothamgolf.com

After an easy start, this 18-hole par 72 course, designed in 1968 by Geoffrey Cornish, gets very challenging. Holes No. 6 through No. 10 all have water, as does No. 13. Other than the first five holes, which are basically open, the course is wooded. At No. 10, a 360-yard par 4, golfers must navigate a narrow fairway and land on an island green. The course length is 6,122 yards.

Most Pocono golf courses allow soft spikes only on their courses. If you have steel spikes on your golf shoes, some pro shops will change them to soft spikes for about $6.00. Ask about course spike policy when you make your reservation.

Amenities include tournaments, memberships, a driving range, practice area, pro shop, clubhouse, snack bar, lockers, and lessons. Greens fees are $35 to ride and $25 to walk on weekdays, reduced to $25 and $18 at twilight, after 3:00 P.M. Weekend rates go up to $48 (no walking) until 1:00 P.M., then, from 1:00 to 3:00 P.M., $35 to ride and $25 to walk. "Late twilight" thereafter, $25 and $20, respectively. Reserved tee times are recommended seven days in advance.

The Resort at Split Rock
One Lake Drive, Lake Harmony
(570) 722-9111, ext. 774
(800) 255-7625
www.splitrockresort.com
Split Rock Resort boasts a 27-hole public course with much to offer. Currently, it consists of the par 72 18-hole North Course and the par 35 9-hole South Course. There are plans to add an additional nine holes to the South Course and a clubhouse to anchor the 36-hole complex. Both additions were under construction in 2004. North Course yardages range from 5,500 yards from the seniors' tees, up to 7,048 yards from "the tips." The North Course does have five sets of tee boxes for the enjoyment of players of all abilities. The North Course is an obvious choice as one of the most challenging and scenic golf courses in northeastern Pennsylvania. The South Course layout is the essence of target golf, with three sets of tee boxes, with yardages ranging from 2,300 to 3,000 yards.

The clubhouse, currently under construction, will boast men's and ladies' locker rooms, an expanded pro shop and merchandise area, a snack shop, an ele-

gant restaurant and bar with panoramic views and extensive cart and club storage areas. Golf membership and golf packages are available. Split Rock is conveniently located only 4 miles from I–80 and the Pennsylvania Turnpike. Call for additional information.

Milford/Lake Wallenpaupack Area

Cliff Park Golf Course and Inn
S.R. 2001, off U.S. Highway 6, Milford
(570) 296-6491
www.cliffparkinn.com
This nine-hole par 35 is a tough course. Good luck breaking par. The course pro likes the 198-yard par 3 No. 3, which travels from an elevated tee to an elevated green. Local seniors love to play here because the course provides short, scenic fairways. Many people choose to walk. At 3,115 yards, the course plays long for nine holes.

The course is on the grounds of the lovely Cliff Park Inn. Opened in 1913, this was the first American golf course started by a woman, Annie Buchanan. Now part of the Delaware Water Gap Recreation Area, it is run by Jamie and Yvonne Klausmann. Lessons, showers, a practice area, a pro shop, a snack bar, and a restaurant/bar are provided at the course. Greens fees are $14 for nine holes and $20 for weekends and holidays, and $20 and $25, respectively, on weekdays. Twilight rates drop to $10. Cart rentals are $15 for 9 holes and $25 for 18. Pull carts and bag rentals are available, but the course does not take tee times, leaving them on a first-come, first-served basis.

Cricket Hill Golf Club
US 6, Hawley
(570) 226-4366
www.crickethillgolf.com
A good short game helps at this 18-hole, par 70, 5,790-yard course. This public course starts very open, but things get much tighter on the back nine. Eleven

i *Golf is still considered a genteel sport, and most Pocono golf courses require "proper attire." Proper attire usually means a collared shirt (no T-shirts or tank tops) and slacks or Bermuda shorts. Of course, in golfer's fashion, weird mixes of plaids are just fine.*

ponds are sprinkled throughout. A popular hole is the par 5, 455-yard No. 12,
which starts with a quick dogleg and then
hops over a pond to a figure-8 green.

Among the amenities are a driving
range, lessons, showers, a practice area, a
pro shop, clubhouse, lockers, and a restau-
rant/bar. Greens fees are $24 for walkers,
and $36 for riders (including a cart) on
weekends; $22 and $34 on weekdays.
After 4:00 P.M., you can play the course for
$12 on weekdays and $14 on weekends.

Red Maple Golf Course
Highway 296, South Canaan
(570) 937-4543
This nine-hole, par 33 provides more tricks
than the average short course. Its 2,300
yards of rolling fairways, water, and trees
keep play interesting. You will need to be
a skillful shot-maker to score well here.
The natural hazards present a surprising
number of potential problems. Do not let
the short yardage fool you into thinking
this is an easy course. A pro shop and a
snack bar are provided. Greens fees are
$8.00 for the first nine holes, $15.00 for 18
holes on weekdays and $9.00 and $17.00,
respectively, on weekends. Carts rent for
$6.00 per person on weekdays for 9 holes
and $15.00 per person for 18 holes. Week-
end cart rates go to $14 per person for 9
holes and $27 per golfer on weekends.
Walking is permitted.

The Country Club at Woodloch Springs
1 Woodloch Drive, Hawley
(570) 685-8075, ext. 4041
www.woodloch.com
Many serious golfers in the Poconos
regard this course as perhaps the most
professional operation in the region for
playability, staff, and facilities. The 18-hole
par 72 course is accessible to guests of
Woodloch Pines resort, property owners
or renters at Woodloch Spring, and guests
of other Pocono resorts as explained in
this chapter's introduction. The course pro
describes the course as challenging, offering "above average" difficulty. Rolling hills,
trees, and creeks are present throughout.

As little of the surrounding countryside as
possible was disturbed during construction of the course in 1992. The total
yardage of 6,127 gives an indication of the
need for some long-driving ability. The
signature hole is No. 14, a 577-yard par 5
monster known as the Hell's Gate Gorge.
To be successful here, golfers must carry a
tee shot of more than 220 yards off a
200-foot drop through the gorge.

Three PGA pros are available for lessons. Amenities include a clubhouse, driving range, practice area, restaurant and
bar, lockers, and a swimming pool. In addition, the impressive facilities of the resort
are explained in our Accommodations
chapter. Greens fees, including cart, are
$70 weekdays and $85 on weekends. You
can also choose to play just nine holes at
$43 on weekdays and $48 on weekends
and holidays. The fees include a mandatory cart, and you are limited to 4.5 hours
on this course, which comes to 15 minutes
a hole. If you can't keep that pace, course
rangers inform you. Golfers must be staying at the resort, and reservations are
strongly suggested.

DRIVING RANGES

Looking for a little practice before tackling
those long Pocono fairways? Here are
some driving ranges that will help you
polish your skills.

Mount Pocono Area

940 Golf 'N' Fun
Highway 940, Pocono Lake
(570) 646-0700
When not on the 275-yard practice range,
golfers may enjoy an 18-hole miniature
golf course, an arcade, and a snack bar.
Group lessons may be arranged. Since
there are 20 tees, you should have no
trouble finding a home on the range. Balls
are obtained from vending machines by
tokens purchased at the office. A $3.00
small token gets the golfer 25 balls;

$10.00 buys four tokens good for 100. Large tokens come in $5.00 denomination only. One token buys 50 balls, and four ($20) give the golfer 250 balls—a bonus of 50 free. Clubs rent for $11, but if you get the four token specials, a club is free. The park is open every day.

West End

Golf Plantation
US 209, Kresgeville
(610) 681-5959

Regarded as one of the best driving ranges in the Poconos, Golf Plantation features covered tees, a putting green, a sand bunker, and a complete pro shop capable of handling all types of club repair. Clubs may be custom fitted with a Sportech swing-analyzing computer. Private lessons and a regularly scheduled golf school provide tips for those looking to improve their game. In addition to the driving range, there is a tougher-than-average miniature golf course. Refreshments are available at the ice cream parlor/snack bar. Rates for golf balls for the range are $4.50 for 40, $6.00 for 80, and $11.00 for 170. Golf Plantation is open every day through late evening during the summer. Plans for the rest of the year are uncertain, call to see if they're open.

Milford/Lake Wallenpaupack Area

Costa's Family Fun Park
US 6, 3 miles east of Lake Wallenpaupack, Lords Valley
(570) 226-8585, (800) 928-4FUN
www.costasfamilyfunpark.com

Costa's provides plenty of entertainment for the entire family while the golfer practices. In addition to the driving range, facilities include batting cages, an 18-hole miniature golf course, two go-kart tracks,

a children's play area, and an arcade. A restaurant and ice cream parlor offer fast food. The driving range has six target greens and 19 Astroturf tees. Baskets of balls are available in three sizes: small, with 28 to 32 balls is $4.00; medium, with 41 to 43 balls is $5.00 and a large, with 53 to 57 balls is $5.75. Clubs, including options for children and left-handed players, are provided free. Hours of operation vary according to season, so call ahead.

Golf Park Plus
Golf Park Drive, off Highway 590
Lake Ariel
(570) 689-4996, (570) 689-0560
www.golfparkplus.com

In addition to a driving range, Golf Park Plus offers bumper boats, go-karts, two 18-hole miniature golf courses, a train ride, paintball, a snack bar, and an arcade. As at 940 Golf 'N' Fun (see previous entry), golf balls are purchased with tokens. Each small token ($3.00) is good for 25 balls; four small tokens ($10.00) buys 100. One large token ($5.00) is good for 50 balls, and four large tokens ($20.00) buys 250—a free bonus of 50. Drivers and irons are available at no charge. Golf Park Plus is open every day.

The driving range, Moss Hollow Creek, is unique in the Poconos because it features eight over-water tees among its 20 Astroturf tees. Even long-hitters will have trouble reaching the far end of the range some 450 yards away. Private and group lessons are available with advance reservations.

GOLF SCHOOLS

You've just been promoted, and your boss tells you that most of your deals will be hammered out on the golf course, so you'd better be competent. Truth is, you've never hit a ball farther than 18 whimsical holes at the minigolf course down the road. You have to learn the game fast. Luckily, we have some world-class golf schools associated with two of our top golf courses.

Mount Pocono Area

The Brian Boyle School of Golf
Skytop Lodge, Highway 390, Skytop
(570) 595-8910
www.skytop.com
Founded in 1999, the Brian Boyle School of Golf runs spring through fall. Emphasis is placed on development of the pre-swing routine for consistent setup and alignment, pivot of the body, and proper weight shift, along with correct wrist cock, resulting in maximum distance and control. The school also stresses chipping, putting, and bunker play to realize your full potential with a dependable short game. The school includes six hours of instruction over two days, range balls, video analysis, instructional material, clubs if needed, and refreshments. The cost is $150, which does not include accommodations at the resort. Classes for juniors, which stress safety, rules, and etiquette as well as technique, are also available for $135.

The Greg Wall Golf School
Pocono Manor Inn & Golf Resort
Highway 314, Pocono Manor
(570) 839-7111
www.poconomanor.com
A professional teaching staff provides 12 hours of instruction over two days. You get instruction manuals, a video analysis of your swing, free greens fees after school each day, club storage and cleaning, a school bag tag, and unlimited practice range balls. The school is open April through July and costs $225 per person. Accommodations at the resort are extra.

West End

Swing's the Thing Golf School
Golf Plantation
Highway 209, Kresgeville
(800) 797-9464, (800) RXSWING
(570) 421-6666
www.swingsthething.com
Two instructors, Dick Farley and Rick McCord, teach here and at Orange Lake Country Club in Orlando, Fla. They have been recognized by Golf magazine as some of the best teachers in the United States. Students receive a stop-action video and textbook as part of their instruction. The 1- to 3-day program includes all greens fees, instruction, lunches, and lodging. Commuters pay $399 for two days without accommodations. The schools are offered May through August. Former students receive preferential registration (space is limited) and discounts.

Delaware Water Gap/ Shawnee-on-Delaware

Tillinghast Golf Academy
1 River Road, Shawnee-on-Delaware
(570) 424-4000
www.shawneeinn.com
Tillinghast Academy is named after A. W. Tillinghast, who designed the 18-hole course at the Shawnee Inn in 1907. It offers golf teaching techniques ranging from a single nine-hole game with the pro at $90 ($100 with lunch), to $450 for training and unlimited use of Shawnee practice facilities, including a new three-hole green. Family packages are available for $700. A two-day, 18-hole schedule with an instructor can be had for $126 per day, or play three days for $114 per day.

OUR NATURAL WORLD

Most people who travel to the Poconos come here to spend time outdoors—with good reason. We have beautiful scenery that offers lots of recreational opportunities, We also have some unique spots. In fact, the Nature Conservancy named the Pocono Mountains one of the world's "Last Great Places."

We've gone on about our natural history and many of our outdoor wonders in other chapters—Parks; Recreation; Winter Sports; Overview; Attractions; and In, On, and Around the Water. In this chapter we look at the birds, the bees, and the bears; the waterfalls and fossils; and one special place you won't want to miss.

BUGS

The first thing you'll need to learn is the "Pocono Wave." On occasional summer days lots of little black gnats will congregate around your face. When you wave them away so they don't fly into your eyes, nose and mouth, you're doing the Pocono Wave.

Aside from throwing foul language at them, Insiders have developed a number of ways to cope with the bugs. Perhaps you've noticed locals standing around with one hand held over their head. It's not a strange affectation; the gnats fly to your highest spot, which is usually your head. If you walk on your hands, they'll fly around your feet; but more practically, if you hold a hand up high, they congregate around it, leaving your mouth free for gossip. Smokers claim that a lit cigarette keeps them away, leaving us to wonder about walking around with a stick of incense like a '60s flower child. Some shops sell punk, which

should do the trick if you can stand the smell. Of course, there's insect repellent, but we're always loathe to put it on our face, where the buggies love to buzz, Don't bother with one of those electric bug zappers. Word is, they kill the moths and the good bugs that eat the ones that bother you, but the biting and annoying kind are not attracted to the zapper.

The other important bug here is the tick. We have both dog and deer ticks, and deer ticks can carry Lyme disease. Make sure you check yourself and your family for ticks after going out in the woods and fields. Many people wear light clothing and tuck their pants into their socks to help prevent tick bites. You'll probably see the ticks if they're crawling on your white pants. Tucking the socks in helps make a barrier against the little horrors. You can also spray your clothing with an insect repellent that's effective against ticks.

If you find a tick on you, grasp it firmly without squeezing and pull it off gently. Other methods of removal—hair spray, nail polish, or alcohol—could release a disease-producing spirochete into your bloodstream, assuming the tick is infected. If you get the tick off within a day, you are not likely to be infected.

Lyme disease is increasing in the area, and you should know the symptoms. Lyme disease can be serious if you don't catch it early. If you're bitten by a Lyme-carrying deer tick (some of which are as small as the period at the end of this sentence), you may develop a rash that looks like a bull's eye around the original bite. Within a week or two, you'll have flu-like symptoms.

If your doctor diagnoses Lyme disease in its early stages, you can take an antibiotic—and that's the end of it. If you miss it at this point—and many people do—you can develop a variety of symptoms including headache, stiff neck, facial paralysis and inflammation, and slowing of the heart, and locally our brand of Lyme often includes Bell's palsy. Those who don't catch it early can go on to lengthy bouts of arthritis as well as permanent heart damage.

All of this scary stuff is to say be aware of ticks, take preventive measures, check yourself after you go outside, and if you suspect you've contracted Lyme disease, discuss it with your doctor immediately. There is a vaccine that has been developed for Lyme disease, but there are some concerns about its side effects. If you're interested in the vaccine, talk to your doctor.

Indoors, although we've had an occasional battle when the ants go marching, we have yet to see a cockroach in the Poconos.

Not all the bugs in the Poconos are horrible. If you're here during the warm weather, you'll see a variety of gorgeous butterflies, moths, and dragonflies. We've seen more different kinds here than anywhere else we've been.

BIRDS

The Poconos are a great place for bird watchers; at least 260 species have been recorded here. You can see clouds of goldfinches hovering around a feeder, watch brightly colored hummingbirds flit through the flowers, observe a rufous-sided towhee digging in a hedge, and hold a mewing conversation with a catbird. If you hear tapping sounds, look for a woodpecker. We have several kinds here, including an occasional enormous pileated woodpecker, which carves holes just its size in old fruit trees. Black-capped chickadees are everywhere, and the tiny blue-gray gnatcatcher makes a rattling sound more like a squirrel than a bird. In the winter, bright red cardinals decorate the hedges like Christmas balls.

If you're interested in the Poconos' natural history, don't miss **The Poconos, An Illustrated Natural History Guide** *by Carl S. Oplinger and Robert Halma. This fascinating book explains the forces of Mother Nature in the region. Watch, too, for naturalist John Serrao's excellent column in the Sunday* **Pocono Record.** *Serrao regularly leads nature walks around the area.*

We have plenty of waterfowl. Every pond, lake, and river has its share of ducks and Canada geese, and you can catch sight of the occasional heron or egret in regional wetlands. Ospreys, once rare, have been reintroduced to the area and are thriving. If you're walking quietly through the woods, you may spot wild turkeys or pheasants. We've seen a hawk lift a mouse right out of the driveway in front of us, and of course, the numerous turkey vultures and crows are doing their best to clear away the roadkill.

The stars of the bird population are the eagles. We have bald eagles and golden eagles. Most people report seeing eagles soaring above the Delaware River, especially at twilight. Take a canoe trip down the river, or drive through the park along the Pennsylvania, New York, and New Jersey banks, stopping anywhere you can get close to the water. With time and patience, chances are good that you'll spot one of these beautiful birds.

The best habitat area for bald eagles is in the northern part of the Poconos. Travel along the Upper Delaware on both sides of the river to try to spot some eagles. The best time to see them is on a cold sunny January day, as many eagles winter in this area, but you may spot one at other times of the year too. Eagles often feed around 7:00 and 11:00 A.M. and 3:00 P.M., all of which are good times to see them.

BEASTS

We have lots of interesting land-bound wildlife in the Poconos too. There's about one black bear per square acre. You certainly won't see a bear every day, nor every week, but if you're in the Poconos, there's a good chance you will see one eventually, and if you do, it's something you'll never forget. The places you're most likely to see a bear are on a country road, at a bird feeder, or in a dumpster—they love to eat garbage.

Should you encounter a bear, don't panic. Don't try to dance with it, but you shouldn't have to run away or play dead, either. Most likely, it will be the first to leave. Attacks by black bears are extremely rare. The only one we've been able to track down is a case in which a woman's unleashed dog frightened the bear, and it responded by biting her face. She was able to make it run away by shouting and waving her arms.

Please don't feed the bears. When bears eat food clearly provided by humans, they lose their fear of us and it increases their chances of getting shot by a hunter or hit by a car. Bears who habitually go after "people food" in the park have to be trapped and relocated or killed, as they present a hazard. If you're camping, don't leave any food where a bear can get it, and make sure the garbage can lid is on tightly. If you're caught feeding a bear, you face substantial fines and up to six months in jail.

The Poconos have tons of white-tailed deer. They're beautiful, they're numerous, and they love to eat our gardens. You will probably see some while you're here, especially at twilight. Be aware that in wooded areas, one might step out directly in front of your car, so drive with caution.

Deer-hunting season, which is in the fall (see our Fishing and Hunting chapter), is a such a big event that they close school on the first day. No self-respecting Pocono male would be caught dead in school on the first day of deer hunting season. Since deer have no natural predators in the Poconos, hunting is the one way we have to control the deer population—aside from hitting them with cars, which is substantially more hazardous than hunting.

Some coyotes and bobcats inhabit the region, but it's unlikely you'll spot any. More likely, however, you'll see foxes and skunks. These animals, though shy, are numerous and not too hard to find.

These mammals are by no means the only ones in the Poconos. We also have rabbits, snowshoe hares, raccoons, otters, beavers (if you're observant, you'll see lots of gnawed trees), minks, bats, shrews, moles, mice, weasels, porcupines, three varieties of squirrel (red, gray, and flying), and groundhogs.

You'll also find two poisonous snakes in the Poconos—the timber rattler and the copperhead. Both have a flat, triangular head, and vertical-slit pupils, although we hope you don't get close enough to look into their eyes. Both snakes are relatively shy and would rather avoid you than bite you. If you're exploring rocky spots and old lumber mills, don't put your hand anywhere you can't see. Snakes like to sun themselves on rocks and other warm spots.

FALL FOLIAGE

Pocono people think that our fall foliage display is even better than New England's. That's because we have a tremendous diversity of terrain and forest type, so we have different trees at different elevations turning color at different times. The month of October in the Poconos is one long light show, with each day getting prettier than the day before and people swearing that the colors are peaking for weeks. Early October is usually the time you'll see color up the mountain, while mid-October is the high time around the river. We have five different forest types and more than 100 species of trees, including maples, birches, tulip-trees, sumac, persimmon, aspen, ash, oaks, cherry, beech, basswood, tamaracks, hickories, black gum, and sassafras, all with their varying shades of color from bright gold to fiery red to deep purple. When the trees all around you are glowing, and the mountain ridge across the river looks like it's on fire, reflecting more gold in the river, you know autumn can't get any prettier. From early September through the month of October you can get a weekly update on the state of the autumn leaves by calling the Pocono Mountain Vacation Bureau's Fall Foliage Hotline, (570) 421-5565, or go online to 800poconos.com.

WATERFALLS

Thirty of Pennsylvania's 75 named waterfalls can be found in the Pocono region. There are two areas where waterfalls are numerous. The eastern edge of the Pocono Plateau, which runs by Skytop, Canadensis, Buck Hill Falls, Mountainhome, Cresco, Mount Pocono, Pocono Manor, and Tannersville, drops 1,000 feet in stages to the lower Poconos. (Of course, we don't see a plateau; we think we see mountains.) Along that eastern edge are lots of waterfalls, but they tend to be on private or resort lands. Farther east, the streams fall a hundred feet or more to the Delaware River, creating a series of waterfalls. Since many of these are on parkland, you can visit them. Following is a list of some of the waterfalls that are accessible to the public.

Delaware Water Gap/ Shawnee-on-Delaware

Bushkill Falls
Bushkill Falls Road, Bushkill
(570) 588-6682
www.bushkillfalls.com
Take U.S. Highway 209 into Bushkill, and follow the signs to these spectacular falls. As this is one of the area's top tourist attractions, you'll pay an admission charge ($8.00 for folks 11 and older, $4.00 for

Mountain laurel, our state flower, is toxic. It is safe to touch but should not be eaten. Ingesting a small portion will cause flu-like symptoms, and large quantities can be fatal. The leaves are poisonous to deer and livestock as well.

kids ages 4 through 10, free for those younger than four, and $7.00 for senior citizens (see our Attractions chapter for more details). What you get is four well-maintained trails, some beautiful waterfalls, and admission to a Native American exhibit that emphasizes the local Lenape culture. When we have a wet season, the falls pound down the rock, roiling and sending a spray that climbs back up the gorge even higher than the falls. Because the nature of a waterfall is to go from a high place to a low place, there are lots and lots of steps here. There are also plenty of benches for the weary. Bushkill Falls has extensive souvenir and gift shops, food, paddleboat rides, miniature golf, and a picnic pavilion. Many people return again and again to see these lovely falls and walk the trails.

Buttermilk Falls
U.S. Highway 209 and Buttermilk Falls Road Marshalls Creek
From the Marshalls Creek exit off Interstate 80, follow US 209 north toward Marshalls Creek. Within about a mile, you'll see several signs pointing to Shawnee. Following the signs to Shawnee, turn right on Buttermilk Falls Road. Pull into the parking lot at the Shawnee Sales Center (immediately on your left) and walk back to the falls near the corner of US 209 and Buttermilk Falls Road. The foamy water accounts for the name. This is a popular spot for bridal pictures.

Shawnee Mill Pond
On the property of Shawnee Falls Studio River Road, Shawnee-on-Delaware
A small but picturesque waterfall can be seen across River Road from the Shawnee

The Power of Water
Creates a Gorgeous Gap

For nearly 170 years, the Delaware Water Gap, often regarded as one of the most striking natural wonders of our country, has been a popular tourist destination. This breathtaking gorge in the Kittatinny Ridge separates Mount Tammany (1,527 feet) on the New Jersey side and Mount Minsi (1,464 feet) on the Pennsylvania side of the Delaware River.

Most likely, moving water wore down and pushed through a weak spot in the ridge over an unimaginable amount of time. The combination of the water cutting downward and rocks on either side thrusting upward created the Gap hundreds of millions of years ago.

The first resort opened near the Delaware Water Gap in 1829. By the end of the 19th century, there were more than 20 places around the Gap to accommodate the vacationers who arrived from surrounding cities to bask in the scenic beauty.

While still magnificent today, the Delaware Water Gap must have been overwhelming to city-bred visitors in the 1800s. In the years before extensive travel, the mountain peaks separated by the large river were the wildest environments many people from New York and Philadelphia had even seen. The mountains were as green as the cityscape was gray and bleak. Try to imagine sitting in a passenger train meandering through the Gap and catching your first sight of vast expanses of trees, rocky cliffs, and water

General Store. Park by the General Store and pick up something to nibble; then cross the road and stand on the concrete bridge, gazing at the millpond and falls. These falls are especially lovely in the spring, when the forsythias and a hillside of daffodils paint the scene with yellows. The first European in the area, Nicholas DePui, settled on this spot. (See our History chapter.) You can read about it on the historic marker, but don't walk over to the falls or the pretty wooden bridge, as they are on private property and you will be trespassing. The home on this property contains Shawnee Falls Studio (see our Arts and Culture chapter) with an excellent art gallery just around the corner from the falls.

Milford/Lake Wallenpaupack Area

Childs Falls
George W. Childs Recreation Site, off Highway 729, near Dingmans Ferry
Turn from US 209 in the Delaware Water Gap National Recreation Area onto Highway 739 following the signs to Dingmans Ferry, and look for signs for the George W. Childs Recreation Site. A path through a

as blue as the sky. It's no wonder Delaware Water Gap was then the second most popular inland tourist destination on the East Coast (Saratoga Springs, N.Y., was the first).

If you're drawn to climbing and hiking the Gap, you'll find it easily accessible. On the Pennsylvania side, a 2.7-mile portion of the Appalachian Trail takes hikers to the summit of Mount Minsi. The trail is slightly steep but well marked. A shorter walk on the New Jersey side leads to the summit of Mount Tammany. This portion of the Appalachian Trail offers more spectacular views, but is also more dangerous—watch young children closely. Hikers can sit on rocky outcrops and view the entire Gap, surrounding towns, and birds of prey including hawks, eagles, and ospreys.

If you climb Mount Tammany, look for prickly pear cacti. While more common in the Southwest, the cactus does grow here and on some cliffs around Milford and Matamoras. It sports beautiful yellow flowers in July.

You also can appreciate the Delaware Water Gap by car—simply pull into one of several scenic overlooks. (See our Attractions chapter.) Locals on lunch break favor Resort Point on Highway 611 just south of the town of Delaware Water Gap. Along the same highway, Point of Gap and Arrow Island are ideal picnicking spots.

During the tourist heyday, Point of Gap was filled with souvenir stands where visitors would pay to look through a telescope at a rock formation resembling a Native American profile on the New Jersey cliffs. Time and erosion have not been kind to the Indian; he is barely recognizable today.

dark hemlock ravine leads you past three waterfalls—Factory Falls, Fulmer Falls, and Deer Leap Falls—as well as the ruins of an old wool mill. Bring a picnic; there's a great pavilion by one of the falls.

Raymondskill Falls
Off US 209, MM 18.5, Milford

Raymondskill is also in the Delaware Water Gap National Recreation Area. Take US 209 through the park to the 18.5-mile marker and look for a sign to the falls. The turn is well marked. There are two parking lots, a fairly new one that has an easy path to the middle pool of the falls, and an older one with a restroom and an easy path to the top of the falls. This is a famous restroom, by the way, as the park service spent $600,000 to revamp the parking lots, redo some trails, and build the outhouse. The papers have trumpeted it as a $600,000 outhouse, and the National Park Service has instituted changes in the way they fund projects as a result of the fuss made over this restroom.

Raymondskill is Pennsylvania's highest waterfall, tumbling 165 feet over mossy shale into two main pools. You can sit at the bottom of the falls breathing the fresh air, being cooled by the water spray and contemplating the mossy rocks, the ferns, the rhododendron, and the many separate rivulets of water cascading into the pool. The path to the bottom of the falls and the path leading from the top to the middle pool can be a little steep, but the paths from the parking lots to the top of the falls and the middle pool are wide and easy.

Please obey the NO SWIMMING signs. Although the upper pools look like lovely spots for a dip, the rocks can become slippery, and people do go over the edge and must be rescued with ropes. No swimming is allowed within 50 feet of the top of any waterfall in the park.

Shohola Falls
Shohola Recreation Area, off U.S. Highway 6, Shohola

Along US 6, about midway between Hawley and Milford, you'll see a parking lot just west of a bridge. It's for a state game land also called the Shohola Recreation Area. Pull in and follow an easy path down to the falls (it's well marked). Shohola Falls is below a dammed lake, plunging over a series of drops and winding its way into a rocky gorge. You can follow the path to a couple of overlooks. Apparently, the falls once was steeper, but it was blasted out to float logs to lumber mills farther downstream. Judging by the number of fishermen in the lake above, the fishing must be excellent. (See our Fishing and Hunting chapter for details.) The recreation area includes picnic tables, trails, and boating.

FOSSILS

The Poconos are full of fossils. All of northeastern Pennsylvania was once part of a shallow sea, and many rocky outcrops in the area are packed with fossilized brachiopods (a double shell that looks like a cross between a scallop and clam with uneven halves), horn coral, crinoid (a ridged stalk that was an animal related to the starfish), bryzoa (moss-like animals), and trilobites. Conveniently, the fossils tend to be in shale, which is easily broken. In some areas, you can find fossilized ferns in coal. The most spectacular fossil, the skeleton of a mastodon, was found in the 1980s in a peat bog near Marshalls Creek. The Marshalls Creek mastodon is on display at the State Museum of Pennsylvania in Harrisburg.

There are some places where you can gather fossils, but don't even think of taking any from the Delaware Water Gap National Recreation Area. If you find any there, observe them and leave them in place. Nothing, except trash, may be removed from the park, and violators are answerable to a federal magistrate who may impose heavy fines. Leave the fossils for the next visitor to enjoy. The National Recreation Area offers a good exhibit of local fossils at the Kittatinny Visitor's Center, off I-80, just over the New Jersey border.

You'll find fossils all over the Poconos, in rocky outcroppings and digging in your garden, but there's one place where you may collect Pocono fossils.

West End

Beltzville State Park
US 209, 5 miles east of Lehighton
(610) 377-0045
www.dcnr.state.pa.us

Pick up a map at the visitors center and look for picnic shelter No. 2, which is near the end of a long, thin parking lot. Walk out past the shelter to the shore of the lake, and start picking up the sand-colored stones. You'll find lots of brachiopod and crinoid fossils, and you may keep what you find. If you get hot and dusty searching for fossils, head over to the swimming beach and jump in the water. (See our In, On, and Around the Water chapter.)

ONE VERY SPECIAL PLACE

Tannersville Cranberry Bog
Cherry Lane and Bog Roads
Tannersville
(570) 629-3061
www.mcconservation.org
The Poconos are replete with special places, and everybody has a spot that is particularly magical to them. However, the Tannersville Cranberry Bog is unlike anything you're likely to have encountered before.

More than 13,000 years ago, the last glaciers retreated from the area. In some places they carved out holes that filled with water but were not connected to a stream or river; thus, they were isolated from any source of running water. These holes became what we call bogs.

The Tannersville Cranberry Bog is the southernmost low-altitude bog of its kind along the eastern seaboard (most similar bogs are up high in the Adirondack Mountains or much farther north in the Canadian wilderness). The Tannersville Bog has been designated as a National Natural Landmark and is being run as an outdoor museum by the Nature Conservancy in cooperation with the Monroe County Environmental Education Center. (See our Parks chapter.)

Tannersville is not a true bog because it receives a little groundwater flow, but its

Poison ivy might be our most common weed. Around here, it's so vigorous, it can grow huge, hairy vines as thick as your arm. Beware! If you think you've touched a poison ivy plant, wash with soap as quickly as possible; you have about 10 minutes before the irritant starts working its evil magic on you.

plants are similar to those found in a true bog. The bog is covered with a floating mat of sphagnum moss, a highly absorbent plant that generates hydrogen, making the water acidic. The sphagnum dies and sinks to the bottom where it decays and becomes peat moss, gradually filling the bog. Because the water is acidic and nutrient-poor, some unusual plants grow here, including two insect-eating species—the pitcher plant, which is large and easily spotted, and the tiny sundew. To make up for a lack of nitrogen in their growing environment, these plants must trap and digest insects. Several other unusual plants also grow here, including orchids, calla lilies, and dwarf mistletoe, a 2-centimeter parasite that grows on black spruce.

The Nature Conservancy has built a floating boardwalk across the bog. Access is limited to preserve the extremely fragile ecosystem. Public bog walks take place on Wednesday afternoons throughout the summer. This is the only time you can visit the bog without making special arrangements; call the listed number to preregister. Walks are led by a naturalist who will help you understand what you are seeing. This place is awesome!

CAMPS AND ⟨❧⟩ CONFERENCE CENTERS

"Hello Muddah/Hello Faddah, Here I am at/Camp Granada . . . ." So went the old Allan Sherman ditty and a host of other goofy tunes and books (*Salute Your Shorts*) and movies (*Meatballs*) depicting life at summer camp as a mosquito-ridden hell run by counselors who took their basic training from Vlad the Impaler.

Too bad Allan Sherman never went to any of the summer camps that dot the Poconos. Unlike the hated "Camp Granada" or the other horror stories of urban mythology, Pocono camps really can be a summer of fun, and many of them offer a child every bit as much education as does the school he or she attends the other nine months of the year.

The Pocono region is home to several camps specifically based on science and the environment, art, religion (denominational and interdenominational), and sports. Scout camps are here, but they are managed and attended according to the councils to which they belong. For more information about scout camps, contact your local council for its camp and its location.

The Pocono region is a great place for camps because of the mountains, hundreds of lakes, and easy access from nearby states via Interstate 80, Interstate 84, and Interstate 81. In fact, as we note in the

"Worship" section of our chapter, this area has been a spot for camp-based activities for religious groups since before the turn of the century.

A word about facilities: Most camps are traditional in setup. Lodges or bungalows have from four to 28 bunks (the exception is the Pocono Soccer Camp held at Maywood College in Scranton and Moravian College in Bethlehem, where campers stay in the college dorms). As a general rule bathroom and shower facilities are shared within a bunk unit. There is always a centralized recreation facility and eating hall. Most camps (again excluding the Pocono Soccer Camp that isn't in a traditional camp environment) have the basic amenities covered in terms of swimming, hiking, tennis, and other sports activities, games, arts and crafts, and some type of boating program. A swimming pool or lake is always available. All, of course, have the advantage of mountaintop, valley, or lakeside views.

All of the particulars about a camp, from camper-to-counselor ratio to the sort of food served, are addressed in color brochures that each camp sends out to prospective campers. Wayne County provides a list of the camps in its area; contact the Wayne County Chamber of Commerce at 742 Main Street, Honesdale, (570) 253-1960.

There are too many camps to list every one—probably 20 for every one we deal with here—and each one has some special cache that differentiates it from others. In this chapter we focus on camps that have programs of special interest or merit. We give information related to programs offered, since if a camp interests you because of its programs, you will want to write or call for its brochures.

i | *Most camps require health forms, so be sure to check the applications for what documents are needed to register, and be sure to call your doctor early to get an appointment to have those forms filled out.*

As for conference centers, the ones we mention here are small and more individualized, for the church group, the family, or even for the single who just wishes to partake in a theme-oriented conference or a personal retreat. The major resorts in the area (covered in our Accommodations chapter) cater to conferences for business needs, such as corporate-executive retreats, team-building seminars, expos, and other exhibition-type gatherings.

The camp specialties we mention here are a sampling of the wide range of options and represent some fine choices and a variety of interests and price ranges. Christian camps and YMCA camps are a lot less expensive than the sports camps that feature guaranteed visits from the Philadelphia '76ers (as does the '76ers Basketball Camp), or coaching by Olympic-status coaches such as those at the International Gymnastics Training Camp.

Costs vary by the type of camp, and prices change each year. A week at an overnight sports camp averages $440 for Sunday to Saturday; the high end is around $825. Educational camps run from $150 a week to $800 a week. Religious overnight camps can run from $215 to $825 a week.

Before choosing a camp in any category, check out what it offers, and try to find out about it from others who have gone there; some camps supply references from past campers' families. Ask what the camp's philosophy is. Find out the qualifications of the director and staff. Ask about the camper-to-counselor ratio. Find out what type of transportation the camp provides and whether it has liability insurance. Inquire about safety procedures, medical procedures, and first aid.

If it's a sports camp, make sure it separates campers by skill level, and find out if it provides an assessment of the child's progress. Also, with sports camps, it might be important to know what other activities are offered. Some sports camps are totally dedicated to the one sport, and no other activities are included, which means your child must really be dedicated to the sport. Two such camps are the Pocono Invitational Basketball Camp and the Pocono Cup Soccer Camp (though swimming pools are available at both facilities).

SPORTS CAMPS

Stroudsburg/East Stroudsburg

International Gymnastics Camp
Golden Slipper Road, Bartonsville
(570) 629-0244
www.international-gym-camp.com
This camp is operated by the International Gymnastics School and headed by All-American gymnast Bruno Klaus. It is considered top-notch because of its facilities and coaching and training staff. The school operates throughout the school year, and the camp is its natural summer extension. Past and present coaching and training staffs have included many World Championship team members and American Olympians—Kurt Thomas, Brandy Johnson, Jim Hartung, Peter Kormann, and Mitch Gaylord to name a few. Abe Grossfeld, a former U.S. Olympic coach, has taught here, as have many international Olympians such as Romanians Constantin Petrescu, Mircea Badelescu, and Lavinia Agache, and Russian Olga Korbut. The facilities are exceptional with five gymnasiums filled with specialized gymnastics apparatus, a lake for swimming, boating, Jet Skiing, a climbing wall, a trapeze, and much, much more after-gymnastics activities. The cabins are modern, and the grounds, beach, trails, and dining hall are all fine. The camp is completely international in flavor, from the decor to the coaches to the young gymnasts who attend.

Aspiring gymnasts, even beginners, are welcome—50 percent of campers are new students to the sport. The staff is very helpful, and safety is a prime value. Staffers work at developing trust and showing respect for each student's individual abilities. The summer camp fee is $660 per week.

International Sports Training Camp
1100 Twin Lake Road, Stroudsburg
(570) 620-2267
www.international-sports.com

This camp is a sister to International Gymnastic Training Camp. It too has excellent coaches, drawn from universities around the country, who specialize in each of the covered sports. For $700, young athletes can spend a week concentrating on basketball, soccer, field hockey, or volleyball. A generalized camp, offering a variety of sports, is available at $825 per week, and discounts on all the camps are granted to those who sign up for two or more weeks.

While camps are dedicated to a specific sport, there is free time each day to take part in some other activities, including horseback riding, Jet Skiing, swimming, mountain biking, archery, and so on.

The facilities include fields for each sport activity, a field house, health center, boathouse, canteen, and cafeteria. Some facilities are shared with the gymnast camp, and all overlook the surrounding lake and the mountains. The sessions last five to seven days and are scheduled from mid-June through August. All camps are open to boys and girls ages 8 to 17 of all skill levels. This camp fills up fast. Some weeks are closed by December, so early registration is highly recommended.

Pocono Invitational Basketball Camp
Featherman Road off Cherry Valley Road, Stroudsburg
(570) 992-6343
www.hoopgroup.com/pocono

This is the oldest, longest-running basketball camp in the country—the summer of 2003 was its 40th season. At one time, this family-pioneered and owned camp was by invitation only, hence the "invitational" in its name. Now it is open to all boys and girls fifth grade and up. This camp is considered a developmental camp, so there is a lot of teaching and

evaluating. It is, however, entirely devoted to practice, lectures, drills, and daily league competition. While there is an Olympic-size pool to cool off in after activities, the focus here, reiterated by its director, is on basketball. Youngsters attending should know that playing basketball is what they will be doing the whole week!

U.S. Women Olympians have trained and taught here, including medallists Nancy Lieberman, Anne Donovan, and Vikki Bullett, and new Olympians Nikki McCray and Carla McGhee. Men players Terry Dehere of the L.A. Nets, Craig Ehlo of the Atlanta Hawks, and Mark Jackson and Rik Smits of the Indiana Pacers also have coached here. The camp notes that its staffers and coaches range from "Margaret Wade to Rene Portland; from Carol Blazejowski to Nancy Lieberman; from Dr. J. to Chris Mullin." Among the alumni of the camp are Kobe Bryant and Tracy McGrady. A week-long session runs $440–$460.

Pocono Cup Soccer Camp
Marywood University, Scranton and Moravian College, Bethlehem
(570) 424-1157

Pocono Cup Soccer Camp is totally dedicated to the serious soccer player. It is held at two area colleges and has overnight or day registration for the sessions, a women's camp with a special staff, and specialized camps. All coaches are top university and college performers, including Jerry Sheska, program director and East Stroudsburg University men's soccer head coach. The program begins at 9:00 A.M. and ends at 10:00 P.M. whether you attend as an overnighter or as a day camper. Many local soccer enthusiasts begin staying as day campers, but as they progress year after year, they decide to stay for the full experience, which includes technical and fitness training all morning, tactics with games and teams in the afternoons, match play and assessment in the evening, and a closing lecture and daily review each night, ending at 10:00 P.M.

Programs here include the Upper Ninety Goalkeeper Camp and Team Weeks that run with the Advanced Weeks. The camps are for boys and girls ages 10 to 18.

Stroudsburg Roller Skating Camp
Big Wheel, Highway 191, Stroudsburg
(570) 992-1949

For one week in August, adult serious artistic dance and figure skaters can learn dance routines, take figure skating seminars, and enjoy the company of other skaters at the annual Stroudsburg Roller Skating Camp at the Big Wheel. According to the book, *The History of Roller Skating* by James Turner, this camp, which has been running since 1979, is the oldest skating camp in the country. Accommodations are at East Stroudsburg University or in a hotel of your choice. Costs range from a little more than $100 for a single day of seminars and skating to a little more than $500 for the complete week of seminars and skating, dorm room, meals, a camp shirt, and group photo. There are several options in between.

EDUCATIONAL CAMPS

Stroudsburg/East Stroudsburg

Monroe County Environmental Education Center
Running Valley Road, Bartonsville
(570) 629-3061
www.mcconservation.org

The center runs many programs including day camps in the summer (see the "Day Camps" section in this chapter) and day classes (see our Kidstuff chapter) throughout the year. However, the center offers a residential Conservation Camp for county residents ages 14 to this year's graduating seniors one week during the summer at a cost of $150. The week is usually in mid-July, and the program is held at Stony Acres Recreation Facility of East Stroudsburg University in Marshalls Creek. The

Dog and deer ticks proliferate in the woods that surround all the camps. When packing those trunks for summer camp, be sure to throw in an insect repellant that repels ticks.

program focuses on conservation-related topics such as forestry, archery, trap shooting, beekeeping, fly fishing, water quality, and taxidermy. Besides the activities at the center, the camp sometimes includes a two-day canoe trip on the Delaware River.

Milford/Lake Wallenpaupack Area

Science Camp Watonka
Wangom Road, Hawley
(570) 226-4779
www.watonka.com

This is a camp for "science-minded boys ages 7 to 15." It has a well-rounded program that includes all the regular camp activities, along with a daily science concentration, selected by the individual camper. The camp sessions cost $3,195 for the first four-week session, $2,895 for the second four-week session, or $5,195 for the entire eight weeks. The camp fee is inclusive; there are no other costs for any activities, insurance, or uniforms. Transportation is the only extra. It is not a summer school; it is an experience with science in well-equipped laboratories and computer labs. The daily lab instruction can be in astronomy, biochemistry, biology, nature, chemistry, computer science, earth science, electronics, ham radio, photography, physics, robotics, video, and more. The computer science lab was one of the first in the country and has programs for beginner, intermediate and advanced computer users. Arts and crafts are also explored in areas such a jewelry making, leather work, woodworking, dramatics, rocketry, and video production.

Sports activities include swimming, sailing, windsurfing, canoeing, cycling, and lifesaving, taught in the camp's lake. Field and court sports include soccer, softball, hockey, badminton, tennis, basketball, and volleyball. There are single-performer sports such as climbing, archery, riflery, minibikes (for age 10 and older), mountain bikes, and trap and skeet shooting. There are many other activities here, including trips to points of interest in the area, hikes, overnight camp-outs, and orienteering. The camp uses the best equipment available, and the staff-to-camper ratio is about one-to-two and a half, which means a lot of close supervision and instruction.

DAY CAMPS

Many of the area day-care centers provide some type of day-camp experience. Also, some recreation departments sponsor programs, and in some townships, day-camp type activities are held in the parks. Your best bet is to check with the township office or schools for possible leads. There are a few day camps that have a particular difference that may be of interest to you, so we'll point those out here.

Delaware Water Gap/ Shawnee-on-Delaware

Pocono Environmental Education Center (PEEC)
Emery Road, Dingmans Ferry
(570) 828-2319
www.peec.org
A weeklong session for children ages 3 to 15 taps into children's curiosity about the natural world. Tadpoles, for ages 3 to 5, with an adult who is at least 16 years old, investigates ponds, insects, and feathered and furry animals. The price is $62 per week. Lifestyles of the Wet and Slimy, for 6 to 9-year-olds, looks under rocks, in the trees, in the sky, and in the pond. There are different programs for returning campers at this level, and each week has a

different theme. To get wet and slimy, you pay $125 for the week. Junior Naturalist, ages 10 to 12, helps your child develop leadership skills while hiking, canoeing, swimming, learning about watersheds, wild animals, and outdoor living skills. This group will do a community project, such as building a beaver baffle. The Senior Naturalist, ages 13 to 15, learn outdoor living skills, and do research and service projects. Junior and Senior Naturalist programs cost $125 per week.

Stroudsburg/East Stroudsburg

Camelbeach Day Camp
Camelback Road, Tannersville
(570) 629-1661
www.camelbeach.com
During the winter, Camelback Ski Area has skiing activities for children, but during the summer it offers a day camp for children ages 5 to 12. Fees start at $95 for a two-day package (minimum of 24 hours advance reservation), $110 for three days, $140 for one week, $260 for two weeks, and $120 for each additional week up to $1,100 for 10 weeks.

The camp runs from 9:00 A.M. to 4:00 P.M., but early drop-off and late pickup can be arranged. The activities include the typical arts and crafts, nature studies, sports and swimming, and the atypical camp activities of Camelbeach Water Park. Tennis instruction is available for an additional fee. For those who are in the area for a summer vacation, it is good to note that you can send your children for two or three days; you don't have to register them for the whole week.

International Day Camp
9020 Bartonsville Woods Road
Stroudsburg
(570) 629-0244
www.gymschool.com
International Day Camp is an affiliate of the International Gymnastics Camp and

International Sports Camp. It shares the same beautiful mountain views and stresses fitness and sports-related activities in the Kindercamp and sports camp. There are a multitude of activities including wall climbing, horseback riding, gymnastics, swimming, and trapezing.

For children, ages 3 to 10, day camps from Monday through Friday cost $225, reduced to $200 for two or more weeks, and $900 for five weeks.

Monroe County Environmental Education Center
8050 Running Valley Road, Bartonsville
(570) 629-3061
www.mcconservation.org

This center offers two one-week camp sessions for children ages 9 to 12 each summer—one in July and one in August. Dubbed "Forest, Fields and Me," each week's program is the same, so children are only allowed to register for one session.

The camps, which cost $75 per child, provide a hands-on experience that includes discovering nature in the forest, fields, and wetlands that comprise the Environmental Center's domain. The camp is limited to 25 campers per session. The daily schedule runs from 9:00 A.M. until 3:30 P.M. The center also offers a variety of day programs for children ages 4 to 9 that encompass one morning or afternoon. These programs begin in late June and run through August.

Monroe County Recreation Department
4221 Manor Drive, Stroudsburg
(570) 992-4343
www.co.monroe.pa.us

In Monroe County, day-camp activities are sponsored in the schools of Pocono Mountain, Pleasant Valley, Stroudsburg, and East Stroudsburg from 9:00 A.M. to 3:00 P.M. late June through July at a cost of $250–$265 per child. The department also provides workshops and seminars at different locations throughout the county, and swimming and tennis lessons. These programs are highly sought-after, so participants must attend for the entire ses-

If you're looking for an overnight camp at an extremely reasonable cost, check with the Girl Scouts and Boy Scouts. These camps usually have wonderful facilities and cost very little. Your scout will be earning badges, too.

sion, and early sign-up is strongly recommended. Summer programs are for students ages 6 to 12.

Stroud Township
1215 North Fifth Street, Stroudsburg
(570) 421-3362
www.township.stroud.pa.us

Stroud Township provides its own day camp program at the Stroudsburg High School for children entering second through seventh grade. It is open from 9:00 A.M. to 3:00 P.M. from late June through July. A half-day program, 9:00 A.M. to noon, is available for children going into first grade. The activities include arts and crafts and sports played on the school's playing fields or in the gym. There are optional swimming lessons for an additional fee. Another day camp, for East Stroudsburg residents, will be held at Dansbury Park in East Stroudsburg. The cost for the Stroudsburg Township camp is $155 for six weeks for the full day and $80 for the half day. The East Stroudsburg camp costs $165 for six weeks for the full day and $85 for the half day.

West End

Beltzville State Park
Pohopoco Drive, Lehighton
(610) 377-9150
www.dcnr.state.pa.us/stateparks/parks

This park offers a popular four-day day camp program, Youth Education Learning Series, for ages 4 to 17. Campers are grouped by age. Touch & Grow, for ages 4 to 5, and Environmental Discovery, for ages 6 to 8, run 9:30 A.M. to 12:30 P.M.; Junior Naturalist, for ages 9 to 13 and

If you're a Pennsylvania resident and your child will be a junior or senior in high school, look into the Pennsylvania Governor's School of Excellence. These intensive five-week programs are held at universities statewide in the sciences, health care, arts, information technology, teaching, international studies, agricultural science, and global entrepreneurship. Admission is extremely competitive so apply early. Go to www.pgse.org for an application.

Conservation Leadership Program, for ages 14 to 17 run 9:30 A.M. to 1:00 P.M. Camp costs $25.00 for the first child in your family and $12.50 for each additional child. Lots of community programs are scheduled April through October. Most of these programs are suitable for all ages. They're free, but you must call ahead to register, as space is limited. Programs are based on nature, taking advantage of the lake and surrounding woods for nature walks and crafts (making things from natural materials), swimming and studies of fish, turtle, or insects in the area. The programs vary, and the park staff suggests you call to find out what's going on when. A program guide is printed in April, and you can request a copy by calling the number above. The summer camp schedule and registration dates are published in the local newspapers (be sure to check the *Pocono Record*) in April. The dates fill up fast, so if you don't see them in the paper, call to find out the schedule.

Champion Sportsplex Summer Camp
9 Pilgrim Way, Brodheadsville
(570) 402-0501
www.championsportsplex.com
Champion Sportsplex offers a three-week serious training camp in Taekwondo for any age of serious practitioner. The training sessions run from 9:00 A.M. to 8:00

P.M., with generous lunch and dinner breaks. There's no arts and crafts or any other camp-type activity—it's all Taekwondo. The cost of the three-week session is $600.

YMCA CAMPS
Stroudsburg/East Stroudsburg

Pocono Family YMCA
809 Main Street, Stroudsburg
(570) 421-2525
www.poconoymca.org
The Pocono Family YMCA offers five Y camps. Camp Hidden Lake, for children going into grades 5 through 7, is run in the Delaware Water Gap National Recreation Area. They offer archery, mountain biking, nature programs, lake swimming, canoeing, hiking, and a field trip each week. Mountaineers Camp, for kids going into grades 1 through 3, at the Y in Cresco, offers creative fun on and off-site, with popcorn wars, a weekly field trip, off-site swimming, and time to run around in their outdoor play area. Summer Fun Camp, for children going into grades 1 through 3, at the Y in Stroudsburg, offers swimming in their indoor pool, a spacious gym for play, and a weekly field trip. Preschool Camp, at the Stroudsburg Y, for ages 3 to 5, offers arts and crafts, music, swimming, games, nature, science, weekly themes, special guests, story time, and snacks. Village People Camp, at the Foxmoor YMCA in Marshalls Creek, is for children going into the first through third grades. They take weekly day trips, swim off-site, do crafts, and run and climb on the Y's outdoor playground. The cost of these camps is $110 per week for Y members and $155 per week for nonmembers. Extended hours for working parents are available—6:30 to 8:00 A.M. is $15 for members and $20 for nonmembers, while 4:00 to 6:30

P.M. is $20 for members and $25 for non-members. Financial assistance is available for those who would otherwise not be able to attend the camp.

Milford/Lake Wallenpaupack Area

Camp Speers-Eljabar
Highway 739, Dingmans Ferry
(570) 828-2329
www.campspeersymca.org
The Pike County YMCA overnight offers eight weeks of overnight camp at its 1,100-acre facility near Dingmans Ferry. All the traditional camp activities are offered. Campers 8 to 16 years old choose three activities from a list that includes canoeing, ropes, fishing, kayaking, newspaper writing, sailing, rocketry, photography, dance, target sports, outdoor living skills, and much more. All campers swim as well. Horseback riding is available for an additional fee. Teens 13 to 16 may also choose adventure trips, including camping, spelunking, rafting, and more. A special mainstreaming program is available for campers with learning and developmental disabilities.

One-week sessions cost $570, while two-week sessions cost $995. Horseback riding costs an additional $110 per week. Campers must be current YMCA members. If your camper is not a member, you may purchase a Camp Speers-Eljabar membership for $40 for an individual or $70 for a family.

CONFERENCE CENTERS/ CAMPS

Some of the listings included here operate as camps during the summer months and as conference and retreat centers during off months. Since all are near ski areas, winter months provide some interesting retreat and conference options.

Delaware Water Gap/ Shawnee-on-Delaware

Kirkridge Retreat Center
2495 Fox Gap Road, Bangor
(610) 588-1793
www.kirkridge.org
An interdenominational Christian retreat and study center, Kirkridge runs seminars on a variety of spiritual, political, and life topics, bringing in clergy, authors, and other heavy thinkers. Columcille (see our Close-up in our Attractions chapter), a park with stones reminiscent of Stonehenge and other Celtic sites, is on the grounds of this center, which is set on a wooded ridge overlooking the Delaware Water Gap. Check out their catalog on the Web or ask to be put on the mailing list so you can attend seminars, such as "Labyrinth," "Thomas Merton and Henry Nouwen, Two Models of the Spiritual Life," and "Making a Living While Making a Difference." Kirkridge also offers occasional trips and study tours, such as "Selma to Montgomery, A Kirkridge Civil Rights Pilgrimage to Alabama."

Kirkridge also opens its facilities as a conference center to outside groups of 10 to 92 people. They offer meeting rooms, a kitchen and dining room, break-out rooms, and double-occupancy bedrooms. You can cook for yourself or arrange for Kirkridge to provide the meals. Group rates are $53 per person per overnight without meals and $82 per person per overnight with meals. Kirkridge also offers units for private retreats.

Paradise Lake Retreat Center
Sugar Mountain Road, Bushkill
(570) 588-6067
www.kidswithapromise.org
This lovely 500-acre center on top of Sugar Mountain in Bushkill accepts religious groups of any age with space for 25 to 200 people. The facility is available for midweek retreats or even daylong retreats. Housing is in log cabins with bunk-style

> *There are camps for special children, too. Camps exist for children with asthma, children who are mourning the loss of someone close to them, and children with developmental and physical disabilities. Check with your doctor and social service agencies to locate the right camp for your special child.*

accommodations that can sleep between 20 and 56 people. There are also single rooms large enough for a whole group and special accommodations for group speakers. The accommodations, food, and facilities are provided; you bring your own speakers and program. Rates depend on the number of people staying and the time of year. Call for more information.

A lake provides boating and swimming, and there's also an outdoor pool. The large gymnasium is a great place for indoor basketball and volleyball. In winter, the mountain provides a fun spot for tubing and tobogganing, and the lake allows for ice-skating. There are numerous trails for hiking.

One of the most interesting features of the camp is a chapel of stone and glass that overlooks the lake. In the summer the center is used as a camp for underprivileged inner-city kids from New York. Rates are on a sliding scale based on the individual family's ability to pay. For further information, call (888) NYC–KIDS.

Stroudsburg/East Stroudsburg

Twin Pines Camp, Conference and Retreat Center
3000 Twin Pines Road, Stroudsburg
(570) 629-2411
www.gospelcom.net
An Evangelical Congregational Church Camp, Twin Pines has camp activities for boys and girls in senior high, junior high,

and grades 1 through 5; special needs students; adults; and family groups. There are sports and music camps, frontier and mountainside camping experiences at outpost camps, and parent and child camps.

Rates average $225 per child per week. Under the Family Camp umbrella, adults stay for $225 each; youth ages 12 to 17, $191; children ages 3 to 11, $158; and toddlers two and younger, $58 each. Discounts are offered for early registration.

The facilities also are available for retreats and conferences throughout the year accommodating up to 70 adults or 110 youth. Twin Pines also operates an extensive retreat and conference center program each year, offering singles' retreats, women's retreats, and more, and accepts groups who wish to be guided in their own experiences.

An interesting addition to this center is the Sweigert Nature Center that is managed by a staff naturalist and displays both mounted and live animals.

Mount Pocono Area

Pocono Plateau Program Center
Highway 191 North, Cresco
(570) 676-3665
www.poconoplateau.org
The 750 acres of forests, lakes, wildlife habitats, and hiking trails offer year-round facilities for Christian retreats, summer camps, and outdoor education classes. Two lakes provide for swimming, boating, and fishing. There are indoor and outdoor recreation pavilions for volleyball, basketball, and other activities such as tetherball and ultimate Frisbee. A children's play area is also part of the complex.

In winter, weather permitting, there is ice-skating on the lake and sledding. You can bring your own retreat here, or you can take part in a Plateau-led retreat for children, young adults, junior and senior high students, and families. Those who choose to camp at the Adventure Site in platform tents have the option of cooking their own meals at the tent site over the fire or on a camp stove.

In summer, several one-week camps are offered, each for a specific age group, with different themes and activities. Mommy and me is a three-day camp for kids 4 to 7 years old, with their moms ($155 for mommy and $125 for me). Campers in a senior high school extreme biking camp travel over 140 miles on bicycles, stopping at sister camps and seeing Pennsylvania in a whole new way.

Most weeklong camps average $280 per camper per week, although those that take you off-site for special activities like golf cost more. Specialty camps include activities like high ropes, rock climbing, performing a musical, golfing, ocean kayaking, whitewater rafting, mountain biking, backpacking, pioneer games, and candle making.

There are also special trip camps to spots like the Grand Canyon, and these vary in price according to transportation and accommodations.

Accommodations include heated lodges, which are available for groups of 9 to 125, with one large bathroom/shower facility for each wing or floor; platform tents at the adventure site for groups of 8 to 72, with bathrooms and hot showers in the Adventure Lodge; and meeting rooms for 12 to 125. Rates vary; call ahead for confirmation.

Spruce Lake Retreat
Highway 447 North, Canadensis
(570) 595-7505, (800) 822-7505
www.sprucelake.org
This Mennonite-owned and operated facility is a year-round adult and children's camp and retreat center. There are 320 acres with streams, waterfalls, wildlife, two small lakes, and hiking trails. During the summer, there are coed children's wilderness expedition and outpost camps at $215 to $235 per child for ages 8 to 18, with a different age level each week. There is even a three-day minicamp for youngsters age eight and nine with a low camper-to-counselor ratio and seven kids

to a tent to ensure a positive camping experience for new campers. Activities for all levels include swimming, paddleboating, minigolf, archery, a climbing tower, music, leather crafts, zipline, soccer, basketball, rocketry, watersliding, and many more exciting activities. Besides children's summer camps, there are youth and adult programs for adventure activities such as wilderness expeditions, challenge-course events, and cross-country ski weekends.

Family, holiday, and seasonal retreats are held here. For Christian schools, the Spruce Lake Outdoor School is an outdoor-classroom education tool. There are residence programs for kids in grades 4 to 12. Programs include hikes, adventure activities, and outdoor skills. The school's programs are centered around an outdoor education center that is specifically designed as a learning and display facility for nature subjects and outdoor class introductions. They also offer spiritual, academic, and social activities for homeschoolers, especially groups of homeschoolers.

This center has varied lodging facilities, conference rooms that accommodate from 20 to 200, wooded campsites with a heated bathhouse, a central dining room with buffet service, and a multipurpose Lakeview Program Center that seats up to 900 people. All meals are provided with the retreat and camping programs. An interesting option here is a bed-and-breakfast program. Reservations are available any time of the year for four types of rooms—motel-style, inn-style, dorm-style, and kitchenette. Nightly rates run from $24 to $34 per adult, depending on style of room. Children staying with their parents cost less.

West End

Camp Streamside
Rossinger Road, Reeders
(570) 629-1902
www.streamside.org
Camp Streamside offers Kids Kamp, Teen Camp, and Pathfinders Wilderness Camp.

This is a Christian-based camp, but it does not represent any particular denomination. It offers all the usual camp activities, but adds a 300-foot waterslide or giant treehouse. Rates are $200–$240 per week. Families can attend camp together at weekend family camps for $61 per person, which includes two nights and all meals. There's even a bus from Philadelphia.

There are fine conference facilities here, and Streamside provides a host for each group during its stay, along with support through equipment and other options.

Mt. Gilead Camp and Conference Center
Mountain Road, off Highway 715
Reeders
(570) 629-0920
www.mtgileadcamp.org

Mt. Gilead is a nondenominational, Christian girls (ages 7–17) camp during the summer and a conference and retreat center the rest of the year. A week at camp costs $250, and additional charges for special programs can cost up to $180. Scholarships are available. Any child signing up for more than one week must pay a $30 weekend stay-over fee.

The camp weeks are organized around a theme—canoeing, "Jiving Jungle," "Blizzard Blast," a wilderness trek, "Get a Clue," "Galaxy Quest," and horseback riding. There is no on-site kitchen staff available throughout the year, so those who wish to set up a retreat or conference weekend must make plans with the center to have meals provided or to bring their own sup-

plies and cooks. Also, there aren't any programs planned; the center is available to those who have their own program in mind and bring speakers and activities with them. This camp is built on very mountainous terrain. It is up the back of Camelback Ski Area, so it is for the hardy and those who enjoy rustic and woodsy surroundings.

Milford/Lake Wallenpaupack Area

Ramah in the Poconos
Off Highway 247, Lake Como
(570) 798-2504
www.ramahpoconos.org

The Conservative Jewish education programs at Ramah are for children in grades 5 through 10. Camp is divided into two four-week sessions or an eight-week session. The programs are sponsored by the Jewish Theological Seminary and offer Hebrew and Judaic programs. Activities include sports, nature, arts, music, dance, and drama. A lake provides for waterfront activities—boating, kayaking, canoeing, sailing, windsurfing, swimming, and fishing—and nature outings, camping, and canoeing trips are scheduled. The camp also offers a 10-day camp for the deaf and hard of hearing. Accommodations are in cabins that sleep 12 to 14, and the kitchen is kosher. Expect to pay approximately $3,300 per child for a four-week session and $5,350 for an eight-week session.

RELOCATION

It's finally happened. After joining the eight million tourists who visit the Poconos every year, you've fallen in love with the place and want to make it your home. In that, you're not alone. You may have a family and you're eager to escape the claustrophobic urban crush to find more breathing space. Or you may be a retiree, in search of a little slice of paradise in which to spend your golden years now that the children are grown and gone and the home in which you've lived for decades suddenly feels too cavernous for two. Whatever goals you may cherish, you'll find them here.

The Pocono region has it all. Autumn colors are so varied and vivid you can almost taste them. Winter whitens some of the best ski resorts in the Northeast and turns the nighttime sky into an array of diamonds on black velvet. Spring calls anglers to pristine lakes and tumbling streams, teeming with fish, and summer brings a horde of golfers to more than 35 rolling green courses, many of them world class.

Where will you settle when you get here? How much will a new home cost you? What amenities are available for your age group? What can you expect by way of child care? How will your spiritual needs be met? In this chapter, encompassing real estate, retirement, health care, child care, and worship, we will try to supply some answers. So look upon your decision to move as the first step in a grand adventure, and read on. The welcome mat has just been laid outside our door.

REAL ESTATE

They come in droves, like refugees fleeing a war zone. Given the problems, both financial and social, now plaguing the neighboring states of New York and New Jersey, the war zone analogy really isn't far from the truth. Property taxes in those states have exploded in recent years, whereas ours, although under increasing pressure from a growing population of schoolchildren, have remained relatively stable. The Poconos, encompassing Monroe, Pike, Wayne, and Carbon Counties, long have been known as the last "bedroom community" west of New York City and north of Philadelphia, but in the last two years they have achieved the possibly dubious distinction of being the fastest growing counties in the state. For that reason, and because of a constantly fluctuating marketplace, hard figures about the number of homes sold and average prices throughout the Poconos are hard to come by. In fact, when the Wayne/Pike County Real Estate Association suffered a computer meltdown in restructuring, it lost all data prior to July 2003. So take what follows as a general guideline and when you're ready to buy, ask your Realtor for a comparative market analysis on homes in the neighborhood in which you want to live.

Available figures indicate that in 2000, 2,718 single-family homes were sold in the region through the Multiple Listing Service used by real estate agencies to find and market homes for newcomers. That was almost double the 1,554 sold via the MLS in 1997, but in 2003, that number exploded to 3,357 in Monroe County alone, with estimates that topped 4,000 in the four-county area. Still, even that increase represents only part of the picture of growth in the Poconos. The four counties have experienced a building boom in new homes in the past few years, and since neither building contractors nor homeowners who put out FOR SALE BY OWNER signs use the MLS system, the number of homes actually sold is far higher. It may be no exaggeration to say that what may be the greatest land rush since the opening of the Oklahoma Territory more than a century ago now is taking place right here in Pennsylvania's own little Garden of Eden.

In 2003, a record 1,634 building permits were issued in Monroe County alone, well ahead of the old record of 1,592 set in 2001. The Pocono Builders Association predicts that 2004 will exceed both previous years, though a growing scarcity of land for development may inhibit construction. The average price of a home constructed in 2003 was $179,000. Newly built homes, however, do carry higher price tags than older homes sold by their owners.

If you're thinking of buying an older home, check out listings in the local newspaper and in any number of real estate booklets available in the area. Then find yourself a Realtor who not only will show you a variety of homes, with their prices, in the Multiple Listing Service, but, when you find your dream home, will get you prequalified for a mortgage loan and supply you with a seller's disclosure revealing any problems with the property under consideration.

Each county has a builders' association, in which members must meet established quality standards and codes, and they must provide a minimum one-year written warranty. Contact the Pocono Builders Association at 556 Main Street, Stroudsburg, (570) 421-9009, for information on certified building companies. Then, after you have selected a builder, ask for references and consult the Better Business

Bureau at (570) 342-5100, or visit their Web site, www.nepa.bbb.org, at which you can enter the name of a business and check them out. Make sure you read all the way to the bottom of the listing. The Web site also has some good advice for those thinking of building a home.

Most Pocono builders offer home and land packages from $80,000 to $180,000. Of course, if you want a fancier home or one that is customized to suit your needs, you'll pay more. Be wary of exceptionally low prices—you'll probably find out too late that those "bargains" don't include many necessities. When you read an ad, note whether or not land is included, and whether a well and septic are part of the package. Land, a well, and a septic system, all necessary if you're building outside a town, can raise the price of a new home substantially. If you're choosing your builder based on advertised prices, you need to factor these items into the equation.

The most popular areas for new home construction are the West End, Mount Pocono and Stroudsburg/East Stroudsburg. Models are on display along U.S. Highway 209 in the West End, US 209 Business from East Stroudsburg to Marshalls Creek, US 209 from the Marshalls Creek exit of Interstate 80 into Marshalls Creek itself, and Highway 611 from Stroudsburg to Mount Pocono.

When buying a home site, make sure the property can accommodate a septic system, because most rural areas lack central water and sewer. If the property does not pass a percolation test—a test of how quickly liquid flows through the soil—you will not be allowed to build. Wetland regulations are strictly enforced and could prevent you from building on that dream lot with the wonderful view and surrounding water. We know people who started building and then had to move their house because they were building too close to a stream. Make sure this is all resolved before that first shovelful of earth is removed. If you have questions about these regulations and tests, contact your township sewage enforcement officer

The total number of people who live within a two-hour drive of the Poconos—those deemed most likely to consider a vacation home—is a staggering 28 million. One-third of the entire population of the United States lives within a six-hour drive of Pike County. Throughout the 1980s and 1990s, Monroe and Pike Counties have ranked first and second in percentage of population growth among Pennsylvania counties.

about the percolation test and your county conservation district for information on wetland regulations.

Wetland regulations protect you as well as the environment. The people who started building too close to the stream would have had a few feet of water on their ground floor during the flood of 1996, had they continued building on the original spot. Others who built before wetland regulations were put into effect have perpetually wet basements or garages.

The population of the Poconos has been increasing at an astounding rate, and the development of our beautiful open spaces is one of the hottest issues here. Open space advocates have organized, and they quickly step in to buy and preserve large tracts of land when they come on the market before developers can obtain them. The conservationists cannot afford bidding wars, however, so must try to persuade sellers to sell to them at appraised value for the sake of the environment. Even so, open space available for construction is dwindling, another factor that is expected to drive real estate prices up in years to come.

If your goal is to buy an existing house, hire a house inspector to evaluate the current state of the structure and its internal systems. Call an inspector after you have made an offer on the property. You can make the agreement of sale contingent upon a favorable inspection. If it's an old house, the inspector is going to find some systems that are not ready to chug along for another 50 years. If you're going to have to replace the roof next year, the price of the house may not seem as attractive to you as it did before. You'll need to consider your love of the house, how much you're willing to spend immediately to make it comfortable, how much you were planning on paying for it, and whether there are other homes that would appeal to you if you don't like what the inspector has to say.

We have excellent public schools throughout the Poconos, although all our school districts are struggling with tremendous increases in student population, and property taxes have been rising fast (see our Education chapter). Governor Ed Rendell and local state legislators have proposed alternative tax systems, including gambling, to bring property taxes down. There are some very good Catholic schools and a handful of private schools, some based on the Montessori system, but private tuition can run as high as $7,000 a year.

Many of our residents commute to New York City, Scranton/Wilkes-Barre, Allentown, Bethlehem, or metropolitan centers in New Jersey. Thousands of them here now depend upon Martz bus lines to get them to work every day. Weather and traffic allowing, it is a 90-minute ride from the toll gate at Delaware Water Gap to New York City's Port Authority. Establishment of a commuter train from Stroudsburg to New York City has been in the works for years, and in 2004 it appeared that the line actually might materialize. The best advice, however, is "Believe it when you see it."

Not all commuters have to rely on physical transportation to live in the Poconos and work in New York City. In this age of information, many work at home, telecommuting via computer and modem. Though there are some skilled professions here, most jobs fall into the range of $10 or less per hour. Check the Sunday classifieds for a look at the local job market. If you're thinking of moving here to establish an innovative business of your own, you'll find many talented, underemployed people looking for good work.

In years past, the majority of homes throughout the Poconos were secondary vacation homes, but primary home sales now dominate the market. Those who live in Delaware Water Gap/Shawnee-on-Delaware and the Stroudsburgs and commute typically desire a home within 20 minutes of the toll bridge on I-80 or the Martz bus park and ride on Highway 611 in Delaware Water Gap. The West End has moved from a secondary to a primary home market. Vacation homes still domii

Before you decide to buy any home, be sure you receive a seller's disclosure listing any flaws or problems the structure might have. Finding out, after you've closed, that the roof leaks, the basement floods, and the electrical system will have to be replaced, can really spoil your day.

nate much of Wayne and Pike Counties. In 2003 the *Pocono Record* reported several sales of at least $200,000 each in Pike, with average home sales topping out at $111,689 in Mount Pocono and $104,701 in Coolbaugh Township. In Monroe County, the market set a record high, with an average sale price of $147,876, up from $131,536 in 2002, but you still can find a decent home in the area in the range of $95,000 to $135,000, and a summer cabin on up to an acre of land for as little as $75,000. If you can afford as much as $200,000, you'll have your pick of almost everything but the mansions, many of which start at the $500,000 level. The most expensive home constructed in 2003 went for $538,000 in Great Bear, the toniest community in the Poconos.

Fluctuations in the boiling real estate market tend to render pricing examples obsolete a month after publication, but in general, in 2004 a decent home could be found in the range of $100,000 to $135,000. Midlevel homes ran from $140,000 to $180,000; high-end, four-bedroom homes generally were priced between $180,000 and 220,000; and there always are a few fine homes and estates ranging from $500,000 up to $3.5 million.

Rentals, on the other hand, increasingly are few and far between. Christine Scrofano, a real estate agent at Wilkins & Associates, one of the few agencies with a specialty in rentals, said early in 2004 that home rentals, where available, run from $950 to $1,200 a month, topping out at $1,500 to $1,600 a month at the high end. Apartments generally rent from $675 to $950 a month. Students of East Strouds-

burg University occupy most of the available rentals near the campus. If you plan to attend the university, be aware that there is a borough ordinance against having more than two unrelated people share a house. East Stroudsburg created this policy to prevent large numbers of students from overcrowding homes and apartments. Most of the apartments above stores on Main Street are occupied by students.

Apartments also are scarce in the West End, Wayne County, and Pike County because developers generally make greater profit using land for home sites than by building apartment complexes. Also, local residents, fearful of increasing demands on overcrowded roads, often oppose facilities that will bring in large numbers of new neighbors.

The Delaware River defines one side of the Poconos, but don't count on finding riverfront property. The Delaware Water Gap National Recreation Area takes up 40 miles of shoreline, so there are few riverfront homes available. If you want water, you're more likely to find lakefront than riverfront. Actually, that's a blessing, because the river has a way of occasionally jumping its banks, and anything in its path can get washed away or at least be left severely damaged. The last major flood we had was in the fall of 2004, when the river rose more than 28.4 feet above its normal level. Before that, the most memorable flood was in summer 1955, when the river rose a terrifying 36.6 feet, destroying whole neighborhoods (see our History chapter). If you have your heart set on riverfront property, head south of Portland along River Road and see if you can spot any FOR SALE signs. If you buy property close to the river or any of its tributaries, find out where the water level topped out during these two storms. You may need flood insurance.

Whatever your motivation or financial condition, you should have no trouble finding a good home in the Poconos. Our developments range from a few that look like Tobacco Road, with owner-built vacation fantasies, to those that sport a solid middle-class look, to a few others that are simply extravagant and full of mansions and miniature estates. The latter may be found in such elegant communities as Great Bear, Country Club of the Poconos, and Blue Mountain Lakes. Similar urban homes grace Sarah, Thomas, and Scott Streets in downtown Stroudsburg. Mid-price, but still occasionally elegant, homes can be found in such communities as Penn Estates, Saw Creek, Winona Lakes, and Lake of the Pines, with a variety of styles and prices scattered throughout small, out-of-the-way communities and rural areas. Neighborhoods and housing communities vary widely in the four-county area, and their characteristics are constantly shifting as the population increases. Here are a few of the highlights.

Neighborhoods and Nearby Communities

DELAWARE WATER GAP/ SHAWNEE-ON-DELAWARE

Delaware Water Gap is close to the river and the Appalachian Trail, while Shawnee, with its water park, golf course, and ski mountain, lies beside the river, bordering the National Recreation Area. They're great places to while away your leisure time, but few properties are available in either location. If you're lucky enough to find a home here, it will cost a little more than a similar place in Stroudsburg or East Stroudsburg. But with a commuter-friendly proximity to I-80 and the sheer beauty of the two towns, it's well worth paying extra.

Marshalls Creek, also close to I-80, has more available real estate, but you'll want to look twice before moving in because there is a perpetual traffic jam from the intersection of US 209 and Highway 402, backing up eastbound and westbound traffic for miles in both directions on weekends. There are side roads and short-

cuts around the congestion, but as more people discover them, they, too, are becoming strangulated. A bypass has been promised by 2007, but work on it has yet to begin. In the latest development, a bureaucratic dustup between PennDot and the Army Corps of Engineers over wetlands protection has stopped the project cold.

Saw Creek, once a vacation development, now is a year-round home to many families. West of US 209 and just south of Bushkill, this enormous, gated community boasts six pools, tennis courts, skiing, a lake, and assorted sporting opportunities. Also off 209 are two of the most expensive private golf communities in the Poconos. Homes in Great Bear Country Club surround an 18-hole golf course (see our Golf chapter) designed by Jack Nicklaus and generally are priced from $500,000 up. At Country Club of the Poconos, town houses, golf villas, lakefront condos, elegant cluster homes, and two restaurants are woven into an 18-hole course designed by Jim Fazio. Prices range from $130,000 to more than $500,000. Farther north, just outside Bushkill, lower home prices can be found in Pocono Ranchlands and Pocono Mountain Lake Estates.

STROUDSBURG/EAST STROUDSBURG

All sorts of Pocono real estate can be found in these connected towns and surrounding communities. Whether you fancy an old Victorian in a downtown setting, an affordable starter home, or a top-shelf estate in a private community, a Realtor can show you something near the Stroudsburgs. There also are some surprising rural parts of both towns where you will find farms and forest dwellings. And, in a couple of areas, there are some city-like neighborhoods. These are small areas, but you want to know if you're moving in next to them. If you're looking at a home, take a walk around the block, and then around the blocks surrounding that block, to make sure you feel comfortable with the neighborhood. Talk to your potential neighbors and ask them about the neighborhood, too. The area around East Stroudsburg University is lovely, and the university offers a lot of cultural programs to the greater community, but not everybody can be happy with having rowdy students on the block.

East Stroudsburg always has had a reputation as a solid, middle-class community. Homes are well maintained, lawns are mowed, and gardens are weeded. In addition to the university, the town hosts the Pocono Medical Center, which boasts a nationally ranked cancer treatment center.

MOUNT POCONO AREA

Much of the real estate in the Mount Pocono area is reasonably priced, compared with neighborhoods in more affluent areas, but the region also boasts some very high-end properties around the towns of Buck Hill Falls, Skytop, Mountainhome, Cresco, and Canadensis, all of which lie along Highway 390 northeast of the town of Mount Pocono. These were some of the earliest resort areas on the mountain, and they contain the most desirable older homes.

Less expensive homes in subdivisions with amenities may be found near Mount Pocono, Tobyhanna, Pocono Summit, Pocono Lake, and Pocono Pines. The market there is a mix of primary and secondary homes, most of which are no more than 20 years old. The majority of new homes in the Poconos are built here and in the West End. The population has increased dramatically in the last decade. As testament to this trend, the Pocono Mountain School District complex in Swiftwater more resembles a university campus than the grounds of a public school, and a second, larger high school has been built.

For those seeking the security of a housing development with amenities ranging from pools, tennis courts, and nine-hole golf courses to fitness centers and restaurants, several upscale communities are available. Lake Naomi, near the village of

Pocono Pines, is featured in *The Ninety-Nine Best Residential and Recreational Communities in America,* by Lester Giese, L. Anne Thornton, and William Kinnaman (published by John Wiley & Sons). The development surrounds a pristine 50-acre lake for swimming, fishing, sailing, or sunning at one of its seven beaches. Lake Naomi offers an excellent restaurant, two pools, a fitness center, tennis courts, a nine-hole golf course, and programs for kids.

Other popular areas for home buyers in search of planned communities include Pinecrest Lake resort in Pocono Pines, Timber Trails, Lake View Estates, Locust Lake Village, Blue Mountain Village, and, on the western edge of the Poconos, Big Bass Lake, north of Gouldsboro. And for skiers, town houses right off the slopes are available at Big Boulder, Jack Frost, Shawnee Mountain, and Camelback. Ask your Realtor for details.

WEST END

These rolling farmlands have become the boom area for building. Developers regularly solicit the remaining farmers to sell their land, and any older farmhouse on at least 50 to 100 acres is snapped up virtually the minute it goes on the market. Usually, the buyer sells the house to fund development of the remaining land as a subdivision. Such projects are common from Sciota to Jim Thorpe. Many are off US 209, which creates some heavy traffic delays, especially on weekends. Some of the more popular developments are Indian Mountain Lakes, Pleasant Valley Estates, and Birch Hollow Estates.

At the southern end of the region, Jim Thorpe has become a major tourist destination along the order of New Hope, Pennsylvania, a Manhattanite's Mecca for antiques and art. The steep, narrow streets are lined with boutiques, antiques shops, and art galleries. Row houses and mansions built for the mine workers and executives, respectively, have been restored. The Greenwich Village flavor of the businesses, the Industrial Revolution era architecture, and the European landscape as the Lehigh River makes a grand entrance through the sweeping Lehigh Gorge create an intoxicating combination that strikes the senses like no other spot in northeastern Pennsylvania. Understandably, many who visit want to live here, and the town has developed a reputation as an artists' community.

Nearby, the town of Lehighton presents a unique real estate situation. Few homes ever reach the open market. Most are passed from generation to generation. The town's residents are loyal to the community and tend to stay in the area.

MILFORD/LAKE WALLENPAUPACK AREA

Milford is a picture-perfect small town, with carefully restored Victorians flanking its tree-lined streets, recalling the old-fashioned American atmosphere of a town in a Ray Bradbury novel. Residents and shop owners pride themselves on preserving the town's old-time character. Walk through the village and admire the gardens and the architecture. Spring, when the lilacs are in bloom, is an especially evocative time in Milford. While there are a fair number of retirees and commuters in Milford, the majority of residences are still vacation homes. Orange County, NY, just east of Milford, is the fastest growing county in New York, so nearby jobs are getting easier to find. Commuters can reach northern New Jersey via Interstate 84, and a train runs into New York City from Port Jervis, NJ, just across the river.

Outside Milford, along U.S. Highways 6 and 209, commercial activity has increased significantly. A Wal-Mart and the Westfall Towne Center shopping complex have opened, and more major projects are planned.

Masthope, in Lackawaxen Township, offers stables, a lake, a swimming pool, and a ski lodge with eight trails (see our Winter Sports chapter). The lodge often hosts big-name entertainment. Masthope was founded by Carl Hope, the same

Buyers looking for waterfront property should visit Wayne County. The high water table in the region has created an unusual number of ponds, streams, and lakes. More than 21 square miles of water are scattered throughout the county. Although Wayne County has more lakes than any other in Pennsylvania, there are no lakes in Sterling Township.

developer who built the town house and timeshare properties around Shawnee.

The most unusual private subdivision in this area is Twin Lakes, near Shohola. The community surrounds two lakes—one of them the largest natural lake in the Poconos—and all the homes, most constructed of stone and log, are at least a century old. Prices generally are on the high side.

Hemlock Farms, the largest private community in the Poconos, is in Lords Valley. Its facilities, security, fire department, and recreation are so extensive that it functions almost as a self-contained town. Recreational amenities include lakes, pools, tennis courts, a country club, health clubs, and playing fields. Other well-regarded developments in the area are Gold Key Lake and Pocono Mountain Woodland Lake.

Some of the most coveted real estate in the Poconos is lakefront property along Lake Wallenpaupack's 52-mile shoreline. This 5,700-acre man-made lake is the focus of a great deal of recreational activity (see our In, On, and Around the Water and Fishing and Hunting chapters). Homes on the shoreline are very pricey, but they drop dramatically as one moves inland.

Three popular communities near the lake are Hidden Lake Estates, Tanglwood Lake Estates, and Fawn Lake Forest. Hidden Lake Estates is a quarter-mile from Lake Wallenpaupack and features its own 40-acre lake. Unlike many subdivisions, lots are large, ranging from 2 to 12 acres.

Existing homes are very high-end. Slightly farther away, Tanglwood Lake Estates has an 18-hole golf course, access to a beach and docking on Lake Wallenpaupack, a small private lake, a health club, and playing fields. Fawn Lake Forest, considered a good second-home community, has access to Lake Wallenpaupack, indoor and outdoor swimming pools, and a clubhouse.

North of Lake Wallenpaupack, lovely Victorians can be found in Hawley and Honesdale, early industrial towns that are beginning to draw more tourists. Many of the old homes still available are suitable for conversion to bed-and-breakfast inns or small shops. Honesdale bears the nickname "Maple City" because in 1847 borough officials planted 1,500 maple trees to provide shade for residents. Many of the same trees, now towering, still decorate the downtown landscape. Hawley and Honesdale are too far away for most New York commuters, but the drive to Scranton or Wilkes-Barre takes about an hour. Commuters to Scranton or Wilkes-Barre also often look at homes in Waymart, Hamlin, or Lake Ariel. Most desirable, and hence, most expensive, are the "cottages," actually minimansions, which were built around the lake as weekend homes by leaders of the then-flourishing coal industry.

Perhaps the most luxurious community in the woods of the Poconos is Woodloch Springs outside Hawley. Set on 400 acres of forest, streams, ponds, meadows, mountains, and wetlands, the very expensive homes are anything but rustic. The development boasts an acclaimed 18-hole golf course at adjoining Woodloch Pines Resort.

In Northern Wayne County, the most rural region in the Poconos, the market is almost exclusively secondary homes, though in the present population explosion in the Poconos, many formerly seasonal cabins are being turned into permanent residences. Most cherished features for those seeking homes here are privacy, view, and water; fishing and hunting in this area are outstanding. The terrain often changes dramatically from rolling hills to heavily wooded mountains. Many residents own horses, and others earn a living boarding them for weekenders.

Real-Estate Agents

Whatever the weight of your pocketbook or taste in lifestyle, it's here for you. There are more than 700 real estate agents in the area to help you find it. Space constraints forbid the listing of all the agencies, but here is a sampling:

Century 21 Millennium
227 North Ninth Street, Stroudsburg
(570) 422-6321, (800) 893-3493

4 Liberty Square Plaza, East Stroudsburg
(570) 223-1310, (800) 459-9190
www.century21millennium.net
This family-run operation maintains two offices in the Poconos specializing in residential and vacation home sales, commercial/industrial properties, and land. Diane Grinaway runs the Stroudsburg office, with 28 full-time agents. Her husband, Bob Grinaway, oversees 12 agents in the East Stroudsburg operation. Between them, the Grinaways have 23 years of combined experience in the real estate business.

Coldwell Banker
1215 North Ninth Street, Stroudsburg
(570) 424-6611, (800) 736-5770
www.cbprre.com
With eight offices and 95 agents, Coldwell Banker is the largest independently owned real estate agency in Monroe County. Coldwell Banker specializes in residential real estate, with a division for vacation rentals. There is a separate office that handles commercial and industrial real estate.

Forney Realty Inc.
US 209 Business, East Stroudsburg
(570) 424-5680, (800) 838-5680
www.forney.poconorealty.com
With 30 years in business, this six-agent office is one of the oldest real estate

Rebuilding Together

Monroe County has a surprise for those who lament that "Christmas comes but once a year." Around here, it comes twice. Christmas in April—Monroe County, which debuted in April 1995, is a nonprofit, chartered organization, and a member of the national nonprofit group, Christmas in April—USA, begun in Midland, Texas.

In April 2002, Christmas in April changed its name, locally and nationally, to Rebuilding Together, but the mission remains the same: to keep low-income, elderly, and disabled homeowners living in warmth, safety, independence, dignity, and decency through home repair and rehabilitation volunteer services. In Monroe County, more than 250 homes have been rehabilitated through the financial and physical aid of local volunteers and businesses. One day each year, these folks devote their time, expertise, materials, money, support, and spirit to help senior citizens continue to live in the dignity they deserve.

In Monroe County, the Christmas in April committee was especially lucky to have many local building and architec-

tural professionals offer their services to make plans and manage and teach the volunteer laborers. Of course, a large number of volunteers were senior citizens—their efforts focused with the help of the Monroe County Senior Clubs, Inc. All work completed has to meet the national Home Safety Checklist guidelines developed by the national organization.

In 2002, 18 local businesses sponsored the project. A sponsor contributes $1,000 or more to the local chapter of Rebuilding Together. That money is used to buy materials for the repairs. Renovations are absolutely free to the chosen seniors. Ramps are built, roofs are put on, bathrooms are repaired, trailer homes are made safe—whatever needs to be done is done through this program. Since its beginning in Midland, Texas, in 1972, Christmas in April/Rebuilding Together has renovated more than 63,000 houses. Monroe County has been a significant part of these statistics. It continues to be part of the group that has found a way to make Christmas come twice a year.

agencies in the Poconos. Pat Forney helped found the Multiple Listing Service in this area. This small agency handles various types of properties, but most of its listings are residential. Agents can show you property in Monroe County, as well as parts of Pike, Carbon, and Northhampton Counties. Forney specializes in personalized service.

The Prudential
US 209, East Stroudsburg
(570) 424-5408
www.ahome4us.com

5023 Route 611, Stroudsburg
(570) 421-2221

Highway 115, Saylorsburg
(570) 992-7277
The Prudential has three independent offices in the area and its agents show

residential properties all over the Poconos. They emphasize training and experience. In the East Stroudsburg office, many agents have more than 20 years in the business. You will find only full-time real estate agents at Prudential offices.

Spread Eagle Realty
447 Office Plaza, 200 Plaza Court Suite A, Highway 447, East Stroudsburg
(570) 425-7725
Spread Eagle Realty, with eight agents, specializes in condominiums and town houses, but they also can show you existing houses or, through their construction/architectural division, help you build your dream home. The agents help you determine what you can afford, then they help you find—or build—the home that's best for you. The three principal brokers have decades of experience in real estate.

Wilkins & Associates Real Estate Inc.
304 Park Avenue
(570) 421-8950, (800) 252-4601
www.wilkins1.com
Tom Wilkins has been running this agency since 1988, and he has built an empire. He has six offices, more than 70 agents, and three divisions: Wilkins & Associates Real Estate handles home sales; Northeast Pennsylvania Management specializes in managing developments, apartment houses, and other types of properties, and Wilkins & Associates Short-Term Department handles weekend, weekly, and seasonal rentals. In fact, they claim to have the largest listing of vacation rentals in the Poconos, including timeshare condos and single homes. Wilkins also is the largest rental agency in the Poconos and has many listings for long-term renters, as well as vacationers.

MOUNT POCONO AREA

Century 21 Genesis
Route 611, Tannersville
(570) 629-1621
Veteran Realtor Joe Narrows is broker of record at this one-stop Tannersville office,

owned by Richard Tate. Tate also owns Mountain Area Abstract, which does business in the same building, making it very handy for Genesis clients. Genesis has 13 real estate agents, active throughout the Poconos.

Mountainlife Real Estate Inc.
Highway 940, Pocono Pines
(570) 646-6600
With three agents, Mountainlife Real Estate is a small, personalized agency. Their sales and rentals stretch from Mount Pocono to Lake Harmony, and they have a good vacation and long-term rental list. This small agency tries very hard to make its customers happy.

RE/MAX
14 Knob Road, Pocono Pines
(570) 646-1776
www.robbaxter.com

9 Pocono Boulevard, Mount Pocono
(570) 839-9191
www.pocono-realestate.com

1111 North Fifth Street, Stroudsburg
(570) 476-2345, (888) 794-5589
www.bobhay.com

Highway 507, Greentown
(570) 676-0695
www.pare.org

Highway 739, Lords Valley
(570) 775-7171

1100 Church Street, Honesdale
(570) 253-9566
www.remax-waynehpa.com
RE/MAX has three independent offices in Monroe County and three more in Pike and Wayne Counties. Rob Baxter, whose great-grandfather, Rufus Wilder Miller, built Lake Naomi for his Pocono Spring Water Company, heads the Pocono Pines office, which specializes in lakefront and higher-end second homes. The firm also has 250 vacation rental homes handled by C.R. Baxter Rentals Unlimited, (800) 962-7368.

RE/MAX emphasizes experience and hires neither beginners nor part-time agents. In this office, agents average 15 years of real estate experience. Because each RE/MAX agent has experience, each is his or her own boss and can design a marketing plan for a specific home without having to submit it to a supervisor.

MILFORD/LAKE WALLENPAUPACK AREA

Century 21 Select Group
US 6, Hawley
(570) 226-1233, (570) 226-1808
(800) 227-1233
www.c21kimax.com
A merger, in 2003, with several small independent agencies left Century 21 Kimax (rechristened Century 21 Select) with eight offices throughout six Pennsylvania counties, including those in the Poconos. The agency, served by 70 Realtors, specializes in second homes in the Lake Wallenpaupack region, as well as offering a good selection of primary homes throughout the region. This company also handles a small listing of vacation rentals.

Davis R. Chant Realtors
106 East Harford, Milford
(570) 296-7717, (800) 372-4268
www.chantre.com
Davis Chant has been in the business for 40 years and has 50 agents in 6 offices in Pennsylvania. They are licensed in three states—New York, New Jersey, and Pennsylvania—and comprise the largest real estate agency in Pike and Wayne Counties. While they have extensive listings in all types of real estate, they have especially strong listings in resort, second home, and commercial properties. Chant also is an excellent agency to call for vacation rentals near Milford or around Lake Wallenpaupack.

RETIREMENT

Not long ago, retirement would have been considered the last chapter in a book of this nature, or in an individual's book of life. Now, for many, it is the first chapter, because as more and more people

Just moved here and can't find friends? Join a club, join a church or temple, or volunteer through the Retired and Senior Volunteer Program (R.S.V.P.). Club meetings are listed in Dignity, *the* Pocono Record's *monthly supplement for seniors. You can also find out more about clubs by calling the Monroe County Area Agency on Aging, (570) 420-3735. To contact R.S.V.P., call (570) 420-3747.*

achieve a healthy age of 100 or more, at 65 or so they finally know what they want to be when they grow up.

The U.S. Census bureau reported in 2000 that centenarians are the fastest-growing segment of our society. The nation now has more than 50,000 citizens 100 or older—up from 3,700 in 1940—and by 2020, it is estimated that the number will have increased to 214,000. That implies a growing demographic group of vigorous senior citizens leading productive lives well into their seventies, eighties, and nineties.

A look around our area will tell you that a lot of those folks are choosing the Poconos as the place to begin their next 40 to 50 years. And never make the mistake of using some outmoded standard of decrepitude as the gauge with which to measure the potential quality of that life span. Our retirees and senior citizens are everywhere these days. You'll see them wherever you go: volunteering as aides in the hospitals, as tutors in the schools, and as ushers at the local playhouses; delivering meals on wheels; acting as friendly visitors; driving their neighbors to and from appointments; or counseling each other in senior centers or government-sponsored programs such as APPRISE, which helps with insurance claims.

Senior citizens here are always in a process of beginning: starting new businesses; developing new senior centers, founding such clubs as the Pocono Singles Club and the Young and the Rest of Us,

RELOCATION

The Monroe County Area Agency on Aging publishes Senior Town Call of Monroe County, *a very useful monthly newsletter. To receive it on a regular basis, call (570) 420-3735 and ask to be placed on the mailing list.*

supporting and managing such organizations as Arts on the Mountain, introducing such new programs as the International Hearing Dog Association, and generally helping ensure quality of life for all residents in the Poconos. If you are looking for an active retirement life, you'll find it in the Poconos, where older adults comprise from 12 to 18 percent of the population in Monroe, Pike, Wayne, and Carbon Counties.

Most seniors live on their own. They are helped by health organizations such as the Visiting Nurses Association (VNA), hospice groups, and other caregiver groups. The area agencies on aging offer support of varying kinds, depending on their charters. Some, such as the Pike County Area Agency on Aging, provide personal care through their own allocations, while others, the Monroe County Area Agency on Aging, for example, work through outside groups. The focus of all the agencies, however, is helping seniors remain independent for as long as possible—a goal most seniors have for themselves.

If you're a retiree just moving to the area, the first place you should call is your local area agency on aging. Agencies provide brochures and pamphlets that outline all the opportunities and aid in the area; including how to volunteer, where to get hospice care; how to obtain identification cards for mass transit; and where to register for classes in driving, wellness, or arts and crafts.

Senior citizens who do not have drivers' licenses can obtain photo identification cards from the Bureau of Driver Licensing in Harrisburg. The credit-card

sized IDs, which must be renewed every four years, show the carrier's photo, name, address, date of birth, and signature. The card actually is available to any Pennsylvania resident 16 or older, but it is an especially handy option for seniors who, for one reason or another, have allowed their drivers' licenses to expire. The cost of a non-driver's ID card is $10. For more information, write to the Photo Identification Program, Bureau of Licensing, P.O. Box 68682, Harrisburg, PA 17106, or call (800) 932-4600. You can also visit their Web site at www.dmv.state.pa.us.

Area Agencies on Aging

The area agencies on aging, which follow state and federal guidelines for required services, are very active in Monroe, Pike, Wayne, and Carbon Counties. They provide opportunities and assistance to meet the many needs of the area's seniors. They also maintain senior centers in each county that serve as meeting places where seniors can play games; have socials; share meals; start clubs; sponsor trips; and participate in agency-sponsored wellness programs, including exercise, health screenings, and lectures. Monroe County even has a coalition of senior clubs, Monroe County Senior Clubs Inc., (570) 629-3407, that serves as a forum for all area senior citizen clubs and sponsors inter-club events.

The American Association of Retired Persons (AARP) sponsors 55/Alive Mature Driver courses at many locations, including the different county centers listed subsequently. These courses are designed to make senior drivers aware of age-related conditions that might affect their driving skills. They will not help a driver with a suspended license renew the privilege, but completing the course can result in an insurance premium reduction. For more information, contact one of the following area agencies on aging:

- Monroe County Area Agency on Aging, 724B Phillips Street, Stroudsburg, (570) 420-3735, maintains four senior centers: Loder Senior Center, 62 Analomink Street, East Stroudsburg, (570) 420-3745; Barrett Senior Center, Barrett Township Ambulance Building, Highway 191, Mountainhome, (570) 595-9141 or (570) 595-6004; Chestnuthill Township Park, Highway 715, Brodheadsville, (570) 992-2916; and Pocono Pines Friendship Center, American Legion Building, old Highway 940, Pocono Lake, (570) 646-9611.
- Pike County Area Agency on Aging, 150 Pike County Boulevard, (570) 775-5550, is responsible for two senior centers. The Blooming Grove senior center is housed in the same building as the Pike County Area Agency on Aging and can be reached at the same phone number; a second center in Bushkill is in the American Legion Building on Mink Pond Road, (570) 588-9923.
- Wayne County area Agency on Aging, 323 10th Street, Honesdale, (570) 253-4262, serves three senior centers: Hawley Senior Citizen Center, V.F.W. Building, Bingham Park, US 6, Hawley, (570) 226-4209; Earl J. Simons Senior Citizen Center, 323 10th Street, Honesdale, (570) 253-4262; and the Hamlin Senior Center, Salem Township Building, Highway 590, Hamlin, (570) 689-3766.
- Carbon County Office on Aging, 401 Delaware Avenue, Third Floor, Palmerton, (610) 824-7830, (800) 441-1315, is responsible for five senior centers. These include Lehighton Senior Center, 243 South Eighth Street, Lehighton, (610) 377-1530; Weatherly Senior Center, Zion Lutheran Church, Third and Fell Streets, Weatherly, (570) 427-8175; Panther Valley Senior Center, Nesquahonong School Apartments, East Catawissa Street, Nesquahonong, (570) 669-9930; Penn/Kidder Senior Center, Highway 903 and Smith Road, Jim Thorpe, (570) 325-4980; and Palmerton Senior Center, Sokol Hall, 452 Lehigh Avenue, Palmerton, (610) 826-4505.

Transportation for Seniors

Specialized transportation for senior citizens is provided in each county through the area agencies on aging. Each agency provides transportation service a little differently, but all rely on a program called Shared Ride, which is partially funded by the Pennsylvania Department on Aging. The department's Harrisburg number is (717) 783-1550. The revenue from the Pennsylvania lottery underwrites the cost of Shared Ride in each county. Ride fees differ among area agencies, depending on the destination. Individuals must show identification to receive a reduced rate. Some drivers are retired senior citizens who work part time for Shared Ride. Please note that Shared Ride is not an emergency service.

Shared Ride is a major asset to Pocono counties because of limited public transportation, which exists only in Monroe County as MC Transit, (570) 839-6282, in Carbon County as Carbon County Community Transit, and in the few privately owned taxi companies. (See our Getting Around chapter for details.) MC Transit provides transportation on the major arteries between Stroudsburg, Mount Pocono, and Brodheadsville. It provides free transportation to seniors during off-peak hours for folks with transit identification cards, which may be obtained at any agency on aging. MC Transit also is the carrier for the Shared Ride program in Monroe County.

Seniors 65 and older may obtain bus passes to ride free on public mass transit on weekends and off-peak hours during the week. Bus routes run from Eagle's Glen in East Stroudsburg and Delaware Water Gap to Tobyhanna State Park, and Saylorsburg and Effort in the West End, with shopping stops at Walmart, downtown Stroudsburg, Stroud Mall, and the Crossings factory outlet complex in Tannersville.

Carbon County Community Transit offers free rides of 35 miles or shorter to senior citizens, aged 65 and older, during off-peak hours. If the trip is longer than 35 miles, seniors must pay $1.00.

Shared Ride requires advance notice. How much notice is needed depends on the particular agency. At minimum, it is 24 hours. Call Shared Ride offices in the following counties for more information: Monroe, (570) 839–8210; Pike, (570) 296–9333; Carbon, (570) 669–6380; and Wayne, (570) 253–4280.

Job Opportunities

There are full-time and part-time jobs available for senior citizens who wish to supplement their retirement income. The area agencies on aging work with seniors to place them in available employment openings. Opportunities vary widely and may surprise you. For information, call your area agency on aging.

Volunteer Opportunities

If you are interested in volunteering, you have many options. In Monroe County, contact the Retired and Senior Volunteer Program (R.S.V.P.), (570) 420–3747, which is affiliated with the national organization, R.S.V.P., a clearing house for organizations that need volunteer help. If you are older than 55, R.S.V.P. will screen you to determine your likes and needs and will put you into their computerized volunteer file. In no time, you will be one of R.S.V.P.'s more than 1,600 volunteers who contribute nearly 200,000 hours a year in Monroe County alone.

Volunteers work in hospitals as dispatchers, porters, and intra-office mail deliverers; in local community-service organizations as the American Cancer Society and American Red Cross; and in

local arts organizations and area historical societies. Local phone directories usually list individual organizations that need volunteer help. Look there if you are interested in contacting a particular group or organization. The possibilities are endless. For more information about volunteer programs, call R.S.V.P.

Continuing Education

Folks who want to enrich their retirement years with continuing education have many options in our area. Classes at East Stroudsburg University can be audited free of charge (without credit toward a degree) but the university has expanded the program well beyond that. (See our Close-up in this chapter for details.) Folks in the northern part of the Poconos may want to look into Penn State Worthington's "Go-60" program. Northampton Community College classes are available for audit only to seniors who live in Northampton County, but they offer several courses specifically for seniors, both at their Tannersville campus and at their main campus in Bethlehem (see our Education chapter for more information). The Monroe County Career and Technical Institute at Bartonsville, (570) 629–2001, offers a variety of courses from automotive technology to nursing (see our Education chapter for details). If transportation is an issue for you, the area agencies on aging can help. Often, seniors live far from the few mass transit options in the area, so transportation for those who don't drive might require planning. (See this chapter's "Transportation for Seniors" section for more information.)

Wellness

Commitment to wellness is a cornerstone of the health programs in this area. Each of the agencies on aging offers free health screenings and exercise classes as part of

ESU Offers Post-College Age Learning Opportunities

One who loves to study never graduates, even after his or her 60th birthday rolls around, and East Stroudsburg University is making sure seniors who wish to expand their minds have plenty of space in which to do it.

Since 1981, the university has allowed senior citizens to enroll in a variety of scholastic programs, tuition-free. You can apply for a senior citizen tuition waiver for the semester in which you wish to participate by calling (570) 422-3540. The tuition-free system, which offers a maximum of six credits, toward no degree, remains in place, but now an even broader curriculum has been added under the aegis of the Older Adult Learning Center, which is affiliated with the Elder Hostel Institute Network. This program isn't free, but it's so reasonable that it might as well be. An annual fee of $35 is required to join the organization; then, for a tuition fee of $25 per term, seniors can enroll for study in an unlimited number of disciplines, such as art, history,

finance, health, sports, philosophy, and writing. All courses and related Learning Center activities are held during daylight hours, with instruction provided by qualified volunteers proficient in their chosen subject. Participants must be retired and, again, no degree is offered.

Apart from the sheer joy of learning without the pressures associated with term papers and exams, the program offers retirees an opportunity to interact with people who share their interests, to explore unfamiliar subjects and broaden their horizons, and to realize the deep satisfaction that comes with discovering new ideas.

It's generally agreed that truly active minds seldom surrender to dementia, and this program emphatically gives the lie to the old saw: you can't teach an old dog new tricks.

For more information, call (570) 422-2854, or e-mail cesmmr@po-box .esu.edu.

the daily opportunities for seniors. Area hospitals also offer programs that promote wellness.

PrimeTime Health promotes the health of older Pennsylvanians as part of a statewide initiative administered through the area agencies on aging. The Monroe County office is on the second floor of the Loder Senior Center, 62 Analomink Street, East Stroudsburg, (570) 420-3746, and

runs screenings, exercise programs, and nutrition and socialization programs. They also offer lectures emphasizing prevention and the management of health problems. Most of the lectures take place at senior centers, but clubs, workplaces, and other organizations may request speakers on health and safety issues.

In Monroe County, Pocono Medical Center is well known for its Older Adult

Exercise Program, which has been running since 1982 and was cited in the 1996 report of the White House Conference on Aging for its recommendations on hospital-based senior wellness programs. The program is sponsored by the hospital's Cardiac Services Department and offers mild progressive stretching and exercise for people 70 and older, two or three times a week, at three locations in the community. Call (570) 476-3357 for more information.

Gnaden Heutten Memorial Hospital in Lehighton offers the New Seasons program for folks 55 and older. New Seasons features free health screenings, health insurance claims, counseling, educational programs, and a coordinator to help you decide what you need. Call (610) 377-7180 to speak with the New Seasons coordinator.

The YMCA also is an important source for wellness programs. The Pocono Family YMCA in Stroudsburg has a wide selection of exercise programs, including arthritis swims and health-specific classes for increasing aerobic capacity. Call (570) 421-2525 for a list of the offerings. In Barrett Township (northwest of Stroudsburg in Mountainhome), older-adult exercise programs are available too. Call (570) 595-2730 for information.

Monroe County Recreation, (570) 992-4343, sponsors some programs for older adults. It schedules lap swim times and other adult swim programs at the area high school pools. Along with the YMCA the Monroe County Area Agency on Aging, Monroe County Recreation sponsors the Senior Fitness Walk each May as a celebration of senior citizen physical fitness.

Retirement-Living Options

As we've noted, independence is a key goal for senior citizens. We do not have a wide range of options for assisted living, personal care, or nursing homes, although there are some, and their services vary. Many seniors live at home with the help of visiting nurse programs or homemaker aid provided through the area agencies on aging or other health care organizations.

Retirement Communities

Blue Mountain Village
4 miles off Highway 33 at Wind Gap exit
Chicola Lake
(610) 381-2222, (888) BLUMT1
www.retirenet.com
At this secluded hideaway, spacious modular homes on full foundations rim a 90-acre lake in the middle of a sylvan setting in the Blue Mountains near Saylorsburg. The 42.5-acre tract is zoned for 110 homes, available to folks older than 55. Amenities include a clubhouse with pool; leisure trails; and a lake stocked with trout, bass, and catfish. Some of the lakeshore homes have decks right over the water so you can walk out on a summer morning and catch your own breakfast. Modular homes at Blue Mountain Village start at around $50,000.

LaBar Village
Village Circle, Stroudsburg
(570) 476-3126
LaBar Village, a housing development for folks older than 55, is on the outskirts of Stroudsburg. Its residents live in town houses on neatly winding lanes surrounding a condominium with community rooms. Security guards are posted at all entrances to the village. There is a community association, and transportation is provided by LaBar Village vans. Condos sell from $95,000 to $140,000, and town houses range from $135,000 to $175,000.

Senior Housing

Senior citizen housing is available at seven Monroe County locations, and more are being added as our population of senior citizens increases. Some are managed on-site, while the Monroe County Housing Authority manages others.

Eligibility for these senior housing options is based on income guidelines, which vary from unit to unit. Look for a range of $16,000 to $28,000 for one person and $19,920 to $33,000 for two people. All must be older than 62. If you are interested in senior housing, realize that current waiting lists at each of the existing complexes are approximately three years long.

Seniors who have their own apartments or who have found a place to live but need financial assistance should look into a program administered by the U.S. Department of Housing and Urban Development, referred to as Section 8—Rental Certificate and Rental Voucher Programs. This program is processed through the housing authority in Monroe County, (570) 421-7770, for families whose income does not exceed 50 percent of the median income for the area. There are other qualifications that give preference to those in displaced situations. Section 8 pays a landlord the difference between what you can afford and the cost of your housing.

Avon Court—Monroe County Housing Authority
1055 West Main Street, Stroudsburg
(570) 421-7770
Avon Court actually is in East Stroudsburg on Day Street across from Dansbury Park, but you must contact the housing authority at the listed number or address for information. Housing is in cottages containing four units. Each unit has a kitchen, living room, bedroom, and bathroom. Avon Court is convenient to the bus and to small stores that make up the East Stroudsburg shopping area. It also is near the Loder Senior Center.

Eagle Valley Senior Housing Apartments
Stokes and Roosevelt Streets
East Stroudsburg
(570) 426-1337

Twenty one-bedroom apartments in a one-story building are administered by a private, nonprofit, low-income housing corporation with the federal Department of Housing and Urban Development. Each apartment has its own entrance and patio, and there is a community room with patio and laundry facilities. A country store across the street offers convenience items, and the bus stops at the corner. It's only a short bus ride to the Stroud Mall and other shopping areas. The library's bookmobile comes through every two weeks.

Limekiln Manor
19 East Kinney Avenue, Mt. Pocono
(570) 839-8613
Limekiln Manor is a mixed age, low-income property developed under the aegis of the U.S. Department of Agriculture Rural Development. The building, just off Highway 611 in Mount Pocono, houses 40 one- and two-bedroom apartments. Communal facilities include a sitting room, some laundry rooms, a patio, picnic tables, and benches. A bus stops at the edge of the property, but Limekiln Manor is within two blocks of lots of businesses, including a grocery store and a movie theater.

The Oaks Senior Community
Highways 390 and 191, Cresco
(570) 595-7856
A cluster of bungalows house four one-bedroom units each in Barrett Township. Grounds are landscaped around a gazebo and a community building. The facility is just off Highways 191 and 390, with some businesses nearby, but no convenience or

The Pocono Record *publishes* Dignity, *a monthly supplement for people who are "50-plus and anything but retiring." Lots of information about area happenings and benefits for seniors is published every month. The Monroe County Area Agency on Aging also puts out a newsletter for seniors. Call (570) 420-3735 to request a copy.*

The Pennsylvania Department of Aging publishes a helpful handbook for senior citizens that's called **Benefits and Rights for Older Pennsylvanians.** *Contact your area agency on aging to obtain a copy.*

food stores. Shared Ride is the only public transportation available.

Shirley Futch Plaza
4 South Kistler Street, East Stroudsburg
(570) 421-1517
This is a lovely, well-maintained senior complex. It has five floors, elevators, and all wheelchair-accessible options. The units are one-bedroom apartments, with kitchenette, living room-dining room combination, and bathroom. Grounds are nice, with tables for picnicking and relaxing. The plaza is right across from Dansbury depot and the Loder Senior Center. The bus stops just outside, and the facility is within walking distance of East Stroudsburg University and a number of small stores.

Westgate Apartments—Monroe County Housing Authority
1055 West Main Street, Stroudsburg
(570) 421-7770
Westgate is across from Stroudsburg High School and Stroudsburg Park. It has five floors of efficiency apartments, with a few one-bedroom apartments. Upper-story apartments have balconies. Grounds are well maintained, with walkways and benches, and a bus stops at the front door. A Wawa convenience store is just up the street, and the center of town is about a 5-block walk away.

Home Health Services

Services provided through home health service agencies include skilled nursing for blood work, catheter care, wound care, IV therapy, EKGs, nutrition counseling physical therapy, speech and occupational therapy, and hospice care. All services are coordinated through health care benefits programs provided by private insurance companies, Medicare, and Medicaid. Fees are based on insurance company guidelines for physician-ordered services. For those in need of further assistance, some fees may be picked up by United Way or other charitable organizations.

We list just a few of the available services for seniors who need help to continue living at home. The number of services is extensive, so contact your area hospital, area agency on aging, or phone directory for others. Here are a few:

The Visiting Nurse Association (VNA), (570) 421-5390, provides hospice services and works with area hospitals and the Monroe County Agency on Aging, (570) 420-3735, which can supply information on other home health care options.

Pocono Eldercare, Highway 390 in Promised Land Village, (570) 676-3359, offers daily or weekly nonmedical in-home assistance. Help with bathing, medication reminders, meals, light housekeeping, shopping, and other nonmedical needs are available 24 hours a day, seven days a week. Eldercare, which also accepts those not yet elderly, serves Monroe, Pike, and Wayne Counties, as well as the Lehigh Valley. The agency also supplies traveling companions for seniors who need help to get to special family events.

In Pike County, arrangements for home health care, including meals for the homebound, are coordinated through the Pike County Area Agency on Aging, (570) 775-5550. The community health nurse arranges in-home assistance for the elderly.

In Wayne County, Wayne Home Health Services, (570) 253-8431, is the key provider for home health needs. The Wayne County Area Agency on Aging, (570) 253-4262 also offers referrals to home health services.

In Carbon County, Carbon County Home Health Care provides personal service and health care to eligible clients as part of Gnaden Heutten Memorial Hospital's health system. Call (610) 377-7157 for service information.

Nursing Homes and Assisted Living

Like home health care agencies, nursing homes and assisted living facilities are too numerous to list here, and your choice may depend upon geography, religion, personal needs, and the feel you get for the place. Contact your area agency on aging (see the previous section).

HEALTH CARE

The Poconos constitute a rural outback in the midst of the otherwise urbanized Eastern Seaboard, but that does not translate into substandard medical care. The region is served by four main not-for-profit hospitals, one of which—the Pocono Medical Center in East Stroudsburg—was cited by Consumers' Checkbook's Guide to Hospitals as having one of the lowest death rates in the nation. The facility placed in the top 256 of 5,500 hospitals surveyed.

The Pocono Medical Center, the winner of several national awards and citations, carries more than 1,100 employees on its payroll and has 180 doctors, covering 30 specialties, on staff.

Pocono Medical Center primarily serves Monroe and Pike Counties. The West End is covered by Gnaden Heutten Memorial Hospital in Lehighton and Palmerton Hospital in Palmerton, while Wayne Memorial Hospital covers the Lake Wallenpaupack area. Walk-in services generally are available through these hospitals' emergency rooms, and all four offer extensive health care services. Major health problems requiring specialists not available in the area are best served at facilities in Scranton, Allentown/Bethlehem, Philadelphia, New York, and Danville, PA, where the Geisinger Medical Center, considered one of the top hospitals in the country, provides many area residents with specialists. Geisinger recently opened a new state-of-the art satellite hospital in Mount Pocono.

There are a few specialization centers, such as Gnaden Heutten, Stepping Stones individualized mental health program, and the Dale and Frances Hughes Cancer Center of the Pocono Health System. Individualized home health care can be provided through the home health and nursing agencies in the area, most of which work in connection with area hospitals or through physicians' offices. These services generally are recommended by doctors. If you need them, your doctor, the hospital, or, if you are a senior citizen, area agencies on aging, will provide you with the needed referrals and information (see the "Retirement" section for more details).

Hospitals have limited ambulance service. Most ambulance service is provided by volunteer and privately owned ambulance corps. Volunteer ambulance services have been the backbone of the Pocono support system for a long time, though private companies are moving into the area and, in some cases, supplanting the volunteer responders. All the volunteer services are run by local responders who are trained EMTs. Trained First Responders are on call for each local ambulance corps. When you move into an area, check with your local hospital or municipal clerk to find out which ambulance group serves your location. The emergency number to call in Monroe, Carbon, and Pike Counties is 911. Dialing 0 for operator will get you emergency care in other locations.

If you're having undiagnosed breathing problems, check your basement or crawl space for mold. Several varieties of mold are endemic in the Poconos, and an allergy to any one of them can be devastating.

Hospitals

STROUDSBURG/EAST STROUDSBURG

Most Monroe County and Pike County doctors are affiliated with Pocono Medical Center. This 192-bed facility provides extensive services in every area of need, from birth to life-threatening illness. Pocono Medical Center's Dale and Frances Hughes Cancer Center is an affiliate of the Jefferson Hospital Network and provides the kind of state-of-the-art radiation, clinical trials, and chemotherapy usually found only in academic health centers. It is considered one of the top cancer treatment facilities on the East Coast. The newly renovated emergency room averages more than 56,000 visits annually, making it one of Pennsylvania's busiest. The Clementine Abeloff Community Health Center provides sick and well child care, and dental care to uninsured and underinsured children up to the age of 18. The hospital also offers many wellness and education programs to the community. The mental health needs of the community also are met through this hospital's Mental Health Services, and its coordination with Mental Health-Mental Retardation (MH-MR) for the Carbon, Monroe, and Pike County areas, a centralized mental health agency, (570) 421-2901 or (800) 338-6467.

Outpatient and ambulatory services, including same-day surgery, are provided through this hospital. The center also maintains and immunization registry, the first of its kind in Pennsylvania.

Each of the hospitals listed here has a referral service. To reach physicians in other locations in eastern Pennsylvania, you can call Eastern Pennsylvania Health Network (EPHN) Physician Finder, 801 Ostrum Street, Bethlehem, (800) 422-7340 or (800) 851-0268.

The Pocono Medical Center has a physician referral service at (800) 851-0268.

Gnaden Heutten Memorial Hospital
211 North 12th Street, Lehighton
(610) 377-1300
www.ghmh.org

Gnaden Heutten Memorial Hospital is the largest and most comprehensive health care facility in Carbon County. The 202-bed hospital offers a wide range of services, including cardiac rehabilitation, physical speech and occupational therapies, same-day surgery, mammography, ultrasound, radiology and nuclear medicine, oncology and chemotherapy, and inpatient and outpatient mental health services.

The Women's Health Center, providing a full scope of women's health services, has offices in Lehighton and Tamaqua and at the Gnaden Heutten Health Center in Brodheadsville, (610) 681-3300. Gnaden Huetten's new "Health Works" Wellness Center offers a state-of-the-art fitness facility and health care education. Call (570) 386-8080 for membership information.

Besides offering a full range of inpatient and outpatient services to residents of Carbon, Monroe, and Schuykill Counties, Gnaden Heutten also offers many educational programs and provides support groups for diabetes, cancer, laryngectomies, arthritis, caregivers, and menopause. Services for older acute-care adults are provided by the New Seasons program. Gnaden Heutten is accredited by the Joint Commission on Accreditation of Hospitals.

Palmerton Hospital
135 Lafayette Avenue, Palmerton
(610) 826-3141
www.palmertonhospital.com

This hospital is a 70-bed, full service acute care facility. It provides emergency, medical/surgical, obstetrical, gynecological, and pediatric care. It is a modern community hospital with advanced technology. The hospital sponsors many outpatient support programs and community service activities.

Outpatient facilities include a modern same-day surgery suite, radiology, nuclear medicine, ultrasound, certified mammography suite, medical laboratory, and extensive cardiology testing, including echocardiology, EKGs, and stress testing. The hospital also provides outpatient physical therapy and has a popular pulmonary and cardiac rehab lab.

Palmerton Hospital is affiliated with St. Luke's Hospital in Bethlehem, a tertiary care center, and is a member of the Eastern Pennsylvania Health Network.

Palmerton also has satellite offices staffed by hospital-affiliated physicians throughout the area. For details, call the hospital switchboard.

MILFORD/LAKE WALLENPAUPACK AREA

Wayne Memorial Hospital
601 Park Street, Honesdale
(570) 253-8100
www.wmh.org
This is a 98-bed, nonprofit, community owned and operated acute care hospital. Wayne Memorial operates two outpatient clinics in Milford, (570) 296-6358, and Stourbridge Mall in Honesdale, (570) 253-7322, and six laboratory and testing centers: Wayne Memorial Hospital (24 hours), (570) 253-8127; Pike County Medical Center, (570) 775-7100; Hamlin Outpatient Center, (570) 689-4670; Lakewood Medical Center, (570) 798-2828; Greentown Family Medical Center, (570) 676-5575; and Marie Cheryle P. Lingat, M.D., (570) 253-0800.

Wayne Memorial is connected to HealthNet, Pennsylvania's Telemedicine Program. This system allows local physicians and patients to consult with specialists in other hospitals via face-to-face teleconferencing all over the country.

The hospital's Home Health Department provides home-health options for at-home care, and a maternity program

called New Beginnings offers the latest in care from labor through delivery in one homelike room. Some other areas of its extensive services are occupational therapy, cardiology, lithotripsy, childbirth education, a laboratory and regional blood bank, community health education, oncology and radiation consultation, social services, surgery sibling education, a progressive care unit, advanced life support, van services, and volunteer ambulance transport. Wayne Memorial Health System includes two facilities designed for long-term care: Wayne Woodlands Manor, a skilled nursing facility and residential rehabilitation center, (570) 488-7130; and Murray Tufts Garrett Manor, an assisted living residence on the banks of the Delaware river, (570) 729-7140. The hospital even offers acupuncture, homeopathic remedies, and advice on alternative therapies at Fair Avenue Medical Center and Greentown Family Medical Center.

Mental Health Services/ Drug and Alcohol Rehabilitation

Most area hospitals provide mental health services. However, there are psychiatric facilities in the surrounding areas. Your physician or psychiatrist is the best source for this help, and consultation is required for referral and admission.

Drug and alcohol problems can be addressed through the Drug and Alcohol Commission, (570) 421-1960, and Greenway Behavioral center (see subsequent entry).

STROUDSBURG/EAST STROUDSBURG

Greenway Center for Behavioral Healthcare Services
Highways 314 and 715, Henryville
(570) 688-9162, (800) 832-6402
This facility offers full drug and alcohol inpatient treatment programs for youth

and adults, including a relapse program for those who have returned to addictive behavior after treatment. There are private counselors, Alcoholics Anonymous meetings, psychodrama groups, recreation therapy, and a full line of insurance-accepted rehabilitation services.

Mental Health-Mental Retardation Program
Carbon-Monroe-Pike Counties
730 Phillips Street, Stroudsburg
(570) 421-2901, (800) 338-6467
Mental Health-Mental Retardation Program, Carbon-Monroe-Pike Counties, is a county agency that operates in each of the counties cited. Counseling is available for children and adults. for MH-MR services, the agency's Family and Child Together program, and the Mental Retardation Department for Monroe and Pike Counties, call (570) 421-2901. The Carbon County office can be reached at (610) 377-0773.

Pocono Medical Center, Mental Health Services
206 East Brown Street, East Stroudsburg
(570) 476-3393
An entire floor at this medical facility is dedicated to mental health patients. Patients can be admitted through the emergency room or an admitting doctor.

Hospice/Hope Services

STROUDSBURG/EAST STROUDSBURG

Visiting Nurse Association/Hospice of Monroe County
500 Independence Drive, East Stroudsburg
(570) 421-5390
Hospice/VNA of Monroe County offers in-home terminal care. The organization is nonprofit, funded through the United Way, and the charge to you is based on your ability to pay.

Alternative/Holistic Health Care

Conventional medicine, with its emphasis on corrective surgery and prescription drugs, is not the only healing discipline being practiced today. Holistic and homeopathic approaches involving a wide range of therapies, from acupuncture to various massage techniques to the metaphysical, are enjoying a growing popularity, and all of them are well represented in the Poconos. There are too many individual practitioners of the various healing arts to mention any of them by name, but there are a few outstanding umbrella organizations under which several disciplines are practiced; they are cited here. Chiropractors, of course, are prevalent throughout the area.

Delaware Water Gap/ Shawnee-on-Delaware

Deerfield Manor Spa
Highway 402 and Coolbaugh Road
Marshalls Creek
(570) 223-0160
This luxury spa (see the related Close-up in our Accommodations chapter) offers a wide range of health and fitness services to clientele who stay anywhere from a weekend to two weeks. The gourmet menu emphasizes low-fat, low-calorie eating. A maximum of 33 guests at any given time stay in 22 rooms, and while most clients are women, increasing numbers of men are making reservations. Services include massages, facials, body wraps, aroma therapy, make-up and color analysis, yoga, t'ai chi, Reiki, hiking, aerobics, body sculpting, gym workouts, mind-body-spirit lectures, swimming, sauna, and Jacuzzi. None of the services offered is covered by health insurance.

Stroudsburg/East Stroudsburg

Wellspring Holistic Center
560 Main Street, Stroudsburg
(570) 421-3708
This group, which holds classes in yoga and QiGong—a Chinese movement therapy similar to t'ai chi—offers teaching and treatment through a wide range of holistic disciplines, including Reiki, which essentially is a laying on of hands to channel universal life energy in nonmanipulative therapy; foot reflexology, craniosacral therapy, and neurofacial release; tae kwon do; pilates; hypnotherapy, and therapeutic dance techniques ranging from belly dancing to Japanese sword dancing. The center also offers training for midwives, a women's circle, and "Music Together," a program of music therapy for children, newborn through age 5.

Shooting for the Moon Holistic Center
Highway 209 North, just past the flea
market, Marshalls Creek
(570) 223-0103
This eclectic new-age shop includes a holistic center emphasizing Reiki, with free Reiki exchange, levels one and two; high yoga and general massage therapies; and classes in aromatherapy, all given by a certified massage therapist and Reiki master. (See our Shopping chapter for more details.)

Important Numbers to Know

GENERAL
- Adult Services Cooperative, (570) 421-3050
- AIDS/HIV Warmline, (570) 688-9716

ABUSE
- Child Abuse Monroe County, (570) 420-3590
- Childline PA Child Abuse Hotline, (800) 932-0313

- Domestic Violence, (570) 421-4200
- Childhelp USA (National Hotline for Child/Adult and Family Violence), (800) 422-4453

CHILDREN
- Children and Youth Services of Monroe County, (570) 420-3590
- National Child Abuse Hotline, (800) 422-4453
- National Youth Crisis Hotline, (800) 442-4673

CRISIS INTERVENTION/SUICIDE
- Crisis Intervention Center—Carbon, Monroe, and Pike Counties, (570) 421-2901, after hours toll free, (800) 338-6467
- Suicide Prevention, (570) 421-2901, after hours hotline, (800) 338-6467

ELDERLY
- Monroe County Area Agency on Aging, (570) 420-3735
- Pike County Area Agency on Aging, (570) 775-5550
- *Elder Abuse:*
  Carbon County, (800) 441-1315
  Monroe County, (570) 420-3735
  Pike County, (800) 233-8911
  Wayne County, (800) 648-9620

MENTAL HEALTH/DRUG AND ALCOHOL
- Alcoholics Anonymous, (570) 424-8532
- Monroe County Drug and Alcohol Commission, (570) 421-1960
- Mental Health-Mental Retardation (MH-MR), Monroe, Pike, and Carbon Counties, (570) 421-2901
- Al-Anon and Alateen, (570) 424-1976
- Narcotics Anonymous:
  Pocono Region, (570) 421-6618
- Monroe County State Health Center (referrals only), (570) 424-3020
- Pennsylvania Substance Abuse Information Center, (570) 787-9761, (800) 582-7746
- Nar-Anon Hotline, (610) 778-2100

If you live in a home with no street address, check with your township as to how to describe your location to emergency fire or ambulance operators. Most townships have numbered maps that show everyone's house. If you have a number, you won't have to spend 10 minutes giving directions to your home. Post the map number on every telephone.

- National Clearinghouse for Alcohol and Drug Information, (800) 729-6686
- The Center for Substance Abuse Treatment Hotline, (800) 662-HELP

SEXUALLY TRANSMITTED DISEASES

- C.D.C. National AIDS Hotline, (800) 342-2437
- Pennsylvania AIDS Factline, (800) 662-6080
- STD Hotline, (800) 227-8922
- Pennsylvania VD Hotline, (800) 462-4966
- Planned Parenthood, (570) 424-8306

WOMEN

- Women's Resources of Monroe County, (570) 421-4200
- Planned Parenthood of Northeastern Pennsylvania, (570) 424-8306
- Rape Crisis, (570) 421-4200

CHILD CARE

Sooner or later, every parent faces the same question: Who will take care of my children while I work or when I'm out sampling the venues in the Nightlife chapter of *The Insiders' Guide?*

The answers you find to the child care question will vary, depending on whether you're looking for care during the working day or need someone to watch over your lambs in the evening. You will choose either a babysitter, who usually comes to your home; family day care, usually a mom who is happy to add your children to her own, for a fee; or a day-care center, licensed and regulated by the state, which may offer more services and have an educational component.

The kind of care you choose depends on your child and your personal needs. A babysitter will take care of all your children, may have a more flexible schedule, and may be talked into doing some housework. If you depend on one individual, though, you may be out of luck when he or she is sick or has other commitments. Day care, therefore, may be your best choice, but approach the option with caution.

Some family-based day-care providers are inspected and licensed by the state. Others are less formal. If you find someone you like, your child will spend the day in a good family atmosphere, theoretically doing the things he or she would do with you if you were home. Children often develop a strong bond with their caregivers, and sometimes caregivers are more experienced parents than new moms and dads and may be good sources of advice. Some caregivers, however, plunk the children in front of the television all day and insist that their pay be under the table so they won't have to declare their income for taxes. In addition to the fact that it's illegal for a caregiver to take money without declaring it as income, you can't claim your rightfully earned tax credits on what you paid. Also, a family-based caregiver may go out of business without warning or may have vacation needs that don't correspond with your own.

Day-care centers work with large groups of children. Here your child has better socialization opportunities, but may not get the individualized attention he or she needs. Many centers teach as well as care for the children. Licensed day-care centers must meet state requirements for health, safety, staffing ratios, and educational programs. This verifies that basic safety and health regulations have been met. The center applies for certification by submitting appropriate paperwork and verifications of faculty size, professional staff, equipment, course of study, and health and safety specifications. Certification is evaluated every year to ensure compliance with state standards.

Standards cover safety, health, quality of care, and education in day-care settings. Safety standards require interior and exterior areas to be free of physical hazards and to be of adequate size for the number of children using the facility. Health standards require that someone certified in first aid and CPR for children be at the facility during all hours of operation. The standards for trained personnel require at least one certified early childhood or elementary teacher be on staff at all times. Also, all day-care workers must accumulate 6 to 12 hours of training annually in first aid and early childhood education.

Many preschool programs run half-day and are geared to at-home parents who want to expose their children to an educational and social environment. Some preschool programs center on specific interests such as music, gymnastics, swimming, or art. In many cases, such centers are not licensed preschools according to state guidelines. A designated preschool or nursery school requires a minimum of two hours of planned instruction each day, and the staff must meet certain education requirements.

When you are looking at day care, ask the following questions:

- Am I comfortable with the caregivers? Do they reflect my views on child care?
- Does anybody smoke in the presence of children? (Not only is smoking a bad example for children; it has been shown that exposure to secondhand smoke increases the incidence of respiratory problems.)
- Do the children sit in front of a television set for long periods of time, or are they actively engaged?
- Is there an open door policy; can I visit at any time?

- How do care providers communicate with the parents? Is it on a regular basis?
- What is the ratio of children to staff?
- Is a schedule visibly posted so that I can check where my child will be and what he or she will be doing?
- Does the facility have accommodations for physically challenged children?
- Does the staff have experience with children with developmental problems?
- Does the staff treat children with respect, and are they able to meet the needs of different types of children?
- If there is a diaper changing area, is there a sink nearby?
- Does the facility look safe and fun?
- Are the snacks and meals nutritious?
- What is the course of action if a child is disobedient?
- Are there lots of age-appropriate play materials?
- Are the facility and its staff licensed?
- Does anyone have first aid or CPR training?
- Does everyone have crime and child abuse clearances?
- Can I talk to other parents who use this caregiver?
- Do the children look happy?

There are too many day-care centers in the area to be specifically detailed here, but there are a number of agencies ready, willing, and able to assist you in finding one that meets your needs. Call any of the following for that assistance.

The Stroudsburg YMCA has before- and after-school programs for children. Activities include help with homework, arts and crafts, sports, and swimming for children up to age 12. School buses for Stroudsburg schools pick the children up and drop them off at the Y. This program fills up fast, so call early if you're interested: (570) 421-2525, ext. 133.

Federally Funded Programs

Head Start
Monroe County, part of Pocono Services for Families and Children
212 West Fourth Street, East Stroudsburg
(570) 421-2711

Carbon County, 150 West Phillips Street
Coaldale
(570) 645-7578

Lackawanna, Pike and Wayne Counties
(Scranton-Lackawanna Human Development Agency)
200 Adams Avenue, 2nd Floor, Scranton
(570) 963-6633
Head Start is a federally funded program that is responsive to community require-ments and needs. Each Head Start pro-gram has locally designed options based on a community needs assessment that can change as the community changes. The program is reviewed by a county board of directors, a policy council, com-munity representatives, and parents par-ticipating in the program.

There are two basic types of pro-grams: combination-based and center-based. Combination-based programs support the home as the learning environ-ment and the parents as teachers within that environment. A Head Start teacher visits the home three times during the month, working with the child and the parents, teaching, reviewing learning tech-niques, and discussing age-appropriate development. Once a month, the child and parents attend a class at the center to bolster peer interaction and developmen-tal skills.

In the center-based program, the child attends classes five days a week for 12 months or four days a week during the regular school year. There are also four home visits a year. This program is usually based on social skills as well as preschool learning skills and development.

Children ages 3 and 4 are eligible for Head Start. It is free for families that meet locally defined income requirements.

In Monroe County, Pocono Services for Families and Children offers many more services, including training to day-care providers and a library of toys for day-care centers to borrow.

State Agencies

Pennsylvania Department of Education, Nonpublic and Private Schools Division
333 Market Street, Harrisburg
(717) 783-6788
www.pde.state.pa.us
The Department of Education licenses preschools and nursery schools, which are defined as half-day programs focusing on education. The department has its own set of requirements and regulations sepa-rate from those of the Department of Welfare and can supply a list of licensed preschools and nursery schools as well as a pamphlet outlining regulations and requirements. The department requires appropriate licensing for any day-care center offering a preschool or nursery school as a half-day adjunct to its day-care program.

Pennsylvania Department of Public Welfare, Daycare Unit
339 South Office Building
100 Lackawanna Avenue, Scranton
(570) 963-4371, (800) 222-2108
www.dpw.state.pa.us
Call or write the Department of Public Welfare to obtain a pamphlet outlining regulations for different day-care situa-tions, as well as a list of all licensed and certified day-care facilities in the area. The agency also provides information about the incidence and nature of verified viola-tions at day-care centers, including any that may have occurred at the one you are considering.

Playgroups, Inc. + Moms + Dads + Kids = Instant Friendships

Donna Fernald moved to the Poconos in 1998. She had young children and knew no one with whom they could play, so she hung up flyers seeking children for a play group. She expected to hear from a few moms, but the response was so enormous that she realized there was a need for such a service, and formed a nonprofit organization to meet it.

Today, Playgroups, Inc. serves 100 families, publishes a newsletter, maintains a Web site, runs many special events, and organizes many small neighborhood play groups. The large events are listed in local publications. A party at Thunder Creek Quarry and an open day at Big Wheel (see our Recreation chapter) are typical, but they also hold a "Mom's Night Out" and a "Dad's Night Out," theme-based educational events, and field trips. The annual family picnic, an old fashioned picnic in the park with hot dogs and hamburgers, races, and lots of games, is a highlight of the Playgroups year. The newsletter has parenting tips, recipes, and announcements about upcoming Playgroups events. Playgroups also runs fundraisers for a number of community projects. Small groups, usually with seven to eight children and their moms, constitute the heart of Playgroups. When you join, they find a group that is close to where you live with children in the same age range as yours.

Typically, the small groups meet weekly, convening at a different member's house each time, but the mothers may decide to meet more often, at a park or, in the case of one group, late enough that the dads can watch the kids while the moms go shopping. Usually, while the children play, the moms get social time, but groups sometimes let a couple of moms watch the children while the others go out. When children enter kindergarten, they graduate from Playgroups, but they often return for parties.

You may think this organization exists primarily for the benefit of the children, but the moms get at least as much out of it. Playgroups, Inc., has helped create a community for many families, especially those who are newcomers to the Poconos.

To contact Playgroups, Inc., call (570) 223-7066, write to P.O. Box 1071, East Stroudsburg, PA 18301, or go to their Web site, www.playgroupsinc.org.

The Pennsylvania State University Cooperative Extension

Some of the extensions will send you lists of registered day-care facilities, newsletters, and pamphlets on parenting. Penn State, a land-grant university, has extensions in every county of Pennsylvania as required by law. Cooperative extensions in Pennsylvania offer courses for day-care providers that prepare individuals to meet state requirements for 12 hours annually of continuing child care education. They also

Inquire about financial aid when investigating day-care centers. Some offer scholarships, most offer discounts for siblings and most accept subsidized payments through certain county and state agencies. You may qualify.

offer courses for those interested in setting up centers and obtaining licenses or certifications.

The Pennsylvania State University Cooperative Extensions in the Pocono region include:

- **Monroe County,** 4499 Highway 611, Stroudsburg, one mile north of the Stroud Mall, (570) 421-6430
- **Pike County,** 506 Broad Street, Milford, (570) 296-3400
- **Wayne County,** Northeastern Child Care Services, 1356 North Washington Avenue, Scranton (this agency also covers Susquehanna County), (800) 559-6020
- **Carbon County,** Carbon County Child Care Agency, 1122 North Street, Jim Thorpe, (570) 325-2226

County Agency

**Childcare Information Services of Monroe County
730 Phillips Street, Stroudsburg
(570) 420-3590, (866) 284-5829**
Childcare Information Services maintains a list of licensed day-care facilities in Monroe County and can help you with referrals to appropriate child care centers.

If babysitting is a real problem in your area, consider starting a babysitting cooperative with other parents. In a cooperative, you sit for someone else's children and receive credit toward having your own kids watched by other parents.

They also help low-income families with reduced-cost child care.

It's a struggle to find babysitters anywhere. As soon as teens are old enough to be responsible, they get jobs at hamburger joints that pay more and provide social opportunities, or they are dating and involved in too many activities to be available to you. If you're moving into the area, start making friends and spotting teens as quickly as you can. Sometimes a friend will recommend a sitter; sometimes the mother of another child doesn't mind taking on yours for a few bucks or a promise that you will return the favor.

If you are staying at a hotel, you can probably find sitters; services are provided at most resorts for about $5.00 per hour, usually with a three-hour minimum. If you're staying at a ski resort, babysitting services are available in the lodge nurseries at reasonable rates of $3.00 to $5.00 an hour. Often, during the week, the service is free (see our Winter Sports chapter for details).

A good solution for intrepid youngsters 4 and older is to sign them up for the ski mountain's young skiers' program. These are usually half- to full-day programs that supervise the children and teach them skiing skills, leaving mom and dad free to tumble down the black diamond trails.

Day Care and Extended Care

Recently, many schools in the Poconos have added latchkey programs to meet the needs of the children of working parents, both before and after school. Prices vary from $18 to $25 a day. To learn if such service is available, with nearby bus stops or centers, call your child's school. As for extended day care, there are too many centers throughout the Poconos to list here. You must visit various centers, talk to the people running them, ask lots of questions, and watch children already enrolled to determine which is right for your child.

WORSHIP

William Penn established Pennsylvania as a place of religious tolerance, which was a rare attitude in his day, but one that explains both the fervor and the diversity of faiths that flocked to the commonwealth in the 300 years following its founding. The very place names of Pennsylvania reflect a rich religious heritage. Where else would you find such a concentration of cities and villages with names such as Bethlehem, Nazareth, Promised Land, Lords Valley, Bethany, Angels, South Canaan, and Mount Bethel—all of which are located either in or in the immediate vicinity of the Poconos?

Religious groups that settled in Pennsylvania in the 1700s include Puritans, Quakers, Dutch Reformed, Moravians, Lutherans, Methodists, Amish, Labadists, Sabbathdayers, and continually emerging splinter groups that found a home in our forests primeval. Among the first denominations represented in the Poconos region were Dutch Reformed, Lutheran, Methodist, Quaker, and Moravian. As the 1800s came to the Poconos, so did Presbyterians, Episcopalians, Wesleyans, more Methodists, African Methodists, Baptists, Shakers, Roman Catholics, Mennonites, and the Salvation Army. The 1900s saw a continuation and resurgence of earlier groups as well as the influx of even more diverse churches and faiths: Byzantine Catholics, Full Gospel Believers, followers of Islam, Hindus, Jews, Jehovah's Witnesses, Mormons; the list goes on to include more than 200 churches, synagogues, and other places of worship representing the religious freedom of thousands of Poconos residents.

An interesting corollary to the foundation of faith-generated settlements was the force of the churches in the social and cultural lives of their members. The socials, holidays (holy days), suppers, picnics, musicales, seminars, speakers' evenings, poetry readings, schools, church sings, revivals, summer camps, and outings were the cultural manna of early residents and later visitors. Today, churches remain an integral part of the social, cultural, and artistic backbone of our communities.

As noted, there are hundreds of churches and faith-related organizations in the Poconos. We do not intend to provide a directory here; you can find most of them listed in the telephone directory. Also, the local newspapers, including the *Pocono Record*, provide listings of services in their Friday and Saturday editions. Walk down any street in any town, drive down any country road, or stop at any backroads crossing, and you're sure to find a church or a sign pointing to one. We mention a few churches of historical note in this chapter. Their influence, past and present, is our focus.

In the Early Days...

Beginning in the early 1700s, congregations of Dutch Reformed, Lutherans, Quakers, Methodists, and Moravians carved homesteads out of the wilderness surrounded by the friendly Native Americans they hoped to convert to Christianity. Their missionary zeal met with much success for at least the first 25 years of interaction with the native inhabitants. Then, as we discuss in our Native Americans and History chapters, the relationship between settlers and Native Americans, missionaries and converts, was seriously damaged in the mid-18th century by the repercussions of the Walking Purchase and the French and Indian War. Native Americans were displaced from their homeland in both instances, and in neither did they go quietly.

Dutch Reformed

Dutch Reformed churches were built as early as 1741 in Shawnee. The first was a log structure that in 1752 was rebuilt with native stone. An interesting design in the architecture of the meeting house was the placement of windows above what was determined as head height to prevent worshippers from being fired upon by Native Americans during services. Today, the site is occupied by the Shawnee Presbyterian Church, which was built in 1853 on Shawnee Church road in Shawnee-on-Delaware.

Another Dutch Reformed Church still stands along US 209 in Dingmans Ferry. The church now is a home, with a Southwestern and import shop in what once was the carriage house.

Moravians

The Moravians exerted a strong presence in the 1740s. They came from settlements in the Bethlehem area to convert the natives. In 1743, they quickly established a mission at Gnadenhuetten ("tents of mercy") near what now is Lehighton. In 1747, they moved to the east side of the Lehigh River to Weissport. Believers started other missions in Stroudsburg, including the Dansbury Mission in 1747, and in the surrounding townships of Gilbert, Polk (Wechequetank), Eldred, and Kunkletown (Meniolagomaka). Much of their movement was halted by the massacre at Gnadenhuetten, the mission that became the first casualty of the French and Indian War. Some activity continued through 1760, but most of the missions were destroyed during that war.

Today, the only existing Moravian congregation in the Poconos is in Canadensis (Canadensis Moravian Church), though many more exist in the Allentown–Bethlehem area. Their contributions are still evident in the presence of renowned Moravian College in Bethle-hem. North of Canadensis, on Highway 390 South, are the remains of the Roemerville Moravian Church, now called the Wayside Gospel Chapel. If you are interested in the history of Moravians in this area, the Monroe County Historical Association, (570) 421-7703, has two volumes of Moravian diaries: *The Dansbury Diaries, 1748–1755* and *The Moravian Travel Diaries*. Another volume in the Historical Association's collection, *Moravians in the Poconos*, was written by Rev. Warren D. Wenger, former pastor of the Canadensis church. This little book describes in homespun detail the various Moravian settlements and any remains of their sites, including cemeteries. The cemetery in which 10 victims of the Gnadenhuetten massacre are buried lies just off Union Street in Lehighton. Wenger gives detailed directions to monuments, cemeteries, and church ruins, and shares interesting tidbits about his Moravian predecessors.

Methodists

Methodists also were a major missionary force in Monroe County. As early as 1788, they were established in the Stroudsburg area. In the 1800s, the Stroudsburg Methodist Church on Main Street, established in 1853 and still in existence, became the nucleus of missionary outreach to Cherry Valley, Paradise, Henryville/Oakland, and Mountainhome. Other circuits included Dutotsburg (present-day Delaware Water Gap) and Mauch Chunk (Jim Thorpe). By 1860, there were 36 Methodist churches in the area. Expansion was stopped by the Civil War. After the war, in 1868, the first African Methodist Church opened in Stroudsburg on Third Street, where it remained until 1900. The church, still standing but long abandoned, is owned by a nonprofit organization that plans to renovate it and restore it to its original condition for use as a library and museum. Today, there are almost 50 Methodist churches in the area, some still standing from the 19th century, such as Cherry Valley Methodist Church in Cherry Valley.

Presbyterians

Around 1814, Presbyterians founded the Middle Smithfield Church in a barn near Marshalls Creek and shared a pastor and elders with the Shawnee Church. In 1823, they built the red brick church still in use in Middle Smithfield Township on US 209 near Marshalls Creek. Another notable Presbyterian church is Church of the Mountain, which still is in use in Delaware Water Gap. The Stroudsburg Presbyterian Church was built in 1830 on Sarah Street on land donated by Daniel and Mary Stroud. The Strouds, who were Quakers, gave land both to Presbyterians and Methodists. Time and again, church records for various denominations reveal that land was donated by a Stroud family member, even though the family was not part of that church. That the Strouds donated land, not only to their own church but to many others, demonstrates the tolerant nature of the people in this area at that time.

Quakers

In the 1800s, the Quakers established two meeting houses in Stroudsburg, one on Ann Street and one in Quaker Alley. Originally one organization, they split over ideological differences. All that remains of their presence is two cemeteries, one on Eighth and Ann Streets and the other in Quaker Alley between Fifth and Sixth Streets. The best-known vestiges of Quaker influence are Buck Hill Falls Manor, Pocono Manor, and Skytop. These summer resorts were opened by Quakers from the Philadelphia area. They included not only beautifully appointed main hotels but also gracious "cottages" that today would be regarded as mansions. These surrounded the main grounds and were owned by

members of their respective Society of Friends groups from Philadelphia. Pocono Lake Preserve was a very quiet camp facility that did not have a resort attached. It was strictly for members only and eschewed the more elegant trappings of the other three. Today, Skytop and Pocono Manor remain prestigious resorts. For more information about them, we recommend *The Growth and Variety of Monroe County Resorts* by Roger A. Dunning; you can find a copy at the Monroe County Historical Association.

Catholics

Catholics started arriving in the Poconos in the late 1800s and now constitute the largest religious denomination in the region. The first Catholic church, St. Matthew's in East Stroudsburg, was established around 1850. Since then, several other Catholic churches have sprung up all over the Poconos. Today, their members are involved in ecumenical activities, renewal liturgies, outreach programs for the homeless and otherwise needy, and various other church-sponsored events.

Judaism

Temple Israel, in Stroudsburg, has served conservative and orthodox Jewish worshippers for 80 years. The synagogue's current congregation consists of 100 families. Temple B'Nai Harim, in Pocono Pines off Highway 940, is the only Reform con-

Temple B'Nai Harim, the only congregation of Reform Judaism in the Poconos, was founded in a coffee shop and, until construction of its new Temple, met ecumenically in Our Lady of the Lake Catholic Church. B'Nai Harim, translated from the Hebrew, is "Children of the Mountains."

gregation in the Poconos. Formed in 1997 with Rabbi Barbra Goldman-Wartell, it now serves 50 families. The only other congregation in the Poconos is the Jewish Fellowship of Hemlock Farms.

Other Churches

Another unique and remarkable "church" is the nondenominational one found at Columcille, a Celtic art and megalith center consisting of massive standing stones similar to the famed ones at Stonehenge in England. Described by its creator, the retired Rev. William Cohea, as "a playground for the spirit," this place of prayer and meditation is south of the Stroudsburgs off Highway 191 on Fox Gap Road. See the related Close-up in our Attractions chapter for details. We also have several Jehovah's Witness Kingdom Halls in the Poconos.

Sponsored Activities

The Poconos became a popular summer vacation spot in the late 1800s, attracting a host of campgrounds, camp meetings, and revivals, sponsored by a variety of church groups. Methodists were the leaders in this field, and their camp meetings became huge events. The most famous of the Methodist camp meeting grounds was at Lake Pauponomy, now Saylors Lake. In 1893, an estimated 5,000 people attended a summertime celebration of prayer, singing, and socializing. Camp meetings

gave religious group members places to vacation together. Churches also sponsored musicals, band concerts, poetry readings, picnics, suppers, and other social outings.

Today, churches in the Poconos still offer members, and anyone else who wants to come, a variety of social activities, and they continue to contribute to and support the arts. Every week in summer, you'll find church-sponsored socials, tasting suppers, strawberry and blueberry festivals, corn and doggie roasts, and square dances. Throughout the year, you can enjoy concerts sponsored by church-related groups. Sunday school classes perform plays, particularly during the holiday seasons and vacation Bible school sessions. Many churches sponsor art events, too, and concerts by young artists are coordinated by music teacher associations and other musical groups within the churches. Some churches lend theatrical groups practice space, and some hold music school programs open to the community in their buildings.

Arts on the Mountain (see our Arts and Culture chapter) grew out of the Trinity Episcopal Church (1896) in Mount Pocono. Artists in all areas participate in dramatic productions as well as opera, art songs, violin concerts, and other music events. To celebrate its centennial in 1996, church members organized the Trinity Centennial Orchestra, which performs its own summer concerts. Arts on the Mountain also presents shows, open and free to the public, featuring local artists.

The Presbyterian Church of the Mountain, in Delaware Water Gap, is a strong supporter of the arts and other activities. It was out of this church—particularly the work of its former pastor, the Rev. William Cohea (see the Columcille Close-up in our Attractions chapter) with local jazz greats Phil Woods, Urbie Green, and others—that the Delaware Water Gap Jazz Festival was born. And from this popular festival came the Jazz Mass CD from the annual event of the same name that is part of the Delaware Water Gap Celebration of the

Arts. Sunday evening concerts are presented all summer long in the outdoor gazebo on the church lawn (inside if it's raining). Church of the Mountain members built and maintain a year-round shelter for Appalachian Trail hikers.

Historic St. Marks' Episcopal Church (see the "Architectural Gems" section of our Attractions chapter) presents an annual concert series, aptly named "Music from Historic St. Mark's Episcopal Church," which consists of church recitals and concerts throughout the year.

Recommended Reading

Many informative books about worship in the Poconos carry titles that do not specifically indicate them as books about churches. The Monroe County Historical Association has an 1886 edition of a massive volume (to which we are greatly indebted) titled *History of Wayne, Pike and Monroe Counties, Pennsylvania,* by Alfred Matthews. It gives detailed accounts of the development of various churches, including who started them and who donated land for their buildings. It is

interesting not only because of its informal style but also because it was written in chronological proximity to the events it describes. The historical association also has history files of many different churches and many other volumes that touch on the influence of places of worship in Poconos history.

Another significant book in the Monroe County Historical Association's collection is the *Guide to Cemeteries and Burial Grounds of Monroe County, Pennsylvania,* compiled by Dale E. Berger. For those who enjoy reading about history and stories detailed on tombstones, or for those searching for long-lost records of dates and births, this book is a good find. It is well-researched, and much of its information about early church histories is culled from the aforementioned *History of Wayne, Pike and Monroe Counties, Pennsylvania,* condensed and described in the present-day context.

Whether you choose to worship in song, through art, or through prayer, and wherever you choose to do so—in churches, among rocks, in synagogues or temples—the Poconos have a place for you. The ideals of religious tolerance espoused by William Penn remain in practice by your hosts and neighbors.

EDUCATION ⬤

In general, the public schools in the Poconos are good. If you prefer private school, your choices are mostly confined to church-affiliated schools and a couple of Montessori-based institutions. A large number of parents homeschool their children. Some of them are dissatisfied with the local alternatives, some have a strong independent streak and see home-based education as one piece of their lifestyle, and some keep their children out of the schools for religious reasons.

Many of the public schools have had to renovate in the last few years and thus have updated their specialized facilities, especially their science and computer labs and their music rooms. Many of the schools participate in the state's artists-in-education program, bringing professional artists to their schools for intensive work with the students. And most of the schools have lots of extracurricular activities that enhance the academic programs offered. In Monroe County, the attendance runs at more than 90 percent, which is high compared to schools in many other areas and may even mean that most of the students are happy to be in school. Standardized test scores are decent, too.

Some Pocono high schools, such as Stroudsburg and East Stroudsburg, cooperate with area colleges so that individual students can take certain courses at a college level. For example, one Stroudsburg High School student whizzed through French, Spanish, and German, so the school arranged for her to take Russian at East Stroudsburg University.

The biggest pressure on the schools is the phenomenal growth in Monroe and Pike counties. Most of the districts are coping and are engaged in major building projects to meet the needs of their growing communities, but most are bursting at the seams. As more students enroll, it has become necessary to raise taxes to fund the increased need for services in the schools. In some districts, we have reached a crisis situation, with property taxes jumping up hundreds of dollars in a single year, elders being taxed out of their homes, the general populace demanding that school districts cut their spending, and parents of students begging the school boards not to cut so much that the quality of education is threatened. A number of money-saving suggestions are being studied, including split-shift schooling, year-round schooling, paying for after-school activities, and more, but thus far, no solutions have been implemented. There has also been serious talk statewide about shifting the taxes away from property and onto some other taxing vehicle, but again, it's still talk.

Because these are large districts covering a variety of communities, they must serve the needs of a range of students. The children of college professors share a classroom with the children of families who have been poor and under-educated for generations. These children are all entitled to an excellent education, and all have limitless potential if they are provided with the proper resources. The schools must have honors programs, regular academic offerings, vocational training for those who do not plan to go to college, and special education for children with special needs.

State law mandates that the schools must provide a student with appropriate education. In other words, if a child is gifted, an individualized education program (a.k.a. IEP) must be devised that will meet her or his needs. In most districts this will include a certain number of hours of "enrichment."

Likewise, if a child has learning differences, which may or may not correspond to differences in intelligence, the school and parents must agree to an IEP that provides the kind of support the child needs to reach full potential.

Many of our special-education programs are excellent, but the parents must be the strongest voice for a child with special needs. Often a child is put into an existing program that may or may not be suitable. If you feel your child is not being adequately served, you must set up a meeting and revise the IEP. Ideally, the parent, who knows his or her child best, can work with the professional educator, who knows what resources are available, to design a good program for that child. Since all children are different, some are better served than others. If you're dissatisfied with the accommodations made for your child's special needs, talk to the school, ask for a meeting, and work to find the right solution.

Special education is expensive. Although the average student costs a district around $7,000 a year, a special-ed program may run as high as $26,000 because a child may need more one-on-one time with an educator, may need special equipment, or may have to be sent to a school that can serve him or her better. Some teachers and administrators resent spending so much money on students who may be less cooperative than the "forgotten" students in the middle. When a child resists learning, many educators dislike using more resources on that child and squeezing the rest of the school's budget. In the long run, though, when a special-ed program works, and a student is able to achieve his or her potential, we taxpayers are probably saving money. That student should be able to find work and, in turn, become a taxpayer, rather than running the risk of needing special services from the state for the rest of his or her life. In fact, many special-ed students grow up to make great contributions to our society.

If you're planning to move to the Poconos, especially if you're moving to Monroe County where you can choose to settle in one of four school districts, take time to get to know the schools. Most of

When it snows, most of the districts are quick to delay or cancel school. If you wake to the slightest bit of snow, check one of the following sources. School closings and delays are broadcast by: WVPO (840 AM), WSBG (93.5 FM), WODG (99.9 FM), WBRE-TV (Channel 28), WFMZ-TV (Channel 69), WNEP-TV (Channel 16), WBRC-TV (Channel 13), and WYOU-TV (Channel 22).

the districts have differences in philosophy, size, curriculum, and student diversity. Make an appointment to talk to the principals of the schools you are considering. Visit, and ask for information on curriculum, class size, extracurricular activities, and the status of the schools' graduates. You may find yourself more attracted to some districts, which can help you narrow down your choices on where to settle.

Kindergarten is not required by law in the State of Pennsylvania, although it is strongly recommended. To enter kindergarten, students must be five or older on or before September 1. To enter first grade, students must be six or older on or before September 1. Proof of age—a birth or baptismal certificate—and immunization records must be presented at the time of registration. You should also bring your child's social security number. Most districts require proof of residency—settlement papers, utility bills, a lease, or a letter from your real estate agent or landlord. In Pennsylvania, children must have a medical examination upon entry into a school as well as during sixth grade and during eleventh grade. Parents are encouraged to have their children examined by a family physician, but some school districts will provide a medical exam if the parents cannot meet this request. Parents are notified of the time and date of the exam and are encouraged to be present. The hepatitis B shot series is required for all students and must be administered before they can enter kindergarten.

*Charter schools—public schools orga-
nized by a group of parents, teachers,
or community members—are growing in
Pennsylvania. Consider one if the regular schools don't work for your child,
but examine it carefully before making a
final decision. Charter schools that
teach over the Internet have been challenged, and some others have closed
suddenly, leaving students high and dry.
Ask lots of questions.*

We have two institutions of higher
education in the Poconos—East Strouds-
burg University and Northampton Com-
munity College's Monroe County Campus.
Just outside the Poconos, colleges and
universities include the University of
Scranton, Lehigh University, Muhlenberg
College, Moravian College, Kutztown Uni-
versity of Pennsylvania, Lafayette College,
Marywood College, Cedar Crest College,
Penn State–Wilkes-Barre/Scranton, King's
College, Wilkes University, and Centenary
College in Hackettstown, NJ.

PUBLIC SCHOOL DISTRICTS

Since so much goes on in each district,
highlighting all the parameters would be
impossible. We'll touch on the main points
and provide you with the numbers to call
for more information. You can also peruse
their Web pages on the Internet. The best
way to get answers to your questions is
by checking out the schools for yourself.
Most principals are happy to meet with
the parents of prospective students.

Sports are important to many in these
school districts. Young athletes can start
soccer and T-ball at 5 years old. Would-be
football stars can join the midget league
in third grade. By the time students are
ready to enter high school, most of them
already have some experience in the
sports they want to play. When the school
district is large, a greater variety of sports

is available. If the district is small, your
child is more likely to be part of the team,
even if he or she is only an average player.

Music resounds in the school districts.
Many of the bands are especially strong,
and they often achieve state and national
recognition.

Instrumental music starts in the fourth
grade in most districts as an elective class
and continues through high school. The
influence of music education is apparent
in the number of students who, after
graduation, continue to participate in
community orchestras, bands, choral societies, and musical productions.

Vocal music is strong here, and students take part in choruses, concert
choirs, swing choirs, musical productions,
and show choirs. The caliber of performance from these groups at every school
is exhilarating. Stage shows put on by
high schools tend to be elaborate and
professional. Tickets sell out quickly.

Each school district has enrichment
programs and honors-level classes as well
as special education accommodations.
Students from the Pocono districts have
been accepted into top colleges and universities.

Extracurricular activities support academic excellence. Those inclined toward
scholarly pursuits can participate in
scholastic scrimmage teams, math scrimmage teams, and forensic competitions in
debate and speech. We have science fairs,
geography fairs, and spelling bees.

The Monroe Career and Technical Institute (www.monroecti.org) supports the
Pocono Mountain, East Stroudsburg,
Stroudsburg, Notre Dame, and Pleasant
Valley school districts. An important project there is the Student-Built House
Project. A typical student-built house has
hardwood floors, a stone fireplace and lots
of luxurious touches. The students have
done everything from the foundation to
the wiring. The homes are part of a development adjoining the school, and all of
them have been sold. Although the homes
are built by students, the instructors hold

them to a higher standard than many builders use, so they are beautifully built.

The school's Allied Health Program provides a health-related curriculum to prepare students for careers in health care services.

To learn more about the school districts, contact them individually at the addresses and phone numbers that follow.

Stroudsburg/East Stroudsburg

East Stroudsburg Area School District
321 North Courtland Street
East Stroudsburg
(570) 424-8500
www.cavalier.net
Six elementary schools, two intermediate schools, and two senior high schools comprise the East Stroudsburg district, which covers 214 square miles of Monroe and Pike counties, serves a student population of more than 7,700, and employs a number of innovative learning projects. Resica Elementary School integrates the arts into all parts of its curriculum and has received statewide recognition for its program. Business Education Partnerships matches representatives from local businesses with math and science classes to enhance instruction. The band program is especially strong, and East Stroudsburg Area High School South's band was one of three in the state to be invited to play at the Pennsylvania Music Educator's Association conference in 2002.

Almost half of the certified staff in the district hold a master's degree or master's equivalency. Because the population of the district is increasing rapidly, a new campus in Lehman Township opened for the 2000–2001 school year. The campus includes an elementary school, an intermediate school, and a high school.

Stroudsburg Area School District
123 Linden Street, Stroudsburg
(570) 421-1990
www.sburg.org
Stroudsburg has a population of approximately 5,200 students. It serves Stroudsburg, Delaware Water Gap, and Hamilton and Stroud townships and includes five elementary schools, an intermediate school, a junior high school, and a high school.

Since growth has been comparatively slow in Stroudsburg, schools in this district have maintained their neighborhood feel. The high school football and wrestling teams are strong, and the music department's productions are always excellent. The small size of the high school gives the average students the chance to participate in all kinds of activities. Even if they're not the greatest basketball players, they can be on the team and play a significant amount of the time. Although athletic, musical, and academic activities draw from a smaller pool of talent than many other schools, they consistently win honors in statewide competitions. In 2002, Stroudsburg High School's science Olympiad team placed first (for the third year in a row) in Northeast Pennsylvania and sixth in a demanding statewide competition.

Mount Pocono Area

Pocono Mountain School District
Pocono Mountain School Road, Swiftwater
(570) 839-7121
www.pmsd.org
The largest of all the school districts, Pocono Mountain has a student population of more than 11,400 and continues to grow. This district includes seven elementary centers, two intermediate schools, two high schools, and a small academy for high school students who have been referred for attendance, disciplinary or other at-risk behaviors. With more than 1,500 computers in the classrooms,

EDUCATION

CLOSE-UP

Homeschooling Is Big in the Poconos

Homeschooling is strongly supported in the Poconos. Those who homeschool their children are staunch advocates of the program and almost militant in their reactions to local school board regulation. There's even an organization that acts as a clearinghouse for homeschoolers. The number of homeschooled children grows as school populations increase. Some homeschool because they have religious objections to public and private school curricula, some because they feel they can meet their child's special needs more effectively at home than in the schools, and some because they want to be with their children and provide the guidance they feel appropriate and necessary for their kids' growth.

Since the 1988 passage of the Home School Bill, homeschoolers have the state's approval if minimum requirements are met and the following guidelines are followed:

- The homeschooled child must be assessed by an evaluator of the parents' choice who has been approved by the district.
- Parents must have high school diplomas and no criminal records.
- Parents must present curriculum plans each year by August 1, outlining their child's goals for the school year.
- The curriculum plan must be approved by the district.
- A log of each day's activities must be kept for each child and submitted to the evaluator.
- Students must receive a full 180 days of schooling.

Some homeschoolers work with other families, providing controlled socialization and allowing each parent to concentrate on those parts of the instruction they know best. Many parents sign up their homeschooled children for athletics and

Pocono Mountain maintains a ratio of one computer to every six students.

The Pocono Mountain High School marching band is especially strong, and in 2001 it took its fifth consecutive first place win in its division of the Atlantic Coast Tournament of Bands. Pocono Mountain High School also runs an innovative cultural program with students involved in all aspects of producing cultural events for the school and the community.

West End

Jim Thorpe Area School District
140 West 10th Street, Jim Thorpe
(570) 325–3691
www.jtasd.k12.pa.us
The Jim Thorpe Area School District, with more than 1,700 students, includes an elementary school, a junior high school, and a high school. Some Wilkes University professors utilize the schools' state-of-the-art computers to teach college

extracurricular activities so they can interact with other kids.

If the homeschooling parent is a certified teacher, all of the requirements for homeschooling are irrelevant. The parent can simply register the child as being tutored at home. Tutoring does not fall under homeschooling guidelines. A new wrinkle in homeschooling is cyber schooling. Under recent state legislation allowing charter schools, independent public schools funded by the state and local school district, a number of cyber schools have been formed on the premise that the student can work at a home computer and interact with instructors over the Internet. The school districts define cyber schools as homeschools, not charter schools, and they contend that cyber schools should be privately funded. There have been court battles and children with uncertain status over this issue. The outcome has not yet been determined.

The Pennsylvania Homeschoolers, a resource for those interested in home-schooling in Pennsylvania, is headed by Dr. Howard Richman. For a newsletter and free catalog of books about home-schooling, send a self-addressed, stamped envelope to RD 2, Box 117, Kittanning, Pennsylvania 16201, or call (724) 783–6512. The Pennsylvania Homeschoolers also run an informative Web page at www.pahomeschoolers.com.

If you look, you can find parents who homeschool their children. Head to the library and look for a parent with a group of kids who should be in school. Many churches have homeschooling families in their parishes or congregations—part of what seems like an underground network—so be sure to inquire.

The bottom line: Many homeschooled students do well. They get high scores on their SATs and are sought by colleges.

The ranks of homeschoolers are swelling. If homeschooling sounds attractive to you, make contact with other homeschoolers, check out the Pennsylvania Homeschoolers Web site and do your research. The education of a child is not a task to take lightly. If you're going to do it, make sure you do it right.

courses. The district offers an extensive technology education menu to its high school students, including laser and fiber optics, aerospace, computer animation, and many other subjects.

Lehighton Area School District
200 Beaver Run Road, Lehighton
(610) 377–4490
www.lehighton.org
Four elementary schools, a middle school, and a high school serve approximately 2,500 students in the district. The Carbon County district has excellent sports programs. The football and track teams consistently compete for regional and state championships. High school students in the district have the opportunity to work in the school's television production studio.

Palmerton Area School District
3533 Fireline Road, Palmerton
(610) 826–7101
www.palmerton.org
Palmerton Area School District, in Carbon County, has approximately 2,080 students

in its two elementary schools, its middle school, and its high school. Vocational programs are supported through classes at the Carbon County Vocation School. Strong football and track programs, a marching band, and club activities round out extracurricular offerings. The growth in this community has been stable, so Palmerton schools have not seen the expansion evident in other Pocono districts.

Not everybody confines themselves to the Poconos for schooling. Some folks send their children to Bethlehem to Moravian Academy or the new Lehigh Valley Charter High School for the Performing Arts.

Pleasant Valley School District
District Administration Offices, School Lane, Brodheadsville
(570) 402-1000
www.pvbears.org
Four elementary schools, an intermediate school, a middle school, and a high school are part of Pleasant Valley School District, which serves approximately 7,000 students. This school system boasts an excellent instrumental music program, with a number of different bands and orchestras. The faculty, with a strong reputation for active involvement, developed an environmental center on the grounds of an elementary center. The elementary schools use a literature-based curriculum to teach language arts. The high school, with a performance-based curriculum, consistently produces students who distinguish themselves academically. Pleasant Valley has maximized their technological abilities. They have not only put their curriculum on line, so that parents can see what their children are learning in school, but they also offer evening technology courses to adults in the district.

Milford/Lake Wallenpaupack Area

Delaware Valley School District
HC 77, Box 379A, Milford, PA 18337
(570) 296-1800
www.dvasdweb.dvasd.k12.pa.us
Three elementary schools, a primary school, two middle schools, and a high school in this growing district in Pike County serve a student population of more than 5,400. The elementary school has its own TV station (DVE-TV, Channel 5) that actively pursues stories in Pike County as well as at places like the United Nations in New York City. A few years ago they covered the Presidents' Summit for America's Future chaired by Colin Powell. This district strongly supports academic scrimmages, science and math fairs, and athletics. In 2002, the Scholastic Bowl team made it to the national championship in New Orleans, while nine Odyssey of the Mind teams competed at the state competition.

Wallenpaupack School District
HC 6, Box 6075, Hawley, PA 18428
(570) 226-4557
www.paupack.ptd.net
Wallenpaupack School District, which covers an area of approximately 325 square miles in Pike and Wayne counties, serves more than 4,000 students in its kindergarten center, primary school (grades K through 2), elementary school (grades K through 6), intermediate school (grades 3 through 5), middle school (grades 6 through 8), and high school (grades 9 through 12). The high school offers on-site vocational training in building trades, power mechanics, allied health, and food service. A cooperative education program combines classroom study with work experience. Wallenpaupack students have won awards in foreign language, art, music, essay, oratorical, and drama competitions as well as in the state Science Olympiad. The district also offers a number of adult enrichment and job training courses in the evening.

PRIVATE SCHOOLS

As noted in this chapter's introduction, you'll find few private schools in the Pocono region, and most are church-affiliated. Many of the private schools, however, are excellent and have turned out to be effective alternatives for students who are not reaching their potential in the public school system.

Delaware Water Gap/ Shawnee-on-Delaware

Blair Academy
1 Park Street, Blairstown, NJ
(908) 362-6121
www.blair.edu
All right, Blairstown is actually about 16 miles east of Delaware Water Gap in New Jersey, but Blair Academy is an alternative for area high school students. The oldest Presbyterian-affiliated boarding school in the nation, Blair offers a demanding and diverse college-preparatory curriculum in classes of no more than 8 to 12 students. The enrollment of about 400 includes more than 100 day-students. Students in the 2003–2004 school year came from 21 different nations. The beautiful, wooded campus has been named a national historic landmark. Blair students are encouraged to participate in extracurricular activities and traditionally go on to prestigious colleges.

Shawnee Academy
River Road, Minisink Hills
(570) 420-8601
Shawnee runs a special education school and an alternative school for day students as well as a completely separate school for full-time residents who are being treated there for mental illness. If your school district feels that they don't have an appropriate program for your child, they may offer Shawnee as a viable alternative. Here, the student learns in a more intensive setting with more staff and more hands-on activities. The school works hard at providing a positive atmosphere for learning. Because Shawnee also includes a residential treatment program, a full spectrum of services can be provided, if needed, including diagnostic assessments, crisis services, and outpatient and home-based mental health treatment. Shawnee currently has 180 students.

St. Paul's Lutheran School
Craig's Meadow Road, Marshalls Creek
(570) 223-7700
This Christian school is open to all faiths. The grades here are pre-kindergarten through first grade, and enrollment is currently 45 students. St. Paul's offers lots of individual instruction. The classes are small, with no more than 10 students to each teacher. Learning is child-centered and proceeds at the individual student's pace.

Stroudsburg/East Stroudsburg

East Stroudsburg Christian Academy
9 Three Point Garden Road
East Stroudsburg
(570) 421-4087
This school is quite small. Enrollment is 85 from pre-kindergarten through grade 12. While the elementary grades work within a traditional classroom, grades seven through 12 have a self-paced study program supervised by a teacher and an aide. The 27-year-old school offers a Bible-based education at reasonable rates. All of its graduates go on to college.

The Growing Concern
Railroad Drive, Tannersville
(570) 629-2754
This Montessori school serves 68 preschool through fourth grade students. The mixed-age classes are small, and children work at their own pace. The Growing Concern has a beautiful building on a lovely, wooded lot. The care the parents and faculty lavish on this school is obvious.

The One-Room Schoolhouse

On almost every country road where an early community once existed, you'll see a small building—usually white and run-down. These buildings once provided the education for thousands of area residents who walked to school—rain or shine, snow or sleet—until well into the 1940s. About that time, several small schools consolidated, beginning the growth of what have become some enormous school districts.

A few restored schoolhouses are maintained by local historical organizations as museums—the Bell School in Cherry Valley and the Dutot School in Delaware Water Gap, among them. On the grounds of the Pocono Mountain School District is a reproduction of a one-room schoolhouse built by Monroe County Vo-Tech students. The furnishings are antique and historically accurate.

Sunday School teachers from St. John's Evangelical Church still use a one-room schoolhouse that was built in 1836.

The Custard School, off Rimrock Road in Bartonsville, has its original blackboards and teacher's desk, although it no longer sits on a platform as it once did.

Attending Custard School was not like going to class today. All classes were taught in one room; grades 1 through 8 studied together. When it was time to give a lesson for a specific grade, students went up to a big bench at the front of the room and sat together, a practice this unique Sunday school still uses. The other students sat at their desks and continued their work—reading, writing, and arithmetic.

Students learned a lot from each other. Since they were together all the time, younger students easily picked up knowledge from older ones, an educational technique that has been reintroduced in some schools today. The older students often taught younger classmates while the teacher worked with others.

Notre Dame Elementary School
78 Ridgeway Street, East Stroudsburg
(570) 421-3651
www.notredameelementary.com
This traditional Catholic elementary school has 350 students in preschool through sixth grade. The school includes three years of Montessori instruction and a choice of half- or full-day kindergarten. The local parishes send their students here. Unaffiliated students are welcome, but the school is popular, and there are waiting lists for every grade. Students

usually go on to Notre Dame High School for grades 7 to 12.

Notre Dame High School
60 Spangenburg Avenue
East Stroudsburg
(570) 421-0466
www.notredamehigh.com
This Catholic college-preparatory school is coeducational with an enrollment of approximately 350 in grades 7 to 12. Its curriculum is that of a traditional Catholic school, although students of other denom-

Resources included books as well as a corner cabinet filled with nature items and pamphlets describing them. Keturah Hartman, a second-generation graduate of Custard School, remembers a large coconut shell filled with coconut that the children would eat when the teacher wasn't looking.

Recess included outdoor games such as "ticleedy over," in which students would throw a ball to each other over the very steep roof. In winter they hiked to the top of the meadow across the road from the school, taking along old boards to ride down the snow-crusted hills.

Classes were small. Hartman was the sole graduate in her eighth-grade class. Graduations were sometimes held in local churches. Each one-room school would send their graduating eighth graders to a general commencement ceremony.

When schools began consolidating in the late 1930s and early 1940s, there was resistance. One teacher in Reeders refused to send her students, yet walked them down to the consolidated school in Tannersville every year to take the required state exams. Often folks felt they were losing the control of their children and their communities by consolidating with others.

Holidays prompted celebrations. Halloween was always a time for mischief. As Hartman remembers, "Every year the boys used to put the teacher's chair on the roof. Sometimes they'd turn over the outhouses." Students and their families attended "box socials." Young ladies brought lunches in fancy, decorated shoeboxes and the young men would bid on the boxes. The winning bid carried with it the privilege of eating with the owner. Schools also held "shadow socials." A sheet was hung, and the girls had their shadows cast on the sheet by a lantern. The boys would bid on the shadows to spend time with the girl.

Most schools in the Pocono region are growing tremendously. Many of the private schools emphasize their small size. Those with fond memories of their one-room schoolhouses agree with the private schools that "small is beautiful."

inations attend. Notre Dame's strong academic reputation means there is always a waiting list, and more than 90 percent of its students go on to college. One of the values of this school is its small size, which ensures faculty and administration get to know every student. Activities include musicals (which are consistently excellent) and athletics, including boys and girls soccer (for which this school is known), baseball, basketball, softball, golf, tennis, and field hockey.

Stroudsburg Seventh-Day Adventist School
West Main Street, Stroudsburg
(570) 421-5577
www.stroudsburgsda.org
Thirty-three students in grades kindergarten to 8 partake in a religious education at the Stroudsburg Seventh-Day Adventist School. Three classrooms, one for grades K through 2, the second for grades 3 through 5, and the third for 6 through 8, echo the teaching methods of the old

> *Bus transportation to private schools must be provided by the district in which you live. If you plan to send your child to private, check with the district for scheduling.*

one-room schoolhouses. Classes are small, and there are no more than 13 students to a teacher. Students who wish to continue a Seventh-day Adventist education go on to Blue Mountain Academy, a boarding high school in Berks County.

Mount Pocono Area

Evergreen Community School
Highways 390 and 191, Cresco
(570) 595-6355
www.evergreencommunityschool.org
The Evergreen Community School, the only private academic school in the area for grades 6 through 12, opened its doors in the fall of 1996. With 45 students, Evergreen emphasizes small classes (never more than a 14-to-1 student/teacher ratio) and a hands-on learning environment utilizing project-oriented teaching methods in conjunction with the latest technology, including Pentium computers with Internet access for research, modeling, and communication. Students progress at their own rate. In place of varsity level sports programs, Evergreen offers lifetime activities, such as golf, tennis, trap, and skeet, horseback riding, yoga, bowling, skiing/snowboarding, ice-skating, and fly fishing.

Monsignor McHugh Elementary School
Highway 191, Cresco
(570) 595-7463
www.monsignormchugh.com
This traditional Catholic elementary school serves more than 480 preschoolers through eighth graders. Students wear uniforms. The faculty consists of mostly laypersons. Most students are from local parishes, but others are welcome too. The

school's atmosphere is upbeat, and the students thrive. Computer learning is emphasized in all grades.

The Oxford School
Highway 314 East, Swiftwater
(570) 839-7367
The Oxford School serves 50 toddlers through first graders. The school offers very small classes (a student-teacher ratio never greater than 10-to-1), a great deal of depth in each subject studied, and a full-day kindergarten. Oxford looks at children's readiness for school rather than their calendar age, so they often accept children in kindergarten and first grade who are younger than those in the public schools.

Tender Treasures Day Care
Route 115 and State Road, Effort
(570) 629-1080
Tender Treasures has 14 students in their kindergarten and first-grade class. Many of their students missed the cutoff date for public school, but are intellectually and socially ready for kindergarten and first grade. Some students, in fact, are gifted, and Tender Treasures works with each student at his or her level rather than making everybody work at a group level. Most of their units are a minimum of six months ahead of the public schools, so when a student graduates from first grade here, he or she is well prepared for second grade at a public or private school. In addition to academics, Tender Treasures emphasizes socialization, manners, and citizenship. Tender Treasures is also a day-care center, so before- and after-school care is provided.

COLLEGES AND UNIVERSITIES

East Stroudsburg University
Normal Street, East Stroudsburg
(570) 422-3211
www.esu.edu
East Stroudsburg is one of 14 universities in the Pennsylvania State System of

Higher Education. It was founded as a normal school, or teacher's college, in 1893. Later it joined the state system and expanded its courses of study, though it still has a heavy emphasis on education as a major. ESU achieved university status in 1983. The university works closely with the community, co-sponsoring math fairs, participating in experimental workshops and projects with different school districts, supporting local organizations' fairs, and providing women's awareness programs. There are approximately 5,100 undergraduates and 1,000 graduate students.

Undergraduate degrees students can earn at ESU include a bachelor's in special education, history, geography, physical education, art, theater, French, philosophy, Spanish, biochemistry, biotechnology, chemical biotechnology, computer science, computer security, earth and space science, environmental studies, general science, marine science, mathematics, media communication and technology, medical technology, physical science, physics, economics, management, political science, social studies, sociology, music, secondary education, English, speech communication, psychology, early-childhood education and elementary education, biology, nursing, speech pathology and audiology, chemistry, allied-health education, restaurant and tourism management, and recreation and leisure services management. Other programs—engineering, pharmacy, medical technology, and podiatry—are offered in conjunction with other universities in the state.

The graduate division offers master's degrees in biology, cardiac rehabilitation and exercise science, computer science, elementary education, general science, health education, health and physical education, history, instructional technology, physical education, political science, public health, reading, secondary education, special education, speech pathology, and audiology. The university also offers certification degrees for prospective principals, superintendents, reading specialists, and special education supervisors.

A night school has been added to serve students who cannot attend during the day (see the Adult Education section below).

Northampton Community College—Monroe Campus
Old Mill Road, Tannersville
(570) 620-9221
www.northampton.edu

The campus is a branch of Northampton Community College in Bethlehem. The enrollment is 1,900 and has grown so fast that they have had to add onto their buildings every couple of years. There are associate degree programs and certifications available at this campus, including accounting, business administration, business management, early childhood education, education, general studies, liberal arts, social work, criminal justice, LPN, Medical Billing Specialist, and electronics technology. The student lounge even has wireless Internet access. Just bring along your laptop and you can log on.

The Monroe campus even has a truck-driving program that provides the various levels of certification for tractor-trailer truck and school bus drivers.

About a third of Northampton's students transfer to four-year colleges, while two-thirds go into the workforce. The small size of the Monroe Campus makes it a particularly good place to start for students who need direction or are returning to college after a hiatus. Class sizes are small—in most cases there's a 19-to-1 student-to-faculty ratio—and teacher accessibility is one of the school's hallmarks. Offerings include adult-education and community-outreach courses for individuals and groups trying to begin new careers.

Students participate in various community and college affairs, and extracurricular activities are expanding. The student body includes a mix of recent high school graduates and returning adults. The college ensures its community affiliation by offering night courses in some area high schools with its regular

and adjunct faculty. They also provide a full range of services in tutoring, career counseling, and job placement.

ADULT EDUCATION
Stroudsburg/East Stroudsburg

East Stroudsburg University
Normal Street, Each Stroudsburg
(570) 422-3311
www.esu.edu
In addition to the regular on-campus continuing education courses, many of them scheduled after 4:00 P.M. to make them more convenient for working adults, 25 to 30 courses are offered off-campus in locations throughout northeastern Pennsylvania. This program is intended to make graduate education more available to professional educators.

Senior citizens may take up to a maximum of six credits a semester, usually two classes, on a noncredit basis, tuition-free at ESU. The university also offers The Older Adult Learning Center (TOALC), in conjunction with Elderhostel. TOALC offers a diverse catalog of courses taught by members of the community.

Monroe Career and Technical Institute
Laurel Lake Road, Bartonsville
(570) 629-2001
www.monroecti.org
This vo-tech school offers extensive adult-education programs, including GED, enrichment courses, and certification programs related to employment options

such as healthcare assistant and technician. Maintenance certifications are available for working with refrigerants.

West End

Carbon County Vocational and Technical
150 West 13th Street, Jim Thorpe
(570) 325-4140
www.carbonaecenter.com
This school offers continuing education programs in enrichment and GED diplomas. It also has federally funded programs targeted to individuals with certain demographics; most notably, for the past 11 years, the school has been the county's site for the New Choices program, which helps displaced single-parent homemakers plan careers.

Milford/Lake Wallenpaupack Area

Delaware Valley Adult and Community
Education (DV-ACE)
940 Twin Lakes Road, Shohola
(570) 296-3615
www.dvasdweb.dvasd.K12.pa.us
This program holds courses for all ages in the public schools. Options include CPR and basic first aid, computers, swimming, day camp, booktalks, math-a-mania, cooking, quilting, aerobics, fishing, and tennis. Course listings are described in brochures that are distributed through local newspapers three times a year.

MEDIA

If you're just visiting the Poconos, you're probably here to get away from it all. But let's face it; nobody wants to get away from all of it. We still need news of the world, and while the Poconos are quite far from the urban mob scene, news and information sources abound.

While the *Pocono Record* is the only daily newspaper in Monroe County, which is considered to be the heart of the Poconos, you'll also find a host of community weeklies and free publications from all over the region as well as a wide range of radio and television stations that, though they may be broadcasting from Scranton, Allentown–Bethlehem, New York, or Philadelphia, come through loud and clear. Newspapers from areas outside the Poconos also can be found on most newsstands. Here is a rundown on some of the available media choices.

NEWSPAPERS AND MAGAZINES

Dailies

The Express-Times
30 North Fourth Street, Easton
(610) 258-7171
pennlive.nj.com/expresstimes
The editor of this 150-year-old daily newspaper characterizes its editorial policy as that of "a vigorously independent troublemaker." The *Express-Times* offers news, sports, and features across international, national, and local spectra—including extensive coverage of the Poconos. The *Express-Times* boasts a daily circulation of 53,000, and it can be found on newsstands throughout the region.

The Morning Call
101 North Sixth Street, Allentown
(610) 820-6500
www.mcall.com
The Morning Call has a daily circulation of 111,594 Monday through Wednesday, 126,181 Thursday through Saturday, and 165,607 on Sunday. The paper existed as a family-owned business from its founding at the turn of the century until 1984 when it was sold to the Times Mirror Company, which also owns the *Los Angeles Times, New York Newsday,* the *Baltimore Sun,* the *Hartford Courant,* the *Stamford Advocate,* and the *Greenwich Times.* The Tribune Company acquired Times Mirror in 2000, adding papers including the *Chicago Tribune* and the *Orlando Sentinel* to the *Morning Call*'s family. The *Morning Call* is a general-circulation daily, carrying national and international news and features, sports, and local news, which is considered its strongest editorial suit.

Though published in Allentown in the Lehigh Valley south of the Poconos, the *Morning Call* covers the Poconos and can be found on virtually every newsstand in the region.

Pocono Record
511 Lenox Street, Stroudsburg
(570) 421-3000
www.poconorecord.com
Acquired in 1946 by Ottaway Newspapers as the *Daily Record,* the *Pocono Record* is published every morning. It is the primary news and advertising publication in Monroe and Pike counties, and it keeps its finger on the pulse of the Poconos with circulation into Wayne, Carbon, and Northampton Counties—even Warren County, New Jersey. Local news coverage,

particularly sports, is very comprehensive. Big city newspaper readers may be surprised at the *Pocono Record*'s national and international coverage, which is supplied by the AP and is minimal. The focus here is local, and the *Record* does local very well.

The *Pocono Record*'s history can be traced back to April 2, 1894, when the *Stroudsburg Daily Times* began publication as a weekly. The earliest newspapers in Monroe County were the *Stroudsburg Gazette* from the early 1800s and its successor, the *Monroe Democrat,* which was founded in 1836.

Called *Pocono Record* since 1965, the newspaper has grown and diversified in recent years. The advertising and editorial offices were completely renovated in 1996. A new printing facility was constructed in Tannersville in 1995. In addition to the daily paper, the *Pocono Record* publishes Dignity, a monthly magazine for "people who are 50 and older and anything but retiring"; the *Mountain Mail*, a monthly that covers the community around Barrett Township; the *Eastern Pocono Community News,* a weekly covering roughly the same area as the East Stroudsburg School District; and the Easy to Read large-print phonebook. The advertising in the *Pocono Record* gives a good indication of local stores and services, and their Web site has an even more extensive guide to local businesses and attractions. Look for restaurant and nightclub advertisements on Friday and Saturday to find out about specials and band schedules.

Circulation figures are 23,000 for Monday through Saturday editions and 26,336 on Sunday.

The Times News
First and Iron Streets, Lehighton
(610) 377-2051

A newspaper with a circulation of 15,218 published daily Monday through Saturday, the *Times News* combines national and international news with reporting from Carbon, Monroe, Lehigh, Schuylkill, and Northampton Counties. Sports, both local and national, are thoroughly covered.

The Wayne Independent
220 Eighth Street, Honesdale
(570) 253-3055
www.wayneindependent.com

National news and syndicated political columns diversify the content of this newspaper, which is published daily Tuesday through Saturday and has a circulation of 4,331. It strikes a comfortable balance between world-event highlights and more extensive reporting on local concerns.

Weeklies/Monthlies

The Gazette
84–88 Fowler Street
Port Jervis, NY
(800) 295-2181

Another weekly owned by Ottaway Newspapers, the *Gazette* hits newsstands in the northern section of the Pocono region every Friday. Much of its coverage is devoted to New York State; however, Pike County information also is provided.

The News Eagle
522 Spring Street, Hawley
(570) 226-4547
www.neagle.com

The largest-circulation newspaper in Pike and Wayne Counties at 6,500 copies, the *News Eagle* is published every Tuesday, Thursday, and Saturday morning. Its content combines syndicated columnists, legal notices, local sports, and regional news. Like the Pike *County Dispatch* (see listing below), it packs a lot of information onto relatively few pages, usually 14.

The Pike County Courier
511 Broad Street, Milford
(570) 296-6397
www.pikecountypa.com

Established in 1990, this monthly boasts a little bit of everything. Scoops and strong opinions on local issues share space with gardening, horoscopes, cooking, music, movie reviews, and fitness columns. The emphasis is placed on Pike County stories written by local authors. Prominent and unique area residents are profiled regularly.

Pike County Dispatch
105 West Catharine Street, Milford
(570) 296-6641
Another newspaper with a long history, the *Dispatch* began publishing in 1826. It is the primary source of news in Pike County. This weekly, published every Thursday morning, with a circulation of 6,000, focuses on community events, church activities, school news, and legal activities. Here is where you will see pictures of the star athlete and scholastic leaders. This is the only newspaper to offer timely news on issues within Pike County. The layout apparently has not changed much in the last 179 years. Pages are packed with narrow columns of type and few photos, like newspapers in the good old days.

The River Reporter
93 Erie Avenue, Narrowsburg, NY
(845) 252-7414
www.riverreporter.com
Southern New York State and northern Pike and Wayne Counties are thoroughly documented in this weekly, printed every Thursday with a circulation of 4,500. Its tagline boasts of the paper's coverage is "spanning three states, five counties, more than 60 communities, and a river." Most of its pages are devoted to issues and news stories. The sports section and automotive column also are extensive.

Weekly Almanac
113 Church Street, Honesdale
(570) 253-9270
Published every Thursday, with a circulation of 5,000, the *Weekly Almanac* provides coverage of Hawley and Honesdale school activities, community events, local sports, and church happenings. Several pages are devoted to editorials and letters to the editor, providing a good idea of where residents stand on local issues.

Freebies

In addition to the aforementioned newspapers, you can pick up many free publications at shop entrances in the Poconos.

The Community Express
P.O. Box 606, Reeders, PA 18352
(570) 476-0601
Restaurant, movie and music reviews, nature, art, and business articles also are included in this "paper for people with a point of view." The paper is published monthly.

Dignity
511 Lenox Street, Stroudsburg
(570) 421-3000
www.dignityonline.com
A product of the *Pocono Record*, *Dignity* is published monthly and caters to the 50-and-older population. It carries columns, profiles of noteworthy older residents and covers events of interest to seniors.

Eastern Pocono Community News
511 Lenox Street, Stroudsburg
(570) 421-3000
www.poconorecord.com
The *Pocono Record* publishes this scrappy newspaper for the eastern Poconos covering the East Stroudsburg School District and Delaware Water Gap. The editor is opinionated and experienced, and sometimes runs whole issues devoted to themes like the freedom of the press in

---

One of the early newspapers in Monroe County was named the **Monroe Democrat,** *which was founded in 1836 to exploit the dominance of that political party in the area.*

Silent Noon

The Pike County Dispatch, in Milford, was founded in 1826 and has been in continuous publication for 179 years. The paper has operated out of its present building since 1915. Up until five years ago, the noon whistle was blown with a button in the newsroom, but the custom ended because, in the words of a staffer, "Nobody blows whistles any more."

high school. School coverage is excellent. Columns by James Dobson, Herb Dennenberg, and some local writers round out the offerings.

Focus
Carriage House Square, Effort
(570) 688-0788
Published weekly, *Focus* features event notices for the southern Poconos and the Slate Belt plus health, home improvement, and real estate columns among its many advertisements.

Mountain Mail
511 Lenox Street, Stroudsburg
(570) 595-6333
This monthly for Barrett Township and the surrounding area is published by the *Pocono Record.* The paper, with a circulation of 8,000, is a real hometown rag, with news of local achievements, a community calendar, and columns covering area history, ecology, volunteers, schools, cooking, business, pets, travel, humor, health, books, and more.

News of the Poconos
211 Main Street, White Haven
(570) 443-9131
Upcoming events and stories on local shops comprise the editorial content of this paper published 10 times each year. Some stories are saddled with byline puns such as an article on an Indian gift shop by Nate Eva Merikan and one on a seafood restaurant by Ivana Lobb Sturr.

News of the Poconos is now part of Journal Newspapers of Pa., Inc., which also publishes the *Journal of the Pocono Plateau, Journal-Valley Views,* the *Herald Journal Mountaintop,* and several custom newspapers for community associations.

The Pocono Shopper
96 South Courtland Street
East Stroudsburg
(570) 421-4800
www.zwire.com
Other than a very interesting history column, horoscope, and press releases on local events, this weekly is designed as a vehicle for local businesses to promote themselves. It is hand-delivered to homes in most of Monroe County and is readily available at the entrances of supermarkets. Other editions are distributed throughout the Poconos. If you want to compare prices at the local supermarkets, this paper is worth a look.

This Week in the Poconos
Highway 940, Pocono Pines
(570) 839-7103
www.thisweek.net
This small magazine with a glossy color cover is packed with information on area shops, restaurants, and attractions and is one of the area's most popular tourist publications. A scan of its pages will provide visitors countless ideas for things to do. It focuses on Monroe County, Jim Thorpe, and the Lake Wallenpaupack area.

RADIO

In the Poconos, where mass transit is anything but massive, and the great outdoors weaves its spell in every season of the year, visitors and natives alike spend a lot of time in their cars. All cars have radios (except, perhaps, some from New York City where signs saying RADIO ALREADY STOLEN are displayed on dashboards). Radios get a workout here. Regional stations, playing a variety of formats, come in loud and clear in most areas, although you may lose stations in the valleys and find them again on the ridges. In addition to local stations, you may find stations from New Jersey, Philadelphia, and even one or two from New York City. To reach their audiences, some stations—such as WVIA, which airs National Public Radio fare— have installed translators throughout the Pocono region to boost their signals. For weather, sports, news, and music—from golden oldies to rock 'n' roll—here is a rundown of the dial.

ADULT CONTEMPORARY

WSBG 93.5 FM
WDNH 95.3 FM
WLEV 100.7 FM
WHCY 106.3 FM
WKRF 107.9 FM
WMGH 105.5 FM
WZZO 95.1 FM

CLASSIC ROCK

WODE 99.9 FM

COLLEGE RADIO

WESS 90.3 FM

COUNTRY

WRNJ 107.1 FM
WDLC 1490 AM
WPSN 1590 AM

EASY LISTENING

WEST 1400 AM
WFMZ 100.7 AM

OLDIES

WGPA 1100 AM
WYNS 1160 AM
WYCY 105.3 FM
WTSX 96.7 FM

PUBLIC RADIO

WVIA 89.9 FM
WRTI 91 FM

ADULT NOSTALGIA

WVPO 840 AM, 960 AM
WDLC 1490 AM

TALK

WDNB 102.1 FM

TELEVISION

Unlike radio signals, which seem to bounce largely unimpeded through the tall forests and rolling hills that make up the Poconos, television is a picky thing, easily blocked by the very geographical features visitors come to see and residents have come to love. As a result, the cable television business is very healthy here, and in recent years, satellite dishes have grown on roofs and walls all over the region. In some areas, a standard rooftop antenna is a workable, if limited, option, but generally, only the wired will win the whole spectrum. For them, here is where the networks can be found.

ABC

WNEP-TV 16
WPVI-TV 6

Even though a good deal of Pocono living is rural, most area residents have access to advanced services such as cable TV, digital cable, high-speed Internet, high-definition TV, and, coming soon, video-on-demand.

CBS
WYOU-TV 22
KYW-TV 3

FOX
WOLF-TV 56

INDEPENDENT
WFMZ-TV 69

LOCAL
WBRC-TV 13

NBC
WBRE-TV 28

PUBLIC TELEVISIONS
WLVT Channel 39
WVIA Channel 44

If you're on a cable, the channels you find these stations on vary, depending on where in the Poconos you are. Go to Blue Ridge Cable TV's Web site (see below) to find out precisely which channel carries which station.

Cable Television

Blue Ridge Cable Television Inc.
613 Third Street, Palmerton
(610) 826–2551
www.brctv.com

This is the cable television provider for the Pocono Mountains area. For information on rates for hookup, call the office closest to you. In addition to cable TV, Blue Ridge offers digital cable TV and cable modem service. The company also has offices at 200 North First Street, Lehighton, (610) 377-2250; 920 Ehler Street, Stroudsburg, (570) 421-0780; 20 West Ridge Street, Lansford, (570) 645-5511; 112 Bennett Avenue, Milford, (570) 296-8200; 115 A Route 940, Pocono Summit, (570) 839–3550; U.S. Highway 209, Gilbert, (610) 681-6100; Highway 29 and Diamond Terrace, Tunkhannock, (570) 836-5422; and U.S. Highway 6, Hawley, (570) 226-4914.

Blue Ridge Cable Television TV 13
936 Elm Street, Lehighton
(610) 826–4060
www.brctv13.com
The most comprehensive locally produced television station in the Poconos, Channel 13 may be picked up by cable viewers in Monroe, Pike, Carbon, Schuylkill, Northampton, Lackawanna, Berks, and Lehigh Counties. At 9:00 A.M., 5:00, 10:00, and 11:00 P.M. daily, *Eyewatch News* provides complete coverage of local news, weather, and sports. Other programs produced in-house discuss money and local legislators. There are also shows on local sports, Nascar, outdoor activities, and even a polka show.

INDEX

ABOUT THE AUTHORS

JANET BREGMAN-TANEY

After nearly a decade of answering letters for philosopher/architect Buckminster Fuller, Janet Bregman-Taney found herself writing features and a consumer column for the *Philadelphia City Paper.* She has since written newspapers-in-education supplements for the *Philadelphia Inquirer,* a newsletter for Rodale Press, and a coloring book for the Philadelphia Orchestra, as well as CD liner notes and a TV pilot. Currently, she is editor of *Dignity,* a monthly magazine for people 50 and older, published by the *Pocono Record.* When not chained to her computer, Janet is a multi-instrumentalist for the Juggernaut String Band, with whom she has traveled extensively in Europe and the Eastern United States, appeared on radio and TV, and recorded four albums. Since moving to the Poconos in 1995, she is convinced that she lives in one of the most magical spots on the planet, and she plans to be here for an unimaginably long time.

Janet Bregman-Taney PETER TANEY

KENNETH R. CLARK

Ken Clark, who served as a feature writer, general assignments reporter, and media critic both for United Press International and the *Chicago Tribune,* was a veteran of 35 years in daily journalism when he retired in 1995. Since then he has found time to write a novel titled *Omega Rising: Adventures in a Parallel Universe,* co-author the *Insiders' Guide to the Pocono Mountains,* and travel the nation in a motor home with his wife, Dorothy. Out of those journeys have come "Highways and Byways—My Way," a series of monthly travel columns for *Dignity* magazine (see our Media chapter). When not on the road, he and Dorothy live in a deep green forest in Marshalls Creek, Pennsylvania, which, ultimately, is the best destination of them all.

Kenneth R. Clark

HELP US KEEP THIS GUIDE UP TO DATE

Every effort has been made by the authors and editors to make this guide as accurate and useful as possible. However, many things can change after a guide is published—phone numbers change, facilities come under new management, etc.

   We would love to hear from you concerning your experiences with this guide and how you feel it could be improved and be kept up to date. While we may not be able to respond to all comments and suggestions, we'll take them to heart and we'll also make certain to share them with the authors. Please send your comments and suggestions to the following address:

   The Globe Pequot Press
   Reader Response/Editorial Department
   P. O. Box 480
   Guilford, CT 06437

Or you may e-mail us at:

   editorial@GlobePequot.com

Thanks for your input, and happy travels!